ST/LEG/SER.C/55

UNITED NATIONS JURIDICAL YEARBOOK 2017

UNITED NATIONS • NEW YORK, 2025

ST/LEG/SER.C/55

UNITED NATIONS PUBLICATION
Sales No. E.25.V.2
ISBN 978-92-1-003535-4
eISBN 978-92-1-107313-3
ISSN 0082-8297
eISSN 2412-1223

CONTENTS

Page

Part Two. Legal activities of the United Nations and related intergovernmental organizations

FOREWORD

By its resolution 1814 (XVII) of 18 December 1962, the General Assembly requested the Secretary-General to publish a *Juridical Yearbook* which would include certain documentary materials of a legal character concerning the United Nations and related intergovernmental organizations, and by its resolution 3006 (XXVII) of 18 December 1972, the General Assembly made certain changes in the outline of the *Yearbook*. The present volume, which is the fifty-fifth of the series, has been prepared by the Codification Division of the Office of Legal Affairs.

Chapters I and II contain selected legislative texts and treaties, or provisions thereof, concerning the legal status of the United Nations and related intergovernmental organizations.

Chapter III contains a general review of the legal activities of the United Nations and related intergovernmental organizations, based on information provided by each organization.

Chapter IV contains selected treaties concerning international law concluded under the auspices of the organizations concerned during the year in question, whether or not they entered into force in that year in view of the sometimes considerable time lag between the conclusion of the treaties and their entry into force.

Chapter V contains selected decisions of administrative tribunals of the United Nations and related intergovernmental organizations.

Chapter VI reproduces selected legal opinions of the United Nations and related intergovernmental organizations.

Chapter VII includes a list of judgments, advisory opinions and selected decisions rendered by international tribunals in 2017.

Chapter VIII contains decisions given in 2017 by national tribunals relating to the legal status of the various organizations.

Finally, the bibliography, which is prepared under the responsibility of the Office of Legal Affairs by the Dag Hammarskjöld Library, lists works and articles of a legal character relating to the work of the United Nations and related intergovernmental organizations.

Several documents published in the *Juridical Yearbook* were supplied by the organizations or Governments concerned at the request of the Secretariat. Treaty provisions, legislative texts and judicial decisions may have been subject to minor editing by the Secretariat.

This volume will appear on the United Nations Juridical Yearbook's website at http://legal.un.org/unjuridicalyearbook/.

ABBREVIATIONS

AMISOM	African Union Mission in Somalia
CCLM	Committee on Constitutional and Legal Matters (FAO)
CLCS	Commission on the Limits of the Continental Shelf
CTBTO	Comprehensive Nuclear-Test-Ban Treaty Organization
CTC	Counter-Terrorism Committee (Security Council)
CTED	Counter-Terrorism Committee Executive Directorate (United Nations)
ECCAS	Economic Community of Central African States
EU	European Union
EUFOR RCA	European Union Force in the Central African Republic
EUFOR ALTHEA	European Union Force ALTHEA
FAO	Food and Agriculture Organization of the United Nations
IAEA	International Atomic Energy Agency
IBRD	International Bank for Reconstruction and Development
ICAO	International Civil Aviation Organization
ICC	International Criminal Court
ICTR	International Criminal Tribunal for Rwanda
ICTY	International Criminal Tribunal for the former Yugoslavia
IFAD	International Fund for Agricultural Development
IGO	Intergovernmental organization
ILC	International Law Commission
ILO	International Labour Organization
IMF	International Monetary Fund
IMO	International Maritime Organization
ITLOS	International Tribunal for the Law of the Sea
ITU	International Telecommunication Union
JBVMM	Joint Border Verification and Monitoring Mechanism (UNISFA)
MEU	Management Evaluation Unit (United Nations)
MINUJUSTH	United Nations Mission for Justice Support in Haiti
MINURSO	United Nations Mission for the Referendum in Western Sahara
MINUSMA	United Nations Multidimensional Integrated Stabilization Mission in Mali
MINUSCA	United Nations Multidimensional Integrated Stabilization Mission in Central African Republic

WMO	World Meteorological Organization
WFP	World Food Programme
WTO	World Trade Organization

Part One

LEGAL STATUS OF THE UNITED NATIONS AND RELATED INTERGOVERNMENTAL ORGANIZATIONS

Chapter I

LEGISLATIVE TEXTS CONCERNING THE LEGAL STATUS OF THE UNITED NATIONS AND RELATED INTERGOVERNMENTAL ORGANIZATIONS

Paraguay

Law No. 5877 that implements the Rome Statute that creates the International Criminal Court*

[…]

Article 32. Privileges and Immunities.

The staff of the International Criminal Court, as well as locally recruited staff, counsels and staff assisting counsels, witnesses, victims, experts before the International Criminal Court and other persons whose presence is required at the seat of the Court, shall enjoy in the territory of the State such privileges and immunities as are necessary for the performance of their functions, under the terms of Article 48 of the Rome Statute and the Agreement on the Privileges and Immunities of the International Criminal Court.

[…]

* Translation from the original in Spanish.

Chapter II

TREATIES CONCERNING THE LEGAL STATUS OF THE UNITED NATIONS AND RELATED INTERGOVERNMENTAL ORGANIZATIONS*

A. Treaties concerning the legal status of the United Nations

1. Status of the Convention on the Privileges and Immunities of the United Nations. Approved by the General Assembly of the United Nations on 13 February 1946**

In 2017, no State acceded to the Convention. As at 31 December 2017, there were 162 States parties to the Convention.***

2. Agreements relating to missions, offices and meetings

(*a*) Agreement between the United Nations and the Government of the Republic of Benin concerning the status of the United Nations Multidimensional Integrated Stabilization Mission in Mali (MINUSMA) in the territory of the Republic of Benin. Cotonou, 8 February 2017****

I. Preamble

The United Nations, acting through the United Nations Multidimensional Integrated Stabilization Mission in Mali ("MINUSMA"), and the Government of Benin ("the Government"), hereinafter referred to jointly as "the Parties" and individually as "the Party",

Recalling Article 105 of the Charter of the United Nations, in particular paragraphs 1 and 2 thereof, pursuant to which "the Organization shall enjoy in the territory of each of its Members such privileges and immunities as are necessary for the fulfilment of its purposes" and "representatives of the Members of the United Nations and officials of the

---

* In light of the large number of treaties concluded, only a selection of the relevant treaties is reproduced herein.

** United Nations, *Treaty Series*, vol. 1, p. 15, and vol. 90, p. 327 (corrigendum to vol. 1).

*** For the list of States parties to the Convention, see *Multilateral Treaties Deposited with the Secretary-General*, available on the website http://treaties.un.org.

**** Entered into force on 8 February 2017 by signature, in accordance with paragraph 57. United Nations registration no. I-54305.

Organization shall similarly enjoy such privileges and immunities as are necessary for the independent exercise of their functions in connection with the Organization",

Considering the Convention on the Privileges and Immunities of the United Nations ("the Convention"), adopted by the General Assembly in its resolution 22 (I) of 13 February 1946, to which the Republic of Benin is a party,

Considering Security Council resolution 2100 (2013) of 25 April 2013, establishing MINUSMA, and the subsequent Security Council resolutions concerning MINUSMA and the situation in Mali, in particular paragraph 20 of resolution 2100 (2013), and paragraph 33 of resolution 2295 (2016) whereby the Security Council:

> "Calls upon Member States, especially those in the region, to ensure the free, unhindered and expeditious movement to and from Mali of all personnel, as well as equipment, provisions, supplies and other goods, which are for the exclusive and official use of MINUSMA, in order to facilitate the timely and cost-effective delivery of the logistical supply of MINUSMA, and in this regard, requests the Secretary-General to take all necessary measures to facilitate the logistical supply of MINUSMA and to consolidate supply routes, including through using alternative routes and relocating MINUSMA's logistics hubs",

Considering that, following consultations between MINUSMA and the Beninese authorities during a mission to Cotonou conducted by the Director of Mission Support of MINUSMA from 19 to 27 August 2015, the Government of the Republic of Benin stands ready to provide the assistance required by the United Nations for the establishment of a new supply route for MINUSMA from the port of Cotonou,

Desiring to establish the legal framework for the activities of MINUSMA in the territory of Benin in order to facilitate the transit of personnel, goods and equipment required by MINUSMA for its operational activities in Mali,

Have agreed as follows:

II. Definitions and classification

1. For the purposes of the present Agreement:

(*a*) "MINUSMA" means the United Nations Multidimensional Integrated Stabilization Mission in Mali, established by Security Council resolution 2100 (2013) of 25 April 2013. MINUSMA comprises:

- (i) The "Special Representative" appointed by the Secretary-General of the United Nations. Except in paragraph 7 (*a*), "Special Representative" in the present Agreement also means any member of MINUSMA who has been delegated functions or authority by the holder of that title. This term also means, including in paragraph 7 (*a*), any member of MINUSMA appointed acting head of MINUSMA by the Secretary-General as a result of the death, resignation or incapacity of the Special Representative;
- (ii) A "civilian component" consisting of United Nations officials and of other persons assigned by the Secretary-General to assist the Special Representative or made available by participating States to serve as part of MINUSMA;
- (iii) A "military component" consisting of military and civilian personnel made available to MINUSMA by participating States at the request of the Secretary-General;

(*b*) "Member of MINUSMA" means the Special Representative of the Secretary-General and any member of the civilian components (including the police component) or military component of MINUSMA, including consultants and experts on mission and personnel made available collectively by contributing States;

(*c*) "Government" means the Government of the Republic of Benin;

(*d*) "Territory" means the territory of Benin, including its airspace;

(*e*) "Participating State" means a State providing personnel, services, equipment, provisions, supplies, materials and other goods, including spare parts and means of transport, to any of the above-mentioned components of MINUSMA;

(*f*) "Convention" means the Convention on the Privileges and Immunities of the United Nations adopted by the United Nations General Assembly on 13 February 1946, to which Benin is a party;

(*g*) "Contractors" means natural or legal persons, other than members of MINUSMA, and their employees and subcontractors engaged by the United Nations to perform services and/or to supply equipment, provisions, supplies, materials and other goods, including spare parts and means of transport, in support of MINUSMA activities, provided that these contractors are not considered third-party beneficiaries of the present Agreement;

(*h*) "Vehicles" means civilian and military vehicles in use by the United Nations and operated by members of MINUSMA, participating States or contractors in support of MINUSMA activities;

(*i*) "Vessels" means civilian and military vessels in use by the United Nations and operated by members of MINUSMA, participating States or contractors in support of MINUSMA activities;

(*j*) "Aircraft" means civilian and military aircraft in use by the United Nations and operated by members of MINUSMA, participating States or contractors in support of MINUSMA activities.

III. Purpose and scope of the present Agreement

2. The present Agreement sets out the legal framework for the activities of MINUSMA and its members and contractors in the territory of Benin and establishes their status and the rights, privileges and immunities of MINUSMA and its members, as well as the facilities granted to MINUSMA specifically for the benefit of its contractors in the performance of the services that they have been engaged to perform exclusively for MINUSMA.

3. Unless specifically provided otherwise, the provisions of the present Agreement, any obligation undertaken by the Government and any privilege, immunity, facility or concession granted to MINUSMA or any of its members or contractors shall apply only in Benin.

IV. Application of the Convention and the status of MINUSMA and its members

4. MINUSMA, as a subsidiary organ of the United Nations whose activities and mandate are aligned with the principles of peace and security of the United Nations, and its property, funds and assets, as well as its members, shall enjoy the rights, privileges,

immunities, exemptions and facilities mentioned in the present Agreement and those provided for in the Convention.

5. Article II of the Convention, which applies to MINUSMA, shall also apply to the property, funds and assets of participating States used in connection with MINUSMA.

6. The Government undertakes to respect the exclusively international status of MINUSMA.

7. In particular, the Government shall grant:

(*a*) The Special Representative, the Deputy Special Representatives, the Force Commander and the Police Commissioner of MINUSMA, together with such high-ranking members of the Special Representative's staff as may be agreed upon with the Government, the status specified in sections 19 and 27 of the Convention, inasmuch as the privileges and immunities therein referred to are those accorded to diplomatic envoys under international law;

(*b*) Officials of the United Nations assigned to the civilian component of MINUSMA and made available to it, as well as United Nations Volunteers assimilated thereto, the privileges and immunities set out in articles V and VII of the Convention;

(*c*) Locally recruited personnel of MINUSMA the immunities pertaining to acts performed by them in their official capacity, exemption from taxation and immunity from national service obligations provided for in article V, section 18, paragraphs (*a*), (*b*) and (*c*), of the Convention;

(*d*) Other personnel participating in missions for MINUSMA, including military observers, military liaison officers and military advisers, members of the United Nations Civilian Police, including members of formed police units, and civilian personnel who are not United Nations officials, the privileges, immunities, exemptions and facilities accorded to experts on mission for the United Nations under articles VI and VII of the Convention;

(*e*) Military personnel of national contingents serving in the military component of MINUSMA immunity from legal process of every kind in respect of any criminal offence that they might commit in Mali or Benin. The personnel concerned shall be subject to the exclusive jurisdiction of the contributing States of which they are nationals in connection with such offences.

8. Immunity from legal process in respect of words spoken or written and all acts performed by members of MINUSMA in their official capacity, including locally recruited personnel, shall continue even after they cease to be members of or employed by MINUSMA and after the expiration of the other provisions of the present Agreement.

9. Members of MINUSMA shall be exempt from taxation on the pay and emoluments received from the United Nations or from a participating State and any income received from outside Benin. Members of MINUSMA shall also be exempt from all other direct taxes, except municipal rates for services enjoyed, and from all registration fees and charges.

10. MINUSMA and its members shall refrain from any action or activity incompatible with the impartial and international nature of their duties or inconsistent with the spirit of the present Agreement. They shall respect all laws and regulations of the host country, including those concerning traffic, security, public order and public decency, as well as contract and labour laws in respect of persons hired by members of MINUSMA privately, outside the scope of their duties for MINUSMA, in Benin. They shall attempt, by means of

appropriate legal mechanisms, to find appropriate solutions to settle disputes of a private law character with third parties in Benin. The Special Representative shall take all appropriate measures to ensure respect for those obligations, as well as the maintenance of good order and discipline among members of MINUSMA and among locally recruited personnel.

V. Entry, residence in Benin and departure from the territory

11. The Government shall grant MINUSMA, its members and its contractors full and complete freedom to enter, reside in and depart freely and unhindered from the Republic of Benin. The same shall apply with regard to their materials, provisions, supplies, equipment and other goods, including spare parts and land vehicles, vessels and aircraft.

12. The Government shall grant special facilities for the speedy processing of formalities for the entry into and departure from the territory of Benin by all members of MINUSMA, including the military component.

13. For that purpose, the Special Representative and members of MINUSMA shall be exempt from passport and visa regulations, immigration inspection and restrictions and the payment of all duties and fees on entering into or departing from the territory of Benin. They shall, however, complete arrival and departure cards. They shall also be exempt from any regulations governing the residence of aliens in the Republic of Benin, including registration, but shall not be considered as acquiring any right to permanent residence or domicile in the Republic of Benin. For the purpose of such entry to the Republic of Benin or departure from the country, the appropriate authorities of Benin shall only require members of MINUSMA to have:

(i) An individual or collective movement order issued by or under the authority of the Special Representative or any appropriate authority of a participating State; and

(ii) a personal identity card, bearing a number and the name and photograph of the holder, issued by the Special Representative (hereinafter "MINUSMA identity card"), except upon first entry, when a United Nations *laissez-passer*, national passport or personal identity card issued by the United Nations or the appropriate authorities of a participating State shall be accepted in lieu of a MINUSMA identity card.

14. The Government shall issue promptly, free of charge and without any restrictions, all necessary visas, permits, authorizations and licences to contractors within three days of the submission of a request.

VI. Travel, means of transport, permits and authorizations

15. The Government shall guarantee full and complete freedom of movement throughout the country for members and contractors of MINUSMA, together with their goods, materials, provisions, supplies, equipment and other goods, including spare parts and means of transport.

16. Aircraft of MINUSMA shall respect security regulations that have been published and specifically communicated to MINUSMA by the civil aviation authority of the Republic of Benin.

17. The Government shall supply MINUSMA with the information necessary to facilitate its movements and ensure the security of its members and contractors, including maps and other information, such as information concerning the location of all hazards and obstacles, as necessary.

18. That freedom shall, with respect to large movements of personnel, equipment, vehicles, vessels or aircraft through airports or on railways, roads used for general traffic or navigable waterways within Benin, be coordinated with the Government.

19. MINUSMA and its members and contractors, together with the vehicles, vessels and aircraft of MINUSMA and its contractors, may use the roads, bridges, canals and other navigable waterways, port facilities, airfields and airspace of Benin without the payment of any form of monetary contributions, dues, tolls, user fees, airport taxes, landing fees, parking fees, overflight fees, port fees or charges, including wharfage and compulsory pilotage charges. However, MINUSMA shall not claim exemption from charges which are in fact charges for services rendered, it being understood that such charges shall be calculated at the most favourable rates.

20. Vehicles, aircraft and vessels of MINUSMA are not subject to licencing and registration by the Government, it being understood that all vehicles, aircraft and vessels shall carry third-party liability insurance.

21. The Government shall grant MINUSMA contractors and their employees the facilities they need in order to deliver all services provided exclusively to MINUSMA or to deliver, for the exclusive use of MINUSMA, materials, provisions, supplies, equipment and other goods, including spare parts and means of transport that MINUSMA or the contractors themselves may require.

22. The Government shall accept as valid permits and licences issued by the Special Representative for the operation by any member of MINUSMA, including locally recruited personnel, of any MINUSMA transport or communications equipment and for the practice of any profession or occupation in connection with the activities of MINUSMA, provided that no licence to drive or pilot MINUSMA transport equipment shall be issued to any person who is not already in possession of an appropriate and valid national licence.

23. The Government shall accept as valid, and where necessary validate, free of charge and without any restrictions, licences and certificates issued by the appropriate authorities in other States in respect of aircraft and vessels, including those operated by contractors exclusively for MINUSMA, provided that such licences and certificates are in conformity with international norms and practices.

24. Without prejudice to the foregoing, the Government further agrees to grant promptly, free of charge and without any restrictions, the necessary authorizations, licences and certificates, where required, for the acquisition, use, operation and maintenance of aircraft and vessels for MINUSMA.

VII. Tax exemptions and customs facilities

25. The Government shall grant MINUSMA and its contractors the right to:

(i) Import by the most convenient and direct means of land, air or maritime transport, free of duty, fees, taxes and other charges, without prohibition or restriction of any kind, all equipment, provisions, supplies, fuel, materials and other goods, including spare parts and means of transport, which are for the exclusive and official use of MINUSMA;

(ii) Clear ex customs and excise warehouse, free of duty, taxes, fees and charges and free of other prohibitions and restrictions, equipment, provisions, supplies, fuel, materials and other goods, including spare parts and means of transport, which are for the exclusive and official use of MINUSMA;

(iii) Export or re-export all goods and equipment, including spare parts and means of transport, all equipment, provisions, supplies, fuel, materials and other goods.

26. The Government shall promptly grant MINUSMA and its contractors, upon presentation by MINUSMA or by contractors of a consignment note, airway bill, cargo manifest or packing list, all necessary authorizations, permits and licences required for the import of equipment, provisions, supplies, fuel, materials and other goods, including spare parts and means of transport, used in support of MINUSMA, including with regard to import by contractors, free of any prohibitions and restrictions and without the payment of monetary contributions, duties, charges or taxes, in particular value-added tax.

27. The Government likewise undertakes to promptly grant all authorizations, permits and licenses required for the purchase or export of goods for which permits and licences are required, including in respect of purchase or export by contractors, free of any prohibitions and restrictions and without the payment of monetary contributions, duties, fees, charges or taxes.

VIII. United Nations flag, markings and identification

28. The Government recognizes the right of MINUSMA to display within Benin the United Nations flag on its headquarters, camps or other premises, aircraft, vehicles, vessels and otherwise as decided by the Special Representative.

29. Vehicles, aircraft and vessels of MINUSMA shall carry a distinctive United Nations identification, which shall be notified to the Government.

IX. Communications

30. With regard to communications, MINUSMA shall enjoy the facilities provided for in article III of the Convention.

31. The Government shall facilitate the establishment and maintenance of MINUSMA communications, including transnational communications, while respecting their privileged nature under the Convention. It recognizes the right of MINUSMA and its members to unrestricted communication by radio (including satellite, mobile and hand-held radio), telephone, email, facsimile or any other means, it being understood that the radio frequencies used shall be determined by MINUSMA in cooperation with the Government as quickly as possible. MINUSMA shall be exempt from any fees for and taxes on the allocation of frequencies. Connections to the local telephone networks shall be made after consultation and in accordance with arrangements with the Government. The use of the above-mentioned networks shall be charged at the most favourable rates.

32. Issues with respect to communications which may arise and which are not specifically provided for in the present Agreement shall be dealt with pursuant to the relevant provisions of the Convention.

X. Financial transactions, import of the personal effects of members of MINUSMA, transport of funds by members of MINUSMA

33. MINUSMA may hold funds and currency of any kind and operate accounts in any convertible currency, freely transfer its funds and currency within the territory of Benin and from one country to another, and freely convert any currency held by it to any other currency.

34. Internationally recruited members of MINUSMA shall have the right to import free of duty their personal effects in connection with their arrival in Benin.

35. MINUSMA and the Government may agree that a special vehicle licencing system, such as the one used for vehicles of members of diplomatic missions or international organizations, shall be used for the personal vehicles of internationally recruited members of MINUSMA serving in Benin, in accordance with the laws in force in Benin.

36. When entering or departing from Benin, members of MINUSMA may take with them such funds as the Special Representative certifies were received in pay and emoluments from the United Nations or from a participating State and are a reasonable residue thereof. Special arrangements may be made for the implementation of the present provisions in the interests of the Government and the members of MINUSMA.

37. The Special Representative shall cooperate with the Government and shall render all assistance within his or her power in ensuring the observance of the customs and fiscal laws and regulations of Benin by the members of MINUSMA, in accordance with the present Agreement.

XI. Premises of MINUSMA

38. The Government shall assist MINUSMA in obtaining the necessary premises for the conduct of its operational and administrative activities. Without prejudice to the fact that all such premises remain Beninese territory, the premises of MINUSMA, and United Nations archives and correspondence, shall be inviolable and subject to the exclusive authority and control of the United Nations. The Government shall guarantee free access to such premises. The Special Representative alone may consent to the entry of any government officials or of any other person not member of MINUSMA to such premises.

XII. Security

39. The Government shall ensure that the provisions of the Convention on the Safety of United Nations and Associated Personnel, adopted by the General Assembly of the United Nations on 9 December 1994, are applied in respect of MINUSMA and its property, assets, members and associated personnel.

40. The Government shall, with all the means at its disposal, take the necessary measures to protect MINUSMA, its property and its members in the exercise of their functions. Without prejudice to the fact that United Nations premises remain under the exclusive authority of the Organization, the Government shall, whenever the need is expressed

by the Special Representative, take the necessary measures to prevent and remedy any intrusion or damage to the premises and property of MINUSMA and any unlawful act that affects members of MINUSMA or associated personnel. The Government shall prevent any disturbance of the peace of MINUSMA and its members and associated personnel, and any violation of their integrity.

41. At the request of the Special Representative, the Government shall provide armed escorts to protect the members of MINUSMA in the exercise of their functions and, if necessary, to protect MINUSMA depots, equipment, vehicles, aircraft and vessels in the Republic of Benin.

XIII. Uniform and arms

42. While performing official duties, military personnel, United Nations military observers, United Nations military liaison officers, military advisers and civilian police components of MINUSMA, including members of formed police units, shall wear the national military or police uniform of their respective States with standard United Nations accoutrements. The wearing of civilian dress by the above-mentioned members of MINUSMA may be authorised by the Special Representative at other times.

43. United Nations Security Officers and Field Service Officers may wear the United Nations uniform.

44. The members of MINUSMA mentioned in this section may possess and carry, in the exercise of their official duties and in accordance with their orders, arms, ammunition and other military equipment and police equipment, including global positioning devices.

45. Apart from officers of close protection missions, MINUSMA agents authorized to bear arms in the exercise of their official duties shall be in uniform whenever they are bearing such arms.

46. MINUSMA and its members mentioned in this section shall be authorized to transport their arms and ammunition to and from the Republic of Mali through the territory of the Republic of Benin, in accordance with practical arrangements to be agreed between the Government and the Special Representative.

XIV. Criminal and civil proceedings in Benin involving members of MINUSMA

47. Should the Government consider that any member of MINUSMA has committed a criminal offence, it shall promptly inform the Special Representative and present to him or her any evidence available to it.

Subject to the provisions of paragraph 7 (*a*):

(*a*) If the accused person is a member of the civilian component or a civilian member of the military component, the Special Representative shall conduct any necessary supplementary inquiry and then agree with the Government whether or not criminal proceedings should be instituted. Failing such agreement, the provisions of paragraph 53 of the model status-of-forces agreement for peace-keeping operations (document A/45/594 of 9 October 1990, hereinafter the "model SOFA"), concerning the submission of disputes to a tribunal of three arbitrators, shall apply. In the event that criminal proceedings are instituted in accordance with the present Agreement, the competent courts and authorities of Benin shall ensure that the member of MINUSMA concerned is brought to trial and tried in accordance with international standards of justice, fairness and due process of law, as set out in the International Covenant on Civil and Political Rights adopted by the General Assembly of the United Nations on 16 December 1966 (hereinafter "the Pact"), to which Benin is a Party. The Government confirms that, in accordance with the Second Optional Protocol to the Covenant, to which Benin is a Party, the death penalty has been abolished in Benin and that accordingly no sentence of death will be imposed in the event of a guilty verdict;

(*b*) Military members of the military component of MINUSMA shall be subject to the exclusive jurisdiction of their respective participating States in respect of any criminal offences which may be committed by them in Benin or Mali.

48. If any civil proceeding is instituted against a member of MINUSMA before any Beninese court, the Special Representative shall be notified immediately, and he or she shall certify to the court whether or not the proceeding is related to the official duties of such member:

(*a*) If the Special Representative certifies that the proceeding is related to official duties, such proceeding shall be discontinued and the provisions of paragraph 51 of the model SOFA, concerning a standing claims commission, shall apply;

(*b*) If the Special Representative certifies that the proceeding is not related to official duties, the proceeding may continue. In that event, the courts and authorities of Benin shall grant the concerned member of MINUSMA the opportunity to exercise his or her rights in accordance with due process of law, and to ensure that the trial is conducted in accordance with international standards of justice, fairness and due process as set out in the Covenant. If the Special Representative certifies that a member of MINUSMA is unable, because of his or her official duties or authorized absence, to protect his or her interests in the proceeding, the court shall, at the defendant's request, suspend the proceeding until the elimination of the disability, but for no more than 90 days. Property of a member of MINUSMA that is certified by the Special Representative to be needed by the defendant for the fulfilment of his or her official duties shall be free from seizure for the enforcement of a judgement. The personal liberty of a member of MINUSMA shall not be restricted in a civil proceeding, whether to enforce a judgement, to compel an oath or for any other reason.

XV. Miscellaneous and final provisions

49. Without prejudice to the provisions of paragraph 48 of the present Agreement, the personnel of MINUSMA, including those recruited internationally, shall strive to amicably settle any disputes of a private law character that may arise with third parties in Benin.

50. The provisions of paragraphs 5 to 11 of General Assembly resolution 52/247, of 26 June 1998, shall apply to third-party claims against the United Nations for damage resulting from or attributable to the presence or activities of MINUSMA or its members in Benin.

51. Any dispute or claim of a private law character to which MINUSMA is a party and over which the courts of Benin do not have jurisdiction because of any provision of the present Agreement shall be settled by a standing claims commission to be established for that purpose. The commission shall be established and operate in accordance with the provisions of paragraph 52 of the model SOFA.

52. Disputes concerning the terms of employment and conditions of service of locally recruited personnel shall be settled by the administrative procedures to be established by the Special Representative.

53. The Special Representative and the Government shall take all necessary measures to ensure close and reciprocal liaison at every appropriate level, including for the purpose of resolving any differences concerning the interpretation of the present Agreement.

54. All differences between the United Nations and the Government arising out of the interpretation or application of the present arrangements which involve a question of principle concerning the Convention and cannot be resolved through dialogue between the parties shall be dealt with in accordance with the procedure set out in section 30 of the Convention.

55. The Special Representative and the Government may conclude supplemental arrangements to the present Agreement.

56. Wherever the present Agreement refers to privileges, immunities and rights of MINUSMA and to the facilities Benin undertakes to provide to MINUSMA and its members, the Government shall have the ultimate responsibility for the implementation and fulfilment of such privileges, immunities, rights and facilities by the appropriate local authorities.

57. The present Agreement shall enter into force on the date of its signature by or for the Secretary-General of the United Nations and the Government.

In witness whereof, the undersigned, being the duly authorized plenipotentiary of the Government and the duly appointed representative of the United Nations, have, on behalf of the Parties, signed the present Agreement.

Done at Cotonou on 8 February 2017, in two original copies in the French language.

For the United Nations	For the Government of the Republic of Benin
[*Signed*] Mahamat Saleh Annadif	[*Signed*] Aurélien A. Agbénonci
Special Representative of the Secretary-General for Mali	Minister for Foreign Affairs and Cooperation

(*b*) Host State Agreement between the United Nations and the Kingdom of the Netherlands concerning the United Nations Office for the Coordination of Humanitarian Affairs—Humanitarian Data Centre. New York, 11 July 2017*

Whereas the United Nations through its Office for the Coordination of Humanitarian Affairs (OCHA) wishes to establish a Humanitarian Data Centre in The Hague, the Kingdom of the Netherlands, to facilitate the implementation of its mandate;

* Entered into force on 11 July 2017 by signature, in accordance with article 38. United Nations registration no. I-54746.

Whereas the Kingdom of the Netherlands wishes to facilitate the work of OCHA in this regard;

Desiring to lay down conditions concerning the privileges, immunities, facilities, and services of and related to the OCHA Humanitarian Data Centre in the territory of the Kingdom of the Netherlands as are necessary for the fulfilment of the purposes of the Centre;

The United Nations and the Kingdom of the Netherlands have agreed as follows:

Part I: General Provisions

Article 1. Use of terms

For the purpose of this Agreement:

(*a*) "Agreement" means this Host State Agreement between the Kingdom of the Netherlands and the United Nations;

(*b*) "host State" means the Kingdom of the Netherlands;

(*c*) "OCHA" means the United Nations Office for the Coordination of Humanitarian Affairs;

(*d*) "Centre" means the OCHA Humanitarian Data Centre in The Hague;

(*e*) "Parties" means the United Nations and the host State;

(*f*) "General Convention" means the Convention on the Privileges and Immunities of the United Nations adopted by the General Assembly of the United Nations on 13 February 1946, to which the Kingdom of the Netherlands acceded on 19 April 1948;

(*g*) "Vienna Convention" means the Vienna Convention on Diplomatic Relations of 18 April 1961, to which the Kingdom of the Netherlands acceded on 7 September 1984;

(*h*) The "Head of the Centre" means the person appointed by the Secretary-General to head the Centre;

(*i*) "officials of the Centre" means the Head of the Centre and staff who are assigned by the Secretary-General to serve as part of the Centre;

(*j*) "experts on mission" means persons, other than officials, who, on a temporary basis, perform missions for the Centre;

(*k*) "interns" means students and recent graduates (degree obtained within the last twelve (12) months) who have been accepted by OCHA into its internship programme for the purpose of performing certain tasks for the Centre without receiving a salary from OCHA. An intern shall in no case fall under the definition of an official of the Centre;

(*l*) "family members forming part of the household" means:

- spouses and registered partners of a staff member of the Centre continuously living with the staff member;
- children of the staff member under the age of 18;
- children of the staff member up to and including the age of 27 provided that they are unmarried, financially dependent on their parents and living continuously with their parent(s) during their posting in the host State; and
- any such member of the immediate family of the staff member of the Centre as may be agreed upon between the host State and the United Nations.

(*m*) "premises" means buildings, parts of buildings and areas, including installations and facilities made available to, maintained, occupied or used by the Centre in the territory of the host State in consultation with the host State, in connection with its functions and purposes;

(*n*) "property" means, without prejudice to the General Convention, all property (be it material, real, or intellectual), assets, and funds belonging to the Centre or held or administered by the Centre in the territory of the host State in furtherance of its functions;

(*o*) "Ministry of Foreign Affairs" means the Ministry of Foreign Affairs of the host State;

(*p*) "competent authorities" means national, provincial, municipal and other competent authorities under the laws, regulations and customs of the host State;

(*q*) "Secretary-General" means the Secretary-General of the United Nations.

Article 2. Establishment of the Centre

1. OCHA shall establish a Centre in the host State, to carry out functions in accordance with the mandate of OCHA set out in United Nations General Assembly resolution 46/182 and subsequent resolutions.

2. The seat of the Centre shall be located in The Hague, the Netherlands.

Article 3. Purpose and scope of this Agreement

This Agreement shall regulate matters relating to or arising out of the establishment and the proper functioning of the Centre in the host State. It shall, *inter alia*, create conditions conducive to the stability and independence of the Centre and facilitate its smooth and efficient functioning.

PART II: STATUS OF THE CENTRE

Article 4. Juridical personality

1. The Centre shall possess full juridical personality in the host State. This shall, in particular, include the capacity:

(*a*) to contract;

(*b*) to acquire and dispose of movable and immovable property; and

(*c*) to institute legal proceedings.

2. For the purpose of this Article, the Centre shall be represented by the Head of the Centre.

Article 5. Privileges, immunities and facilities

1. The Centre shall enjoy, in the territory of the host State, such privileges, immunities and facilities as are necessary for the fulfilment of its purposes.

2. The General Convention shall apply to the Centre and the archives of the Centre. Furthermore, the Centre shall enjoy the privileges, immunities and facilities set out in this Agreement.

Article 6. Inviolability of the premises

1. The premises shall be inviolable. The competent authorities shall ensure that the Centre is not dispossessed and/or deprived of all or any part of its premises without its express consent.

2. The competent authorities shall not enter the premises to perform any official duty, except with the express consent, or at the request of the Head of the Centre, or an official designated by him or her. Judicial actions and the service or execution of legal process, including the seizure of private property, cannot be enforced on the premises except with the consent of, and in accordance with conditions approved by, the Head of the Centre, or an official designated by him or her.

3. In case of fire or other emergency requiring prompt protective action, or in the event that the competent authorities have reasonable cause to believe that such an emergency has occurred or is about to occur on the premises, the consent of the Head of the Centre, or an official designated by him or her, to any necessary entry into the premises shall be presumed if neither of them can be contacted in time.

4. Subject to paragraphs 1, 2 and 3 of this Article, the competent authorities shall take the necessary action to protect the premises against fire or other emergency.

5. The Centre shall prevent its premises from being used as a refuge by persons who are avoiding arrest or the proper administration of justice under any law of the host State.

Article 7. Protection of the premises and their vicinity

1. The competent authorities of the host State shall exercise due diligence to ensure that the security and tranquility of the premises are not impaired by any person or group(s) of persons attempting unauthorized entry into or onto the premises or creating disturbances in the immediate vicinity. As may be required for this purpose, the host State shall provide adequate police protection on the boundaries and in the vicinity of the premises.

2. If so requested by the Head of the Centre, or an official designated by him or her, the competent authorities shall, in consultation with the Head of the Centre, or an official designated by him or her, to the extent it is deemed necessary by the competent authorities, provide adequate protection, including police protection, for the preservation of law and order on the premises and for the removal of persons therefrom.

3. The Centre shall provide the competent authorities with all information relevant to the security and protection of the premises.

Article 8. Law and authority on the premises

1. The premises of the Centre shall be under the control and authority of the Centre, as provided for in this Agreement.

2. Except as otherwise provided in this Agreement or the General Convention, the laws and regulations of the host State shall apply on the premises.

3. The Centre shall apply United Nations rules and regulations as are necessary for the carrying out of its functions. No laws or regulations of the host State which are inconsistent with the rules and regulations of the United Nations under this paragraph shall, to the extent of such inconsistency, be applicable on the premises.

4. Any dispute between the Centre and the host State as to whether a rule or regulation of the United Nations comes within the ambit of this Article or as to whether a law or regulation of the host State is inconsistent with a rule or regulation of the United Nations under this Article shall promptly be settled by the procedure under Article 34 of this Agreement. Pending such settlement, the rule or regulation that is the subject of the dispute shall apply and the law or regulation of the host State shall be inapplicable on the premises to the extent that the Centre claims it to be inconsistent with the rule or regulation in question.

Article 9. Public services for the premises

1. The competent authorities shall secure, upon the request of the Head of the Centre, or an official designated by him or her, on fair and equitable conditions, the public services needed by the Centre such as, but not limited to, postal, telephone, telegraphic services, any means of communication, electricity, water, gas, sewage, collection of waste, fire protection, local transportation and cleaning of public streets, including snow removal.

2. In cases where the services referred to in paragraph 1 of this Article are made available to the Centre by the competent authorities, or where the prices thereof are under their control, the rates for such services shall not exceed the lowest comparable rates accorded to essential agencies and organs of the host State.

3. In case of any interruption or threatened interruption of any such services, the Centre shall be accorded the priority given to essential agencies and organs of the host State, and the host State shall take steps accordingly to ensure that the work of the Centre is not prejudiced.

4. Upon request of the competent authorities, the Head of the Centre, or an official designated by him or her, shall make suitable arrangements to enable duly authorized representatives of the appropriate public services to inspect, repair, maintain, reconstruct and relocate utilities, conduits, mains and sewers on the premises under conditions which shall not unreasonably disturb the carrying out of the functions of the Centre.

Article 10. Flags, emblems and markings

The Centre shall be entitled to display the United Nations' flags, emblems and markings on its premises and to display its flag on vehicles used for official purposes.

Article 11. Funds, assets and other property

1. The Centre, its funds, assets and other property, wherever located and by whomsoever held, shall enjoy immunity from every form of legal process, except insofar as in any particular case the Secretary-General has expressly waived its immunity. It is understood, however, that no waiver of immunity shall extend to any measure of execution.

2. Funds, assets and other property of the Centre, wherever located and by whomsoever held, shall be immune from search, seizure, requisition, confiscation, expropriation and any other form of interference, whether by executive, administrative, judicial or legislative action.

3. To the extent necessary to carry out the functions of the Centre, funds, assets and other property of the Centre, wherever located and by whomsoever held, shall be exempt from restrictions, regulations, controls or moratoria of any nature.

Article 12. Inviolability of archives, documents and materials

The archives of the Centre, and all papers and documents in whatever form, and materials being sent to or from the Centre, held by the Centre or belonging to it, wherever located and by whomsoever held, shall be inviolable.

Article 13. Facilities and immunities in respect of communications

1. The Centre shall have the right to operate all appropriate means of communication, including electronic means of communication, and shall have the right to use codes or ciphers for its official communications and correspondence. The official communications and correspondence of the Centre shall be inviolable.

2. The Centre shall have the right to dispatch and receive correspondence and other materials or communications by courier or in sealed bags, which shall enjoy the same privileges, immunities and facilities as diplomatic couriers and bags.

3. No censorship shall be applied to the official communications or correspondence of the Centre. Such immunity from censorship shall extend to printed matter, photographic and electronic data communications and other forms of communication as may be used by the Centre. The Centre shall have the right to operate radio, satellite and other telecommunication equipment on the United Nations-registered frequencies or frequencies allocated to it by the host State in accordance with its national procedures. The host State shall endeavour to allocate to the Centre, to the extent possible, frequencies for which it has applied.

Article 14. Freedom of financial assets from restrictions

Without being restricted by financial controls, regulations, notification requirements in respect of financial transactions, or moratoria of any kind, the Centre:

(*a*) may hold and use funds, gold or negotiable instruments of any kind and maintain and operate accounts in any currency and convert any currency held by it into any other currency;

(*b*) shall be free to transfer its funds, gold or currency from one country to another, or within the host State; and

(*c*) may raise funds in any manner which it deems desirable, except that with respect to the raising of funds within the host State, the Centre shall obtain the concurrence of the competent authorities.

Article 15. Exemption from taxes and duties for the Centre and its property

1. Within the scope of its official activities, the Centre, its assets, income and other property shall be exempt from:

(*a*) all direct taxes, whether levied by national, provincial or local authorities, which includes, *inter alia*, corporation tax;

(*b*) import and export taxes and duties (belastingen bij invoer en uitvoer);

(*c*) motor vehicle tax (motorrijtuigenbelasting);

(*d*) tax on passenger motor vehicles and motorcycles (belasting van personenauto's en motorrijwielen);

(*e*) value added tax (omzetbelasting) paid on goods and services supplied on a recurring basis or involving considerable expenditure;

(*f*) excise duties (accijnzen) included in the price of alcoholic beverages and hydrocarbons such as fuel oils and motor fuels, as well as chemical supplies;

(*g*) real property transfer tax (overdrachtsbelasting);

(*h*) insurance tax (assurantiebelasting);

(*i*) energy tax (energiebelasting);

(*j*) tax on mains water (belasting op leidingwater); and

(*k*) any other taxes and duties of a substantially similar character as the taxes provided for in this paragraph, levied in the host State subsequent to the date of entry into force of this Agreement.

2. The exemptions provided for in paragraph 1, subparagraphs *e*) through *k*), of this Article may be granted by way of a refund. These exemptions shall be applied in accordance with the formal requirements of the host State. These requirements, however, shall not affect the general principles laid down in paragraph 1 of this Article.

3. Goods acquired or imported under the terms set out in paragraph 1 of this Article shall not be sold, let out, given away or otherwise disposed of in the host State, except in accordance with conditions agreed upon with the host State.

4. The Centre shall not claim exemption from taxes which are, in fact, no more than charges for public utility services provided at a fixed rate according to the amount of services rendered and which can be specifically identified, described and itemized.

Article 16. Exemption from import and export restrictions

The Centre shall be exempt from all restrictions on imports and exports in respect of articles imported or exported by the Centre for its official use and in respect of its publications.

Part III: Privileges, Immunities and Facilities Accorded to Persons under this Agreement

Article 17. Privileges, immunities and facilities of the Head of the Centre

1. The Head of the Centre, together with members of his or her family forming part of the household who are not nationals or permanent residents of the host State, shall enjoy the privileges, immunities, exemptions and facilities accorded to heads of diplomatic missions in accordance with international law and in particular under the General Convention and the provisions of the Vienna Convention. He or she shall, *inter alia*, enjoy:

(*a*) personal inviolability, including immunity from arrest or detention or any other restriction of their liberty and from seizure of their personal baggage;

(*b*) immunity from criminal, civil and administrative jurisdiction;

(*c*) inviolability of all papers and documents in whatever form and materials;

(*d*) immunity from national service obligations;

(*e*) exemption from immigration restrictions and alien registration;

(*f*) exemption from taxation on salaries, emoluments and allowances paid to them in respect of their employment with OCHA;

(*g*) the same privileges in respect of currency and exchange facilities as are accorded to diplomatic agents;

(*h*) the same immunities and facilities in respect of their personal baggage as are accorded to diplomatic agents;

(*i*) the right to import free of duties and taxes, except payments for services, their furniture and effects at the time of first taking up their post in the host State, and to re-export their furniture and effects free of duties and taxes to their country of destination upon separation from OCHA;

(*j*) for the purpose of their communications with the Centre, the right to receive and send papers in whatever form; and

(*k*) the same repatriation facilities in time of international crisis as are accorded to diplomatic agents under the Vienna Convention.

2. The Head of the Centre shall continue to be accorded immunity from legal process of every kind in respect of words which were spoken or written and all acts which were performed in his or her official capacity even after he or she ceased to perform his or her functions for the Centre.

3. With respect to the inheritance and gift tax, which depends upon residence, periods during which the Head of the Centre is present in the host State for the discharge of his or her functions shall not be considered as periods of residence.

4. The host State shall not be obliged to exempt from income tax pensions or annuities paid to former Heads of the Centre and the members of their family forming part of the household.

5. Persons referred to in this Article who are nationals or permanent residents of the host State shall enjoy within the host State only the privileges, immunities and facilities under Article V, Section 18 and Article VII of the General Convention, together with the following modifications and supplementary provisions:

(*a*) immunity from legal process of every kind in respect of words spoken or written and all acts performed by them in their official capacity, which immunity shall continue to be accorded even after they have ceased to perform their functions for the Centre;

(*b*) inviolability of all official papers and documents in whatever form and materials;

(*c*) exemption from taxation on salaries, emoluments and allowances paid to them in respect of their employment with OCHA;

(*d*) for the purpose of their communications with the Centre the right to receive and send papers in whatever form; and

(*e*) the right to import free of duties and taxes, except payments for services, their furniture and effects at the time of first taking up their post in the host State.

6. Persons referred to in paragraph 5 of this Article shall not be subjected by the host State to any measure which may affect the free and independent performance of their functions for the Centre.

Article 18. Privileges, immunities and facilities of the other officials of the Centre

1. Officials of the Centre shall enjoy such privileges, immunities and facilities as are necessary for the independent performance of their functions. They shall enjoy privileges and immunities accorded to officials of the United Nations under Articles V and VII of the General Convention, including as modified and supplemented below:

(*a*) immunity from legal process of every kind in respect of words spoken or written and all acts performed by them in their official capacity, which immunity shall continue to be accorded even after they have ceased to perform their functions for the Centre;

(*b*) immunity from seizure and inspection of official baggage;

(*c*) inviolability of all official papers and documents in whatever form and materials;

(*d*) immunity from national service obligations;

(*e*) together with members of their family forming part of the household, exemption from immigration restrictions and alien registration;

(*f*) exemption from taxation on salaries, emoluments and allowances paid to them in respect of their employment with OCHA;

(*g*) the same privileges in respect of currency and exchange facilities as are accorded to the officials of comparable rank of diplomatic missions established in the host State;

(*h*) exemption from inspection of personal baggage, unless there are serious grounds for believing that the baggage contains articles the import or export of which is prohibited by law or controlled by the quarantine regulations of the host State; an inspection in such a case shall be conducted in the presence of the official concerned;

(*i*) together with members of their family forming part of the household, the same repatriation facilities in time of international crisis as are accorded to diplomatic agents under the Vienna Convention; and

(*j*) the right to import free of duties and taxes, except payments for services, their furniture and effects at the time of first taking up their post in the host State, and to re-export their furniture and effects free of duties and taxes to their country of destination upon separation from the Centre.

2. In addition to the privileges, immunities and facilities listed in paragraph 1 of this Article, officials of the Centre of P-5 level and above, together with members of their family forming part of the household who are not nationals or permanent residents of the host State, shall be accorded the same privileges, immunities and facilities as the host State accords to diplomatic agents of comparable rank of the diplomatic missions established in the host State in conformity with the Vienna Convention.

3. In addition to the privileges, immunities and facilities listed in paragraph 1 of this Article, officials of the Centre of P-4 level and below, together with members of their family forming part of the household who are not nationals or permanent residents of the host State, shall be accorded the same privileges, immunities and facilities as the host State accords to members of the administrative and technical and service staff of diplomatic missions established in the host State, in conformity with the Vienna Convention, provided that the immunity from criminal jurisdiction shall not extend to acts performed outside the course of their official duties.

4. With respect to the inheritance and gift tax, which depends upon residence, periods during which officials are present in the host State for the discharge of their functions shall not be considered as periods of residence.

5. The host State shall not be obliged to exempt from income tax pensions or annuities paid to former officials of the Centre and the members of their family forming part of the household.

6. Persons referred to in this Article who are nationals or permanent residents of the host State shall enjoy only the privileges, immunities and facilities under Article V, Section 18, and Article VII of the General Convention, including as modified and supplemented below:

(*a*) immunity from legal process of every kind in respect of words spoken or written and all acts performed by them in their official capacity, which immunity shall continue to be accorded even after they have ceased to perform their functions for the Centre;

(*b*) inviolability of all official papers and documents in whatever form and materials;

(*c*) exemption from taxation on salaries, emoluments and allowances paid to them in respect of their employment with OCHA; and

(*d*) the right to import free of duties and taxes, except payments for services, their furniture and effects at the time of first taking up their post in the host State.

7. Persons referred to in paragraph 6 under this Article shall not be subjected by the host State to any measure which may affect the free and independent performance of their functions for the Centre.

Article 19. Experts on mission for the Centre

1. Experts on mission for the Centre shall enjoy the privileges and immunities, exemptions and facilities as are necessary for the independent performance of their functions for the Centre, and in particular, shall enjoy the privileges and immunities, exemptions and facilities under Articles VI and VII of the General Convention.

2. Experts on mission for the Centre shall be provided by the Head of the Centre with a document certifying that they are performing functions for the Centre and specifying a time period for which their functions will last. This certificate shall be withdrawn prior to its expiry if the expert on mission for the Centre is no longer performing functions for the Centre.

Article 20. Employment of family members of officials of the Centre

1. Members of the family forming part of the household of an official of the Centre shall be authorized to engage in gainful employment in the host State for the duration of the term of office of the official concerned.

2. Members of the family forming part of the household of an official of the Centre who obtain gainful employment shall enjoy no immunity from criminal, civil or administrative jurisdiction with respect to matters arising in the course of or in connection with such employment. However, any measures of execution shall be taken without infringing the inviolability of their person or of their residence, if they are entitled to such inviolability.

3. In case of the insolvency of a person aged under eighteen (18) with respect to a claim arising out of gainful employment of that person, the Centre shall seek to ensure that the official of the Centre of whose family the person concerned is a member, meets their

private legal obligations that arise in this connection, and where necessary, the Secretary-General shall give prompt attention to a request for a waiver in this regard.

4. The employment referred to in paragraph 1 of this Article shall be in accordance with the legislation of the host State, including fiscal and social security legislation.

Article 21. Interns

1. Within eight (8) days after the commencement of an internship in the host State, the Centre shall request the Ministry of Foreign Affairs to register any intern in accordance with paragraph 2 of this Article.

2. Without prejudice to the applicable rules of the European Union with regard to the rights of citizens of a member state of the European Union, the European Economic Area, or Switzerland or their family members, the Ministry of Foreign Affairs shall register interns for a maximum period of six (6) months, provided that the Centre supplies the Ministry of Foreign Affairs with a declaration signed by them, accompanied by adequate proof, to the effect that:

(*a*) the intern entered the host State in accordance with the applicable immigration procedures;

(*b*) the intern has sufficient financial means for living expenses and for repatriation, as well as sufficient medical insurance (including coverage of costs of hospitalization for at least the duration of the internship plus one (1) month) and third party liability insurance, and shall not be a charge on the public purse in the host State;

(*c*) the intern shall not engage in gainful employment in the host State during his or her internship other than as an intern for the Centre;

(*d*) the intern shall not bring any family members to reside with him or her in the host State other than in accordance with the applicable immigration procedures; and

(*e*) the intern shall leave the host State within fourteen (14) days after the end of the internship, unless he or she is otherwise authorized to stay in the host State in accordance with the applicable immigration legislation.

3. In exceptional circumstances, the maximum period of six (6) months mentioned in paragraph 2 of this Article, may be extended once by a maximum period of six (6) months. However, the total period of the internship shall not exceed a period of one (1) year.

4. The Centre shall not incur liability for damage resulting from non-fulfilment of the conditions of the declaration referred to in paragraph 2 of this Article by interns registered in accordance with that paragraph.

5. Under this Agreement, interns shall not enjoy privileges, immunities and facilities within the host State.

Article 22. Personnel recruited locally and not otherwise covered by this Agreement, including such personnel assigned to hourly rates

Personnel recruited locally and assigned to hourly rates by OCHA and not otherwise covered by this Agreement shall be accorded immunity from legal process in respect of words spoken or written and all acts performed by them in their official capacity for the

Centre. The terms and conditions of employment of such individuals shall be in accordance with the relevant Regulations of OCHA.

Part IV: Waiver Of Privileges, Immunities, and Facilities

Article 23. Waiver of immunities

1. The privileges, immunities and facilities provided for in Articles 17, 18 and 19 of this Agreement are granted in the interests of the Centre and not for the personal benefit of the persons themselves.

2. The Secretary-General shall have the right and duty to waive the immunity granted under this Agreement of any person in any case where, in his opinion, the immunity would impede the course of justice and can be waived without prejudice to the interests of the Centre.

Part V: Cooperation between the Centre and the Host State

Section 1: General

Article 24. General cooperation between the Centre and the host State

1. Whenever this Agreement imposes obligations on the competent authorities, the ultimate responsibility for the fulfilment of such obligations shall rest with the Government of the host State.

2. The host State shall promptly inform the Centre of the office designated to serve as the official contact point and to be primarily responsible for all matters in relation to this Agreement, as well as of any subsequent changes in this regard.

3. The Head of the Centre, or an official designated by him or her, shall serve as the official contact point for the host State and shall be primarily responsible for all matters in relation to this Agreement. The host State shall be informed promptly about this designation and of any subsequent changes in this regard.

Article 25. Cooperation with the competent authorities

1. The Centre shall cooperate at all times with the competent authorities to facilitate the proper administration of justice and the enforcement of the laws of the host State, to secure the observance of police regulations and to prevent the occurrence of any abuse in connection with the privileges, immunities and facilities accorded under this Agreement.

2. The Centre and the host State shall cooperate on security matters, taking into account the public order and national security interests of the host State.

3. Without prejudice to their privileges, immunities and facilities, it is the duty of all persons enjoying such privileges, immunities and facilities to respect the laws and regulations of the host State and not to interfere in the internal affairs of the host State.

4. The Centre shall cooperate with the competent authorities responsible for health, safety at work, electronic communications and fire prevention.

5. The Centre shall observe all security directives as agreed with the host State, as well as all directives of the competent authorities responsible for fire prevention regulations.

Article 26. Notification and Identification Cards

1. With respect to officials, the Centre shall promptly, but within eight (8) days, notify the host State of their date of appointment. With respect to interns, the Centre shall promptly, but within eight (8) days, notify the host State of the date of acceptation of such persons into the internship programme of OCHA.

2. The Centre shall promptly, but within eight (8) days, notify the host State of the date of hiring of experts on missions, the date of hiring of persons in the personal employ of officials, and the date of hiring of personnel recruited locally in accordance with Article 22 of this Agreement.

3. In order to facilitate the entry and stay of the persons mentioned below, the Centre will promptly, and preferably no later than eight (8) days after the date of their first arrival in the host State, inform the host State of:

(*a*) the presence of officials of the Centre;

(*b*) the presence of members of the family forming part of the household of officials of the Centre;

(*c*) the presence of experts on mission;

(*d*) the presence of interns;

(*e*) the presence of persons in the personal employ of those referred to in subparagraph (*a*) of this paragraph;

(*f*) the date of the arrival of the persons referred to in subparagraphs (*a*), (*b*), (*c*), (*d*), and (*e*) of this paragraph.

4. With respect to the persons referred to in paragraphs 2 and 3 of this Article, the Centre shall promptly, but within eight (8) days, notify the host State of their final departure or the termination of their functions or their involvement with OCHA.

5. With respect to members of the family forming part of the household of officials of the Centre, the Centre shall, where appropriate, promptly, but within eight (8) days, notify the host State once a person has ceased to form part of the household.

6. With respect to persons in the personal employ of officials, the Centre shall, where appropriate, promptly, but within eight (8) days, notify the host State once a person is no longer in the personal employ of officials.

7. The host State shall issue an identity card which shall serve to identify the holder in relation to the competent authorities, to:

(*a*) officials of the Centre who are assigned to serve in the host State;

(*b*) members of the family forming part of the household of the persons referred to in paragraph 3(*a*) of this Article;

(*c*) interns, provided that they have been registered in accordance with Article 21(2) of this Agreement;

(*d*) experts on mission, provided that the Ministry of Foreign Affairs has been supplied with the document referred to under Article 19(2) of this Agreement;

(*e*) persons referred to in paragraph 3(*e*) of this Article.

8. Upon request, the host State shall issue an identity card which shall serve to identify the holder in relation to the competent authorities to personnel recruited locally in accordance with Article 22 of this Agreement.

9. At the final departure of the persons referred to in paragraphs 2 and 3 of this Article or when these persons have ceased to perform their functions, the identity card referred to in paragraph 7 and 8 of this Article shall be promptly, and not later than within fifteen (15) days, be returned by the Centre to the Ministry of Foreign Affairs. In case persons who have ceased to perform their functions are not able to return the identity card referred to in paragraph 7 and 8 of this Article within the specified time period, the Ministry of Foreign Affairs shall be consulted immediately.

Article 27. Social security regime

The social security systems of the United Nations offer coverage comparable to the coverage under the legislation of the host State. Accordingly, officials of the Centre to whom the aforementioned scheme applies shall be exempt from the social security provisions of the host State. Consequently, officials of the Centre shall not be covered against the risks described in the social security provisions of the host State.

SECTION 2: VISAS, PERMITS AND OTHER DOCUMENTS

Article 28. Entry, stay and departure

1. For purposes of official business of the persons listed below and the family members forming part of their household, the host State shall facilitate their entry into its territory, their departure from its territory and their transit to or from the premises of the Centre:

(*a*) the Head of the Centre;

(*b*) other officials of the Centre;

(*c*) experts on mission;

(*d*) interns.

2. This Article shall not prevent the requirement of reasonable evidence to be provided by the Centre to establish that persons claiming the treatment provided for in this Article fall under one of the categories in paragraph 1 above.

3. Visas which may be required by persons referred to in this Article shall be granted without charge and as promptly as possible.

4. Without prejudice to the provisions of the General Convention, all the aforementioned persons who are entitled to the privileges and immunities under this Agreement, shall enjoy these privileges and immunities from the moment they enter the territory of the host State to take up their posts or to undertake official Centre-related duties and shall come to an end within a reasonable period after the expiry or termination of their contracts of employment or completion of their Centre-related duties.

Article 29. Laissez-passer *and United Nations Certificate*

1. The host State shall recognize and accept the United Nations *laissez-passer* as a valid travel document. Where applicable, the host State further agrees to issue any required visas in the United Nations *laissez-passer.*

2. The host State shall recognize and accept in accordance with the provisions of Section 26 of the General Convention the United Nations certificate issued to persons travelling on the business of the Centre.

3. Holders of a *laissez-passer* or a certificate indicating that they are travelling on the business of the Centre shall be granted facilities for speedy travel.

Article 30. Driving licence

1. During their period of employment with the Centre, officials of the Centre, as well as members of their family forming part of the household and persons in the personal employ of those referred to in Article 26 paragraph 3(*a*) of this Agreement, shall be allowed to obtain from the host State a driving licence on presentation of their valid foreign driving licence or to continue to drive using their own valid foreign driving licence, provided they are in possession of an identity card issued by the host State in accordance with Article 26 of this Agreement.

2. During the period of their assignment, any person issued an identity card by the host State shall be allowed to continue to drive using their own valid foreign driving licence.

Section 3: Security, Safety and Protection of Persons Referred to in this Agreement

Article 31. Security, safety and protection of persons referred to in this Agreement

1. Without prejudice to the privileges, immunities and facilities granted under this Agreement, the competent authorities shall take effective and adequate action which may be required to ensure the security, safety and protection of persons referred to in this Agreement, indispensable for the proper functioning of the Centre, free from interference of any kind.

2. The Centre shall cooperate with the competent authorities with a view to facilitating the observance by all persons referred to in this Agreement of the directives necessary for their security and safety, as given to them by the competent authorities.

3. Without prejudice to their privileges, immunities and facilities, it is the duty of all persons referred to in this Agreement to observe the directives necessary for their security and safety, as given to them by the competent authorities.

Part VI: Final Provisions

Article 32. Supplementary arrangements and agreements

The Centre and the host State may, for the purpose of implementing this Agreement or of addressing matters not foreseen in this Agreement, make supplementary arrangements and agreements as appropriate.

Article 33. Settlement of disputes with third parties

OCHA shall make provisions for appropriate modes of settlement of:

(*a*) disputes arising out of contracts and other disputes of a private law character to which the Centre is a party; and (*b*) disputes involving any person referred to in this Agreement who, by reason of his or her official position or function in connection with the Centre, enjoys immunity, if such immunity has not been waived by the Secretary-General.

Article 34. Settlement of differences on the interpretation or application of this Agreement or supplementary arrangements or agreements

1. All differences arising out of the interpretation or application of this Agreement or supplementary arrangements or agreements between the Parties shall be settled by consultation, negotiation or other agreed mode of settlement.

2. If the difference is not settled in accordance with paragraph 1 of this Article within three months following a written request by one of the Parties to the difference, it shall, at the request of either Party, be referred to a Tribunal of three arbitrators. Each Party shall appoint one arbitrator, and the two arbitrators so appointed shall appoint a third, who shall be the chairperson of the Tribunal. If, within thirty days of the request for arbitration, a Party has not appointed an arbitrator, or if, within fifteen (15) days of the appointment of two arbitrators, the third arbitrator has not been appointed, either Party may request the President of the International Court of Justice to appoint the arbitrator referred to. The Tribunal shall determine its own procedures, provided that any two arbitrators shall constitute a quorum for all purposes, and all decisions shall require the agreement of any two arbitrators. The expenses of the Tribunal shall be borne by the Parties as assessed by the Tribunal. The arbitral award shall contain a statement of the reasons on which it is based and shall be final and binding on the Parties.

Article 35. Application

This Agreement shall apply to the part of the Kingdom of the Netherlands in Europe only.

Article 36. Amendments and review

1. This Agreement may be amended by mutual written consent of the Parties.

2. This Agreement shall be reviewed at the request of either Party.

Article 37. Interpretation of the Agreement, the General Convention and the Vienna Convention

1. This Agreement shall be interpreted in light of its primary purpose of enabling OCHA through opening and maintaining its Centre in the host State to fully and efficiently discharge its responsibilities and fulfil its purposes.

2. The provisions of this Agreement shall be complementary to the provisions of the General Convention and the Vienna Convention, the latter Convention only insofar as it is relevant for the diplomatic privileges, immunities and facilities accorded to the appropriate categories of persons referred to in this Agreement. Insofar as any provision of this Agreement and any provisions of the General Convention and the Vienna Convention relate to the same subject matter, each of these provisions shall be applicable and neither shall narrow the effect of the other.

Article 38. Entry into force and termination

1. This Agreement shall enter into force on the day of its signature.

2. This Agreement shall cease to be in force by mutual consent of the Parties, or if the Centre is removed from the territory of the host State or upon completion of the Centre's mandate, except for such provisions as may be applicable in connection with the orderly termination of the operations of the Centre in the host State and the disposition of its property therein, as well as provisions granting immunity from legal process of every kind in respect of words spoken or written or all acts performed in an official capacity under this Agreement.

In Witness Whereof, the undersigned, duly authorized thereto, have signed this Agreement.

Done at New York, on [11 July 2017], in duplicate, in the English language.

For the United Nations	For the Kingdom of the Netherlands
[*Signed*]	[*Signed*]

(*c*) Exchange of letters constituting an agreement between the United Nations and the Hashemite Kingdom of Jordan concerning the activities in Jordan of the United Nations Office of the Special Envoy for Yemen. New York, 23 March 2017 and 28 July 2017*

I

23 March 2017

Excellency,

1. I have the honour to refer to the Agreement on the Implementation Mechanism for the Transition Process in Yemen in Accordance with the Initiative of the Gulf Cooperation Council ("the Agreement"), signed in Riyadh on 23 November 2011, which requests the Secretary-General to "provide continuous assistance, in cooperation with other agencies, for the implementation of this Agreement".

2. I also have the honour to refer to United Nations Security Council resolutions 2014 (2011) of 21 October 2011, 2051 (2012) of 12 June 2012, 2140 (2014) of 26 February 2014, 2201 (2015) of 15 February 2015, 2204 (2015) of 25 February 2015, 2216 (2015) of 14 April 2015 and 2266 (2016) of 24 February 2016, by which the Council requested the Secretary-General to continue his good offices role with respect to the situation in Yemen. In its resolution 2051 (2012), the Security Council also welcomed the political engagement of the United Nations through a small presence in Yemen, consisting of a team of experts, to support the implementation of the transition process and to provide advice to the parties in conjunction with the Government of Yemen, in particular in support of the National Dialogue process.

3. I have the further honour to refer to the letter dated 18 June 2012 from the Secretary-General addressed to the President of the Security Council (S/2012/469), in

* Entered into force on 28 July 2017 by the exchange of the said letters, in accordance with their provisions. United Nations registration no. I-54810.

which the Secretary-General announced his intention to establish an Office of the Special Envoy for Yemen ("OSE-Yemen"), with a presence in Yemen to, *inter alia*, exercise the Secretary-General's good offices with a view to facilitating Yemen's transition and assisting in the implementation of the Agreement

4. I have the honour, moreover, to refer to the letter dated 24 May 2016 from the Secretary-General to the President of the Security Council (S/2016/488), in which the Secretary-General stated his intention to strengthen OSE-Yemen in order to undertake a number of functions and to move OSE-Yemen to Amman as soon as practicable, while maintaining the presence of OSE-Yemen in Sanaa. In a letter dated 26 May 2016 (S/2016/489), the President of the Security Council informed the Secretary-General that the members of the Security Council had taken note of the information contained in the letter of the Secretary-General and the proposed arrangement expressed therein.

5. If the temporary relocation of the headquarters of OSE-Yemen to Amman is acceptable to your Government, 1 trust that, consistently with its obligations pursuant to Article 2, paragraph 5, and Article 105 of the Charter of the United Nations, your Government will accord to OSE-Yemen and to its assets and members those rights, privileges and immunities, facilities and exemptions, that are necessary for the effective fulfilment of its functions. In this regard, 1 wish to propose that your Government accord to OSE-Yemen, its property, funds and assets and to its members the privileges and immunities, exemptions and facilities provided for in the Convention on the Privileges and Immunities of the United Nations of 13 February 1946 (the "Convention"), to which Jordan acceded on 3 January 1958 without any reservation—Facilities as provided herein are also required for the contractors and their employees engaged by the United Nations or OSE-Yemen to perform services exclusively for OSE-Yemen and/or supply exclusively to OSE-Yemen equipment, provisions, supplies, materials and other goods in support of OSE-Yemen (hereinafter referred to as "United Nations contractors").

6. I propose, in particular, that your Government extend to:

(*a*) the Special Envoy of the Secretary-General for Yemen, the Director of OSE-Yemen, the Chief of Staff of OSE-Yemen and such other high-ranking members of OSE-Yemen as may be agreed between the United Nations and the Government, the privileges and immunities, exemptions and facilities which are enjoyed by diplomatic envoys in accordance with international law;

(*b*) the officials of the United Nations assigned to serve with OSE-Yemen, the privileges and immunities to which they are entitled under Articles V and VII of the Convention. Officials of Jordanian nationality or with permanent residency status in Jordan shall enjoy only those privileges and immunities provided for in Section 18 of the Convention;

(*c*) Experts (other than United Nations officials) performing missions for OSE-Yemen shall be accorded the privileges and immunities provided for under Article VI and Section 26, Article VII of the Convention.

Without prejudice to the above, all members of OSE-Yemen, as listed in paragraph 6 (*a*), (*b*) and (*c*) above, shall enjoy immunity from legal process in respect of all words spoken and written and all acts performed by them in discharging their official duties.

7. The United Nations shall, from time to time, notify the Government of the names of the members of OSE-Yemen as listed in paragraph 6 (*a*), (*b*) and (*c*) above. It shall also

notify the Government of any changes in their status. The United Nations shall inform the Government of the names of the members of OSE-Yemen in advance of their official travel to Jordan unless, for reasons beyond its control, it is not practically possible for the United Nations to do so.

8. The Secretary-General shall have the right and duty to waive the immunity of any member of OSE-Yemen as listed in paragraph 6 (*a*), (*b*) and (*c*) above where, in his opinion, the immunity would impede the course of justice and can be waived without prejudice to the interests of the United Nations.

9. United Nations contractors, other than local contractors, shall be accorded repatriation facilities in time of crisis and their services provided to OSE-Yemen shall be exempt from direct taxes in Jordan. However, contractors will not be exempt from taxes which are, in fact, no more than charges for public utility services.

10. The privileges and immunities necessary for the fulfilment of the functions of OSE-Yemen also include:

(i) freedom of entry and exit without undue delay or hindrance of the members of OSE-Yemen as listed in paragraphs 6 (*a*), (*b*) and (*c*) above as well as OSE-Yemen's property, supplies, equipment, spare parts and means of transport and, to that end, prompt issuance by the Government, free of charge and without any restrictions, of all necessary visas, residency permits, licenses and permits. The Government shall, in accordance with its national law, allow United Nations contractors, their property, supplies, equipment, spare parts and means of transport, freedom of entry and exit without undue delay or hindrance and shall speedily process free of charge all requests for visas, licenses and permits without restrictions;

(ii) freedom of movement of its members and United Nations contractors, their property, equipment and means of transport, which shall as appropriate be coordinated with the Government OSE-Yemen, its members, United Nations contractors when providing services to OSE-Yemen, and their vehicles and aircraft shall use roads, bridges, canals, and other waters, port facilities and airfields without the payment of dues, tolls, landing fees, parking fees, overflight fees, port fees and charges, including wharfage charges. However, exemption from charges which are limited in amount to the approximate cost of services rendered will not be claimed;

(iii) the right to import, free of duty or other restrictions, equipment (including, *inter alia*, telecommunications equipment), provisions, supplies and other goods which are for the exclusive and official use of OSE-Yemen;

(iv) the right to re-export free of duty or other restrictions or otherwise dispose of equipment, as far as it is still usable, all unconsumed provisions, supplies and other goods so imported or cleared ex customs and excise warehouse which are not transferred, or otherwise disposed of, on terms and conditions to be agreed upon with the Government or an entity nominated by the Government;

(v) issuance without undue delay by the Government of all necessary authorizations, permits and licenses for the importation or re-exportation or purchase of equipment, provisions, supplies, materials and other goods used in support of OSE-Yemen, including in respect of importation or re-exportation or purchase by United Nations contractors in support of OSE-Yemen, free of any restrictions and without payment of duties, charges or taxes including value-added tax;

(vi) the right to be issued with diplomatic license plate numbers for the operation of vehicles used in support of OSE-Yemen, and acceptance by the Government of driving permits or licenses issued by the United Nations for the operation of those vehicles;

(vii) acceptance by the Government, or where necessary validation without delay by the Government, free of charge and without any restriction, of licenses and certificates already issued by appropriate authorities in other States in respect of aircraft used in support of OSE-Yemen; issuance without delay by the Government, free of charge and without any restrictions, of necessary authorizations, licenses and certificates, where required, for the acquisition, use, operation and maintenance of aircraft used in support of OSE-Yemen; it being understood that aircraft used in support of OSE-Yemen shall comply with the applicable international regulations and standards;

(viii) the right to fly the United Nations flag and place distinctive United Nations identification on premises, vehicles and aircraft used in support of OSE-Yemen;

(ix) the right to enjoy in the territory of Jordan for its official communications treatment not less favourable than that accorded by the Government to any other Government OSE-Yemen shall have the right to communicate by radio, satellite or other forms of communication with United Nations Headquarters and between the various offices and to connect with the United Nations radio and satellite network, and to communicate by telephone, facsimile and other electronic data systems. The frequencies on which the communication by radio will operate shall be decided upon on terms and conditions to be agreed with the Government;

(x) the right to make arrangements through its own facilities for the processing and transport of private mail addressed to or emanating from members of OSE-Yemen. The Government shall be informed, prior to the setting up of such arrangements, of their nature and details. It shall not interfere with or apply censorship to the mail of OSE-Yemen or its members.

11. The Government shall assist OSE-Yemen, as necessary, in obtaining such areas for headquarters or other premises as may be necessary for the conduct of the operational and administrative activities of OSE-Yemen. Without prejudice to the fact that all such premises remain Jordanian territory, they shall be inviolable.

12. The Government undertakes to assist OSE-Yemen as far as possible in obtaining equipment, provisions, supplies, materials and other goods and services from local sources required for its subsistence and operations. In respect of equipment, provisions, supplies, materials and other goods purchased locally by OSE-Yemen or by United Nations contractors for the official and exclusive use of OSE-Yemen, the Government shall make appropriate administrative arrangements for the remission or return of any excise or tax payable as part of the price. The Government shall exempt OSE-Yemen and United Nations contractors from general sales taxes in respect of all local purchases made exclusively for

official OSE-Yemen purposes. In making purchases on the local market, OSE-Yemen shall, on the basis of observations made and information provided by the Government in that respect, avoid any adverse effect on the local economy.

13. The Government shall take all appropriate measures to ensure the security of members of OSE-Yemen as listed in paragraphs 6 (*a*), (*b*) and (*c*) above. In particular it shall take all appropriate steps to protect members of OSE-Yemen, their equipment and premises from attack or any action, that prevents them from discharging their mandate. OSE-Yemen and its members shall cooperate to the fullest extent possible with the Government in this regard. This is without prejudice to the fact that all premises of OSE-Yemen are inviolable.

14. The Government confirms that its national law defines certain crimes that would apply to the acts set out below and which are punishable by appropriate penalties:

(*a*) a murder, kidnapping or other attack upon the person or liberty of an individual;

(*b*) a violent attack upon official premises;

(*c*) a violent attack upon the private accommodation or the means of transportation of any individual likely to endanger his or her person or liberty;

(*d*) a threat to commit any such attack with the objective of compelling a physical or juridical person to do or to refrain from doing any act;

(*e*) an attempt to commit any such attack; and

(*f*) an act constituting participation as an accomplice in any such attack, or in an attempt to commit such attack, or in organizing or ordering others to commit such attack.

15. Jordan, in accordance with and to the extent provided for under its national laws, shall exercise jurisdiction over the crimes set out in paragraph 14 above committed against members or premises of OSE-Yemen: (*a*) when the crime was committed in its territory; (*b*) when the alleged offender is one of its nationals; (*c*) when the alleged offender, other than a member of OSE-Yemen, is present in its territory, unless it has extradited such a person to the State on whose territory the crime was committed, or to the State of his or her nationality, or to another State that has jurisdiction over the crime.

16. The Government shall, in accordance with and to the extent provided for under the national laws, submit to its competent authorities for the purposes of prosecution under its national laws without exception and without delay cases involving persons accused of crimes described in paragraph 14 above committed against members or premises of OSE-Yemen who are present within its territory (if the Government does not extradite them), as well as cases involving those persons that are subject to its criminal jurisdiction who are accused of other crimes in relation to OSE-Yemen or its members which, if committed in relation to the forces of the Government or against the local civilian population, would have rendered such acts crimes liable to prosecution. Those authorities shall take their decision in the same manner as in the case of any other offence of a similar level of gravity under the laws of Jordan and under the same conditions.

17. OSE-Yemen and its members as listed in paragraphs 6 (*a*), (*b*) and (*c*) above shall, in so far as it is consistent with the provisions of this Agreement, respect all local laws and regulations.

18. It is further understood that operative paragraphs 5–11, inclusive, of General Assembly resolution 52/247 of 26 June 1998 apply in respect of third-party claims against the United Nations resulting from or attributable to OSE-Yemen or the activities of its members.

19. Any dispute between the United Nations and the Government concerning the interpretation or application of this Agreement, except for a dispute that is regulated by Section 30 of the Convention or Section 32 of the Convention on the Privileges and Immunities of the Specialized Agencies, shall be resolved by negotiations or other agreed mode of settlement.

20. Without prejudice to existing agreements regarding their legal status and operations in Jordan, the above-mentioned arrangements may, as appropriate, be extended to specific Specialized and related Agencies and offices, funds and programmes of the United Nations, their property, funds and assets and their officials and experts on mission that are established in Jordan to perform functions in relation to OSE-Yemen, provided that this is done with the written consent of the Special Envoy, the Specialized or related Agency or office, fund or programme concerned and the Government.

21. If the above provisions meet with your approval, I would propose that this letter and your reply thereto constitute an agreement between the United Nations and the Government of Jordan with immediate effect. This Agreement shall remain in force for one year and is automatically renewed thereafter unless terminated by either party in writing giving at least 60 days' notice. This Agreement may be supplemented by additional agreements, assurances, or understandings.

I would like to take this opportunity to express my gratitude to the Government of Jordan for the support provided to OSE-Yemen in facilitating its tasks.

Please accept, Excellency, the assurances of my highest consideration.

Yours sincerely,

[*Signed*] Jeffrey Feltman
Under-Secretary-General for Political Affairs

II

SC/ME/7/1188
July 28th, 2017

Excellency,

I have the honour to refer to your letter of 23 March 2017 (DPA/MEWAD/2017/04551) concerning the activities in Jordan of the United Nations Office of the Special Envoy for Yemen.

In reply, I have the honour to confirm that the terms of your proposal are acceptable to the Government of Jordan.

Consequently, your letter and this reply thereto shall constitute an agreement between the Government of Jordan and the United Nations with immediate effect.

Please accept, Excellency, the assurances of my highest consideration.

[*Signed*] Sima Babous
Ambassador
Permanent Representative

III

23 March 2017

Excellency,

In connection with the proposed exchange of letters between the United Nations and the Government of Jordan concerning the activities in Jordan of the United Nations Office of the Special Envoy for Yemen (OSE-Yemen), I should like, on behalf of the United Nations, to state the following:

(i) OSE-Yemen, its members and contractors shall exercise their freedom of movement in Jordan in accordance with the exclusion zones and security concerns of the Government of Jordan;

(ii) OSE-Yemen will carry out its functions in accordance with its mandate and will not be involved in the political activities of the Yemeni community based in Jordan;

(iii) The maximum number of international staff of OSE-Yemen who are to be deployed to Amman in 2017 is not expected to exceed 70. This number is subject to change, depending on the operational requirements of OSE-Yemen and the decisions of the General Assembly. The United Nations will inform your Government at the beginning of each calendar year of the maximum number of international staff who, it is envisaged, will be deployed to Amman during the course of that year; and

(iv) Meetings with the parties to the situation in Yemen and events organized by OSE-Yemen involving such parties shall only take place in Jordan with the prior approval of, and subject to arrangements to be agreed with, your Government. OSE-Yemen will inform the Government in advance of the names of the participants.

If the foregoing meets with your approval, I would propose that this letter and your reply thereto constitute a supplementary agreement to the exchange of letters between the United Nations and the Government of Jordan concerning the activities in Jordan of the United Nations Office of the Special Envoy for Yemen.

Please accept, Excellency, the assurances of my highest consideration.

[*Signed*] Jeffrey Feltman
Under-Secretary-General for Political Affairs

IV

SC/ME/7/1189

July 28th, 2017

Excellency,

I have the honour to refer to your letter dated 23 March 2017 (DPA/MEWAD/2017/4551) in connection with the proposed exchange of letters between the United Nations and the Government of Jordan concerning the activities in Jordan of the United Nations Office of the Special Envoy for Yemen.

In reply, I have the honour to confirm that the terms of your letter are acceptable to the Government of Jordan.

Consequently, your letter and this reply thereto shall constitute a supplementary agreement to the exchange of the above-mentioned letters between the Government of Jordan and the United Nations concerning the activities in Jordan of the United Nations Office of the Special Envoy for Yemen.

Please accept, Excellency, the assurances of my highest consideration.

[*Signed*] SIMA BABOUS
Ambassador
Permanent Representative

(*d*) Memorandum of understanding between the Argentine Republic and the United Nations on south-south and triangular cooperation for achieving the 2030 agenda. Building innovative and inclusive partnerships. Buenos Aires, 7 September 2017*

The Argentine Republic, represented by the Ministry of Foreign Affairs and Worship (hereinafter referred to as the "Argentine Republic") and the United Nations, represented by the Department of Economic and Social Affairs (hereinafter referred to as "United Nations");

Desiring to make arrangements concerning the organization of the Development Cooperation Forum (DCF) Argentina Republic High-level Symposium on "South-South and Triangular Cooperation for achieving the 2030 Agenda. Building Innovative and Inclusive Partnerships" and a series of pre-meetings and side events (hereinafter referred to as "the Symposium");

Have reached the following understanding:

1. The Symposium will be organized by the Argentine Republic in cooperation with the United Nations and will be held from 6 to 8 September 2017 at the San Martin Palace in Buenos Aires, Argentine Republic. The Symposium is within the scope of General Assembly Resolutions 61/16 of 20 November 2006 on the Strengthening of the Economic and Social Council and 70/299 of 29 July 2016 on Follow-up and review of the 2030 Agenda for Sustainable Development at the global level.

2. The Symposium will be attended by the following participants:

(*a*) Up to 120 representatives from governments, United Nations system organizations and other multilateral institutions, civil society, academia, parliaments, local governments, philanthropic organizations and the private sector;

(*b*) The President of the United Nations Economic and Social Council (ECOSOC);

(*c*) Up to 9 officials from the United Nations; and

(*d*) Up to 20 representatives from the Argentine Republic and other national stakeholders.

---

* Entered into force on 7 September 2017 by signature, in accordance with paragraph 15. United Nations registration no. I-54718.

3. The maximum number of participants will be 150. The final list of participants will be determined by the United Nations in consultation with the Argentine Republic prior to the holding of the Symposium.

4. The Symposium will be conducted in English, French and Spanish.

5. The United Nations will be responsible for:

(*a*) The provision of substantive and logistical support before, during and after the Symposium, including the preparation of the appropriate documentation and the report of the Symposium in consultation with the Argentine Republic;

(*b*) The sending of official invitations to participants, as specified in paragraphs 2(*a*), 2(*b*) and 2(*d*).

6. The Argentine Republic will provide at its own cost, the following:

(*a*) The issuance of round-trip airline tickets and the payment of terminal expenses and daily subsistence allowance in accordance with the prevailing United Nations rates as set by the International Civil Service Commission for; (i) the President of the United Nations Economic and Social Council (ECOSOC) as specified in 2(*b*); and (ii) for up to 9 officials from the United Nations as specified in 2(*c*), as agreed between the Argentine Republic and the United Nations;

(*b*) The issuance of round-trip airline tickets and the payment of terminal expenses and daily subsistence allowance for up to 40 funded participants from among the participants as specified in paragraph 2 (*a*) in accordance with the rates established in the Argentinian law;

(*c*) Transportation arrangements between the airport and the hotel for high-level participants, President of the United Nations Economic and Social Council (ECOSOC) and Under-Secretary-General for Economic and Social Affairs, as agreed between the Argentine Republic and the United Nations;

(*d*) Local staff to assist with the planning and any necessary administrative, logistical and technical support during the Symposium, including for: (i) set-up of the Symposium and side event rooms (technical and audio components, seating, nameplates, etc.); (ii) reproduction of symposium materials before and during the Symposium, as agreed between the Argentine Republic and the United Nations and taking into account paragraph 5(*a*); and (iii) registration of participants, issuance of badges and other related secretarial and conference services;

(*e*) Event planner to coordinate all aspects of the organization of the symposium; support team to provide support in the preparation and follow-up of the symposium; media personnel team for press briefings and media stakeout; ushers/usherettes to assist and guide symposium participants; and photographers/videographers to cover the symposium;

(*f*) One or two professional moderators to prepare for the symposium and assist in moderating the discussions during the Symposium;

(*g*) Symposium premises and facilities, including one large conference room, one medium-sized conference room, four small break-out rooms, one multi-functional room; technical equipment, conference services and other requirements; audio-video recording of all the Symposium; language and translation of background documentation; and interpretation in English, French and Spanish;

(*h*) Hospitality during the Symposium, including breakfasts, coffee breaks, luncheons and dinners, as agreed between the Argentine Republic and the United Nations;

(*i*) Office for the use by the President of ECOSOC and Under-Secretary-General for Economic and Social Affairs and office space for other officials from the United Nations (3 separate rooms) with computers, printer, internet access, international telephone lines or equivalent, photocopying equipment and stationery, as agreed between the Argentine Republic and the United Nations.

7. The cost of transportation (air fares, terminal expenses), local accommodation, daily subsistence allowance, and other related costs for the rest of the participants as specified in paragraphs 2(*a*) and 2(*d*) are not covered under paragraph 6(*a*) and it will be the responsibility of the participants and their respective organizations.

8. Except for making factual statements concerning the Symposium, the Argentine Republic will not use the name, including any abbreviation thereof, or emblem of the United Nations, for any purposes whatsoever without the prior written approval of the United Nations. Under no circumstances will authorization be granted to use the name or emblem of the United Nations for commercial purposes. Any communication materials related to the Symposium (*i.e.*, press release, press statements, banners, signage, brochures, posters, folders and other related materials) will be subject to review and prior approval between the Argentine Republic and the United Nations.

9. The Argentine Republic confirms that the representatives of States, officials of the United Nations and of other United Nations Specialized Agencies, and experts on missions to the Symposium will be accorded such privileges, immunities, facilities and courtesies as are necessary for performing their functions in connection with the Symposium, in accordance with the Convention on the Privileges and Immunities of the United Nations (hereinafter referred to as "the General Convention") and the Convention on the Privileges and Immunities of the Specialized Agencies (hereinafter referred to as "the Specialized Agencies Convention"), as well as in accordance with customary international law. In particular, representatives of States will enjoy the privileges and immunities accorded under Article IV of the General Convention. The experts on missions to the Symposium shall enjoy the privileges and immunities accorded to experts on mission for the United Nations under articles VI and VII of the General Convention. Officials of the United Nations participating in or performing functions in connection with the Symposium shall enjoy the privileges and immunities provided under articles V and VII of the General Convention. Officials of the Specialized Agencies participating in the Symposium shall be accorded the privileges and immunities provided under articles VI and VIII of the Specialized Agencies Convention.

10. The Argentine Republic confirms that visas and unimpeded entry into and exit from the Argentine Republic will be granted at no cost to the representatives of States, officials of the United Nations and of other United Nations Specialized Agencies, all participants and experts on missions participating in the Symposium who hold an Official or Diplomatic Passport. The Argentine Republic agrees that the UN shall bear no costs for visas and entry permits, where required.

11. The Argentine Republic will provide, at its own expense, such protection as may be required to ensure the safety of the participants and the effective functioning of the Symposium in an atmosphere of security.

12. The Argentine Republic will be responsible for dealing with any action, claim or other demand against the United Nations or its officials and arising out of:

(*a*) injury to persons or damage to or loss of property in the Symposium premises that are provided by or are under the control of the Argentine Republic for the Symposium;

(*b*) injury to persons or damage to or loss of property caused by, or incurred in using the transportation services provided by or under the control of the Argentine Republic;

(*c*) the employment for the Symposium of personnel provided or arranged by the Argentine Republic.

And the Argentine Republic will indemnify and hold harmless the United Nations and its officials in respect of any such action, claim or other demand.

13. This Memorandum may be amended with the mutual written consent of the Argentine Republic and the United Nations.

14. Except for a dispute concerning privileges and immunities, which will be subject to Section 30 of the Convention on the Privileges and Immunities of the United Nations, any differences arising out of the interpretation or application of this Memorandum will be settled amicably through consultations and negotiations by the Argentine Republic and the United Nations, unless in any case it is agreed by the Argentine Republic and the United Nations to have recourse to another mode of settlement.

15. This Memorandum will come into effect on the date of signature and remain in effect for the duration of the Symposium and for such additional period as is necessary for its preparation and for all matters relating to any of its provisions to be settled.

Signed on September 2017, in duplicate in English language.

For the Argentine Republic	For the United Nations Department of Economic and Social Affairs
[*Signed*] JORGE MARCELO-FAURIE	[*Signed*] LIU ZHENMIN
Minister of Foreign Affairs and Worship	Under-Secretary-General for Economic and Social Affairs

(*e*) Agreement between the United Nations and the Government of the Republic of Colombia concerning the status of the United Nations Verification Mission in Colombia. New York, 19 October 2017*

I. DEFINITIONS

For the purpose of the present Agreement the following definitions shall apply:

* Entered into force 19 October 2017 by signature, in accordance with section XI . United Nations registration no. I-54745.

(*a*) "the Mission" means the United Nations Verification Mission in Colombia, established in accordance with Security Council resolution 2366 (2017) of 10 July 2017;

(*b*) "Special Representative" means the Special Representative of the Secretary-General and Head of the United Nations Verification Mission in Colombia appointed by the Secretary-General of the United Nations. Any reference to the Special Representative in this Agreement shall, except in paragraph 23, include any member of the Mission to whom he or she delegates a specified function or authority. It shall also include, including in paragraph 23, any member of the Mission whom the Secretary-General may designate as acting Head of Mission of the Mission following the death or resignation of the Special Representative;

(*c*) "member of the Mission" means:

(i) the Special Representative;

(ii) officials of the United Nations assigned to serve with the Mission;

(iii) United Nations Volunteers recruited through the United Nations Volunteer programme assigned to serve with the Mission;

(iv) unarmed international observers assigned to serve with the Mission pursuant to Security Council resolutions 2366 (2017) [of 10 July 2017], 2377 (2017) of 14 September 2017 and 2381 (2017) of 5 October 2017;

(v) other persons assigned to perform missions for the Mission and who fall within the scope of Article VI of the Convention.

(*d*) "the Government" means the Government of the Republic of Colombia;

(*e*) "the territory" means the territory of the Republic of Colombia;

(*f*) "the Convention" means the Convention on the Privileges and Immunities of the United Nations adopted by the General Assembly of the United Nations on 13 February 1946, to which the Republic of Colombia is a Party;

(*g*) "contractors" means persons, other than members of the Mission, engaged by the United Nations, including juridical as well as natural persons and their employees and sub-contractors, to perform services for the Mission or to supply equipment, provisions, supplies, fuel, materials or other goods, including spare parts and means of transport, in support of the Mission activities. Exemptions and facilities that are to be accorded with respect to the provision of such services and the supply of such goods must be solicited by the Mission. Such contractors shall not be considered beneficiaries of the present Agreement;

(*h*) "vehicles" means vehicles of the United Nations and operated by members of the Mission or contractors in support of the Mission activities;

(*i*) "aircraft" means aircraft of the United Nations and operated by members of the Mission or contractors in support of the Mission activities;

(*j*) "vessels" means maritime or riverine vessels of the United Nations and operated by members of the Mission or contractors in support of the Mission activities;

(*k*) "Standard Basic Assistance Agreement" means the Agreement between the Government of Colombia and the United Nations Development Programme concerning assistance by the United Nations Development Programme to the Government of Colombia, which was signed on 29 May 1974 and entered into force on 23 January 1975.

II. Application of the Present Agreement

2. Unless specifically provided otherwise, the provisions of the present Agreement and any obligation undertaken by the Government and any privilege, immunity, exemption, facility or concession granted to the Mission or to any member of the Mission or to contractors, when solicited by the Mission, shall apply in Colombia only.

III. Application of the Convention

3. The Mission, its property, funds and assets and its members shall enjoy the privileges and immunities, exemptions and facilities specified in the present Agreement, as well as those provided for in the Convention.

IV. Status of the Mission

4. The Mission and its members shall refrain from any action or activity incompatible with the impartial and international nature of their duties or inconsistent with the spirit of the present Agreement. The Mission and its members shall respect all local laws and regulations. The Special Representative shall take all appropriate measures to ensure the observance of these obligations.

5. The Government undertakes to respect the exclusively international nature of the Mission.

United Nations flag, markings and identification

6. The Government recognizes the right of the Mission to display the United Nations flag on its headquarters and other premises, on its vehicles and vessels and otherwise as decided by the Special Representative.

7. Vehicles, aircraft and vessels of the Mission shall carry a distinctive United Nations identification, which shall be notified to the Government.

Communications

8. The Mission shall enjoy the facilities in respect of communications that are provided for in Article III of the Convention. Issues with respect to communications which may arise and which are not specifically provided for in the present Agreement shall be dealt with pursuant to the relevant provisions of the Convention.

9. Subject to the provisions of paragraph 8:

(*a*) the Mission shall have the right to install and to operate radio sending, receiving and repeater stations, as well as satellite systems, in order to connect appropriate points within the territory of Colombia with each other and with United Nations offices in other countries and to exchange telephone, voice, facsimile and other electronic data with the United Nations global telecommunications network. Such telecommunication services shall be operated in accordance with the International Telecommunication Convention and Regulations. The frequencies on which such services may operate shall be decided upon in cooperation with the Government. If no decision has been reached fifteen (15) working days after the matter has been raised by the Mission with the Government, the Government shall immediately allocate suitable frequencies to the Mission for this purpose. The Mission shall be exempt from any and all taxes on the allocation of frequencies for this purpose, as well as from any and all taxes on, and all fees for, their use. However, the Mission will not claim exemption from fees which are in fact no more than charges for services rendered;

(*b*) the Mission shall enjoy, within the territory of Colombia, the right to unrestricted communication by radio (including satellite, mobile and hand-held radio), telephone, electronic mail, facsimile or any other means, and of establishing the necessary facilities for maintaining such communications within and between premises of the Mission, including the laying of cables and land lines and the establishment of fixed and mobile radio sending, receiving and repeater stations. The frequencies on which the radio may operate and the areas of land on which sending, receiving and repeater stations may be erected shall be decided upon in cooperation with the Government. If no decision has been reached fifteen (15) working days after the matter has been raised by the Mission with the Government, the Government shall immediately allocate suitable frequencies or land, as the case may be, to the Mission for these purposes. The Mission shall be exempt from any and all taxes on the allocation of frequencies for this purpose, as well as from any and all taxes on, and any and all fees for, their use. However, the Mission will not claim exemption from fees which are in fact no more than charges for services rendered. Connections with local telephone and electronic data systems may be made only after consultation and in accordance with arrangements made with the Government;

(*c*) the Mission shall have the right to disseminate to the public in Colombia and to the public abroad information relating to its mandate through electronic media, including websites, social media, webcasts, data feeds and online and messaging services. The content of data disseminated through such media shall be under the exclusive editorial control of the Mission and shall not be subject to any form of censorship. The Mission shall be exempt from any prohibitions or restrictions regarding the production or dissemination of such data, including any requirement that permits be obtained or issued for such purposes;

(*d*) the Mission shall have the right to disseminate to the public in Colombia information relating to its mandate through official printed materials and publications, which the Mission may produce itself or through private publishing companies in Colombia. The content of such materials and publications shall be under the exclusive editorial control of the Mission and shall not be subject to any form of censorship. The Mission shall be exempt from any prohibitions or restrictions regarding the production or the publication or dissemination of such official materials and publications, including any requirement that permits be obtained or issued for such purposes. This exemption shall also apply to private publishing companies in Colombia which the Mission may use for the production, publication or dissemination of such materials or publications;

(*e*) the Mission may make arrangements through its own facilities for the processing and transport of private mail addressed to or emanating from members of the Mission. The Government shall be informed of the nature of such arrangements and shall not interfere with or apply censorship to the mail of the Mission or its members. In the event that postal arrangements applying to private mail of members of the Mission are extended to transfer of currency or the transport of packages and parcels, the conditions under which such operations are conducted shall be agreed with the Government.

Travel and transport

10. The Mission, its members and contractors, together with their property, equipment, provisions, supplies, fuel, materials and other goods, including spare parts, as well as vehicles and aircraft, including the vehicles and aircraft of contractors used exclusively in the performance of services for the Mission, shall enjoy full freedom of movement without delay throughout Colombia by the most direct route possible for the purpose of executing the tasks defined in the Mission's mandate and without the need for travel permits or prior authorization or notification, except in the case of movements by air, which shall comply with the generally applicable procedural requirements for flight planning and operations within the airspace of Colombia as promulgated, and as specifically notified to the Mission, by the civil aviation authority of Colombia. The Government shall, where necessary, provide the Mission with maps and other information, where available, including maps of and information on the location of minefields and other dangers and impediments, which may be useful in facilitating the Mission's movements and ensuring the safety and security of its members.

11. Vehicles, aircraft, and vessels shall not be subject to registration or licensing by the Government, it being understood that copies of all relevant certificates issued by appropriate authorities in other States in respect of aircraft shall be provided by the Mission to the civil aviation authority of Colombia and that all vehicles, vessels and aircraft shall carry third party insurance. The Mission shall provide the Government, from time to time, with updated lists of the Mission vehicles.

12. The Mission and its members and contractors, as well as vehicles, aircraft, and vessels, including vehicles, aircraft and vessels of its contractors used exclusively in the performance of services for the Mission, may use roads, bridges, ferries, waterways, airfields, airspace and port facilities without the payment of any form of monetary contributions, dues, tolls, user fees or charges, including airport taxes, landing fees, parking fees, overflight fees, port fees or charges, including wharfage and compulsory pilotage charges. However, the Mission will not claim exemption from charges which are in fact charges for services rendered. Exemptions and facilities that are to be accorded pursuant to this paragraph must be solicited by the Mission.

Privileges and immunities of the Mission

13. The Mission, as a subsidiary organ of the United Nations, enjoys the status, rights, privileges and immunities, exemptions and facilities of the United Nations pursuant to and in accordance with the Convention. The Government recognizes in particular:

(*a*) The right of the Mission, including through contractors, to import, by the most convenient and direct route by land, sea or air, free of duty, taxes, fees and charges and free of prohibitions and restrictions, equipment, provisions, supplies, fuel, materials and other goods which are for the exclusive and official use of the Mission;

(*b*) The right of the Mission, including through contractors, to clear ex customs and excise warehouse, free of duty, taxes, fees and charges and free of prohibitions and restrictions, equipment, provisions, supplies, fuel, materials and other goods which are for the exclusive and official use of the Mission;

(*c*) The right of the Mission, including through contractors, to re-export or otherwise dispose of all usable items of property and equipment and all unconsumed provisions, supplies, materials, fuel and other goods which have previously been imported, cleared ex customs and excise warehouse or purchased locally for the exclusive and official use of the Mission and which are not transferred, or otherwise disposed of, on terms and conditions to be agreed upon, to the competent local authorities of Colombia.

To the end that such importation, clearances, transfer or exportation may be effected with the least possible delay, a mutually satisfactory procedure, including documentation, shall be agreed between the Mission and the Government at the earliest possible date.

Exemptions and facilities that are to be accorded pursuant to this paragraph must be solicited by the Mission.

For the purposes of this paragraph, neither the Mission nor contractors will claim exemption from fees and charges which are in fact no more than charges for services rendered.

V. Facilities for the Mission and its Contractors

Premises required for conducting the operational and administrative activities of the Mission

14. The Government shall provide, without cost to the Mission where possible, and in agreement with the Special Representative, for the duration of the Mission's mandate and for such time thereafter as may be strictly required for the orderly winding down of the Mission's activities, such areas for headquarters and other premises as may be necessary for the conduct of the operational and administrative activities of the Mission, including the establishment of the necessary facilities for maintaining communications in accordance with paragraph 9. Without prejudice to the fact that all such premises remain territory of Colombia, they shall be inviolable and subject to the exclusive control and authority of the United Nations. The Government shall guarantee unimpeded access to such United Nations premises.

15. The Government undertakes to assist the Mission in obtaining and making available, where applicable, water, sewerage, electricity and other facilities. Where such utilities or facilities are not provided free of charge, payment shall be made by the Mission on terms to be agreed with the competent authority. The Mission shall be responsible for the maintenance and upkeep of facilities so provided. In the event of interruption or threatened interruption of service, the Government undertakes to give, as far as is within its powers, the same priority to the needs of the Mission as to essential government services.

16. The Mission shall have the right, where necessary, to generate, within its premises, electricity for its use and to transmit and distribute such electricity. It shall also have the right, where necessary, to construct water wells and waste water treatment systems within its premises for its own use.

17. Any government official or any other person seeking entry to the Mission premises shall obtain the permission of the Special Representative.

Provisions, supplies and services, and sanitary arrangements

18. The Government agrees to grant promptly, upon presentation by the Mission of a bill of lading, airway bill, cargo manifest or packing list, all necessary authorizations, permits and licenses required for the import of equipment, provisions, supplies, fuel, materials

and other goods for the exclusive and official use of the Mission, including in respect of import by contractors, free of any prohibitions and restrictions and without the payment of monetary contributions or duties, fees, charges or taxes, including value-added tax. The Government likewise agrees to grant promptly all necessary authorizations, permits and licenses required for the purchase or export of such goods, including in respect of purchase or export by contractors, free of any prohibitions and restrictions and without the payment of monetary contributions, duties, fees, charges or taxes. Special arrangements shall be made between the Government and the Mission for the implementation of the present paragraph.

19. The Government undertakes to assist the Mission as far as possible in obtaining equipment, provisions, supplies, fuel, materials and other goods and services from local sources required for its subsistence and operations. In respect of equipment, provisions, supplies, fuel, materials and other goods and services purchased locally by the Mission or by contractors for the official and exclusive use of the Mission, the Government shall make appropriate administrative arrangements for the exemption of any excise, tax or monetary contribution payable as part of the price. Upon request by the Mission, the Government shall exempt the Mission and contractors from general sales taxes in respect of all local purchases for the exclusive and official use of the Mission. In making purchases on the local market, the Mission shall, on the basis of observations made and information provided by the Government in that respect, avoid any adverse effect on the local economy.

20. For the proper performance of the services in support of the Mission provided by contractors, other than by nationals of Colombia resident in Colombia, the Government agrees to provide such contractors with facilities for their entry into and departure from Colombia, without delay or hindrance, and for their residence in Colombia, as well as for their repatriation in time of crisis. For this purpose, the Government shall promptly issue to such contractors, free of charge and without any restrictions, all necessary visas, licenses and permits. The Mission's contractors, other than nationals of Colombia resident in Colombia, shall be accorded the necessary facilities and privileges in regard to services and goods provided to the Mission for its official and exclusive use. Exemptions and facilities that are to be accorded pursuant to this paragraph must be solicited by the Mission.

21. The Mission and the Government shall cooperate with respect to sanitary services and shall extend to each other their fullest cooperation in matters concerning health, particularly with respect to the control of communicable diseases, in accordance with international conventions.

Recruitment of local personnel

22. The Mission may recruit locally such personnel as it requires. Upon the request of the Special Representative, the Government undertakes to facilitate the recruitment of qualified local staff by the Mission.

VI. Status of the Members of the Mission

Privileges and immunities

23. The Special Representative, the Deputy Special Representative of the Secretary-General, the Chief of Staff, the chief international observer and members of the Mission of equivalent ranks as notified by the Special Representative shall have the status specified in

Sections 19 and 27 of the Convention and shall be accorded the privileges and immunities, exemptions and facilities there provided.

24. Officials of the United Nations assigned to serve with the Mission remain officials of the United Nations entitled, subject to paragraph 27, to the privileges and immunities, exemptions and facilities set out in Articles V and VII of the Convention.

25. United Nations Volunteers recruited through the United Nations Volunteer programme assigned to serve with the Mission shall be assimilated to officials of the United Nations assigned to serve with the Mission and shall accordingly enjoy the privileges and immunities, exemptions and facilities set out in Articles V and VII of the Convention.

26. International observers and personnel other than United Nations officials whose names are for that purpose notified to the Government by the Special Representative shall be considered as experts on mission within the meaning of Article VI of the Convention and shall enjoy the privileges, immunities, exemptions and facilities set out in that Article and in Article VII.

27. Members of the Mission shall be exempt from taxation on the pay and emoluments received from the United Nations. Members of the Mission other than locally recruited personnel shall also be exempt from taxation on any income received from outside Colombia, as well as from all other direct taxes, except municipal rates for services enjoyed, and from all registration fees and charges.

28. Members of the Mission, other than those recruited locally, shall have the right to import free of duty their personal effects in connection with their arrival in Colombia. They shall be subject to the laws and regulations of Colombia governing customs and foreign exchange with respect to personal property not required by them by reason of their presence in Colombia with the Mission. The Government shall, as far as possible, give priority for the speedy processing of entry and exit formalities for members of the Mission, other than those recruited locally, upon prior written notification. On departure from Colombia, members of the Mission, other than those recruited locally, may, notwithstanding the above-mentioned exchange regulations, take with them such funds as the Special Representative certifies were received in pay and emoluments from the United Nations and are a reasonable residue thereof. Special arrangements shall be made for the implementation of the present provisions in the interests of the Government and the members of the Mission.

29. The Special Representative shall cooperate with the Government and shall render all assistance within his or her power in ensuring the observance of the customs and fiscal laws and regulations of Colombia by members of the Mission, in accordance with the present Agreement.

30. Privileges and immunities are granted to members of the Mission in the interests of the United Nations and not for the personal benefit of the individuals themselves. The Secretary General of the United Nations shall have the right and the duty to waive the immunity of any member of the Mission in any case where, in his or her opinion, the immunity would impede the course of justice and can be waived without prejudice to the interests of the United Nations.

Entry, residence and departure

31. The Special Representative and members of the Mission shall, whenever so required by the Special Representative, have the right to enter into, reside in and depart from Colombia.

32. The Government undertakes to facilitate the entry into and departure from Colombia, without delay or hindrance, of the Special Representative and members of the Mission and shall be kept informed of such movements. For this purpose, the Special Representative and members of the Mission shall be exempt from passport and visa regulations and immigration inspection and restrictions, as well as from payment of any taxes, fees or charges on entering into or departing from Colombia. Members of the Mission shall also be exempt from any regulations governing the residence of aliens in Colombia, including registration and residence and work permits, but shall not be considered as acquiring any right to permanent residence or domicile in Colombia.

33. For the purpose of such entry or departure, members of the Mission shall only be required to have a personal numbered identity card issued in accordance with paragraph 34 of the present Agreement, except in the case of first entry into Colombia, when the United Nations laissez passer, national passport or personal identity card issued by the United Nations shall be accepted in lieu of the said identity card.

Identification

34. The Special Representative shall issue to each member of the Mission before or as soon as possible after such member's first entry into Colombia, as well as to all locally recruited personnel, and to contractors, a numbered identity card, showing the bearer's name and photograph. Except as provided for in paragraph 33 of the present Agreement, such identity card shall be the only document required of a member of the Mission.

35. Members of the Mission, as well as its locally recruited personnel and contractors, shall be required to present, but not to surrender, their Mission identity cards upon the demand of an appropriate official of the Government.

Uniforms and arms

36. United Nations Security Officers may wear the United Nations uniform. United Nations Security Officers may possess and carry items of security equipment, including global positioning devices, while on official duty in accordance with their orders within the premises of the Mission. When doing so, they must wear the United Nations uniform, except as otherwise provided in paragraph 37.

37. United Nations close protection officers and United Nations Security Officers serving in close protection details may carry firearms and ammunition and wear civilian clothes while performing their official functions.

38. The Mission shall keep the Government informed of the number and the types of firearms carried by United Nations close protection officers and United Nations Security Officers serving in close protection details and of the names of the officers carrying them.

Permits and licenses

39. The Government agrees to accept as valid, without tax or fee, a permit or license issued by the Special Representative for the operation by any member of the Mission of any [of] the Mission vehicle or vessel or for the practice of any profession or occupation in connection with the functioning of the Mission, provided that no such permit or license

shall be issued to any member of the Mission who is not already in possession of an appropriate and valid national or international permit or license for the purpose concerned.

40. The Government agrees to accept as valid, and where necessary promptly to validate, free of charge and without any restrictions, licenses and certificates already issued by appropriate authorities in other States in respect of aircraft and vessels, including those operated by contractors exclusively for the Mission. Without prejudice to the foregoing, the Government further agrees to grant promptly, free of charge and without any restrictions, necessary authorizations, licenses and certificates, where required, for the acquisition, use, operation and maintenance of aircraft and vessels.

41. The Government further agrees to accept as valid, without tax or fee, permits or licenses issued by the Special Representative to United Nations close protection officers and to United Nations Security Officers serving in close protection details who are members of the Mission for the carrying or use of firearms or ammunition in strict connection with the functioning of the Mission.

Arrest and transfer of custody and mutual assistance

42. The Special Representative shall take all appropriate measures to ensure the maintenance of discipline and good order among members of the Mission. To this end, United Nations Security Officers shall patrol the areas provided for headquarters and other premises of the Mission and areas where its members are deployed. Elsewhere, such personnel shall be employed only subject to arrangements with the Government and in liaison with it in so far as such employment is necessary to maintain discipline and order among members of the Mission.

43. The personnel mentioned in paragraph 42 above may apprehend any other person caught in flagrante delicto on the premises of the Mission. Such other person shall be delivered immediately to the nearest appropriate official of the competent authority of the Republic of Colombia for the purpose of dealing with any offence or disturbance on such premises.

44. Subject to the provisions of paragraphs 23 and 26, competent authorities of the Republic of Colombia may:

(*a*) take into custody any member of the Mission when so requested by the Special Representative and consistent with Colombian law; or

(*b*) apprehend a member of the Mission caught in flagrante delicto in the commission or attempted commission of a criminal offence. Such person shall be delivered immediately, together with any item collected, to the nearest appropriate representative of the Mission, after which the provisions of paragraph 49 shall apply.

45. The Mission shall afford to the competent authorities of the Republic of Colombia the widest possible measure of assistance in connection with investigations or court proceedings carried out by Colombia or by other States in respect of criminal offences committed in the territory of Colombia. The competent authorities of the Republic of Colombia shall afford to the Mission the widest possible measure of assistance in connection with administrative investigations or proceedings in respect of such offences. Assistance afforded pursuant to the present paragraph may include taking statements from other persons, the collection and production of evidence and, if possible, the handing over of items connected with an offence. The handing over of any such items may be made

subject to their return on the terms specified by the authority delivering them. When assistance is provided pursuant to the present paragraph on a confidential basis, the other party shall take the necessary measures to ensure that such confidentiality is respected and maintained. Each party shall notify the other of the disposition of any case in the outcome of which the other may have an interest or in which there has been a transfer of custody under the provisions of paragraphs 43 or 44.

Safety and security

46. The Government shall ensure that the provisions of the Convention on the Safety of United Nations and Associated Personnel (the "Safety Convention") and its Optional Protocol, to both of which Colombia is party, are applied to and in respect of the Mission, its members and their equipment and premises.

47. Upon the request of the Special Representative, the Government shall provide such security as necessary to protect the Mission, its members and their equipment during the exercise of their functions. The Government shall also, upon request of the Special Representative, provide such assistance to the Mission as may be necessary for the evacuation of members of the Mission and their equipment from rural areas in the event of medical emergency or an emergency threatening their security.

Jurisdiction

48. Members of the Mission shall be immune from legal process in respect of words spoken or written and all acts performed by them in their official capacity. Such immunity shall continue even after they cease to be members of or employed by or for the Mission and after the expiration of the other provisions of the present Agreement.

49. Should the Government consider that any member of the Mission has committed a criminal offence, it shall promptly inform the Special Representative and present to him or her any information available to it. Subject to the provisions of paragraph 23, the Special Representative shall determine whether or not the conduct of the member of the Mission concerned is related to his or her official duties and whether he or she is therefore immune from legal process. If the Special Representative determines that the member of the Mission is immune from legal process and the Secretary-General does not waive that immunity, criminal proceedings may not be instituted against that member with respect to the criminal offence concerned. If the Government disagrees with the determination of the Special Representative, the question shall be resolved as provided in paragraph 55 of the present Agreement. If the Special Representative determines that the member of the Mission is not immune from legal process or that he or she is immune but the Secretary-General waives that immunity, criminal proceedings may be instituted against that member with respect to the criminal offence concerned. In the event that criminal proceedings are instituted in accordance with the present Agreement, the courts and authorities of Colombia shall ensure that the member of the Mission concerned is prosecuted, brought to trial and tried in accordance with international standards of justice, fairness and due process of law, as set out in the International Covenant on Civil and Political Rights (the "Covenant"), to which Colombia is a Party. The Government confirms that, in accordance with the Second Optional Protocol to the Covenant, to which Colombia is a

Party, the death penalty has been abolished in Colombia and that accordingly no sentence of death will be imposed or carried out in the event of a guilty verdict.

50. If any civil proceeding is instituted against a member of the Mission before any court of Colombia, the Special Representative shall be notified immediately and he or she shall certify to the court whether or not the proceeding is related to the official duties of such member.

(*a*) If the Special Representative certifies that the proceeding is related to official duties, such proceeding shall be discontinued and the provisions of paragraph 53 of the present Agreement shall apply;

(*b*) If the Special Representative certifies that the proceeding is not related to official duties, the proceeding may continue in accordance with the national laws of Colombia. In that event, the courts and authorities of Colombia shall grant the member of the Mission concerned sufficient opportunity to safeguard his or her rights in accordance with due process of law and shall ensure that the suit is conducted in accordance with international standards of justice, fairness and due process of law, as set out in the Covenant. If the Special Representative certifies that a member of the Mission is unable, because of his or her official duties or authorized absence, to protect his or her interests in the proceeding, the Government shall, without intervening as a party in such proceedings and at the Special Representative's request, support by means of an official communication a request that the court afford the defendant sufficient time to arrange for his or her representation and appearance at the proceedings. The personal liberty of a member of the Mission shall not be restricted in a civil proceeding, whether to enforce a judgement, decision or order, to compel an oath or for any other reason.

Deceased members

51. The Special Representative or the Secretary-General of the United Nations shall have the right to take charge of and dispose of the body of a member of the Mission who dies in Colombia, as well as that member's personal property located within Colombia, in accordance with United Nations procedures.

VII. Limitation of Liability of the United Nations

52. Third party claims for property loss or damage or for personal injury, illness or death arising from or directly attributed to the Mission and which cannot be settled through the internal procedures of the United Nations shall be settled by the United Nations in the manner provided for in paragraph 53 of the present Agreement, provided that the claim is submitted within six months following the occurrence of the loss, damage or injury or, if the claimant did not know or could not reasonably have known of such loss, damage or injury, within six months from the time he or she had discovered the loss, damage or injury, but in any event not later than one year after the termination of the mandate of the Mission. Upon determination of liability as provided in this Agreement, the United Nations shall pay compensation within such financial limitations as have been approved by the General Assembly in its resolution 52/247 of 26 June 1998.

VIII. Settlement of Disputes

53. Except as provided in paragraph 55, any dispute or claim of a private law character to which the Mission or any member thereof is a party and over which the courts of Colombia do not have jurisdiction because of any provision of the present Agreement shall be settled by a standing claims commission to be established for that purpose at the request of the Government. One member of the commission shall be appointed by the Secretary-General of the United Nations, one member by the Government and a chairman jointly by the Secretary-General and the Government. If no agreement as to the chairman is reached within thirty (30) days of the appointment of the first member of the commission, the President of the International Court of Justice may, at the request of either the Secretary-General of the United Nations or the Government, appoint the chairman. Any vacancy on the commission shall be filled by the same method prescribed for the original appointment, provided that the thirty-day period there prescribed shall start as soon as there is a vacancy in the chairmanship. The commission shall determine its own procedures, provided that any two members shall constitute a quorum for all purposes (except for a period of thirty days after the creation of a vacancy) and all decisions shall require the approval of any two members. The awards of the commission shall be final. The awards of the commission shall be notified to the parties and, if against a member of the Mission, the Special Representative or the Secretary-General of the United Nations shall use his or her best endeavours to ensure compliance.

54. Disputes concerning the terms of employment and conditions of service of locally recruited personnel, as members of the Mission, shall be settled by the regulations, rules and procedures of the United Nations.

55. All other disputes between the Mission and the Government concerning the interpretation or application of the present Agreement that are not settled by negotiation shall, unless otherwise agreed by the parties, be submitted to a tribunal of three arbitrators. The provisions relating to the establishment and procedures of the claims commission set out in paragraph 53 shall apply, *mutatis mutandis*, to the establishment and procedures of the tribunal. The decisions of the tribunal shall be final and binding on both parties.

56. All differences between the United Nations and the Government arising out of the interpretation or application of the present arrangements which involve a question of principle concerning the Convention shall be dealt with in accordance with the procedure of section 30 of the Convention.

IX. Supplemental Arrangements

57. The Special Representative and the Government may conclude supplemental arrangements to the present Agreement.

X. Liaison

58. The Ministry of Foreign Affairs of the Government of Colombia shall act as the main liaison agency for all dealings between the Government of Colombia and the Mission. The Special Representative and the Government shall take appropriate measures to ensure close and reciprocal liaison at every appropriate level.

XI. Miscellaneous Provisions

59. Wherever the present Agreement refers to privileges, immunities, exemptions and rights of the Mission and to facilities Colombia undertakes to provide to the Mission, the Government shall have the ultimate responsibility for the implementation and fulfilment of such privileges, immunities, exemptions, rights and facilities by the appropriate local authorities.

60. The Government shall consider any imports and exports of goods and services, or purchases of goods and services made locally by the United Nations Development Programme (UNDP) for the benefit of the Mission to fall within the scope of, and to benefit from the facilities and exemptions provided in, the Standard Basic Assistance Agreement.

61. The present Agreement shall enter into force immediately upon signature.

62. The present Agreement shall remain in force until the departure of the final element of the Mission from Colombia, except that:

(*a*) the provisions of paragraphs 46, 48, 51, 55 and 56 shall remain in force;

(*b*) the provisions of paragraphs 52 and 53 shall remain in force until all claims made in accordance with the provisions of paragraph 52 have been settled.

In Witness Whereof, the undersigned, being the duly appointed representative of the United Nations and the duly authorized plenipotentiary of the Government, have, on behalf of the Parties, signed the present Agreement.

Done at New York on the 19 day of October Two Thousand and Seventeen, in duplicate, in the English and Spanish languages. In the case of any inconsistency, the text in the English language shall prevail.

For the United Nations	For the Government of the Republic of Colombia
[*Signed*] Jeffrey Feltman	[*Signed*] María Emma Mejía Vélez
Under-Secretary-General for Political Affairs	Permanent Representative of the Republic of Colombia to the United Nations in New York

3. United Nations Office for Project Services

Agreement between the Government of the Republic of Serbia and the United Nations Office for Project Services concerning the establishment of an Office for the United Nations Office for Project Services in Belgrade, Republic of Serbia. Belgrade, 30 May 2017, and Copenhagen, 30 May 2017*

This Agreement is entered between the Government of the Republic of Serbia and the United Nations Office for Project Services ("UNOPS") in order to define the status of the UNOPS Office in the Republic of Serbia ("Host Country");

Whereas UNOPS was established as a separate and identifiable entity by the United Nations General Assembly decision 48/501 of 19 September 1994 to provide, *inter alia*, management and other support services for the benefit of the Member States of the United Nations, impartially, efficiently and on a cost reimbursement basis;

Whereas UNOPS is an integral part of the United Nations, whose status, privileges and immunities are governed by the Convention on the Privileges and Immunities of the United Nations, adopted by the General Assembly of the United Nations on 13 February 1946, to which the Republic of Serbia acceded on 12 March 2001, without reservation;

Whereas UNOPS expresses its wish to establish an office in Belgrade, Republic of Serbia;

Whereas the Host Country has agreed that UNOPS establishes its seat in Belgrade, Republic of Serbia, for the benefit of its people;

Now, Therefore the Host Country and UNOPS have entered into this Agreement in a spirit of friendly co-operation:

Article I. Definitions

1. For the purposes of this Agreement,

(*a*) "Archives" means all records, correspondence, documents, manuscripts, computer records, still and motion pictures, film and sound recordings, and any other records belonging to or held by the Office in furtherance of its functions;

(*b*) "Executive Director" means the Executive Director of UNOPS, who is responsible and accountable to the Secretary-General of the United Nations for all UNOPS functions, activities, and services;

(*c*) "Experts on mission" means persons, other than Officials of the Office, appointed by and accountable to UNOPS to perform missions at the request of or on behalf of the Office in accordance with Article VI and Section 26 of the Article VII of the General Convention;

(*d*) "General Convention" means the Convention on the Privileges and Immunities of the United Nations adopted by the General Assembly on 13 February 1946, to which the Republic of Serbia is a party;

(*e*) "Head of the Office" means the official appointed by the Executive Director of UNOPS as the Director in charge of the Office in the Host Country;

(*f*) "Host Country" means the Republic of Serbia;

* Entered into force 30 May 2017 by notification, in accordance with article XXII. United Nations registration no. I-54720.

(*g*) "Office" means the UNOPS Office in the Host Country;

(*h*) "Officials of the Office" means all of the UNOPS staff members assigned to the Office irrespective of their nationality, with the exception of those who are locally recruited and paid hourly rates, as provided for in United Nations General Assembly resolution 76(1) of 7 December 1946;

(*i*) "Party" means UNOPS or the Host Country, individually;

(*j*) "Parties" means UNOPS and the Host Country, collectively;

(*k*) "Premises of the Office" means the building or part of building occupied or used permanently or temporarily by the Office in accordance with this Agreement and with the approval of the Host Country, issued by the Ministry of Foreign Affairs of the Republic of Serbia;

(*l*) "Property of the Office" means all property, including funds, income and other assets belonging to or held or administered by the Office in furtherance of its functions;

(*m*) "Secretary-General" means the Secretary-General of the United Nations;

(*n*) "Telecommunications" means any emission, transmission or reception of written or verbal information, images, sound or information of any nature by wire, radio, satellite, optical, fibre or any other electronic or electromagnetic means.

Article II. Establishment of the Office

The seat of the Office shall be established in Belgrade, Republic of Serbia, to permit UNOPS to carry out its activities and services.

Article III. Juridical Personality

1. The Office shall possess juridical personality in the Republic of Serbia. It shall have the capacity:

(*a*) to contract;

(*b*) to acquire and dispose of immovable and movable property;

(*c*) to institute legal proceedings;

2. For the purposes of this agreement, the Office shall be represented by the Head of the Office.

Article IV. Purpose and Scope of the Agreement

1. (*a*) This Agreement regulates the status of the Office in the Host Country, in particular of its premises, officials and experts on mission;

(*b*) The modalities of assistance rendered by the Office to the Host Country shall be determined in separate project specific agreements between the Office and the Host Country.

Article V. Application of the General Convention

The General Convention shall be applicable to the Office, its archives, property, and telecommunications and to its officials and experts on mission assigned to the Office in the Host Country.

Article VI. Inviolability of the Office

1. The premises of the Office and its property, archives and telecommunications, wherever located and by whomsoever held, shall be inviolable and enjoy immunity from search, requisition, confiscation, expropriation and any other form of interference, whether by executive, administrative, judicial or legislative action except when in a particular case such immunity has been expressly waived in accordance with the General Convention. However, no waiver of immunity from legal process shall extend to any measure of execution.

2. No officer or official of the Host Country or person exercising any public authority within the Host Country, shall enter the premises of the Office to perform any duties therein except with the consent of, and under the conditions approved by the Head of the Office. In case of a fire or other emergency requiring prompt protection action, the consent of the Head of the Office to any necessary entry into the premises shall be presumed if he or she cannot be reached in time.

3. The premises of the Office can be used for meetings, seminars, exhibitions and other related purposes which are organized by the Office or other United Nations entities.

Article VII. Security and Protection

The competent authorities shall ensure the security and protection of the premises of the Office and exercise due diligence to ensure that the tranquillity of the Office premises is not disturbed by the unauthorized entry of persons or groups of persons from outside or by disturbances in its immediate vicinity.

Article VIII. Communications Facilities

1. The Office shall enjoy, for its official communications, treatment not less favorable than that accorded by the Host Country to any other accredited diplomatic mission in the Host Country, in the matter of priorities, rates and taxes on mails, cables, telegrams, radiograms, telephotos, telephone and other communication and press rates for information to the press and radio.

2. The Host Country shall secure the inviolability of the official communications of the Office, whatever the means of the communications employed, and shall not apply any censorship to such communications.

3. The Office shall have the right to operate communication equipment, including satellite facilities and to use codes and to dispatch and receive correspondence by couriers and bags. The bags must bear visibly the emblem of the United Nations, UNOPS or any other United Nations entity and may contain only documents or articles intended for official use, and the courier shall be provided with a courier certificate issued by the United Nations, UNOPS or any other United Nations entity.

Article IX. Funds, Assets and Other Property

1. The Office, its funds, assets and other property, wherever located and by whomsoever held, shall enjoy immunity from every form of legal process except when in a particular case such immunity has expressly been waived in accordance with the General Convention. It is understood, however, that no waiver of immunity shall extend to any measure of execution.

2. The property and assets of the Office shall be exempt from restrictions, regulations, controls and moratoria of any nature.

3. Without being restricted by financial controls, regulations or moratoria of any kind, the Office:

(*a*) may hold and use funds, currency or negotiable instruments of any kind and maintain and operate accounts in any currency and convert any currency held by it into any other currency;

(*b*) shall be free to transfer its funds or currency from the Host Country to another country, or within the Host Country, to the United Nations or any other agency; and

(*c*) shall enjoy the most favorable, legally available rate of exchange for its financial transactions.

Article X. Exemption from Taxes, Duties, Import or Export Restrictions

The Office, its assets, funds and other property shall enjoy:

(*a*) Exemption from all direct taxes and levies, fees, tolls and duties, with the exception of charges for the usage of public utilities;

(*b*) Exemption from customs duties, charges and all other levies, as well as from restrictions on the import or export of materials imported or exported by the Office for its official use;

(*c*) Exemption from all restrictions on the import or export of publications, still and moving pictures, films, tapes, diskettes and sound recordings imported, exported or published by the Office within the framework of its official activities.

Article XI. Officials of the Office

1. Officials shall be granted the privileges, immunities and facilities specified in Articles V and VII of the General Convention.

2. In accordance with the provisions of Section 17 of the General Convention, the Host Country shall be periodically informed of the names of the Officials assigned to the Office.

Article XII. Head of the Office

1. The Head of Office shall be the principal channel of communication with the Host Country on all UNOPS matters. Further to the identification of the Head of Office by the Executive Director to the Government, the Head of Office shall have full responsibility and ultimate authority for the UNOPS activities and services in all its aspect in the Host Country. The Head of Office shall maintain liaison on behalf of UNOPS with the appropriate organs of the Host Country, and shall inform it of the policies, criteria and procedures of UNOPS. The Head of Office shall assist the Host Country, as may be required, in the preparation of requests for UNOPS assistance.

2. Without prejudice to the provisions of the above Article, the Head of the Office shall enjoy during his or her residence in the Host Country the privileges, immunities and facilities granted to heads of accredited foreign missions to the Host Country.

3. The privileges, immunities and facilities referred to above shall also be accorded to a spouse and dependent members of the family of the Head of Office.

Article XIII. Experts on Mission

Experts on mission who are appointed by and accountable to UNOPS to perform missions for the Office shall be granted the privileges, immunities and facilities specified in Article VI and Section 26 of the Article VII of the General Convention.

Article XIV. Waiver of Immunity

Privileges and immunities referred to in this Agreement are granted in the interest of the United Nations and not for the personal benefit of the persons to which such privileges and immunities are being granted. The right and the duty to waive the immunity of these persons, in any case where it can be waived without prejudice to the interests of the United Nations shall lie with the Secretary-General of the United Nations.

Article XV. Entry into, exit from, movement and sojourn within the Host Country

All persons referred to in this Agreement shall have the right of unimpeded entry into, exit form, sojourn and free movement within the Host Country. Visas, entry permits or licenses, where required, shall be granted as promptly as possible and free of charge.

Article XVI. United Nations Laissez-Passer, *Certificates and Visas*

1. The Host Country shall recognize and accept the United Nations *laissez-passer* issued to Officials of the Office and any other United Nations entity as a valid travel document.

2. In accordance with the provisions of Section 26 of the General Convention, the Host Country shall recognize and accept the United Nations certificate issued to Experts on Mission and other persons travelling on business for UNOPS or any other person travelling on the business of the United Nations.

3. All persons referred to in this Agreement shall be granted facilities for speedy travel. Visas, entry permits or licenses, where required, shall be granted free of charge and as promptly as possible to the persons referred to in this Agreement, their dependents and other persons invited to the Office in connection with the official work and activities of the Office.

Article XVII. Identification Cards

1. Once notified by the Head of the Office, the Host Country shall issue identification cards to all persons referred to in this Agreement, certifying their status under this Agreement.

2. Upon the demand of an authorized official of the Host Country, persons referred to in this Agreement shall be required to present, without having to surrender, their identification cards.

Article XVIII. Flags, Emblem and Markings

The Office shall be entitled to display the United Nations flag, logo, emblem and markings in the Office premises and on vehicles used for official purposes.

Article XIX. Cooperation with the Host Country

1. Without prejudice to the privileges and immunities accorded by this Agreement, it is the duty of all persons enjoying such privileges and immunities to respect the laws and regulations of the Host Country, and not to interfere in the internal affairs of the Host Country.

2. Without prejudice to the privileges and immunities referred to in this Agreement, the Office shall cooperate at all times with the Host Country to facilitate the proper administration of justice, secure the observance of police regulations and prevent the occurrence of any abuse in connection with the facilities, privileges and immunities accorded to persons referred to in the present Agreement.

Article XX. Supplemental Agreements

1. Arrangements of an administrative and financial nature concerning the Office may be made by supplemental agreements, as appropriate.

2. The Parties may enter into any other supplemental agreements as the Parties may deem appropriate.

Article XXI. Settlement of disputes

Any dispute between the Office and the Host Country arising out of, or relating to this Agreement which is not settled by negotiation or another agreed mode of settlement, shall, at the request of either Party, be submitted to an arbitral tribunal of three arbitrators. Each Party shall appoint one arbitrator, and the two arbitrators so appointed shall appoint a third, who shall be the chairperson of the Tribunal. If, within sixty (60) days of the request for arbitration, a Party has not appointed an arbitrator, or if, within thirty (30) days of the appointment of two arbitrators, the third arbitrator has not been appointed, either Party may request the President of the International Court of Justice to appoint the arbitrator referred to. The Tribunal shall determine its own procedures. The fees and expenses of the Tribunal shall be borne by the Parties as assessed by the Tribunal. The arbitral award shall contain a statement of the reasons on which it is based and shall be final and binding on the Parties.

Article XXII. Final Provisions

1. This Agreement may be modified by written agreement between the Parties hereto.

2. This Agreement may be terminated by either Party by written notice to the other and shall terminate three months after receipt of such notice. Notwithstanding any such notice of termination, this Agreement shall remain in force to allow the completion of the Office's operations of in the Host Country, the liquidation of its properties, to settle all pending matters relating to the implementation of this Agreement and the resolution of any dispute between the Parties in relation to this Agreement.

3. The obligations assumed by the Host Country shall survive the termination of this Agreement, to the extent necessary to permit orderly withdrawal of the property and archives, of the Office and of its officials, expert on missions and other relevant persons under this Agreement.

4. This agreement shall be signed in English and Serbian languages. The English version shall prevail in the event of any inconsistences.

5. This Agreement shall be subject to the signature of both Parties. It shall enter into force after UNOPS receives the notification from the Host Country confirming that it has been ratified in accordance with its internal procedures.

In Witness Whereof, the undersigned, duly appointed representatives of the Parties, have signed the present Agreement between the Government of the Republic of Serbia and the United Nations Office for Project Services on this 30 day of May 2017 in Belgrade, and on this … of … 2017 in Copenhagen, in four originals, two copies in English and two copies in Serbian language.

For the Government of the Republic of Serbia	For the United Nations Office for Project Services
[*Signed*]	[*Signed*]
The First Deputy Prime Minister and Minister of Foreign Affairs	Under-Secretary General and Executive Director

4. United Nations Human Settlements Programme

Agreement between the United Nations, represented by the United Nations Human Settlements Programme (UN-HABITAT) and the Government of the Republic of Tunisia on the establishment of a country office in the Republic of Tunisia. Paris, 16 May 2017*

Considering that the United Nations Human Settlements Programme (UNHSP), or UN-Habitat, was originally established as the United Nations Centre for Human Settlements (Habitat) in accordance with United Nations General Assembly resolution 32/162 of 19 December 1977. The Centre, located in Nairobi, Kenya, was subsequently transformed into a subsidiary organ of the General Assembly pursuant to resolution 56/206 of 21 December 2001 (known as "UN-Habitat"). This body is the agency responsible for coordinating human settlements activities within the United Nations system and the focal point for the monitoring, evaluation and implementation of the Habitat Agenda. It also manages the human settlements tasks in section 21 of the Agenda. In addition it is responsible for promoting and consolidating collaboration with partners, including local authorities, private companies and non-governmental organizations, for the implementation of the Habitat Agenda and the achievement of the Millennium Development Goals, in particular target 7.D: to achieve, by 2020, a significant improvement in the lives of at least 100 million slum dwellers,

---

* Entered into force 16 May 2017 by signature, in accordance with article XXVI. United Nations registration no. I-54847.

Considering that the Government of the Republic of Tunisia, hereinafter referred to as "the Government", after consultation with UN-Habitat, wishes to promote international cooperation in the field of habitat and urban development in the Republic of Tunisia,

Considering that consultations have taken place between UN-Habitat and the Government of the Republic of Tunisia (hereinafter referred to as "the Government") with a view to establishing in the city of Tunis a UN-Habitat Country Office in the Republic of Tunisia (hereinafter referred to as the "Office"),

Considering that the Government has agreed with UN-Habitat to establish the Office in the Republic of Tunisia in the city of Tunis with a view to promoting international co-operation in the field of habitat and urban development in the Republic of Tunisia,

Wishing to note, through this Agreement, all matters that may relate to the establishment and proper functioning of the Office,

The United Nations, represented by UN-Habitat, and the Government of the Republic of Tunisia (hereinafter referred to as "the Parties") have agreed as follows:

Article I. Definitions

1. For the purposes of this Agreement:

(*a*) "Host Country" means the Government of the Republic of Tunisia;

(*b*) "Government" means the Government of the Republic of Tunisia;

(*c*) "Head of the Office" means the official in charge of the Office;

(*d*) "Experts on mission" means persons, other than United Nations officials, who perform missions at the request of or on behalf of the Country Office or other United Nations entity;

(*e*) "Officials" means all staff members of the Country Office, irrespective of nationality, with the exception of those who are recruited locally and are assigned to hourly rates, as provided for in General Assembly resolution 76 (I) of 7 December 1946;

(*f*) "Persons providing services" means contractors, field experts, volunteers, consultants, as well as legal and natural persons and their employees;

(*g*) "Convention" means the Convention on the Privileges and Immunities of the United Nations, adopted by the United Nations General Assembly on 13 February 1946, to which [the Host Country] is a party;

(*h*) "Competent authorities" means central, local and other authorities under the law of the Host Country;

(*i*) "Premises of the Office" means the building, and structures or portions thereof, that at any given moment are physically occupied by the Office or used for meetings convened [in the Republic of Tunisia] by the Office, or any other land or any other buildings that may from time to time be made part of the headquarters, on a temporary or permanent basis, in accordance with this Agreement or a supplementary agreement concluded with the Republic of Tunisia;

(*j*) "Archives of the County Office" means all records, correspondence, documents, manuscripts, computer records, still or moving images, films and sound recordings belonging to or held by the Country Office for the performance of its functions;

(*k*) "Property of the Country Office" means all property of the Office, including funds, income and other assets belonging to the Office or held or administered by the Office for the performance of its functions;

(*l*) "Secretary-General" means the Secretary-General of the United Nations; and

(*m*) "Telecommunications" means any issuance, transmission or receipt of written or verbal information, images, sound or any other information by cable, radio, satellite, optical fibre or any other electronic or electromagnetic means.

Article II. Purpose of the Agreement

1. This Agreement sets out the basic conditions and procedures for the establishment and functioning of the Country Office, as well as its status and the status of its staff and premises, and the framework for cooperation with the Government.

2. It covers all the assistance to be provided by UN-Habitat in that regard.

3. This Agreement also applies to project documents and other texts drawn up by the Parties by mutual agreement to define the aim of such assistance and the respective responsibilities of the Parties.

Article III. Establishment of the Office

1. The Country Office shall have its headquarters in Tunis, Republic of Tunisia.

2. The Government shall ensure that the treatment accorded to the Country Office is equal and identical to that accorded to any other foreign mission accredited to the Host Country.

3. All buildings and premises, located in Tunis or in another governorate of the Republic of Tunisia, that are, with the consent of the Government, used for meetings, seminars, training courses, symposiums, workshops or similar activities organized by the United Nations shall be temporarily considered premises of the Office. This agreement shall apply *mutatis mutandis* to all meetings, seminars, training courses, symposiums, workshops and other activities for their duration.

4. The Country Office shall strive to:

(*a*) promote international and regional cooperation to advance the implementation of the New Urban Agenda;

(*b*) obtain, in cooperation with UN-Habitat headquarters, the funds necessary for the development and implementation of activities in the Republic of Tunisia;

(*c*) promote and implement the operational activities of UN-Habitat in the Republic of Tunisia;

(*d*) cooperate with regional and international organizations, the national Government and local authorities;

(*e*) organize international and regional conferences on human settlements issues, to which participants from all States Members of the United Nations shall be invited; and

(*f*) promote the implementation in the Republic of Tunisia of the global programmes and international campaigns of UN-Habitat.

5. Juridical personality

(*a*) The Office shall possess juridical personality in the Host Country. It shall have the capacity:

(i) To contract;

(ii) To acquire and dispose of immovable and movable property; and

(iii) To institute legal proceedings.

(*b*) For the purposes of this Agreement, the Country Office shall be represented by the Head of the Office.

Article IV. Assessed financial contribution to programme and other costs

1. The Government shall transfer to the technical cooperation account of UN-Habitat an annual amount of $100,000 (one hundred thousand United States dollars) to cover the costs of the Office, staff and temporary staff, excluding international communications costs.

2. The amount of the contribution intended to cover UN-Habitat costs shall be determined in accordance with the regulatory procedures of the United Nations.

3. The Government shall provide to the Office of UN-Habitat, free of charge and as soon as possible following the entry into force of this Agreement, appropriate premises in the vicinity of the Ministry of Housing. Such premises must meet the United Nations minimum operating security standards relating to security and protection.

4. The Government shall transfer to UN-Habitat an amount of $50,000 (fifty thousand United States dollars) for the purposes of establishing the Office and purchasing a vehicle to be used by staff of the Office.

5. The funds transferred to UN-Habitat shall be managed in accordance with UnitedNations rules of procedure and financial regulations

Article V. Inviolability of the Country Office

1. The premises of the Country Office shall be inviolable. The property, funds and assets of the Office, wherever located and by whomsoever held, shall be immune from search, requisition, confiscation, expropriation and any other form of interference, whether by executive, administrative, judicial or legislative action.

2. The competent authorities shall not enter the premises of the Country Office except with the express consent of and under the conditions approved by the Head of the Office. In the event of fire or other emergency requiring urgent protection measures, the consent of the Head of the Office to any necessary entry into the premises shall be presumed if he or she cannot be reached in time.

3. The premises of the Office may be used for meetings, seminars, exhibitions and other similar activities organized by the Office, the United Nations or other related organizations.

4. The records and archives of the Country Office, and in general all documents belonging to it or held by it, shall be inviolable, wherever located and by whomsoever held.

Article VI. Security and protection

1. The competent authorities shall ensure the security and protection of the premises of the Country Office in accordance with the established and recognized regulations for diplomatic and foreign missions in the country.

2. The competent authorities shall take, as appropriate, specific measures required to adequately ensure the security, safety and protection of persons referred to in this Agreement, indispensable for the proper functioning of the Country Office, free from interference of any kind.

Article VII. Public services

1. The competent authorities shall facilitate, at the request of the Head of the Office and under conditions not less favourable than those accorded by the Government to any accredited diplomatic mission in the country, access to the public services required by the Country Office, including, but not limited to, public networks and communications services.

2. In the event that the public services referred to in paragraph (*a*) above are provided to the Country Office by the competent authorities, or where the prices of those services are regulated by the competent authorities, the rates charged shall not exceed the lowest comparable rates accorded to accredited diplomatic missions in the country.

3. In case of *force majeure* resulting in a complete or partial disruption of the abovementioned services, the Country Office shall, for the performance of its functions, be accorded the same priority as essential public agencies and organs.

4. The provisions of this Article shall not prevent the reasonable application of fire protection or sanitary regulations of the Host Country.

Article VIII. Communications

1. The Country Office shall enjoy in respect of its official communications treatment not less favourable than that accorded by the Government to any diplomatic mission or nongovernmental organization in the matter of installation and operation, priorities, rates and taxes for the following forms of communication in particular: telegrams, telefaxes, satellite links, telephone, electronic mail and other communications; and rates for information to the press and radio.

2. The Government shall ensure the inviolability of the official communications and correspondence of the Office, whatever the means of communication employed, and shall impose no censorship on such communications or correspondence.

3. The Office has the right to operate communications equipment, in particular satellite communications equipment, to use cables and to dispatch and receive its correspondence by mail or sealed bag, which shall have the same privileges and immunities as diplomatic mail and bags.

Article IX. Funds, assets and other property

1. The Office, its property, funds and assets, wherever located and by whomsoever held, shall enjoy immunity from legal process except to the extent that the Secretary-General

of the United Nations expressly waives that immunity in a particular case. It is, however, understood that no waiver of immunity shall extend to any enforcement measure.

2. The property and assets of the Country Office cannot be restricted by financial controls, regulations or moratoriums of any kind, and the Country Office may:

(*a*) Hold and use funds, currency and negotiable instruments of any kind, have and operate accounts in any currency and convert any currency held by it into any other currency;

(*b*) Transfer its funds or currency from one country to another or within any country; and

(*c*) Enjoy the most favourable legally available rate of exchange for its financial transactions.

Article X. Exemption from taxes, customs duties and restrictions on imports and exports

1. The Country Office, its funds, assets, income and other property shall be exempt from:

(*a*) All direct and indirect taxes and levies, including value added tax; it is understood, however, that the Country Office will not claim exemption from taxes which are no more than charges for public services that are rendered by the competent authorities or by a company under the laws and regulations of the Host Country at a rate fixed according to the amount of services provided and that can be specifically defined, described and itemized;

(*b*) Customs duties, prohibitions and restrictions on articles imported or exported by the Country Office for its official use; it is understood that articles imported under such exemptions will not be sold in the Host Country except under conditions agreed with the competent authorities; and

(*c*) Customs duties and prohibitions and restrictions on imports and exports in respect of publications, still and moving images, films, tapes, audio devices and sound recordings exported or published by the Office within the framework of its official activities.

Article XI. Participation in United Nations meetings

1. Representatives of members of the United Nations invited to meetings, seminars, training courses, symposiums, workshops and similar activities organized by the Country Office, the Organization or other related organizations shall, while exercising their functions, enjoy the privileges and immunities set out in article IV of the Convention.

2. The Government, in accordance with relevant United Nations principles and practices and this Agreement, shall secure complete freedom of expression for all participants in meetings, seminars, training courses, symposiums, workshops and similar activities organized by the Country Office and other relevant organizations. All participants and persons exercising functions in connection with meetings, seminars, training courses, symposiums, workshops and similar activities organized by the Country Office and other related organizations shall enjoy such privileges, immunities and facilities as are necessary for their participation and the independent exercise of their functions. In particular, all participants and persons exercising functions in connection with meetings, seminars, training courses, symposiums, workshops and similar activities organized by the Country Office and other related organizations shall enjoy immunity from legal process in respect of words spoken or written and acts done by them in connection with such meetings, seminars, training courses, symposiums, workshops and similar activities.

Article XII. Privileges and immunities

1. The Convention referred to in Article I of this Agreement shall apply *mutatis mutandis* to the Office and its property, funds and assets, officials, experts on mission and persons providing services in the Host Country.

A. *Head of the Office and high-ranking officials*

1. The Head of the Office shall enjoy the privileges, immunities, exemptions and facilities normally accorded to the heads of diplomatic missions to the Host Country. Furthermore, without prejudice to the other provisions of this Agreement, all officials in the Country Office at the P/L-5 level or higher shall enjoy the privileges, immunities and facilities accorded to diplomatic staff at missions to the Host Country. Their names shall be included on the diplomatic list.

2. The privileges, immunities and facilities referred to in paragraph 1 above shall also be accorded to the spouses and dependent family members of the officials concerned.

B. *Status of the officials of the Country Office*

1. The officials of the Country Office shall enjoy the following privileges, immunities and facilities within the Host Country:

(*a*) Immunity from legal process in respect of words spoken or written and all acts done by them in their official capacity; such immunity shall continue to be accorded to them after termination of their employment with the United Nations;

(*b*) Immunity from personal arrest or detention and from seizure of their personal and official effects and baggage, except in cases of flagrante delicto; in such cases, the appropriate authorities shall immediately inform the Head of the Office of the arrest or detention or of the seizure;

(*c*) Exemption from taxation on United Nations salaries and emoluments; exemption from taxes on all their income and property, and those of their spouses and dependent family members, provided that such income derives from sources outside the Host Country and that such property is located outside the Host Country;

(*d*) Exemption from military service and all national service obligations;

(*e*) Exemption in respect of themselves, their spouses and dependent family members from immigration restrictions and alien registration;

(*f*) The same privileges in respect of exchange facilities as are accorded to the officials of comparable ranks forming part of diplomatic missions to the Host Country;

(*g*) The same protection and the same repatriation facilities for themselves, their spouses and dependent family members in time of international crisis as are accorded to diplomatic envoys;

(*h*) The right to import, free of customs taxes and other fees, in one or more consignments:

— Limited quantities of certain articles intended for personal use or consumption that may not be gifted or sold;

— A motor vehicle, free of customs and excise duties, including value added tax, in accordance with the regulations applicable in the Host Country, to diplomatic representatives to the country and/or members of international organizations who live in the country; the right to import a motor vehicle shall be renewed every three years; a vehicle imported in accordance with these provisions may be sold under conditions agreed with the Host Country; and

— The right to export, upon cessation of their employment in the Host Country, their furniture and personal effects, including motor vehicles, free of duties and taxes.

2. Officials who are nationals of or who have permanent resident status in the Host Country shall enjoy the privileges and immunities set out in section 18 of the Convention referred to in article I of this Agreement.

3. In accordance with section 17 of the Convention, the names of the officials shall from time to time be made known to the competent authorities.

C. Experts on mission

1. Experts (other than officials) performing missions for the United Nations shall enjoy, during the period of their missions, including the time spent on journeys, the privileges and immunities set out in articles VI and VII of the Convention.

2. Experts on mission shall be exempt from taxation on the salaries and emoluments paid by the Office and may enjoy other privileges, immunities and facilities agreed by the Parties.

3. Experts on mission who are nationals of or who have permanent resident status in the Host Country shall enjoy only the privileges and immunities set out in articles VI and VII of the Convention.

Article XIII. Persons providing services

1. The Government shall accord to all persons providing services to or on behalf of the Country Office the same privileges and immunities as are accorded to the officials of the Country Office.

Article XIV. Staff recruited locally and assigned to hourly rates

1. The conditions of employment for persons recruited locally and assigned to hourly rates shall be governed by the resolutions, decisions, regulations and rules, and policies of relevant United Nations bodies.

2. Staff recruited in the Host Country who are assigned to hourly rates to provide services to the Country Office shall be immune from legal process in respect of words spoken or written and all acts performed by them in their official capacity. Such immunity shall continue to be accorded to them after termination of their employment with the United Nations.

Article XV. Waiver of immunity

1. The privileges and immunities referred to in the articles above are accorded to the persons concerned solely in the interests of the United Nations and not for the personal benefit of the individuals themselves. The Secretary-General shall have the right and the duty to waive the immunity of those persons in any case where, in his opinion, the immunity would impede the course of justice and can be waived without prejudice to the interests of the United Nations.

Article XVI. Freedom of movement

1. All persons referred to in this Agreement, including participants in meetings (seminars, training courses, symposiums, workshops and similar activities) shall be authorized to enter, exit, stay unimpeded and move freely in the Host Country.

2. Visas and entry permits shall, as necessary, be issued free of charge and as promptly as possible.

Article XVII. Laissez-passer: *certificates and visas*

1. The Government shall recognize and accept United Nations *laissez-passer* issued to Officials as valid travel documents:

(*a*) In accordance with section 26 of the Convention, the competent authorities shall recognize and accept certificates issued by the United Nations for experts on mission and other persons travelling on the business of the United Nations;

(*b*) All persons referred to in this Agreement shall be granted facilities for speedy travel. Visas and entry and exit permits shall, as required, be issued free of charge to persons referred to in this Agreement, their dependents and all other persons invited by the Country Office as part of the official activities of the Office; and

(*c*) Similar facilities to those specified in paragraph (*b*) above shall be accorded to experts on mission and other persons who, though not holders of United Nations *laissez-passer*, are recognized by the Office as travelling on official business of the United Nations.

Article XVIII. Identification

1. At the request of the Head of the Office, the Government shall issue to persons referred to in this Agreement identification documents required to confirm their status under this Agreement.

2. Persons referred to in this Agreement shall be required to show, but not to hand over, their identification documents to any authorized Government official who requests to see them.

Article XIX. Flags, emblems and markings

1. The Country Office may fly or display flags and/or emblems of the United Nations on its premises and official vehicles.

Article XX. Social security

1. The United Nations Joint Staff Pension Fund shall enjoy legal capacity in the Host Country and the same exemptions, privileges and immunities as the United Nations itself. Benefits received from the Pension Fund shall be exempt from taxation.

2. The United Nations and the Government agree that, since officials of the Organization are covered by the Staff Regulations and Rules of the United Nations, including article VI thereof, which establishes a comprehensive regime for social security, the United Nations, the Country Office and its staff members, irrespective of nationality, shall be exempt from the application of the laws of the Host Country relating to the coverage of and mandatory contributions to its social security schemes while exercising their functions in connection with the United Nations.

3. The provisions of paragraph 1 above shall apply *mutatis mutandis* to the family members forming part of the households of the persons referred to in that paragraph, unless they are employed or self-employed in the Host Country or receive social security benefits from the Host Country.

Article XXI. Access to the labour market for family members and issuance of visas and residence permits to household employees

1. The Government shall undertake to grant work permits to the spouses of officials of the Country Office and their 21-year-old or economically dependent children.

2. The Government shall undertake to issue visas and residence permits and all other documents, as necessary, to the household employees of officials of the Country Office as promptly as possible.

3. The Government shall undertake to help, to the extent possible, officials, experts on missions and persons providing services to obtain residential accommodation.

Article XXII. Cooperation between the Government and the United Nations

1. Without prejudice to their recognized privileges and immunities, the persons who enjoy these privileges and immunities shall be required to abide by the laws of the Host Country and to refrain from any interference in the internal affairs of the Host Country.

2. The United Nations shall cooperate at all times with the competent authorities to facilitate the proper administration of justice, ensure the enforcement of police regulations and prevent the occurrence of any abuse in connection with the privileges, immunities and facilities mentioned in this Agreement.

Article XXIII. Responsibility

1. The Government shall bear all risks of operations carried out under this Agreement.

2. In particular, the Government shall be required to deal with any claims resulting from operations under this Agreement or that are directly attributable to it which may be brought by third parties against the Organization, its officials, experts on mission, persons providing services or participants in meetings, seminars, training courses, symposiums, workshops and similar activities organized by the Office or a related organization, and it shall indemnify and exonerate the United Nations and its personnel in respect of such claims, unless the Parties agree that the claim or liability was caused by gross negligence or intentional harm.

Article XXIV. Supplementary agreements

1. Administrative and financial arrangements concerning the Country Office may be made, as needed, through supplementary agreements.

2. The Parties may conclude any other supplementary agreement they deem necessary.

Article XXV. Settlement of disputes

1. Any dispute between the parties arising from or relating to this Agreement that is not settled by negotiations or any other agreed mode of settlement shall be referred at the request of either party to a tribunal of three arbitrators, one of whom shall be appointed by

the Secretary-General of the United Nations, one to be appointed by the Government and the third, who shall be the Chair, to be chosen by the two other arbitrators. If either Party fails to appoint an arbitrator within three months of the appointment of the arbitrator by the other Party, or if the first two arbitrators should fail to appoint the Chair within three months of the appointment of the second arbitrator, the President of the International Court of Justice shall nominate such arbitrators at the request of either party. Except as otherwise agreed by the parties, the tribunal shall adopt its own rules of procedure, provide for the reimbursement of its members and the distribution of expenses between the parties, and take all decisions by a two-thirds majority. Its decisions on all questions of procedure and substance shall be final and, even if rendered in default of one of the parties, be binding on both of them.

Article XXVI. Final provisions

1. It is the understanding of the Parties that, if the Host Country enters into an agreement with an intergovernmental organization containing terms and conditions more favourable than those under this Agreement, such terms and conditions shall be extended to the Office, at its request, by means of a supplemental agreement. The implementation of this Agreement must not conflict with existing and former national laws and international instruments in this area and shall have no effect whatsoever on the sovereignty and security of the State.

2. This agreement may be modified by mutual consent through an exchange of letters in which the Parties express their intention to that effect.

3. This Agreement shall remain in force for an unlimited period. Either Party may terminate this agreement by written notification to the other Party. In such a case, this Agreement shall expire 12 months from the date of receipt of such notification. The obligations assumed by the Government shall remain in effect following the termination of the Agreement for the period of time necessary to permit the orderly withdrawal of the property, funds and assets of the Office and the resolution of any pending dispute in accordance with article XXV of this Agreement.

4. This Agreement shall enter into force on the date on which it is signed by both Parties.

5. This Agreement was concluded and signed at Paris, France, on 16 May 2017, in two originals in the French language and two originals in the Arabic language, the two versions being identical and authentic.

For the Government of the Republic of Tunisia	For the United Nations, represented by UN-Habitat
[*Signed*] Mohamed Salah Arfaoui	[*Signed*] Joan Clos
Minister of Infrastructure, Housing and Spatial Planning	Executive Director

B. Treaties concerning the legal status of intergovernmental organizations related to the United Nations

1. Convention on the Privileges and Immunities of the Specialized Agencies*

In 2017, Brunei Darussalam acceded to the Convention and undertook to apply the provisions of the Convention to the International Monetary Fund. As at 31 December 2017, there were 128 States parties to the Convention.**

2. International Labour Organization

On 20 January 2017, an agreement concerning the status of the International Labour Organization in Côte d'Ivoire was concluded and entered provisionally into force.*** The Agreement will enter into force definitely upon the Government's notification of the completion of its internal procedures providing for the final approval of the Agreement.

3. Food and Agriculture Organization

(*a*) Agreements regarding the establishment of FAO Representations and Offices

The legal status, privileges and immunities enjoyed by FAO offices, its personnel and assets are confirmed in agreements concluded with the host countries. An agreement concerning the establishment of an FAO Representation was concluded with the Republic of South Sudan on 21 June 2017. An agreement was also concluded with the United Mexican States on 13 October 2017 for the transformation of the FAO Representation into an FAO Partnership and Liaison Office, as well as with the Republic of Costa Rica on 27 January 2017 amending the existing Host Country Agreement to allow for multiple accreditations of the designated FAO Representative to cover a number of FAO offices in the region. Finally, an agreement was concluded on 21 August 2017 with the Republic of Armenia. This agreement, which operates alongside the existing agreement concerning the establishment of the FAO Representation in Armenia, addresses delivery of technical assistance within that country.

(*b*) Agreements for hosting meetings of FAO Bodies

For the purpose of holding international conferences and meetings of FAO bodies outside FAO Headquarters and premises, FAO normally concludes agreements specifying

---

* United Nations, *Treaty Series*, vol. 33, p. 261.

** For the list of the States parties to the Convention, see *Multilateral Treaties Deposited with the Secretary-General*, available on the website of the Treaty Section of the United Nations Office of Legal Affairs: http://treaties.un.org.

*** Not reproduced herein. For the text, see https://www.ilo.org/dyn/legprot/en/f?p=2200:10002:13334682749328::NO:10002:P10002_COUNTRY_ID:103023:NO.

the privileges and immunities and other facilities that the Organization and participants (delegations and observers) will enjoy for the purpose of the meeting, and to address any potential liabilities of the Organization. These agreements are based on a standard Memorandum of Responsibilities. During 2017, Memoranda of Responsibilities were concluded with Austria, Brazil, Canada, Finland, France, Germany, Ireland, Korea, Mali, Mexico, Montenegro, Norway, Oman, Panama, Paraguay, Poland, Rwanda, Slovenia, Switzerland, Tanzania, and Turkey for hosting sessions of FAO Governing and Statutory Bodies to be held in 2017 and 2018.

(*c*) Agreements concerning FAO technical assistance activities

In accordance with Article XVI of the FAO Constitution, and in line with longstanding practice, a number of agreements were concluded with FAO members concerning technical assistance activities to be conducted within those States. A significant number of contribution agreements were also concluded with resource partners to support these technical assistance activities.

The application of fiscal exemptions to technical assistance activities continued to be a matter of particular attention in 2017. For example, the FAO was requested to clarify to a local tax authority the meaning of "important purchases" of goods and services provided to the Organization within the context of the principle of remission or return of the amount of Value-Added Tax under the relevant international treaties. The Organization also addressed an increasing number of requests aimed at applying regional and/or national sanctions regimes to the FAO, as well as national money laundering and counterterrorism provisions. Moreover, in 2017 several resource partners raised questions concerning the applicability of national freedom of information laws.

In all the above cases, the FAO has sought to maintain its status as a UN Common System Organization and the privileges and immunities it enjoys under the FAO Constitution, the 1947 Convention on Privileges and Immunities of the Specialized Agencies ("CPISA"), and relevant bilateral agreements, noting that its technical assistance activities are official functions of the Organization as reflected in Article I of the FAO Constitution.

(*d*) Employment-related matters

During 2017, the FAO continued to address claims by staff and non-staff personnel before national authorities concerning employment-related matters. Many of these matters related to the payment of benefits, including social security benefits, on the basis of national legislation.

The FAO maintained the established position of the UN System. In these cases, the FAO recalled its immunity from every form of legal process, the international character of the employment relationship between the Organization and its personnel, the application of the Organization's rules—as distinct from national laws and procedures—to the employment contracts, and the provision for alternative dispute settlement mechanisms under the Organization's legal framework.

4. United Nations Educational, Scientific and Cultural Organization

For the purpose of holding international conferences on the territory of member States, UNESCO concluded various agreements that contained the following provisions concerning the legal status of the Organization:

"Privileges and Immunities

The Government of [name of the State] shall apply, in all matters relating to this meeting, the provisions of the Convention on the Privileges and Immunities of the Specialized Agencies of the United Nations as well as Annex IV thereto to which it has been a party from [date].

In particular, the Government shall not place any restriction on the entry into, sojourn in, and departure from the territory of [name of the State] of all persons, of whatever nationality, entitled to attend the meeting by virtue of a decision of the appropriate authorities of UNESCO and in accordance with the Organization's relevant rules and regulations.

Damage and accidents

As long as the premises reserved for the meeting are at the disposal of UNESCO, the Government of [name of State] shall bear the risk of damage to the premises, facilities and furniture and shall assume and bear all responsibility and liability for accidents that may occur to persons present therein. The [name of State] authorities shall be entitled to adopt appropriate measures to ensure the protection of the participants, particularly against fire and other risks, of the above-mentioned premises, facilities and furniture. The Government of [name of State] may also claim from UNESCO compensation for any damage to persons and property caused by the fault of staff members or agents of the Organization."

In 2017, for such agreements, UNESCO decided to include the following new provision concerning security and safety:

"Security

The Government of (Country) shall be responsible for providing at its expense, such police protection and security as may be required to ensure the efficient functioning of all pre-session meetings, meetings and sessions of the main conferences and any other meetings linked to the event, in a calm and serene ambiance and without interference of any kind.

Such police service shall be under the direct supervision and control of a senior officer to be designated by the Government of (Country). He/she shall work in close coordination and cooperation, including at distance, with the senior security liaison officer and Event Security Coordinator (ESC) appointed by UNESCO for this purpose, so as to ensure a proper atmosphere of security and tranquility. Mr/Madame XXX, Field Security Coordination Officer and Deputy Chief of Security, has been assigned to act as point of contact and is UNESCO's event security coordinator for this activity. On the Host Country side, Mr/Madame XXX will act as its designated Senior Security Officer (SSO).

In accordance with the UNDSS Framework for Accountability, the UN Designated Official for (Country) is responsible for the security of United Nations personnel, premises, and assets throughout the country and must be kept informed throughout the process. The name of the responsible officers for security shall be communicated to UNDSS by respectively the Host Country and UNESCO, not later than a month before the event.

Security within and outside the Conference Premises shall be the responsibility of the host country, in close coordination and collaboration with UNESCO."

5. United Nations Industrial Development Organization

(*a*) Grant agreement between UNIDO and the United States Agency for International Development regarding implementation of a project in Morocco entitled "H2O Maghreb Partnership Project", signed on 28 April 2017*

ATTACHMENT B—PROGRAM DESCRIPTION

LEGAL FRAMEWORK

The project will be governed by the provisions of the Standard Basic Cooperation Agreement between the Kingdom of Morocco and UNIDO concluded on 6th September 1988 in Vienna.

ATTACHMENT C—STANDARD PROVISIONS

II. REQUIRED AS APPLICABLE STANDARD PROVISIONS FOR COST-TYPE AWARDS TO PUBLIC INTERNATIONAL ORGANIZATIONS

4. *Reporting of Foreign Taxes (UN) (April 2011)*

The recipient is not subject to taxation of activities implemented under the award based on its privileges and immunities as a public international organization (PIO). However, should it be obligated to pay value-added taxes or customs duties related to the award, the recipient must notify the USAID Agreement Officer's Representative (AOR).

(*b*) Basic cooperation agreement between UNIDO and the Government of Iraq, signed on 30 June 2017

Article X. Privileges and Immunities

1. The Government shall apply to UNIDO, including its organs, property, funds and assets, and to its officials, including the UNIDO Representative in Iraq, and his or her staff in the country, the provisions of the Convention on the Privileges and Immunities of the United Nations, except that if the Government has acceded in respect of UNIDO to the Convention on the Privileges and Immunities of the Specialized Agencies, the Government shall apply the provisions of the latter Convention, including Annex XVII thereof relating to UNIDO.

2. The Representative and his or her staff in the country shall be granted such additional privileges and immunities as may be necessary for the effective exercise of their official functions. In particular, the Representative shall enjoy the same privileges and immunities as the Government accords to diplomatic envoys in accordance with international law.

3. (*a*) Except as the Government and UNIDO may otherwise agree in Project Documents relating to specific projects, the Government shall grant all persons, other than

* Entered into force on 28 April 2017.

Government nationals employed locally, performing services on behalf of UNIDO, who are not covered by paragraphs 1 and 2 above, the same privileges and immunities as are granted to officials under Section 18 or 19, respectively, of the Conventions on the Privileges and Immunities of the United Nations or of the Specialized Agencies, as applicable;

(*b*) For purposes of the instruments on privileges and immunities referred to in the preceding parts of this Article:

(i) All papers and documents relating to a project in the possession or under the control of the persons referred to in sub-paragraph 3 (*a*) above shall be deemed to be documents belonging to UNIDO; and

(ii) Equipment, materials and supplies brought into, or purchased, or leased by those persons within the country for purposes of a project shall be deemed to be the property of UNIDO.

4. The expression "persons performing services" as used in Articles X, XI and XIV of this Agreement includes volunteers, consultants and juridical as well as natural persons and their employees. It includes governmental or nongovernmental organizations or firms which UNIDO may retain to implement or to assist in the implementation of UNIDO assistance to a project and their employees. Nothing in this Agreement shall be construed to limit the privileges, immunities or facilities conferred upon such organizations or firms or their employees in any other instrument.

(*c*) Contribution arrangement between UNIDO and the Department of Natural Resources of Canada regarding implementation of a project entitled "Support and operation of the Clean Energy Ministerial's (CEM) Energy Management Working Group (EMWG)", signed on 7 and 8 November 2017*

9. Privileges and Immunities

9.01 Nothing in or related to this Contribution Arrangement will be deemed to constitute any waiver, express or implied, of the immunities, privileges, exemptions and facilities enjoyed by the Participants under international law, international Conventions or Arrangements; or the domestic legislation and laws of the Recipient's Member States."

(*d*) Letter of agreement between UNIDO and the Swiss Confederation, through the State Secretariat for Economic Affairs regarding implementation of a project entitled "Global Quality and Standards Programme", signed on 27 November 2017**

19. Nothing in or relating to this Agreement shall be deemed a waiver of any of the privileges and immunities of UNIDO and no provision of this Agreement shall be interpreted or applied in a manner, or to an extent, inconsistent with such privileges and immunities.

* Entered into force on 8 November 2017.

** Entered into force on 27 November 2017.

(*e*) Trust fund agreement between UNIDO and the Federal Ministry of Science, Research and Economy of the Republic of Austria regarding implementation of a project entitled "Private Financing Advisory Network", signed on 5 December 2017*

ANNEX A—PROJECT DOCUMENT

8. LEGAL CONTEXT

It is expected that each set of activities to be implemented in the target countries will be governed by the provisions of the Standard Basic Cooperation Agreement concluded between the Government of the recipient country concerned and UNIDO or—in the absence of such an agreement—by one of the following: (i) the Standard Basic Assistance Agreement concluded between the recipient country and UNDP, (ii) the Technical Assistance Agreements concluded between the recipient country and the United Nations and specialized agencies, or (iii) the Basic Terms and Conditions Governing UNIDO Projects.

6. International Criminal Court

(*a*) Rome Statute of the International Criminal Court**

On 27 October 2017, Burundi's withdrawal from the Rome Statute of the International Criminal Court (the "Rome Statute") took effect.

(*b*) Amendment(s) to the Rome Statute

On 14 December 2017, at its 12th plenary meeting, the Assembly of States Parties ("ASP") adopted three amendments to article 8(2)(*b*) and to article 8(2)(*e*) of the Rome Statute, which are subject to ratification or acceptance and shall enter into force in accordance with article 121(5) of the Rome Statute.

(i) *Amendment to be inserted as article 8(2)(b)(xxvii) and article 8(2)(e)(xvi) of the Rome Statute*

"Employing weapons, which use microbial or other biological agents, or toxins, whatever their origin or method of production;".

(ii) *Amendment to be inserted as article 8(2)(b)(xxviii) and article 8(2)(e)(xvii) of the Rome Statute*

"Employing weapons the primary effect of which is to injure by fragments which in the human body escape detection by X-rays;".

* Entered into force on 5 December 2017.

** United Nations, *Treaty Series*, vol. 2187, p. 3.

(iii) *Amendment to be inserted as article 8(2)(b)(xxix) and article 8(2)(e)(xviii) of the Rome Statute*

"Employing laser weapons specifically designed, as their sole combat function or as one of their combat functions, to cause permanent blindness to unenhanced vision, that is to the naked eye or to the eye with corrective eyesight devices;".

(*c*) Ratification/Acceptance of amendments to the Rome Statute

(i) *Amendment to article 8(2)(e) of the Rome Statute*

Portugal, Argentina, Panama and State of Palestine ratified the amendment to article 8 of the Rome Statute* on 11 April, 28 April, 6 December and 29 December 2017, respectively.

(ii) *Amendments on the crime of aggression to the Rome Statute of the International Criminal Court*

Portugal, Argentina and Panama ratified the amendments to the Rome Statute on the crime of aggression on 11 April, 28 April and 6 December 2017, respectively.**

(iii) *Amendment to article 124 of the Rome Statute*

Portugal and Austria ratified the amendment to article 124 of the Rome Statute on 11 April and 22 September, respectively. The Netherlands accepted the amendment on 20 March 2017.***

(*d*) Agreement on the Privileges and Immunities of the ICC

On 17 January 2017, Peru ratified the Agreement on the Privileges and Immunities of the ICC. On 17 May 2017, the Republic of Moldova acceded to the Agreement on the Privileges and Immunities of the ICC.****

---

* The amendment entered into force in accordance with article 121(5) of the Rome Statute on 26 September 2012.

** United Nations, *Treaty Series*, vol. 2922, p.199.

*** In accordance with article 121(4) of the Rome Statute, the amendment has not yet entered into force.

**** United Nations, *Treaty Series*, vol. 2271, p. 3.

Part Two

LEGAL ACTIVITIES OF THE UNITED NATIONS AND RELATED INTERGOVERNMENTAL ORGANIZATIONS

Chapter III

GENERAL REVIEW OF THE LEGAL ACTIVITIES OF THE UNITED NATIONS AND RELATED INTERGOVERNMENTAL ORGANIZATIONS

A. General review of the legal activities of the United Nations

1. Membership of the United Nations

As of 31 December 2017, the number of Member States of the United Nations was 193.

2. Peace and Security

(*a*) Peacekeeping missions and operations[1]

(i) *Peacekeeping missions and operations established in 2017*

Haiti

The United Nations Mission for Justice Support in Haiti (MINUJUSTH) was established by Security Council resolution 2350 (2017) of 13 April 2017, upon completion of the mandate of the United Nations Stabilization Mission in Haiti (MINUSTAH), for an initial period of six months, from 16 October 2017 until 15 April 2018. MINUJUSTH was established to assist the Government of Haiti to further develop the Haitian National Police (HNP); to strengthen Haiti's rule of law institutions, including the justice and prisons; and to promote and protect human rights.

(ii) *Changes in the mandate and/or extensions of time limits of ongoing peacekeeping operations or missions in 2017*

a. Cyprus

The United Nations Peacekeeping Force in Cyprus (UNFICYP) was established by Security Council resolution 186 (1964) of 4 March 1964.[2] The Security Council decided

[1] The missions and operations are listed in chronological order as per their date of establishment.

[2] For more information on UNFICYP, see https://unficyp.unmissions.org. See also the reports of the Secretary-General on the United Nations operation in Cyprus for the period from 16 December 2016 to 22 June 2017 (S/2017/586), from 23 June to 18 December 2017 (S/2018/25) and from 19 December 2017 to 20 June 2018 (S/2018/676).

to extend the mandate of UNFICYP by resolutions 2338 (2017) of 26 January 2017 and 2369 (2017) of 27 July 2017, until 31 July 2017 and 31 January 2018, respectively.

b. Syrian Arab Republic and Israel

The United Nations Disengagement Observer Force (UNDOF) was established by Security Council resolution 350 (1974) of 31 March 1974.[3] The Security Council renewed the mandate of UNDOF by resolutions 2361 (2017) of 29 June 2017 and 2394 (2017) of 21 December 2017 until 31 December 2017 and 30 June 2018, respectively.

c. Lebanon

The United Nations Interim Force in Lebanon (UNIFIL) was established by Security Council resolutions 425 (1978) and 426 (1978) of 19 March 1978.[4] Following a request by the Lebanese Foreign Minister, presented in a letter dated 25 July 2017 addressed to the Secretary-General, the Secretary-General recommended the Security Council to consider the renewal of UNIFIL for a further period of one year.[5] The Security Council decided to extend the mandate of UNIFIL by resolution 2373 (2017) of 30 August 2017, until 31 August 2018.

d. Western Sahara

The United Nations Mission for the Referendum in Western Sahara (MINURSO) was established by Security Council resolution 690 (1991) of 29 April 1991.[6] By resolution 2351 (2017) of 28 April 2017, the Security Council decided to extend the mandate of MINURSO until 30 April 2018.

e. Democratic Republic of the Congo[7]

The United Nations Organization Mission in the Democratic Republic of the Congo (MONUC) was established by Security Council resolution 1279 (1999) of 30 November

---

[3] For more information on UNDOF, see https://undof.unmissions.org. See also the reports of the Secretary-General on the United Nations Disengagement Observer Force (UNDOF) for the period from 18 November 2016 to 1 March 2017 (S/2017/230), from 2 March to 16 May 2017 (S/2017/486), from 17 May to 9 September 2017 (S/2017/810), from 10 September to 24 November 2017 (S/2017/1024) and from 25 November 2017 to 23 February 2018 (S/2018/244).

[4] For more information on UNIFIL, see https://unifil.unmissions.org. See also the twenty-fifth semi-annual report of the Secretary-General to the Security Council on the implementation of Security Council resolution 1559 (2004) (S/2017/374), the twenty-sixth semi-annual report of the Secretary-General to the Security Council on the implementation of Security Council resolution 1559 (2004) (S/2017/867), and the reports of the Secretary-General on the implementation of Security Council resolution 1701 (2006) (S/2017/201, S/2017/591, S/2017/964 and S/2018/210).

[5] Letter dated 7 August 2017 from the Secretary-General addressed to the President of the Security Council (S/2017/680).

[6] For more information MINURSO, see https://minurso.unmissions.org. See also the reports of the Secretary-General on the situation concerning Western Sahara for the period from 19 April 2016 to 10 April 2017 (S/2017/307) and from 10 April 2017 to 28 March 2018 (S/2018/277).

[7] See subsection (*f*) (iii) below on sanctions concerning the Democratic Republic of the Congo.

1999. As of 1 July 2010, MONUC was renamed United Nations Organization Stabilization Mission in the Democratic Republic of the Congo (MONUSCO).[8]

Acting under Chapter VII of the United Nations Charter, the Security Council, by its resolution 2348 (2017) of 31 March 2017, extended the mandate of MONUSCO until 31 March 2018 including, on an exceptional basis and without creating a precedent or any prejudice to the agreed principles of peacekeeping, its Intervention Brigade. The Security Council also decided, taking into account the recommendations of the Secretary General in his report S/2017/206, that MONUSCO's authorized troop ceiling would be comprised of 16,215 military personnel, 660 military observers and staff officers, 391 police personnel, and 1,050 personnel of formed police units. The Security Council further decided that the mandate of MONUSCO should include, with priority, tasks concerning: (*a*) protection of civilians; (*b*) implementation of the 31 December 2016 agreement and support to the electoral process; and (*c*) protection of the United Nations. Further, the Security Council authorized MONUSCO to pursue tasks concerning (*a*) stabilisation and Disarmament, Demobilization and Reintegration (DDR); (*b*) Security Sector Reform (SSR); (*c*) sanctions regime; and (*d*) mining activities.

f. Liberia[9]

The United Nations Mission in Liberia (UNMIL) was established by Security Council resolution 1509 (2003) of 19 September 2003.[10] By resolution 2333 (2016) of 23 December 2016, the Security Council had extended the mandate of UNMIL for a final period until 30 March 2018. In the statement by the President of the Security Council of 24 July 2017 (S/PRST/2017/11), the Security Council commended the overall progress towards restoring peace, security, and stability in Liberia and welcomed the Liberia Peacebuilding Plan, entitled 'Sustaining Peace and Securing Development'.

[8] See Security Council resolution 1925 (2010) of 28 May 2010. For more information on MONUSCO see https://monusco.unmissions.org. See also the reports of the Secretary-General on the United Nations Organization Stabilization Mission in the Democratic Republic of the Congo (S/2017/206, S/2017/565, and S/2017/824), the reports of the Secretary-General on the implementation of the Peace, Security and Cooperation Framework for the Democratic Republic of the Congo and the Region (S/2017/208 and S/2017/825), the report of the Secretary-General on the implementation of the political agreement of 31 December 2016 in the Democratic Republic of the Congo (S/2017/435), the Special report of the Secretary-General on the strategic review of the United Nations Organization Stabilization Mission in the Democratic Republic of the Congo (S/2017/826), and the statements of the President of the Security Council of 4 January 2017 (S/PRST/2017/1) and 26 July 2017 (S/PRST/2017/12).

[9] See subsections (*f*) (ii) below on sanctions concerning Liberia.

[10] For more information on UNMIL, see http://unmil.unmissions.org. See also the thirty-third progress report of the Secretary-General on the United Nations Mission in Liberia covering the period since 15 November 2016 until 16 June 2017 (S/2017/510), the final progress report of the Secretary-General on the United Nations Mission in Liberia covering the period since 16 June 2017 until 30 March 2018 (S/2018/344), and the letter dated 4 April 2017 from the Secretary-General addressed to the President of the Security Council, setting out a peacebuilding plan to direct the role of the United Nations system and other relevant partners in supporting the transition of Liberia (S/2017/282).

g. Republic of the Sudan (Darfur)[11]

The African Union-United Nations Hybrid Operation in Darfur (UNAMID) was established and authorized by Security Council resolution 1769 (2007) of 31 July 2007.[12] By resolution 2363 (2017) of 29 June 2017, the Security Council decided to extend the mandate of UNAMID until 30 June 2018.

By the same resolution, it decided that from the date of adoption of this resolution until six months thereafter ("phase one"), UNAMID's authorised ceiling for troops and police should be reduced to consist of up to 11,395 military personnel, 2,888 police personnel including individual police officers and members of formed police units. The Security Council further decided, from 31 January 2018, to further reduce UNAMID's troop and police ceiling, taking into account the recommendations in the Special Report ("phase two"), and that by 30 June 2018, UNAMID's authorised ceiling for troops and police should be reduced to consist of up to 8,735 military personnel and 2,500 police personnel including individual police officers and members of formed police units, unless the Security Council decided to adjust the scope and pace of the reduction.

h. Republic of the Sudan and Republic of South Sudan (Abyei)[13]

The United Nations Interim Security Force for Abyei (UNISFA) was established by Security Council resolution 1990 (2011) of 27 June 2011.[14] The Security Council decided to extend the mandate of UNISFA, as set out in paragraph 2 of resolution 1990 (2011) and modified by resolution 2024 (2011) and paragraph 1 of resolution 2075 (2012), by resolution 2352 (2017) of 15 May 2017 and resolution 2386 (2017) of 15 November 2017, until 15 November 2017 and 15 May 2018, respectively.

Acting under Chapter VII of the Charter of the United Nations, the Council, in resolutions 2352 (2017) and 2386 (2017), also decided to extend until 15 November 2017 and 15 May 2018, respectively, the tasks of UNISFA, as set out in paragraph 3 of resolution 1990 (2011), and determined that, for the purposes of paragraph 1 of resolution 2024 (2011), support to the operational activities of the Joint Border Verification and Monitoring Mission (JBVMM) should include support to the *Ad Hoc* Committees.

By resolution 2386 (2017), the Council also decided to extend until 15 April 2018 UNISFA's mandate modification set forth in resolution 2024 (2011) and paragraph 1 of resolution 2075 (2012), and further decided that this should be the final such extension unless the parties took the specific measures. The Council also decided to maintain the authorized troop ceiling of 4,791 until 15 April 2018, and further decided that as of 15 April 2018,

---

[11] See subsection (*f*) (v) below on sanctions concerning the Republic of Sudan.

[12] For more information on UNAMID, see http://unamid.unmissions.org. See also the reports of the Secretary-General on UNAMID (S/2017/250, S/2017/503, S/2017/746, S/2017/907 and S/2017/1113), the special report of the Secretary-General and the Chairperson of the African Union Commission on the African Union-United Nations Hybrid Operation in Darfur on UNAMID (S/2017/437) and the assessment of the status of implementation of the Doha Document for Peace in Darfur in the next 60-day report on the African Union-United Nations Hybrid Operation in Darfur (UNAMID) (Letter) (S/2017/747).

[13] See subsection (*f*) (v) and (xiii) below on sanctions concerning the Republic of Sudan and the Republic of South Sudan, respectively.

[14] For more information on UNISFA, see https://unisfa.unmissions.org.

the authorized troop ceiling should decrease to 4,235, unless it decided to extend the mandate modification set forth in resolution 2024 (2012) and paragraph 1 of resolution 2075 (2012), in accordance with paragraphs 2 and 9.

i. Republic of South Sudan[15]

The United Nations Mission in the Republic of South Sudan (UNMISS) was established by the Security Council in resolution 1996 (2011) of 8 July 2011.[16] By resolution 2392 (2017) of 14 December 2017, the Security Council, acting under Chapter VII of the Charter of the United Nations, decided to extend the mandate of UNMISS through 15 March 2018.

j. Mali[17]

The United Nations Multidimensional Integrated Stabilization Mission in Mali (MINUSMA) was established by Security Council resolution 2100 of 25 April 2013.[18] By resolution 2364 (2017) of 29 June 2017, the Security Council, acting under Chapter VII of the Charter of the United Nations, decided to extend the mandate of MINUSMA until 30 June 2018.

By the same resolution, the Security Council decided that MINUSMA should continue to comprise up to 13,289 military personnel and 1,920 police personnel, and requested the Secretary General to take the necessary steps to expedite force and asset generation, as well as deployment. The Council also decided that the strategic priority of MINUSMA would remain to support the implementation by the Government, the *Plateforme* and *Coordination* armed groups, as well as by other relevant Malian stakeholders, of the Agreement on Peace and Reconciliation in Mali, in particular its political and security aspects, notably the gradual restoration and extension of State authority.

k. Central African Republic[19]

The United Nations Multidimensional Integrated Stabilization Mission in the Central African Republic (MINUSCA) was established by Security Council resolution 2149 (2014)

---

[15] See subsection (*f*) (xiii) below on sanctions concerning the Republic of South Sudan.

[16] For more information on UNMISS, see http://unmiss.unmissions.org. See also the reports of the Secretary-General on South Sudan (S/2017/224, S/2017/505, S/2017/784 and S/2017/1011), the letter dated 17 April 2017 from the Secretary-General addressed to the President of the Security Council (S/2017/328) and the statements by the President of the Security Council of 23 March 2017 (S/PRST/2017/4) and of 14 December 2017 (S/PRST/2017/25).

[17] See subsection (*f*) (xiv) below on sanctions concerning Mali.

[18] For more information on MINUSMA, see https://minusma.unmissions.org. See also the reports of the Secretary-General on the situation in Mali (S/2017/271, S/2017/478, S/2017/811 and S/2017/1105), the Fifteenth report on the support provided by French forces to the United Nations Multidimensional Integrated Stabilization Mission in Mali between 1 December 2016 and 1 March 2017 (Letter) and the Seventeenth report on the support provided by French forces to the United Nations Multidimensional Integrated Stabilization Mission in Mali between 1 June and 1 September 2017 (Letter).

[19] See subsection (*e*)(*c*) below concerning actions of Member States authorized by the Security Council, and subsection (*f*) (xi) below on sanctions concerning the Central African Republic.

of 10 April 2014.[20] By resolution 2387 (2017) of 15 November 2017, the Security Council decided to extend the mandate of MINUSCA until 15 November 2018.

By the same resolution, the Council decided to authorise an increase of 900 military personnel in addition to the military personnel authorized by paragraph 24 of resolution 2301 (2016) in order to increase MINUSCA's flexibility and mobility to improve the efficient implementation of its full mandate and, in particular, the protection of civilians task provided at paragraph 42 (*a*), thereby resulting in an authorized troop ceiling of 11,650 military personnel, including 480 Military Observers and Military Staff Officers, 2,080 police personnel, including 400 Individual Police Officers, as well as 108 corrections officers. The Council also decided that the mandate of MINUSCA should include the following priority tasks: (*a*) protection of civilians; (*b*) good offices and support to the peace process, including national reconciliation, social cohesion and transitional justice; (*c*) facilitate the creation of a secure environment for the immediate, full, safe and unhindered delivery of humanitarian assistance; and (*d*) protection of the United Nations.

(iii) *Other ongoing peacekeeping operations or missions*

a. India and Pakistan

The United Nations Military Observer Group in India and Pakistan (UNMOGIP) was established by resolutions 39 (1948) and 47 (1948) of 20 January and 21 April 1948 respectively, in order to supervise, in the State of Jammu and Kashmir, the ceasefire between India and Pakistan, as well as to observe, to the extent possible, developments pertaining to the strict observance of the ceasefire of 17 December 1971 and to report thereon to the Secretary-General.[21] UNMOGIP continued to operate in 2017.

b. Middle East

The United Nations Truce Supervision Organization (UNTSO) was established by Security Council resolution 50 (1948) on 29 May 1948 in order to supervise the observation of the truce in Palestine. [22] UNTSO continued to operate in 2017.

c. Kosovo

The United Nations Interim Administration Mission in Kosovo (UNMIK) was established by resolution 1244 (1999) on 10 June 1999, and was mandated to help ensure conditions for a peaceful and normal life for all inhabitants of Kosovo and advance regional stability in the western Balkans.[23] UNMIK continued to operate in 2017.

---

[20] For more information on MINUSCA, see https://minusca.unmissions.org. See also the reports of the Secretary-General on the situation in the Central African Republic (S/2017/94, S/2017/473 and S/2017/865), the United Nations Multidimensional Integrated Stabilization Mission in the Central African Republic (MINUSCA) Letter, and the statements of the President of the Security Council dated 4 April 2017 (S/PRST/2017/5) and 13 July 2017 (S/PRST/2017/9).

[21] For more information on UNMOGIP, see https://unmogip.unmissions.org.

[22] For more information on UNTSO, see http://untso.unmissions.org.

[23] For more information on UNMIK, see https://unmik.unmissions.org. See also the reports of the Secretary-General on UNMIK (S/2017/95/Rev.1, S/2017/387, S/2015/579, S/2017/640 and S/2017/911).

(iv) *Peacekeeping missions or operations concluded in 2017*

a. Côte d'Ivoire[24]

The United Nations Operation in Côte d'Ivoire (UNOCI) was established by Security Council resolution 1528 (2004) of 27 February 2004.[25] By its resolution 2284 (2016), the Security Council had extended the mandate of UNOCI for a final period, until 30 June 2017, and requested the Secretary-General to provide, by 31 January 2017, an update on the implementation of the mandate and its phased drawdown, including the continued transition of its security responsibilities to the Government of Côte d'Ivoire. The final progress report of the Secretary-General on the United Nations Operation in Côte d'Ivoire of 31 January 2017 (S/2017/89) presented major developments since 31 March 2016 and an update on the drawdown and transition of UNOCI. In the statement of the President of the Security Council of 30 June 2017 (S/PRST/2017/8), the Security Council noted that UNOCI was completing its mandate on 30 June 2017 and commended the achievements made by Côte d'Ivoire since 2004.

b. Haiti

The United Nations Stabilization Mission in Haiti (MINUSTAH) was established by Security Council resolution 1542 (2004) of 30 April 2004.[26] By resolution 2350 (2017) of 13 April 2017, the Security Council, acting under Chapter VII of the Charter of the United Nations, decided to extend the mandate of MINUSTAH for a final period of six months and that the Mission should close by 15 October 2017. The Security Council also decided that the military component of MINUSTAH should gradually drawdown during the final six-month period, fully withdrawing from Haiti by 15 October 2017. The Security Council established the United Nations Mission for Justice Support in Haiti (MINUJUSTH) for an initial period of six months, from 16 October 2017 until 15 April 2018.

(*b*) Political and peacebuilding missions

(i) *Political and peacebuilding missions established in 2017*

Colombia

The United Nations Verification Mission in Colombia (the Verification Mission) was established by Security Council resolution 2366 (2017) of 10 July 2017, for an initial period of 12 months, headed by a Special Representative of the Secretary-General of the United Nations.[27] By the same resolution, the Council decided further that the Verification

---

[24] See subsection (*f*) (iv) below on sanctions concerning Côte d'Ivoire.

[25] For more information on UNOCI, see https://onuci.unmissions.org.

[26] For more information on MINUSTAH, see https://minustah.unmissions.org. See also the reports of the Secretary-General on the United Nations Stabilization Mission in Haiti and the United Nations Mission for Justice Support in Haiti (S/2017/223; S/2017/604; and S/2017/840) as well as the statement of the President of the Security Council of 17 October 2017 (S/PRST/2017/20).

[27] For more information on the Verification Mission, see https://colombia.unmissions.org. See also the "Final Agreement for Ending the Conflict and Building a Stable and Lasting Peace" (the Final Agreement) (S/2017/272) between the Government of Colombia and the Revolutionary Armed Forces of

Mission should verify implementation by the Government of Colombia and FARC-EP of section 3.2 and 3.4 of the Final Agreement as called for in section 6.3.3 of the Final Agreement, including the process of political, economic and social reincorporation of the FARC-EP; the implementation of personal and collective security guarantees; and comprehensive programmes on security and protection measures for communities and organisations in the territories, and should include the required regional and local verification. It decided also that the Verification Mission should begin all verification activities on 26 September 2017, immediately after completion of the mandate of the United Nations Mission in Colombia established by resolution 2261 (2016), and that that would commence the initial 12-month period.

By resolution 2377 (2017) of 14 September 2017, the Security Council welcomed the Secretary-General's report S/2017/745 and approved the recommendations therein regarding the size, operational aspects and mandate of the United Nations Verification Mission in Colombia.

A request was made by the Government of Colombia and the National Liberation Army (ELN) on 29 September 2017 in a Joint Communiqué for the United Nations to participate as the international component and coordinator of a monitoring and verification mechanism (MVM), comprised of representatives of the Government of Colombia, the ELN, the United Nations and the Catholic Church, to verify compliance with the temporary bilateral ceasefire. By Security Council resolution 2381 (2017) of 6 October 2017, the Council decided that the Verification Mission should, on a temporary basis until 9 January 2018, participate in and coordinate the work of the MVM, as outlined in the Joint Communiqué, in order to: (i) verify compliance with the temporary, bilateral, national ceasefire with the ELN at the national, regional and local level; (ii) endeavour to prevent incidents through enhanced coordination between the parties and resolution of disagreements; (iii) enable timely response by the parties to incidents; and (iv) verify and report publicly and to the parties on compliance with the ceasefire.

(ii) *Changes in the mandate and/or extensions of the time limits of ongoing political and peacebuilding missions in 2017*

a. Afghanistan[28]

The United Nations Assistance Mission in Afghanistan (UNAMA) was established by Security Council resolution 1401 (2002) of 28 March 2002.[29] On 17 March 2017, the

Colombia (FARC-EP) and the letter dated 7 June 2017 from the President of Colombia on behalf of the Government of Colombia and FARC-EP (S/2017/481) requesting a second special political mission for a period of three years, renewable if necessary, in accordance with section 6.3.3 of the Final Agreement. In addition, see the reports of the Secretary-General on the Verification Mission (S/2017/745, S/2017/1117, and S/2017/830) and the statements of the President of the Security Council on Colombia of 11 May 2017 (S/PRST/2017/6) and of 5 October 2017 (S/PRST/2017/18).

[28] See subsection (*f*) (ix) on sanctions concerning Afghanistan.

[29] For more information on UNAMA, see http://unama.unmissions.org. See also the reports of the Secretary-General on the situation in Afghanistan and its implications for international peace and security, (S/2017/189, S/2017/508, S/2017/783 and S/2017/1056) and the Special report on the strategic review of the United Nations Assistance Mission in Afghanistan of 10 August 2017 (S/2017/696).

Security Council decided by resolution 2344 (2017) to extend the mandate of UNAMA until 17 March 2018.

In the same resolution, the Council decided further that UNAMA and the Special Representative of the Secretary General, within their mandate and in a manner consistent with Afghan sovereignty, leadership and ownership, would continue to lead and coordinate the international civilian efforts, in full cooperation with the Government of Afghanistan and in accordance with the London, Kabul, Tokyo and Brussels Conferences Communiqués and the Bonn Conference Conclusions, with a particular focus on priorities that were laid out in the resolution.

b. Iraq

The United Nations Assistance Mission for Iraq (UNAMI) was established by Security Council resolution 1500 (2003) of 14 August 2003.[30] By resolution 2367 (2017) of 14 July 2017, the Security Council decided to extend the mandate of UNAMI until 31 July 2018. It decided further, by the same resolution, that the Special Representative of the Secretary General and UNAMI, at the request of the Government of Iraq, and taking into account the letter from the Minister of Foreign Affairs of Iraq to the Secretary General (S/2017/518), should continue to pursue their mandate as stipulated in resolution 2299 (2016).

c. Guinea Bissau[31]

The United Nations Integrated Peacebuilding Office in Guinea-Bissau (UNIOGIBIS) was established by Security Council resolution 1876 (2009) of 26 June 2009.[32] By resolution 2343 (2017) of 23 February 2017, the Security Council decided to extend the mandate of UNIOGIBIS for a period of 12 months beginning on 1 March 2017 until 28 February 2018.

d. Libya[33]

The United Nations Support Mission in Libya (UNSMIL) was established by Security Council resolution 2009 (2011) of 16 September 2011.[34] By resolution 2376 (2017) of 14 September 2017, the Security Council decided to extend the mandate of UNSMIL until 15 September 2018, under the leadership of the Special Representative of the Secretary General, as an integrated special political mission, in full accordance with the principles of national ownership to exercise mediation and good offices to support: (i) an inclusive

---

[30] For more information on the activities of UNAMI, see http://www.uniraq.org. See also the thirteenth, fourteenth, fifteenth and sixteenth reports of the Secretary-General pursuant to paragraph 4 of resolution 2107 (2013) (S/2017/73, S/2017/371, S/2017/569 and S/2017/880, respectively), the reports of the Secretary-General pursuant to resolution 2299 (2016) (S/2017/75, S/2017/357 and S/2017/592) and the report of the Secretary-General pursuant to resolution 2367 (2017) (S/2017/881).

[31] See subsection (*f*) (x) below on sanctions concerning Guinea-Bissau.

[32] For more information on UNIOGBIS, see http://uniogbis.unmissions.org. See also the reports of the Secretary-General on developments in Guinea-Bissau and the activities of UNIOGBIS (S/2017/111, S/2017/695 and S/2017/715) as well as the statement of the President of the Security Council on the situation in Guinea-Bissau of 13 September 2017 (S/PRST/2017/17).

[33] See subsection (*f*) (viii) below on sanctions concerning Libya.

[34] For more information on UNSMIL, see https://unsmil.unmissions.org. See also the reports of the Secretary-General on UNSMIL (S/217/283 and S/2017/726).

political process within the framework of the Libyan Political Agreement; (ii) continued implementation of the Libyan Political Agreement; (iii) consolidation of the governance, security and economic arrangements of the Government of National Accord (GNA); and (iv) subsequent phases of the Libyan transition process;

By resolution 2376 (2017), the Security Council decided further that UNSMIL, within operational and security constraints, should undertake the following tasks: (i) support to key Libyan institutions; (ii) support, on request, for the provision of essential services, and delivery of humanitarian assistance and in accordance with humanitarian principles; (iii) human rights monitoring and reporting; (iv) support for securing uncontrolled arms and related materiel and countering their proliferation; and (v) coordination of international assistance, and provision of advice and assistance to the GNA led efforts to stabilize post conflict zones, including those liberated from Da'esh.

e. Somalia[35]

The United Nations Assistance Mission in Somalia (UNSOM) was established by Security Council resolution 2102 (2013) of 2 May 2013 under the leadership of a Special Representative of the Secretary-General.[36] By resolution 2346 (2017) of 23 March 2017 and resolution 2358 (2017) of 14 June 2017, the Security Council decided to extend the mandate of UNSOM as set out in paragraph 1 of resolution 2158 (2014) until 16 June 2017 and 31 March 2018, respectively.

(iii) *Other ongoing political and peacebuilding missions in 2017*

a. Middle East

The Office of the United Nations Special Coordinator for the Middle East Peace Process (UNSCO), established by the Secretary-General on 1 October 1999,[37] continued to operate throughout 2017.[38]

b. Lebanon

The Office of the United Nations Special Coordinator for Lebanon (UNSCOL) was established in 2000 as the Personal Representative of the Secretary-General for Southern Lebanon.[39] The mandate was expanded to include coordination of United Nations political activities for the whole of Lebanon and the title changed to Personal Representative

---

[35] See subsection (*f*) (i) below on sanctions concerning Somalia.

[36] For more information on UNSOM, see https://unsom.unmissions.org. See also the reports of the Secretary-General on Somalia (S/2017/21, S/2017/408, S/2017/751 and S/2017/1109) and the letter dated 5 May 2017 from the Secretary-General addressed to the President of the Security Council on the review of the United Nations presence in Somalia after the 2016 electoral process (S/2017/404).

[37] Exchange of letters between the Secretary-General and the Security Council (S/1999/983 and S/1999/984).

[38] For more information on UNSCO, see https://unsco.unmissions.org.

[39] S/2000/718.

for Lebanon in 2005,[40] and Lebanon and to Special Coordinator for Lebanon in 2007,[41] respectively. UNSCOL continued to operate throughout 2017.[42]

c. Central Asia

The United Nations Regional Centre for Preventive Diplomacy for Central Asia (UNRCCA) was established on 10 December 2007 by a letter dated 7 May 2007 from the Secretary-General to the President of the Security Council (S/2007/279). UNRCCA continued to function throughout 2017.[43]

d. Central African region

The United Nations Regional Office for Central Africa (UNOCA), located in Libreville, Gabon, was established in August 2010 on the basis of an exchange of letters between the Secretary-General and the Security Council.[44] UNOCA began its operations on 2 March 2011 and continued its operations throughout 2017 after its mandate had been extended in 2015 until 31 of August 2018.[45]

e. African Union

The United Nations Office to the African Union (UNOAU) was established by the General Assembly in resolution 64/288 of 24 June 2010, *inter alia* to enhance the partnership between the United Nations and the African Union. UNOAU continued to function throughout 2017.[46]

f. West Africa and the Sahel

The new United Nations Office for West Africa and the Sahel (UNOWAS), was established in January 2016 on the basis of an exchange of letters between the Secretary-General and the Security Council, merging the former Office of the Special Envoy for the Sahel (OSES) and the United Nations Office for West Africa (UNOWA).[47] UNOWAS began its operations on 12 February 2016 and continued its operations throughout 2017.

---

[40] Letter dated 17 November 2005 from the Secretary-General to the President of the Security Council (S/2005/726).

[41] Letter dated 8 February 2007 from the Secretary-General to the President of the Security Council (S/2007/85).

[42] For more information on the activities UNSCOL, see http://unscol.unmissions.org.

[43] For more information on UNRCCA, see http://unrcca.unmissions.org.

[44] For more information about UNOCA, see https://unoca.unmissions.org. See also the reports on the situation in Central Africa and the activities of the United Nations Regional Office for Central Africa (S/2017/465 and S/2017/995).

[45] Exchange of letters between the Secretary-General and the President of the Security Council (S/2015/554 and S/2015/555).

[46] For more information on UNOAU, see https://unoau.unmissions.org.

[47] Letter dated 28 January 2016 from the President of the Security Council addressed to the Secretary-General (S/2016/89). For more information about UNOWAS, see https://unowas.unmissions.org/. See also the reports of the Secretary-General on the activities of the United Nations Office for West Africa and the Sahel (S/2017/563 and S/2017/1104).

(iv) *Political and peacebuilding missions concluded in 2017*

Colombia

By resolution 2261 (2016) of 25 January 2016, the Security-Council established a political mission to Colombia to participate, for a period of 12 months, as the international component and coordinator in the tripartite mechanism to monitor and verify the definitive bilateral ceasefire and cessation of hostilities between the Government of Colombia and the FARC-EP, foreseen for the Final Peace Agreement between the Government of Colombia and the FARC-EP.[48] By resolution 2307 (2016) of 13 September 2016, the Security Council subsequently approved the recommendations submitted by the Secretary-General in report S/2016/729 regarding the size, operational aspects and mandate of the Mission. In 2017, the mandate of this mission was replaced by the United Nations Verification Mission, established by the Security Council by resolution 2366 (2017) of 10 July 2017.

(*c*) Other bodies

(i) *Cameroon-Nigeria Mixed Commission*

The Cameroon-Nigeria Mixed Commission was established by the Secretary-General, pursuant to a Joint Communiqué of the Presidents of Nigeria and Cameroon adopted in Geneva on 15 November 2002, to facilitate the implementation of the 10 October 2002 ruling of the International Court of Justice on the Cameroon-Nigeria boundary dispute.[49] The mandate of the Mixed Commission included supporting the demarcation of the land boundary and delineation of the maritime boundary, facilitating the withdrawal and transfer of authority along the boundary, addressing the situation of affected populations and making recommendations on confidence-building measures. The Mixed Commission continued its work in 2017.[50]

(ii) *Monitoring mechanism for Syria*

The United Nations monitoring mechanism for Syria was established by Security Council resolution 2165 of 14 July 2014 to monitor, under the authority of the United Nations Secretary-General and with the consent of the relevant neighbouring countries of Syria, the loading of all humanitarian relief consignments of the United Nations humanitarian agencies and their implementing partners at the relevant United Nations facilities.[51] By resolution 2393 (2017) of 19 December 2017, the Security Council decided to renew its

---

[48] For more information about the United Nations Mission to Colombia see https://colombia.unmissions.org/en.

[49] *Land and Maritime Boundary between Cameroon and Nigeria (Cameroon* v. *Nigeria: Equatorial Guinea intervening), Judgment, I. C. J. Reports 2002*, p. 303.

[50] For more information on the Commission's work in 2017, see the exchange of letters between the Secretary-General and the President of the Security Council (S/2017/78, S/2017/79, S/2017/1034 and S/2017/1035).

[51] For more information on the Monitoring Mechanism, see the report of the Secretary-General on the revised estimates relating to the programme budget for the biennium 2016–2017 under sections 27, Humanitarian assistance, and 36, Staff assessment, United Nations Monitoring Mechanism (A/70/726)

decisions in paragraphs 2 and 3 of Security Council resolution 2165 (2014) for a further period of twelve months, until 10 January 2019.

(iii) *Organisation for the Prohibition of Chemical Weapons—United Nations Joint Investigative Mechanism*

The Organisation for the Prohibition of Chemical Weapons—United Nations Joint Investigative Mechanism (OPCW-JIM) was established following Security Council resolution 2235 (2015) of 7 August 2015. The OPCW-JIM ceased functioning on 17 November 2017, following the one-year mandate renewal decided on in resolution 2319 (2016) of 17 November 2016.[52]

(iv) *United Nations Security Management System Board of Inquiry—Group of Experts in Kananga, Democratic Republic of the Congo*

The United Nations Security Management System Board of Inquiry was established by the Under-Secretary-General for Safety and Security, in consultation with the Executive Office of the Secretary-General and the Under Secretaries-General for Political and Legal Affairs. The Board was convened on 24 April 2017, following a security incident resulting in the deaths of two members of two members of the Group of Experts on the Democratic Republic of Congo in Kananga, Democratic Republic of the Congo in March 2017. It conducted a field visit from 6 to 17 June 2017 and submitted its report on 2 August 2017. In view of the seriousness of the events, the Secretary-General communicated a summary of the internal report to the Security Council on 15 August 2017.[53]

(*d*) Missions of the Security Council

(i) *Lake Chad Basin Region*

In a letter dated 27 January 2017, the President of the Security Council informed the Secretary-General that the Council had decided to send a mission to Lake Chad Basin region (Cameroon, Chad, Niger and Nigeria) from 1 to 7 March 2017, outlining in an annex the mission's terms of reference.[54]

The mission to the Lake Chad Basin Region would, *inter alia*, assess the security situation in the countries of the Lake Chad Basin, namely Cameroon, Chad, the Niger and Nigeria, in particular the threat posed by the terrorist groups Boko Haram and Islamic State in Iraq and the Levant (ISIL, also known as Da'esh), and the potential impact on the wider region.

---

[52] For more information, see the reports of the OPCW-JIM, S/2017/131, S/2017/552 and S/2017/904. See also the letter dated 18 May 2017 from the Secretary-General addressed to the President of the Security Council (S/2017/440).

[53] Latter dated 15 August 2017 from the Secretary-General addressed ot the President of the Security Council (S/2017/713), Annex.

[54] Letter dated 1 March 2017 from the President of the Security Council addressed to the Secretary-General (S/2017/181). For more information, see the report of the Security Council mission to the Lake Chad Basin region (Cameroon, Chad, Niger and Nigeria), 1–7 March 2017 (S/2017/403).

(ii) *Haiti*

In a letter dated 15 June 2017, the President of the Security Council informed the Secretary-General that the Council's decision to send a mission to Haiti from 22 to 24 June 2017, outlining in an annex to the letter the mission's terms of reference.[55] The Security Council would carry out its mission to Haiti in the context of its resolution 2350 (2017).

The objectives of the mission were to reaffirm the support of the Security Council to the Government and people of Haiti to strengthen their country and institutions, in order to contribute to the stability and development of Haiti; to conduct a review of the implementation of resolution 2350 (2017), focusing on the successful conclusion and closure of the United Nations Stabilization Mission in Haiti (MINUSTAH) and the smooth transition between MINUSTAH and the United Nations Mission for Justice Support in Haiti (MINUJUSTH), including the orderly and progressive drawdown of the military component; and to identify on the ground the necessary requirements for the successful implementation of the mandate of MINUJUSTH.

(iii) *Ethiopia*

In a letter dated 1 September 2017, the President of the Security Council informed the Secretary-General that the Council had decided to send a mission to Ethiopia from 6 to 8 September 2017, outlining in an annex to the letter the mission's terms of reference.[56]

The objectives of the mission were, *inter alia*, to hold informal consultations regarding the partnership between the African Union and the United Nations, funding for African Union peace and security activities and post-conflict peacebuilding.

The objectives also included holding joint consultative meetings: to exchange views on how to build on recent political and security achievements to realize the objective of a secure, stable and prosperous Somalia, in particular through support for security sector reform and institution-building; to discuss the security and humanitarian situation in South Sudan and what steps the African Union and the United Nations Security Council can take to help achieve a genuine and sustainable ceasefire and facilitate the revitalization of the political process towards a lasting solution through inclusive dialogue; to discuss the threat posed by terrorism, particularly the terrorist attacks perpetrated by Boko Haram and the Islamic State in Iraq and the Levant (ISIL, also known as Da'esh), as well as the dire humanitarian situation in the Lake Chad Basin region, including large-scale displacement, and the risk of famine in the region; and to discuss the mobilization and implementation of regional and international support to assist the conflict-affected populations of the region and its respective Governments in their efforts to respond to these challenges.

---

[55] Letter dated 15 June 2017 from the President of the Security Council addressed to the Secretary-General (S/2017/511). See also the report of the Security Council mission to Haiti (22 to 24 June 2017) (S/PV.7994).

[56] Letter dated 1 September 2017 from the President of the Security Council addressed to the Secretary-General (S/2017/757). See also the report of the Security Council mission to Ethiopia (6 to 8 September 2017) (S/2017/1002).

(iv) *Sahel*

In a letter dated 16 October 2017, the President of the Security Council informed the Secretary-General about the Council's decision to send a mission to the Sahel region through visits to Mali, Mauritania and Burkina Faso, outlining in an annex to the letter the mission's terms of reference.[57] The mission would be carried out within the framework of Security Council resolutions 2359 (2017), 2364 (2017) and 2374 (2017) and in accordance with information given in the Press Statement issued as SC/12955 (2017).

The mission aimed, *inter alia*, to assess the situation in the Group of Five Sahel States, including regarding the level and the nature of the threat posed by terrorism and transnational organized crime (including arms and drug trafficking, the smuggling of migrants, trafficking in persons), and explore means to provide support in confronting those threats on national, sub-regional and regional levels.

The mission's objectives included also, *inter alia*, to underline that lasting peace and security in the Sahel region would not be achieved without a full, effective and inclusive implementation of the Agreement on Peace and Reconciliation in Mali; to urge the parties to accelerate the implementation of the Agreement; to underline the establishment of a new sanctions regime concerning Mali; and to call on the members of the Agreement Monitoring Committee and other relevant international partners to sustain their support to the implementation of the Agreement.

(*e*) Action of Member States authorized by the Security Council

(i) *Côte d'Ivoire*

French forces had initially been authorized, for a period of 12 months, by Security Council resolution 1528 (2004) of 27 February 2004 to use all necessary means in order to support UNOCI. By its resolution 2284 (2016), the Security Council had extended the mandate of the UNOCI for a final period, until 30 June 2017. On 31 January 2017, the Secretary-General provided an update on the implementation of the mandate of UNOCI and its phased drawdown, including the continued transition of its security responsibilities to the Government of Côte d'Ivoire, with a view to completing the mandate.[58]

(ii) *Bosnia and Herzegovina*

The European Union Force Althea (EUFOR ALTHEA) was initially authorized by Security Council resolution 1575 (2004) of 22 November 2004.[59] By its resolution 2384 (2017)

---

[57] Letter dated 16 October 2017 from the President of the Security Council addressed to the Secretary-General (S/2017/871). See also the report of the Security Council mission to the Sahel region (19 to 22 October 2017) (S/PV.8077).

[58] For more information on the United Nations Operation in Côte d'Ivoire, see Final progress report of the Secretary-General on the United Nations Operation in Côte d'Ivoire (S/2017/89).

[59] For more information on the European Union military mission in Bosnia and Herzegovina (EUFOR), see: https://www.euforbih.org/, and the forty-seventh to forty-ninth reports of the High Representative for Implementation of the Peace Agreement on Bosnia and Herzegovina (S/2015/300, S/2015/841 and S/2016/663, annexes, respectively).

of 7 November 2017, the Security Council, acting under Chapter VII of the Charter of the United Nations, authorized the Member States acting through or in cooperation with the European Union to establish for a further period of twelve months a multinational stabilization force (EUFOR ALTHEA). It also decided to renew the authorization provided by paragraph 11 of resolution 2183 (2014) for Member States acting through or in cooperation with NATO to continue to maintain a NATO Headquarters, both as a legal successor to SFOR under unified command and control.

The Security Council further authorized those Member States to take all necessary means to effect the implementation of and to ensure compliance with annexes 1-A and 2 of the Peace Agreement,[60] and to take all necessary measures to ensure compliance with the rules and procedures governing command and control of airspace over Bosnia and Herzegovina with respect to all civilian and military air traffic. Moreover, it authorized Member States to take all necessary means, at the request of either EUFOR ALTHEA or the NATO Headquarters, in defence of the EUFOR ALTHEA or NATO presence respectively, and to assist both organizations in carrying out their missions. It also recognized the right of both EUFOR ALTHEA and the NATO presence to take all necessary measures to defend themselves from attack or threat of attack.

(iii) *Somalia*[61]

The African Union Mission in Somalia (AMISOM) was initially authorized by the Security Council, acting under Chapter VII of the Charter of the United Nations, in resolution 1744 (2007) of 20 February 2007.[62] By resolutions 2355 (2017) of 26 May 2017 and 2372 (2017) of 30 August 2017, respectively, the Security Council, acting under Chapter VII of the Charter of the United Nations, decided to authorize the Member States of the African Union to maintain the deployment of AMISOM until 31 August 2017 and 31 May 2018, respectively. By resolution 2372 (2017), it also decided to reduce the level of uniformed AMISOM personnel to a maximum level of 21,626 by 31 December 2017. The Security Council further decided, by the same resolution, that AMISOM should be authorized to take all necessary measures, in full compliance with participating States' obligations under international humanitarian law and international human rights law, and in full respect for the sovereignty, territorial integrity, political independence and unity of Somalia, to carry out its mandate.

By resolution 2372 (2017) the Council also decided to authorize AMISOM to pursue the following strategic objectives: enabling the gradual handing over of security responsibilities from AMISOM to the Somali security forces contingent on abilities of the Somali security forces and political and security progress in Somalia; reducing the threat posed by Al Shabaab and other armed opposition groups; and assisting the Somali security forces to provide security for the political process at all levels as well as stabilization, reconciliation

---

[60] General Framework Agreement for Peace in Bosnia and Herzegovina and the Annexes thereto, attachment to letter dated 29 November 1995 from the Permanent Representative of the United States of America to the United Nations addressed to the Secretary-General (S/1995/999).

[61] With regard to acts of piracy off the coast of Somalia, see subsection (*k*) below.

[62] For more information AMISOM, see http://amisom-au.org. See also the letter dated 25 July 2017 from the Secretary-General addressed to the President of the Security Council concerning the African Union Mission in Somalia (AMISOM) (S/2017/653).

and peacebuilding in Somalia. It also decided to authorize AMISOM to carry out certain priority tasks to achieve those objectives.

(iv) *Central African Republic*

French forces had initially been authorized by the Security Council in resolution 2127 (2013) of 5 December 2013 to take all necessary measures to support the African-led International Support Mission in the Central African Republic (MISCA) and, by resolution 2149 (2014) of 10 April 2014, to use all necessary means to provide operational support to elements of MINUSCA, from the commencement of the activities of MINUSCA until the end of its mandate. By resolution 2387 (2017) of 15 November 2017 and acting under Chapter VII of the Charter of the United Nations, the Security Council authorised the French forces, within the provisions of their existing bilateral agreement with the CAR and the limits of their capacities and areas of deployment, at the request of the Secretary General, to use all the means to provide operational support to elements of MINUSCA when under serious threat.

(v) *Mali*

French forces had initially been authorized by Security Council resolution 2164 (2014) of 25 June 2014 to use all necessary means to intervene in support of elements of MINUSMA when under imminent and serious threat upon request of the Secretary-General. By resolution 2364 (2017) of 29 June 2017 and acting under Chapter VII of the Charter of the United Nations, the Security Council decided to extend this authorization until the end of MINUSMA's mandate as authorized in the resolution.

(vi) *Syrian Arab Republic*

By resolution 2165 (2014) of 14 July 2014, the Security Council, underscoring the obligations of Member States under Article 25 of the Charter of the United Nations, authorized United Nations humanitarian agencies and their implementing partners to use routes across conflict lines and the border crossings of Bab al-Salam, Bab al-Hawa, Al Yarubiyah and Al-Ramtha, in addition to those already in use, in order to ensure that humanitarian assistance reaches people in need throughout Syria through the most direct routes, with notification to the Syrian authorities. In resolution 2393 (2017) of 19 December 2017, the Security Council, underscoring the obligations of Member States under Article 25 of the Charter of the United Nations, decided to renew the authorization for a further period of twelve months, until 10 January 2019.[63]

---

[63] See also resolution 2254 (2015) of 18 December 2015, in which the Security Council, *inter alia*, endorsed the "Vienna Statements" in pursuit of the full implementation of the Geneva Communiqué of 30 June 2012, as the basis for a Syrian-led and Syrian-owned political transition in order to end the conflict in Syria. See further the reports of the Secretary-General on the implementation of Security Council resolutions 2139 (2014) and 2165 (2014) and 2191 (2014) (S/2015/48, S/2015/124, S/2015/206, S/2015/264, S/2015/368, S/2015/468, S/2015/561, S/2015/651, S/2015/698, S/2015/813, S/2015/862 and S/2015/962) and the statements of the President of the Security Council dated 24 April 2015 (S/PRST/2015/10) and 17 August 2015 (S/PRST/2015/15).

(*f*) Sanctions imposed under Chapter VII of the Charter of the United Nations[64]

(i) *Somalia and Eritrea*

The Security Council Committee established pursuant to resolution 751 (1992) of 24 April 1992 concerning Somalia was mandated to oversee the general and complete arms embargo imposed by Security Council resolution 733 (1992) and to undertake the tasks set out by the Security Council resolutions 751 (1992), 1356 (2001) and 1844 (2008). Following the adoption of resolution 1907 (2009), which imposed a sanctions regime on Eritrea and expanded its mandate, the Committee decided on 26 February 2010 to change its name to "Security Council Committee pursuant to resolution 751 (1992) and 1907 (2009) concerning Somalia and Eritrea".[65] The Security Council Committee submitted, on 26 December 2017, a report on its work in 2017 to the Security Council.[66]

By resolution 2385 (2017) of 14 November 2017, the Security Council, acting under Chapter VII of the Charter of the United Nations, reaffirmed the existing arms embargo on Somalia. By the same resolution, the Security Council further reaffirmed the existing arms embargo on Eritrea.

By the same resolution, it decided to renew the provisions set out in paragraph 2 of resolution 2142 (2014) until 15 November 2018 and reiterated that the arms embargo should not apply to deliveries of weapons, ammunition or military equipment or the provision of advice, assistance or training, intended solely for the development of the Security Forces of the Federal Government of Somalia, to provide security for the Somali people, except in relation to deliveries of the items set out in the annex of resolution 2111 (2013).

By the same resolution, it expressed concern that the charcoal trade provided significant funding for Al-Shabaab, and in that context reiterated paragraphs 11 to 21 of resolution 2182 (2014), and further decided to renew the provisions set out in paragraph 15 of resolution 2182 (2014) until 15 November 2018. It decided also that until 15 November 2018 and without prejudice to humanitarian assistance programmes conducted elsewhere, the measures imposed by paragraph 3 of resolution 1844 (2008) should not apply to the payment of funds, other financial assets or economic resources necessary to ensure the timely delivery of urgently needed humanitarian assistance in Somalia.

By the same resolution, it also decided to extend until 15 December 2018 the mandate of the Somalia and Eritrea Monitoring Group as set out in paragraph 13 of resolution 2060 (2012) and updated in paragraph 41 of resolution 2093 (2013) and expressed its intention to review the mandate and take appropriate action regarding the further extension no later than 15 November 2018.[67]

---

[64] For more information on the sanction regimes established by the Security Council, see the Council's website relating to subsidiary organs at http://www.un.org/en/sc/subsidiary/.

[65] The expanded mandate of the Committee is delineated in paragraph 18 of resolution 1907 (2009), paragraph 13 of resolution 2023 (2011) and paragraph 23 of resolution 2036 (2012).

[66] Report of the Security Council Committee pursuant to resolutions 751 (1992) and 1907 (2009) concerning Somalia and Eritrea (S/2017/1088).

[67] See the Somalia report of the Monitoring Group on Somalia and Eritrea pursuant to Security Council resolution 2317 (2016) (S/2017/924) and the Report of the Monitoring Group on Somalia and Eritrea pursuant to Security Council resolution 2317: Eritrea (2016) (S/2017/925).

(ii) *Democratic Republic of the Congo*

The Security Council Committee established pursuant to resolution 1533 (2004) of 12 March 2004 to oversee the relevant sanctions measures and to undertake the tasks set out by the Security Council in paragraph 15 of resolution 1807 (2008), paragraph 6 of resolution 1857 (2008) and paragraph 4 of resolution 1896 (2009), continued its operations in 2017 and submitted, on 29 December 2017, a report on its work in 2017 to the Security Council.[68]

By resolution 2360 (2017) of 21 June 2017, the Security Council, acting under Chapter VII of the Charter of the United Nations, decided, *inter alia*, to renew until 1 July 2018 the measures as set out in paragraphs 1 to 6 of resolution 2293 (2016). It also decided to expand the sanctions designation criteria to cover individuals and entities engaging in or providing support for acts that included planning, directing, sponsoring or participating in attacks against the United Nations Organization Stabilization Mission in the Democratic Republic of the Congo (MONUSCO) peacekeepers or United Nations personnel, including members of the Group of Experts. In the same resolution, the Security Council decided to extend until 1 August 2018 the mandate of the Group of Experts established pursuant to resolution 1533 (2004).

(iii) *Republic of the Sudan*

The Security Council Committee established pursuant to resolution 1591 (2005) of 29 March 2005, to oversee the relevant sanctions measures concerning the Sudan and to undertake the tasks set out by the Security Council in sub-paragraph 3 (*a*) of the same resolution, continued its operations in 2017 and submitted, on 29 December 2017, a report on its work in 2017 to the Security Council.[69]

By resolution 2340 (2017) of 8 February 2017, the Security Council, acting under Chapter VII of the Charter of the United Nations, decided to extend the mandate of the Panel of Experts, originally appointed pursuant to resolution 1591 (2005), until 12 March 2018, and expressed its intent to review the mandate and take appropriate action regarding further extension no later than 12 February 2018.[70]

(iv) *Democratic People's Republic of Korea*

The Security Council Committee established pursuant to resolution 1718 (2006) on 14 October 2006, to oversee the relevant sanctions measures concerning the Democratic People's Republic of Korea (DPRK) and to undertake the tasks set out in paragraph 12 of that same resolution and in resolutions 1874 (2009), 2087 (2013) and 2094 (2013), continued

---

[68] Report of the Security Council Committee established pursuant to resolution 1533 (2004) concerning the Democratic Republic of the Congo (S/2017/1103).

[69] Report of the Security Council Committee established pursuant to resolution 1591 (2005) concerning the Sudan (S/2017/1081).

[70] See the final report of the Panel of Experts submitted in accordance with paragraph 2 of resolution 2265 (2016) (S/2017/22) and the final report of the Panel of Experts submitted in accordance with paragraph 2 of resolution 2340 (2017) (S/2017/1125).

its operations in 2017 and submitted, on 29 December 2017, a report on its work to the Security Council.[71]

By resolution 2345 (2017) of 23 March 2017, the Security Council, acting under Article 41 of Chapter VII of the Charter of the United Nations, decided to extend until 24 April 2018 the mandate of the Panel of Experts, as specified in paragraph 26 of resolution 1874 (2009) and modified in paragraph 29 of resolution 2094 (2013), decided that this mandate should apply also with respect to the measures imposed in resolution 2321 (2016), and expressed its intent to review the mandate and take appropriate action regarding further extension no later than 24 March 2018.[72]

By resolution 2356 (2017) of 2 June 2017, the Security Council decided to apply the measures specified in paragraph 8(*d*) of resolution 1718 (2006), adding 14 individuals and four entities or to any individuals or entities acting on their behalf or at their direction and to entities owned or controlled by them.

By resolution 2371 (2017) of 5 August 2017, the Security Council decided to extend the effects of measures specified in paragraph 8(*d*) of resolution 1718 (2006), to nine individuals and four entities. It also adjusted the measures from such resolution, designating additional goods, conventional arms-related items, materials, equipment, goods and technology. It also directed the Committee to undertake its tasks to this effect and report to the Security Council within 30 days of the adoption of the resolution. The Resolution added that the Committee may designate vessels that were related to the activities prohibited by prior resolutions, and Member States Shall prohibit the entry of such vessels into their ports, unless required in case of emergency or for humanitarian reasons, consistent with such resolutions.[73] The Security Council further decided, among others, that the DPRK shall not supply, sell or transfer directly or indirectly seafood, lead and lead ore, and that all States shall prohibit the procurement of such items from the DPRK by their nationals. It decided that States shall prohibit the opening of new joint ventures or cooperative entities with DPRK entities or individuals or the expansion of existing joint ventures, whether or not acting on behalf of the government of the DPRK, unless approved by the Committee. It also decided that the mandate of the Committee and of the Panel of Experts shall also apply with respect to the measures imposed in its resolution. It decided to authorize all Member States to seize and dispose of items the supply, sale, transfer or export is prohibited by the resolutions abovementioned, as well as any obligation of parties to the Non-Proliferation Treaty, the Convention on the Prohibition of the Development, Production, Stockpiling and Use of Chemical Weapons and on Their Development of 29 April 1997, and the Convention on the Prohibition of the Development, Production and Stockpiling of Bacteriological (Biological) and Toxin Weapons and on Their Destruction of 10 April 1972.

By resolution 2375 (2017) of 11 September 2017, the Security Council acting under Chapter VII of the Charter of the United Nations decided to apply the measures specified in paragraph 8(*d*) of resolution 1718 (2006) to an additional individual and three entities, designating additional WMD-related dual-use items, additional convention arm-related

[71] Report of the Security Council Committee established pursuant to resolution 1718 (2006) (S/2017/1129).

[72] See the report of the Panel of Experts submitted pursuant to resolution 1874 (2009) (S/2015/131).

[73] See Security Council Resolutions 1718 (2006), 1874 (2009), 2087 (2013), 2094 (2013), 2270 (2016), 2321 (2016), 2356 (2017) and 2224 (2017).

items, materials, equipment, goods and technology. It also decided to apply the measures imposed by paragraph 6 of resolution 2371 (2016) on vessels transporting prohibited items from the DPRK, and called Member States to take actions to give effect to such measures.

By resolution 2397 (2017) of 22 December 2017, the Security Council, acting under Chapter VII of the Charter of the United Nations, and taking measures under Article 41, extended the measures specified in paragraph 8(*d*) of resolution 1718 (2006) to 16 individuals and one entity. It decided that all Member States shall prohibit the direct or indirect supply, sale or transfer to the DPRK of all crude oil, all refined petroleum products and that the DPRK shall not procure such products. Nonetheless, it decided that such measures would not apply to refined petroleum products, including diesel and kerosene, in the aggregate amount of up to 500,000 barrels during a period of twelve months beginning on January 1, 2018, and for a twelve-month periods thereafter, under certain conditions. It also decided that the DPRK shall not supply, sell or transfer certain food and agricultural products, machinery, electrical equipment, earth and stone including magnesite and magnesia, wood and vessels and that States shall prohibit the procurement of such products, as well as of all industrial machinery, transportation vehicles and iron, steel and other metals. It excluded the provision of spare parts needed to maintain the operation of DPRK commercial civilian passenger aircraft. It also decided that the mandate of the Committee and of the Panel of Experts shall also apply with respect to the measures imposed in its resolution.

(v) *Libya*

The Security Council Committee established pursuant to resolution 1970 (2011) concerning Libya to oversee the relevant sanctions measures continued its operations in 2017 and submitted, on 29 December 2017, a report on its work in 2017 to the Security Council.[74]

In resolution 2362 (2017) of 29 June 2017, the Security Council, acting under Chapter VII of the Charter of the United Nations, decided to extend until 15 November 2018 the authorizations provided by and the measures imposed by resolution 2146 (2014), relating to prevention of illicit oil exports, and decided further that the authorisations provided by and the measures imposed by that resolution should apply with respect to vessels loading, transporting, or discharging petroleum, including crude oil and refined petroleum products, illicitly exported or attempted to be exported from Libya.

In the same resolution, the Security Council, acting under Chapter VII of the Charter of the United Nations, reaffirmed that the travel ban and asset freeze measures specified in paragraphs 15, 16, 17, 19, 20 and 21 of resolution 1970 (2011), as modified by paragraphs 14, 15 and 16 of resolution 2009 (2011), and decided that, in addition to the acts listed in paragraph 11 (*a*)–(*f*) of resolution 2213 (2015), such acts may also include but are not limited to planning, directing, sponsoring, or participating in attacks against United Nations personnel, including members of the Panel of Experts established by paragraph 24 of resolution 1973 (2011) and modified by resolutions 2040 (2012), 2146 (2014), 2174 (2014), 2213 (2015) and the resolution in question, 2362 (2017).

---

[74] Report of the Security Council Committee established pursuant to resolution 1970 (2011) concerning Libya (S/2017/1086).

By the same resolution, the Security Council decided to extend until 15 November 2018 the mandate of the Panel of Experts, established by paragraph 24 of resolution 1973 (2011) and modified by resolutions 2040 (2012), 2146 (2014), 2174 (2014), and 2213 (2015) and decided that the Panel's mandated tasks should remain as defined in resolution 2213 (2015) and should also apply with respect to the Measures updated in that resolution.[75] It also decided that the Panel should provide to the Council an interim report on its work no later than 28 February 2018, and a final report to the Council, after discussion with the Committee, no later than 15 September 2018 with its findings and recommendations.

By resolution 2292 (2016) of 14 June 2016 and acting under Chapter VII of the Charter of the United Nations, the Security Council decided to authorize all Member States, in those exceptional and specific circumstances for a period of 12 months, to inspect on the high seas off the coast of Libya, of vessels that were believed to be carrying arms or related materiel to or from Libya, in violation of the arms embargo and, upon discovery of prohibited items, to seize and dispose of such items. In resolution 2357 (2017) of 12 June 2017, the Council decided to extend the authorizations as set out in resolution 2292 for a further 12 months from the date of the adoption of resolution 2357 (2017).

(vi) *Afghanistan*

The Security Council Committee established pursuant to resolution 1988 (2011) on 17 June 2011, to oversee the relevant sanctions measures and to undertake the tasks set out by the Security Council in paragraph 30 of the same resolution, continued its operations in 2017 and submitted, on 29 December 2017, a report on its work in 2017 to the Security Council.[76]

In resolution 2344 (2017) of 17 March 2017, the Security Council decided to extend until 17 March 2018 the mandate of the United Nations Assistance Mission in Afghanistan (UNAMA), as defined in its resolutions 1662 (2006), 1746 (2007), 1806 (2008), 1868 (2009), 1917 (2010), 1974 (2011), 2041 (2012), 2096 (2013), 2145 (2014), 2210 (2015), 2274 (2016) and paragraphs 5 and 6 of resolution 2344 (2017).

(vii) *Guinea-Bissau*

The Security Council Committee established pursuant to resolution 2048 (2012) on 18 May 2012, to monitor the implementation of the measures imposed by resolution 2048 (2012), designate the individuals subject to the measures and consider requests for exemptions, continued its operations in 2017 and submitted, on 29 December 2017, a report on its work in 2017 to the Security Council.[77] By resolution 2343 (2017), the Security Council decided to request the Secretary-General to submit to the Security council regular reports on the implementation of the measures established pursuant to resolution 2048 (2012),

[75] Final report of the Panel of Experts in accordance with paragraph 13 of resolution 2278, established pursuant to resolution 1973 (2011) (S/2017/466).

[76] Report of the Security Council Committee established pursuant to resolution 1988 (2011) (S/2017/1083).

[77] Report of the Security Council Committee established pursuant to resolution 2048 (2012) concerning Guinea-Bissau (S/2017/1120). See also the Report of the Secretary-General on the progress made with regard to the stabilization of and restoration of constitutional order in Guinea-Bissau (S/2017/715).

and also decided to review such sanctions measures, seven months from the adoption of resolution 2343 (2017).

(viii) *Central African Republic*

The Security Council Committee established pursuant to resolution 2127 (2013) of 5 December 2013 to undertake the tasks set out by the Security Council in paragraph 57 of the same resolution continued its operations in 2017 and submitted, on 29 December 2017, a report on its work in 2017 to the Security Council.[78]

By resolution 2339 (2017), the Security Council decided that until 31 January 2018, all Member States shall continue to take the necessary measures to prevent the direct or indirect supply, sale or transfer to the Central African Republic from or through their territories or by their nationals, or using their flag vessels or aircraft, of arms and related materiel of all types, including weapons and ammunition, military vehicles and equipment, paramilitary equipment, and spare parts for the aforementioned, and technical assistance, training, financial or other assistance, related to military activities or the provision, maintenance or use of any arms and related materiel, including the provision of armed mercenary personnel whether or not originating in their territories. It also provided certain exceptions. In the same resolution, it also authorized and decided that all Member States shall, upon discovery of the abovementioned items, seize, register and dispose such times.

In such resolution, the Security Council also decided that until 31 January 2018, all Member States shall continue to take the necessary measures to prevent the entry into or transit through their territories of individuals designated by the Committee, as well as to freeze assets owned or controlled by individuals or entities designated by the Committee. It encouraged measures such as States to report such departures or attempted entries into their territories and urged the authorities of the Central African Republic to ensured that fraudulent travel documents are removed from circulation. It decided to allow certain exceptions to this regime, as listed in the resolution.

It also decided that the mandate of the Committee would apply with respect to the measures imposed in paragraphs 54 and 55 of resolution 2127 (2013) and paragraphs 30 and 32 of resolution 2134 (2014) extended by this resolution. The Security Council also decided to extend the mandate of the Panel of Experts until 28 February 2018, and specified that its mandate should include the tasks as listed in the resolution.

In resolution 2387 (2017) 15 November 2017, the Security Council authorized the United Nations Multidimensional Integrated Stabilization Mission in the Central African Republic (MINUSCA) to monitor the implementation of the measures renewed and modified by paragraph 1 of resolution 2339 (2017), and to seize and collect arms and any related material covered by the measures imposed in the same resolution. It also requested Requests MINUSCA to destroy, as appropriate, the weapons and ammunitions of disarmed combatants in keeping with its effort to seize and collect arms and related materiel the supply, sale or transfer of which violate the measures imposed by paragraph 1 of resolution 2339 (2017).

---

[78] Report of the Security Council Committee established pursuant to resolution 2127 (2013) concerning the Central African Republic (S/2017/1090).

(ix) *Yemen*

The Security Council Committee established pursuant to resolution 2140 (2014) of 26 February 2014, to monitor the implementation of the measures imposed by the resolution, continued its operations in 2017 and submitted, on 29 December 2017, a report on its work in 2017 to the Security Council.[79]

By resolution 2342 (2017) of 235 February 2017, the Security Council, decided to renew until 26 February 2018 the measures imposed by paragraphs 11 and 15 of resolution 2140 (2014), reaffirms the provisions of paragraphs 12, 13, 14 and 16 of resolution 2140 (2015), and further reaffirms the provisions of paragraphs 14 to 17 of resolution 2216 (2015); applicable to individuals or entities designated by the Committee or in the annex to resolution 2216 (2015).

It also decided to extend until 28 March 2018 the mandate of the Panel of Experts as set out in the resolutions mentioned above. In the same resolution, the Security Council decided to urge all parties and Member States and international organizations to ensure cooperation with the Panel of Experts and called upon Member States to report to the Committee on the steps they had taken to implement the measures imposed.

(x) *South Sudan*

In resolution 2206 (2015) of 3 March 2015, the Security Council decided to establish a Committee of the Security Council consisting of all the members of the Council to monitor the implementation of the measures imposed by the resolution.[80]

By resolution 2353 (2017) of 24 May 2017, the Security Council, acting under Article 41 of Chapter VII of the Charter of the United Nations, decided to renew until 31 May 2018, the travel and financial measures imposed by paragraphs 9 and 12 of resolution 2206 (2015). By resolution 2353 (2017), the Security Council also decided that the Panel of Experts should provide to the Council, after discussion with the Committee, an interim report by 1 December 2017, a final report by 1 May 2018, and, except in the months when these reports were due, updates each month, and expressed its intention to review the mandate and take appropriate action regarding the further extension of the mandate no later than 31 May 2018.

(xi) *Mali*

In resolution 2374 (2017) of 5 September 2017, the Security Council decided to establish, in accordance with rule 28 of its provisional rules of procedure, a Committee of the Security Council consisting of all the members of the Council (herein "the Committee"), to undertake to following tasks: (*a*) to monitor implementation of the measures imposed in paragraphs 1 and 4 of the resolution; (*b*) to designate those individuals and entities subject to the measures imposed by paragraph 4, to review information regarding those

[79] Report of the Security Council Committee established pursuant to resolution 2140 (2014) (S/2017/1097). For more information about the situation in Yemen, see the statement of the President of the Security Council dated 15 June 2017 (S/PRST/2017/7).

[80] See Report of the Security Council Committee established pursuant to resolution 2206 (2015) concerning South Sudan (S/2017/1093).

individuals, and to consider requests for exemptions in accordance with paragraph 5 of the resolution; (*c*) to designate those individuals subject to the measures imposed by paragraph 1, to review information regarding those individuals, and to consider requests for exemptions in accordance with paragraph 2 of the resolution; (*d*) to establish such guidelines as may be necessary to facilitate the implementation of the measures imposed above; (*e*) to encourage a dialogue between the Committee and interested Member States and international, regional and subregional organizations, in particular those in the region, including by inviting representatives of such States or organizations to meet with the Committee to discuss implementation of the measures; (*f*) to seek from all States and international, regional and sub-regional organizations whatever information it may consider useful regarding the actions taken by them to implement effectively the measures imposed above; and (*g*) to examine and take appropriate action on information regarding alleged violations or non-compliance with the measures contained in the resolution.

By the same resolution, the Council requested the Secretary-General to create, for an initial period of thirteen months from the adoption of the resolution, in consultation with the Committee, a group of up to five experts, under the direction of the Committee, and to make the necessary financial and security arrangements to support the work of the Panel, expressed its intent to consider the renewal of this mandate no later than 12 months after the adoption of this resolution, and decided that the Panel should carry out a number of tasks.

Also by the same resolution, the Council decided that, for an initial period of one year from the date of the adoption of that resolution, all Member States should take the necessary measures to prevent the entry into or transit through their territories of individuals designated by the Committee. It also decided that, for an initial period of one year from the date of the adoption of the resolution, all Member States should freeze without delay all funds, other financial assets and economic resources which were on their territories, which were owned or controlled, directly or indirectly, by the individuals or entities designated by the Committee, or by individuals or entities acting on their behalf or at their direction, or by entities owned or controlled by them, and decided further that all Member States should ensure that any funds, financial assets or economic resources are prevented from being made available by their nationals or by any individuals or entities within their territories, directly or indirectly to or for the benefit of the individuals or entities designated by the Committee.

(*g*) Terrorism

(i) *General Assembly*

On 7 December 2017, the General Assembly, upon the recommendation of the Sixth Committee, adopted resolution 72/123 entitled "Measures to eliminate international terrorism", and resolution 72/127 entitled "Observer status for the Eurasian Group on Combating Money Laundering and Financing of Terrorism in the General Assembly", without a vote.

On 19 December 2017, the General Assembly also adopted resolution 72/165 entitled "International Day of Remembrance and Tribute to the Victims Terrorism", without a vote. On the same day, the General Assembly also adopted resolution 72/180, entitled "Protecting human rights and fundamental freedoms while countering terrorism", without a vote. The Assembly, *inter alia*, reaffirmed that States must ensures that any measure taken to combat terrorism complies with their obligations under international law, in particular, international human rights law, refugee law and humanitarian law, and called upon States to take measures to abide by their international human rights obligations and to protect the victims of terrorism, including with regard to their access to justice.

On 19 December 2017, the General Assembly also adopted Resolution 72/194 entitled "Technical assistance for implementing the international conventions and protocols related to counter-terrorism", where it, *inter alia*, urged Member States to consider becoming parties to exiting conventions and protocols related to counter-terrorism, and encouraged them to continue to promote effective coordination of local authorities. In the same resolution, the Assembly requested the United Nations Office on Drugs and Crime, upon request and within its mandate, to enhance and continue to provide legal assistance for building the capacity of Member States to become parties and implement international conventions and protocols and enhancing cooperation in developing appropriate criminal responses to prevent the financing, mobilization, travel, recruitment, organization and radicalization of foreign terrorist fighters, including gender perspectives into criminal justice responses to terrorism.

On 24 December 2017, the General Assembly adopted resolution 72/246 entitled "Effects of terrorism on the enjoyment of human rights Statement of financial implications (A/72/680)" by a vote of 95 in favour to one against and 58 abstentions. In that resolution, the Assembly, *inter alia*, reaffirmed its commitment to the United Nations Global Counter-Terrorism Strategy as adopted in its resolution 60/288 and recognized the need to redouble efforts for even attention paid to and even implementation of the pillars of such strategy. It also called upon Member States to remain alert to the use of information and communications technology for terrorist purposes and to cooperated to counter violent extremist propaganda and incitement to violence on the Internet and social media.

(ii) *Security Council counter-terrorism and non-proliferation committees*

a. Security Council Committee pursuant to resolutions 1267 (1999), 1989 (2011) and 2253 (2015) concerning ISIL (Da'esh), Al-Qaida and associated individuals, groups, undertakings and entities

The 1267 Committee was first established by Security Council resolution 1267 (1999) of 15 October 1999 and set forth a sanctions regime concerning the Taliban. The regime was modified and strengthened by subsequent resolutions, including resolutions 1333 (2000), 1390 (2002), 1455 (2003), 1526 (2004), 1617 (2005), 1735 (2006), 1822 (2008), 1904 (2009), 1989 (2011) and 2253 (2015) so that the sanctions measures would be applicable to designated individuals and entities associated with Al-Qaida, wherever located. The Committee continued its operations in 2017 and submitted, on 20 December 2017, a report on its work in 2017 to the Security Council.[81]

On 24 May 2017, the Security Council adopted resolution 2354 (2017), where it welcomed a document of the Counter-Terrorism Committee containing a proposal for a comprehensive international framework to counter terrorist narratives, with recommended guidelines and good practices to effective counter the ways that ISIL (Da'esh), Al Qaida and

[81] Report of the Security Council Committee pursuant to resolutions 1267 (1999) and 1989 (2011) and 2253 (2015) concerning Al-Qaida and associated individuals and entities (S/2017/1084).

associated individuals, groups, undertakings and entities use their narratives to encourage, motivate, and recruit others to commit terrorist acts.[82] The Council decided to direct the Counter Terrorism Committee, with the support of the Counter-Terrorism Executive Directorate and in consultation with the Counter-Terrorism Implementation Task Force to continue to identify good practices, review legal measures taken by States, work with other agencies and contribute to efforts of the United Nations to develop models to counter terrorist narratives both online and offline.

By resolution 2368 (2017) of 20 July 2017, the Security Council, acting under Chapter VII of the Charter of the United Nations, decided that all States should take certain measures as imposed by paragraph 8 (*c*) of resolution 1333 (2000) paragraphs 1 and 2 of resolution 1390 (2002), and paragraphs 1 and 4 of resolution 1989 (2011), with respect to ISIL, Al-Qaida, and associated individuals, groups, undertakings and entities. Such measures included, among others, the freezing of assets, a travel ban, and an arms embargo. The Council also included a list of acts or activities indicating that an individual, group, undertaking or entity is eligible for inclusion in the ISIL (Da'esh) & Al-Qaida Sanctions List.

By resolution 2379 (2017) of 21 September 2017, the Security Council reiterated its condemnation of all violations of humanitarian law, and acts of terrorism and requested the Secretary-General to establish an Investigative Team, headed by a Special Adviser, to support domestic efforts to hold ISIL (Da'esh) accountable by collecting, preserving, and storing evidence in Iraq of acts that may amount to war crimes, crimes against humanity and genocide committed by the terrorist group ISIL (Da'esh) in Iraq. The Security Council further emphasized that the Team should be impartial, independent and credible and should act consistent with the Terms of Reference which set out the framework in which the Team will operate, the Charter of the United Nations and United Nations best practice, and relevant international law including international human rights law. The Security Council further requested that after the approval of the Terms of Reference, the Secretary-General should undertake without delay the steps, measures and arrangements necessary for the speedy establishment and full functioning of the Investigative Team.

On 21 December 2017, the Security Council adopted resolution 2396 (2017), where it called Member States to prevent the movement of terrorists by border controls, and to notify upon travel, arrival or deportation of captured individuals whom they have reasonable grounds to believe are terrorists. In the same resolution, it also decided that Member States shall require airlines operating in their territories to provide advance passenger information systems to detect the departure or attempted travel of foreign terrorist fighters and individuals designated by the Committee established under resolutions 1267 (1999), 1989 (2011) and 2253 (2015). It also decided that Member States shall develop watch lists or databases of known and suspected terrorists for use by law enforcement to screen travellers and conduct risk assessment and encouraged Member States to share such information and facilitate capacity building and technical assistance. The Council also directed the Committee to continue to devote special focus to the threat posed by foreign terrorist fighters, specifically those associated with ISIL, ANF and all groups, undertakings and entities associated with Al-Qaida.

---

[82] See Letter dated 26 April 2017 from the Chair of the Security Council Committee established pursuant to resolution 1373 (2001) concerning counter-terrorism addressed to the President of the Security Council (S/2017/375).

b. Counter-Terrorism Committee

The Counter-Terrorism Committee (CTC) was established pursuant to Security Council resolution 1373 (2001) of 28 September 2001, in the wake of the 11 September terrorist attacks in the United States of America, to bolster the ability of United Nations Member States to prevent terrorist acts both within their borders and across regions.[83] By resolution 1535 (2004) of 26 March 2004, the Security Council established the Counter-Terrorism Committee Executive Directorate (CTED) to assist the work of the CTC and coordinate the process of monitoring the implementation of resolution 1373 (2001).

The Security Council, in resolution 2341 (2017) adopted on 13 February 2017 recalled its decision in resolution 1373 (2001) that all States shall establish terrorist acts as serious criminal offences in domestic laws and regulations and called upon all Member States to ensure that they have established criminal responsibility for terrorist attacks intended to destroy or disable critical infrastructure, as well as the planning of, training for, and financing of and logistical support for such attacks. It also called upon Member States to explore means to exchange relevant information and establish or strengthen partnerships with stakeholders to share information and experience to prevent, protect, mitigate, investigate respond to and recover damage from terrorist attacks on critical infrastructure facilities. In the same decision, the Security Council also directed the CTC, with the support of the CTED to continue with their mandated to examine the efforts of Member States to protect critical infrastructure from terrorist attacks, while implementing resolution 1373 (2001).

On 2 August 2017, the Security Council adopted resolution 2370 (2017) where, among other measures, it reaffirmed its decision in resolution 1373 (2001) that all States shall refrain from providing any form of support to entities or persons involved in terrorist acts and emphasized the importance of Member States taking measures to prevent the illicit trafficking of weapons to terrorists in conflict areas, as it stressed the importance of assisting States to enable them to monitor and control stockpiles of small and light weapons to prevent terrorists from acquiring them. In the same decision, it also directed the Counter Terrorism Committee to continue examining Member States efforts to eliminate the supply of weapons to terrorists, as relevant to the implementation of resolution 1373 (2001) to identify good practices and vulnerabilities.

The Security Council, by resolution 2395 (2017) of 21 December 2017, *inter alia* underlined the overarching objective of the CTC to ensure full implementation of resolution 1373 (2001), deciding that CTED will continue to operate as a special political mission under the policy guidance of the CTC for the period ending 31 December 2021 and that an interim review would be conducted on 31 December 2019.

The Security Council, by resolution 2396 (2017) of 21 December 2017, *inter alia* reaffirmed its resolution 1373 (2001), in particular its decisions that all States shall establish terrorist acts as serious criminal offenses in domestic laws and regulation. It also reiterated and clarified some of the obligations imposed by resolution 1373 (2001).

---

[83] See also Security Council resolution 1624 (2005) of 14 September 2005 and the statement of the President of the Security Council dated 29 May 2015 (S/PRST/2015/11).

c. 1540 Committee (non-proliferation of weapons of mass destruction to non-State actors)

On 28 April 2004, the Security Council adopted resolution 1540 (2004) by which it decided that all States would refrain from providing any form of support to non-State actors that attempt to develop, acquire, manufacture, possess, transport, transfer or use nuclear, chemical or biological weapons and their means of delivery, and established a Committee to report on the implementation of the same resolution. The mandate of the Committee was subsequently extended by resolutions 1673 (2006), 1810 (2008) and 1977 (2011) of 20 April 2011 until 25 April 2021. The Committee continued its operations in 2017 and submitted, on 9 and 29 December 2016, a final document on the 2016 comprehensive review of the status of implementation of resolution 1540 (2004)[84] and a review of the implementation of resolution 1540 (2004) in 2016 to the Security Council,[85] respectively.

In resolution 2325 (2016) of 15 December 2016, the Security Council, acting under Chapter VII of the Charter of the United Nations, decided that the 1540 Committee would continue to submit to the Security Council its Programme of Work, before the end of each January, and would brief the Security Council in the first *quarter* of each year. It also decided that the 1540 Committee should continue to intensify its efforts to promote the full implementation by all States of resolution 1540 (2004). The Programme of work of the Committee for the period from 1 February 2017 to 31 January 2018 was submitted to the Security Council on 10 February 2017.[86]

(*h*) Humanitarian law and human rights in the context of peace and security

(i) *Children and armed conflict*

The Security Council Working Group on Children and Armed Conflict was established by Security Council resolution 1612 (2005) to review reports of the monitoring and reporting mechanism concerning on children armed conflict listed in the annexes to the Secretary-General's report on children and armed conflict.[87]

In a Statement on 31 October 2017 made by its President,[88] the Security Council took note of the 16th report of the Secretary General on children and armed conflict[89] and the recommendations contained therein. The Security Council further reiterated its commitment to address the widespread impact of armed conflict on children, as an important aspect of any comprehensive strategy to resolve conflict and sustain peace and stressed the importance of adopting a broad strategy of conflict prevention.

The Security Council further reiterated its deep concern about attacks in armed conflict that had affected children and called upon all parties to armed conflict to allow and

---

[84] Report of the Security Council Committee established pursuant to resolution 1540 (2004) (S/2016/1038).

[85] Review of the implementation of resolution 1540 (2004) for 2016 (S/2016/1127).

[86] Letter dated 10 February 2017 from the Chair of the Security Council Committee established pursuant to resolution 1540 (2004) addressed to the President of the Security Council (S/2017/126).

[87] A/59/659–S/2005/72.

[88] Statement by the President of the Security Council of 31 October 2017 (S/PRST/2017/21).

[89] See also the Report of the Secretary-General on Children and armed conflict (S/2017/821).

facilitate safe, timely and unhindered humanitarian access to children. It also welcomed the continued strengthening of the Monitoring and Reporting mechanism as requested by its resolutions 1612 (2005), 1882 (2009), 1998 (2011), 2143 (2014) and 2225 (2015) and commends the role of UNICEF and other United Nations entities at the field level.

(ii) *Women and peace and security*[90]

In resolution 2343 (2017) of 23 February 2017 Security Council emphasized the important role of women in the prevention and resolution of conflicts and in peacebuilding, as recognized in resolution 1325 (2000) and in subsequent resolutions on women, peace and security. In the same resolution, the Council affirmed that the United Nations Integrated Peacebuilding Office in Guinea-Bissau and the Special Representative would continue to provide support to the Government of Guinea-Bissau to incorporate a gender perspective into peacebuilding, in line with Security Council resolutions 1325 (2000), 1820 (2008) and 2242 (2015), as well as a national action plan on Gender to ensure the involvement, representation and participation of women at all levels.

In resolution 2344 (2017) of 17 March 2017, the Security Council reiterated the importance of increasing the functionality, professionalism and accountability of the Afghan security sector in line with resolution 1325 (2000) and its successor resolutions on Women, Peace and Security. In resolution 2359 (2017) of 21 June 2017, the Security Council emphasized the important role of women in the prevention and resolution of conflicts and in peacebuilding, as recognized in resolution 1325 (2000), and underlines that a gender perspective should be taken into account in implementing all aspects of the strategic concept of operations of the G5 Sahel joint force.

In resolution 2367 (2017) of 14 July 2017, the Security Council, *inter alia*, encouraged the Government of Iraq to reinvigorate its efforts to promote and protect the rights of women and reaffirming its resolutions 1325 (2000), 1820 (2008), 1888 (2009), 1889 (2009), 1960 (2010), 2106 (2013), 2122 (2013) and 2242 (2015) on women, peace, and security and reiterating the need for the full, equal, and effective participation of women, reaffirming the key role women can play in re-establishing the fabric of society. The Security Council stressed the need for their full political participation, including in upcoming elections and the Independent High Electoral Commission, stabilization planning, political decision making, local and national reconciliation and peace processes, and expressed concern for the lack of implementation of Iraq's National Action Plan of 2014 in accordance with resolution 1325 (2000) as well as the lack of a national entity responsible for its implementation.

In resolution 2376 (2017) of 14 September 2017, the Security Council, *inter alia*, urged the full, equal and effective participation of women in all activities relating to the democratic transition, conflict resolution and peacebuilding in Libya, and called on the Libyan authorities to prevent and respond to sexual violence in conflict, including addressing impunity for sexual violence crimes in line with relevant Security Council resolutions, including resolutions 1325 (2000), 2106 (2013), 2122 (2013), 2242 (2015) and 2331 (2016).

---

[90] For more information on the legal activities of the United Nations as it relates to women, see section 6 sub-section (*e*) of the present chapter.

In resolution 2378 (2017) of 20 September 2017, the Security Council recalled resolution 1325 (2000) and recognized the indispensable role of women in United Nations peacekeeping, including supporting the critical role that women play in all peace and security efforts, including those to prevent and resolve conflict and mitigate its impact, welcoming efforts to incentivize greater numbers of women in military and police deployed in United Nations peacekeeping operations and recalling its resolution 2242 (2015) and its aspiration to increase the number of women in military and police contingents of United Nations peacekeeping operations.

(iii) *Protection of civilians in armed conflict*

In resolution 2352 (2017) of 15 May 2017, the Security Council, *inter alia*, underscored the mandate on the protection of civilians of the United Nations Interim Security Force for Abyei as set out in paragraph 3 of resolution 1990 (2011) included taking the necessary actions to protect civilians under imminent threat of physical violence, irrespective of the source of such violence, and commending UNISFA's efforts in that regard. In resolution 2360 (2017) of 21 June 2017, the Security Council recalled all its relevant resolutions on women and peace and security, on children and armed conflict, and on the protection of civilians in armed conflicts, also recalling the conclusions of the Security Council Working Group on Children and Armed Conflict pertaining to the parties in armed conflict of the Democratic Republic of the Congo adopted on 18 September 2014.[91]

In resolution 2363 (2017) of 29 June 2017, the Security Council, *inter alia*, reiterated its demand that all parties to the conflict in Darfur immediately end violence, including attacks on civilians, peacekeepers and humanitarian personnel, emphasized that those responsible for violations of international humanitarian law and violations and abuses of human rights must be held accountable and that the Government of Sudan bears the primary responsibility to protect civilians within its territory and subject to its jurisdiction, including protection from crimes against humanity and war crimes, recalled resolution 2117 (2013) and expressed concern at the continued threats to civilians posed by unexploded ordnance.

In resolution 2365 (2017) of 30 June 2017, the Security Council urged parties to armed conflicts to protect civilian population, including children from the threats posed by landmines, explosive remnants of war and improvised explosive devices and, encouraged the international community to advocate and support efforts to clear these devices, to provide risk education, and to conduct risk reduction activities, as well as to provide assistance for the care, rehabilitation, and economic and social reintegration of victims and persons with disabilities.

In resolution 2372 (2017) of 30 August 2017, the Security Council underlined the importance of respect for international humanitarian law and the protection of civilians, especially women and children, as well as relevant Security Council resolutions, by all actors in Somalia.

In resolution 2378 (2017) of 20 September 2017, the Security Council reaffirmed that States bear the primary responsibility for protection of civilians throughout their whole territory while mindful of the important role United Nations peacekeeping operations play

91 S/AC.51/2014/3.

in this regard and further recognized the role that regional and subregional organizations can play in the protection of civilians, and in particular women and children affected by armed conflict, as well as in the prevention of and response to sexual and gender-based violence in armed conflicts and post-conflict situations.

In resolution 2387 (2017) of 15 November 2017, the Security Council, *inter alia*, recalled its previous resolutions on the protection of civilians in armed conflict, including 2286 (2016) and 1894 (2009); its resolutions on Children and Armed Conflict including 2225 (2015) and its resolutions on Women, Peace and Security including 2106 (2013) and 2242 (2015), and calling upon all parties in the CAR to engage with the Special Representative on Children and Armed Conflict and the Special Representative on Sexual Violence in Conflict.

(iv) *Small arms and light weapons*

In resolution 2370 (2017) of 2 August 2017, the Security Council recognized the need for Member States to undertake appropriate measures consistent with international law to address the illicit trafficking in small arms and light weapons, in particular to terrorists, also urging Member States to fully implement the "Programme of Action to Prevent, Combat and Eradicate the Illicit Trade in Small Arms and Light Weapons in All Its Aspects" and the International Tracing Instrument to assist in preventing terrorist from acquiring small and light weapons, in particular in conflict and post-conflict areas.

In 2017, the Secretary-General provided a follow up report to Security Council resolution 2220 (2015) entitled "Small arms and light weapons".[92] Among other issues, it urged States to consider ratifying or acceding to the Arms Trade Treaty and the United Nations Convention against Transnational Organized Crime and its Protocols, including the Protocol against the Illicit Manufacturing of and Trafficking in Firearms, Their Parts and Components and Ammunitions.

(v) *Youth*

In resolution 2358 (2017) of 14 June 2017, the Security Council, *inter alia*, reaffirmed the important role of women and youth in the prevention and resolution of conflicts, and in peacebuilding and stressed the importance of their participation in all efforts for the maintenance and promotion of peace and security.

(*i*) Comprehensive assessment of United Nations peace operations

In a statement by the President of the Security Council of 21 December 2017,[93] the Security Council, *inter alia*, reaffirmed the primary responsibility of national authorities in identifying, driving and directing activities to sustain peace and reiterated its commitment to enhance the effectiveness of the United Nations in addressing conflict at all stages. The Security Council also underscored the critical importance of improving the accountability,

---

[92] S/2017/1025.

[93] S/PRST/2017/27.

transparency and performance of United Nations peace operations, took note of the intention of the Secretary-General to conduct reviews of peacekeeping missions.

(*j*) Review of the Peacebuilding Architecture

In a statement by the President of the Security Council of 21 December 2017,[94] the Security Council, *inter alia*, acknowledged the importance of the coordination, coherence and cooperation with the Peacebuilding Commission, and expressed its intention to regularly request, deliberate and draw upon the specific, strategic and targeted advice of the Peacebuilding Commission, including to assist with the longer-term perspective required for sustaining peace being reflected in the formation, review and drawdown of peacekeeping operations and special political missions mandates.

(*k*) Piracy

In resolution 2383 (2017) of 7 November 2017, the Security Council, welcoming the report of the Secretary-General submitted pursuant to Security Council resolution 2316 (2016) on the implementation of that resolution and on the situation with respect to piracy and armed robbery at sea off the coast of Somalia,[95] and acting under Chapter VII of the Charter of the United Nations, decided, for a further period of twelve months from the date of the resolution, to renew the authorizations as set out in paragraph 14 of resolution 2316 (2016) granted to States and regional organizations cooperating with Somali authorities in the fight against piracy and armed robbery at sea off the coast of Somalia, for which advance notification had been provided by Somali authorities to the Secretary-General.

The Security Council further decided that the arms embargo on Somalia imposed by paragraph 5 of resolution 733 (1992) and further elaborated upon by paragraphs 1 and 2 of resolution 1425 (2002) and modified by paragraphs 33 to 38 of resolution 2093 (2013) did not apply to supplies of weapons and military equipment or the provision of assistance destined for the sole use of Member States, international, regional, and subregional organizations undertaking such measures.

The Security Council also called upon all States to criminalize piracy under their domestic law and to favourably consider the prosecution of suspected, and imprisonment of those convicted, pirates apprehended off the coast of Somalia, and their facilitators and financiers ashore, consistent with applicable international law, including international human rights law, and decided to keep those matters under review, including, as appropriate, the establishment of specialized anti-piracy courts in Somalia with substantial international participation and/or support as set forth in resolution 2015 (2011).

(*l*) Migrant smuggling and human trafficking

By resolution 2380 (2017) of 5 October 2017, the Security Council, acting under Chapter VII of the Charter of the United Nations, condemned all acts of migrant smuggling

---

[94] S/PRST/201/27.

[95] S/2017/859.

and human trafficking into, through and from the Libyan territory and off the coast of Libya. It decided, *inter alia*, to renew the authorizations as set out in paragraphs 7, 8, 9 and 10 of resolution 2240 (2015) for a period of twelve months and reaffirmed that the authorizations provided in paragraphs 7 and 8 of such resolution apply only with respect to the situation of migrant smuggling and human trafficking on the high seas off the coast of Libya. The Security Council further emphasized that all migrants, including asylum seekers, should be treated with humanity and dignity and that their rights should be fully respected, urging all States in this regard to comply with their obligations under international law, including international human rights law and international refugee law, as applicable.

In resolution 2388 (2017) of 21 November 2017, the Security Council reaffirmed its condemnation of all acts of instances of trafficking in persons, especially women and children. It urged Member States to consider as a priority ratifying or acceding to the United Nations Convention against Transnational Organized Crime and its supplementing Protocol to Prevent, Suppress and Punish Trafficking in Persons, Especially Women and Children, as well as all relevant international instrument. Additionally, it called upon Member States, *inter alia*, to make efforts to investigate, disrupt and dismantle networks engaging in trafficking in persons in areas affected by armed conflict, and to collect evidence of human trafficking.

The Security Council reiterated its condemnation of all acts of trafficking, in particular, the sale or trade in persons undertaken by the "Islamic State of Iraq and the Levant" (ISIL, also known as Da'esh), including of Yazidis and other persons belonging to religious and ethnic minorities, and of any such trafficking in persons crimes and other violations and abuses committed by Boko Haram, Al-Shabaab, the Lord's Resistance Army, and other terrorist or armed groups for the purpose of sexual slavery, sexual exploitation, and forced labour.

By the same resolution, the Security Council requested the Secretary-General to further explore, as appropriate, links between the trafficking of children in conflict situations, with a view to addressing all violations and abuses against children in armed conflict. It also requested the Secretary-General, in consultation with Member States, to ensure, where appropriate, that training of relevant personnel of special political and peacekeeping missions include, specific information enabling them, within their mandates, to identify, confirm, respond to and report on situations of trafficking in persons.

3. Disarmament and related matters[96]

(*a*) Disarmament machinery

(i) *Disarmament Commission*

The United Nations Disarmament Commission, a subsidiary organ of the General Assembly with a general mandate on disarmament questions, comprises all member States of the United Nations.

[96] For more information about disarmament and related matters see *The United Nations Disarmament Yearbook*, vol. 42, 2017 (United Nations Publication, Sales No.: E.18.IX.5, for part I, and Sales No.: E.18.IX.7, for part II), which is also available at: https://www.un.org/disarmament/publications/yearbook/.

The Commission held its organizational session for 2017 in New York on 13 February 2017.[97] The Commission then held six plenary meetings at the United Nations Headquarters from 3 to 21 April 2017.[98] The Commission had before it the report of the Conference on Disarmament on its 2016 session [99] and other documentation submitted by the Secretary-General,[100] as well as other documents submitted by Member States dealing with substantive questions.[101]

At its 367th meeting on 21 April 2017, the Commission adopted, by consensus, the reports of the Commission and its subsidiary bodies to be submitted to the General Assembly.[102]

(ii) *Conference on Disarmament*

The Conference on Disarmament, established in 1979 as the single multilateral disarmament negotiating forum of the international community, was a result of the First Special Session on Disarmament of the United Nations General Assembly in 1978.

The Conference was in session from 23 January to 31 March, 15 May to 30 June and 31 July to 15 September 2017, during which it held 32 formal plenary meetings and six informal plenary meetings.[103] At its 1402nd plenary meeting on 24 January 2017, the Conference adopted its agenda for the 2017 session,[104] which included, *inter alia*, the items "Cessation of the nuclear arms race and nuclear disarmament", "Prevention of nuclear war, including all related matters", "Prevention of an arms race in outer space", "Effective international arrangements to assure non-nuclear-weapon States against the use or threat of use of nuclear weapons", "New types of weapons of mass destruction and new systems of such weapons", "Comprehensive programme of disarmament" and "Transparency in armaments".

Throughout the 2017 session, successive presidents of the Conference conducted intensive consultations with a view to reaching consensus on a programme of work on the basis of relevant proposals, but no consensus was reached on a programme of work for the 2017 session.[105] On 14 September 2017, the Conference adopted its annual report and transmitted it to the General Assembly for its consideration.[106]

(iii) *General Assembly*

In 2017, the General Assembly adopted, on the recommendation of the First Committee, multiple resolutions concerning institutional activities relating to disarmament machinery.

---

[97] *Official Records of the General Assembly, Seventy-Second Session, Supplement No. 41* (A/72/42), para. 2.

[98] *Ibid*., para. 5.

[99] *Official Records of the General Assembly, Seventy-First Session, Supplement No. 27* (A/71/27).

[100] See A/CN.4/211.

[101] *Official Records of the General Assembly, Seventy-Second Session, Supplement No. 41* (A/72/42), para. 15.

[102] *Ibid*., para. 17.

[103] *Official Records of the General Assembly, Seventy-Second Session, Supplement No. 27* (A/72/27), paras. 2–3.

[104] *Ibid*., paras. 12–13.

[105] *Ibid*., para. 20.

[106] *Ibid*., para. 58.

On 4 December 2017, the General Assembly adopted resolutions 72/23 entitled "Prohibition of the development and manufacture of new types of weapons of mass destruction and new systems of such weapons: report of the Conference on Disarmament" by a recorded vote of 180 in favour, to 3 against, without abstentions; resolution 72/46 entitled "Relationship between disarmament and development", without a vote; 72/60 entitled "United Nations Regional Centre for Peace and Disarmament in Africa", without a vote; resolution 72/61 entitled "United Nations Regional Centre for Peace, Disarmament and Development in Latin America and the Caribbean", without a vote; resolution 72/62 entitled "United Nations Regional Centre for Peace and Disarmament in Asia and the Pacific", without a vote; resolution 72/63 entitled "Regional confidence-building measures: activities of the United Nations Standing Advisory Committee on Security Questions in Central Africa" without a vote; resolution 72/64 entitled "United Nations regional centres for peace and disarmament", without a vote; resolution 72/65 entitled "Report of the Conference on Disarmament", without a vote; and resolution 72/66 entitled "Report of the Disarmament Commission", without a vote.

On the same date, the General Assembly also adopted, by a recorded vote of 181 in favour to 3 against and no abstentions, resolution 72/49 entitled "Convening of the fourth special session of the General Assembly devoted to disarmament".

(*b*) Nuclear disarmament and non-proliferation issues

In 2017, several preparatory meetings and conferences were held on nuclear disarmament and non-proliferation matters.

On 20 September 2017, the Conference on Facilitating the Entry into Force of the Comprehensive Nuclear-Test-Ban-Treaty, 1996 (CTBT),[107] was held in New York.[108] Foreign ministers and other high-level representatives met at the United Nations Headquarters in New York to discuss concrete measures to facilitate the entry into force of the CTBT. In their Final Declaration, the ratifying States and other States signatories affirmed that a universal and effectively verifiable Treaty constituted a fundamental instrument in the field of nuclear disarmament and non-proliferation and also affirmed the vital importance and urgency of the entry into force of the CTBT.[109]

The International Atomic Energy Agency (IAEA) held its sixty first General Conference of Member States from 18 to 22 September 2017 in Vienna.[110] The Conference adopted 16 resolutions and 3 decisions [111] relating to the work of IAEA in key areas, including on measures to strengthen international cooperation in nuclear, radiation, transport and waste safety, nuclear security; strengthening the Agency's activities related to nuclear science, technology and applications; implementation of the Agreement between the Agency and the Democratic People's Republic of Korea; and application of IAEA safeguards in the Middle East.

---

[107] General Assembly resolution A/50/245 of 17 September 1996. For the text of the treaty, see A/50/127.

[108] For more information see https://www.ctbto.org/the-treaty/article-xiv-conferences/afc2017/.

[109] See https://www.ctbto.org/fileadmin/user_upload/Art_14_2017/CTBT_Art_XIV_2017_6.pdf.

[110] For more information see https://www.iaea.org/about/policy/gc/gc61.

[111] GC(61)/RES/DEC(2017).

(i) *General Assembly*

On 10 November 2017, the General Assembly adopted, without reference to a Main Committee, resolution 72/5 entitled "Report of the International Atomic Energy Agency", without a vote.

On 4 December 2017, the General Assembly adopted, upon the recommendation of the First Committee, several resolutions concerning nuclear weapons and non-proliferation issues: resolution 72/22 entitled "African Nuclear-Weapon-Free Zone Treaty", without a vote; resolution 72/24 entitled "Establishment of a nuclear-weapon-free zone in the region of the Middle East", without a vote; resolution 72/25 entitled "Conclusion of effective international arrangements to assure non-nuclear-weapon States against the use or threat of use of nuclear weapons', by a recorded vote of 125 to none, with 62 abstentions; resolution 72/29 entitled "Follow-up to nuclear disarmament obligations agreed to at the 1995, 2000 and 2010 Review Conferences of the Parties to the Treaty on the Non-Proliferation of Nuclear Weapons", by a recorded vote of 118 in favour to 44 against, with 17 abstentions; resolution 72/30 entitled "Humanitarian consequences of nuclear weapons", by a recorded vote of 141 in favour to 15 against, with 27 abstentions; resolution 72/31 entitled "Taking forward multilateral nuclear disarmament negotiations", by a recorded vote of 125 in favour to 39 against, with 14 abstentions; resolution 72/37 entitled "Ethical imperatives for a nuclear-weapon-free world" by a vote of 130 in favour, to 36 against and 15 abstentions; resolution 72/38 entitled "Nuclear disarmament", by a recorded vote of 119 in favour to 41 against, with 20 abstentions; resolution 72/39 entitled "Towards a nuclear weapon-free world: accelerating the implementation of nuclear disarmament commitments", by a vote of 137 in favour to 31 against and 16 abstentions; resolution 72/41 entitled "Reducing nuclear danger" by 124 votes in favour to 49 against and 11 abstentions; resolution 72/42 entitled "Measures to prevent terrorists from acquiring weapons of mass destruction", without a vote; resolution 72/45 entitled "Nuclear-weapon-free southern hemisphere and adjacent areas", by a recorded vote of 149 in favour to 5 against, with 29 abstention; resolution 72/50 entitled "United action with renewed determination towards the total elimination of nuclear weapons", by a recorded vote of 156 in favour to 4 against and 24 abstentions; resolution 72/58 entitled "Follow-up to the advisory opinion of the International Court of Justice on the legality of the threat or use of nuclear weapons", by a recorded vote of 131 in favour to 31 against, with 18 abstentions; resolution 72/59 entitled "Convention on the Prohibition of the Use of Nuclear Weapons", by a recorded vote of 123 in favour to 50 against and 10 abstentions; resolution 72/67 entitled "The risk of nuclear proliferation in the Middle East", by a recorded vote of 157 in favour to 5 against, with 20 abstentions; and resolution 72/70 entitled "Comprehensive Nuclear-Test-Ban Treaty", by a recorded vote of 180 in favour to 1 against, with 4 abstentions.

On 24 December 2017, the General Assembly adopted resolution 72/521 entitled "Follow-up to the 2013 high-level meeting of the General Assembly on nuclear disarmament Statement of financial implications (A/72/673)", by a recorded vote of 114 in favour to 30 against and 14 abstentions.

(ii) *Security Council*

In 2017, the Security Council adopted five resolutions relating to nuclear disarmament and non-proliferation issues. In resolutions 2345 (2017) of 23 March 2017, the

Security Council recalled the report of the Panel of Experts established pursuant to resolution 1874 (2009) concerning the nuclear and ballistic missile-related activities carried out by the Democratic People's Republic of Korea[112] and decided, *inter alia*, to extend until 24 April 2018 the mandate of the Panel of Experts and expressed its intent to further review the mandate to take appropriate action regarding further extension. Resolutions 2356 (2017) of 2 June 2017, 2371 (2017) of 5 August 2017, 2375 (2017) of 11 September 2017 and 2397 (2017) of 22 December 2017 related to nuclear tests conducted by the Democratic People's Republic of Korea in violation of several Security Council resolutions.

(*c*) Biological and chemical weapons issues

(i) *Biological Weapons Convention*

Pursuant to the final document of the Eighth Review Conference of the States Parties[113] to the Convention on the Prohibition of the Development, Production and Stockpiling of Bacteriological (Biological) and Toxin Weapons and on their Destruction, 1972 (Biological Weapons Convention), [114] the Meeting of the States Parties was held in Geneva from 4 to 8 December 2017.

(ii) *Chemical Weapons Convention*

The twenty-second session of the Conference of the States Parties to the Convention on the Prohibition of the Development, Production, Stockpiling and Use of Chemical Weapons and on their Destruction, 1992 (Chemical Weapons Convention)[115] was held in the Hague, from 27 November to 1 December 2017. The Conference considered, *inter alia*, the status of implementation of the Chemical Weapons Convention, fostering of international cooperation for peaceful purposes in the field of chemical activities, the OPCW Programme for Africa and the engagement with chemical industry and the scientific community. On 1 December 2017, the Conference considered and adopted the report of its twentieth-second session.[116]

The membership of the Organization for the Prohibition of Chemical Weapons (OPCW) remained as 192 States parties in 2017.

(iii) *General Assembly*

On 4 December 2017, the General Assembly adopted three resolutions relating to biological and chemical weapons in 2017, resolution 72/28 entitled "Role of science and technology in the context of international security and disarmament", without a vote; resolution 72/43, entitled "Implementation of the Convention on the Prohibition of the Development, Production, Stockpiling and Use of Chemical Weapons and on Their Destruction", by a recorded vote of 159 in favour to 7 against, with 14 abstentions; and resolution 72/71

---

[112] S/2017/150.

[113] See the Final Document of the Eighth Review Conference (BWC/CONF.VIII/4).

[114] United Nations, *Treaty Series*, vol. 1015, p. 164.

[115] United Nations, *Treaty Series*, vol. 1974, p. 45.

[116] C-22/5.

entitled "Convention on the Prohibition of the Development, Production and Stockpiling of Bacteriological (Biological) and Toxin Weapons and on Their Destruction", without a vote.

(iv) *Security Council*

On 5 August 2017, the Security Council adopted resolution 2371 (2017) concerning non-proliferation and the Democratic People's Republic of Korea. The Council, acting under Chapter VII of the Charter, *inter alia*, recalled paragraph 24 of resolution 2270 (2016) and decided that the Democratic People's Republic of Korea shall not deploy or use chemical weapons and called upon such State to accede to the Convention on the Prohibition of the Development, Production, Stockpiling and Use of Chemical Weapons and Their Destruction, and then to immediately comply with its provisions.

On 11 September 2017, the Security Council adopted resolution 2375 (2017) concerning non-proliferation and the Democratic People's Republic of Korea. The Council, acting under Chapter VII of the Charter, *inter alia*, decided to authorize and noted that Member States shall seize and dispose items the supply, sale transfer, or export is prohibited by Security Council resolutions 1718 (2006), 1874 (2009), 2087 (2013), 2094 (2013), 2270 (2016), 2321 (2016), 2356 (2017), 2371 (2017), as well as under various disarmament treaties, including the Convention on the Prohibition of the Development, Production, Stockpiling and Use of Chemical Weapons and on Their Development of 29 April 1997, and the Convention on the Prohibition of the Development, Production and Stockpiling of Bacteriological (Biological) and Toxin Weapons and on Their Destruction of 10 April 1972.

(*d*) Conventional weapons issues

(i) *International Trade in Conventional Arms*

The Third Conference of States Parties to the Arms Trade Treaty (ATT)[117] was held in Geneva from 11 to 15 September 2017 in Geneva, Switzerland. Three preparatory meetings were held on 16 February, 7 April and 1 June 2017 in Geneva, Switzerland. A number of decisions were adopted by the Conference, concerning, *inter alia*, mandating the Treaty Secretariat to establish and maintain a database of States parties' national points of contact. On 15 September 2017, the Conference adopted its final report.[118]

On 4 December 2017, the General Assembly, on the recommendation of the First Committee, adopted resolution 72/40 entitled "Assistance to States for curbing the illicit traffic in small arms and light weapons and collecting them", without a vote; resolution 72/44 entitled "The Arms Trade Treaty", by a recorded vote of 155 in favour to none against, with 29 abstentions; and resolution 72/57 entitled "The illicit trade in small arms and light weapons in all its aspects", without a vote.

[117] United Nations, *Treaty Series*, registration no. 523373.

[118] ATT/CSP3/2017/SEC/184/Conf.FinRep.Rev1.

(ii) *Other conventional weapons issues*

On 4 December 2017, the General Assembly, on the recommendation of the First Committee, adopted eight other resolutions dealing with conventional arms issues: resolution 72/32 entitled "Compliance with non-proliferation, arms limitation and disarmament agreements and commitments" by a vote of 173 in favour to 1 against and 11 abstentions; resolution 72/35 entitled "Conventional arms control at the regional and subregional levels", by a recorded vote of 184 to 1, with 2 abstentions; resolution 72/36 entitled "Countering the threat posed by improvised explosive devices", without a vote; resolution 72/53 entitled "Implementation of the Convention on the Prohibition of the Use, Stockpiling, Production and Transfer of Anti-Personnel Mines and on Their Destruction", by a recorded vote of 167 in favour to none against, with 17 abstentions; resolution 72/54 entitled "Implementation of the Convention on Cluster Munitions", by a recorded vote of 142 in favour to 2 against, with 36 abstentions; resolution 72/55 entitled "Problems arising from the accumulation of conventional ammunition stockpiles in surplus, without a vote; and resolution 72/68 entitled "Convention on Prohibitions or Restrictions on the Use of Certain Conventional Weapons Which May Be Deemed to Be Excessively Injurious or to Have Indiscriminate Effects", without a vote. On 7 December 2017, the General Assembly, on the recommendation of the Fourth Committee, adopted resolution 72/75 entitled "Assistance in mine action", without a vote.

In resolution 2365 (2017) of 30 June 2017, the Security Council, *inter alia*, expressed concerned over the threat that landmines, explosive remnants of war and improvised explosive devices pose to civilians, refugees returning to their homes, as well as to peacekeepers, humanitarian personnel, civilian personnel, and law enforcement personnel, and called all parties to armed conflicts to protect civilian population and to end immediately and effectively the use of explosive devices in violation of international humanitarian law.

(iii) *Other international conferences and meetings*

The Seventh Meeting of States Parties to the Convention on Cluster Munitions, 2008,[119] was held from 4 to 6 September 2017 in Geneva.[120] During the thematic discussions, participants in the Meeting welcomed the ratifications of the Convention by Benin and Madagascar, and the submission of a progress report by Germany in its capacity as President.

With regard to the Protocol on Prohibitions or Restrictions on the Use of Mines, Booby-Traps and Other Devices, as amended on 3 May 1996 (Amended Protocol II)[121] annexed to the Convention on Conventional Weapons, the Nineteenth Annual Conference of the High Contracting Parties to Amended Protocol II was held on 21 November 2017 in Geneva. The Conference, *inter alia*, decided that the Group of Experts of the High Contracting Parties to CCW Amended Protocol II would continue to exchange information on a voluntary basis on national measures, best practices and lessons learned on the following topics related to improvised explosive devices: (*a*) general features of such devices, including new types; (*b*) methods of humanitarian clearance of these devices; and (*c*) methods to protect civilians. The Conference also decided that the Group would continue discussions on how to

[119] United Nations, *Treaty Series*, vol. 2688, p.39.

[120] CCM/MSP/2017/12.

[121] United Nations, *Treaty Series*, vol. 2048, p. 93.

facilitate effective voluntary sharing of information to help counter the illicit use of these weapons. The conference adopted its report at the second plenary meeting.[122]

The 2017 Meeting of the High Contracting Parties to the Convention on Certain Conventional Weapons was held in Geneva from 22 to 24 November 2017. On emerging technologies in the area of lethal autonomous weapon systems, the High Contracting Parties agreed on the proposed mandate for the continuation of the Group of Government Experts on this issue in 2018. Meeting participants welcomed the "Conclusions and recommendations" as reflected in the report of the Group of experts.[123]

The Eleventh Conference of the High Contracting Parties to Protocol V on Explosive Remnants of War was held in Geneva on 20 November 2017.[124] The Conference welcomed that Afghanistan consented to be bound by Protocol V and also welcomed the efforts undertaken by the Secretary-General of the United Nations, President of the Eleventh Conference, organizations, CCW Sponsorship Programme, and Implementation Support Unit to promote universalization of Protocol V. The conference decided that in 2018 the work under Protocol V was to focus on the clearance of explosive remnants of war, to complete the consideration of Article 4 and to continue national reporting. At its second plenary meeting, on 20 November the Conference adopted its final document.

The Sixteenth Meeting of the States Parties to the Convention on the Prohibition of the Use, Stockpiling, Production and Transfer of Anti-personnel Mines and on Their Destruction, 1997 (Mine-Ban Convention)[125] was held in Vienna from 18 to 21 December 2017. The Meeting considered reports on the work of the Convention's four committees, and two panel discussions were held. The first panel was entitled "20 Years of Success: Fulfilling the Promise of the Convention by 2025", the second panel was entitled "Keeping People at the Heart of the Convention: Effective Victim Assistance".

States parties welcomed the accession of Sri Lanka to the Convention and took note of the establishment of the informal working group on the universalization of the Convention. The Meeting participants also considered and took note of the reports of the Convention committees. They welcomed the announcement by Belarus on the completion of its article 4 obligations (stockpile destruction) and by Algeria on the completion of its article 5 responsibilities (mine clearance). During the meeting, the States parties granted the extension requests by Angola, Ecuador, Iraq, Thailand and Zimbabwe for completing the destruction of anti-personnel mines in mined areas,[126] and expressed concern for the situation in Ukraine since 2014 and welcomed the commitment by Ukraine to continue to engage with the Committee on Article 5 Implementation. At its final plenary session, on 21 December 2017, the Meeting adopted its final report.[127]

---

[122] CCW/AP.II/CONF.19/4.

[123] CCW/GGE.1/2017/3.

[124] CCW/P.V/CONF/2017/5.

[125] United Nations, *Treaty Series*, vol. 2056, p. 211.

[126] APLC/MSP.7/2016/L.3 and APLC/MSP.7/2006/5, para. 27.

[127] APLC/MSP.16/2017/11.

(*e*) Regional disarmament activities of the United Nations

(i) *Africa*

In 2017, the United Nations Regional Centre for Peace and Disarmament in Africa (UNREC) continued to assist, upon request, Member States and intergovernmental and civil society organizations in Africa to promote disarmament, peace and security.[128] The Centre continued to support Member States by providing assistance to control small arms and light weapons through capacity-building for civilian authorities, defence and security forces. The Centre continued to implement a project funded by the European Union on physical security and stockpile management in Sahel and carried out two workshops in each of the five States participating in the programme (Burkina Faso, Chad, Mali, Mauritania, Niger and Nigeria). The Centre provided assistance in preventing the diversion of such weapons, in particular to non-State armed groups and terrorist groups, pursuant to Security Council resolution 2178 (2014).

The Centre began a project aimed at increasing participation of women at all levels of decision-making in disarmament processes by helping in capacity building activities with civil society organizations to support the implementation of Security Council resolutions 1325 (2000), 2349 (2017) and 2370 (2017). The Centre also continued to raise awareness of African Member States of issues relating to weapons of mass destruction, in particular by assisting in implementing disarmament and non-proliferation instruments, such as the Convention on the Prohibition of the Development, Production and Stockpiling of Bacteriological (Biological) and Toxin Weapons and on Their Destruction and Security Council resolution 1540 (2004) on the non-proliferation of weapons of mass destruction and their means of delivery to non-State actors.

UNREC participated with the African Union Commission in the organization of a consultative meeting in N'Djamena in May 2017 on the Treaty and its implementation in Central Africa. Other partners included the United Nations Office on Drugs and Crime, the Economic Community of Central African States, the Regional Centre on Small Arms in the Great Lakes Region, the Horn of Africa and Bordering States and the Small Arms Survey.

The Assembly of the African Union adopted the "Roadmap for Silencing the Guns by 2020" at its twenty-eight ordinary session held in Addis Ababa on 30 and 31 January. The Southern African Development Community participated in the 693rd meeting of the Peace and Security Council of the African Union, held on 14 June 2017, and addressed the African Union Master Roadmap of Practical Steps to Silence the Guns in Africa by 2020. Additionally, the African Union and the Organization for the Prohibition of Chemical Weapons organized a workshop on "Strengthening International and Regional Partnerships for Effective Chemical Weapons Convention Implementation in Africa" on 13 and 14 November in Addis Ababa.

During 2017, UNREC continued its capacity building efforts with Lake Chad Basin countries affected by Boko Haram to prevent the diversion of small arms and light weapons to foreign terrorist fighters. Acting within the framework of the Counter Terrorism Implementation Task Force and in support of Security Council resolution 2178 (2014),

---

[128] For more information, see the reports of the Secretary-General on the United Nations Regional Centre for Peace and Disarmament (A/72/97 (for the period from July 2016 to June 2017) and A/73/151 (for the period from July 2017 to June 2018)).

UNREC conducted a train-the-trainer course in November for 27 participants from the beneficiary countries, as well as experts from other African countries. From 18 to 20 December 2017, UNREC also organized a capacity-building workshop to promote gender perspectives in disarmament, non-proliferation and arms control processes in the Lake Chad basin.

Other activities included the forty-fourth meeting of the United Nations Standing Advisory Committee on Security Questions in Central Africa held in Yaoundé from 29 May to 2 June 2017. The secretariat of the Economic Community of Central African States (ECCAS), acting as a designated subregional coordination and monitoring mechanism for the Kinshasa Convention, which entered into force on 8 March 2017, prepared a five-year plan of action for implementing the Convention, thereby contributing towards a stable security environment conducive to the economic development of ECCAS States members.

(ii) *Asia and the Pacific*

The United Nations Regional Centre for Peace, Disarmament and Development in Asia and the Pacific (UNRCPD) continued its promotion of disarmament, non-proliferation and arms control programmes in the region throughout 2017.[129]

Regional Centre organized two expert review events, for Kyrgyzstan and Uzbekistan, to assess the progress in the development and implementation of their national action plans, which were held in Vienna, in March and May 2017. It also contributed to a regional consultative meeting on preventing arms diversion, organized by the United Nations Institute for Disarmament Research, held in Bangkok, in March 2017, and to the United Nations Office on Drugs and Crime expert group meeting on education for justice, held in Vienna, in March 2017, to develop recommendations for university courses on preventing the illicit trafficking of firearms and armed violence and establishing and maintaining gun-free zones. It organized two expert review events in Vienna in September 2017 for Mongolia and Tajikistan in order to assess the progress made by the two countries in developing and implementing their national action plans. Regional Centre further undertook projects relating to the implementation of Security Council resolution 1540 (2004).

In 2017, the Centre held the twenty-seventh United Nations Conference on Disarmament Issues in cooperation with the Government of Japan, the Prefecture of Hiroshima and the City of Hiroshima. The Conference was entitled "Towards Realizing a World Free of Nuclear Weapons—Paving the Way to Achieve the Common Goal", and focused on prospects for nuclear disarmament and non-proliferation in light of the recent adoption of the Treaty on the Prohibition of Nuclear Weapons, ongoing preparations for the 2020 Review Conference of the Parties to the Treaty on the Non-Proliferation of Nuclear Weapons and other developments.[130]

In 2017, ASEAN continued to make progress in its implementation of the Treaty on the Southeast Asia Nuclear Weapon-Free Zone. At the meeting of ASEAN Foreign

---

[129] For more information, see the reports of the Secretary-General on the United Nations Regional Centre for Peace, Disarmament and Development in Asia and the Pacific (A/72/98, A/72/98/Corr.1 (for the period from 1 July 2016 to 30 June 2017) and A/73/126 (for the period from 1 July 2017 to 30 June 2018)).

[130] *The United Nations Disarmament Yearbook*, vol. 41 (Part II), 2016 (United Nations publication, Sales No.: E.17.IX.4), pp. 148–149.

Ministers in Manila on 5 August 2017, participants agreed to extend the Plan of Action to implement the Treaty for another five-year period (2018–2022).

The ninth Inter-Sessional Meeting on Non-Proliferation and Disarmament of the ASEAN Regional Forum, held in Auckland, New Zealand in March 2017, discussed Security Council resolutions relating to the Democratic People's Republic of Korea, the role of the Panel of Experts of the Security Council Committee established pursuant to resolution 1718 (2006) and the implementation of related sanctions by United Nations Member States. [131]

(iii) *Latin America and the Caribbean*

The United Nations Regional Centre for Peace, Disarmament and Development in Latin America and the Caribbean (UNLIREC) continued its technical, legal and training activities to support the efforts by States in the region in their implementation of disarmament, arms control and non-proliferation instruments and adherence to international standards and norms in those fields during 2017.[132] The Regional Centre also assisted States in the region in their implementation of Security Council resolution 1540 (2004), in particular with regard to issues relating to national legislation, maritime border security, combating proliferation financing and national action plans. With the adoption of the 2030 Agenda for Sustainable Development, the Regional Centre aligned its activities to support the realization of the Sustainable Development Goals, in particular Goal 16 ("Promote peaceful and inclusive societies for sustainable development, provide access to justice for all and build effective, accountable and inclusive institutions at all levels"). Furthermore, the Regional Centre also continued its efforts to promote the participation of women in disarmament, arms control and non-proliferation initiatives, in line with General Assembly resolution 65/69 on women, disarmament, non-proliferation and arms control.

(iv) *General Assembly*

On 4 December 2017, upon the recommendation of the First Committee, the General Assembly adopted without a vote the following resolutions dealing with regional disarmament: resolution 72/33 entitled "Confidence-building measures in the regional and subregional context"; resolution 72/34 entitled "Regional disarmament"; resolution 72/60 entitled "United Nations Regional Centre for Peace and Disarmament in Africa"; resolution 72/61 entitled "United Nations Regional Centre for Peace, Disarmament and Development in Latin America and the Caribbean"; resolution 72/62 entitled "United Nations Regional Centre for Peace and Disarmament in Asia and the Pacific"; resolution 72/63 entitled "Regional confidence-building measures: activities of the United Nations Standing Advisory Committee on Security Questions in Central Africa"; resolution 72/64 entitled "United Nations regional centres for peace and disarmament"; and resolution 72/69 entitled "Strengthening of security and cooperation in the Mediterranean region".

---

[131] *The United Nations Disarmament Yearbook*, vol. 42 (Part II), 2017 (United Nations publication, Sales No.: E.17.IX.7), pp. 156–157.

[132] For more information, see reports of the Secretary-General on the United Nations Regional Centre for Peace, Disarmament and Development in Latin America and the Caribbean (A/72/99 (for the period from July 2016 to June 2017) and A/73/127 (for the period from July 2017 to June 2018)).

On the same day, upon the recommendation of the First Committee, the Assembly also adopted resolution 72/21 entitled "Implementation of the Declaration of the Indian Ocean as a Zone of Peace", with 132 votes in favour to 3 against and 46 abstentions, and resolution 72/35 entitled "Conventional arms control at the regional and subregional levels", by a recorded vote of 184 to 1, with 2 abstentions.

(*f*) Outer space (disarmament aspects)

The thirty-seventh session of the Inter-Agency Meeting on Outer Space Activities (UN-Space) was held on 24 August 2017 in Geneva. The session, organized by the Office for Outer Space Affairs and hosted in coordination with the World Health Organization, focused, foremost, on the use of space technology within the United Nations system and its potential contribution to UNISPACE+50. The agenda of the thirty-sixth session of UN-Space, as adopted, and the list of participants are contained in annexes I and II.[133]

In 2017, UN-Space agreed that the upcoming report of the Secretary-General on the coordination of space-related activities within the United Nations system: directions and anticipated results for the period 2018–2019, to be submitted for consideration by the Committee at its sixty-first session, in 2018, should focus on reinforcing synergies in efficiency measures in the use of space science, technology and applications within the United Nations system in support of global development efforts.[134] It was also agreed that there would be a workshop, to be held in New York in the second half of 2018, to consider public/private partnership models and cooperation with the private sector to increase the use of space science, technology and applications for economic growth and sustainable development, as well as the legal and ethical aspects of cooperation models involving non-State actors. UN-Space also agreed to establish a global financing facility to enable deeper engagement of United Nations entities in cross-sectoral activities relating to the use of space science, technology, information and applications.[135]

The sixtieth session of the Committee on the Peaceful Uses of Outer Space, was held from 7 to 16 June 2017.[136]

General Assembly

On 4 December 2017, the General Assembly, upon the recommendation of the First Committee, adopted the following resolutions with regard to disarmament activities in outer space: resolution 72/26 entitled "Prevention of an arms race in outer space", by a recorded vote of 182 to 0, with 3 abstentions; resolution 72/27 entitled "No first placement of weapons in outer space", by a recorded vote of 131 to 4, with 48 abstentions.

On 7 December 2017, the General Assembly adopted, upon the recommendation of the Fourth Committee, resolution 72/77 entitled "International cooperation in the peaceful

---

[133] See Report of the Inter-Agency Meeting on Outer Space Activities (UN-Space) on its thirty-seventh session, A/AC.105/1143.

[134] A/AC.105/1143, para. 14.

[135] *Ibid*., para. 19.

[136] Final Document of the sixtieth session of the Committee on the Peaceful Uses of Outer Space A/72/20.

uses of outer space", without a vote; and resolution 72/79 entitled "Consideration of the fiftieth anniversary of the United Nations Conference on the Exploration and Peaceful Uses of Outer Space", without a vote.

On 24 December 2017, the General Assembly adopted resolution 72/250 entitled "Further practical measures for the prevention of an arms race in outer space: Statement of financial implications (A/72/679)", by a recorded vote of 108 in favour to 5 against and 47 abstentions.

(*g*) Other disarmament measures and international security

General Assembly

On 4 December 2017, the General Assembly, upon the recommendation of the First Committee, adopted resolution 72/47, entitled "Observance of environmental norms in the drafting and implementation of agreements on disarmament and arms control" without a vote; resolution 72/48, entitled "Promotion of multilateralism in the area of disarmament and non-proliferation" by a recorded vote of 130 to 4, with 51 abstentions.

On 20 December 2017, the General Assembly adopted resolution 72/199 entitled "Restructuring of the United Nations peace and security pillar", without a vote.

4. Legal aspects of peaceful uses of outer space

(*a*) Legal Subcommittee on the Peaceful Uses of Outer Space

The Legal Subcommittee on the Peaceful Uses of Outer Space held its fifty-sixth session at the United Nations Office in Vienna from 27 March to 7 April 2017.[137]

Under the agenda item "Information on the activities of international intergovernmental and non-governmental organizations relating to space law", the Subcommittee, *inter alia*, welcomed information received from international intergovernmental and non-governmental organizations and agreed that it was important to continue the exchange of information on recent developments in the area of space law between the Subcommittee and such organizations should once again be invited to report to the Subcommittee, at its fifty-seventh session, on their activities relating to space law.

With regard to United Nations treaties on outer space, the Subcommittee reconvened its Working Group on the Status and Application of the Five United Nations Treaties on Outer Space and endorsed the report of the Chair of the Working Group on 6 April 2017.[138] The view was expressed that there was a complementary relationship between the United Nations treaties on outer space, which were the foundation of international space law, and the more flexible, non-legally binding instruments such as resolutions, guidelines and principles, which were more appropriate for prompt reaction to current developments in outer space activities. It was also expressed that the universal adherence to the Outer Space Treaty, the Rescue Agreement, Liability Convention and Registration Convention

---

[137] For the Report of the Legal Subcommittee, see A/AC.105/1122.

[138] See Report of the Chair of the Working Group on the Status and Application of the Five United Nations Treaties on Outer Space, A/AC.105/C.2/L.301/Add.1, Annex I.

and their underlying principles was important at the present time when the international community was developing new norms of behaviour to govern space activities.[139]

Regarding matters related to the definition and delimitation of outer space and the character and utilization of geostationary orbit, the Subcommittee reconvened its Working Group on the Definition and Delimitation of Outer Space and endorsed the report of the Working Group on 6 April 2017.[140]

Regarding the agenda item entitled "National legislation relevant to the peaceful exploration and use of outer space", the Subcommittee agreed that the discussions under the item were important and that they enabled States to gain an understanding of existing national regulatory frameworks, share experiences on national practices and exchange information on national legal frameworks, and encouraged Member States to continue to submit to the Secretariat texts of their national space laws and regulations and to provide updates and inputs for the schematic overview of national regulatory frameworks for space activities.[141]

Under the agenda item "Capacity-building in space law", the Subcommittee noted with satisfaction that the Office for Outer Space Affairs had updated the directory of education opportunities in space law,[142] including with information on available fellowships and scholarships, and recommended that States members and permanent observers of the Committee inform the Subcommittee, at its fifty-seventh session, of any action taken or planned at the national, regional or international level to build capacity in space law.[143]

As for agenda item "Review and possible revision of the Principles Relevant to the Use of Nuclear Power Sources in Outer Space", *inter alia*, the Legal Subcommittee noted the successful completion of the multi-year workplan of the Working Group on the Use of Nuclear Power Sources in Outer Space of the Scientific and Technical Subcommittee, for the period 2014–2017,[144] and noted with satisfaction the endorsement by the Scientific and Technical Subcommittee of the new multi-year workplan of the Working Group for the period 2017–2021.[145]

Some delegations expressed the view that the Principles should be reviewed with a view to developing binding international standards, while others mentioned that such revision was envisaged in the Principles, that certain technological advances should be taken into account and that reference frameworks for radiological protection had evolved.[146] That view was complemented by another one expressing that the focused work of the Working Group under its completed workplan has demonstrated that the Safety Framework provided a comprehensive and sufficient foundation of guidance for Member States and international intergovernmental space organizations to develop and operate their own space applications using nuclear power sources in a safe manner.

---

139 *Ibid.*, paras. 82–83.

140 See Report of the Chair of the Working Group on the Definition and Delimitation of Outer Space, A/AC.105/1122, Annex II.

141 *Ibid.*, paras. 122–123.

142 A/AC.105/C.2/2017/CRP.10.

143 A/AC.105/1122, paras. 135–136.

144 A/AC.105/1065, Annex II, para. 9.

145 A/AC.105/1138, para. 237, and annex II, para. 9.

146 A/AC.105/1122, paras. 142–143.

The view was expressed that the use of applications using nuclear power sources should be in conformity with international law, the Charter of the United Nations and United Nations treaties and principles on outer space. This view was then complemented with another one which expressed that it was important to monitor the effectiveness of the implementation of the Safety Framework.[147]

Under the agenda item "General exchange of information and views on legal mechanisms relating to space debris mitigation measures, taking into account the work of the Scientific and Technical", the Subcommittee agreed that States members of the Committee and international intergovernmental organizations having permanent observer status with the Committee should be invited to further contribute to the compendium of space debris mitigation standards adopted by States and international organizations by providing or updating the information on any legislation or standards adopted with regard to space debris mitigation, using the template provided for that purpose. The Subcommittee also agreed that all other States Members of the United Nations should be invited to contribute to the compendium, and encouraged States with such regulations or standards to provide information on them.[148]

Under agenda item "General exchange of information on non-legally binding United Nations instruments on outer space", the Subcommittee welcomed the compendium "Information on an updated compendium on mechanisms adopted by States and international organizations in relation to non-legally binding United Nations instruments on outer space"[149] as a valuable contribution to facilitate the exchange of views and sharing of information.

Regarding the agenda item "General exchange of views on the legal aspects of space traffic management", the Subcommittee noted that space environment was becoming increasingly complex and congested, owing to the growing number of objects in outer space, the diversification of actors in outer space and the increase in space activities. It was noted that such factors increased the chances of potential collisions in outer space and that space traffic management could be considered in that context. Several views were expressed, *inter alia*, that there was a need to develop comprehensive traffic management regulations under the ITU Radio Regulations.[150] Another view expressed was that a system of space traffic management rules could facilitate the practical application of a fault-based liability regime by defining a standard of care and due diligence for activities in outer space, against which behaviours of space actors could be assessed to establish fault.[151]

On the agenda item entitled "General exchange of views on the application of international law to small satellite activities", the Subcommittee agreed that the continuation of its work under this item would provide valuable opportunities for addressing a number of topical issues relating to international and national policy and regulation measures regarding the use of small satellites by various actors.[152] The Subcommittee agreed that consideration of the draft questionnaire on the application of international law to small-satellite

---

[147] *Ibid.*, paras. 144–149.

[148] *Ibid.*, para. 173.

[149] A/AC.105/C.2/2017/CRP.21.

[150] A/AC.105/1122, para. 201.

[151] *Ibid.*, para. 203.

[152] *Ibid.*, para. 207.

activities[153] should be considered by the Working Group on the Status and Application of the Five United Nations Treaties on Outer Space.[154]

On the agenda item entitled "General exchange of views on potential legal models for activities in exploration, exploitation and utilization of space resources", some delegations expressed the view that in the light of the increasing participation of the private sector in space activities, an international legal framework developed in a multilateral forum that clearly defined and guided commercial activities in outer space could play an important role in expanding the use of outer space, and stimulate space activities and that such a framework was required to provide legal security.[155] Another view was expressed that the regulation of private sector actors in outer space was consistent with a State's international obligations under the Outer Space Treaty and with half a century of practice under the Treaty, and the consistently stated positions of some States.[156]

Regarding the agenda item "Review of international mechanisms for cooperation in the peaceful exploration and use of outer space", the Subcommittee reconvened its Working Group on the Review of International Mechanisms for Cooperation in the Peaceful Exploration and Use of Outer Space and endorsed the report of the Chair of the Working Group. On 6 April 2017, the Subcommittee endorsed the report of the chair of the Working Group.[157] The Subcommittee agreed that the review of the mechanisms for cooperation in space activities had assisted States in understanding the different approaches to cooperation in space activities and contributed to the further strengthening of regional, interregional and international cooperation in the exploration and peaceful uses of outer space. In that regard, the Subcommittee noted that 2017, the final year of consideration of the agenda item under its workplan, would coincide with the fiftieth anniversary of the Outer Space Treaty.[158]

Concerning future work, the Subcommittee agreed that five single issues/items for discussion, entitled "Review and possible revision of the Principles Relevant to the Use of Nuclear Power Sources in Outer Space", "General exchange of information on non legally binding United Nations instruments on outer space", "General exchange of views on the legal aspects of space traffic management", "General exchange of views on the application of international law to small-satellite activities" and "General exchange of views on potential legal models for activities in exploration, exploitation and utilization of space resources", should be retained on the agenda of the Subcommittee at its fifty-seventh session.[159] The Subcommittee further decided that a new single issue/item for discussion, entitled "General exchange of information and views on legal mechanisms relating to space debris mitigation and remediation measures, taking into account the work of the Scientific and Technical Subcommittee", should be included on the agenda at its fifty-seventh session.[160]

---

153 A/AC.105/C.2/2017/CRP.11.

154 A/AC.105/1122, para. 220.

155 *Ibid.*, para. 228.

156 *Ibid.*, para. 245.

157 *Ibid.*, Annex III.

158 *Ibid.*, para. 266.

159 *Ibid.*, para. 269.

160 *Ibid.*, para. 270.

(*b*) General Assembly

In 2017, the General Assembly adopted four resolutions relating to the legal aspects of the peaceful uses of outer space. On 4 December 2017, upon the recommendation of the First Committee, the General Assembly adopted resolution 72/56 entitled "Transparency and confidence-building measures in outer space activities" without a vote. On 7 December 2017, upon the recommendation of the Fourth Committee, the Assembly adopted resolution 72/77 entitled "International cooperation in the peaceful uses of outer space" without a vote; resolution 72/78 entitled "Declaration on the fiftieth anniversary of the Treaty on Principles Governing the Activities of States in the Exploration and Use of Outer Space, including the Moon and Other Celestial Bodies", without a vote; and resolution 72/79 entitled "Consideration of the fiftieth anniversary of the United Nations Conference on the Exploration and Peaceful Uses of Outer Space", without a vote.

5. Human Rights[161]

(*a*) Sessions of the United Nations human rights bodies and treaty bodies

(i) *Human Rights Council*

The Human Rights Council, established in 2006,[162] meets as a quasi-standing body in three annual regular sessions and additional special sessions as needed. Reporting to the General Assembly, its agenda and programme of work provide the opportunity to discuss all thematic human rights issues and human rights situations that require the attention of the Assembly.

The Council's mandate includes the review on a periodic basis of the fulfilment of the human rights obligations of all Member States, including the members of the Council, over a cycle of four years through the universal periodic review.[163] The Council also assumed the thirty-eight country and thematic special procedures existing under its predecessor, the

---

[161] This section covers the resolutions adopted, if any, by the Security Council, the General Assembly and the Economic and Social Council. It also includes a selective coverage of the legal activities of the Human Rights Council, in particular activities of Special Rapporteurs and selected resolutions on specific human rights issues. Other legal developments in human rights may be found under the section in the present chapter entitled "Peace and security". The present section does not cover resolutions addressing human rights issues arising in particular States, nor does it cover in detail the legal activities of the treaty bodies (namely, the Human Rights Committee, the Committee on Economic, Social and Cultural Rights, the Committee on the Elimination of Racial Discrimination, the Committee on the Elimination of Discrimination Against Women, the Committee Against Torture, the Committee on the Rights of the Child, the Committee on the Protection of the Rights of All Migrant Workers and Members of their Families and the Committee on the Rights of Persons with Disabilities). Detailed information and documents relating to human rights are available on the website of the Office of the United Nations High Commissioner for Human Rights at http://www.ohchr.org.

[162] General Assembly resolution 60/251 of 15 March 2006. For further details on its establishment, see the United Nations Juridical Yearbook, 2006, chap. III, section 5.

[163] The first universal periodic review cycle covered the period 2008–2011. The second universal periodic review cycle covered the period 2012–2016. The third universal periodic review cycle commenced in 2017 and run through 2022. For a list of States included and calendar of review sessions, see the section Universal Periodic Review at the homepage of the Human Rights Council at http://www.ohchr.org.

Commission on Human Rights, while reviewing the mandate and criteria for the establishment of these special procedures.[164] Moreover, based on the previous "1503 procedure", the confidential complaint procedure of the Council allows individuals and organizations to continue to bring complaints revealing a consistent pattern of gross and reliably attested violations of human rights to the attention of the Council.[165]

In 2017, the Human Rights Council held its thirty-fourth, thirty-fifth and thirty-sixth regular sessions[166] and its twenty-seventh special session on "Human rights situation of the minority Rohingya Muslim population and other minorities in the Rakhine State of Myanmar".[167]

(ii) *Human Rights Council Advisory Committee*

The Human Rights Council Advisory Committee was established pursuant to Human Rights Council resolution 5/1 of 18 June 2007.[168] The Advisory Committee is composed of eighteen experts, and functions as a think-tank for the Council, working under its direction and providing expertise in the manner and form requested by the Council, focusing mainly on studies and research-based advice, suggestions for further enhancing its procedural efficiency, as well as further research proposals within the scope of the work set out by the Council. The Advisory Committee held its eighteenth session from 20 to 24 February 2017 and its nineteenth session from 7 to 11 August 2017 in Geneva.[169]

(iii) *Human Rights Committee*

The Human Rights Committee was established under the International Covenant on Civil and Political Rights of 1966[170] to monitor the implementation of the Covenant and its Optional Protocols[171] in the territory of States parties. The Committee held its 119th session from 6 to 29 March 2017, its 120th session from 3 to 28 July 2017 and its 121st session from 16 October to 10 November 2017 in Geneva.[172] The Committee did not adopt a general comment in 2017.

---

[164] Human Rights Council decision 1/102 of 30 June 2006.

[165] More detailed information on the mandate, work and methods of the Human Rights Council is available at the homepage of the Human Rights Council at http://www.ohchr.org/.

[166] For the reports of the Human Rights Council on its thirty-fourth and thirty-fifth sessions, see *Official Records of the General Assembly, Seventy-second Session, Supplement No. 53* (A/72/53). For the report of the Human Rights Council on its thirty-sixth session, see *ibid., Seventy-second Session, Supplement No. 53A* (A/72/53/Add.1).

[167] For the report of the Human Rights Council on its twenty-seventh special session, see *ibid., Seventy-third Session, Supplement No. 53* (A/73/53).

[168] The Human Rights Council Advisory Committee replaced the Sub-Commission for the Promotion and Protection of Human Rights as the main subsidiary body of the Human Rights Council.

[169] For the reports of the Advisory Committee on its eighteenth and nineteenth sessions, see A/HRC/AC/18/2 and A/HRC/AC/19/2, respectively.

[170] United Nations, *Treaty Series*, vol. 999, p. 171.

[171] Optional Protocol to the International Covenant on Civil and Political Rights, *ibid.*; and Second Optional Protocol to the International Covenant on Civil and Political Rights, *ibid.*, vol. 1642, p. 414.

[172] For the report of the Human Rights Committee on its 119th session, see *Official Records of the General Assembly, Seventy-second Session, Supplement No. 40* (A/72/40). For the reports of the Human Rights

(iv) *Committee on Economic, Social and Cultural Rights*

The Committee on Economic, Social and Cultural Rights was established by the Economic and Social Council[173] to monitor the implementation of the International Covenant on Economic, Social and Cultural Rights of 1966[174] by its State parties. The Committee held its sixtieth, sixty-first and sixty-second sessions in Geneva from 20 to 24 February, from 29 May to 23 June, and from 18 September to 6 October 2017, respectively.[175] The Committee adopted general comment No. 24 (2017) on State obligations under the Covenant in the context of business activities.[176]

(v) *Committee on the Elimination of Racial Discrimination*

The Committee on the Elimination of Racial Discrimination was established under the International Convention on the Elimination of All Forms of Racial Discrimination of 1966[177] to monitor the implementation of this Convention by its States parties. The Committee held its ninety-second, ninety-third and ninety-fourth sessions in Geneva from 24 April to 12 May, from 31 July to 25 August, and from 20 November to 8 December 2017, respectively.[178] The Committee did not adopt a general recommendation in 2017.

(vi) *Committee on the Elimination of Discrimination against Women*

The Committee on the Elimination of Discrimination against Women was established under the Convention on the Elimination of All Forms of Discrimination against Women of 1979[179] to monitor the implementation of this Convention by its States parties. The Committee held its sixty-sixth, sixty-seventh and sixty-eighth sessions in Geneva from 13 February to 3 March, from 3 to 21 July, and from 23 October to 17 November 2017, respectively.[180] The Committee adopted general recommendation No. 35 (2017) on gender-based violence against women, updating general recommendation No. 19,[181] and general recommendation No. 36 (2017) on the right of girls and women to education.[182]

Committee on its 120th and 121st sessions, see *ibid., Seventy-third Session, Supplement No. 40* (A/73/40).

173 Economic and Social Council resolution 1985/17 of 28 May 1985.

174 United Nations, *Treaty Series*, vol. 993, p. 3.

175 For the reports of the sixtieth, sixty-first, and sixty-second sessions, see *Official Records of the Economic and Social Council, 2018, Supplement No. 2* (E/2018/22).

176 E/C.12/GC/24.

177 United Nations, *Treaty Series*, vol. 660, p. 195.

178 For the report of the ninety-second session, see *Official Records of the General Assembly, Seventy-second Session, Supplement No. 18* (A/72/18). For the reports of the ninety-third and the ninety-fourth sessions, see *ibid., Seventy-third Session, Supplement No. 18* (A/73/18).

179 United Nations, *Treaty Series*, vol. 1249, p. 13.

180 For the report of the sixty-sixth session, see *Official Records of the General Assembly, Seventy-second Session, Supplement No. 38* (A/72/38). For the reports of the sixty-seventh and sixty-eighth sessions, see *ibid., Seventy-third Session, Supplement No. 38* (A/73/38).

181 CEDAW/C/GC/35.

182 CEDAW/C/GC/36.

(vii) *Committee against Torture*

The Committee against Torture was established under the Convention against Torture and Other Cruel, Inhuman or Degrading Treatment or Punishment of 1984[183] to monitor the implementation of this Convention by its States parties. The Committee held its sixtieth, sixty-first and sixty-second sessions in Geneva from 18 April to 12 May, from 24 July to 11 August, and from 6 November to 6 December 2017, respectively.[184] The Committee adopted general comment No. 4 (2017) on the implementation of article 3 of the Convention in the context of article 22,[185] which replaced general comment No. 1 (1997).

The Subcommittee on Prevention of Torture, established in October 2006 under the Optional Protocol to the Convention against Torture and Other Cruel, Inhuman or Degrading Treatment or Punishment,[186] held its thirty-first, thirty-second and thirty-third sessions from 13 to 17 February, from 12 to 16 June, and from 13 to 17 November 2017, respectively.[187]

(viii) *Committee on the Rights of the Child*

The Committee on the Rights of the Child was established under the Convention on the Rights of the Child of 1989[188] to monitor the implementation of this Convention by its States parties. The Committee held its seventy-fourth, seventy-fifth and seventy-sixth sessions in Geneva from 16 January to 3 February, from 15 May to 2 June, and from 11 to 29 September 2017, respectively.[189] The Committee adopted general comment No. 21 (2017) on children in street situations.[190] The Committee also adopted joint general comments No. 22 and No. 23 (2017) with the Committee on the Protection of the Rights of All Migrant Workers and Members of Their Families, on the general principles regarding the human rights of children in the context of international migration,[191] and on State obligations regarding the human rights of children in the context of international migration in countries of origin, transit, destination and return,[192] respectively.

---

[183] United Nations, *Treaty Series*, vol. 1465, p. 85.

[184] For the report of the sixtieth session, see *Official Records of the General Assembly, Seventieth-second Session, Supplement No. 44* (A/72/44). For the reports of the sixty-first and sixty-second sessions, see *ibid., Seventy-third Session, Supplement No. 44* (A/73/44).

[185] CAT/C/GC/4.

[186] United Nations, *Treaty Series*, vol. 2375, p. 237.

[187] For details of the thirty-first, thirty-second and thirty-third sessions, see the eleventh annual report of the Subcommittee (CAT/C/63/4).

[188] United Nations, *Treaty Series*, vol. 1577, p. 3.

[189] For the reports of the seventy-fourth, seventy-fifth and seventy-sixth sessions, see *Official Records of the General Assembly, Seventy-third Session, Supplement No. 41* (A/73/41).

[190] CRC/C/GC/21.

[191] CMW/C/GC/3-CRC/C/GC/22.

[192] CMW/C/GC/4-CRC/C/GC/23.

(ix) *Committee on the Protection of the Rights of All Migrant Workers and Members of Their Families*

The Committee on the Protection of the Rights of All Migrant Workers and Members of Their Families was established under the International Convention for the Protection of the Rights of All Migrant Workers and Members of Their Families of 1990[193] to monitor the implementation of this Convention by its States parties in their territories. The Committee held its twenty-sixth and twenty-seventh sessions in Geneva from 3 to 13 April and from 4 to 13 September 2017, respectively.[194] The Committee adopted joint general comments No. 3 and No. 4 (2017) with the Committee on the Rights of the Child on the human rights of children in the context of international migration.[195]

(x) *Committee on the Rights of Persons with Disabilities*

The Committee on the Rights of Persons with Disabilities was established under the Convention on the Rights of Persons with Disabilities of 2006[196] and its 2006 Optional Protocol[197] to monitor the implementation of the Convention and the Optional Protocol by States parties. The Committee held its seventeenth and eighteenth sessions in Geneva from 20 March to 12 April and from 14 to 31 August 2017, respectively.[198] The Committee adopted general comment No. 5 (2017) on living independently and being included in the community.[199]

(xi) *Committee on Enforced Disappearances*

The Committee on Enforced Disappearances was established under the International Convention for the Protection of All Persons from Enforced Disappearance of 2006[200] to monitor the implementation of this Convention by its State parties. The Committee held its twelfth and thirteenth sessions in Geneva from 6 to 17 March and from 4 to 15 September 2017, respectively.[201] The Committee did not adopt a general comment in 2017.

---

[193] United Nations, *Treaty Series*, vol. 2220, p. 3.

[194] For the report of the twenty-sixth session, see *Official Records of the General Assembly, Seventy-second Session, Supplement No. 48* (A/72/48). For the report of the twenty-seventh session, see *ibid., Seventy-third Session, Supplement No. 48* (A/73/48).

[195] See subsection (*a*)(viii) above.

[196] United Nations, *Treaty Series*, vol. 2515, p. 3.

[197] *Ibid.*, vol. 2518, p. 283.

[198] For the reports of the seventeenth and eighteenth sessions, see *Official Records of the General Assembly, Seventy-fourth Session, Supplement No. 55* (A/74/55).

[199] CRPD/C/GC/5.

[200] General Assembly resolution 61/177 of 20 December 2006, annex.

[201] For the report of the twelfth session, see *Official Records of the General Assembly, Seventy-second Session, Supplement No. 56* (A/72/56). For the report of the thirteenth session, see *ibid., Seventy-third Session, Supplement No. 56* (A/73/56).

(*b*) Racism, racial discrimination, xenophobia and related intolerance

(i) *Human Rights Council*

The Special Rapporteur on contemporary forms of racism, racial discrimination, xenophobia and related intolerance, Mr. Mutuma Ruteere, submitted two reports to the Human Rights Council. The first report, submitted pursuant to General Assembly resolution 71/179, addressed developments and summarized general trends with regard to the continuing human rights and democratic challenges posed by extremist political parties, movements and groups.[202] The second report, submitted pursuant to Human Rights Council resolution 34/35, was the final report of the Special Rapporteur to the Council.[203] In the report, the Special Rapporteur provided a summary of the activities undertaken during the period under review and an overview of the thematic work undertaken by the mandate since its creation, and analysed the challenges of combating racism, xenophobia and discrimination in the context of countering terrorism.

The United Nations High Commissioner for Human Rights submitted a report to the Human Rights Council, pursuant to Council resolution 32/17, on the impact of multiple and intersecting forms of discrimination and violence in the context of racism, racial discrimination, xenophobia and related intolerance on the full enjoyment of all human rights by women and girls.[204]

The Working Group of Experts on People of African Descent submitted a consolidated annual report to both the General Assembly and the Human Rights Council.[205]

On 24 March 2017, the Human Rights Council adopted, without a vote, resolution 34/32 entitled "Combating intolerance, negative stereotyping and stigmatization of, and discrimination, incitement to violence and violence against, persons based on religion or belief", resolution 34/33 entitled "Establishment of a forum on people of African descent", and resolution 34/35 entitled "Mandate of the Special Rapporteur on contemporary forms of racism, racial discrimination, xenophobia and related intolerance". On the same day, the Council adopted resolution 34/34 entitled "Mandate of the Intergovernmental Working Group on the Effective Implementation of the Durban Declaration and Programme of Action" by a recorded vote of 46 to 1, with no abstentions. The Council also adopted resolution 34/36 entitled "Elaboration of complementary standards to the International Convention on the Elimination of All Forms of Racial Discrimination" by a recorded vote of 31 to 4, with 12 abstentions.

On 23 June 2017, the Council adopted, without a vote, resolution 35/30 entitled "Consideration of the elaboration of a draft declaration on the promotion and full respect of human rights of people of African descent".

On 29 September 2017, the Council adopted, without a vote, resolution 36/23 entitled "Mandate of the Working Group of Experts on People of African Descent". On the same day, the Council adopted resolution 36/24 entitled "From rhetoric to reality: a global call

---

[202] A/HRC/35/42.

[203] A/HRC/35/41.

[204] A/HRC/35/10.

[205] A/HRC/36/60; A/72/319.

for concrete action against racism, racial discrimination, xenophobia and related intolerance" by a recorded vote of 32 to 5, with 10 abstentions.

Ms. E. Tendayi Achiume was appointed by the Council as Special Rapporteur on contemporary forms of racism, racial discrimination, xenophobia and related intolerance in September 2017 and took up her functions on 1 November 2017.

(ii) *General Assembly*

The Special Rapporteur on contemporary forms of racism, racial discrimination, xenophobia and related intolerance, Mr. Mutuma Ruteere, submitted two reports to the General Assembly. The first report addressed the implementation of General Assembly resolution 71/179 on combating glorification of Nazism and other practices that contribute to fuelling contemporary forms of racism, racial discrimination, xenophobia and related intolerance, based on views collected from Governments and non-governmental organizations.[206] In the second report, submitted pursuant to General Assembly resolution 71/181, the Special Rapporteur analysed the challenges linked to combating racism, xenophobia and discrimination in the context of counter-terrorism.[207]

The Secretary-General submitted two reports to the General Assembly. The first report entitled "Programme of activities for the implementation of the International Decade for People of African Descent" presented an overview of the enjoyment of human rights by women and girls of African descent, drawing from the work of international human rights mechanisms as well as responses from key stakeholders.[208] The second report, entitled "A global call for action for the total elimination of racism, racial discrimination, xenophobia and related intolerance and the comprehensive implementation of and follow-up to the Durban Declaration and Programme of Action", submitted pursuant to General Assembly resolution 71/181, addressed the implementation of that resolution, based on information from Member States and other stakeholders.[209] The Secretariat also transmitted the report of the group of independent eminent experts on the implementation of the Durban Declaration and Programme of Action.[210]

On 19 December 2017, on the recommendation of the Third Committee, the General Assembly adopted resolution 72/156 entitled "Combating glorification of Nazism, neo-Nazism and other practices that contribute to fuelling contemporary forms of racism, racial discrimination, xenophobia and related intolerance", by a recorded vote of 133 to 2, with 49 abstentions, and resolution 72/157 entitled "A global call for concrete action for the total elimination of racism, racial discrimination, xenophobia and related intolerance and the comprehensive implementation of and follow-up to the Durban Declaration and Programme of Action", by a recorded vote of 133 to 10, with 43 abstentions.

---

[206] A/72/291.

[207] A/72/287.

[208] A/72/323.

[209] A/72/324.

[210] A/72/285.

(c) Right to development and poverty reduction

(i) *Right to development*

a. Human Rights Council

In March 2017, Mr. Saad Alfarargi was appointed by the Human Rights Council, pursuant to Council resolution 33/14, as Special Rapporteur on the right to development. The Special Rapporteur took up his role on 1 May 2017 and submitted a report to both the General Assembly and the Human Rights Council, which presented an outline of the preliminary strategy regarding his work under the mandate, his approach to engagement with stakeholders, and his methods of work.[211]

The Working Group on the Right to Development submitted a report on its eighteenth session to the Human Rights Council.[212]

The Secretary-General and the United Nations High Commissioner for Human Rights submitted a consolidated report on the right to development to both the General Assembly and the Human Rights Council.[213] The report summarized the activities of the Office of the United Nations High Commissioner for Human Rights (OHCHR) on the promotion and realization of the right to development covering the period from June 2016 to May 2017, and provided an analysis of the implementation of the right to development, taking into account existing challenges and making recommendations on how to overcome them.

On 22 June 2017, the Human Rights Council adopted resolution 35/21 entitled "The contribution of development to the enjoyment of all human rights", by a recorded vote of 30 to 13, with 3 abstentions.[214] On 28 September 2017, the Council adopted resolution 36/9 entitled "The right to development", by a recorded vote of 31 to 11, with 4 abstentions.

b. General Assembly

On 19 December 2017, on the recommendation of the Third Committee, the General Assembly adopted resolution 72/167 entitled "The right to development", by a recorded vote of 140 to 10, with 38 abstentions.

(ii) *Poverty reduction*

a. Human Rights Council

The Special Rapporteur on extreme poverty and human rights, Mr. Philip Alston, submitted a report to the Human Rights Council pursuant to Council resolution 26/3.[215] The report analyzed, from the perspective of international human rights law, the approach of replacing or supplementing existing social protection systems with a universal basic income.

[211] A/HRC/36/49; A/72/163.

[212] A/HRC/36/35.

[213] A/HRC/36/23; A/72/201.

[214] One delegation did not cast a vote.

[215] A/HRC/35/26.

On 22 June 2017, the Council adopted, without a vote, resolution 35/19 entitled "Extreme poverty and human rights". On 23 June 2017, the Council adopted, without a vote, resolution 35/28 entitled "The Social Forum".[216]

b. General Assembly

The Special Rapporteur on extreme poverty and human rights, Mr. Philip Alston, submitted a report to the General Assembly pursuant to Human Rights Council resolution 35/19.[217] The report analysed the civil and political rights of people living in poverty within the frameworks of human rights and development.

The Secretary-General submitted a report, entitled "Implementation of the Second United Nations Decade for the Eradication of Poverty (2008–2017)", pursuant to General Assembly resolution 71/241.[218] The report discussed progress in and challenges to poverty eradication, evaluated the implementation of the Decade, and concluded with recommendations to maintain the momentum generated by the implementation of the Decade in the context of the 2030 Agenda for Sustainable Development.

On 20 December 2017, on the recommendation of the Second Committee, the General Assembly adopted, without a vote, resolution 72/233 entitled "Implementation of the Second United Nations Decade for the Eradication of Poverty (2008–2017)".

(*d*) Right of peoples to self-determination

(i) *Universal realization of the right of peoples to self-determination*

a. Human Rights Council

On 24 March 2017, the Human Rights Council adopted resolution 34/29 entitled "Right of the Palestinian people to self-determination", by a recorded vote of 43 to 2, with 2 abstentions.

b. General Assembly

In accordance with General Assembly resolution 71/183, the Secretary-General submitted a report on the right of peoples to self-determination.[219]

On 19 December 2017, on the recommendation of the Third Committee, the General Assembly adopted resolution 72/159 entitled "Universal realization of the right of peoples to self-determination", without a vote, and resolution 72/160 entitled "The right of the Palestinian people to self-determination", by a recorded vote of 176 to 7, with 4 abstentions.

---

[216] For the report of the Co-Chair-Rapporteurs of the 2017 Social Forum, see A/HRC/37/74. See also Human Rights Council resolution 32/27 of 1 July 2016.

[217] A/72/502.

[218] A/72/283.

[219] A/72/317.

(ii) *Mercenaries*

a. Human Rights Council

The Working Group on the use of mercenaries as a means of violating human rights and impeding the exercise of the right of peoples to self-determination submitted its report to the Human Rights Council, presenting an overview of the findings of a global study conducted from 2013 to 2016 on national legislation on private military and security companies.[220]

On 28 September 2017, the Council adopted resolution 36/3 entitled "The use of mercenaries as a means of violating human rights and impeding the exercise of the right of peoples to self-determination", by a recorded vote of 32 to 15, with no abstentions.

b. General Assembly

In accordance with Commission on Human Rights resolution 2005/2 and Human Rights Council resolution 33/4, the Secretary-General transmitted the report of the Working Group on the use of mercenaries as a means of violating human rights and impeding the exercise of the right of peoples to self-determination to the General Assembly.[221]

On 19 December 2017, on the recommendation of the Third Committee, the General Assembly adopted resolution 72/158 entitled "Use of mercenaries as a means of violating human rights and impeding the exercise of the right of peoples to self-determination", by a recorded vote of 128 to 51, with 6 abstentions.

(*e*) Economic, social and cultural rights

Human Rights Council

On 23 March 2017, the Human Rights Council adopted resolution 34/4 entitled "Question of the realization in all countries of economic, social and cultural rights", without a vote.

(i) *Right to food*

a. Human Rights Council

The Special Rapporteur on the right to food, Hilal Elver, submitted a report to the Human Rights Council concerning the effects of pesticides on the right to food.[222]

On 23 March 2017, the Human Rights Council adopted, as orally revised, resolution 34/12 entitled "The right to food", by a vote of 30 to 1, with 16 abstentions.

b. General Assembly

The Secretary-General transmitted to the General Assembly the interim report of the Special Rapporteur on the right to food, submitted pursuant to General Assembly Resolution 70/154.[223] The report focused on the right to food in conflict situations.

---

[220] A/HRC/36/47.

[221] A/72/286.

[222] A/HRC/34/48.

[223] A/72/188.

On 19 December 2017, upon recommendation of the Third Committee, the General Assembly adopted resolution 72/173 entitled "The right to food" without a vote. On 20 December, upon recommendation of the Second Committee, the General Assembly adopted resolution 72/238 entitled "Agriculture development, food security and nutrition", with 185 votes in favour, to one against and no abstentions.

(ii) *Right to education*

a. Human Rights Council

The Special Rapporteur on the right to education, Ms. Koumba Boly Barry, submitted her annual report to the Human Rights Council pursuant to its resolutions 8/4 and 26/17.[224] The report addressed issues and challenges to the right to education through non-formal education.

On 22 June 2017, the Human Rights Council adopted resolution 35/2 entitled "The right to education: follow-up to Human Rights Council resolution 8/4", without a vote. On the same day, the Human Rights Council also adopted resolution 35/22 entitled "Realizing the equal enjoyment of the right to education by every girl", without a vote.

b. General Assembly

The Secretary-General transmitted to the General Assembly the report of the Special Rapporteur on the right to education,[225] which focused on the role of equity and inclusion in the right to education.

(iii) *Right to adequate standard of living, including adequate housing*

a. Human Rights Council

The Special Rapporteur on adequate housing as a component of the right to an adequate standard of living, and on the right to non-discrimination in this context, Ms. Leilani Farha, submitted her report to the Human Rights Council.[226] The Special Rapporteur focused on the "financialization of housing" and its impact on human rights.

On 23 March 2017, the Human Rights Council adopted resolution 34/9 entitled "Adequate housing as a component of the right to an adequate standard of living, and the right to non-discrimination in this context", without a vote.

b. General Assembly

The Secretary-General transmitted to the General Assembly the report of the Special Rapporteur on adequate housing as a component of the right to an adequate standard of living, and on the right to non-discrimination in this context,[227] which focused on the right to housing of persons with disabilities.

---

[224] A/HRC/35/24.

[225] A/72/496.

[226] A/HRC/34/51.

[227] A/72/128.

(iv) *Access to safe drinking water and sanitation*

a. Human Rights Council

In accordance with Human Rights Council resolution 27/7 and 33/10 of 2016, the Special Rapporteur on the human right to safe drinking water and sanitation, Mr. Léo Heller, submitted his report to the Human Rights Council.[228] The report focused on the regulation of water and sanitation services in the context of the realization of human rights and discussed the role that regulatory frameworks can play in the implementation of these human rights at the national level.

b. General Assembly

The Secretary-General transmitted to the General Assembly the report of the Special Rapporteur on the human right to safe drinking water and sanitation, Mr. Léo Heller, submitted pursuant to General Assembly Resolution 64/292 and Human Rights Council resolution 18/1.[229] The report complemented the Special Rapporteur's first report on the realization of the human rights to water and sanitation in development cooperation.

(v) *Right to health*

a. Human Rights Council

The Special Rapporteur on the right of everyone to the enjoyment of the highest attainable standard of physical and mental health, Mr. Dainius Puras, submitted a report to the Human Rights Council.[230] In his report, the Special Rapporteur focused on the right to mental health and some of the challenges and opportunities, where he called for a shit in the paradigm, based on the recurrence of human rights obligations in mental health settings, often affecting persons with intellectual, cognitive and psychosocial disabilities.

On 23 June 2017, the Human Rights Council adopted, without a vote, resolution 35/23 entitled "The right of everyone to the enjoyment of the highest attainable standard of physical and mental health in the implementation of the 2030 Agenda for Sustainable Development". On 28 September 2017, the Human Rights Council adopted, without a vote, resolution 36/13 entitled "Mental health and human rights".

b. General Assembly

The Secretary-General transmitted to the General Assembly the report of the Special Rapporteur on the right of everyone to the enjoyment of the highest attainable standard of physical and mental health.[231] In the report, the Special Rapporteur referred to the effect of corruption on good governance, the rule of law, development and the equitable enjoyment of all human rights, including the right to health. The report focused on forms of

---

[228] A/HRC/36/45.

[229] A/72/127.

[230] A/HRC/35/21.

[231] A/72/137.

corruption and practices which undermine principles of medical ethics and social justice, as well as transparent health-care provision.

(vi) *Cultural rights*

a. Human Rights Council

The Special Rapporteur in the field of cultural rights, Ms. Karima Bennoune, submitted her report to the Human Rights Council.[232] The report addressed the phenomena of fundamentalism and extremism and their grave impact on the enjoyment of cultural rights. She stresses that these are human rights issues requiring a human rights-based response, which she outlines. In the report, the Special Rapporteur argued that cultural rights can play a key role in combating fundamentalism and extremism. The Special Rapporteur also submitted to the Human Rights Council a report on her mission to Cyprus carried out from 24 May to 2 June 2016.[233]

On 23 March 2017, the Human Rights Council adopted resolution 31/12, entitled "Promotion of the enjoyment of the cultural rights of everyone and respect for cultural diversity", without a vote.

b. General Assembly

The Secretary-General transmitted to the General Assembly the report of the Special Rapporteur in the field of cultural rights.[234] The report built on previous reports concerning diverse forms of fundamentalism and extremism as threats to cultural rights and their impact on the cultural rights of women.

(*f*) Civil and political rights

(i) *Torture*

a. Human Rights Council

The Special Rapporteur on torture and other cruel, inhuman or degrading treatment or punishment, Mr. Nils Melzer, submitted his report to the Human Rights Council.[235] In the report, the Special Rapporteur provided an overview of the activities of the mandate during the reporting cycle, including country visits carried out by the previous Special Rapporteur, Mr. Juan Méndez. The new Special Rapporteur outlined his thematic priorities and vision for his mandate.

On 24 March 2017, the Human Rights Council adopted, without a vote, resolution 34/19 entitled "Torture and other cruel, inhuman or degrading treatment or punishment: mandate of the Special Rapporteur".

---

[232] A/HRC/34/56.

[233] A/HRC/34/56/Add.1.

[234] A/72/155.

[235] A/HRC/34/54.

b. General Assembly

The Secretary-General transmitted to the General Assembly the Report of the Special Rapporteur on torture and other cruel, inhuman or degrading treatment or punishment.[236] The report addressed the circumstances in which the extra-custodial use of force by State agents could amount to torture, or other cruel, inhuman or degrading treatment or punishment and how the prohibition of such treatment applies to the development, acquisition, trade and use of weapons in law enforcement.

On 19 December 2017, upon recommendation of the Third Committee, the General Assembly adopted resolution 72/163 entitled "Torture and other cruel, inhuman or degrading treatment or punishment", without a vote.

(ii) *Arbitrary detention, persons deprived of liberty, and extrajudicial, summary and arbitrary execution*

a. Human Rights Council

The Special Rapporteur on extrajudicial, summary or arbitrary executions, Ms. Agnes Callamard submitted her report to the Human Rights Council, pursuant to Human Rights Council resolution 26/12.[237] The report considered key elements of a gender-sensitive perspective to the mandate and showed that violations of the right to life may also stem from the deprivation of basic conditions that guarantee life, such as access to essential health case.

On 22 June 2017, the Human Rights Council adopted resolution 35/15 entitled "Mandate of the Special Rapporteur on extrajudicial, summary or arbitrary executions", without a vote.

b. General Assembly

The Secretary-General transmitted to the General Assembly the report of the Special Rapporteur on extrajudicial, summary or arbitrary executions,[238] in which she focused on the mass casualties of refugees and migrants, where she addressed killings by both State and non-State actors.

(iii) *Enforced disappearances and missing persons*

a. Human Rights Council

The Working Group on Enforced or Involuntary Disappearances submitted its annual report to the Human Rights Council,[239] which provided information on the activities of, and communications and cases examined between 19 May 2016 and 17 May 2017.

On 28 September 2017, the Human Rights Council adopted resolution 36/6, without a vote.

---

[236] A/72/178.

[237] A/HRC/35/23.

[238] A/72/335.

[239] A/HRC/36/39.

b. General Assembly

Pursuant to General Assembly resolution 70/160, the Secretary-General submitted to the General Assembly a report entitled "International Convention for the Protection of All Persons from Enforced Disappearance",[240] containing information on the activities carried out in relation to the implementation of the resolution by Member States, the Secretary-General, the United Nations High Commissioner for Human Rights and her Office, the Committee on Enforced Disappearances, the Working Group on Enforced or Involuntary Disappearances and intergovernmental and non-governmental organizations.

The Committee on Enforced Disappearances also submitted the reports of its eleventh and twelfth sessions to the General Assembly.[241]

On 19 December 2017, the General Assembly adopted, upon recommendation of the Third Committee, resolution 72/183 entitled "International Convention for the Protection of All Persons from Enforced Disappearance", without a vote.

(iv) *Integration of human rights of women and a gender perspective*[242]

a. Human Rights Council

The Special Rapporteur on violence against women, its causes and consequences, Ms. Dubravka Šimonović, submitted a report to the Human Rights Council.[243] The report considered key elements of a human rights-based approach to integrated services and protection measures on violence against women, with a focus on shelters and protection orders.

The Working Group on the issue of discrimination against women in law and in practice also submitted a report to the Human Rights Council.[244] The Report contained a compendium of good practices in the elimination of discrimination against women.

The Office of the United Nations High Commissioner for Human Rights also submitted a report to the Council.[245] The report addressed developments concerning human rights bodies and mechanisms and activities carried out by the Office of the United Nations High Commissioner for Human Rights that contribute to the promotion and full application of the provisions of the United Nations Declaration on the Rights of Indigenous Peoples, and follow-up on the effectiveness of the Declaration.

On 22 June 2017, the Human Rights Council adopted, without a vote, resolution 35/10 entitled "Accelerating efforts to eliminate violence against women: engaging men and boys in preventing and responding to violence against all women and girls" and resolution 35/18 entitled "Elimination of discrimination against women and girls".

---

[240] A/72/280.

[241] A/72/56.

[242] For more information on the rights of women, see section 6 of this chapter.

[243] A/HRC/35/30.

[244] A/HRC/35/29.

[245] A/HRC/36/22.

b. General Assembly

The Secretary General submitted to the General Assembly the report of the Special Rapporteur on violence against women its causes and consequences.[246] The report discussed the adequacy of the international legal framework on violence against women, and the Special Rapporteur reported on the answers received from women's rights regional mechanisms and the Committee on the Elimination of Discrimination against Women and presented responses received from civil society following her call for input on the issue.

On 19 December 2017, the General Assembly adopted, upon recommendation of the Third Committee, resolution 72/147 entitled "Follow-up to the Fourth World Conference on Women and full implementation of the Beijing Declaration and Platform for Action and the outcome of the twenty-third special session of the General Assembly", without a vote. On the same day the General Assembly also adopted, upon recommendation of the Third Committee, resolution 72/148 entitled "Improvement of situation of women and girls in rural areas" and resolution 72/149 entitled "Violence against women migrant workers", without a vote.

On 20 December 2017, the General Assembly adopted, upon recommendation of the Second Committee resolution 72/233 entitled "Women in development", without a vote.

(v) *Trafficking*

a. Human Rights Council

The Special Rapporteur on trafficking in persons, especially women and children, Ms. Maria Grazia Giammarinaro, submitted her annual report to the Human Rights Council.[247] In the report, the Special Rapporteur focused on the efforts of multi-stakeholder initiatives and industry coalitions to address, through voluntary standards, trafficking in supply chains. The Special Rapporteur analysed challenges in adopting voluntary standards and assurance processes that facilitate the detection of trafficking in persons.

On 22 June 2017, the Human Rights Council adopted resolution 35/5 entitled "Mandate of the Special Rapporteur on trafficking in persons, especially women and children" without a vote.

b. General Assembly

The Secretary-General transmitted to the General-Assembly the joint report of the Special Rapporteur on the sale and sexual exploitation of children, including child prostitution, child pornography and other child sexual abuse material, Maud de Boer-Buquicchio, and the Special Rapporteur on trafficking in persons, especially women and children, Maria Grazia Giammarinaro.[248] The report provided a study of the vulnerabilities of children to sale, trafficking, and other forms of exploitation in situations of conflict and humanitarian crisis, and contained recommendations aimed at reducing such vulnerabilities and enhancing the protection of children.

On 27 September 2017, the General Assembly adopted resolution 72/1 entitled "Political declaration on the implementation of the United Nations Global Plan of Action

---

[246] A/72/134.

[247] A/HRC/35/37.

[248] A/72/164.

to Combat Trafficking in Persons", without a vote. On 19 December 2017, upon recommendation of the Third Committee, the General Assembly adopted resolution 72/195 entitled "Improving the coordination of efforts against trafficking in persons" without a vote.

(vi) *Freedom of religion or belief, expression and assembly*

a. Human Rights Council

The Special Rapporteur on freedom of religion or belief, Mr. Ahmed Shaheed, presented his first report identifying challenges and presenting an outline of methods of work and priorities as guiding framework for his mandate.[249]

The Special Rapporteur on the promotion and protection of the right to freedom of opinion and expression, Mr. David Kaye, submitted his annual report to the Council.[250] The report focused on the role played by private actors engaged in the provision of internet and telecommunications access.

The Special Rapporteur on the rights to freedom of peaceful assembly and of association, Ms. Annalisa Ciampi, presented the final thematic report of former Special Rapporteur Maina Kiai, who finalized her mandate on 30 April 2017.[251] The Report focused on the ways in which associational groupings improved societies and, in turn, advanced global peace, human development and respect for human rights. The report underscored the imperative of an enabling civic environment and the exercise of the rights to freedom of peaceful assembly and of association in achieving these aspirations.

On 23 March 2017, the Human Rights Council adopted resolution 34/10, entitled "Freedom of religion or belief" without a vote. On 24 March 2017, the Human Rights Council adopted resolution 34/18 entitled "Freedom of opinion and expression: mandate of the Special Rapporteur on the promotion and protection of the right to freedom of opinion and expression", without a vote.

On 24 March 2017, the Human Rights Council adopted resolution 34/32 entitled "Combating intolerance, negative stereotyping and stigmatization of, and discrimination, incitement to violence and violence against, persons based on religion or belief", without a vote.

b. General Assembly

The Secretary-General transmitted to the General Assembly the interim report of the Special Rapporteur on freedom of religion or belief, in accordance with General Assembly resolution 71/196.[252] In his report, the Special Rapporteur referred to the increase in religious intolerance and the gap between international commitments to combat intolerant acts and national practices.

---

[249] A/HRC/34/50.

[250] A/HRC/35/22.

[251] A/HRC/35/28.

[252] A/72/365.

The Secretary-General submitted to the General Assembly a report on steps taken by States to combat intolerance, negative stereotyping, stigmatization, discrimination, incitement to violence and violence against persons, based on religion or belief.[253]

The Secretary-General transmitted to the General Assembly the report of the Special Rapporteur on the promotion and protection of the right to freedom of opinion and expression.[254] The report provided an assessment of the state of access to information with regard to the activities of international organizations. The Secretary-General transmitted to the General Assembly the report of the Special Rapporteur on the rights to freedom of peaceful assembly and of association.[255] The report outlined the vision of the mandate of the new Special Rapporteur, Ms. Annalisa Ciampi, building on the work of the previous Special Rapporteur.

On 19 December 2017, upon recommendation of the Third Committee, the General Assembly adopted resolution 72/176 entitled "Combating intolerance, negative stereotyping, stigmatization, discrimination, incitement to violence and violence against persons, based on religion or belief" and resolution 72/177 entitled "Freedom of religion or belief", without a vote.

(vii) *Right to life*

Human Rights Council

The High Commissioner for Human Rights submitted a report of the high-level panel discussion on the question of death penalty, held on 1 March 2017.[256]

On 29 September 2017, the Human Rights Council adopted resolution 36/17 entitled "The question of the death penalty" by a recorded vote of 27 to 13 with 7 abstentions.

(viii) *Right to privacy*

a. Human Rights Council

The Special Rapporteur on the right to privacy, Mr. Joseph A. Cannataci, submitted a report to the Human Rights Council,[257] which focused governmental surveillance activities from a national and international perspective.

On 23 March 2017, the Human Rights Council adopted resolution 34/7 entitled "The right to privacy in the digital age", without a vote.

b. General Assembly

The Secretary-General transmitted to the General Assembly the report of the Special Rapporteur on the right to privacy.[258] The report provided a summary of activities

[253] A/72/381.

[254] A/72/350.

[255] A/72/135.

[256] A/HRC/36/27.

[257] A/HRC/34/60.

[258] A/72/540.

undertaken during 2016 and 2017 and an interim report of the Thematic Action Streams TASK Force on Big Data and Open Data established by the Special Rapporteur.

(ix) *Right to truth*

a. Human Rights Council

The Special Rapporteur on the promotion of truth, justice, reparation and guarantees of non-recurrence, Mr. Pablo de Greiff, submitted two reports to the Human Rights Council. The first report focused on the participation of victims in transitional justice measures.[259] The second report focused on transitional justice in weakly institutionalized post-conflict settings.[260]

On 28 September 2017, the Human Rights Council adopted resolution 36/7 entitled "Special Rapporteur on the promotion of truth, justice, reparation and guarantees of non-recurrence", without a vote.

b. General Assembly

The Secretary-General transmitted to the General Assembly the report of the Special Rapporteur on the promotion of truth, justice, reparation and guarantees of non-recurrence.[261] The report proposed the development of a substantive, comprehensive framework approach to prevention.

(*g*) Rights of the child

a. Human Rights Council

The Special Representative of the Secretary-General for Children and Armed Conflict, Ms. Leila Zerrougui, submitted her annual report to the Human Right Council.[262] In the report, the Special Representative referred to the activities undertaken in discharging her mandate and the progress achieved in addressing grave violations against children, and explored the challenges in strengthening the protection of children affected by armed conflict and set out recommendations to States.

The Special Representative of the Secretary-General on Violence against Children, Ms. Marta Santos Pais, submitted her annual report to the Human Rights Council.[263] The report provided an overview of initiatives and developments to safeguard the right of children to be free from violence. The report also referred to the implementation of the 2030 Agenda for Sustainable Development and its target to end all forms of violence against children.

The Special Rapporteur on the sale of children, child prostitution and child pornography, Ms. Maud de Boer-Buquicchio provided an overview of her activities since

---

[259] A/HRC/34/62.

[260] A/HRC/36/50.

[261] A/72/523.

[262] A/HRC/34/44.

[263] A/HRC/34/45.

March 2016 and included a thematic study on illegal adoptions and recommendations to address such phenomenon.[264]

The Human Rights Council Advisory Committee submitted its final report entitled "Global issue of unaccompanied migrant children and adolescents and human rights."[265]

The United Nations High Commissioner for Human Rights submitted three reports to the Council. The first report contained information on the expert workshop on the impact of existing strategies and initiatives to address child, early and forced marriage.[266] The second report contained an analytical study on the relationship between climate change and the full enjoyment of the rights of the child,[267] and the third report contained a summary report on a panel discussion on the adverse impact of climate change on States' efforts to realize the rights of the child and related policies, lessons learned and good practices.[268]

On 24 March 2017, the Human Rights Council adopted resolution 34/16 entitled "Rights of the child: protection of the rights of the child in the implementation of the 2030 Agenda for Sustainable Development", without a vote. On 22 June 2017, the Human Rights Council adopted without a vote resolution 35/5 entitled "Mandate of the Special Rapporteur on trafficking in persons, especially women and children", and resolution 35/16 entitled "Child, early and forced marriage in humanitarian settings". On 28 September 2017, the Human Rights Council adopted resolution 36/5 entitled "Unaccompanied migrant children and adolescents and human rights", without a vote.

b. General Assembly

The Secretary-General submitted a report on the rights of the child, containing information on the status of the Convention on the Rights of the Child, with a focus on violence against children.[269]

The Secretary-General transmitted to the General Assembly the joint report of the Special Rapporteur on the sale of children, child prostitution and child pornography and the Special Rapporteur on trafficking in persons, especially women and children.[270] The report described the activities undertaken under both mandates and studied the vulnerabilities of children to sale, trafficking and other forms of exploitation in situations of conflict and humanitarian crisis.

On 19 December 2017, the General Assembly adopted, upon recommendation of the Third Committee, resolution 72/154 entitled "the girl child", without a vote. On 24 December 2017, the General Assembly, upon recommendation of the Third Committee, adopted resolution 72/245 entitled "rights of the child", without a vote.

---

[264] A/HRC/34/55.

[265] A/HRC/36/51.

[266] A/HRC/35/5.

[267] A/HRC/35/13.

[268] A/HRC/35/14.

[269] A/72/356.

[270] A/72/164.

c. Security Council

On 17 March 2017, the Security Council adopted resolution 2344 (2017), in which it addressed the impact of the situation in Afghanistan on both women and children.

On 31 March 2017, the Security Council adopted resolution 2348 (2017) in which it addressed the impact of the conflict in the Democratic Republic of the Congo on children, and resolution 2349 (2017) in which it addressed peace and security in Africa and the effect on the women and children.

(*h*) Migrants

a. Human Rights Council

The Special Rapporteur on the human rights of migrants, Mr. François Crépeau, submitted his report to the Human Rights Council, in accordance with Human Rights Council resolution 26/19. [271] In the report, the Special Rapporteur proposed the development of an agenda within the framework of the United Nations, in parallel to the 2030 Agenda for Sustainable Development, to be known as the 2035 agenda for facilitating human mobility.

On 24 March 2017, the Human Rights Council adopted as orally revised without a vote, resolution 34/21 entitled "Human rights of migrants: mandate of the Special Rapporteur on the human rights of migrants", without a vote. On 22 June 2017, the Human Rights Council adopted resolution 35/17 entitled "Protection of the human rights of migrants: the global compact for safe, orderly and regular migration", without a vote. On 28 September 2017, the Human Rights Council adopted as orally revised resolution 36/5 entitled "Unaccompanied migrant children and adolescents and human rights", without a vote.

b. General Assembly

The Secretary-General transmitted to the General Assembly the report of the Special Rapporteur on human rights of migrants,[272] which the Special Rapporteur proposed the development of an agenda within the framework of the United Nations, to be known as the 2035 agenda for facilitating human mobility.

On 19 December 2017, upon recommendation of the Third Committee, the General Assembly adopted resolution 72/149 entitled "violence against women migrant workers" and resolution 72/179 entitled "Protection of migrants", without a vote.

(*i*) Internally displaced persons

a. Human Rights Council

The Special Rapporteur on the human rights of internally displaced persons, Ms. Cecilia Jimenez-Damary, submitted his annual report to the Human Rights Council.[273] The report provided an overview of the activities undertaken by the previous Special

---

[271] A/HRC/35/25.

[272] A/72/173.

[273] A/HRC/35/27.

Rapporteur, Mr. Chaloka Beyani and the outline of the strategic priorities and working practices of the new Special Rapporteur.

b. General Assembly

The Secretary-General transmitted to the General Assembly the report of the Special Rapporteur on the human rights of internally displaced persons.[274] The report provided a summary of the thematic priorities of the work of the Special Rapporteur. In particular, the Special Rapporteur considered how national authorities and their national and international humanitarian, development and human rights partners can enhance the participation of internally displaced persons in decisions affecting them in all phases of internal displacement.

On 7 December 2017, the General Assembly adopted, upon recommendation of the Fourth Committee, resolution 72/81 entitled "Persons displaced as a result of the June 1967 and subsequent hostilities", without a vote. On 19 December 2017, the General Assembly adopted, upon recommendation of the Third Committee, resolutions 72/152 entitled "Assistance to refugees, returnees and displaced persons in Africa", and 72/182 entitled "Protection of and assistance to internally displaced persons", without a vote.

(*j*) Minorities

a. Human Rights Council

The Special Rapporteur on minority issues, Ms. Rita Izsák, submitted her report to the Human Rights Council,[275] which provided an overview of some major challenges and emerging issues relating to the rights of persons belonging to national or ethnic, religious and linguistic minorities and reflected on the work of the Forum on Minority Issues during her mandate.

On 23 March 2017, the Human rights Council adopted resolution 34/6 entitled "Mandate of the Special Rapporteur on minority issues", without a vote.

b. General Assembly

The Secretary-General transmitted to the General Assembly the report of the Special Rapporteur on minority issues.[276] The report provided an overview of the main activities carried out by the Special Rapporteur during her mandate of six years, including a summary of thematic reports, communications, country visits, the Forum on Minority Issues and other relevant issues.

On 19 December 2017, upon recommendation of the Third Committee, the General Assembly adopted resolution 72/184 entitled "Effective promotion of the Declaration on the Rights of Persons Belonging to National or Ethnic, Religious and Linguistic Minorities", without a vote.

---

[274] A/72/202.

[275] A/HRC/34/53.

[276] A/72/165.

(*k*) Indigenous issues

a. Human Rights Council

The Special Rapporteur on the rights of indigenous peoples, Ms. Victoria Tauli Corpuz, submitted her report to the Human Rights Council.[277] In the report, the Special Rapporteur provided a thematic study on the impacts of climate change and climate finance on the rights of indigenous peoples.

The United Nations High Commissioner for Human Rights also submitted a report to the Council on the rights of indigenous peoples.[278]

The Expert Mechanism on the Rights of Indigenous Peoples submitted its annual report covering its activities during the tenth session in Geneva from 10 to 14 July 2017.[279]

The Expert Mechanism also submitted a report to the Human Rights Council entitled "Good practices and challenges, including discrimination, in business and in access to financial services by indigenous peoples, in particular indigenous women and indigenous persons with disabilities",[280] and a study concerning such good practices.[281]

On 28 September 2017, the Human Rights Council adopted, without a vote, resolution 36/14 entitled "Human rights and indigenous peoples".

b. General Assembly

The Secretary-General transmitted to the General Assembly the report of the Special Rapporteur on the rights of indigenous peoples.[282] In the report, the Special Rapporteur provided an assessment of the Assessment of the implementation of the United Nations Declaration on the Rights of Indigenous Peoples on the occasion of its tenth anniversary.

On 19 December 2017, the General Assembly adopted resolution 72/155 entitled "Rights of indigenous peoples", on the recommendation of the Third Committee and without a vote.

(*l*) Terrorism and human rights

a. Human Rights Council

The Special Rapporteur on the promotion and protection of human rights and fundamental freedoms while countering terrorism, Mr. Ben Emmerson, submitted his sixth and final report to the Human Rights Council.[283] In the report, the Special Rapporteur assessed the developments that have taken place in connection with the principal issues addressed in each of his previous thematic reports, and made recommendations for reform of the United Nations institutional architecture for addressing issues related to human rights and counter-terrorism.

---

[277] A/HRC/36/46.

[278] A/HRC/36/22.

[279] A/HRC/36/57.

[280] A/HRC/36/56.

[281] A/HRC/36/53.

[282] A/72/186.

[283] A/HRC/34/61.

The United Nations High Commissioner for Human Rights also a report to the Human Rights Council concerning the negative effects of terrorism on the enjoyment of all human rights and fundamental freedoms.[284]

On 23 March 2017, the Human Rights Council also adopted resolution 34/8 entitled "Effects of terrorism on the enjoyment of all human rights", by a recorded vote of 28 to 25 with 4 abstentions. On 23 June 2017, the Human Rights Council adopted resolution 35/34 entitled "Protection of human rights and fundamental freedoms while encountering terrorism", without a vote.[285]

b. General Assembly

The Secretary-General submitted a report to the Assembly entitled "Promotion and protection of human rights and fundamental freedoms while countering terrorism".[286]

The Secretary General transmitted the report of the newly appointed Special Rapporteur on the promotion and protection of human rights and fundamental freedoms while countering terrorism, Ms. Fionnuala Ní Aoláin.[287] In the report, the new Special Rapporteur identified four substantive areas of interest falling within the mandate: the proliferation of permanent states of emergency and the normalization of exceptional national security powers within ordinary legal systems; the need for greater clarity in respect of the legal relationships between national security regimes and international legal regimes (human rights, international humanitarian law and international criminal law) as well as the relationship of human rights to the emergence of stand-alone international security regimes regulating terrorism and counter-terrorism; the advancement of greater normative attention focused on the gendered dimensions of terrorism and counter-terrorism; and the advancement of the rights and the protection of civil society in the fight against terrorism.

On 4 December 2017, upon the recommendation of the First Committee and without a vote, the General Assembly adopted resolution 72/42 entitled "Measures to prevent terrorists from acquiring weapons of mass destruction". On 7 December 2017, upon recommendation of the Sixth Committee, the General Assembly adopted resolution 72/123 entitled "Measures to eliminate international terrorism" without a vote.

c. Security Council

On 13 February 2017, the Security Council adopted resolution 2341 (2017) which, *inter alia*, encouraged all States to make concerted and coordinated efforts, including through international cooperation, to raise awareness, to expand knowledge and understanding of the challenges posed by terrorist attacks, to improve preparedness for such attacks against critical infrastructure, and called upon Member States to consider developing or further improving their strategies for reducing risks to critical infrastructure from terrorist attacks, which should include, *inter alia*, assessing and raising awareness of the relevant risks, taking preparedness measures, including effective responses to such attacks,

[284] A/HRC/34/30.

[285] A/HRC/RES/35/34.

[286] A/72/316.

[287] A/72/495.

as well as promoting better interoperability in security and consequence management, and facilitating effective interaction of all stakeholders involved.

On 20 July 2017, the Security Council adopted resolution 2368 (2017) which reaffirmed that those responsible for committing, organizing or supporting terrorist acts must be held accountable. On 2 August 2017, the Security Council adopted resolution 2370 (2017) on the threats to international peace and security caused by terrorist acts, which urged Member States to act cooperatively to prevent terrorists from acquiring weapons, while respecting human rights and fundamental freedoms and stressed the importance of cooperation with civil society and the private sector.

On 21 December 2017, the Security Council adopted resolution 2396 (2017) which, *inter alia*, encouraged Member States to collaborate in the pursuit of developing and implementing effective counter-narrative strategies as part of the efforts against terrorism.

(*m*) Persons with disabilities

a. Human Rights Council

The Special Rapporteur on the rights of persons with disabilities, Ms. Catalina Devandas-Aguilar submitted her annual report to the Human Rights Council focusing on the access to rights-based support for persons with disabilities.[288]

On 22 June 2017, the Human Rights Council adopted as orally revised resolution 35/6 entitled "Special Rapporteur on the Rights of persons with disabilities", without a vote.

b. General Assembly

The Secretary-General transmitted the report of the Special Rapporteur on the rights of persons with disabilities, which examined the challenges experienced by girls and young women with disabilities in relation to their sexual and reproductive health and rights.[289]

On 19 December 2017, upon the recommendation of the Third Committee, the General Assembly adopted resolution 71/165 entitled "Implementation of the Convention on the Rights of Persons with Disabilities and the Optional Protocol thereto: situation of women and girls with disabilities" with 187 votes in favour and no abstentions.

(*n*) Contemporary forms of slavery

a. Human Rights Council

The Special Rapporteur on contemporary forms of slavery, including its causes and consequences, Ms. Urmila Bhoola, presented her report to the Human Rights Council, which focused on the right of access to justice and legal remedies for slavery, institutions and practices similar to slavery, servitude and forced labour.[290]

---

[288] A/HRC/34/58.

[289] A/72/133.

[290] A/HRC/36/43.

b. General Assembly

The Secretary General transmitted the report of the Special Rapporteur on contemporary forms of slavery, including its causes and consequences,[291] which discussed how the continued prevalence of contemporary forms of slavery can be seen as a symptom of the weaknesses in the efforts to achieve sustainable development and analysed the Sustainable Development Goals and discusses how the formulation of the 2030 Agenda for Sustainable Development and the inclusion of a specific target on slavery present a historic opportunity.

The Secretary-General submitted to the General Assembly a report on United Nations Voluntary Trust Fund on Contemporary Forms of Slavery,[292] which provided an overview of the work of the Trust Fund, in particular the recommendations for grants to beneficiary organizations that were adopted by the Board of Trustees of the Fund at its twenty-first session, held in Geneva from 28 November to 2 December 2016.

(*o*) Environment and human rights[293]

Human Rights Council

The Special Rapporteur on the human rights obligations related to environmentally sound management and disposal of hazardous substances and waste, Mr. Başkut Tuncak, submitted his report to the Human Rights Council.[294] In the report, the Special Rapporteur prepared guidelines for good practices in relation to the human rights obligations related to the environmentally sound management and disposal of hazardous substances and wastes.

The Special Rapporteur on the issue of human rights obligations relating to the enjoyment of a safe, clean, healthy and sustainable environment, Mr. John Knox, submitted his report to the Human Rights Council.[295] The report focused on the human rights obligations relating to the conservation and sustainable use of biological diversity, and discussed the importance of ecosystem services and biodiversity for the full enjoyment of human rights.

On 24 March 2017, the Human Rights Council adopted resolution 34/20 entitled "Human rights and the environment", without a vote. On 22 June 2017, the Human Rights Council also adopted resolution 35/20 entitled "Human rights and climate change", without a vote. On 28 September 2017, the Human Rights Council adopted resolution 36/15 entitled "Mandate of the Special Rapporteur on the implications for human rights of the environmentally sound management and disposal of hazardous substances and waste", without a vote.

---

[291] A/72/139.

[292] A/72/229.

[293] For more information on the environment, see section 8 of this chapter.

[294] AHRC/36/41.

[295] A/HRC/34/49.

(*p*) Business and human rights

a. Human Rights Council

The open-ended intergovernmental working group on transnational corporations and other business enterprises with respect to human rights presented its report of the second session which took place from 24 to 28 October 2016.[296]

The Working Group on the issue of human rights and transnational corporations and other business enterprises submitted its report to the Human Rights Council,[297] which focused on opportunities for small and medium-sized enterprises in the implementation of the Guiding Principles on Business and Human Rights.

The Secretariat transmitted the summary of discussions of the fifth session of the Forum on Business and Human Rights, held in Geneva from 14 to 16 November 2016, to the Human Rights Council.[298]

On 22 June 2017, the Human Rights Council adopted resolution 35/7 entitled "Business and human rights: mandate of the Working Group on the issue of human rights and transnational corporations and other business enterprises", without a vote.

b. General Assembly

The Secretary-General transmitted to the General Assembly the report of the Working Group on the issue of human rights and transnational corporations and other business enterprises,[299] which addressed the concept of access to effective remedies under the Guiding Principles on Business and Human Rights and clarified the interrelationship between the right to effective remedy, access to effective remedy, access to justice and corporate accountability.

(*q*) Promotion and protection of human rights

(i) *International promotion and protection*

a. Human Rights Council

The Independent Expert on human rights and international solidarity, Ms. Virginia Dandan, submitted her report to the Human Rights Council.[300] In the report, the Independent Expert proposed a draft declaration on the right to international solidarity, and an overview of the work of the mandates since its establishment in 2005.

---

[296] A/HRC/34/47.

[297] A/HRC/35/32.

[298] A/HRC/35/34, The Chair of the Forum prepared a summary of the discussions of the Forum on 2016 (A/HRC/FBHR/2016/2).

[299] A/72/162.

[300] A/HRC/35/35.

The United Nations High Commissioner for Human Rights submitted to the Council a report on the workshop on regional arrangements for the promotion and protection of human rights.[301]

The Independent Expert on the promotion of a democratic and equitable international order, Mr. Alfred de Zayas, submitted his report to the Council,[302] which focused on the impact of the financial and economic policies pursued by international organizations and other institutions, in particular the World Bank and the International Monetary Fund, on a democratic and equitable international order.

On 23 March 2017, the Human Rights Council adopted resolution 34/11 entitled "The negative impact of the non-repatriation of funds of illicit origin on the enjoyment of human rights, and the importance of improving international cooperation" by a recorded vote of 30 to 1 with 16 abstentions. On 24 March 2017, the Human Rights Council adopted, without a vote, resolution 34/17 entitled "Regional arrangements for the promotion and protection of human rights", and resolution 34/41 entitled "Human rights, democracy and the rule of law", without a vote.

On 22 June 2017, the Human Rights Council adopted resolution 35/1 entitled "Seventieth anniversary of the Universal Declaration of Human Rights and twenty-fifth anniversary of the Vienna Declaration and Programme of Action", without a vote, resolution 35/3 entitled "Human rights and international solidarity" by a recorded vote of 32 to 15 with no abstentions, and resolution 35/4 entitled "Promotion of the right to peace" by a recorded vote of 32 to 11, with 4 abstentions. On the same day, the Human Rights Council adopted resolution 35/8 entitled "Enhancement of international cooperation in the field of human rights", by a recorded vote of 32 to 3 with 12 abstentions.

On 28 September 2017, the Human Rights Council adopted resolution 36/4 entitled "Mandate of the independent expert on the promotion of a democratic and equitable international order" with a recorded vote of 32 to 15, with no abstentions. On 29 September 2017, the Human Rights Council adopted resolution 36/21 entitled "Cooperation with the United Nations, its representatives and mechanisms in the field of human rights", by a vote of 28 to none, with 19 abstentions, and resolution 36/28 entitled "Enhancement of technical cooperation and capacity-building in the field of human rights", without a vote. On the same day, the Human Rights Council also adopted resolution 36/29 entitled "Promoting international cooperation to support national human rights follow-up systems, processes and related mechanisms, and their contribution to the implementation of the 2030 Agenda for Sustainable Development", without a vote.

b. General Assembly

The Secretary-General transmitted to the General Assembly the report of the Independent Expert on human rights and international solidarity.[303] The report outlines the draft declaration on the right of international solidarity and discussed the implications of the right to international solidarity in the achievement of goal 17 of the 2030 Agenda for

---

301 A/HRC/34/23.

302 A/HRC/36/40.

303 A/72/171.

Sustainable Development, namely, to strengthen the means of implementation and revitalize the global partnership for sustainable development.

The Secretary-General also transmitted the interim report of the Independent Expert on the promotion of a democratic and equitable international order, which examined the impact of the conditionality of loans from the International Monetary Fund on development and human rights.[304]

On 7 December 2017, upon the recommendation of the Fourth Committee and without a vote, the General Assembly adopted resolution 72/77 entitled "International cooperation in the peaceful uses of outer space". On 11 December 2017, without reference to a Main Committee, the General Assembly adopted resolution 72/132 entitled "International cooperation on humanitarian assistance in the field of natural disasters, from relief to development", and resolution 72/136 entitled "Promotion of interreligious and intercultural dialogue, understanding and cooperation for peace", without a vote.

On 19 December 2017, the General Assembly, upon recommendation of the Third Committee, adopted resolutions 72/169 entitled "Enhancement of international cooperation in the field of human rights", and 72/171 entitled "Strengthening United Nations action in the field of human rights through the promotion of international cooperation and the importance of non-selectivity, impartiality and objectivity", without a vote, resolution 72/172 entitled "Promotion of a democratic and equitable international order", by a recorded vote of 129 to 54 with 5 abstentions, and resolution 72/198 entitled and resolution 72/198 entitled "International cooperation to address and counter the world drug problem", without a vote.

On 20 December 2017, upon the recommendation of the Second Committee and without a vote, the General Assembly adopted resolution 72/207 entitled "Promotion of international cooperation to combat illicit financial flows in order to foster sustainable development", and resolution 72/206 entitled "Financial inclusion for sustainable development".

(ii) *Ombudsman, mediator and other national human rights institutions*

a. Human Rights Council

The United Nations High Commissioner for Human Rights submitted a report entitled "Summary of the panel discussion on promoting international cooperation to support national human rights follow-up systems and processes", which provided information of the meeting held on 9 November 2016, during the twenty-sixth session of the Working Group on the Universal Periodic Review.

On 23 June 2017, the Human Rights Council adopted resolution 35/32 entitled "National policies and human rights", without a vote.

b. General Assembly

The Secretary-General submitted to the General Assembly a note referring to the report on national institutions for the promotion and protection of human rights,[305] which

[304] A/72/187.

[305] A/72/277.

refers to the activities undertaken by the Office of the United Nations High Commissioner for Human Rights to establish and strengthen national human rights institutions.

On 19 December 2017, upon the recommendation of the Third Committee, the General Assembly adopted resolution 72/186 entitled "The role of the Ombudsman, mediator and other national human rights institutions in the promotion and protection of human rights", without a vote.

(iii) *Right to promote and protect universally recognized human rights*

a. Human Rights Council

The Special Rapporteur on the situation of human rights defenders, Mr. Michel Forst, submitted his annual report to the Human Rights Council.[306] In his report, the Special Rapporteur focused on the activities carried out between June 2014 and March 2017.

On 23 March 2017, the Human Rights Council adopted resolution 34/5 entitled "Mandate of the Special Rapporteur on the situation of human rights defenders", without a vote.

b. General Assembly

The Secretary-General transmitted to the General Assembly a report of the Special Rapporteur on the situation of human rights defenders.[307] The report highlighted the lack of accountability for the adverse human rights impacts of business activities in human rights defenders, who are exposed to attacks from States and business-related actors.

(*r*) Miscellaneous

(*i*) *Human rights and good governance*

The Special Rapporteur on the independence of judges and lawyers, Mr. Diego García-Sayán, submitted his first annual report to the Human Rights Council, in which he presented his perspective on the mandate and an overview of the work of his predecessors.[308]

On 22 June 2017 the Human Rights Council adopted resolution 35/11 entitled "Mandate of the Special Rapporteur on the independence of judges and lawyers", without a vote, and resolution 35/12 entitled "Independence and impartiality of the judiciary, jurors and assessors, and the independence of lawyers" and resolution 35/15 entitled "Mandate of the Special Rapporteur on extrajudicial, summary or arbitrary executions", without a vote.

---

306 A/HRC/34/52.

307 A/72/170.

308 A/HRC/35/31.

(ii) *Effects of economic reform policies and foreign debt on the full enjoyment of all human rights, particularly economic, social and cultural rights*

a. Human Rights Council

The Independent Expert on the effects of foreign debt and other related international financial obligations of States on the full enjoyment of all human rights, particularly economic, social and cultural rights, Mr. Juan Pablo Bohoslavsky, submitted two reports to the Human Rights Council. The first report focused on labour rights in the context of economic reform and austerity measures.[309] The second report focused on the economic, social and cultural rights on his mission to institutions of the European Union.[310]

On 23 March 2017, the Human Rights Council adopted resolution 34/3 entitled "Mandate of the Independent Expert on the effects of foreign debt and other related international financial obligations of States on the full enjoyment of all human rights, particularly economic, social and cultural rights" by a recorded vote of 31 to 16 with no abstentions. On 23 June 2017, the Human Rights Council adopted resolution 35/25 entitled "The negative impact of corruption on the enjoyment of human rights", without a vote.

b. General Assembly

The Secretary-General transmitted a report of the Independent Expert on the effects of foreign debt and other related international financial obligations of States on the full enjoyment of all human rights, particularly economic, social and cultural rights, which studied the human rights implications of debt disputes being submitted to international investment arbitration.

On 20 December 2017, upon the recommendation of the Second Committee, the General Assembly adopted resolution 72/204 entitled "External debt sustainability and development", without a vote.

(iii) *Unilateral coercive measures*

a. Human Rights Council

The Special Rapporteur on the negative impact of unilateral coercive measures on the enjoyment of human rights, Mr. Idriss Jazairy, submitted his report to the Human Rights Council, in which he described the activities undertaken between July 2016 and June 2017 and the issues relating to remedies and redress for victims of unilateral coercive measures, on the basis of a review, assessment and evaluation of the various mechanisms available to victims.[311]

On 24 March 2017, the Human Rights Council adopted resolution 34/10 entitled "Human rights and coercive measures" by a recorded vote of 30 to 15 with 1 abstention.

b. General Assembly

The Secretary-General transmitted to the General Assembly the report of the Special Rapporteur on the negative impact of unilateral coercive measures on the enjoyment of

---

[309] A/HRC/34/57.

[310] AHRC/34/57/Add.1.

[311] A/HRC/36/44.

human rights.[312] The report, the Special Rapporteur reviewed key developments regarding unilateral sanctions applied to certain countries and addressed certain aspects of the issue of extraterritoriality in relation to unilateral sanctions.

On 19 December 2017, upon the recommendation of the Third Committee, the General Assembly adopted resolution 72/168 entitled "Human rights and unilateral coercive measures", by a recorded vote of 134 to 53, without abstentions.

(iv) *Human rights of older persons*

The Independent Expert on the enjoyment of all human rights by older persons, Ms. Rosa Kornfeld-Matte, submitted her report to the Council, which examined the impact of assistive and robotics technology, artificial intelligence and automation on the human rights of older persons.[313]

On 22 June 2017, the Human Rights Council adopted, as orally revised, resolution 35/13 entitled "Protection of the family: role of the family in supporting the protection and promotion of human rights of older persons", by a recorded vote of 30 to 12 with 5 abstentions.

(v) *Other issues*

On 23 March 2017, the Human Rights Council adopted, without a vote, resolutions 34/14 entitled "Right to work" and 34/15 entitled "birth registration and the right of everyone to recognition everywhere as a person before the law". On 22 June 2017, the Human Rights Council adopted, without a vote, resolution 35/14 entitled "Youth and human rights". On 23 June 2017, the Human Rights Council adopted resolution 35/24 entitled "Human rights in cities and other human settlements", without a vote. On 29 September 2017, the Human Rights Council adopted resolution 36/22 entitled "Promotion and protection of the human rights of peasants and other people working in rural areas", by a recorded vote of 34 to 2 with 11 abstentions.

6. Women[314]

(*a*) United Nations Entity for Gender Equality and the Empowerment of Women (UN-Women)

UN-Women was established by the General Assembly pursuant to resolution 64/289 of 2 July 2010 as a composite entity to function as a secretariat with the additional role of leading, coordinating and promoting the accountability of the United Nations system in

[312] A/72/370.

[313] A/HRC/36/48.

[314] This section covers the Security Council, the General Assembly, the Economic and Social Council, and the Commission on the Status of Women and the United Nations Entity for Gender Equality and the Empowerment of Women (UN-Women). For more detailed information and documents regarding this topic generally, see the website of UN-Women at https://www.unwomen.org/. For information regarding women and human rights, see Chapter III section A.5(*a*)(vi) and section A.5(*f*) iv).

its work on gender equality and the empowerment of women.[315] The Executive Board of UN-Women held four meeting sessions in New York in 2017,[316] during which it adopted four decisions: decision 2017/1 entitled "The elaboration of the UN-Women Strategic Plan 2018–2021"; decision 2017/2 entitled "Annual Report of the Under-Secretary-General/Executive Director on the implementation of the Strategic Plan 2014–2017"; decision 2017/3 entitled "Report on the evaluation function of the United Nations Entity for Gender Equality and the Empowerment of Women, 2016" and decision 2017/4 entitled "Report on internal audit and investigation activities for the period from 1 January to 31 December 2016".

(*b*) Commission on the Status of Women

The Commission on the Status of Women was established by the Economic and Social Council in its resolution 11 (II) 21 June 1946 as a functional commission to deal with questions relating to gender equality and the advancement of women. It is the principal global policy-making body in this field and prepares recommendations for and reports to the Economic and Social Council on the promotion of women's rights in political, economic, civil, social and educational fields.

The Commission held its sixty-first session in New York from 13 to 24 March 2017.[317] In accordance with Economic and Social Council resolution 2016/3, the priority theme of the Commission was "Women's economic empowerment in the changing world of work". It also considered as its review theme "Challenges and achievements in the implementation of the Millennium Development Goals for women and girls", evaluating progress in the implementation of the agreed conclusions of its fifty-eighth session. In addition, the Commission discussed, as a focus area, "Empowerment of indigenous women".

During its sixty-first session, the Commission adopted resolution 61/1 of 24 March 2017 entitled "Preventing and eliminating sexual harassment in the workplace".

(*c*) Economic and Social Council

On 7 June 2017, the Economic and Social Council adopted resolution 2017/9 entitled "Mainstreaming a gender perspective into all policies and programmes in the United Nations system" and resolution 2017/10 entitled "Situation of and assistance to Palestinian women".

---

[315] It consolidated the mandates and functions of the Office of the Special Adviser on Gender Issues and Advancement of Women, the Division for the Advancement of Women, the United Nations Development Fund for Women and the International Research and Training Institute for the Advancement of Women.

[316] See the reports of the Executive Board of UN-Women: Report on the election of the Bureau and on the first regular session, 16 January and 14 February 2017 (UNW/2017/1); Report on the annual session of 2017, 27 to 28 June 2017(UNW/2017/5; Report on the second regular session of 2017, 29 to 30 August 2017(UNW/2017/11) and the Report of the joint meeting of the Executive Boards of UNDP/UNFPA/UNOPS, UNICEF, UN-Women and WFP 19 June 2017.

[317] For report of the Commission on the Status of Women on its sixty-first session, see *Official Records of the Economic and Social Council, 2017, Supplement No.7* (E/2017/27-E/CN.6/2017/21).

(*d*) General Assembly

On 19 December 2017, the General Assembly adopted, on the recommendation of the Second Committee and without a vote, resolution 72/147 entitled "Follow-up to the Fourth World Conference on Women and full implementation of the Beijing Declaration and Platform for Action and the outcome of the twenty-third special session of the General Assembly"; resolution 72/148 entitled "Improvement of the situation of women and girls in rural areas"; resolution 72/149 entitled "Violence against women migrant workers" and resolution 72/154 entitled "the girl child".

On the same day, the Assembly adopted, on the recommendation of the Third Committee, resolution 72/162 entitled "Implementation of the Convention on the Rights of Persons with Disabilities and the Optional Protocol thereto: situation of women and girls with disabilities", by a recorded vote of 187 to 0, with no abstentions.

On 20 December 2017, the General Assembly adopted, on the recommendation of the Second Committee and without a vote, resolution 72/234 entitled "Women in development".

(*e*) Security Council[318]

On 15 June 2017, the President of the Security Council issued a statement in connection with the Council's consideration of the item "The situation in the Middle East",[319] in which it called upon the parties to ensure at least 30 percent representation of women in peace negotiations and called upon the United Nations to regularly report on consultations with women leaders and women's organizations in line with resolution 2122(2013). On 21 December 2017, the President of the Council adopted a statement in connection with the Council's consideration of the item "United Nations peacekeeping operations", where the Security Council reaffirmed the primary responsibility of national governments and authorities in identifying strategies for sustaining peace and emphasized that "inclusivity, including by ensuring full and effective participation of women, is key to advancing national peacebuilding processes and objectives in order to ensure that the needs of all segments of society are taken into account".[320]

7. Humanitarian matters

(*a*) Economic and Social Council

On 27 June 2017, the Economic and Social Council adopted resolution 2017/14 entitled "Strengthening of the coordination of emergency humanitarian assistance of the United Nations", without a vote.

---

[318] See also section III.A.2(*h*)(ii) on women, peace and security.

[319] S/PRST/2017/7

[320] S/PRST/2017/27

(*b*) General Assembly

On 4 December 2017, the General Assembly, upon the recommendation of the First Committee, adopted resolution 72/30 entitled "Humanitarian consequences of nuclear weapons", by a recorded vote of 141 to 15, with 27 abstentions.

On 7 December 2017, the General Assembly, upon the recommendation of the Fourth Committee, adopted resolution 72/85 entitled "Applicability of the Geneva Convention relative to the Protection of Civilian Persons in Time of War, of 12 August 1949, to the Occupied Palestinian Territory, including East Jerusalem, and the other occupied Arab territories" by a recorded vote of 157 to 7, with 10 abstentions.

On 11 December 2017, the General Assembly, without reference to a Main Committee and without a vote, adopted resolution 72/131 entitled "Safety and security of humanitarian personnel and protection of United Nations personnel"; resolution 72/132 entitled "International cooperation on humanitarian assistance in the field of natural disasters, from relief to development"; resolution 72/133 entitled "Strengthening of the coordination of emergency humanitarian assistance of the United Nations" and resolution 72/134 entitled "Assistance to Palestinian People".

On 20 December 2017, the General Assembly adopted, upon the recommendation of the Second Committee and without a vote, resolution 72/218 entitled "Disaster risk reduction".

8. Environment

(*a*) United Nations Climate Change Conference in Bonn

The United Nations Climate Change Conference was held in Bonn, Germany, from 6 to 17 November 2017. The twenty-third session of the Conference of States Parties to the United Nations Framework Convention on Climate Change (COP23), 1992,[321] the thirteenth session of the Conference of the Parties serving as the meeting of Parties to the Kyoto Protocol (CMP13), 1997,[322] and the second part of the first session of the Conference of the Parties serving as the meeting of the Parties to the Paris Agreement (CMA 1.2) were held during the Conference. At the Conference, States met to advance the aims and ambitions of the Paris Agreement and achieve progress on its implementation guidelines.[323]

The Conference of States Parties to the United Nations Framework Convention on Climate Change adopted 22 decisions and 1 resolution.[324] The Conference of the Parties serving as the meeting of Parties to the Kyoto Protocol adopted seven decisions and one resolution.[325]

---

321 United Nations, *Treaty Series,* vol. 1771, p. 107.

322 *Ibid.*, vol. 2303, p. 107.

323 For the list of decisions and resolutions, see the report of the Conference (FCCC/KP/CMP/2017/7 and Add.1 and Add.2).

324 For the report of the Conference of the Parties, see FCCC/CP/2017/11 and Add.1 and Add.2.

325 For the report of the Conference of the Parties, see FCCC/KP/CMP/2017/7/ and Add.1.

(*b*) Economic and Social Council

The High-level Political Forum on Sustainable Development (HLPF), United Nations central platform for follow-up and review of the 2030 Agenda for Sustainable Development and the Sustainable Development Goals, provides for the full and effective participation of all States Members of the United Nations and States members of specialized agencies. The meeting of the high-level political forum on sustainable development in 2017 convened under the auspices of the Economic and Social Council, was held from Monday, 10 July, to Wednesday, 19 July 2017; including the three-day ministerial meeting of the forum from Monday, 17 July, to Wednesday, 19 July 2017. The theme was "Eradicating poverty and promoting prosperity in a changing world".

In accordance with paragraph 84 of the 2030 Agenda, Member States have decided that the HLPF shall carry out regular voluntary reviews of the 2030 Agenda which will include developed and developing countries as well as relevant United Nations entities and other stakeholders. The reviews were State-led, involving ministerial and other relevant high-level participants, and provide a platform for partnerships, including through the participation of major groups and other relevant stakeholders. In 2017, 43 countries have volunteered to present their national voluntary reviews to the HLPF.[326]

On 20 April 2017, the Council adopted resolution 2017/4 entitled "United Nations strategic plan for forests 2017–2030 and quadrennial programme of work of the United Nations Forum on Forests for the period 2017–2020" without a vote. On 7 June 2017, the Council adopted resolution 2017/7 entitled "Work of the Statistical Commission pertaining to the 2030 Agenda for Sustainable Development", without a vote, and resolution 2017/8 entitled "United Nations Inter-Agency Task Force on the Prevention and Control of Non-communicable Diseases", without a vote. On 8 June 2017 the Council adopted resolution 2017/11 entitled "Social dimensions of the New Partnership for Africa's Development" (tackles the environment and other subjects), without vote, and resolution 2017/13 entitled "Work of the Committee of Experts on the Transport of Dangerous Goods and on the Globally Harmonized System of Classification and Labelling of Chemicals", without a vote. On 8 July 2017, the Economic and Social Council adopted resolution 2017/24 entitled "Human settlements", without a vote.

(*c*) General Assembly

During the seventy-first session, on 2 February 2017, the Assembly adopted resolution 71/276 entitled "Report of the open-ended intergovernmental expert working group on indicators and terminology relating to disaster risk reduction", without reference to a Main Committee and without a vote. On 27 April 2017, the Assembly adopted resolution 71/285 entitled "United Nations strategic plan for forests 2017–2030" and resolution 71/286 entitled "United Nations forest instrument", without reference to a Main Committee and without a vote. On 6 July 2017, the General Assembly adopted resolution 71/312 entitled "Our ocean, our future: call for action" and resolution 71/313 entitled

[326] The High-level Political Forum, United Nations central platform for follow-up and review of the 2030 Agenda for Sustainable Development and the Sustainable Development Goals, provides for the full and effective participation of all States Members of the United Nations and States members of specialized agencies, https://sustainabledevelopment.un.org/hlpf/2017

"Work of the Statistical Commission pertaining to the 2030 Agenda for Sustainable development", without reference to a Main Committee and without a vote. On 11 September 2017, the General Assembly adopted resolution 71/326 entitled "Tackling illicit trafficking in wildlife", without reference to a Main Committee and without a vote.

During the seventy-second session, on 4 December 2017, the Assembly adopted resolution 72/47 entitled "Observance of environmental norms in the drafting and implementation of agreements on disarmament and arms control" and resolution 72/52 entitled "Prohibition of the dumping of radioactive wastes", upon the recommendation of the First Committee and without a vote. On 7 December 2017, the General Assembly adopted resolution 72/76 entitled "Effects of atomic radiation", upon the recommendation of the Fourth Committee and without a vote. On 19 December, the Assembly adopted resolution 72/141 entitled "Implementation of the outcome of the World Summit for Social Development and of the twenty-fourth special session of the General Assembly", upon the recommendation of the Third Committee and by a recorded vote of 184 to 2, with 0 abstentions.

On 20 December 2017, the General Assembly, upon the recommendation of the Second Committee and without a vote, adopted the following resolutions: resolution 72/211 entitled "World Bee Day"; resolution 72/212 entitled "Strengthening the links between all modes of transport to achieve the Sustainable Development Goals"; resolution 72/213 entitled "International cooperation and coordination for the human and ecological rehabilitation and economic development of the Semipalatinsk region of Kazakhstan"; resolution 72/214 entitled "Sustainable tourism and sustainable development in Central America"; resolution 72/217 entitled "Follow-up to and implementation of the SIDS Accelerated Modalities of Action (SAMOA) Pathway and the Mauritius Strategy for the Further Implementation of the Programme of Action for the Sustainable Development of Small Island Developing States"; resolution 72/218 entitled "Disaster risk reduction"; resolution 72/219 entitled "Protection of global climate for present and future generations of humankind"; resolution 72/220 entitled "Implementation of the United Nations Convention to Combat Desertification in Those Countries Experiencing Serious Drought and/or Desertification, Particularly in Africa"; resolution 72/221 entitled "Implementation of the Convention on Biological Diversity and its contribution to sustainable development"; resolution 72/222 entitled "Education for sustainable development in the framework of the 2030 Agenda for Sustainable Development"; resolution 72/223 entitled "Harmony with Nature"; resolution 72/225 entitled "Combating sand and dust storms"; resolution 72/226 entitled "Implementation of the outcomes of the United Nations Conferences on Human Settlements and on Housing and Sustainable Urban Development and strengthening of the United Nations Human Settlements Programme (UN-Habitat)"; resolution 72/228 entitled "Science, technology and innovation for development"; resolution 72/231 entitled "Follow-up to the Fourth United Nations Conference on the Least Developed Countries"; resolution 72/232 entitled "Follow-up to the second United Nations Conference on Landlocked Developing Countries"; resolution 72/233 entitled "Implementation of the Second United Nations Decade for the Eradication of Poverty (2008–2017)"; resolution 72/235 entitled "Human resources development" and resolution 72/239 entitled "United Nations Decade of Family Farming (2019–2028)".

On the same day, the Assembly, upon recommendation of the Second Committee, also adopted the following resolutions: resolution 72/203 entitled "International financial system and development", by a recorded vote of 180 to 2, and no abstentions; resolution 72/209 entitled "Oil slick on Lebanese shores", by a recorded vote of 163 to 7, with 9 abstentions; resolution 72/215 entitled "Agricultural technology for sustainable development", by a recorded vote of 152 to 1, with 29 abstentions; resolution 72/216 entitled "Implementation of Agenda 21, the Programme for the Further Implementation of Agenda 21 and the outcomes of the World Summit on Sustainable Development and of the United Nations Conference on Sustainable Development", by a recorded vote of 131 to 48, with 4 abstentions; resolution 72/224 entitled "Ensuring access to affordable, reliable, sustainable and modern energy for all", by a recorded vote of 183 to 2, with 1 abstention; resolution 72/227 entitled "Role of the United Nations in promoting development in the context of globalization and interdependence", by a recorded vote of 184 to 2, and no abstentions; resolution 72/229 entitled "Culture and sustainable development", by a recorded vote of 185 to 2, and no abstentions; resolution 72/238 entitled "Agriculture development, food security and nutrition", by a recorded vote of 185 to 1, and no abstentions.

On 22 December 2017, the General Assembly adopted resolution 72/242 entitled "Impact of rapid technological change on the achievement of the Sustainable Development Goals" and resolution 72/249 entitled "International legally binding instrument under the United Nations Convention on the Law of the Sea on the conservation and sustainable use of marine biological diversity of areas beyond national jurisdiction Statement of financial implications (A/72/677)", without reference to a Main Committee and without a vote.

9. Law of the Sea

(*a*) Reports of the Secretary-General

Pursuant to paragraph 351 of General Assembly resolution 71/257 of 23 December 2016, the Secretary-General submitted a comprehensive report on oceans and the law of the sea[327] to the General Assembly at its seventy-second session under the agenda item entitled "Oceans and the law of the sea".

The first part of the report[328] was prepared to facilitate discussions on the topic of focus of the eighteenth meeting of the United Nations Open-ended Informal Consultative Process on Oceans and the Law of the Sea (Informal Consultative Process), namely "The effects of climate change on oceans". The report provided an overview of the climate change and related changes in the atmosphere: key drivers affecting oceans. It also addressed the environmental, economic and social impacts of ocean warming and acidification; as well as current action and further needs with regard to cooperation and coordination in addressing the effects of climate change and related changes in the atmosphere on oceans.

The second part of the report[329] provided information on the legal and policy framework for oceans, namely the United Nations Convention on the Law of the Sea[330] (the "Convention"), and other legal and policy instruments such as Transforming our world: the 2030 Agenda for Sustainable Development.[331] It also addressed issues in relation to

---

[327] A/72/70 and A/72/70/Add.1.

[328] A/72/70.

[329] A/72/70/Add.1.

[330] United Nations, *Treaty Series*, vol. 1833, p. 3.

[331] A/72/70/Add.1, II (B), (paras. 17, 18 and 19).

people at sea,[332] shipping and maritime security,[333] challenges and opportunities for the conservation and sustainable use of the oceans and their resources,[334] and strengthening implementation through integrated and cross-sectoral approaches.[335]

(*b*) Consideration by the General Assembly

(i) *Oceans and law of the sea*

The General Assembly considered the agenda item entitled "Oceans and the law of the sea" on 6 July 2017 and on 5 and 24 December 2017, having before it the following documents: the report of the Secretary-General,[336] the reports on the work of the *Ad Hoc* Working Group of the Whole on the Regular Process for Global Reporting and Assessment of the State of the Marine Environment, including Socioeconomic Aspects (the Regular Process),[337] and of the United Nations Open-ended Informal Consultative Process on Oceans and the Law of the Sea (the Informal Consultative Process) at its eighteenth meeting,[338] and on the twenty-seventh meeting of the Meeting of States Parties to the Convention.[339]

On 6 July 2017, the General Assembly, without reference to a Main Committee, adopted resolution 71/312 entitled "Our ocean, our future: call for action", without a vote.

On 5 December 2017, the General Assembly, without reference to a Main Committee, adopted resolution 72/73 entitled "Oceans and the law of the sea", by a recorded vote of 128 to 1, with 3 abstentions.

On 24 December 2017, the General Assembly, without reference to a Main Committee, adopted resolution 72/249 entitled "International legally binding instrument under the United Nations Convention on the Law of the Sea on the conservation and sustainable use of marine biological diversity of areas beyond national jurisdiction", without a vote.

(ii) *Sustainable fisheries*

On 5 December 2017, the General Assembly also considered the agenda item entitled "Oceans and the law of the sea: sustainable fisheries, including through the 1995 Agreement for the Implementation of the Provisions of the United Nations Convention on the Law of the Sea of 10 December 1982 relating to the Conservation and Management of Straddling Fish Stocks and Highly Migratory Fish Stocks, and related instruments".

On the same day, the General Assembly, without reference to a Main Committee, adopted resolution 72/72 entitled "Sustainable fisheries, including through the 1995 Agreement for the Implementation of the Provisions of the United Nations Convention

---

[332] *Ibid.*, Chapter III.

[333] *Ibid.*, Chapter IV.

[334] *Ibid.*, Chapter V.

[335] *Ibid.*, Chapter VI.

[336] A/72/70 and Add.1.

[337] A/72/89.

[338] A/72/95.

[339] SPLOS/316.

on the Law of the Sea of 10 December 1982 relating to the Conservation and Management of Straddling Fish Stocks and Highly Migratory Fish Stocks, and related instruments", by a recorded vote of 126 to 1, with 3 abstentions.

(iii) *Preparatory Committee established by General Assembly resolution 69/292*

The third and fourth sessions of the Preparatory Committee established by General Assembly resolution 69/292: Development of an international legally binding instrument under the United Nations Convention on the Law of the Sea on the conservation and sustainable use of marine biological diversity of areas beyond national jurisdiction took place from 27 March to 7 April 2017 and 10 to 21 July 2017, respectively, at the United Nations Headquarters in New York. These sessions considered issues relating to marine genetic resources, including questions on the sharing of benefits; measures such as area-based management tools, including marine protected areas; environmental impact assessments; and capacity-building and the transfer of marine technology. The Preparatory Committee has also dealt with a number of cross-cutting issues relating to the scope of application of the instrument, its objective, its relationship with UNCLOS and other instruments, institutional arrangements, clearing-house mechanism, financial resources and issues, compliance, settlement of disputes and responsibility and liability.

In accordance with resolution 69/292, at the end of its fourth session, the Preparatory Committee adopted its report to the General Assembly.[340]

(*c*) Consideration by the Meeting of States Parties to the United Nations Convention on the Law of the Sea

The twenty-seventh Meeting of States Parties was held at United Nations Headquarters from 12 to 16 June 2017.[341] It took note of reports presented by the International Tribunal on the Law of the Sea as well as of the information related to the activities of the International Seabed Authority and the Commission on the Limits of the Continental Shelf (CLCS). On 14 June 2017, the Meeting proceeded with the election of seven members of the Tribunal to fill the seats of those members whose terms of office expires on 30 September 2017.[342] On the same day, the Meeting proceeded with the election of 20 members of the CLCS.[343] However, owing to a lack of nominations from the Group of Eastern European States, the twenty-seventh Meeting was not in position to fill one last vacant seat at the CLCS.[344]

The Meeting also considered the report submitted by the Secretary-General under article 319 of the Convention.[345] In their deliberation under the agenda item entitled "Report of the Secretary-General under article 319 for the information of States parties on issues of a general nature, relevant to States parties, which have arisen with respect

---

[340] See A/AC.287/2017/PC.4/2.

[341] See SPLOS/316.

[342] See *ibid.*, para. 71.

[343] See *ibid.*, para. 82.

[344] See *ibid.*, paras. 83–86.

[345] See the Report of the Secretary-General (A/72/70 and A/72/70/Add.1).

to the United Nations Convention on the Law of the Sea", States parties welcomed the work of the Preparatory Committee established by the General Assembly in its resolution 69/292 entitled "Development of an international legally binding instrument under the United Nations Convention on the Law of the Sea on the conservation and sustainable use of marine biological diversity of areas beyond national jurisdiction". States parties addressed, *inter alia*, the important role of the Convention in achieving sustainable development, including in meeting Sustainable Development Goal 14 of the 2030 Agenda, the crucial role of fisheries in ensuring food security, the importance of tackling illegal, unreported and unregulated fishing, and the recent entry into force of the Port State Measures Agreement. States parties also addressed the impact of climate change on the marine environment and the need for national, regional and global, cross sectoral and integrated initiatives to address that challenge, the impact of marine pollution, including microplastics, and illegal, unreported and unregulated fishing, as well as the need for increased commitment to marine environmental protection. Moreover, the Meeting addressed the role of capacity-building in combating maritime security threats, including piracy, armed robbery and trafficking, capacity-building as an essential component of the global response to climate change and the situation in the South China Sea region.

10. Crime prevention and criminal justice[346]

(*a*) Conference of the States Parties to the United Nations Convention against Corruption

The seventh session of the Conference of the States Parties to the United Nations Convention against Corruption was held in Vienna from 6 to 10 November 2017.[347] The Conference adopted 8 resolutions and 1 decision.

(*b*) Commission on Crime Prevention and Criminal Justice (CCPJ)

The Commission on Crime Prevention and Criminal Justice was established by the Economic and Social Council in its resolution 1992/1 of 6 February 1992 as a functional commission to deal with a broad scope of policy matters in this field, including combating national and transnational crime, covering organized crime, economic crime and money laundering; promoting the role of criminal law in environmental protection, crime prevention in urban areas, including juvenile crime and violence; and improving the efficiency and fairness of criminal justice administration systems. Aspects of these principal themes are selected for discussion at each of its annual sessions. The Commission also provides substantive and organizational direction for the quinquennial United Nations Congress on Crime Prevention and Criminal Justice.

[346] For more detailed information and documents regarding this topic generally, see the website of the United Nations Office on Drugs and Crimes at https://www.unodc.org.

[347] For the report of the Conference of the States Parties to the United Nations Convention against Corruption on its seventh session, see CAC/COSP/2017/14.

The Commission held its regular and reconvened twenty-sixth session from 22 to 26 May 2017 and 7 to 8 December 2017,[348] respectively. The main theme for the twenty-sixth session of the Commission was "Comprehensive and integrated crime prevention strategies: public participation, social policies and education in support of the rule of law".

(*c*) Economic and Social Council

On 20 April 2017, the Economic and Social Council, upon recommendation of the Committee of Experts on International Cooperation on Tax Matters, adopted resolution 2017/3 entitled "United Nations code of conduct on cooperation in combating international tax evasion".

On 6 July 2017, the Economic and Social Council, upon recommendation of the Commission on Crime Prevention and Criminal Justice, adopted the following resolutions and decisions: resolution 2017/15 entitled "Follow-up to the Thirteenth United Nations Congress on Crime Prevention and Criminal Justice and preparations for the Fourteenth United Nations Congress on Crime Prevention and Criminal Justice"; resolution 2017/16 entitled "Promoting the practical application of the United Nations Standard Minimum Rules for the Treatment of Prisoners (the Nelson Mandela Rules)"; resolution 2017/17 entitled "Technical assistance for implementing the international conventions and protocols related to counter-terrorism", recommending their adoption by the General Assembly; resolution 2017/18 entitled "Implementation of the United Nations Global Plan of Action to Combat Trafficking in Persons"; resolution 2017/19 entitled "Promoting and encouraging the implementation of alternatives to imprisonment as part of comprehensive crime prevention and criminal justice policies"; decision 2017/235 entitled "Report of the Commission on Crime Prevention and Criminal Justice on its reconvened twenty-fifth session" and decision 2017/237 entitled "Report of the Commission on Crime Prevention and Criminal Justice on its twenty-sixth session and provisional agenda for its twenty-seventh session".

(*d*) General Assembly

On 4 May 2017, the General Assembly adopted resolution 71/287 entitled "Modalities, format and organization of the high-level meeting of the General Assembly on the appraisal of the United Nations Global Plan of Action to Combat Trafficking in Persons", without reference to a Main Committee and without a vote.

On 15 June 2017, the General Assembly adopted resolution 71/291 entitled "Strengthening the capability of the United Nations system to assist Member States in implementing the United Nations Global Counter-Terrorism Strategy", without reference to a Main Committee and without a vote. On 28 August 2017, the Assembly adopted resolution 71/319 entitled "Draft outcome document of the high-level meeting of the General Assembly on the appraisal of the United Nations Global Plan of Action to Combat Trafficking in Persons", without reference to a Main Committee and without a vote.

On 6 September 2017, the Assembly adopted resolution 71/322 "Strengthening and promoting effective measures and international cooperation on organ donation and

---

[348] See *Official Records of the Economic and Social Council, 2017, Supplement No. 10* and *ibid., Supplement No. 10A (E/2017/30/Add.1)*.

transplantation to prevent and combat trafficking in persons for the purpose of organ removal and trafficking in human organs", without reference to a Main Committee and without a vote. On 27 September 2017, the General Assembly adopted resolution 72/1 entitled "Political declaration on the implementation of the United Nations Global Plan of Action to Combat Trafficking in Persons", without reference to a Main Committee and without a vote.

On 19 December 2017, the General Assembly adopted, on the recommendation of the Third Committee and without a vote, five resolutions under the agenda item 107 entitled "Crime prevention and criminal justice", namely resolution 72/192 entitled "Follow-up to the Thirteenth United Nations Congress on Crime Prevention and Criminal Justice and preparations for the Fourteenth United Nations Congress on Crime Prevention and Criminal Justice"; resolution 72/193 entitled "Promoting the practical application of the United Nations Standard Minimum Rules for the Treatment of Prisoners (the Nelson Mandela Rules)"; resolution 72/194 entitled "Technical assistance for implementing the international conventions and protocols related to counter-terrorism"; resolution 72/195 entitled "Improving the coordination of efforts against trafficking in persons"; and resolution 72/196 entitled "Strengthening the United Nations crime prevention and criminal justice programme, in particular its technical cooperation capacity".

On 20 December 2017, the Assembly adopted, resolution 72/207 entitled "Promotion of international cooperation to combat illicit financial flows in order to foster sustainable development", upon the recommendation of the Second Committee and without a vote.

11. International drug control

(*a*) Commission on Narcotic Drugs

The Commission on Narcotic Drugs (CND) was established by the Economic and Social Council in its resolution 9 (I) of 16 February 1946, to assist the Council in supervising the application of the international drug control treaties. In 1991, the General Assembly expanded the mandate of the Commission to enable it to function as the governing body of the United Nations Office of Drugs and Crime. The Economic and Social Council resolution 1999/30 of 28 July 1999 requested the Commission to structure its agenda with two distinct segments: a normative segment for discharging treaty-based and normative functions; and an operational segment for exercising the role of the governing body of the United Nations Office of Drugs and Crime.

The regular and reconvened sixtieth session of the Commission was held in Vienna from 13 to 17 March 2017 and from 8 to 9 December 2017.[349] The Commission adopted one draft resolution to be recommended by the Economic and Social Council for adoption by the General. It also recommended five draft decisions for adoption by the Economic and Social Council. It further brought another nine resolutions and 13 decisions to the attention of the Economic and Social Council, the text of which is available in the report of the Commission.

---

[349] For the report of the sixtieth session of the Commission on Narcotic Drugs, see *Official records of the Economic and Social Council* 2017, Supplement No. 8, and Supplement No. 8A (E/2017/28 and E/2017/28/Add.1).

(*b*) Economic and Social Council

On 6 July 2017, the Economic and Social Council adopted resolution 2017/20 entitled "Promoting the implementation of the United Nations Guiding Principles on Alternative Development and related commitments on alternative development and regional, interregional and international cooperation on development-oriented, balanced drug control policy addressing socioeconomic issues", on the recommendation of the Commission on Narcotic Drugs.

(*c*) General Assembly

On 19 December 2017, the General Assembly adopted, on the recommendation of the Third Committee and without a vote, resolution 72/197 entitled "Promoting the implementation of the United Nations Guiding Principles on Alternative Development and related commitments on alternative development and regional, interregional and international cooperation on development-oriented, balanced drug control policy addressing socioeconomic issues" and resolution 72/198 entitled "International cooperation to address and counter the world drug problem".

12. Refugees and displaced persons

(*a*) Executive Committee of the Programme of the United Nations High Commissioner for Refugees[350]

The Executive Committee of the Programme of the United Nations High Commissioner for Refugees (UNHCR) was established by the Economic and Social Council in 1958 and functions as a subsidiary organ of the General Assembly, reporting to it through the Third Committee. The Executive Committee meets annually in Geneva to review and approve the programmes and budget of the UNHCR and its intergovernmental and non-governmental partners. The sixty-eighth plenary session of the Executive Committee was held in Geneva from 2 to 6 October 2017.[351]

(*b*) General Assembly

On 1 June 2017, the General Assembly adopted, without reference to a Main Committee, resolution 71/290 entitled "Status of internally displaced persons and refugees from Abkhazia, Georgia, and the Tskhinvali region/South Ossetia, Georgia", by a recorded vote of 80 to 14, with 61 abstentions.

---

[350] For detailed information and documents regarding this topic generally, see the website of the UNHCR at https://www.unhcr.org.

[351] For the report of the United Nations High Commissioner for Refugees on the activities of his Office, see *Official Records of the General Assembly, Seventieth-second Session, Supplement No. 12* (A/72/12). For the report of the sixty-eighth session of the Executive Committee of the High Commissioner's Programme, see *Official Records of the General Assembly, Seventieth-second Session, Supplement No. 12A* (A/72/12/Add.1).

On 7 December 2017, the Assembly adopted, on the recommendation of the Fourth Committee, resolution 72/80 entitled "Assistance to Palestine refugees", by a recorded vote of 162 to 1, with 12 abstentions; resolution 72/81 entitled "Persons displaced as a result of the June 1967 and subsequent hostilities", by a recorded vote of 158 to 7, with 10 abstentions; resolution 72/82 entitled "Operations of the United Nations Relief and Works Agency for Palestine Refugees in the Near East", by a recorded vote of 162 to 6, with 7 abstentions; and resolution 72/83, entitled "Palestine refugees' properties and their revenues", by a recorded vote of 159 to 7, with 9 abstentions.

On 19 December 2017, the General Assembly adopted, on the recommendation of the Third Committee and without a vote, resolution 72/150 entitled "Office of the United Nations High Commissioner for Refugees", resolution 72/151 entitled "Enlargement of the Executive Committee of the Programme of the United Nations High Commissioner for Refugees", and resolution 72/152 entitled "Assistance to refugees, returnees and displaced persons in Africa".

On 19 December 2017 the General Assembly adopted, on the recommendation of the Third Committee and without a vote, resolution 72/149 entitled "Violence against women migrant workers"; and resolution 72/179 entitled "Protection of migrants".

13. International Court of Justice[352]

(*a*) Organization of the Court

At the end of 2017, the composition of the Court was as follows:

President: Ronny Abraham (France);

Vice-President: Abdulqawi Ahmed Yusuf (Somalia);

Judges: Hisashi Owada (Japan), Peter Tomka (Slovakia), Mohamed Bennouna (Morocco), Antônio Augusto Cançado Trindade (Brazil), Christopher Greenwood (United Kingdom), Xue Hanqin (China), Joan E. Donoghue (United States of America), Giorgio Gaja (Italy), Julia Sebutinde (Uganda), Dalveer Bhandari (India), Patrick Lipton Robinson (Jamaica), James Richard Crawford (Australia) and Kirill Gevorgian (Russian Federation).

The Registrar of the Court was Mr. Philippe Couvreur (Belgium); the Deputy-Registrar was Mr. Jean-Pelé Fomété (Cameroon).

The Chamber of Summary Procedure, comprising five judges, including the President and Vice-President, and two substitutes, which is established annually by the Court in accordance with Article 29 of the Statute of the International Court of Justice to ensure the speedy dispatch of business, was composed as follows:

Members:

President: Ronny Abraham;

Vice-President: Abdulqawi Ahmed Yusuf;

---

[352] For more information about the Court, see the reports of the International Court of Justice to the General Assembly, *Official Records of the General Assembly, Seventieth-second Session, Supplement No. 4* (A/72/4) (for the period 1 August 2016 to 31 July 2017) and *ibid., Seventy-third Session, Supplement No. 4* (A/73/4) (for the period 1 August 2017 to 31 July 2018). See also the website of the Court at https://www.icj-cij.org.

Judges: Xue Hanqin, Joan E. Donoghue, and Giorgio Gaja.

Substitute members:

Judges: Antônio Augusto Cançado Trindade and Kirill Gevorgian.

(*b*) Jurisdiction of the Court[353]

As of 31 December 2017, 73 States had recognized the compulsory jurisdiction of the Court, as contemplated by Article 36, paragraph 2, of the Statute. On 21 August 2017, a new declaration recognizing the compulsory jurisdiction of the Court was deposited by Equatorial Guinea.

(*c*) General Assembly

On 26 October 2017, the General Assembly adopted, without reference to a Main Committee, decision 72/509 in which it took note of the report of the International Court of Justice for the period from 1 August 2016 to 31 July 2017.

22 June 2017, the General Assembly adopted, without reference to a Main Committee, resolution 71/292 entitled "Request for an advisory opinion of the International Court of Justice on the legal consequences of the separation of the Chagos Archipelago from Mauritius in 1965", by a recorded vote of 94 to 15, with 65 abstentions.

On 4 December 2017, the Assembly adopted, on the recommendation of the First Committee, resolution 72/58 entitled "Follow-up to the advisory opinion of the International Court of Justice on the legality of the threat or use of nuclear weapons", by a recorded vote of 131 to 31, with 18 abstentions.

14. International Law Commission[354]

(*a*) Membership of the Commission[355]

The membership of the International Law Commission at its sixty-ninth session consisted of Mr. Ali bin Fetais Al-Marri (Qatar), Mr. Carlos J. Argüello Gómez (Nicaragua), Mr. Bogdan Aurescu (Romania), Mr. Yacouba Cissé (Côte d'Ivoire), Ms. Concepción Escobar Hernández (Spain), Ms. Patrícia Galvão Teles (Portugal), Mr. Juan Manuel Gómez-Robledo (Mexico), Mr. Claudio Grossman Guiloff (Chile), Mr. Hussein A. Hassouna (Egypt), Mr. Mahmoud D. Hmoud (Jordan), Mr. Huikang Huang (China), Mr. Charles Chernor Jalloh

---

[353] For further information regarding the acceptance of the compulsory jurisdiction of the International Court of Justice, see chapter I.4 of *Multilateral Treaties Deposited with the Secretary-General*, available on the website https://treaties.un.org/Pages/ParticipationStatus.aspx.

[354] Detailed information and documents relating to the work of the International Law Commission may be found on the Commission's website at https://legal.un.org/ilc/.

[355] Pursuant to article 10 of the Statute of the International Law Commission, the election of the members of the Commission for a five-year term, beginning on 1 January 2017 (until 31 December 2021), took place by secret ballot, at the 40th meeting of the General Assembly at its seventy-first session, held on 3 November 2016. However, due to Covid-19 Pandemic, the General Assembly, on 12 August 2020, decided to postpone the seventy-second session of the Commission to 2021. This decision had an impact on the mandate of the members of the Commission which was extended until the end of 2022.

(Sierra Leone), Mr. Roman A. Kolodkin (Russian Federation), Mr. Ahmed Laraba (Algeria), Ms. Marja Lehto (Finland), Mr. Shinya Murase (Japan), Mr. Sean D. Murphy (United States of America), Mr. Hong Thao Nguyen (Viet Nam), Mr. Georg Nolte (Germany), Ms. Nilüfer Oral (Turkey), Mr. Hassan Ouazzani Chahdi (Morocco), Mr. Ki Gab Park (Republic of Korea), Mr. Chris Maina Peter (United Republic of Tanzania), Mr. Ernest Petrič (Slovenia), Mr. Aniruddha Rajput (India), Mr. August Reinisch (Austria), Mr. Juan José Ruda Santolaria (Peru), Mr. Gilberto V. Saboia (Brazil), Mr. Pavel Šturma (Czech Republic), Mr. Dire D. Tladi (South Africa), Mr. Eduardo Valencia-Ospina (Colombia), Mr. Marcelo Vázquez-Bermúdez (Ecuador), Mr. S. Amos Wako (Kenya), Mr. Michael Wood (United Kingdom of Great Britain and Northern Ireland).

(*b*) Sixty-ninth session of the International Law Commission

The International Law Commission held the first part of its sixty-ninth session from 1 May to 2 June 2017, and the second part of the session from 3 July to 4 August 2017, at its seat at the United Nations Office at Geneva.[356] The Commission continued its consideration of the following topics: "Crimes against humanity", "Provisional application of treaties", "Protection of the atmosphere", "Immunity of State officials from foreign criminal jurisdiction", "Peremptory norms of general international law (*jus cogens*)", "Succession of States in respect of State responsibility", "Protection of the environment in relation to armed conflicts".

In relation to the topic "Crimes against humanity", the Commission had before it the third report of the Special Rapporteur.[357] As a result of its consideration of the topic at the present session, the Commission adopted, on first reading, a draft preamble, 15 draft articles and a draft annex, together with commentaries thereto, on crimes against humanity. The Commission decided, in accordance with articles 16 to 21 of its statute, to transmit the draft articles, through the Secretary-General, to Governments, international organizations and others, for comments and observations, with the request that such comments and observations be submitted to the Secretary-General by 1 December 2018.[358]

As regards to the topic "Provisional application of treaties", the Commission referred draft guidelines 1 to 4 and 6 to 9, provisionally adopted by the Drafting Committee in 2016, back to the Drafting Committee, with a view to having a consolidated set of draft guidelines, as provisionally worked out thus far, prepared. The Commission subsequently provisionally adopted draft guidelines 1 to 11, as presented by the Drafting Committee at the current session, with commentaries thereto.[359]

As regards to the topic "Protection of the atmosphere", the Commission had before it the fourth report of the Special Rapporteur.[360] Following the debate in the Commission, which was preceded by an informal dialogue with atmospheric scientists organized by the Special Rapporteur, the Commission decided to refer the four draft guidelines, as contained in the Special Rapporteur's fourth report, to the Drafting Committee. The

[356] For the report of the International Law Commission on the work at its sixty-ninth session, see *Official Records of the General Assembly, Seventy-second Session Supplement No. 10 (A/72/10).*

[357] A/CN.4/704.

[358] *Official Records of the General Assembly, Seventy-second Session Supplement No. 10 (A/72/10)*, chap. IV.

[359] *Ibid.*, chap. V.

[360] A/CN.4/705 and Corr.1.

Commission considered the report of the Drafting Committee and provisionally adopted draft guideline 9 and three preambular paragraphs, together with commentaries thereto.[361]

With respect to the topic "Immunity of State officials from foreign criminal jurisdiction", the Commission continued its consideration of the fifth report of the Special Rapporteur, which had commenced during the sixty-eighth session.[362] Following the plenary debate, the Commission referred draft article 7, as proposed by the Special Rapporteur in her fifth report, to the Drafting Committee. Upon its consideration of the report of the Drafting Committee, the Commission voted to adopt draft article 7, an annex to the draft articles and a footnote to two of its headings, together with commentaries thereto.[363]

With regard to the topic "Peremptory norms of general international law (*jus cogens*)", the Commission had before it the second report of the Special Rapporteur.[364] The Commission subsequently decided to refer draft conclusions 4 to 9, as contained in the report of the Special Rapporteur, to the Drafting Committee, and decided to change the title of the topic from "*Jus cogens*" to "Peremptory norms of general international law (*jus cogens*)", as proposed by the Special Rapporteur. The Commission subsequently took note of the interim report of the Chairperson of the Drafting Committee on draft conclusions 2 and 4 to 7 provisionally adopted by the Committee, which was submitted to the Commission for information.[365]

As regards the topic "Succession of States in respect of State responsibility", the Commission decided to include the topic in its programme of work, and to appoint Mr. Pavel Šturma as Special Rapporteur. The Commission had before it the first report of the Special Rapporteur.[366] Following the debate in plenary, the Commission decided to refer draft articles 1 to 4, as contained in the report of the Special Rapporteur, to the Drafting Committee. The Commission subsequently took note of the interim report of the Chairperson of the Drafting Committee on draft articles 1 and 2 provisionally adopted by the Committee, which was submitted to the Commission for information.[367]

With respect to the topic "Protection of the environment in relation to armed conflicts", the Commission established a Working Group on the topic, chaired by Mr. Marcelo Vázquez-Bermúdez. The Working Group had before it the draft commentaries prepared by the former Special Rapporteur, even though she was no longer with the Commission, on draft principles 4, 6 to 8, and 14 to 18 provisionally adopted by the Drafting Committee at the sixty-eighth session of the Commission, and taken note of by the Commission at the same session. The Working Group focused its discussion on the way forward. Upon consideration of the oral report of the Chairperson of the Working Group, the Commission decided to appoint Ms. Marja Lehto as Special Rapporteur.[368]

---

[361] *Official Records of the General Assembly, Seventy-second Session Supplement No. 10 (A/72/10)*, chap. VI.

[362] A/CN.4/701.

[363] *Official Records of the General Assembly, Seventy-second Session Supplement No. 10 (A/72/10)*, chap. VII.

[364] A/CN.4/706

[365] *Official Records of the General Assembly, Seventy-second Session Supplement No. 10 (A/72/10)*, chap. VIII.

[366] A/CN.4/708.

[367] *Ibid.*, chap. IX.

[368] *Ibid.*, chap. X.

Also, at its sixty-ninth session, the Commission decided to include in its long-term programme of work the topics "General principles of law" and "Evidence before international courts and tribunals".[369]

Finally, the Commission recommended to hold its seventieth anniversary commemorative event during its seventieth session in 2018.[370]

(*c*) Sixth Committee

The Sixth Committee of the General Assembly considered the agenda item "Report of the International Law Commission on the work of its sixty-ninth session" at its 18th to 26th and 30th meetings, from 23 to 27 and on 31 October and 1 and 10 November 2017.[371] The Chair of the International Law Commission at its sixty-ninth session introduced the report of the Commission on the work of that session: chapters I to V and XI at the 18th meeting, on 23 October, chapters VI and VII at the 22nd meeting, on 26 October, and chapters VIII to X at the 25th meeting, on 31 October.[372]

At the 30th meeting, on 10 November, the representative of Peru, on behalf of the Bureau, introduced a draft resolution entitled "Report of the International Law Commission on the work of its sixty-ninth session"[373] and orally revised operative paragraph 38 to include the date for the commencement of the debate on the report of the Commission. The Committee decided under item 121 "Revitalization of the work of the General Assembly" that the date would be 22 October 2018.[374]At the same meeting, the Committee adopted draft resolution, as orally revised, without a vote.[375]

(*d*) General Assembly

On 18 December 2017, the General Assembly adopted, on the recommendation of the Sixth Committee and without a vote, resolution 72/116 entitled "Report of the International Law Commission on the work of its sixty-ninth session". The Assembly expressed its appreciation to the International Law Commission for the work accomplished at its sixty-ninth session and recommended that the Commission continue its work on the topics in its current programme, taking into account the comments and observations of Governments, whether submitted in writing or expressed orally in debates in the Sixth Committee. The Assembly also took note with appreciation of the recommendation of the Commission, in its report, regarding the commemoration of its seventieth anniversary in 2018, and encouraged States to make voluntary contributions to the trust fund for the Office of Legal Affairs to support the promotion of international law in order to facilitate the commemoration.

---

[369] *Ibid.*, chap. XI., sect. B.1 and annexes A and B.

[370] *Ibid.*, chap. XI, sect. B.

[371] For the report of the Sixth Committee, see A/72/460. For the summary records, see A/C.6/72/SR.18–26, and 30.

[372] For the ILC report, see *Official Records of the General Assembly, Seventy-second Session Supplement No. 10 (A/72/10).*

[373] A/C.6/72/L.21.

[374] A/72/482.

[375] A/C.6/72/L.21.

Furthermore, the Assembly decided that the next session of the Commission should be held at United Nations Headquarters in New York from 30 April to 1 June 2018, which will coincide with the commemoration of the seventieth anniversary of the Commission, and at the United Nations Office at Geneva from 2 July to 10 August 2018.

15. United Nations Commission on International Trade Law

(*a*) Fiftieth session of the Commission

The United Nations Commission on International Trade Law (UNCITRAL) held its fiftieth session in Vienna from 3 June to 21 July 2017 and adopted its report on 14, 20, and 21 July 2017.[376]

At the session, the Commission finalized and adopted the UNCITRAL Model Law on Electronic Transferable Records with an Explanatory Note,[377] and the Guide to Enactment of the UNCITRAL Model Law on Secured Transactions.[378]

The Commission had before it the reports of Working Group IV (Electronic Commerce) on its fifty-fourth session and on its fifty-fifth session. The Commission was informed that, at the fifty-fifth session of the Working Group, there was general agreement on the view that the suggested work on identity management and trust services on the one hand, and on cloud computing on the other, were different in scope and content.[379] The Commission reaffirmed the mandate given to the Working Group at its forty-ninth session, in 2016. It also agreed to revisit that mandate at its next session, in particular if the need arose to prioritize between the topics or to give a more specific mandate to the Working Group as regards its work in the area of identity management and trust services. The Secretariat was requested to consider convening expert group meetings as it deemed necessary to expedite the work in both areas and ensure the productive use of conference resources by the Working Group. States and international organizations were invited to share with the Working Group and the Secretariat their expertise in the areas of work assigned to the Working Group.[380]

With respect to the work of the Working Group I (MSMEs), the Commission had before it the reports of Working Group I on the work of its twenty-seventh and twenty-eighth sessions outlining progress on the two topics on its current work agenda: (*a*) The creation of a simplified business entity; and (*b*) Key principles of business registration.[381] The Commission commended the Working Group for the progress it had made on the two topics and welcomed the potential completion of the draft legislative guide on key principles of a business registry for possible adoption at its fifty-first session. The Commission also noted that the legislative texts resulting from the current work of the Working Group on those

---

[376] *Official Records of the General Assembly, seventy-second session, Supplement No. 17* (A/72/17), paras. 1 and 14. For the membership of the United Nations Commission on International Trade Law, see para. 4.

[377] *Ibid*., para. 115.

[378] *Ibid*., para. 216.

[379] *Ibid*., para. 117.

[380] *Ibid*., para. 127.

[381] *Ibid*., para. 230.

two topics should be published, including electronically, and in the six official languages of the United Nations, and be disseminated to Governments and other interested bodies.[382]

With respect to the work of Working Group II on the issue of enforcement of international settlement agreements resulting from conciliation proceedings, the Commission considered the reports of the Working Group on its sixty-fifth session, and sixty-sixth session. The Commission expressed its satisfaction with the progress made by the Working Group and the support provided by the Secretariat and requested the Working Group to complete the work expeditiously.[383]

Regarding the future work in the area of international dispute settlement, the Commission recalled that, at its forty-ninth session, in 2016, it had considered three topics for possible future work: concurrent proceedings, the preparation of a code of ethics for arbitrators, and possible reform of the investor State dispute settlement regime.[384] During the current session the Commission decided to entrust Working Group III with a broad mandate to work on the possible reform of investor-State dispute settlement. In line with the UNCITRAL process, Working Group III would, in discharging that mandate, ensure that the deliberations, while benefiting from the widest possible breadth of available expertise from all stakeholders, would be Government-led, with high-level input from all Governments, consensus-based and fully transparent. The Working Group would proceed to: (*a*) first, identify and consider concerns regarding investor-State dispute settlement; (*b*) second, consider whether reform was desirable in the light of any identified concerns; and (*c*) third, if the Working Group were to conclude that reform was desirable, develop any relevant solutions to be recommended to the Commission.[385]

With respect to the work of the Working Group V on insolvency law, the Commission commended the Working Group for the progress that was being made with its current work agenda, in particular for rising to the technical challenge posed by the various topics under consideration and for finding appropriate solutions. The Commission also requested the Secretariat to reflect, in its publications programme, the decisions to mandate work on those topics and to take any other measures necessary to ensure future publication of final texts resulting from that work, including in electronic form and in the six official languages of the United Nations.[386]

The Commission considered the legal developments in the area of public procurement and infrastructure development[387], the endorsement of texts of other organizations namely the Uniform Rules for Forfaiting of the International Chamber of Commerce and adopted at its 1059th meeting, on 14 July 2017, a decision by which it recommended the use of the rules above-mentioned. [388]

[382] *Ibid.*, para. 235.

[383] *Ibid.*, para. 239.

[384] *Ibid.*, para. 241.

[385] *Ibid.*, para. 264.

[386] *Ibid.*, para. 271.

[387] *Ibid.*, paras.272–276.

[388] *Ibid.*, paras. 277–279.

The Commission also considered, *inter alia*, its technical assistance to law reform activities,[389] the promotion of ways and means of ensuring a uniform interpretation and application of UNCITRAL legal texts,[390] the status and promotion of UNCITRAL legal texts,[391] measures aimed at coordination and cooperation with other organizations active in the field of international trade law, [392] the commemoration of the fiftieth anniversary of UNCITRAL[393], the role of UNCITRAL in promoting the rule of law at the national and international levels[394] and the work programme of the Commission.[395]

(*b*) Sixth Committee

The Sixth Committee considered the item "Report of the United Nations Commission on International Trade Law on the work of its fiftieth session" at its 10th, 17th, and 21st meetings, on 9, 20 and 25 October 2017.[396] For its consideration of the item, the Committee had before it the report of the United Nations Commission on International Trade Law on the work of its fiftieth session.[397]

At the 10th meeting, on 9 October, the Chair of the United Nations Commission on International Trade Law at its fiftieth session introduced the report of the Commission on the work of its fiftieth session.

At its 17th meeting, on 20 October 2017, the representative of Austria, on behalf of several States, introduced a draft resolution entitled "Report of the United Nations Commission on International Trade Law on the work of its fiftieth session"[398]. At the same meeting, the representative of Austria, on behalf of the Bureau, introduced a draft resolution entitled "Model Law on Electronic Transferable Records of the United Nations Commission on International Trade Law"[399]. At its 21st meeting, 25 October 2017, the Committee adopted the two draft resolutions without a vote.

(*c*) General Assembly

On 7 December 2017, the General Assembly adopted, upon the recommendation of the Sixth Committee, resolution 72/113 entitled "Report of the United Nations Commission on International Trade Law on the work of its fiftieth session" and resolution 72/114 entitled

---

[389] *Ibid.*, paras. 280–284.

[390] *Ibid.*, paras. 297–304.

[391] *Ibid.*, paras. 305–329.

[392] *Ibid.*, paras. 330–359.

[393] *Ibid.*, paras. 365–420.

[394] *Ibid.*, paras. 421–441.

[395] *Ibid.*, paras. 442–443.

[396] For the report of the Sixth Committee, see A/72/458. For the summary records, see A/C.6/72/SR.10, 17 and 21.

[397] *Official Records of the General Assembly, Seventy-second session, Supplement No. 17* (A/72/17).

[398] A/C.6/72/L.10.

[399] A/C.6/72/L.11.

"Model Law on Electronic Transferable Records of the United Nations Commission on International Trade Law", without a vote.

16. Legal questions dealt with by the Sixth Committee and other related subsidiary bodies of the General Assembly

During the seventy-second session of the General Assembly, the Sixth Committee (Legal), in addition to the topics discussed above concerning the International Law Commission and the United Nations Commission on International Trade Law, considered a wide range of topics. The work of the Sixth Committee and of other related subsidiary organs is described below, together with the relevant resolutions and decisions adopted by the General Assembly in 2017.[400] The resolutions and decisions of the General Assembly described in this section were all adopted, without a vote, during the seventy-second session, on 7 December 2017, on the recommendation of the Sixth Committee.[401]

(*a*) Criminal accountability of United Nations officials and experts on mission

The item entitled "Comprehensive review of the whole question of peacekeeping operations in all their aspects" was included in the agenda of the General Assembly at its nineteenth session, in February 1965, when the General Assembly established the Special Committee on Peacekeeping Operations that was to undertake a comprehensive review of the whole question of peacekeeping operations in all their aspects.[402]

At its sixty-first session, in 2006, the General Assembly decided that the agenda item entitled "Comprehensive review of the whole question of peacekeeping operations in all their aspects", which had been allocated to the Special Political and Decolonization Committee (Fourth Committee), should also be referred to the Sixth Committee for discussion of the report of the Group of Legal Experts on ensuring the accountability of United Nations staff and experts on mission with respect to criminal acts committed in peacekeeping operations,[403] submitted pursuant to General Assembly resolution 59/300.[404] At the same session, the General Assembly decided to establish an *ad hoc* committee, for the purpose of considering the report of the Group of Legal Experts, in particular its legal aspects and to report on its work to General Assembly under the agenda item

[400] For further information and documents regarding the work of the Sixth Committee and the other related subsidiary organs of the General Assembly mentioned in this section, see https://www.un.org/en/ga/sixth/72/72_session.shtml.

[401] The Sixth Committee adopts drafts resolutions, which it recommends for adoption by the General Assembly. These draft resolutions are contained in the reports of the Sixth Committee to the General Assembly on the various agenda items. The Sixth Committee reports also contain information concerning the relevant documentation on the consideration of the items by the Sixth Committee.

[402] General Assembly resolution 2006 (XIX) of 18 February 1965.

[403] A/60/980.

[404] General Assembly decision 61/503A of 13 September 2006.

entitled "Criminal Accountability of United Nations officials and experts on mission".[405] The Assembly had previously considered this item annually since its sixty-second session.

(i) *Sixth Committee*

During the seventy-second session of the General Assembly, the Sixth Committee considered the item at its 8th, 9th and 30th meetings, on 6 October and on 10 November 2017.[406] For its consideration of the item, the Committee had before it the report of the Secretary-General on this topic.[407]

At the 30th meeting, on 10 November 2017, the representative of Pakistan, on behalf of the Bureau, introduced a draft resolution entitled "Criminal accountability of United Nations officials and experts on mission", which the Committee adopted without a vote.[408]

(ii) *General Assembly*

On 7 December 2017, the General Assembly adopted resolution 72/112 entitled "Criminal accountability of United Nations officials and experts on mission" without a vote. The General Assembly, *inter alia*, decided to organize another briefing at the seventy-third session with a view to furthering discussion on measures that could be taken to help to ensure the accountability of United Nations officials and experts on mission and prevent future crimes. The Assembly reiterated its request to the Secretary-General to report to it at its seventy-third session on the implementation of the resolution. It also reiterated its decision that the consideration of the report of the Group of Legal Experts, in particular its legal aspects, shall be continued during its seventy-third session in the framework of a working group of the Sixth Committee, while including the item in the provisional agenda of the seventy-third session.

(*b*) United Nations Programme of Assistance in the Teaching, Study, Dissemination and Wider Appreciation of International Law

The United Nations Programme of Assistance in the Teaching, Study, Dissemination and Wider Appreciation of International Law was established by the General Assembly at its twentieth session in 1965,[409] to provide direct assistance in the field of international law, as well as through the preparation and dissemination of publications and other information relating to international law. The General Assembly authorized the continuation of

---

[405] The *Ad Hoc* Committee on criminal accountability of United Nations officials and experts on mission was established by General Assembly resolution 61/29 of 4 December 2006. The *Ad Hoc* Committee held two sessions at United Nations Headquarters in New York, from 9 to 13 April 2007 and from 7 to 9 and on 11 April 2008. For more information, see https://legal.un.org/committees/.

[406] For the report of the Sixth Committee, see A/72/457. For the summary records, A/C.6/72/SR.8, 9 and 30.

[407] A/72/205.

[408] A/C.6/72/L.18

[409] General Assembly resolution 2099 (XX) of 20 December 1965. For further information on the Programme of Assistance, see https://legal.un.org/poa/.

the Programme of Assistance annually until its twenty-sixth session, biennially until its sixty-fourth session and annually thereafter.

In the performance of the functions entrusted to him by the General Assembly, the Secretary-General is assisted by the Advisory Committee on the United Nations Programme of Assistance in the Teaching, Study, Dissemination and Wider Appreciation of International Law, the members of which are appointed by the General Assembly.

(i) *Sixth Committee*

The Sixth Committee considered the item at its 16th and 30th meetings on 16 October and 10 November 2017.[410] For its consideration of the item, the Committee had before it the Report of the Secretary-General.[411]

At the 30th meeting, on 10 November, the representative of Ghana, on behalf of the Bureau, introduced a draft resolution entitled "United Nations Programme of Assistance in the Teaching, Study, Dissemination and Wider Appreciation of International Law",[412] which the Committee adopted without a vote.

(ii) *General Assembly*

On 7 December 2017, the General Assembly adopted resolution 72/115 entitled "United Nations Programme of Assistance in the Teaching, Study, Dissemination and Wider Appreciation of International Law". In the resolution, the General Assembly noted with satisfaction that resources have been provided under the programme budget for the organization of the United Nations Regional Courses in International Law on an annual basis and the further development of the United Nations Audiovisual Library of International Law. The Assembly also authorized the Secretary-General to carry out the activities specified in his report in 2018 and 2019, including the following activities to be financed from provisions in the regular budget: the International Law Fellowship Programme and the United Nations Regional Courses in International Law for Africa, for Asia-Pacific and for Latin America and the Caribbean, with a minimum of 20 fellowships for each course; the Audiovisual Library of International Law, including its continuation and further development; and the dissemination of legal publications and lectures of the Audiovisual Library to developing countries to the extent that there are sufficient resources. The General Assembly requested the Secretary-General to continue to include resources under the proposed programme budget for the biennium 2020–2021 for those activities.

(*c*) Expulsion of aliens

At its sixty-ninth session, in 2014, the General Assembly, under the item entitled "Report of the International Law Commission on the work of its sixty-sixth session", considered chapter IV of the report of the Commission, which contained the draft articles

---

[410] For the report of the Sixth Committee, see A/72/459. For the summary records, see A/C.6/72/SR.16 and 30.

[411] A/72/517.

[412] A/C.6/72/L.19.

on the expulsion of aliens together with a recommendation, in paragraph 42, that the Assembly: (*a*) take note of the draft articles on the expulsion of aliens in a resolution, annex the articles to the resolution and encourage their widest possible dissemination; and (*b*) consider, at a later stage, the elaboration of a convention on the basis of the draft articles. The Assembly welcomed the conclusion of the work of the Commission on the expulsion of aliens, took note of the recommendation of the International Law Commission contained in paragraph 42 of its report and decided that the consideration of this recommendation would be continued at the seventy-second session.[413]

(i) *Sixth Committee*

The Sixth Committee considered the item at its 14th, 15th, 25th and 28th meetings, respectively on 12, 13 and 31 October 2017, and 3 November 2017.[414]

At the 25th meeting, on 31 October 2017, the representative of Paraguay, on behalf of the Bureau, introduced a draft resolution entitled "Expulsion of aliens".[415] At its 28th meeting, on 3 November 2017, the Committee adopted the draft resolution, without a vote.

(ii) *General Assembly*

On 7 December 2017, the General Assembly adopted resolution 72/117 entitled "Expulsion of aliens". The General Assembly took note of the articles on the expulsion of aliens presented by the International Law Commission and decided to include in the provisional agenda of its seventy-fifth session an item entitled "Expulsion of aliens", with a view to examining, *inter alia*, the question of the form that might be given to the articles or any other appropriate action.

(*d*) Report of the Special Committee on the Charter of the United Nations and on the Strengthening of the Role of the Organization

(i) *Special Committee on the Charter of the United Nations and on the Strengthening of the Role of the Organization*[416]

The item entitled "Need to consider suggestions regarding the review of the Charter of the United Nations" was included in the agenda of the twenty-fourth session of the General Assembly, in 1969, at the request of Colombia.[417]

At its twenty-ninth session, in 1974, the General Assembly decided to establish an *ad hoc* committee on the Charter of the United Nations to consider any specific proposals that

---

[413] A/RES/69/119.

[414] For the report of the Sixth Committee, see A/72/461. For the summary records, see A/C.6/72/SR.14, 15, 25 and 28.

[415] A/C.6/72/L.13.

[416] For more information, see the website of the Special Committee on the Charter of the United Nations and on the Strengthening of the Role of the Organization, available from https://legal.un.org/committees/charter/.

[417] A/7659.

Governments might make with a view to enhancing the ability of the United Nations to achieve its purposes, as well as other suggestions for the more effective functioning of the United Nations that might not require amendments to the Charter.[418]

Meanwhile, another item, entitled "Strengthening of the role of the United Nations with regard to the maintenance and consolidation of international peace and security, the development of cooperation among all nations and the promotion of the rules of international law in relations between States", was included in the agenda of the twenty-seventh session of the General Assembly, at the request of Romania.[419]

At its thirtieth session, the General Assembly decided to reconvene the *ad hoc* committee as the Special Committee on the Charter of the United Nations and on the Strengthening of the Role of the Organization, to examine suggestions and proposals regarding the Charter and the strengthening of the role of the United Nations with regard to the maintenance and consolidation of international peace and security, the development of cooperation among all nations and the promotion of the rules of international law.[420] Since its thirtieth session, the General Assembly has considered the report of the Special Committee annually.

The Special Committee met at United Nations Headquarters from 21 February to 1 March 2017 and considered the items "Maintenance of international peace and security", "Peaceful settlement of disputes", "*Repertory of Practice of United Nations Organs* and *Repertoire of the Practice of the Security Council*" and "Working methods of the Special Committee and identification of new subjects".[421]

(ii) *Sixth Committee*

The Sixth Committee considered the item at its 12th, 13th, 25th and 28th meetings, on 10, 11 and 31 October and on 3 November 2017.[422]

At the 25th meeting, on 31 October, the representative of Lesotho, on behalf of the Bureau, introduced a draft resolution entitled "Report of the Special Committee on the Charter of the United Nations and on the Strengthening of the Role of the Organization".[423] At the 28th meeting, on 3 November, the Committee adopted the draft resolution without a vote.

(iii) *General Assembly*

On 7 December 2017, the General Assembly adopted resolution 72/118 entitled "Report of the Special Committee on the Charter of the United Nations and on the Strengthening of the Role of the Organization". The Assembly, *inter alia*, requested the Special Committee

---

[418] General Assembly resolution 3349 (XXIX) of 17 December 1974.

[419] A/8792.

[420] General Assembly resolution 3499 (XXX) of 15 December 1975.

[421] For the report of the Special Committee, see *Official Records of the General Assembly, Seventy-second Session Supplement No.* 33 (A/72/33).

[422] For the report of the Sixth Committee, see A/72/462. For the summary records, see A/C.6/72/SR.12, 13, 25 and 28.

[423] A/C.6/72/L.12.

to consider the question of the maintenance of international peace and security in all its aspects and the question of the implementation of the provisions of the Charter of the United Nations relating to assistance to third States affected by the application of sanctions, as well as to keep on its agenda the question of the peaceful settlement of disputes between States. Moreover, the Assembly decided to undertake an annual thematic debate in the Special Committee to discuss the means for the settlement of disputes, and invite Member States to focus their comments at the next session of the Special Committee on the subtopic "Exchange of information on State practices regarding the use of negotiation and enquiry".

(*e*) The rule of law at the national and international levels

This item was included in the provisional agenda of the sixty-first session of the General Assembly, in 2006, at the request of Liechtenstein and Mexico.[424] The General Assembly had previously considered the item annually since its sixty-first session.

(i) *Sixth Committee*

The Sixth Committee considered the item at its 5th, 6th, 7th, 8th and 30th meetings, on 4, 5 and 6 October and on 10 November 2017.[425] For its consideration of the item, the Committee had before it the report of the Secretary-General on strengthening and coordinating United Nations rule of law activities.[426]

At the 30th meeting, on 10 November 2017, the representative of Liechtenstein, on behalf of the Bureau, introduced a draft resolution entitled "The rule of law at the national and international levels".[427] At the same meeting, the Committee adopted the draft resolution without a vote.

(ii) *General Assembly*

On 7 December 2017 the General Assembly adopted resolution 72/119 entitled "The rule of law at the national and international levels". The General Assembly decided to include this item in the provisional agenda of its seventy-third session and invited Member States to suggest possible subtopics for future Sixth Committee debated, for inclusion in the forthcoming annual report, with a view to assisting the Sixth Committee in choosing future subtopics.

(*f*) The scope and application of the principle of universal jurisdiction

This item was included in the provisional agenda of the sixty-fourth session of the General Assembly, in 2009, at the request of the United Republic of Tanzania on behalf of

---

[424] A/61/142.

[425] For the report of the Sixth Committee, see A/72/463. For the summary records, see A/C.6/72/SR.5, 6, 7, 8 and 30.

[426] A/72/268.

[427] A/C.6/72/L.17.

the Group of African States.[428] The General Assembly had previously considered the item annually since its sixty-fourth session.

(i) *Sixth Committee*

The Sixth Committee considered the item at its 13th, 14th, 28th and 30th meetings, on 11 and 12 October and on 3 and 10 November 2017.[429] For its consideration of the item, the Committee had before it the reports of the Secretary-General submitted to the General Assembly at its sixty-fifth to seventy-second sessions.[430]

At its 1st meeting, on 2 October, the Committee established a working group pursuant to General Assembly resolution 71/149 to continue to undertake a thorough discussion of the scope and application of the principle of universal jurisdiction. In its resolution 71/149, the Assembly decided that the Working Group should be open to all Member States and that relevant observers to the Assembly would be invited to participate in its work. The Working Group held two meetings, on 12 and 18 October. At its 28th meeting, on 3 November, the Committee heard and took note of the oral report of the Chair of the Working Group.[431]

At the 30th meeting, on 10 November, the representative of Kenya, on behalf of the Bureau, introduced a draft resolution entitled "The scope and application of the principle of universal jurisdiction".[432] At the same meeting, the Committee adopted the draft resolution without a vote.

(ii) *General Assembly*

In resolution 72/120 of 7 December 2017, the General Assembly, *inter alia*, invited Member States and relevant observers, as appropriate, to submit, before 28 April 2018, information and observations on the scope and application of universal jurisdiction, including, where appropriate, information on the relevant applicable international treaties, their national legal rules and judicial practice. The Assembly further requested the Secretary-General to prepare and submit to it, at its seventy-third session, a report based on such information and observations. The Assembly decided that the Working Group should be open to all Member States and that relevant observers to the General Assembly would be invited to participate in the work of the Working Group, and included the topic in the provisional agenda of its seventy-third session.

(*g*) Effects of armed conflicts on treaties

At its sixty-sixth session, in 2011, the General Assembly, under the item entitled "Report of the International Law Commission on the work of its sixty-third session", considered

---

[428] A/63/237/Rev.1.

[429] For the report of the Sixth Committee, see A/72/464./460. For the summary records, see A/C.6/72/SR.13, 14, 28 and 30.

[430] A/65/181, A/66/93 and Add.1, A/67/116, A/68/113, A/69/174, A/70/125, A/71/111, and A/72/112.

[431] See A/C.6/72/SR.28.

[432] A/C.6/72/L.23.

chapter VI of the report of the Commission which contained the draft articles on effects of armed conflicts on treaties together with a recommendation that the Assembly take note of the draft articles and that it consider, at a later stage, the elaboration of a convention on the basis of the draft articles. The Assembly took note of the articles, the text of which was annexed to resolution 66/99, and commended them to the attention of Governments without prejudice to the question of their future adoption or other appropriate action.

At its sixty-ninth session, in 2014, the General Assembly once again commended the articles on the effects of armed conflicts on treaties to the attention of Governments without prejudice to the question of their future adoption or other appropriate action. It requested the Secretary-General to invite Governments to submit written comments on any future action regarding the articles. The Assembly decided to include the item in the provisional agenda of its seventy-second session, with a view to examining, *inter alia*, the question of the form that might be given to the articles.[433]

(i) *Sixth Committee*

The Sixth Committee considered the item at its 17th, 28th and 29th meetings, on 20 October and on 3 and 6 November 2017, respectively.[434] At the 28th meeting, on 3 November, the representative of the Czech Republic, on behalf of the Bureau, introduced a draft resolution entitled "Effects of armed conflicts on treaties".[435] At its 29th meeting, on 6 November, the Committee adopted the draft resolution without a vote.

(ii) *General Assembly*

On 7 December 2017, the General Assembly adopted resolution 72/121 entitled "Effects of armed conflicts on treaties". The Assembly emphasized the value of the articles on the effects of armed conflicts on treaties in providing guidance to States, and invites States to use the articles as a reference whenever appropriate.

(*h*) Responsibility of international organizations

At its sixty-sixth session, in 2011, the General Assembly, under the item entitled "Report of the International Law Commission on the work of its sixty-third session", considered chapter V of the report of the Commission, which contained the draft articles on responsibility of international organizations together with a recommendation that the Assembly take note of the draft articles and that it consider, at a later stage, the elaboration of a convention on the basis of the draft articles. The Assembly took note of the articles, the text of which was annexed to resolution 66/100 of 9 December 2011, and commended them to the attention of Governments and international organizations without prejudice to the question of their future adoption or other appropriate action.

---

[433] General Assembly resolution 69/125 of 10 December 2014.

[434] For the report of the Sixth Committee, see A/72/465. For the summary records, see A/C.6/72/SR.17, 28 and 29.

[435] A/C.6/72/L.15.

At its sixty-ninth session, the General Assembly requested the Secretary-General to invite Governments and international organizations to submit their written comments on any future action regarding the articles. It also requested the Secretary-General to prepare an initial compilation of decisions of international courts, tribunals and other bodies referring to the articles and to invite Governments and international organizations to submit information on their practice in that regard. It further requested him to submit that material to the Assembly at its seventy-second session.[436]

(i) *Sixth Committee*

The Sixth Committee considered the item at its 15th and 30th meetings, on 13 October and 10 November 2017.[437] At the 30th meeting, on 10 November 2017, the representative of Brazil, on behalf of the Bureau, introduced a draft resolution entitled "Responsibility of international organizations".[438] At the same meeting, the Committee adopted draft without a vote.

(ii) *General Assembly*

On 7 December 2017, the General Assembly adopted resolution 72/122 entitled "Responsibility of international organizations". The Assembly decided to include this item in the provisional agenda of its seventy-fifth session with a view to examining, *inter alia*, the question of the form that might be given to the articles.

(*i*) Measures to eliminate international terrorism

This item was included in the agenda of the twenty-seventh session of the General Assembly in 1972, further to an initiative of the Secretary-General.[439] At that session, the General Assembly decided to establish the *ad hoc* committee on International Terrorism, consisting of 35 members.[440]

At its fifty-first session, the General Assembly approved the Declaration to Supplement the 1994 Declaration on Measures to Eliminate International Terrorism and established an Ad Hoc Committee to elaborate an international convention for the suppression of terrorist bombings and, subsequently, an international convention for the suppression of acts of nuclear terrorism, to supplement related existing international instruments, and thereafter to address means of further developing a comprehensive legal framework of conventions dealing with international terrorism.[441] Through the work of the Committee, the Assembly has so far adopted three counter-terrorism instruments.

---

[436] General Assembly resolution 69/126. A/RES/69/126.

[437] For the report of the Sixth Committee, see A/72/466. For the summary records, see A/C.6/72/SR.15 and 30.

[438] A/C.6/72/L.22.

[439] A/8791 and Add.1 and Add.1/Corr.1.

[440] General Assembly resolution 3034 (XXVII) of 18 December 1972.

[441] General Assembly resolution 51/210.

At its seventy-first session, the General Assembly decided to recommend that the Sixth Committee, at the seventy-second session of the Assembly, establish a working group with a view to finalizing the process on the draft comprehensive convention on international terrorism as well as discussions on the item included in its agenda by resolution 54/110 concerning the question of convening a high-level conference under the auspices of the United Nations.[442]

(i) *Sixth Committee*

The Sixth Committee considered the item at its 1st, 2nd, 3rd, 4th, 5th, 28th and 30th meetings, from 2 to 4 October and on 3 and 10 November 2017.[443] For its consideration of the item, the Committee had before it the report of the Secretary-General on measures to eliminate international terrorism.[444]

Pursuant to General Assembly resolution 71/151 of 13 December 2016, at its 1st meeting, on 2 October, the Committee established a working group with a view to finalizing the process on the draft comprehensive convention on international terrorism, as well as discussions on the item included in its agenda by General Assembly resolution 54/110 concerning the question of convening a high-level conference under the auspices of the United Nations. The Working Group was open to all States Members of the United Nations or members of the specialized agencies or of the International Atomic Energy Agency. The Working Group held three meetings, as well as informal consultations, on 16, 20 and 31 October. At its 28th meeting, on 3 November, the Committee heard and took note of the oral report by the Chair of the Working Group on the work of the Working Group and on the results of the informal consultations held during the current session.[445]

At the 30th meeting, on 10 November, the representative of Canada, on behalf of the Bureau, introduced a draft resolution entitled "Measures to eliminate international terrorism".[446] At the same meeting, the Committee adopted the draft resolution without a vote.

(ii) *General Assembly*

On 7 December 2017, the General Assembly adopted resolution 72/123 entitled "Measures to eliminate international terrorism". The Assembly, *inter alia*, decided to recommend that the Sixth Committee, at the seventy-third session of the General Assembly, establish a working group with a view to finalizing the process on the draft comprehensive convention on international terrorism as well as discussions on the item included in its agenda by General Assembly resolution 54/110, while encouraging all Member States to redouble their efforts during the intersessional period towards resolving any outstanding issues.

---

[442] General Assembly resolution 71/151.

[443] A/C.6/72/SR.1, 2, 3, 4, 5, 28 and 30. For the report of the Sixth Committee, see A/72/467. For the summary records, see A/C.6/72/SR.1, 2, 3, 4, 5, 28 and 30.

[444] A/72/111, and A/72/111/Add.1.

[445] See A/C.6/72/SR.28.

[446] A/C.6/72/L.14.

(*j*) Revitalization of the work of the General Assembly

This item, which was included in the agenda of the forty-sixth session of the General Assembly in 1991, had originally been proposed for inclusion in the draft agenda of that session by the President of the General Assembly at its forty-fifth session.[447] The General Assembly had previously considered the question at its forty-sixth to forty-eighth, fifty-second to fifty-third, and fifty-fifth[448] to seventy-first sessions.

At its seventy-first session, the General Assembly considered the item jointly with the item entitled "Implementation of the resolutions of the United Nations". The Assembly also approved the provisional programme of work and timetable of the First Committee for 2017,[449] and the proposed programme of work and timetable of the Special Political and Decolonization Committee (Fourth Committee),[450] the programmes of work of the Second Committee (decision 71/543) and the Third Committee[451] and the provisional programme of work of the Sixth Committee (decision 71/528) for the seventy-second session of the Assembly.

At its 2nd plenary meeting, on 15 September 2017, the General Assembly, on the recommendation of the General Committee, decided to allocate the item to all the Main Committees for the purpose of discussing their working methods and considering and taking action on their respective tentative programmes of work for the seventy-third session of the General Assembly.

(i) *Sixth Committee*

The Sixth Committee considered the item at its 29th meeting, on 6 November 2017.[452] At the 29th meeting, on 6 November, the Chair introduced a draft decision containing the provisional programme of work of the Committee for the seventy-third session of the General Assembly, as proposed by the Bureau.[453] At the 30th meeting, on 10 November 2017, the Committee adopted the draft decision.

(ii) *General Assembly*

In its decision 72/528, the General Assembly noted that the Sixth Committee has decided to adopt the provisional programme of work for the seventy-third second session of the General Assembly, as proposed by the Bureau.

---

[447] See General Assembly decision 45/461 of 16 September 1991.

[448] At its fifty-fourth session, the General Assembly decided to defer consideration of the item (General Assembly decision 54/491).

[449] General Assembly decision 71/518.

[450] General Assembly decision 71/522.

[451] General Assembly decision 71/538.

[452] For the report of the Sixth Committee, see A/72/482. For the summary records, see A/C.6/72/SR.29 and 30.

[453] A/C.6/72/L.24.

(*k*) Administration of justice at the United Nations

The General Assembly considered the item at its fifty-fifth to fifty-ninth and sixty-first to seventy-first sessions, in the framework of both the Fifth and Sixth Committee, with the aim of introducing a new system for handling internal disputes and disciplinary matters in the United Nations.

At its sixty-second session, the General Assembly decided to establish: (*a*) a two-tier formal system of administration of justice, comprising a first instance United Nations Dispute Tribunal and an appellate instance United Nations Appeals Tribunal; (*b*) the Office of Administration of Justice, comprising the Office of the Executive Director and the Office of Staff Legal Assistance and the Registries for the United Nations Dispute Tribunal and the United Nations Appeals Tribunal; (*c*) a single integrated and decentralized Office of the Ombudsman for the United Nations Secretariat, funds and programmes with branches in several duty stations and a new mediation division; (*d*) the Internal Justice Council; and (*e*) the Management Evaluation Unit in the Office of the Under-Secretary-General for Management.[454]

At its sixty-third session, the General Assembly adopted the statutes of the United Nations Dispute Tribunal and the United Nations Appeals Tribunal; it also decided that those Tribunals would be operational as of 1 July 2009; and further decided that all persons who had access to the Office of the Ombudsman under the previous system would also have access to the new informal system.[455] The statutes have been amended at subsequent sessions.[456]

Outstanding legal matters have been considered by the Sixth Committee in the ensuing years. These matters included, *inter alia*, the rules of procedure of the two tribunals, the scope *ratione personae* of the administration of justice system and the scope and functioning of the Office of Staff Legal Assistance (OSLA).

At the seventy-first session, as set out in a letter from the Chair of the Sixth Committee,[457] the Sixth Committee considered the legal aspects of the reports of the Secretary-General and of the Internal Justice Council on the administration of justice at the United Nations and the report of the Secretary-General on the activities of the Office of the United Nations Ombudsman and Mediation Services. The Committee also had before it the report of the Interim Independent Assessment Panel on the system of administration of justice at the United Nations and the report of the Secretary-General on the findings and recommendations of the Interim Independent Assessment Panel and revised estimates relating to the programme budget for the biennium 2016–2017. The Sixth Committee drew the attention of the Fifth Committee to a number of specific issues relating to the legal aspects of those reports.

---

[454] General Assembly resolution 62/228.

[455] General Assembly resolution 63/253.

[456] General Assembly resolutions 66/237, 69/203, 70/112 and 71/266.

[457] See A/C.5/71/10, annex.

(i) *Sixth Committee*

The Sixth Committee considered the item at its 11th and 21st meetings, on 9 and 25 October 2017.[458] For its consideration of the item, the Committee had before it the report of the Secretary-General on the activities of the Office of the United Nations Ombudsman and Mediation Services,[459] the report of the Secretary-General on the administration of justice at the United Nations,[460] and the report of the Internal Justice Council on the administration of justice at the United Nations.[461]

At the 21st meeting, on 25 October 2017, the Committee received a report on the results of the informal consultations and authorized its Chair to send a letter to the President of the General Assembly with a request that it be brought to the attention of the Chair of the Fifth Committee and circulated as a document of the General Assembly. The letter was circulated as an annex to the document A/C.5/72/10.

(ii) *General Assembly*

On 24 December 2017, the General Assembly adopted resolution 72/256 entitled "Administration of justice at the United Nations", without a vote, on the recommendation of the Fifth committee. The Assembly, *inter alia*, took note of the reports of the Secretary-General on administration of justice at the United Nations and on the activities of the Office of the United Nations Ombudsman and Mediation Services,[462] the note by the Secretary-General transmitting the report of the Interim Independent Assessment Panel on the system of administration of justice at the United Nations, the report of the Secretary-General on the findings and recommendations of the Interim Independent Assessment Panel on the system of administration of justice at the United Nations, and revised estimates relating to the programme budget for the biennium 2016–2017, the report of the Internal Justice Council on administration of justice at the United Nations[463] and the related report of the Advisory Committee on Administrative and Budgetary Questions.[464] The Assembly also endorsed the conclusions and recommendations contained in the report of the Advisory Committee.

(*l*) Report of the Committee on Relations with the Host Country

(i) *Committee on Relations with the Host Country*

The Committee on Relations with the Host Country was established by the General Assembly at its twenty-sixth session, in 1971.[465] In 2017, the Committee was composed of the following 19 Member States: Bulgaria, Canada, China, Costa Rica, Côte

---

458 For the summary records of the Sixth Committee, see A/C.6/72/SR.11 and 21.

459 A/72/13871/157.

460 A/72/20471/164.

461 A/72/21071/158.

462 A/72/138.

463 A/72/210.

464 A/72/7/Add.19. A/71/707.

465 General Assembly resolution 2819 (XXVI) of 15 December 1971.

d'Ivoire, Cuba, Cyprus, France, Honduras, Hungary, Iraq, Libya, Malaysia, Mali, Russian Federation, Senegal, Spain, United Kingdom of Great Britain and Northern Ireland and the United States of America.

In 2017, the Committee held the following meetings: the 280th, on 25 January 2017; the 281st meeting, on 27 April 2017; the 282nd meeting, on 13 July 2017; the 283rd meeting, on 6 September 2017; the 284th meeting, on 2 October 2017; and the 285th meeting, on 20 October 2017. During its meetings, the Committee considered a number of topics, namely (i) entry visas issued by the host country; (ii) host country activities: activities to assist members of the United Nations community; and (iii) other matters. At its 285th meeting, on 20 October 2017, the Committee approved a number of recommendations and conclusions, which were contained in chapter IV of its report.[466]

(ii) *Sixth Committee*

The Sixth Committee considered the item at its 27th and 30th meetings on 2 and 10 November 2017.[467] The Chair of the Committee on Relations with the Host Country introduced the report of the Committee.[468]

At the 30th meeting, on 10 November 2017, the representative of Cyprus, on behalf of the Bureau, introduced the draft resolution entitled "Report of the Committee on Relations with the Host Country".[469] At the same meeting, the Committee adopted the draft resolution without a vote.

(iii) *General Assembly*

On 7 December 2017, General Assembly adopted resolution 72/124 entitled "Report of the Committee on Relations with the Host Country". The Assembly, *inter alia*, endorsed the recommendations and conclusions contained in the report of the Committee on Relations with the Host Country and decided to include the item entitled "Report of the Committee on Relations with the Host Country" in the provisional agenda of its seventy-third session.

(*m*) Observer Status in the General Assembly

(i) *Sixth Committee*

The Committee considered requests for observer status in the General Assembly for the Cooperation Council of Turkic-speaking States, for the Eurasian Economic Union in the General Assembly, for the Community of Democracies in the General Assembly, for the International Network for Bamboo and Rattan, for the ASEAN+3 Macroeconomic Research Office in the General Assembly, for the Eurasian Group on Combating Money Laundering and Financing of Terrorism, for the Ramsar Convention on Wetlands

---

[466] *Official Records of the General Assembly, Seventy-second session, Supplement No. 26* (A/72/26), chap. IV.

[467] For the report of the Sixth Committee, see A/72/124. For the summary records, see A/C.6/72/SR.27 and 30.

[468] A/72/26.

[469] A/C.6/72/L.20.

Secretariat in the General Assembly, for the Global Environment Facility, and for the Fund for the Development of the Indigenous Peoples of Latin America and the Caribbean in the General Assembly at its 11th, 15th, 28th, and 29th meetings on 9, 13 October and, 3 and 6 November 2017.[470]

(ii) *General Assembly*

In its resolutions 72/125, 72/126, 72/127 and 72/128 the General Assembly granted observer status to the International Network for Bamboo and Rattan in the General Assembly, to the ASEAN+3 Macroeconomic Research Office in the General Assembly, the Eurasian Group on Combating Money Laundering and Financing of Terrorism in the General Assembly, and the Fund for the Development of the Indigenous Peoples of Latin America and the Caribbean in the General Assembly

By its decisions 72/523, 72/524, 72/525, 72/526, and 72/527, the General Assembly decided to defer a decision on the request for observer status for the Cooperation Council of Turkic-speaking States in the General Assembly, the Eurasian Economic Union in the General Assembly, and the Community of Democracies in the General Assembly, the Ramsar Convention on Wetlands Secretariat in the General Assembly, and the Global Environment Facility in the General Assembly respectively, to its seventy-third session.

[470] For the reports of the Sixth Committee, see A/72/470, A/72/471, A/72/472, A/72/473, A/72/474, A/72/475, A/72/476, A/72/477, and A/72/468, respectively. For the summary records, see A/C.6/72/SR.11, 15, 28 and 29.

17. *Ad hoc* international criminal tribunals[471]

(*a*) Organization of the International Criminal Tribunal for the former Yugoslavia

(i) *Organization of the International Criminal Tribunal for the former Yugoslavia*[472]

During the reporting period, Judge Carmel Agius (Malta) and Judge Liu Daqun (China) continued to serve as President and Vice-President of the Tribunal, respectively. Serge Brammertz (Belgium) continued to serve as Prosecutor and John Hocking (Australia) as Registrar.

During the reporting period, there was one Trial Chamber, composed of Judges Orie (presiding), Flügge (Germany) and Moloto (South Africa).

At the end of 2017, seven permanent judges from seven countries served at the Tribunal: Carmel Agius (President, Malta), Liu Daqun (Vice-President, China), Alphons Orie (Netherlands), Fausto Pocar (Italy), Theodor Meron (United States of America), Moloto (South Africa) and Christoph Flügge (Germany).

(ii) *Composition of the Appeals Chamber*

At the end of 2017, the composition of the Appeals Chamber was as follows: Carmel Agius (Presiding, Malta), Liu Daqun (China), Fausto Pocar (Italy), Theodor Meron (United States of America), Bakone Justice Moloto (South Africa), and Burton Hall (Bahamas) who served as an *ad hoc* Appeals Chamber judge.[473]

(iii) *Organization of the International Residual Mechanism for Criminal Tribunals*[474]

By resolution 1966 (2010) of 22 December 2010, the Security Council, acting under Chapter VII of the Charter of the United Nations, decided to establish the International

[471] This section covers the International Criminal Tribunal for the former Yugoslavia which closed its doors on the 31st of December 2017 and the International Residual Mechanism for Criminal Tribunals, established by Security Council resolutions 827 (1993) of 25 May 1993 and 1966 (2010) of 22 December 2010, respectively. Further information regarding the judgments of the International Criminal Tribunal for Yugoslavia and the International Residual Mechanism for Criminal Tribunal is contained in chapter VII of this publication.

[472] For more information, see, for the period 1 August 2016 to 31 July 2017, the twenty-fourth and final annual report of the International Tribunal for the Prosecution of Persons Responsible for Serious Violations of International Humanitarian Law Committed in the Territory of the Former Yugoslavia since 1991, dated 1 August 2017 (A/72/266–S/2017/662). See also the assessment and report of Judge Carmel Agius, President of the International Tribunal for the Former Yugoslavia, provided to the Security Council pursuant to paragraph 6 of Security Council resolution 1534 (2004) covering the period from 18 November 2016 to 17 May 2017 (S/2017/436, annex I) and the Report of Serge Brammertz, Prosecutor of the International Tribunal for the Former Yugoslavia, provided to the Security Council under paragraph 6 of Security Council resolution 1534 (2004) (S/2017/436, annex II).

[473] See A/72/266–S/2017/662.

[474] For more information on the Mechanism, see, for the period 1 July 2016 to 30 June 2017, the fifth annual report of the International Residual Mechanism for Criminal Tribunals (A/72/261–S/2017/661);

Residual Mechanism for Criminal Tribunals ("the Mechanism") with two branches, the branch for the ICTR which commenced functioning on 1 July 2012 and the branch for the ICTY which commenced functioning on 1 July 2013, to carry out a number of essential functions of the Tribunals after their closure. By the same resolution, the Security Council also decided to adopt that Statute of the Mechanism, contained in the annex.

At the end of 2017, the President of the Mechanism was Judge Theodor Meron (United States), the Prosecutor was Serge Brammertz (Belgian), and the Registrar was Olufemi Elias (Nigeria).[475]

(*b*) General Assembly

On 27 December 2017, the General Assembly adopted, on the recommendation of the Fifth Committee and without a vote, resolution 72/257 entitled "Financing of the International Tribunal for the Prosecution of Persons Responsible for Serious Violations of International Humanitarian Law Committed in the Territory of the Former Yugoslavia since 1991", and resolutions 72/258 and 72/258 *B* entitled "Financing of the International Residual Mechanism for Criminal Tribunals".

(*c*) Security Council

On 31 December 2017, the Security Council issued a press Statement on the Closure of the International Criminal Tribunal for the Former Yugoslavia. The Security Council recalled resolution 827 (1993) which established the ICTY, and marked its closure on 21 December 2017, recalling that the Residual Mechanism for Criminal Tribunals was established to carry out the residual functions of the ICTY and the International Criminal Tribunal for Rwanda, as set out in the Statute of the Residual Mechanism.[476]

---

and for the period 1 July 2017 to 30 June 2018, the sixth annual report of the International Residual Mechanism for Criminal (A/73/289–S/2018/569).

[475] See the sixth annual report of the International Residual Mechanism for Criminal (A/73/289–S/2018/569).

[476] See SC/13151-L/3274.

B. General review of the legal activities of intergovernmental organizations related to the United Nations

1. International Labour Organization[477]

(a) Adoption of a Recommendation and resolutions, and withdrawal or abrogation of six Conventions, by the International Labour Conference during its 106th Session (Geneva, June 2017)[478]

At its 106th Session, the International Labour Conference adopted one international labour Recommendation and decided to abrogate or withdraw six international labour Conventions. It also adopted eight resolutions of which three are highlighted below.

(i) *Recommendation concerning employment and decent work for peace and resilience*

The Employment and Decent Work for Peace and Resilience Recommendation, 2017 (No. 205), which supersedes the Employment (Transition from War to Peace) Recommendation, 1944 (No. 71), provides guidance to ILO members in addressing work issues in crisis situations arising from conflicts or disasters. Based on the same premise as Recommendation No. 71—the fundamental role of employment and social justice in promoting lasting peace and in stabilizing societies torn by conflict—Recommendation No. 205 expands the original scope of Recommendation No. 71 to include internal conflicts and disasters. It broadens and updates the guidance on employment and several other elements of the Decent Work Agenda, taking into account the contemporary context and nature of crises as well as the experience gained by the ILO and the international community in crisis response since 1944.

Recommendation No. 205 provides guidance to members on the measures to be taken to generate employment and decent work for the purposes of prevention, recovery, peace and resilience with respect to crisis situations arising from conflicts and disasters. Its scope of application extends to all workers and jobseekers, and to all employers, in all sectors of the economy directly or indirectly affected by crisis situations. It also concerns workers and persons in volunteer work engaged in crisis response, including in the immediate response.

Recommendation No. 205 invites members to consider 14 guiding principles in taking measures to prevent and respond to crisis situations. These principles recognize the need to promote full, productive, freely chosen employment and decent work, and to respect, promote and realize the fundamental principles and rights at work, other human rights and other relevant international labour standards. They emphasize the importance of good governance, social dialogue, national reconciliation and a just transition to an

---

[477] For official documents and more information in the International Labour Organization, see http://ilo.org.

[478] The texts adopted at the 106th Session (2017) of the International Labour Conference are available in English, French and Spanish at: https://www.ilo.org/ilc/ILCSessions/106/reports/texts-adopted/lang--en/index.htm

environmentally sustainable economy. They highlight the need to respect national laws and use local knowledge, capacity and resources. They affirm the need to combat discrimination and to pay special attention to population groups and individuals who have been made particularly vulnerable by the crisis. They call for international solidarity, burden- and responsibility-sharing and cooperation, and for close coordination and synergies between humanitarian and development assistance.

The Recommendation encourages members to adopt a phased multi-track approach in implementing crisis response strategies, including immediate emergency measures and long-term measures. It offers practical guidance for designing and implementing crisis prevention and response measures in a range of policy areas, while acknowledging the diversity of national circumstances and priorities. In particular, it elaborates on measures for employment and income generation and for sustainable enterprises; rights, equality and non-discrimination; education, vocational training and guidance; social protection; labour law, labour administration and labour market information; and social dialogue and the role of employers' and workers' organizations. It also provides guidance on migrants affected by crises and on refugees and returnees. Importantly, the Recommendation elaborates on actions to prevent, mitigate and prepare for crises in ways that support economic and social development and decent work. It particularly emphasizes the need for strengthened international cooperation and increased complementarity between humanitarian and development initiatives, and it calls on the ILO to play a leading role in crisis response centred on employment and decent work.

(ii) *Resolution concerning employment and decent work for peace and resilience*

The 106th Session of the Conference also adopted the resolution concerning employment and decent work for peace and resilience, which invites governments, employers and workers to give full effect to Recommendation No. 205. It requests the ILO Director-General to promote cooperation and partnerships with other relevant international and regional organizations in support of coordinated policies and initiatives for promoting employment and decent work for prevention and response to crises arising from conflicts and disasters.

(iii) *Abrogation of four and withdrawal of two international labour Conventions*

At its 106th Session (2017), the International Labour Conference decided at its last session in June 2017 to abrogate the following four international labour Conventions: Night Work (Women) Convention, 1919 (No. 4); Minimum Age (Trimmers and Stokers) Convention, 1921 (No. 15); Night Work (Women) Convention (Revised), 1934 (No. 41); and Hours of Work and Rest Periods (Road Transport) Convention, 1939 (No. 67). The Conference also decided to withdraw the following two Conventions: Protection against Accidents (Dockers) Convention, 1929 (No. 28) and Minimum Age (Non-Industrial Employment) Convention (Revised), 1937 (No. 60).

These decisions came twenty years after the adoption of a constitutional amendment to article 19 of the ILO Constitution, which empowers the Conference to put an end, by two-thirds majority and upon recommendation by the Governing Body, to a Convention in force if it appears that it has lost its purpose or that it no longer makes a useful contribution to attaining the objectives of the Organization. The procedure for abrogation applies to Conventions which are in force. The procedure for withdrawal applies to Conventions which have never entered into force or are no longer in force due to denunciations, and to Recommendations.

By terminating the legal effects of the six obsolete Conventions *vis-à-vis* the Organization the Conference contributes to the current process aimed at ensuring that the Organization has a robust and up-to-date body of labour standards serving as a global reference.

(iv) *Resolution concerning fair and effective labour migration governance*

At its 106th Session (June 2017), the International Labour Conference conducted a general discussion on addressing the governance challenges for fair and effective labour migration,[479] with particular reference to labour migration governance at the national, bilateral, regional and interregional levels, and to fair recruitment.[480]

The ILO general discussion aimed at providing guidance to strengthen the ILO's work and impact in the field of labour migration, and to enhance the capacity of ministries of labour and employers' and workers' organizations to engage in dialogue and to influence evidence-based policy formulation and implementation of fair migration governance.[481]

The Conference discussed the benefits and risks inherent in labour migration and identified the key elements of fair and effective labour migration governance, the thematic areas that warrant special attention, and other priorities for ILO action.

The Conference adopted a resolution and conclusions that acknowledge that governance of labour migration requires a comprehensive, integrated and 'whole of government' approach nationally, and strong cooperation across migration corridors and regions. Areas warranting special attention by the ILO include international labour standards, skills, fair recruitment, data and statistics, social protection, freedom of association, temporary labour migration, irregular labour migration, bilateral and multilateral agreements, and collaboration with relevant institutions that deal with labour migration.

(v) *Resolution concerning the second recurrent discussion on fundamental principles and rights at work*

At its 106th Session (June 2017), the International Labour Conference conducted a second recurrent discussion on the strategic objective of fundamental principles and rights at work, in accordance with the follow-up to the ILO Declaration on Fundamental Principles and Rights at Work, 1998 and the ILO Declaration on Social Justice for a Fair Globalization, 2008, to consider how the Organization should respond to the realities and

---

[479] ILO: *Addressing governance challenges in a changing labour migration landscape*, Report IV, ILC, 106th Session, 2017, Geneva. Available at: http://www.ilo.org/ilc/ILCSessions/106/reports/reports-to-the-conference/WCMS_550269/lang--en/index.htm.

[480] ILO: *Fair migration: Setting an ILO agenda*, Report of the ILO Director General, Report I(B), ILC, 103rd Session, 2014, Geneva. Available at: http://www.ilo.org/ilc/ILCSessions/103/reports/reports-to-the-conference/WCMS_242879/lang--en/index.htm

[481] See ILO report of the Director-General, *Fair Migration: Setting an ILO Agenda*, https://www.ilo.org/wcmsp5/groups/public/---ed_norm/---relconf/documents/meetingdocument/wcms_242879.pdf.

needs of its members. The Conference adopted a resolution and conclusions containing a framework for action for the effective and universal respect, promotion and realization of fundamental principles and rights at work for the period 2017–23.

(vi) *Other resolutions adopted by the International Labour Conference*

The following resolutions were also adopted by the International Labour Conference:

- Resolution concerning the arrears of contributions of Kyrgyzstan.
- Resolution concerning the adoption of the Programme and Budget for 2018–19 and the allocation of the budget of income among member States.
- Resolution concerning the scale of assessments of contributions to the budget for 2018.
- Resolution concerning the composition of the Administrative Tribunal of the International Labour Organization.
- Resolution concerning the financial report and audited consolidated financial statements for the year ended 31 December 2016.

(*b*) The Standards Review Mechanism Tripartite Working Group

The Standards Review Mechanism Tripartite Working Group (SRM TWG)[482] held its third meeting in September 2017. During this meeting, the SRM TWG reviewed 19 international labour Conventions and Recommendations concerning occupational safety and health (general provisions and specific risks) and made corresponding recommendations. In addition, the SRM TWG adopted a three-classification system of "up to date", "requiring further action to ensure continued and future relevance" and "outdated" instruments for the purposes of its work in reviewing international labour Conventions and Recommendations.

In November 2017, the ILO Governing Body, on the basis of the recommendations of the SRM TWG, took a number of decisions.[483] In relation to the review of the 19 instruments on occupational safety and health, the Governing Body decided that eight instruments were classified as up to date, ten instruments were classified as requiring further action to ensure their continued and future relevance, and one instrument (Prevention of Industrial Accidents Recommendation, 1929 (No. 31) was classified as out of date. The Governing Body decided to place on the agenda of the 109th Session (2020) of the

---

[482] The Standards Review Mechanism is an in-built mechanism of the ILO standards policy, established by the Governing Body in 2011. It is part of a series of actions taken by the ILO to ensure that it has a clear, robust and up-to-date body of international labour standards serving as a global reference. The SRM operates through a working group composed of representatives of the ILO tripartite constituents. The mandate of the SRM Tripartite Working Group (SRM TWG) is to undertake a review of international labour standards and to make recommendations to the Governing Body on the status of the standards examined, the identification of gaps in coverage, including those requiring new standard and practical and time-bound action as appropriate.

[483] ILO Governing Body 331st Session, Geneva, 26 October-9 November 2017, Minutes GB.331/PV/Draft, para. 723 and "The Standards Initiative: Report of the third meeting of the Standards Review Mechanism Tripartite Working Group", GB.331/LILS/2.

Conference the item of the withdrawal of Recommendation No. 31.[484] In addition, the Governing Body requested the Office to prepare, for consideration for inclusion at the earliest dates possible in future agendas of the International Labour Conference, proposals for possible standard-setting items: on biological hazards and ergonomics, recognizing the regulatory gaps identified in that regard; on the consolidation of the instruments concerning chemical hazards; and on the revision of the instruments concerning guarding of machinery. The Governing Body also adopted the SRM TWG's recommendations on additional non-normative follow-up, including promotional campaigns and technical assistance on issues including asbestos and prevention of major industrial accidents, and the publication of technical guidelines.

(*c*) Guidance documents submitted to the Governing Body of the International Labour Office

(i) *Guidelines on Decent Work and Socially Responsible Tourism*

At its 331st Session (October 2017), the Governing Body of the ILO authorized the publication of the Guidelines on Decent Work and Socially Responsible Tourism, adopted by a meeting of experts in February 2017.[485] The guidelines serve as a reference document for ILO constituents and other stakeholders engaged in the design and implementation of interventions on the promotion of decent work and full and productive employment in the tourism sector with a view to enhancing its sustainability and contributing to the achievement of the Sustainable Development Goals. They are intended for use by all those who are engaged in promoting full and productive employment and decent work in the tourism sector at international, national, regional, local and enterprise level, including governments, policy-makers, employers' and workers' organizations, intergovernmental organizations and non-governmental organizations.

(ii) *Code of Practice on Safety and Health in Ports*

At its 329th Session (March 2017), the Governing Body of the ILO authorized the publication of the Code of Practice on Safety and Health in Ports, adopted by the Meeting of Experts in November 2016.[486]

The Code of Practice text revises and updates the 2005 edition of the ILO code of practice safety and health in ports. The Code is intended to be a concise set of recommendations based on good practice in the industry.

---

[484] ILO Governing Body 331st Session, Geneva, 26 October-9 November 2017, Minutes GB.331/PV/Draft, para. 28 and "Proposal for the withdrawal of the Prevention of Industrial Accidents Recommendation, 1929 (No. 31)", GB.331/INS/2(Add.)

[485] ILO Governing Body, 331st Session, Geneva, 26 October-9 November 2017, Minutes, GB.331/PV, para. 589. The text of the Guidelines on decent work and socially responsible tourism is available at https://www.ilo.org/wcmsp5/groups/public/---ed_dialogue/---sector/documents/normativeinstrument/wcms_546337.pdf

[486] ILO Governing Body, 329th Session, Geneva, 9–24 March 2017, Minutes, GB.329/PV, para. 512. The text of the Code of Practice on safety and health in ports (Revised 2016) is available at https://www.ilo.org/wcmsp5/groups/public/---ed_dialogue/---sector/documents/normativeinstrument/wcms_546257.pdf

(*d*) Special Tripartite Committee established under Article XIII of the Maritime Labour Convention, 2006 (MLC, 2006)

In March 2016, the Governing Body endorsed the establishment of a Working Group of the Special Tripartite Committee (STC) established under Article XIII of the Maritime Labour Convention, 2006 (MLC, 2006) to examine issues related to the protection of seafarers' wages when the seafarer is held captive on or off the ship as a result of acts such as piracy or armed robbery, and to prepare proposals including an amendment to the Code of the MLC, 2006, to address these issues; and to recommend improvements to the process for preparing proposals for amendments to the Code of the MLC, 2006, for consideration by the STC in accordance with article XV of the Convention and article 11 of the Standing Orders of the STC, to promote their earlier and fuller consideration by member States and representative organizations of seafarers and shipowners.

At is meeting in April 2017, the Working Group adopted a set of proposals in relation to the protection of seafarers' wages when the seafarer is held captive on or off the ship as a result of acts of piracy or armed robbery against ships. Concerning the issue of improvements to the process for preparing proposals for amendment to the Code of the MLC, 2006, the Working Group adopted a draft template and resolution.[487]

(*e*) Legal Advisory Services and Training

With respect to international labour standards, in 2017, the ILO provided technical assistance in reporting and other international labour standards related obligations, including capacity building, assistance with implementation and reform of national legislation, to 39 countries. Assistance included training on the content of selected international labour standards; research to generate information on the status of implementation of international labour standards, including legislative gap analyses; advice on elements that will enable tripartite constituents to take the relevant decisions aiming at full implementation; legal advice on the revision or drafting of legislation and regulations in the light of the supervisory bodies' comments; and strengthening the data collection and reporting capacity of tripartite constituents. The ILO also organised legal training courses at the interregional, regional, sub regional and national levels in collaboration with its International Training Centre in Turin.

(*f*) Committee on Freedom of Association

At its last meetings (March and June 2017), the Committee on Freedom of Association had before it more than 193 cases concerning 52 countries from all parts of the world, for which it presented interim or final conclusions, or for which the examination was adjourned pending the arrival of information from governments (381st and 382nd Reports). Many of these cases have been before the Committee on more than one occasion. Moreover, 66 new cases have been submitted to it since the last meeting of the Committee of Experts. The Committee on Freedom of Association has drawn the attention of the Committee of

---

[487] Final report, Meeting of the Working Group of the Special Tripartite Committee established under Article XIII of the Maritime Labour Convention, 2006 (MLC, 2006), STCMLC/WG/2017/5

Experts to the legislative aspects of Cases Nos 2694 (Mexico), 2723 (Fiji), 3019 (Paraguay), 3021 (Turkey), 3117 (El Salvador), 3148 (Ecuador), 3160 (Peru), 3172 (Bolivarian Republic of Venezuela), 3178 (Bolivarian Republic of Venezuela) and 3203 (Bangladesh).

(*g*) Representations submitted under article 24 of the ILO Constitution and complaints made under article 26 of the ILO Constitution

In 2017, the Governing Body considered the developments in 15 representations submitted under article 24 of the ILO Constitution by industrial associations of employers or workers, alleging that a member State that has ratified a Convention has failed to secure within its jurisdiction the effective observance of that Convention.

The Governing Body also considered the developments in three complaints (Guatemala, Qatar and the Bolivarian Republic of Venezuela) made under article 26 of the Constitution alleging that a member State that has ratified a Convention is not securing its effective observance.

2. Food and Agriculture Organization of the United Nations[488]

(*a*) Membership

As of 31 December 2017, the membership of the Food and Agricultural Organization of the United Nations (FAO) remained unchanged at 194 members, two associate members and one member organization.

(*b*) Constitutional and general legal matters

(i) *Governing Bodies*

The Governing Bodies of FAO comprise the Conference, the Council, the Programme Committee, the Finance Committee, the Committee on Constitutional and Legal Matters, the Technical Committees referred to in article V, paragraph 6 (*b*) of the Constitution and the Regional Conferences (*i.e.* for Africa, Asia and the Pacific, Europe, Latin America and the Caribbean, and the Near East).

In 2017, the 40th Session of the Conference was convened. Among a broad range of matters that it addressed, the Conference adopted Resolution 13/2017 concerning qualifications for the office of Independent Chairperson of the Council.[489] Reaffirming the validity and relevance of its previous Resolution 9/2009 on the same subject,[490] and recalling the recom-

[488] For official documents and more information on the Food and Agriculture Organization of the United Nations, see http://www.fao.org.

[489] Report of the 40th Session of the Conference (Rome, 8–13 July 2017), Resolution 13/2017, paragraph 80. The Conference amended its previous Resolution 9/2009, adopted at its 36th Session (Rome, 18–23 November 2009).

[490] See the Report of the 36th Session of the Conference (Rome, 18–23 November 2009), Resolution 9/2009 on the Implementation of the Immediate Plan of Action on the Independent Chairperson of the Council.

mendations in the Final Report of the Independent Review of FAO Governance Reforms,[491] the Conference amended paragraph 2) of its Resolution 9/2009 to include the "knowledge of the functioning of FAO Governing Bodies" among the qualifications that candidates should possess to be nominated for the office of the Independent Chairperson of the Council.

The Conference also adopted Resolution 15/2017 on the filing and recording of the FAO Constitution with the United Nations Secretariat further to a request made by the United Nations Treaty Section under Article 102 of the Charter of the United Nations. The matter was submitted to the Conference because there is no express provision under the FAO legal framework requiring or authorizing the registration or recording and filing of the FAO Constitution with the UN. The Conference authorized the Director General to transmit the FAO Constitution and related instruments to the United Nations Treaty Section for filing, recording and subsequent publication in the United Nations Treaty Series, as recommended by the Committee on Constitutional and Legal Matters (CCLM) at its 102nd Session.[492]

Moreover, the Conference adopted the proposed Amendment to Rule XXV paragraph 6 (*a*) of the General Rules of the Organization.[493] The amendment resulted in the elimination of "airmail" as a method of dispatch of the provisional agenda of the Council to member Nations and Associate members. The decision is part of the implementation of the FAO "PaperSmart" approach, which is in line with measures presently being introduced throughout the United Nations System to increase efficiency and accessibility and reduce the amount of paper used for official documentation and correspondence.

Finally, during 2017, a number of processes began which are likely to have constitutional and legal implications and which will be addressed by the FAO Governing Bodies in the course of 2018.

(ii) *Committee on Constitutional and Legal Matters*

During 2017, the 104th and 105th Sessions of the Committee on Constitutional and Legal Matters (CCLM) were held. During these sessions, the CCLM considered and reviewed a number of substantive constitutional matters and draft resolutions. These included the proposed Amendments to the Agreement for the Establishment of a Commission for Controlling the Desert Locust in the Central Region; the relevant Resolution was subsequently approved by the Council at its 156th Session in 2017.

---

[491] Report of the 39th Session of the Conference (Rome, 6–13 June 2015), Resolution 7/2015, and documents C 2015/26, Rev. 1 on Assessment of the Independent Review of FAO Governance Reforms and C 2015/25 on Independent Review of FAO Governance Reforms.

[492] Report of the 102nd Session of the CCLM (Rome, 14–16 March 2016), paragraph 14. The recommendation was endorsed by the Council at its 154th Session (Rome 30 May–3 June 2016) and submitted to the Conference for approval.

[493] Report of the 40th Session of the Conference (Rome, 3–8 July 2017), Resolution 14/2017. The proposal was reviewed by the CCLM at its 104th Session (Rome, 13–15 March 2017) and subsequently endorsed by the Council, at its 156th Session (Rome, 24–28 April 2017).

(*c*) Treaties, Commissions and other Statutory Bodies established under the auspices of the FAO

As of 31 December 2017, the FAO Director-General exercised Depositary functions in respect of seventeen multilateral treaties adopted under article XIV of the FAO Constitution and nineteen multilateral treaties concluded outside the framework of FAO.[494]

(i) *Entry into force of treaties and amendments thereto*

In 2017, no new treaties were adopted or entered into force. As noted at paragraph (*b*) ii above, amendments to the Agreement for the Establishment of a Commission for controlling the Desert Locust in the Central Region were approved and entered into force on 25 April 2017, aimed at enabling the Commission to strengthen its capacity to react in case of locust outbreaks, which constitutes a major concern for member countries of the Commission.

(ii) *Depositary actions*

During 2017, a total of 19 depositary actions concerning treaties deposited with the Director General of FAO by States were recorded. These actions related to the 1951 International Plant Protection Convention, the 1956 Plant Protection Agreement for the Asia and Pacific Region, the 1966 International Convention for the Conservation of Atlantic Tunas, the 1994 Convention for the Establishment of Lake Victoria Fisheries Organization, the 1991 Regional Convention on Fisheries Cooperation Among African States Bordering the Atlantic Ocean, the 2000 Agreement for the Establishment of the International Organization for the Development of Fisheries and Aquaculture in Europe (EUROFISH), the 2001 International Treaty on Plant Genetic Resources for Food and Agriculture, the 2006 Southern Indian Ocean Fisheries Agreement, and the 2009 Agreement on Port State Measures to Prevent, Deter and Eliminate Illegal, Unreported and Unregulated Fishing.[495]

(*d*) FAO's digital strategy and use of cloud-based solutions

In the course of 2017, the FAO approved a new Digital Strategy, which included—among other things—the use of cloud-based services for storage and/or processing of some the FAO data. In addition to its existing mechanisms for addressing potential risks (the conduct of ex-ante risk assessments on the proposed solutions from the perspective of privileges and immunities, IT security and data protection), the FAO developed a standard "Cloud Solutions" Annex to be appended to its General Terms and Conditions for Services for contracts with cloud computing service providers. The Annex aims to

[494] This does not include the FAO Constitution, bilateral agreements adopted under article 15 of the International Treaty on Plant Genetic Resources for Food and Agriculture and treaties that are no longer in force.

[495] Information on depositary actions regarding multilateral treaties adopted pursuant article XIV of the FAO Constitution and their status is available at: http://www.fao.org/legal/treaties/treaties-under-article-xiv/en/. Information on depositary actions regarding multilateral treaties concluded outside the FAO framework in respect of which the FAO Director-General exercises depositary functions and their status is available at: http://www.fao.org/legal/treaties/treaties-outside-fao-framework/en/.

introduce mandatory conditions addressing the specific risks arising from the use of cloud services (for example, national laws related to data disclosure).

(*e*) Information provided by FAO to, and in collaboration with, other United Nations System entities (LEGN)

The FAO Legal Office continued the work on contract farming providing guidance to farmers and their organizations as well as to national regulators. In 2017, FAO published the "Legal aspects of contract farming agreements—Synthesis of the UNIDROIT/FAO/IFAD Legal Guide on Contract Farming", which summarizes the findings of the UNIDROIT/FAO/IFAD 2015 Legal Guide on Contract Farming by in non-technical language. In addition, FAO published two briefs, one aimed at farmers and one at regulators. Together with technical colleagues, the Legal Office co-organized regional and national workshops on the legal and economic aspects of contract farming in Laos, Ethiopia, Albania and Sri Lanka. In collaboration with the International Institute for Sustainable Development (IISD), the Legal Office contributed to the creation of model contracts for contract farming operations.

In 2017, FAO Legal Office started a collaboration with UNEP, the Commonwealth and UNFCCC in the development of a climate change legal toolkit; an online platform combining a legislative database with an interactive assessment process for national policy makers. Within the same year, a beta version of the toolkit was completed in anticipation of FAO's contribution to the development of a module on agriculture that combines agriculture, fisheries and forestry legislation.

FAO also commenced a broad study on economic, environmental and social sustainability in agriculture and natural resource law in collaboration with UNEP, while UNEP commenced a study focusing on sustainable land management in collaboration with FAO.

FAO Legal Office supported "training of trainers" activities led by the Secretariat of the International Plant Protection Convention (IPPC), a FAO treaty, on the application of a Phytosanitary Capacity Evaluation tool (PCE).

In addition, FAO collaborated with the World Organization for Animal Health (OIE) in the preparation of a programme for joint activities in the area of veterinary legislation.

FAO has been working with United Nations Environment since 2010 to develop guidance on the role of national legislation in addressing chemicals and pesticides based on the recommendations of the International Code of Conduct on Pesticide Management and its implementing Guidelines. In 2017, FAO provided substantial input for the development of implementing Guidelines on chemicals legislation.

During 2017, FAO also continued its collaboration with the World Health Organization (WHO) and the OIE in the development of tripartite resources on Antimicrobial Resistance (AMR), including Guidelines for the Assessment of National legislation related to AMR.

FAO cooperated with the Office of the United Nations High Commissioner for Human Rights (UNHCHR) and academic institutions in creating awareness on the human rights-based approach to the governance and development of small-scale fisheries, and its relationship with food security and the Sustainable Development Goals (SDGs). To this end, two side events were organised within the annual sessions of the Committee on World Food Security and the Maritime Research Conference.

An EU-funded Programme on Sustainable Wildlife Management was launched in 2017, at the initiative of the African, Caribbean and Pacific Group of States (ACP) Secretariat. This Programme is jointly managed by a consortium of partners comprising FAO, the Centre de coopération internationale en recherche agronomique pour le développement (CIRAD), the Centre for International Forestry Research (CIFOR) and the Wildlife Conservation Society (WCS). The FAO Legal Office is leading the legal activities under the Programme, supporting the development of legal frameworks that safeguard the rights of wildlife-dependent communities and individuals along the wild meat value chain, prevent the depletion of wildlife resources, and generate long-term health and economic benefits.

FAO also started a collaboration with the United Nations Office on Drugs and Crime (UNODC) in relation to Illegal Unreported and Unregulated (IUU) fishing, wildlife crime and crimes relating to or associated with fishing activities (*e.g.* Document fraud, trafficking, etc.). This collaboration covers legislative reviews, the delivery of technical assistance and the planning of awareness raising events.

FAOLEX—an online repository of national legislation and policies relating to FAO's mandate which is administered and maintained by LEGN—enhanced its existing data-sharing agreements by syndicating its content to additional websites managed by external partners, notably UrbanLex (http://urbanlex.unhabitat.org/) by UN-Habitat, and CoopLex (http://cooplex.coop/) by the International Co-operative Alliance.

(*f*) Legislative assistance (LEGN)

In its effort to build a world without hunger, FAO provides technical legal assistance in the drafting of legal instruments, the formulation of model laws, legislative reviews, setting-up of implementation infrastructure and oversight mechanism, strengthening of institutional frameworks, and the development of practical legal tools. The Development Law Branch (LEGN) of the FAO Legal Office (LEG) continued to fulfil its mandate to provide legal advice and legislative assistance on sustainable agriculture and management of natural resources to FAO member Nations. To this end, LEGN supported information sharing, carried out legal research, contributed to capacity development, and offered support to the development and implementation of international instruments. In 2017, LEGN provided legal support to over 80 national, regional and global projects. Under these projects, LEGN provided technical legal assistance in:

- 47 countries and territories on animal and plant health and production, food safety and quality. These include 12 on animal health and production,[496] 11 on food safety,[497]

[496] Mongolia, Suriname, Georgia, West Bank and Gaza Strip, Samoa, Barbados, Ghana, Kenya, Djibouti, Somalia, Cote D'Ivoire and Laos.

[497] West Bank and Gaza Strip, Malawi, Nepal, Bangladesh, Sao Tome and Principe, Madagascar, Micronesia, Tonga, Samoa, Honduras and Barbados.

8 on phytosanitary legislation,[498] 5 countries on antimicrobial resistance,[499] 5 on organic production,[500] 3 on pesticides[501] and 3 on seed legislation;[502]

- 40 countries on fisheries, including 20 on the implementation of the Port States Measures Agreement (PSMA),[503] 9 on illegal unreported and unregulated (IUU) fishing,[504] and 4 on sustainable small-scale fisheries;[505]
- 15 countries on forestry[506] and 4 on sustainable wildlife management;[507]
- 9 countries on food security and nutrition, including 4 on the right to food,[508] 3 on food security[509] and 2 on school food and nutrition;[510]
- 5 countries on the implementation of the Voluntary Guidelines for the Responsible Governance of Land, Forests and Fisheries in the context of national food security (VGGTs);[511]
- 3 countries on the legal aspects of decent rural youth employment.[512]

Selected examples of legislative assistance by FAO are as follows:

- The FAO Legal Office is providing legal services in relation to regulatory frameworks to address antimicrobial resistance (AMR). Research is being conducted in the various legal areas that could have an impact on AMR, including comparative analysis of legislation on veterinary medicinal products, pesticides, food safety, feed, aquatic and terrestrial animal health and production, environment and waste, and water. The analysis of legal instruments relevant for AMR was supported in five countries across Asia and Africa, providing the Governments with potential entry-points for regulatory intervention.
- LEGN was part of a multidisciplinary team of FAO specialists in fisheries, aquaculture and international law which provided support to the Latin American and Caribbean Parliament (PARLATINO) in the adoption of the world's first Model Law on Small-Scale Fisheries. The Model Law integrates *inter alia* FAO's Code of Conduct for

---

[498] Georgia, West Bank and Gaza Strip, Uzbekistan, Ukraine, Madagascar, Somalia, Barbados and Nicaragua.

[499] Ghana, Kenya, Tanzania, Zimbabwe and Cambodia.

[500] Uzbekistan, Azerbaijan, Kazakhstan, Russia and Tajikistan.

[501] Cape Verde, Guinea Bissau and Sao Tome and Principe.

[502] Azerbaijan, Mongolia, Uzbekistan.

[503] Bahamas, Cambodia, Costa Rica, Cuba, Ecuador, Gabon, Guinea, Guyana, Mozambique, Myanmar, Palau, Papua New Guinea, Somalia, South Africa, Sri Lanka, Sudan, Thailand, Tonga, Vanuatu.

[504] Cambodia, Costa Rica, Ecuador, Papua New Guinea, Sri Lanka, Thailand, St. Vincent and the Grenadines, Trinidad and Tobago.

[505] Bahamas, Cambodia, Chile, and Costa Rica.

[506] Cote d'Ivoire, Madagascar, Kenya, Timor-Leste, Rwanda, Democratic Republic of Congo, Kenya, Pakistan, Papua New Guinea, Jordan, Seychelles, Comoros, Guinea Bissau, Guinea Conakry, and Mauritania.

[507] Georgia, Democratic Republic of Congo, Republic of Congo and Gabon.

[508] Costa Rica, Panama, Uruguay and Nepal.

[509] Cape Verde, Panama and Dominican Republic.

[510] Guatemala and Sao Tome and Principe.

[511] Gabon, Republic of Congo, Macedonia, Ukraine and Mongolia.

[512] Guatemala, Senegal, and Uganda.

Responsible Fisheries, the Voluntary Guidelines for Securing Sustainable Small-Scale Fisheries in the Context of Food Security and Poverty Eradication, and the Voluntary Guidelines on the Responsible Governance of Tenure of Land, Fisheries and Forests in the Context of National Food Security. In addition, in 2017, LEGN started to develop standard guidelines on legislation to address climate change in the context of food and agriculture. These activities are being carried out in collaboration with the newly established Climate, Biodiversity, Land and Water (CBL) Department, and take into account the developments at the 23rd Session of the Conference of Parties to the United Nations Framework Convention on Climate Change (UNFCCC) recognizing the role of agriculture and food security in the international climate agenda.

(*g*) Legislative studies, Legal Papers Online and other technical papers (LEGN)

In 2017, the FAO Legal Office published several legislative studies, Legal Papers and collaborated in the preparation of other technical papers, as reflected in the Bibliography. The FAO also continued to improve and expand the content and functionalities of FAOLEX (http://faolex.fao.org/) with the addition of 9,100 legislative texts and 950 policies.

3. United Nations Educational, Scientific and Cultural Organization[513]

(*a*) International regulations

(i) *Entry into force of instruments previously adopted*

In 2017, no multilateral conventions or agreements adopted under the auspices of the United Nations Educational, Scientific and Cultural Organization (UNESCO) entered into force.

(ii) *Instruments adopted by the General Conference of UNESCO at its 39th session (30–14 November 2017)*[514]

As requested in its 37th session (2013), the 39th session of the General Conference adopted the *Recommendation on Science and Scientific Researchers* (39 C/Resolution 85) which supersedes the 1974 Recommendation on the Status of Scientific Researchers.

At its 39th session, the General Conference adopted also the *Declaration of Ethical Principles in relation to Climate Change* (39 C/Resolution 86).

---

[513] For official documents and more information on the United Nations Educational, Scientific and Cultural Organization, see http://www.unesco.org.

[514] The texts of all UNESCO standard-setting instruments adopted by the General Conference, as well as the list of States parties to the conventions and agreements, can be found on UNESCO's website at the following address: http://www.unesco.org/legal_instruments.

(iii) *Proposals concerning the preparation of new instruments*

The General Conference, at its 39th session, invited the Director-General to continue the process of elaborating the draft global convention on the recognition of higher education qualifications and submit to it at its 40th session the final progress report and draft text of that global convention, for adoption (39 C/Resolution 81).

Following a preliminary study submitted to the 201st session of the Executive Board (April 2017), the 39th session of the General Conference invited the Director-General to submit to it, at its 40th session (2019), a draft text of a recommendation on open educational resources (39 C/Resolution 44).

(iv) *Proposals concerning the preparation of revised instruments*

At its 39th session, the General Conference decided to convene during the 2018–2019 biennium an international conference of States with a view to view to examining and adopting amendments to the 1974 Regional Convention on the Recognition of Studies, Diplomas and Degrees in Higher Education in Latin America and the Caribbean (39 C/Resolution 82).

The 39th session of the General Conference also requested the Director-General to submit to the Executive Board at its 204th session (April 2018) a proposal for the convening of an international conference of States for the adoption of the revised text of the 1978 Convention on the Recognition of Studies, Diplomas and Degrees in Higher Education in the Arab States (39 C/Resolution 83).

(*b*) Human Rights

Examination of cases and questions concerning the exercise of Human Rights coming within UNESCO's fields of competence.

The Committee on Conventions and Recommendations met in private sessions at UNESCO Headquarters from 19 to 21 April 2017 and from 4 to 6 October 2017 in order to examine communications which had been transmitted to it in accordance with decision 104 EX/3.3 of the Executive Board.

At its April 2017 session, the Committee examined 12 communications of which three were examined with a view to determining their admissibility or otherwise, six were examined as to their substance and three were examined for the first time. The examination of the other 12 communications were deferred. The Committee presented its report to the Executive Board at its 201st session.

At its October 2017 session, the Committee examined 12 communications of which five were examined with a view to determining their admissibility or otherwise, six were examined as to their substance and one was examined for the first time. Three communications were struck from the list because they were considered as having been settled. The examination of the other nine communications were deferred. The Committee presented its report to the Executive Board at its 202nd session.

4. World Health Organization[515]

(a) Institutional and administrative matters

(i) *Election of new Director-General*

At the 70th World Health Assembly, Dr. Tedros Adhanom Ghebreyesus was appointed as Director-General of the World Health Organization (WHO), following the conduct of a secret ballot. This was the first time that the revised procedural framework concerning the election of the WHO Director-General was applied. One of the main characteristics of the new framework is that the World Health Assembly appoints the Director-General from a slate of three candidates nominated by the Executive Board. In this context, the 70th World Health Assembly, also decided to use a paper-based voting system for the appointment of the Director-General and decided, in accordance with Rule 119 of the Rules of Procedure of the World Health Assembly, to adopt changes to its Rules of Procedure to improve the efficiency of paper-based voting. (WHA70(6))

(ii) *Amendments to Basic Documents and Staff Rules*

The Executive Board at its 140th session adopted two resolutions with respect to the proposed amendments to the Staff Regulations and amendments to the Staff Rules, with effect from 1 January 2017: concerning the remuneration of staff in the professional and higher categories, concerning definitions, recruitment incentive, salaries, dependants' allowances, the mobility incentive and related allowances and grants, recruitment policies, assignment to duty, within-grade increase, home leave, the failure to exercise entitlement, expenses on death, abolition of post and Appendix 1 of the Staff Rules. Further the World Health Assembly confirmed the amendment of Appendix 2 of the Staff Rules concerning the education grant, travel of staff members and their spouses and children. (EB140.R8)

The Executive Board also recommended to the 70th World Health Assembly to adopt a resolution regarding adjustments in the remuneration of staff in ungraded posts, with effect of 1 January 2017. (EB140.R9) The 70th World Assembly adopted the recommendations of the Executive Board with regard to remuneration of staff in ungraded posts and of the Director-General. (WHA70.10)

(iii) *Programme budget 2018/2019*

In 2017, the World Health Assembly approved the programme of work as outlined in the proposed programme budget 2018—2019 and the budget of US$ 4421.5 million for the financial year 2018—2019. (WHA70.5)

---

[515] For official documents and more information on the World Health Organization, see https://www.who.int.

(*b*) Other Normative Developments and Activities

(i) *International Health Regulations (2005) ("IHR (2005)")*

The 15 June 2017 marked the 10th anniversary of the entry into force of the International Health Regulations (IHR) (2005).

In 2017, the WHO Director-General convened, in accordance with article 47 of the IHR (2005), the 12th, 13th, 14th and 15th meetings of the Emergency Committee concerning ongoing events and context involving the transmission and international spread of poliovirus. The public health emergency of international concern declared for poliovirus in 2014 continued in 2017 and temporary recommendations were updated following each meeting.

In decision WHA70(11), the 70th World Health Assembly requested the Director-General:

(*a*) to develop, in full consultation with member States, including through the regional committees, a draft five-year global strategic plan to improve public health preparedness and response (…) and

(*b*) to continue to pursue and strengthen efforts to support member States in the full implementation of the IHR (2005), including through building their core public health capacities.

The above-mentioned draft five-year global strategic plan was developed and published on the public WHO website on 11 December 2017 and includes a draft decision for the consideration of the World Health Assembly to endorse the plan and to continue to report annually to the Assembly on the implementation of the Regulations using the self-assessment reporting tool.[516]

(ii) *Supporting National Law Reform Efforts on WHO-mandated Topics*

During 2017, WHO Headquarters, Regional and Country Offices have continued to provide advice to member States on the development, evaluation and implementation of laws related to health. In particular, technical support was provided to member States in the areas of universal health coverage, infectious disease control, food safety, tobacco control, the promotion of healthy diets, substance abuse, mental health, urban health and the elimination of unsafe abortion.

In particular, WHO was involved in the revision of immigration law in China to ensure non-discrimination based on a person's HIV status. WHO also provided support in the introduction of laws on taxing sugar-sweetened beverages including in the Philippines, Brunei Darussalam and Sri-Lanka. WHO continued to engage in the development of national action plans such as the National Food Policy and Action Plan for Antimicrobial Resistance for 2017—2022 in the Maldives. WHO further supported the Philippines, Palau and Sierra Leone in their efforts to reform legislation related to mental health.

(iii) *Noncommunicable Diseases*

In 2017 Dr. Tedros Adhanom Ghebreyesus, Director-General of the World Health Organization (WHO), announced the establishment of a new High-level Global Commission on Noncommunicable Diseases (NCDs).

---

[516] See document EB 142/10.

The Montevideo Roadmap 2018–2030 on NCDs as a Sustainable Development Priority was adopted by the member States represented at the WHO Global Conference on NCDs which took place from 18 to 20 October 2017 and was hosted by the President of Uruguay.

(iv) *Cooperation with other agencies and organizations*

The World Health Assembly agreed to a five-year action plan under which WHO will collaborate with the International Labour Organization and the Organization for Economic Cooperation and Development in the area of health employment and inclusive economic growth. (WHA70.6)

WHO also provided technical input in the drafting of the United Nations Human Rights Council Resolution on Mental Health and Human Rights (A/HRC/36/L.25) which was adopted by the Council in September 2017.

The WHO collaborates with the Secretariat of the Convention on Biological Diversity through a joint work programme. The Nagoya Protocol on Access to Genetic Resources and Fair and Equitable Sharing of Benefits Arising from their Utilization, which entered into force in 2014, is of particular relevance to the work of WHO. In January 2017, the Secretariat provided a study on the public health implications of the implementation of the Nagoya Protocol to the Executive Board, which the Board noted. (EB140(5)). The World Health Assembly, at its 70th session, requested the Director-General, among other things, to continue to support "the strengthening of regulatory capacities" and "to continue consultations with the secretariat of the Convention on Biological Diversity and other relevant international organizations" (WHA70(10)).

5. International Monetary Fund[517]

(*a*) Membership

(i) *Accession to membership*

No new countries became members of the International Monetary Fund (IMF) in 2017. As of 31 December 2017, the membership of the IMF consisted of 189 member countries.

(ii) *Status and Obligations under Article VIII or Article XIV of the IMF's Articles of Agreement*

Under article VIII, Sections 2, 3, and 4 of the IMF's Articles of Agreement, members of the IMF may not, without the IMF's approval (i) impose restrictions on the making of payments and transfers for current international transactions; or (ii) engage in any discriminatory currency arrangements or multiple currency practices. Notwithstanding these provisions, pursuant to article XIV, Section 2 of the IMF's Articles of Agreement, when a member joins the IMF, it may notify the IMF that it intends to avail itself of the transitional arrangements under Article XIV of the IMF's Articles of Agreement that allow the member to maintain and adapt to changing circumstances the restrictions on

[517] For documents and more information on the International Monetary Fund, see http://www.imf.org.

payments and transfers for current international transactions that were in effect on the date on which it became a member. Article XIV of the IMF's Articles of Agreement does not, however, permit a member, after it joins the IMF, to introduce new restrictions on the making of payments and transfers for current international transactions without the IMF's approval. The total number of countries that have accepted the obligations of article VIII, Sections 2, 3, and 4, as of December 31, 2017, was 171. Eighteen countries continued to avail themselves of the transitional arrangements under article XIV.

(iii) *Overdue Financial Obligations to the IMF*

As of December 31, 2017, members with protracted arrears (*i.e.*, financial obligations that are overdue by six months or more) involving the general resources of the IMF were Somalia and Sudan. In addition, Somalia and Sudan have protracted overdue Trust Fund and/or Structural Adjustment Facility obligations not involving the general resources of the IMF. Article XXVI, Section 2(*a*) of the IMF's Articles of Agreement provides that if "a member fails to fulfil any of its obligations under this Agreement, the [IMF] may declare the member ineligible to use the general resources of the [IMF]." Such declarations of ineligibility were in place at end-December 2017 with respect to Somalia and Sudan, whose arrears are subject to sanctions under article XXVI.

(*b*) Key Policy Decisions of the IMF

In 2017, the IMF took steps to move ahead with a number of major policy reforms that would allow it to meet the evolving needs of its members and to adjust to changes in the global economy, as follows:

(i) *Governance Issues in Member Countries*

On July 21, 2017, in response to the International Monetary and Financial Committee's request to review IMF engagement on governance issues, the Executive Board of IMF discussed a staff paper on "The Role of the Fund in Governance Issues—Review of the Guidance Note—Preliminary Considerations". Against a growing recognition that systemic corruption can undermine prospects for delivering sustainable and inclusive growth, the paper assessed the extent to which corruption has been appropriately addressed in the IMF's work in member countries in both economic reviews and Fund-supported programs. The paper examined the implementation of the 1997 Guidance Note on The Role of the IMF in Governance Issues in the period since the last such review was conducted in 2004.

In general, the review found that considerable progress has been made in implementing the 1997 Guidance Note. Executive Directors appreciated the various initiatives introduced by the Fund to promote good governance in member countries, including the Fund's extensive work on helping countries to improve public financial management; establish standards and codes in fiscal and monetary areas; conduct financial sector assessments; strengthen central bank governance; improve the quality, timeliness, and transparency of statistical data; and assess frameworks for anti-money laundering and combating the financing of terrorism. They noted that, while these efforts were not specifically targeted at corruption, they played an important role in helping to limit opportunities for corruption.

The review also found that there has been significant coverage of corruption issues in many country reports, and, where countries were implementing Fund-supported programs, Fund engagement was even deeper and more granular.

The review also pointed to several areas where Fund engagement could be strengthened, including: (1) establishing a better method of assessing the extent of corruption and its macroeconomic impact; (2) developing more concrete and granular policy advice to help governments tackle corruption; (3) providing more candid assessments on the scale and cost of corruption when it is undermining macroeconomic performance; and (4) ensuring evenhanded treatment of corruption issues across countries. Directors noted that, despite progress under the 1997 Guidance Note, there remains significant scope to strengthen Fund engagement, including regarding the coverage of corruption in Fund engagement, which has varied significantly across countries, even among those facing broadly comparable corruption challenges. They noted that, while such cross-country differences may be justified (for example, reflecting different policy priorities and concerns), it is important to adhere to the principle of uniformity of treatment, including by justifying the basis for focusing on corruption in individual cases in light of country-specific circumstances. To address the identified areas, Directors called for a follow-up staff paper with proposals for more specific guidance, for the Executive Board to consider in 2018.

(ii) *Use of Third-Party Indicators*

On November 10, 2017, the Executive Board of the IMF discussed a staff paper on "Use of Third-Party Indicators in Fund Reports". The use of comparative indicators developed by other organizations ("third-party indicators" or "TPIs"), already used in core areas of Fund surveillance, is increasing in emerging macro-critical areas to inform country-specific analysis across time and cross-country comparisons, measuring concepts such as business environment, competitiveness, quality of governance, as well as progress toward social development goals.

Executive Directors took note of recent experiences in the Fund and other international organizations, which indicated that TPIs have been useful in facilitating cross-country comparisons, identifying evidence to help inform analysis and complement assessments in areas where an institution may not gather its own primary data. While Directors recognized that staff's use of TPIs is consistent with the Executive Board's guidance in areas where internal expertise is lacking or limited, they noted that the varied qualities of TPIs currently used by staff present challenges and risks to the Fund's credibility.

Directors welcomed the proposed framework, which consists of principles-based guidance for staff; an "Indicators Digest" as an internal, centralized quality assessment database; and an internal review process to ensure best practice in Fund reports. Directors noted that this approach provides room for staff judgment and flexibility to make progress on surveillance priorities while avoiding flawed analysis and reputational risks. Directors endorsed the three complementary principles for best practice—(i) transparency in the selection and interpretation of the indicators; (ii) robustness, to promote TPIs as one of many inputs and use of multiple indicators and sources to measure similar concepts; and (iii) presentation of the views of stakeholders. In applying these principles, staff would consider a number of factors, including the assurances of integrity, methodological soundness, accuracy, reliability, and accessibility of TPIs, and compiler's characteristics (*e.g.*, is it an international organization with a broad membership). In applying the framework for use of TPIs, Directors attached particular importance to their judicious and evenhanded use based on macro-criticality, and considerations of country-specific contexts in interpreting results. They stressed that TPIs should not replace—but rather supplement—an open, candid, robust, and well-documented discussion with the authorities.

(iii) *Recent Trends in Correspondent Banking Relationships*

Following up on a Staff Discussion Note on the withdrawal of correspondent banking relationships (CBRs) issued in June 2016, the Executive Board of the IMF discussed the staff report "Recent Trends in Correspondent Banking Relationships-Further Considerations" on April 12, 2017.

Executive Directors emphasized the importance of CBRs in facilitating global trade and remittances and supporting economic growth and development. They also underlined the importance of strengthened, coordinated, and collective efforts on the part of all stakeholders, and highlighted the important role of the Fund through its surveillance and capacity development activities and its efforts to facilitate international dialogue.

Despite some withdrawal in CBRs, Directors noted that cross border payments have generally remained stable, and economic activity has been largely unaffected. However, in a limited number of countries, particularly small and fragile states, there has been a concentration of cross border flows through fewer CBRs or alternative arrangements. Directors noted that the drivers of CBR withdrawal are multiple, interrelated, and vary case by case.

Directors supported a continued active role for the Fund to monitor risks and advise its membership on policies to help tackle the adverse impacts from CBR pressures, and endorsed the multipronged approach to support member countries outlined in the staff paper, including surveillance and data collection, FSAP assessments, and capacity development. Directors noted that a severe loss of CBRs stemming from policymaking challenges across a range of areas could require deeper Fund engagement. In such cases involving balance of payments difficulties, a Fund supported program could be considered to help restore external and domestic imbalances and would be expected to take place within existing lending frameworks.

(iv) *Ensuring Financial Stability in Countries with Islamic Banking*

On February 3, 2017, the Executive Board of the IMF held its first formal discussion on Islamic banking (IB) and adopted a set of proposals on the role that the Fund should play in this area. These proposals, and the case for adopting them, are contained in the staff paper "Ensuring Financial Stability in Countries with Islamic Banking" and the accompanying country case studies paper. Further work on this topic is expected in 2018.

The IMF has been providing technical advice to member countries on IB issues for the past 20 years and has been cooperating with relevant standards setters and international organizations on efforts to develop supplementary standards for IB in areas that are not covered by existing international standards. IB continues to grow rapidly, in size and complexity, contributing to financial deepening and inclusion in many countries. However, Executive Directors noted that the growth of IB and its complexities pose new challenges and unique risks for regulatory and supervisory authorities. Against this background, Directors called for stronger efforts to establish a policy framework and environment that promote financial stability and sound development of IB, particularly for countries in which IB has become systemically important.

Directors emphasized the importance of having in place robust IB-specific resolution regimes and other financial safety nets for countries in which IB operates. Noting the slow progress achieved in these areas, they underscored the importance of additional work in collaboration with relevant international bodies on the design of legal regimes and institutional arrangements for effective IB resolution, deposit insurance schemes and anti-money laundering and combating the financing of terrorism, as well as adapting the conventional lender-of-last-resort framework to cover IB. Directors also agreed on the importance of the availability of high-quality liquid assets for IB, and having in place relevant central banking liquidity facilities and instruments, Directors concurred that the emergence in recent years of hybrid financial products in Islamic banking may have brought some benefits, but also raise financial stability concerns.

(v) *Establishment of the Policy Coordination Instrument*

On July 14, 2017, the Executive Board of the IMF approved the establishment of a new non-financing Policy Coordination Instrument (PCI) to further strengthen the Global Financial Safety Net (GFSN) and enhance the effectiveness of the Fund's toolkit. The decision follows a series of discussions by the Executive Board on the adequacy of the GFSN.

The new instrument, which is a form of technical assistance, is designed to help countries unlock financing from official and private donors and creditors, as well as demonstrate a commitment to a reform agenda. It will enable a policy dialogue between the Fund and countries, monitoring of economic developments and policies, as well as Board endorsement of those policies. Executive Directors generally agreed that policies supported under the PCI should meet the standard required under an upper credit tranche (UCT) financial arrangement with the Fund. The key design features draw on fund financing arrangements and the Policy Support Instrument, with some differences. These include no eligibility criteria (it is open to the full membership), a more flexible review schedule, and a review-based approach for monitoring of conditionality. Directors generally agreed that a review-based approach to monitoring program conditionality could help alleviate stigma and streamline the review process while preserving the UCT standard and the Executive Board's judgment regarding its decision to complete a review.

(vi) *Cooperation with Other Organizations*

a. Collaboration Between Regional Financing Arrangements and the Fund

On July 26, 2017, and as part of the broader discussion on strengthening the Global Financial Safety Net (GFSN), the Executive Board of the IMF discussed a paper called "Collaboration Between Regional Financing Arrangements and the Fund". The paper proposed modalities for collaboration—across capacity development, surveillance, and lending. Building on past co-lending experience, it outlined operational principles to help guide future co-lending between the Fund and the various Regional Financing Arrangements (RFAs).

Executive Directors agreed that stronger Fund-RFA collaboration would bring substantial mutually-reinforcing benefits, including promoting early engagement, exploiting complementarities, increasing the firepower, and mitigating contagion. Directors underlined the importance of sharing technical information between the Fund and RFAs, conditional on reciprocity and confidentiality assurances. Directors also concurred that a more structured dialogue with RFAs would help enhance transparency, predictability, and effectiveness of collaboration in an increasingly multi-layered GFSN, with the Fund at its centre.

Directors endorsed six operational principles to guide future Fund-RFA collaboration: respect for the independence of the Fund and the RFA, engagement by each institution in accordance with its mandate and technical expertise, early and ongoing cooperation, consistency between the institutions in supporting single program belonging to the member country, even-handedness in engagement across RFAs and between RFA members and other Fund members, and maintenance of the Fund's preferred creditor status. They welcomed the fact that these principles were grounded in actual Fund-RFA co-financing experience and, at the same time, are generally in line with the existing high-level G20 principles. Directors noted that co-financing by the Fund would proceed only when the member's program, including the macroeconomic framework and conditionality, is consistent with the Fund's lending policies, and that the Fund's role in program design and monitoring would be independent of the share of overall financing it provides.

b. Transmittal Policy: The Exchange of Documents Between the Fund and Other Organizations

On November 10, 2017, the Executive Board of the IMF amended the Transmittal Policy to expand access to IMF documents by other international organizations and currency unions.

Under the Transmittal Policy, originally adopted in 1990, the Fund has transmitted certain Executive Board documents to other international organizations and currency unions. However, some gaps in this framework had emerged over time, resulting in similar organizations having uneven access to Fund documents. The amendments adopted in 2017 seek to ensure a consolidated, even-handed approach to the transmittal of Fund documents to international organizations and currency unions. In particular, international organizations may now receive a wider range of documents, including complete documentation of Fund-supported programs, shortly after consideration by the Executive Board. Currency union central banks and executive bodies may now receive a wide range of Board documents shortly after issuance to the Executive Board and prior to Board consideration.

6. International Civil Aviation Organization[518]

(*a*) Depositary actions in relation to multilateral air law instruments

A total of 88 depositary actions by States were recorded during 2017. A chronological record of States that signed, ratified, acceded, accepted or adhered to multilateral air law instruments during 2017 can be found on the website[519] of the International Civil Aviation Organization (ICAO) as part of the Legal Affairs and External Relations Bureau's Treaty Collection, where status lists of international air law instruments are continually updated.

(*b*) Activities of ICAO in the legal field

(i) *Remotely Piloted Aircraft*

A study was presented to the 36th Session of the Legal Committee (30 November to 3 December 2015) on the issue of liability as it relates to Remotely Piloted Aircraft (RPA), which concluded that the existing international legal liability regime in its current state is legally adequate.

The Committee concluded that other aspects of RPA operations might still merit continued consideration of an international framework and expressed broad support for a questionnaire to States, both as a means of gathering information on national RPAs legislation, and as a means to identify potentially relevant international legal issues. This questionnaire (State letter LE 4/63-16/77) was distributed on 29 August 2016 and called on States to submit their responses by 31 October 2016. These responses will be analysed and a report presented to the 37th Session of the Legal Committee in September 2018.

(ii) *Determination of the Status of an Aircraft—Civil/State*

At the fifth Meeting of its 203rd Session in November 2014, the Council agreed to add the item "Determination of the status of an aircraft—Civil/State" to the Work Programme of the Legal Committee. During the 36th Session of the Legal Committee, in response to working paper LC/36 WP/2-6—State/Civil Aircraft Definition and Its Impact on Aviation, the Committee concluded that a questionnaire should be sent out inquiring about the practical problems States are facing due to the classification of "Civil/State aircraft".

Consistent with the Committee's recommendations, the questionnaire (State Letter LE 4/50-16/86) was distributed on 1 November 2016 and called on States to submit their responses by 1 February 2017. These responses will be analysed and reported to the 37th Session of the Legal Committee in September 2018.

---

[518] For official documents and more information on the international Civil Aviation Organization, see https://www.icao.int.

[519] https://www.icao.int/secretariat/legal/Pages/ChronologicalRecord.aspx.

(iii) *Settlement of Differences*

a. Brazil and United States (2016)

On 2 December 2016, Brazil (the Applicant) presented to ICAO an Application and Memorial pursuant to article 84 of the Convention on International Civil Aviation (Chicago Convention), seeking a decision of the Council on a disagreement with the United States (the Respondent) relating "to the interpretation and application of the Convention and its Annexes following a collision, on September 29th 2006, of the air carrier Boeing 737-8EH operating a regular flight GLO 1907, and air jet Legacy EMB-135BJ operating a flight by ExcelAire Services Inc."

On 27 March 2017, the Respondent submitted a Statement of preliminary objection to the Application. On 19 May 2017, the Applicant submitted Comments on the Statement of preliminary objection. After hearing the parties, the Council, at the ninth Meeting of its 211th Session, decided with 4 votes in favour, 19 against and 11 abstentions, not to accept the Respondent's preliminary objection. The Council further decided to invite the parties to continue their direct negotiations and also requested the President of the Council to be available to provide his good offices as Conciliator during such negotiations. The Respondent subsequently filed its Counter-memorial on 31 August 2017.

At the eighth Meeting of its 212th Session in 2017, the Council considered a progress report on negotiations. The Council endorsed an agreement reached between the two parties to suspend the filing of a Reply by the Applicant to the Respondent's Counter-memorial in order to allow for further consultations among them.

b. Request submitted under Article 54 n) of the Chicago Convention

At the tenth Meeting of its 211th Session, the Council considered and approved a request, submitted by Qatar pursuant to article 54 n) of the Chicago Convention, to schedule an extraordinary session for the consideration of the actions of Bahrain, Egypt, Saudi Arabia and the United Arab Emirates to close their airspace to aircraft registered in Qatar. On 31 July 2017, following its consideration of the item, the Council rendered a decision urging all ICAO member States to continue to collaborate, in particular, to promote the safety, security, efficiency and sustainability of international civil aviation.

c. Qatar and Bahrain, Egypt, Saudi Arabia and the United Arab Emirates (2017)—Application (A)

On 30 October 2017, Qatar presented Application (A) and its corresponding Memorial under the terms of article 84 of the Chicago Convention. Bahrain, Egypt, Saudi Arabia and the United Arab Emirates were named as Respondents. The said Application (A) and its corresponding Memorial relate to a disagreement on the "interpretation and application of the Chicago Convention and its Annexes" following the referenced announcement by the Governments of the Respondents on 5 June 2017 "with immediate effect and without any previous negotiation or warning, that Qatar-registered aircraft are not permitted to fly to or from the airports within their territories and would be barred not only from their respective national air spaces, but also from their Flight Information Regions (FIRs) extending beyond their national airspace even over the high seas". On 15 November 2017, the Council fixed a time-limit of 12 weeks for the filing of Counter-memorials by the Respondents with respect to Application (A).

d. Qatar and Bahrain, Egypt and the United Arab Emirates (2017)—Application (B)

On 30 October 2017, Qatar also presented Application (B) and its corresponding Memorial under the terms of article II, Section 2 of the International Air Services Transit Agreement (Transit Agreement) and Chapter XVIII of the Chicago Convention. Bahrain, Egypt and the United Arab Emirates were named as Respondents. Application (B) relates to a disagreement on the "interpretation and application" of the Transit Agreement, following the referenced announcement by the Governments of the Respondents on 5 June 2017 "with immediate effect and without any previous negotiation or warning, that Qatar-registered aircraft are not permitted to fly to or from the airports within their territories and are barred from their respective national air spaces". On 15 November 2017, the Council fixed a time-limit of 12 weeks for the filing of Counter-memorials by the Respondents with respect to Application (B).

(iv) *Legal Issues Relating to Unruly Passengers*

Further to the *Protocol to Amend the Convention on Offences and Certain Other Acts Committed on Board Aircraft* (Montréal, 2014) and pursuant to the resolution adopted by the Diplomatic Conference, the Task Force on Legal Aspects of Unruly Passengers was established in 2015 to update ICAO Circular 288 (*Guidance Material on the Legal Aspects of Unruly/Disruptive Passengers*) to include a more detailed list of offences and other acts, as well as to make consequential changes to the Circular arising from the adoption of the Protocol. The Task Force held three meetings to review the contents of the Model Legislation on Certain Offences Committed on Board Civil Aircraft and ICAO Circular 288. It will report its work, including the new draft of Model Legislation, to the 37th Session of the Legal Committee in September 2018.

(v) *Safety Aspects of Economic Liberalization and Article 83 bis of the Chicago Convention*

An advance version of the ICAO *Manual on the Implementation of Article 83 bis* was published in English in June 2017. Work continued on the article 83 *bis* Task Force recommendations, as endorsed by the Council at the seventh meeting of its 207th Session, with preparatory work advancing on the establishment of an interactive web-based registration and publication system for article 83 *bis* agreements. Related amendments to Annex 6 (*Operation of Aircraft*) to the Chicago Convention are under consideration by the Air Navigation Commission.

(vi) *Implementation of Article 21 of the Chicago Convention*

Under the item "Implementation of Article 21 of the Chicago Convention" of the General Work Programme of the Legal Committee, a Task Force was established and it held its first meeting in Montréal in September 2017.

The Task Force acknowledged that, for purposes of registration of aircraft, the meaning of the concept of "ownership" of aircraft differed among States. Nevertheless, the Task Force agreed not to recommend any amendments to article 21 in an attempt to define "ownership" to conform to any of the prevailing systems. Further, the Task Force expressed the view that States should not be required to adjust their domestic rules and regulations for the purpose of harmonizing the meaning of ownership and agreed to develop some recommendations to make the differences in the concept of "ownership" more transparent. A better understanding of differences between registration systems around the world would facilitate, in many contracting States, the registration of aircraft transferred from other States.

The Task Force will support the development of a new ICAO Aircraft Registry System and consider the idea of developing a "Model Certificate of De-registration of Aircraft" for inclusion in Annex 7—*Aircraft Nationality and Registration Marks*. A second meeting of the Task Force is scheduled to be held in Montréal in April 2018.

(vii) *New Understanding between ICAO and Quebec*

Recommendation of the Committee on Relations with the Host Country (RHCC) was considered on 14 November 2017 by the Council in order to approve the new *Understanding between the Government of Quebec and ICAO concerning the Immunities, Exemptions and Courtesy Privileges extended to the Organization, its Officials, to Member States and to Members of a Permanent Representation to the Organization*, intended to supersede the current Understanding between ICAO and Quebec signed in 1994. It agreed that the President seek by correspondence the Representatives' final approval for its signature by the Secretary General, which was completed on 19 December 2017.

(viii) *International Interests in Mobile Equipment (Aircraft Equipment)*

On behalf of the Council in its capacity as the Supervisory Authority of the International Registry, the Secretariat monitored the operation of the Registry to ensure that it functions efficiently in accordance with article 17 of the Convention on International Interests in Mobile Equipment (Cape Town Convention). In July, the Council approved the Fourth Report of the Supervisory Authority to the Contracting States to the Cape Town Convention and the Protocol to the Convention on International Interests in Mobile Equipment on Matters specific to Aircraft Equipment (Aircraft Protocol). The Report was issued on 30 August by State Letter LE 3/41.2-IND/17/14. As of 31 December 2017, there were 68 parties to the Cape Town Convention and the Aircraft Protocol.

(ix) *Tuvalu—192nd member State of ICAO*

On 19 October 2017, Tuvalu deposited with the Government of the United States, its notification of adherence to the Convention on International Civil Aviation. The adherence took effect on 18 November 2017, making Tuvalu the newest member State of ICAO and bringing the number of member States to 192.

(x) *Entry into Force of the Beijing Protocol 2010*

On 28 November 2017, the conditions for the entry into force of the Protocol Supplementary to the Convention for the Suppression of Unlawful Seizure of Aircraft, done at Beijing on 10 September 2010 (Beijing Protocol) were fulfilled by the deposit with ICAO of the 22nd instrument of ratification by the Government of the Republic of Uganda. The Protocol entered into force on 1 January 2018.

(xi) *Promotion of the Ratification of the International Air Law Instruments*

The President of the Council and the Secretary General of ICAO continued to promote ratification of international air law instruments during their visits to member States and meetings with high-level government officials in 2017.

A State letter was issued on 20 January 2017 encouraging States to ratify the Protocols Amending Articles 50 (*a*) and 56 of the Convention on International Civil Aviation, signed at Montréal on 6 October 2016. Additionally, two State letters were issued on 2 March 2017 encouraging States to ratify the Beijing instruments (Convention on the Suppression of Unlawful Acts Relating to International Civil Aviation (2010) and the Protocol Supplementary to the Convention for the Suppression of Unlawful Seizure of Aircraft (2010)) and the Convention for the Unification of Certain Rules for International Carriage by Air, done at Montréal on 28 May 1999 (Montreal Convention of 1999).

The Legal Affairs and External Relations Bureau facilitated a legal seminar for Africa, organized by the Eastern and Southern Africa ICAO Regional Office, to promote the Beijing instruments and the Protocol to Amend the Convention on Offences and Certain Other Acts Committed on Board Aircraft (Montréal Protocol of 2014). The Montreal Convention of 1999, the Cape Town Convention and its Aircraft Protocol of 2001 and the Protocols amending Articles 50 (*a*) and 56 of the Convention on International Civil Aviation were also covered at the legal seminar. The legal seminar, held on 27 and 28 November 2017, was attended by 54 participants from 21 African States and two regional safety organizations.

7. Universal Postal Union[520]

(*a*) Agreements concluded by the Universal Postal Union

On 27 March 2017, the Universal Postal Union (UPU) concluded a cooperation agreement with the Association of European Public Postal Operators (POSTEUROP) concerning GHG emissions, CO2eq and use of the UPU's Online Solution for Carbon Analysis and Reporting (OSCAR). The agreement was concluded with the aim of strengthening their mutual cooperation on sustainable development activities.

On 27 March 2017, the UPU and the United Nations amended the agreement concluded on 4 September 2014 regarding the implementation of projects and tools arising from the analysis of big postal data, with the aim of extending its duration until 31 December 2018.

On 29 June 2017, the UPU concluded a cooperation agreement with the Coöperatieve Vereniging International Post Corporation UA (IPC) concerning the development and

[520] For official documents and more information on the Universal Postal Union, see http://www.upu.int.

promotion of international postal services in UPU member countries as well as the improvement and promotion of innovative solutions in the postal industry.

On 12 September 2017, the UPU concluded a cooperation agreement with the Asian-Pacific Postal Union concerning operational readiness for e-commerce and postal payment services development, e-services as well as postal development in the Asia-Pacific region (copy enclosed).

On 7 November 2017, the UPU and the United Nations Framework Convention on Climate Change signed a joint declaration in relation to offsetting of greenhouse gas emissions associated with the operations of the UPU.

(*b*) Establishment of formal relations between the UPU and other entities

In March 2017, the Council of Administration (CA) of the UPU examined and approved the establishment of formal relations between the UPU and VISA Inc. in order to foster both parties' cooperation in the field of financial inclusion and digital financial services in UPU member countries.

(*c*) Amendments to the Regulations to the Universal Postal Convention

In March 2017, the Postal Operations Council of the UPU examined and approved certain proposed amendments to the Regulations to the Universal Postal Union Convention (one of the Acts of the UPU as defined in article 22 of its Constitution). The amendments entered into force between January and April 2018.

8. World Meteorological Organization[521]

(*a*) Membership

In 2017, the membership of the World Meteorological Organization (WMO) remained unchanged at 185 member States and 6 territories.

(*b*) Agreements and other arrangements concluded in 2017

(i) *Agreements with States*

a. Arab States of the Gulf

Memorandum of Understanding between the WMO and the Secretariat of the Cooperation Council for the Arab States of the Gulf (GCC) concerning cooperation in matters of mutual interest. The Memorandum of Understanding was signed on 27 February 2017.

[521] For official documents and more information on the World Meteorological Organization, see https://public.wmo.int/en.

b. Burkina Faso

Letter of Agreement between the WMO and the "Agence Nationale de la Météorologie" (ANAM) concerning cooperation in the project "Strengthening national capacities for Early Warning Systems (EWS)". The Letter of Agreement was signed on 26 September and 3 October 2017.

c. China

Memorandum of Understanding between the WMO and the China Meteorological Administration (CMA) regarding the International Coordination Office of the High-impact Weather Project. The Memorandum of Understanding was signed on 11 May 2017.

Letter of Intent between the WMO and the China Meteorological Administration (CMA) to promote regional meteorological cooperation and co-build the Belt and Road. The Letter of Intent was signed on 14 May 2017.

d. Costa Rica

Agreement between the WMO and the Government of Costa Rica regarding the arrangements for the seventeenth session of the WMO Regional Association IV (North America, Central America and the Caribbean). The Agreement was signed on 2 March 2017.

e. Croatia

Letter of Agreement between the WMO and the "Drzavni Hidrometorololslci Zavod Republike Hrvatske" (DHMZ) concerning the preparation for the establishment of a project office in Croatia. The Letter of Agreement was signed on 15 June 2017.

f. France

Memorandum of Understanding between the WMO and "Météo-France" concerning cooperation in matters of mutual interest. The Memorandum of Understanding was signed on 27 January and 6 February 2017.

g. Indonesia

Letter of Agreement between the WMO and the Agency for Meteorology, Climatology and Geophysics of the Republic of Indonesia (BMKG) regarding the secondment of employee of BMI€G to WMO. The Letter of Agreement was signed on 15 March 2017.

Agreement between the WMO and the Government of Indonesia regarding the arrangements for the seventeenth session of the Commission for Atmospheric Sciences (CA-17) and the fifth session of the Joint WMO/IOC Technical Commission for Oceanography and Marine Meteorology (JCOMM-5). The Agreement was signed on 29 August 2017.

h. Italy

Memorandum of Understanding between the WMO and the Ministry of Environment, Land and Sea Protection of Italy concerning cooperation on WMO HYCOS projects and HydroSOS. The Memorandum of Understanding was signed on 15 December 2017.

i. Netherlands

Memorandum of Understanding between the WMO and the "Koninklijk Nederlands Meteorologisch Instituut" (KNMI) concerning cooperation in matters of mutual interest. The Memorandum of Understanding was signed on 27 January and 3 February 2017.

j. Norway

Memorandum of Understanding between the WMO and the Norwegian Meteorological Service (Met Norway) concerning cooperation in matters of mutual interest. The Memorandum of Understanding was signed on 27 January and 1 February 2017.

k. Republic of Korea

Memorandum of Understanding between the WMO and the Korea Research Institute of Stands and Science for provision of a Central Calibration Laboratory (CCL) for dimethyl sulphide (DMS) to the WMO, Global Atmosphere Watch Programme. The Memorandum of Understanding was signed on 18 and 21 December 2017.

l. Republic of Singapore

Agreement between the WMO and the Government of the Republic of Singapore regarding the Legal Status and the Functioning of the WMO Regional Office for Asia and the South-West Pacific. The Agreement was signed on 21 August 2017.

m. Switzerland

Memorandum of Understanding between the WMO and the Swiss Confederation represented by "MeteoSwiss" concerning financial support for the translation of the International Cloud Atlas into the official languages of the WMO. The Memorandum of Understanding was signed on 13 and 18 December 2017.

Memorandum of Understanding between the WMO and the Swiss Confederation represented by "the Federal Office for the Environment (FOEN)" regarding the contribution to the IG3IS Trust Fund for 2017–2020. The Memorandum of Understanding was signed on 14 and 18 December 2017.

Memorandum of Understanding between the WMO and the Swiss Confederation represented by "the Federal Office of Meteorology and Climatology MeteoSwiss" regarding the contribution to the IG3IS Trust Fund for 2017–2020. The Memorandum of Understanding was signed on 14 and 18 December 2017.

Agreement between the WMO and the Swiss Confederation represented by "the Swiss Federal Department of Foreign Affairs" regarding the granting of a core contribution to the establishment and the general functioning of the Integrated Global Greenhouse Gas Information System (IG3IS) office in Geneva for 2018 until 2020. The Agreement was signed on 14 and 19 December 2017.

(ii) *Agreements with the United Nations*

a. Food and Agriculture Organization of the United Nations (FAO)

Framework Memorandum of Understanding between the WMO and the FAO concerning cooperation in matters of mutual interest in relation to weather, water and climate. The Framework Memorandum of Understanding was signed on 16 June 2017.

b. FAO and Norwegian Refugee Council (NRC)

Extension of the Memorandum of Understanding between the WMO, the FAO and the NRC concerning the hosting arrangements for deployment of experts to the FAO Representation in Dalcar, Senegal. The Extension of the Memorandum of Understanding was signed on 23, 28 August and 5 September 2017.

c. International Telecommunication Union (ITU)

Memorandum of Understanding between the WMO and the ITU concerning cooperation in matters of mutual interest (Arrangements for the Publication of the Handbook on the Use of Radio Spectrum for Meteorology (2017)). The Memorandum of Understanding was signed on 12 April 2017.

d. United Nations (UN)

Arrangement between the WMO and the United Nations concerning the extending competence of the United Nations Appeals Tribunal. This Arrangement was signed on 30 June and 18 July 2017.

e. Secretariat of the United Nations Framework Convention on Climate Change (UNFCC)

Framework Memorandum of Understanding between the WMO and the UNFCC concerning cooperation in matters of mutual interest. The Framework Memorandum of Understanding was signed on 6 November 2017.

f. United Nations Development Programme (UNDP)

Memorandum of Understanding between the WMO and UNDP concerning the extension of their cooperation in matters of mutual interest. The Memorandum of Understanding was signed on 21 September 2017.

g. UNDP and Norwegian Refugee Council (NRC)

Letter of Understanding between the WMO, UNDP in Niger and the NRC concerning the hosting by UNDP of a NRC Standby Expert to WMO. The Letter of Understanding was signed on 15 June, 25 July, and 27 August 2017.

(iii) *Agreements with other intergovernmental organizations, non-governmental organizations and entities*

a. Herzen State Pedagogical University of Russia

Memorandum of Understanding between the WMO and the Herzen State Pedagogical University concerning cooperation in training language professionals. The Memorandum of Understanding was signed on 27 February and 17 May 2017.

b. International Bank for Reconstruction and Development and the International Development Association (World Bank)

Memorandum of Understanding between the WMO and the World Bank concerning cooperation in matters of mutual interest. The Memorandum of Understanding was signed on 20 March 2017.

c. Universitat Rovira i Virgili (URV), Spain

Addendum to Memorandum of Understanding between the WMO and URV concerning cooperation in matters of mutual interest (Centre for Climate Change). The Addendum to Memorandum of Understanding was signed on 16 and 30 June 2017.

d. International Air Transport Association (IATA)

Working Arrangement between the WMO and IATA concerning cooperation on the Operation of the AMDAR Programme. The Working Arrangement was signed 7 July 2017.

e. Economic interest Grouping of European National Meteorological Services (EUMETNET), European Centre for Medium-Range Weather Forecasts (ECMWF) and the European Organization for the Exploitation of Meteorological Satellites (EUMETSAT)

Memorandum of Understanding between the WMO, EUMETNET, ECMWF and EUMETSAT concerning the joint liaison office with the European Institutions in Brussels. The Memorandum of Understanding was signed on 11 and 28 September and 4 and 11 October 2017.

f. Disaster Prevention Research Institute, Kyoto University (DPRI-KU)

Memorandum of Understanding between the WMO and DPRI-ITU regarding Fellowship Program. The Memorandum of Understanding was signed on 4 and 10 October 2017.

g. IHE Delft Institute for Water Education (IHE Delft)

Memorandum of Understanding between the WMO and IHE Delft regarding Fellowship. The Memorandum of Understanding was signed on 4 and 10 October 2017.

h. University of Geneva (UNIGE)

Cooperation Agreement between the WMO and UNIGE concerning cooperation in the area of translation, the exchange of information and student internships. The Cooperation Agreement was signed on 5 and 17 October 2017.

i. World Energy and Meteorology Council (WEMC)

Memorandum of Understanding between the WMO and the WEMC concerning collaboration to support countries in developing Climate Services for Energy. The Memorandum of Understanding was signed on 27 November and 7 December 2017.

j. Stockholm Environment Institute (SEI)

Memorandum of Understanding between the WMO and the SEI concerning cooperation in matters of mutual interest. The Memorandum of Understanding was signed on 22 November and 18 December 2017.

k. International Groundwater Resources Assessment Center (IGRAC)

Memorandum of Understanding between the WMO and the IGRAC concerning cooperation in matters of mutual interest. The Memorandum of Understanding was signed on 7 and 22 December 2017.

9. United Nations Industrial Development Organization[522]

Information on agreements and other arrangements concluded in 2017 is available in Appendix G to the 2017 Annual Report of the United Nations Industrial Development Organization (UNOD).[523]

10. Preparatory Commission for the Comprehensive Nuclear-Test-Ban Treaty Organization (CTBTO)[524]

(*a*) Membership

The Preparatory Commission for the CTBTO is composed of States Signatories to the 1996 Comprehensive Nuclear-Test-Ban Treaty (CTBT). By the end of 2017, the CTBT had 183 States signatories.

In order for the Treaty to enter into force, ratification by the following eight States is needed: China, Democratic People's Republic of Korea, Egypt, India, Islamic Republic of Iran, Israel, Pakistan, and United States of America.

---

[522] For official documents and more information on the United Nations Industrial Development Organization, see http://www.unido.org.

[523] Available at https://www.unido.org/resources/publications/flagship-publications/annual-report/annual-report-2017.

[524] For official documents and more information on the Preparatory Commission for the Comprehensive Nuclear-Test-Ban Treaty Organization, see http://www.ctbto.org.

(*b*) Legal status, privileges and immunities and international agreements

In addition to the Headquarters Agreement, legal status, privileges and immunities are granted to the Commission through "Facility Agreements" concluded with each of the 89 States which are hosting one or more of the 337 monitoring facilities comprising the International Monitoring System (IMS) foreseen to be established under the CTBT. In 2017, a total of 49 facility agreements have been concluded out of which 41 have entered into force.

Pursuant to the decision of the Commission in 2006 to exceptionally allow IMS data to be shared with tsunami warning centres approved as such by the Intergovernmental Oceanographic Commission of UNESCO,[525] fifteen such agreements have now been concluded: Australia, France, Greece, Indonesia, Japan, Malaysia, Myanmar, Philippines, Portugal, Republic of Korea, Russian Federation, Thailand, Turkey and two with the United States of America, based on the model approved by the Commission.

To provide for the necessary privileges and immunities and arrangements for the conduct of workshops or training courses outside of Austria, eight Exchanges of Letters were concluded with host States.

(*c*) Legislative Assistance Activities

Pursuant to paragraph 18 of the Annex to the 1996 Resolution Establishing the Preparatory Commission, the Provisional Technical Secretariat of the Preparatory Commission continued to provide advice and assistance upon request to States in three areas: (*a*) legal and technical information about the CTBT in order to facilitate signature or ratification of the Treaty; (*b*) legal and administrative measures necessary for the implementation of the Treaty; and (*c*) national measures necessary to enable activities of the Preparatory Commission during the preparatory phase, in particular those related to the provisional operation of the IMS.

The Secretariat continued to provide comments and assistance in 2017 on legal assistance requests from States parties or from within the Secretariat. It also maintains a Legislation Database on its website (www.ctbto.org) to facilitate the exchange of information on national implementing legislation as well as other documentary assistance tools, including the Legislation Questionnaire.

11. International Atomic Energy Agency[526]

(*a*) Membership

In 2017, Saint Vincent and the Grenadines became a member State of the International Atomic Energy Agency (IAEA). By the end of the year, there were 169 Member States.

---

[525] *United Nations Juridical Yearbook 2006* United Nations Publication, Sales No. E.09.V1), p. 256.

[526] For official documents and more information on the International Atomic Energy Agency, see http://www.iaea.org.

(*b*) Multilateral treaties under IAEA auspices

(i) *Convention on the Physical Protection of Nuclear Material*[527]

In 2017, Myanmar became a party to the Convention. By the end of the year, there were 155 parties.

(ii) *Amendment to the Convention on the Physical Protection of Nuclear Material*[528]

In 2017, Bangladesh, Bolivia, Costa Rica, Ecuador, Madagascar, Monaco, Myanmar, Namibia, and Senegal became parties to the Amendment. By the end of the year, there were 115 parties.

(iii) *Convention on Early Notification of a Nuclear Accident*[529]

In 2017, Madagascar became a party to the Convention. By the end of the year, there were 121 parties.

(iv) *Convention on Assistance in the Case of a Nuclear Accident or Radiological Emergency*[530]

In 2017, Madagascar and Niger became a party to the Convention. By the end of the year, there were 115 parties.

(v) *Convention on Nuclear Safety*[531]

In 2017, Cuba, Madagascar, Myanmar, Niger, and the Syrian Arab Republic became parties to the Convention and Serbia deposited an instrument of accession thereto. By the end of the year, there were 83 parties and one contracting State.

(vi) *Joint Convention on the Safety of Spent Fuel Management and on the Safety of Radioactive Waste Management*[532]

In 2017, Cuba, Madagascar, and Niger became parties to the Convention and Serbia deposited an instrument of accession thereto. By the end of the year, there were 76 parties and one contracting State.

---

527 United Nations, *Treaty Series*, vol. 1456, p. 101.

528 *IAEA International Law Series*, No. 2, 2006.

529 United Nations, *Treaty Series*, vol. 1439, p. 275.

530 *Ibid.*, vol. 1457, p. 133.

531 *Ibid.*, vol. 1963, p. 293.

532 *Ibid.*, vol. 2153, p. 303.

(vii) *Vienna Convention on Civil Liability for Nuclear Damage*[533]

In 2017, the status of the Convention remained unchanged with 40 parties.

(viii) *Optional Protocol Concerning the Compulsory Settlement of Disputes*[534]

In 2017, the status of the Protocol remained unchanged with two parties.

(ix) *Protocol to Amend the Vienna Convention on Civil Liability for Nuclear Damage*[535]

In 2017, the status of the Protocol remained unchanged with 13 parties.

(x) *Joint Protocol Relating to the Application of the Vienna Convention and the Paris Convention*[536]

In 2017, the status of the Convention remained unchanged with 28 parties.

(xi) *Convention on Supplementary Compensation for Nuclear Damage*[537]

In 2017, Canada became a Party to the Convention. By the end of the year, there were ten parties.

(xii) *Regional Co-operative Agreement for Research, Development and Training Related to Nuclear Science and Technology, 2017*

The Fifth Agreement to Extend the 1987 Regional Co-operative Agreement for Research, Development and Training Related to Nuclear Science and Technology (RCA)[538] expired on 11 June 2017 and was replaced by the Regional Co-operative Agreement for Research, Development and Training Related to Nuclear Science and Technology, 2017 (2017 RCA), which is of unlimited duration. By the end of 2017, the following 15 States were parties to the 2017 RCA: Australia, Bangladesh, India, Indonesia, Japan, Republic of Korea, Malaysia, Mongolia, Myanmar, New Zealand, Pakistan, Palau, Singapore, Thailand, and Viet Nam.

---

[533] *Ibid.*, vol. 1063, p. 265.

[534] *Ibid.*, vol. 2086, p. 94.

[535] *Ibid.*, vol. 2241, p. 270.

[536] *Ibid.*, vol. 1672, p. 293.

[537] *Ibid.*, registration no. 52722.

[538] IAEA, document INFCIRC/167/Add.23.

(xiii) *African Regional Co-operative Agreement for Research, Development and Training Related to Nuclear Science and Technology (AFRA)—(Fifth Extension)*[539]

In 2017, Burkina Faso, Cameroon, the Central African Republic, Congo, Ethiopia, Gabon, Malawi, Mali, Rwanda, and Sierra Leone became parties to the Fifth Extension of the Agreement. By the end of the year, there were 37 parties.

(xiv) *First Agreement to Extend the Co-operation Agreement for the Promotion of Nuclear Science and Technology in Latin America and the Caribbean (ARCAL)*[540]

In 2017, Belize and Jamaica became parties to the Agreement. By the end of the year, there were 21 parties.

(xv) *Co-operative Agreement for Arab States in Asia for Research, Development and Training Related to Nuclear Science and Technology (ARASIA)—(Second Extension)*[541]

In 2017, the status of the Agreement remained unchanged with nine parties.

(xvi) *Agreement on the Establishment of the ITER International Fusion Energy Organization for the Joint Implementation of the ITER Project*[542]

In 2017, the status of the Agreement remained unchanged with seven parties.

(xvii) *Agreement on the Privileges and Immunities of the ITER International Fusion Energy Organization for the Joint Implementation of the ITER Project*[543]

In 2017, the status of the Agreement remained unchanged with six parties.

(*c*) Safeguards Agreements

In 2017, no new Safeguards Agreements pursuant to the Treaty on the Non-Proliferation of Nuclear Weapons (NPT) entered into force. Croatia acceded to the Safeguards Agreement,[544] and the Protocol Additional[545] thereto between the non-nuclear-weapon States of the European Atomic Energy Community (Euratom), Euratom and the IAEA. In addition, a Safeguards Agreement pursuant to the NPT and a Protocol Additional

[539] *Ibid.*, document INFCIRC/377 and INFCIRC/377/Add.20 (fifth extension).

[540] *Ibid.*, document INFCIRC/582 and INFCIRC/582/Add.4 (extension of the agreement).

[541] *Ibid.*, document INFCIRC/613 and INFCIRC/613/Add.3 (second extension).

[542] *Ibid.*, document INFCIRC/702.

[543] *Ibid.*, document INFCIRC/702.

[544] Reproduced in IAEA Document INFCIRC/193/Add.29.

[545] Reproduced in IAEA Document INFCIRC/193/Add.30.

thereto were signed by Liberia abut had not yet entered into force as of December 2017. An agreement with Pakistan[546] for the application of safeguards in connection with the supply of two nuclear power stations entered into force on 3 May 2017.

During 2017, Protocols Additional to the Safeguards Agreements pursuant to the NPT between the IAEA and Honduras,[547] Senegal[548] and Thailand[549] entered into force.

(*d*) Revised supplementary agreements concerning the provision of technical assistance by the IAEA (RSA)

In 2017, Congo and Swaziland signed an RSA with the IAEA. By the end of the year, there were 134 States parties to an RSA.

(*e*) Other Treaties to which IAEA is a party

The Agreement between the International Atomic energy Agency and the Government of the Republic of Kazakhstan regarding the Establishment of the Low Enriched Uranium Bank of the International Atomic Energy Agency in the Republic of Kazakhstan entered into force on 31 January 2017.

The Agreement between the International Atomic Energy Agency and the Government of the Russian Federation regarding the transit of low enriched uranium to the Low Enriched Uranium Bank of the International Atomic Energy Agency in the Republic of Kazakhstan, through the territory of the Russian Federation, entered into force on 31 May 2017.

The Agreement between the International Atomic Energy Agency and the Government of the People's Republic of China regarding the transit of low enriched uranium to the Low Enriched Uranium Bank of the International Atomic Energy Agency in the Republic of Kazakhstan and from the Low Enriched Uranium Bank of the International Atomic Energy Agency in the Republic of Kazakhstan, through the territory of the People's Republic of China, was signed on 5 April 2017.

In August 2017, the IAEA Low Enriched Uranium Bank Storage Facility at the Ulba Metallurgical Plant in Ust-Kamenogorsk, Kazakhstan, was officially inaugurated.

(*f*) IAEA legislative assistance activities

In 2017, the Agency continued to provide legislative assistance to its member States. Country specific bilateral legislative assistance was provided to 20 member States through written comments and advice on drafting national nuclear legislation. The Agency also reviewed the legislative framework of newcomer countries as part of Integrated Nuclear Infrastructure Review missions. Short-term scientific visits to Agency Headquarters were organized for a number of individuals, allowing fellows to gain further practical experience in nuclear law.

---

[546] Reproduced in IAEA Document INFCIRC/920.

[547] Reproduced in IAEA Document INFCIRC/235/Add.1.

[548] Reproduced in IAEA Document INFCIRC/276/Add.1.

[549] Reproduced in IAEA Document INFCIRC/241/Add.1.

The Agency organized the seventh session of the Nuclear Law Institute in Baden, Austria, from 2 to 13 October 2017. The comprehensive two-week course, which uses modern teaching methods based on interaction and practice, is designed to meet the increasing demand by IAEA member States for legislative assistance and to enable participants to acquire a solid understanding of all aspects of nuclear law, as well as to draft, amend or review their national nuclear legislation. 64 participants from 53 IAEA member States attended the training.

Four sub-regional workshops on nuclear law were conducted for African member States in Arusha, United Republic of Tanzania (13–17 March) and in Vienna, Austria (31 July–4 August), for member States of Latin America and the Caribbean in San Ignacio, Belize (25–28 April), and for European member States in Vienna, Austria (6–10 December). One hundred eleven participants from 63 member States attended these workshops. National workshops and training courses on nuclear law were also organized in four member States. The workshops and courses addressed all aspects of nuclear law and provided a forum for an exchange of views on topics relating to the corresponding international legal instruments.

(*g*) Conventions

(i) *Convention on Nuclear Safety (CNS)*

The Seventh Review Meeting of the Contracting Parties of the Convention on Nuclear Safety (CNS) was held at IAEA Headquarters from 27 March to 7 April 2017. The plenary sessions of the Meeting focused on (i) challenges which were identified at the Sixth Review Meeting as a result of learning following the Fukushima Daiichi nuclear power station accident; (ii) a "peer review of the incorporation of appropriate technical criteria and standards used by contracting parties for addressing the principles of the Vienna Declaration on Nuclear Safety in national requirements and regulations"; (iii) major common issues arising from the Country Group discussions *i.e.* safety culture, international peer reviews, legal framework and independence of the regulatory body, financial and human resources, knowledge management, supply chain, managing the safety of ageing nuclear facilities and plant life extension, emergency preparedness, stakeholder consultation and communication; and (iv) challenges faced by non-nuclear power countries and embarking countries in complying with the obligations under the CNS.

Several proposals to improve the peer review process under the CNS were also approved at the Meeting, relating, *inter alia*, to issuing a survey at each Review Meeting to evaluate the effectiveness of the changes to the review process, continuing having topical sessions during future Review Meetings and organizing regional CNS workshops for countries with no nuclear power reactors.

For the first time, States that have signed, but not yet ratified, accepted or approved the CNS (Signatory States) were invited to attend selected parts of the Meeting. These sessions were also webcasted for the first time. In another first, all National Reports were made publicly available after the meeting on the IAEA website.

(ii) *Joint Convention on the Safety of Spent Fuel Management and on the Safety of Radioactive Waste Management (Joint Convention)*

The Third Extraordinary Meeting of the Contracting Parties to the Joint Convention was held at the IAEA Headquarters from 16 to 17 May 2017. At the Meeting, the contracting parties discussed several proposals related to promotional activities, national reports and review meetings, which had been the outcome of a Consultancy Meeting held in October 2016 to discuss feedback from contracting parties to improve the review process. Contracting parties also discussed proposals relating to the procedure of identifying overarching issues during Country Group sessions, the implementation of the definition of "Good Practices", time management at the Review Meetings, and the issue of transboundary movement and multinational disposal of spent fuel and radioactive waste. Contracting parties further agreed to amend the Guidelines regarding the Review Process, so that the Secretariat will make publicly available each National Report, 90 days after the Review Meeting, unless the contracting party concerned notifies the Secretariat otherwise.

The Organizational Meeting for the Sixth Review Meeting of the Contracting Parties to the Joint Convention was held at the IAEA Headquarters from 18 to 19 May 2018. At the Meeting, the contracting parties, *inter alia*, elected the officers of the Sixth Review Meeting that will be held from 21 May to 1 June 2018 and decided on the establishment and composition of altogether eight country groups. They also decided to have two sequential topical sessions at the Sixth Review Meeting, the first one focussing on disused sealed radioactive sources and the second one dedicated to general safety issues, challenges and public acceptance aspects associated with the long-term storage of higher level radioactive waste. Contracting parties further agreed to invite the States that have signed, but not yet ratified, accepted or approved the Joint Convention (Signatory States) to attend selected parts of the Sixth Review Meeting.

(iii) *Promotional activities related to the CNS and to the Joint Convention*

In order to mark the 20th anniversary of the adoption of the Joint Convention (on 5 September 1997), a side event was organized by the IAEA, on 18 September 2017, in the margins of the 61st session of the IAEA General Conference. During the event, several experts involved in the drafting and review process of the Joint Convention, together with representatives of five contracting parties to the Joint Convention—Canada, Cuba, Finland, Ghana and Japan—shared their views with a broader audience on the Joint Convention's history, review process and prospects.

As the CNS and the Joint Convention represent major cornerstones in the international legal framework for nuclear safety, the IAEA has been working towards encouraging universal adherence to and implementation of these Conventions. As part of these efforts, in addition to the regular outreach, tailored promotional activities, such as bilateral meetings and regional workshops, were carried out in 2017. In this context, a Workshop to promote the CNS and the Joint Convention, for member States from Asia and Latin America, was held from 21 to 23 November 2017 in Vienna, with experts from Bolivia, Malaysia, Mongolia, Paraguay, Philippines Singapore and Thailand attending the event. Further, a Workshop to promote the Joint Convention, for member States in the African region, was held from 5 to 7 December 2017 in Rabat, Morocco with experts from Burkina Faso, Egypt, Mali, Sudan and Uganda attending the event.

(iv) *The Convention on the Physical Protection of Nuclear Material (CPPNM) and its Amendment*

A Technical Meeting of the Representatives of States parties to the CPPNM and the CPPNM Amendment was held from 9 to 10 November 2017 at the IAEA Headquarters in Vienna and was attended by 72 participants from 50 parties to the CPPNM and its Amendment. The participants discussed matters such as the efforts towards universalisation of the CPPNM Amendment as well as full implementation through the development and strengthening of member States' legislative and regulatory framework for nuclear security, and improvements to the mechanisms for information sharing. Discussions relating to the preparation of the 2021 Conference of the States parties to the CPPNM Amendment to review the implementation of the Convention were also held.

The IAEA organised, in cooperation with the World Institute for Nuclear Security, the World Nuclear Transport Institute and the International Criminal Police Organization, the International Conference on the Physical Protection of Nuclear Material and Nuclear Facilities, from 13 to 17 November 2017 at the IAEA Headquarters in Vienna. The Conference was attended by more than 650 participants from 95 member States and 10 international organizations. Six main panel sessions addressed a range of topics, including the universalisation and implementation of the CPPNM and its Amendment, the legislative and regulatory framework for the protection of nuclear material in use, storage and transport and for nuclear facilities, developing and sustaining a physical protection regime for nuclear material in use, storage and transport and for nuclear facilities, protection against unauthorized removal of nuclear material during use, storage and transport and sabotage of nuclear material and nuclear facilities, and international and regional cooperation. The Conference also included technical sessions addressing, *inter alia*, international transport, identification and assessment of threats, planning and preparedness for and response to nuclear security events and risk-based physical protection and measures.

(*h*) Civil liability for nuclear damage

The International Expert Group on Nuclear Liability (INLEX) continues to serve as the Agency's main forum for questions related to nuclear liability. The 17th Meeting of INLEX took place in Vienna, Austria in May 2017. The Group reiterated the possible exclusion of certain low risk installations from the scope of application of the liability conventions with specific reference to the case of installations being decommissioned and of installations for the disposal of certain types of low-level radioactive waste. In this respect, the Group concluded that there is no need to exclude any such installations from the scope of application of the revised Vienna Convention on Civil Liability for Nuclear Damage and of the Convention on Supplementary Compensation for Nuclear Damage. The Group also discussed other liability issues relating to disposal facilities, to transportable nuclear power plants and to the transport of nuclear material, as well as the scope of application of the nuclear liability conventions regarding radioactive products or waste. However, the Group felt that these issues required a more detailed analysis, and agreed to consider them further at its next meeting.

In addition, two regional workshops on civil liability for nuclear damage were conducted—one in Montevideo, Uruguay for Latin American countries, and another one in Accra, Ghana for African countries considering launching a nuclear power programme. Both events provided the participants with information on the existing international nuclear liability regimes and advised them on the development of national implementing legislation.

12. Organization for the Prohibition of Chemical Weapons[550]

(*a*) Membership

In 2017, the number of States parties to the Chemical Weapons Convention (CWC) remained unchanged, namely 192.

(*b*) Legal status, privileges and immunities and international agreements

During 2017, the OPCW continued to negotiate privileges and immunities agreements with member States in accordance with paragraph 50 of article VIII of the CWC. As a result, the privileges and immunities agreement with Bahrein, Cambodia and Romania, concluded by the Executive Council in 2017, were signed on 29 June 2017, 12 October 2017 and 6 September 2017 respectively. The agreements are yet to be ratified and have therefore not yet entered into force.

During 2017, the OPCW also concluded a number of international agreements, including, *inter alia*, facility agreements, voluntary contribution agreements, exchange of letters, and memoranda of understanding, which entail substantial undertakings at the policy level or that are intended to facilitate the day-to-day work of the Technical Secretariat in support of the objectives of the CWC.

(*c*) Legislative assistance activities

Throughout 2017, the Technical Secretariat of the OPCW continued to render assistance upon request to States parties that have yet to adopt legislative and other measures to implement their obligations under the CWC, as well as to States parties wishing to update their legal framework. The OPCW continued to provide tailor-made assistance on national implementation of the Convention, pursuant to: (*a*) subparagraph 38(*e*) of article VIII of the CWC; (*b*) the decision on national implementation measures of article VII obligations adopted by the Conference of the States parties ("the Conference") at its Fourteenth Session (C-14/DEC.12, dated 4 December 2009); and (*c*) paragraph 9.103(*c*) of the Report of the Third Special Session of the Conference of the States parties to Review the Operation of the Chemical Weapons Convention (RC 3/3*, dated 19 April 2013).

In carrying out these efforts, the Technical Secretariat of the OPCW also acted in accordance with the decisions of the Conference regarding the implementation of article VII obligations (C-8/DEC.16, dated 24 October 2003; C-10/DEC.16, dated 11 November 2005; C-11/DEC.4, dated 6 December 2006; C-12/DEC.9, dated 9 November 2007; C-13/DEC.7, dated 5 December 2008 and C-14/DEC.12, dated 4 December 2009). These decisions focused

[550] For official documents and more information on the Organization for the Prohibition of Chemical Weapons, see http://www.opcw.org.

on, amongst other things, the obligations of States parties to designate or establish a National Authority to serve as national focal point for effective liaison with the OPCW and other States parties, as required by paragraph 4 of article VII of the CWC, and the steps necessary to enact national implementing legislation, including penal legislation and administrative measures to implement the CWC, as required by paragraph I of article VII of the CWC.

In the course of 2017, one additional State Party informed the Secretariat that it had designated a National Authority. With a total of 190 States parties having designated a National Authority, there are only two States parties which have not yet fulfilled the requirement under article VII (4) of the CWC to designate or established a National Authority. Additionally, with regard to the adoption of the necessary legislative and/or administrative measures, 153 States parties (78%) have submitted the text of their implementing legislation. Of these, as of 31 July 2017, 122 States parties (64%) have legislation covering all initial measures. This number increased by four States parties during the course of 2017.

As required under article VII (5) of the CWC, 160 States parties (83%) have submitted information to the Secretariat on the legislative and administrative measures they have taken to implement various aspects of the CWC as of 31 July 2017, out of which 142 States parties (74%) have provided a copy of the relevant texts.

The Technical Secretariat continued to maintain contacts with States parties with which it had built a relationship through technical assistance programmes and consultations. A number of draft laws as well as existing legislation were reviewed by the Technical Secretariat upon request by States parties in the process of developing or updating their legal framework.

The Technical Secretariat continued to maintain formal and informal working contacts with States parties with which it had built a relationship through technical assistance programmes and consultations. A number of draft laws as well as existing legislation were reviewed by the Technical Secretariat upon request by States parties in the process of developing or updating their legal framework.

The Technical Secretariat participated in and organised events aimed at assisting States parties in the effective implementation of the Convention, such as global and regional annual meetings for National Authorities and legal workshops. Two sessions of the Internship Programme for Legal Drafters and National Authorities' Representatives were organized during the course of the year, in which 10 experts from 5 States parties participated and prepared the initial texts of their draft implementing legislation along with action plans for their adoption. A sub-regional workshop for Legal Drafters and National Authority Representatives from States parties in the Caribbean and Central America was held in Barbados in March 2017 and was attended by seven States parties. The Secretariat also supported a national legal workshop in Georgia in May 2017. Representatives from relevant ministries attended the workshop in order to address gaps in Georgia's legal and regulatory framework of the Convention.

Following the 2016 pilot event in Africa, the Secretariat organized three Stakeholders Forums in September and November 2017 for States parties in Africa, Asia and GRULAC. The Forums were aimed at assisting States parties in achieving progress in the adoption of implementing legislation and at facilitating the sharing of good practices and experiences. The three Stakeholders Forums were participated in by 36 States parties along with the representatives of international and regional organizations. Finally, two sessions of the Influential Visitors Programme were implemented in 2017—with Namibia in April 2017, and with Nigeria in October 2017. High-level officials from Namibia and Nigeria were invited to the OPCW Headquarters and attended a series of meetings to sensitise them on Convention-related issues. As follow-up to the visit by the high-level delegation from Namibia, a National Workshop on the Chemical Weapons Convention was organized by the National Authority of Namibia in Windhoek, Namibia in December 2017, with the aim of increasing understanding and awareness of senior policy makers of Namibia on the CWC and on the urgency of adopting national implementing legislation thereon.

13. World Trade Organization[551]

(*a*) Membership

In 2017, the World Trade Organization (WTO) membership counted 164 members. No new members joined the Organization during the year.

(i) *WTO accessions*

Applications for WTO membership are examined in individual Accession Working Parties, which are established by the Ministerial Conference/General Council. The legal framework of WTO accessions is set out in article XII of the Marrakesh Agreement Establishing the World Trade Organization. As a result of bilateral and multilateral negotiations with WTO members, acceding States/separate customs territories undertake trade liberalizing commitments on market access; specific commitments on WTO rules; and agree to comply with the WTO Agreement.

(ii) *On-going accessions in 2017*

In 2017, the following States/separate customs territories were in the process of acceding to the WTO (in alphabetical order):

1. Algeria
2. Andorra
3. Azerbaijan
4. Belarus
5. Bhutan*
6. Bosnia and Herzegovina
7. Comoros, Union of the*
8. Equatorial Guinea*
9. Ethiopia*
10. Islamic Republic of Iran
11. Iraq
12. Lebanese Republic
13. Libya
14. Sao Tomé and Principe*
15. Serbia
16. Somalia*
17. South Sudan*
18. Sudan*
19. Syrian Arab Republic
20. The Bahamas
21. Timor-Leste*
22. Uzbekistan

* Least Developed Countries (9).

[551] For official documents and more information on the World Trade Organization, see http://www.wto.org.

In the year under review, progress in various accession processes was registered as follows:

- Seven Working Party meetings were held on the accessions of Azerbaijan (one meeting), Belarus (two meetings), Iraq (one meeting, informal) the Union of the Comoros (two meetings), and Sudan (two meetings). In addition, three meetings addressed specific accession-related technical issues in the area of agriculture. These were on the accessions of Azerbaijan (one meeting), Belarus (one meeting), and Sudan (one meeting);
- A Working Party on the accession of South Sudan was established by the 11th WTO Ministerial Conference, on 13 December 2017;
- Progress on the documentary front included circulation of Memoranda on the Foreign Trade Regime (MFTR) for the Working Parties on the accession of Timor-Leste and Sudan (revision).
- Factual Summaries of Points Raised were prepared by the Secretariat for the Working Parties of the Union of the Comoros and Sudan. Elements of a draft Report of the Working Party were prepared by the Secretariat for the Working Parties of Belarus and the Union of the Comoros. Draft Reports were prepared, revised and circulated by the Secretariat for four Working Parties: Azerbaijan (one revision), Belarus (first edition), Bosnia and Herzegovina (one revision) and, the Lebanese Republic (one revision).

(*b*) Dispute Settlement

The General Council convenes as the Dispute Settlement Body (DSB) to deal with disputes arising under the Marrakesh Agreement Establishing the World Trade Organization; the multilateral trade agreements covering trade in goods, trade in services, and trade-related aspects of intellectual property rights; and, under a specific decision, the plurilateral trade agreement on government procurement. The DSB has the sole authority to establish dispute settlement panels, adopt panel and Appellate Body reports, maintain surveillance over the implementation of recommendations and rulings contained in such reports, and authorize suspension of concessions in the event of non-compliance with those recommendations and rulings.

(i) *Requests for consultations received and panels established*

During 2017, the DSB received 17 requests for consultations (the first formal step in dispute settlement proceedings) pursuant to article 4 of the Understanding on Rules and Procedures Governing the Settlement of Disputes (DSU). The DSB established ten new adjudication panels. The DSB established panels in the following disputes:

- United States—Certain Measures Relating to the Renewable Energy Sector (DS510) complaint by India;
- China—Domestic Support for Agricultural Producers (DS511) complaint by the United States;
- Russia—Measures Concerning Traffic in Transit (DS512) complaint by Ukraine;
- Morocco—Anti-Dumping Measures on Certain Hot-Rolled Steel from Turkey (DS513) complaint by Turkey;

- European Union—Measures Related to Price Comparison Methodologies (DS516) complaint by China;
- China—Tariff Rate Quotas for Certain Agricultural Products (DS517) complaint by the United States;
- India—Certain Measures on Imports of Iron and Steel Products (DS518) complaint by Japan;
- Canada—Measures Concerning Trade in Commercial Aircraft (DS522) complaint by Brazil;
- United States—Countervailing Measures on Certain Pipe and Tube Products (Turkey) (DS523) complaint by Turkey;
- United Arab Emirates—Measures Relating to Trade in Goods and Services, and Trade-Related Aspects of Intellectual Property Rights (DS526) complaint by Qatar.

(ii) *Appellate Body and Panel reports adopted by the DSB*

In 2017, the DSB adopted the following nine panel reports covering ten disputes and five Appellate Body reports covering five disputes:

- European Union—Anti-Dumping Measures on Imports of Certain Fatty Alcohols from Indonesia (DS442) complaint by Indonesia (Panel and Appellate Body reports);
- United States—Certain Methodologies and their Application to Anti-Dumping Proceedings Involving China (DS471) complaint by China (Panel and Appellate Body reports);
- Russian Federation—Measures on the Importation of Live Pigs, Pork and Other Pig Products from the European Union (DS475) complaint by the European Union (Panel and Appellate Body reports);
- Indonesia—Importation of Horticultural Products, Animals and Animal Products (DS477) complaint by New Zealand (Panel and Appellate Body reports);
- Indonesia—Importation of Horticultural Products, Animals and Animal Products (DS478) complaint by the United States (Panel and Appellate Body reports);
- Canada—Anti-Dumping Measures on Imports of Certain Carbon Steel Welded Pipe from The Separate Customs Territory of Taiwan, Penghu, Kinmen and Matsu (DS482) complaint by Chinese Taipei (Panel and Appellate Body reports); China—Anti-Dumping Measures on Imports of Cellulose Pulp from Canada (DS483) complaint by Canada (Panel report);
- Indonesia—Measures Concerning the Importation of Chicken Meat and Chicken Products (DS484) complaint by Brazil (Panel report);United States—Conditional Tax Incentives for Large Civil Aircraft (DS487) complaint by the European Union (Panel and Appellate Body reports); European Union—Measures Affecting Tariff Concessions on Certain Poultry Meat Products (D492) complaint by China (Panel report).

(c) Amendments to the WTO Agreement

(i) *Entry into force of the Protocol Amending the TRIPS Agreement*

The Protocol Amending the TRIPS Agreement entered into force on 23 January 2017. The amendment, which incorporates a flexibility on patents and public health, inserted a new article 31*bis* into the Agreement as well as an Annex and Appendix. The amendment replaced the 2003 waiver for members that have accepted the amendment. Members who are yet to accept the amendment currently have until 31 December 2019 to do so (document WT/L/1024). For them the waiver will continue to apply until a member accepts the amendment and it takes effect for it.

(ii) *Agreement on Trade Facilitation*

The Agreement on Trade Facilitation entered into force on 22 February 2017 when the WTO obtained acceptance of the Agreement from two-thirds of its 164 members. This Protocol of Amendment, which was officially opened for acceptance on 27 November 2014, inserts the Agreement on Trade Facilitation into the WTO Agreement. The Agreement seeks to expedite the movement, release and clearance of goods across borders.

(iii) *Trade Policy Review Mechanism*

The WTO General Council adopted a decision (document WT/L/1014) pursuant to article X:8 of the WTO Agreement to amend the English, French, and Spanish versions of paragraph C(ii) of the Trade Policy Review Mechanism (TPRM) contained in Annex 3 to the WTO Agreement. The decision changes the cycle of reviews according to which a member participates in a trade policy review every two, four or six years, depending on the size of its economy, to three, five or seven years, respectively. This new arrangement will be phased in, starting from 2019. This is the first amendment to the TPRM since it was established in 1989 under the GATT and made permanent under the WTO as part of the 1994 Uruguay Round agreements.

(iv) *Civil Aircraft Agreement*

On 26 April 2017, the European Union accepted the Protocol Amending the Annex to the Agreement on Trade in Civil Aircraft (document TCA/9). In accordance with its paragraph 3, the Protocol entered into force for the European Union on 26 May 2017.

14. International Criminal Court[552]

(*a*) Situations under preliminary examinations[553]

Before the International Criminal Court (ICC) Office of the Prosecutor (OTP) opens an investigation in a certain situation, the OTP conducts a preliminary examination in order to determine whether a situation meets the legal criteria established by the Rome Statute and if there is a reasonable basis to proceed with an investigation. Pre-Trial Chamber III (PTC III) has interpreted "reasonable basis" as a "sensible or reasonable justification for a belief that a crime falling within the jurisdiction of the Court has been or is being committed".[554]

(i) *The Situation in Gabon*

Gabon deposited its instrument of ratification to the Rome Statute on 20 September 2000. Pursuant to article 14 of the Statute, the State submitted a referral to the Court on 21 September 2016 for crimes committed in its territory since May 2016, with no end-date.[555] On 29 September 2016, the Prosecutor announced the opening of a preliminary examination for crimes allegedly committed in the context and the aftermath of the presidential elections of 27 August 2016. In June 2017, the OTP conducted its first mission to Libreville, where it met with political and judicial authorities, as well as with the Prosecutor General and the Public Prosecutors of Libreville. The OTP is in the process of assessing whether the information available provides a reasonable basis to believe that the alleged crimes fall within the subject matter jurisdiction of the Court.

(ii) *The Situation in Palestine*

On 1 January 2015, the Government of Palestine lodged a declaration under article 12(3) of the Rome Statute accepting the jurisdiction of the Court over alleged crimes committed "in the occupied Palestinian territory, including East Jerusalem, since June 13, 2014". Palestine additionally acceded to the Statute on 2 January 2015, which entered into force for Palestine on 1 April 2015. During the reporting period, the OTP continued to analyse information pertaining to the Court's jurisdiction in Palestine, as well as crimes allegedly committed by both parties to the 2014 Gaza conflict and crimes allegedly committed in the West Bank, including East Jerusalem since 13 June 2014. The OTP continued to closely follow relevant developments in the region, and held multiple meetings with relevant stakeholders at the seat of the Court, including government officials and civil society representatives.

---

[552] For official documents and more information on the International Criminal Court, see http://www.icc-cpi.int.

[553] Main Source: The Office of the Prosecutor, "Report on Preliminary Examination Activities 2017", 4 December 2017, available at: https://www.icc-cpi.int/itemsDocuments/2017-PE-rep/2017-otp-rep-PE_ENG.pdf.

[554] *Situation in the Republic of Burundi*, Public Redacted Version of "Decision Pursuant to Article 15 of the Rome Statute on the Authorization of an Investigation into the Situation in the Republic of Burundi", ICC-01/17-X-9-US-Exp, 25 October 2017 (ICC-01/17-9-Red), 9 November 2017, para. 30.

[555] Requête aux Fins de Renvoi d'une Situation par un Etat Partie auprès du Procureur de la Cour Pénale Internationale, 20 Septembre 2016, available at: https://www.icc-cpi.int/iccdocs/otp/Referral-Gabon.pdf.

(iii) *The Situation in Ukraine*

On 17 April 2014, the Government of Ukraine lodged a declaration under article 12(3) of the Rome Statute accepting the jurisdiction of the Court over alleged crimes committed on its territory from 21 November 2013 to 22 February 2014. On 25 April 2014, the Prosecutor opened a preliminary examination of the situation in Ukraine. On 8 September 2015, the Government of Ukraine lodged a second declaration under article 12(3) of the Statute accepting the exercise of jurisdiction of the Court in relation to alleged crimes committed on its territory from 20 February 2014 onwards, with no end-date. During the reporting period, the OTP continued its analysis of whether alleged crimes relating to the situation in Crimea and the fighting in eastern Ukraine fall within the jurisdiction of the Court, as well as analysed new information and allegations received concerning the crimes allegedly committed in the context of the Euromaidan events. The OTP also continued engaging with a variety of relevant stakeholders, both through consultations held at the seat of the Court and during two missions to Ukraine, in April and September 2017.

(iv) *The Situation in Colombia*

Colombia deposited its instrument of accession to the Statute on 5 August 2002 along with a declaration under article 124 of the Statute excluding war crimes from the jurisdiction of the Court for a 7-year period. The preliminary examination of the situation in Colombia, which was opened in 2004, remains ongoing. During the reporting period, the OTP continued to engage with Colombian authorities to obtain additional information on relevant investigative steps and prosecutorial activities national authorities have undertaken. The Prosecutor conducted her first visit to Bogota in September 2017, where she met senior officials from the executive and the judiciary, including President Juan Manuel Santos. Upon invitation by the President of the Constitutional Court of Colombia, on 18 October 2017, the Prosecutor submitted to the Constitutional Court an Amicus Curiae brief summarising the Office's views on certain aspects of the Legislative Act 01 of 2017 and Law 1820 of 2017 (Amnesty Law). The OTP also continued to assess relevant national proceedings relating to extrajudicial killings, known as "false positives", sexual and gender-based crimes and forced displacement, and analysed the provisions set forth in the implementing legislation of the Special Jurisdiction for Peace.

(v) *The Situation in Guinea*

Guinea deposited its instrument of accession to the Statute on 14 July 2003. The preliminary examination of the situation in Guinea, which was opened in 2009, remains ongoing, and the OTP has continued to conduct the admissibility assessment. In particular, the OTP continued to assess the Guinean authorities' efforts to conduct genuine national proceedings into the 28 September 2009 events. In March 2017, the OTP conducted its fourteenth mission to Conakry to obtain detailed information on the investigative steps taken by the panel of judges and gauge the prospect of organising a trial within a reasonable timeframe. Following the completion of the national investigation, the OTP has continued to closely examine any potential obstacle to genuine accountability and to support the organization of a fair and impartial trial by engaging with national authorities and other relevant stakeholders.

(vi) *The Situation in Iraq/United Kingdom*

The situation in Iraq/UK has been under preliminary examination since 13 May 2014, when the Prosecutor announced the re-opening of the preliminary examination of the situation in Iraq, previously concluded in 2006, following submission of additional relevant information on the alleged crimes. Iraq is not a State Party to the Rome Statute, but this situation has focussed on allegations of crimes committed by the nationals of the United Kingdom, which has been a State Party since 4 October 2001. Following a thorough factual and legal assessment of the information available, the OTP confirmed its previous conclusions that there is a reasonable basis to believe that members of the UK armed forces committed war crimes within the jurisdiction of the Court against persons in their custody. In the light of this conclusion, the OTP has continued its assessment of admissibility, including complementarity and gravity. During the reporting period, the OTP continued to engage with the relevant national authorities, including through high level meetings of the Prosecutor and Deputy Prosecutor. As part of its close scrutiny of relevant developments at the national level, the Office conducted its third mission to the UK from 13 to 14 February 2017.

(vii) *The Situation in Nigeria*

Nigeria deposited its instrument of ratification of the Statute on 27 September 2001. The preliminary examination of the situation Nigeria, which was opened in 2010, remains ongoing. During the reporting period, the OTP continued to gather information on Nigerian national proceedings related to the identified potential cases involving the commission of alleged crimes against humanity and war crimes, respectively, by Boko Haram and Nigerian security forces. To this end, the OTP engaged with the Nigerian authorities as well as other relevant stakeholders to identify any pending impunity gaps. In May 2017, the Prosecutor also travelled to Abuja, where she met with Acting President Yemi Osinbajo and relevant civil and military authorities, including the Minister of Foreign Affairs and the Minister of Defence.

(*b*) Completed Preliminary Examinations

(i) *The Situation in the Islamic Republic of Afghanistan*

On 10 February 2003, Afghanistan acceded to the Rome Statute accepting the Court's jurisdiction over crimes committed on its territory or by its nationals; the Statute entered into force on 1 May 2003. In 2007, the Prosecutor opened a preliminary examination of the situation in Afghanistan.

On 20 November 2017, following the completion of the preliminary examination, the Prosecution filed a request[556] to Pre-Trial Chamber III for authorisation to open an investigation with respect to alleged crimes committed on the territory of Afghanistan in the period since 1 May 2003, as well as other alleged crimes that have a nexus to the armed conflict in Afghanistan and were committed on the territory of other States parties since 1 July 2002.

---

[556] Public Redacted Version of "Request for authorisation of an investigation pursuant to article 15", ICC-02/17-7-Conf-Exp (20 November 2017), ICC-02/17-7-Red (20 November 2017).

While the consideration of the request is still ongoing at the end of the reporting period, the victims of the alleged crimes have been called to submit representations to the Court's judges.[557]

(ii) *The Situation of Registered Vessels of Comoros, Greece, and Cambodia*

In 2014, the Prosecutor decided not to proceed to an investigation of the situation due to lack of sufficient gravity. As a response to an application filed by representatives of the Government of Comoros, on 16 July 2015, Pre-Trial Chamber I ("PTC I") requested the Prosecutor to reconsider her decision pursuant to article 53(3) of the Rome Statute. Pursuant to Rule 108(2) of the Court's Rules of Procedure and Evidence, the Prosecutor is obliged to review her decision. On 6 November 2015, the Appeals Chamber, by majority, dismissed *in limine* the Prosecutor's appeal against the PTC's request on the basis that it was not a decision "with respect to […] admissibility" within the meaning of article 82(1) (*a*) of the Statute.[558] On 29 November 2017, the Prosecutor notified PTC I of her "final decision", as required by Rule 108(3).[559] Having carried out a thorough review of all the submissions made and all the information available, including information newly made available in 2015–2017, the Prosecutor remained of the view that the information available did not provide a reasonable basis to proceed with an investigation. The final decision filed with the Court provided extensive reasoning in support of this conclusion.

(*c*) Situations under investigation

(i) *The Situation in Burundi*

Burundi deposited its instrument of ratification to the Rome Statute on 21 September 2004. On 25 April 2016, the Prosecutor opened a preliminary examination of the situation in Burundi since 26 April 2015 for crimes committed both in and outside Burundi by Burundian nationals. On 27 October 2016, Burundi submitted an official notification of withdrawal from the Statute,[560] which became effective on 27 October 2017. On 25 October 2017, the Pre-Trial Chamber observed that the Court retains jurisdiction over any crime within its jurisdiction up to and including 26 October 2017, regardless of Burundi's withdrawal.[561] Moreover, Burundi has a duty to cooperate with the Court for the purpose of this investigation since the investigation was authorised on 25 October 2017, prior to the date on which the withdrawal became effective for Burundi. This obligation to cooperate remains in

[557] Afghanistan situation: How victims and their representatives can submit their views to ICC Judges, 20 November 2017, available at: https://www.icc-cpi.int/Pages/item.aspx?name=171120-vprs-inf-afgh.

[558] *Situation on Registered Vessels of the Union of the Comoros, the Hellenic Republic of Greece and the Kingdom of Cambodia*, Notice of Appeal of "Decision on the request of the Union of the Comoros to review the Prosecutor's decision not to initiate an investigation", ICC-01/13-34, 27 July 2015.

[559] Notice of Prosecutor's Final Decision under Rule 108 (3), ICC-01/13, 29 November 2017.

[560] Letter from the Secretary General of the United Nations, *Withdrawal: Burundi*, C.N.805.2016. TREATIES-XVIII.10 (Depositary Notification), 28 October 2016, available at: https://treaties.un.org/doc/Publication/CN/2016/CN.805.2016-Eng.pdf. See also article 127(1) of the Rome Statute.

[561] Public Redacted Version of "Decision Pursuant to Article 15 of the Rome Statute on the Authorization of an Investigation into the Situation in the Republic of Burundi", ICC-01/17-X-9-US-Exp (25 October 2017), ICC-01/17-9-Red, 9 November 2017.

effect for as long as the investigation lasts and encompasses any proceedings resulting from the investigation. Burundi accepted those obligations when ratifying the Statute.

(ii) *The Situation in Georgia*

Georgia ratified the Rome Statute on 5 September 2003. Following the outbreak of international conflict between Georgia and Russia in South Ossetia, the Prosecutor announced on 14 August 2008 the commencement of a preliminary examination for crimes committed in the context of the conflict, between 1 July and 10 October 2008. On 27 January 2016, PTC I authorized the Prosecutor to proceed with an investigation of crimes against humanity and war crimes, during the international conflict, in and around South Ossetia.[562]

With the purpose to build on the existing legal obligations of the State and to facilitate the ongoing investigations in the country, the Court, on 25 July 2017, signed an agreement with the Government of Georgia.[563] During the reporting period, the investigation in Georgia was still ongoing.

(iii) *The Situation in the Central African Republic*

The Central African Republic (CAR) ratified the Rome Statute on 3 October 2001 and referred the first situation in its territory in December 2004. Two cases are currently before the Court:

- *The Prosecutor* v. *Jean-Pierre Bemba Gombo*, ICC-01/05-01/08 (Appeal phase).
- *The Prosecutor* v. *Jean-Pierre Bemba Gombo, Aimé Kilolo Musamba, Jean-Jacques Mangenda Kabongo, Fidèle Babala Wandu and Narcisse Arido.*

In the second case, Trial Chamber VII sentenced Mr. Bemba to a total of one additional year imprisonment (to the total of 18 years imprisonment imposed by Trial Chamber III), Mr. Kilolo to a total of 2 years and 6 months' imprisonment, Mr. Mangenda to a total of 2 years' imprisonment, Mr. Arido to a total of 11 months' imprisonment and Mr. Babala to a total of 6 months' imprisonment.[564]

(iv) *The Situation in the Central African Republic II*

In May 2014, CAR referred the second situation to the Court on the basis of alleged war crimes and crimes against humanity committed in the context of renewed violence in its territory as of 1 August 2012.[565] The investigation opened on 24 September 2014 and during the reporting period the OTP's investigations were ongoing.

---

[562] *Situation in Georgia*, Decision on the Prosecutor's Request for Authorization of an Investigation (with a Separate Opinion of Judge Kovacs), ICC-01/15-12, 27 January 2016.

[563] ICC signs cooperation agreement with government of Georgia, 27 July 2017, available at: https://www.icc-cpi.int/Pages/item.aspx?name=pr1327.

[564] Decision on sentences pursuant to article 76 of the Rome Statute, ICC-01/05-01/13-2123-Corr, 22 March 2017.

[565] See Referral of the Central African Republic, annexed to the Decision Assigning the Situation in the Central African Republic II to Pre-Trial Chamber II, ICC-01/14-1-Anx1, 18 June 2014.

(v) *The Situation in Côte d'Ivoire*

On 18 April 2003, Côte d'Ivoire ratified the Statute and lodged a declaration pursuant to article 12(3) accepting the jurisdiction of the Court for crimes committed as of 19 September 2002. On 3 October 2011, PTC III authorized the opening of a *proprio motu* investigation.[566] Two cases are currently before the Court:

- *The Prosecutor* v. *Laurent Gbagbo and Charles Blé Goudé*, ICC-02/11-01/15 (Trial phase).
- *The Prosecutor* v. *Simone Gbagbo*, ICC-02/11-01/12 (Execution of the warrant of arrest pending).

(vi) *The Situation in Mali*

Mali deposited its instrument of ratification of the Statute on 16 August 2000. In July 2012, Mali referred to the Court the situation in its territory since January 2012. The investigation opened on 6 January 2013 leading to the arrest and trial of Mr. Ahmed Al Faqi Al Mahdi. Pre Trial Chamber I issued an arrest warrant on 18 September 2015. On 27 September 2016, Trial Chamber VIII found Mr. Ahmed Al Faqi Al Mahdi guilty following a guilty plea, and he was sentenced to 9 years.[567] Trial Chamber VIII issued a reparations order of 2.7 million euros against Mr. Ahmed Al Faqi Al Mahdi in expenses of individual and collective reparations for the community of Timbuktu.

- *The Prosecutor* v. *Ahmad Al Faqi Al Mahdi*, ICC-01/12-01/15-236 (Reparations Order).

(vii) *The Situation in Libya*

Libya is not a State Party to the Rome Statute. On 26 February 2011, the United Nations Security Council with Resolution 1970 unanimously referred the situation in Libya to the ICC for crimes committed as of 15 February 2011. The investigation opened in March 2011. An arrest warrant for Mr. Saif Al-Islam Gaddafi was issued on 27 June 2011. Mr. Gaddafi has not been brought to Court's custody yet. Arrest warrants were also issued against Mr. Muammar Gaddafi (whose case was terminated on 22 November 2011, following his death), and against Mr. Abdullah Al-Senussi.

Arrest Warrants by PTC I

On 8 May 2017, the Prosecutor renewed her call before the United Nations Security Council for the effective arrest of Mr. Gaddafi and his surrender to the Court.[568]

- *The Prosecutor* v. *Saif Al-Islam Gaddafi*, ICC-02/04-01/15 (Execution of arrest warrant pending).

---

[566] *Situation in the Republic of Côte d'Ivoire*, Corrigendum to "Decision Pursuant to Article 15 of the Rome Statute on the Authorisation of an Investigation into the Situation in the Republic of Côte d'Ivoire", ICC-02/11-14-Corr, 15 November 2011.

[567] *The Prosecutor* v. *Ahmad Al Faqi Al Mahdi*, Judgment and Sentence, ICC-01/12-01/15, 27 September 2016.

[568] OTP, Statement of the Prosecutor of the International Criminal Court, Fatou Bensouda, to the United Nations Security Council on the situation in Libya, 9 May 2017, available at: https://www.icc-cpi.int/Pages/item.aspx?name=170509-otp-stat-lib.

During the reporting period, two new arrest warrants were issued, against Mr. Al-Tuhamy Mohamed Khaled (on 24 April 2017) and Mr. Mahmoud Mustafa Busayf Al-Werfalli (on 15 August 2017).

- *The Prosecutor* v. *Al-Tuhamy Mohamed Khaled*, ICC-01/11-01/13 (Execution of arrest warrant pending).
- *The Prosecutor* v. *Mahmoud Mustafa Busyf Al-Werfalli*, ICC-01/11-01/17-2 *(Execution of arrest warrant pending)*.

Case of Abdullah Al-Senussi

The case of Mr. Abdullah Al-Senussi was deemed inadmissible by the Appeals Chamber on 24 July 2014. However, on 21 February 2017, the United Nations Support Mission in Libya,[569] issued a full report on the trial of Mr. Al-Senussi before the Libyan Supreme Court.[570] The report concluded that the trial failed to meet the international fair trial standards. In the light of the above report and the full Libyan trial judgment, the Prosecutor has expressed her intention to determine whether new facts have arisen in order to re-open an investigation in accordance with articles 19(10) and 17(2)(*c*) of the Rome Statute.[571]

(viii) *The Situation in the Republic of Kenya*

Kenya ratified the Statute on 15 March 2005. On 31 March 2010, PTC II authorized a *proprio motu* investigation for crimes committed between 1 June 2005 and 26 November 2009.[572] In this situation, the case of Uhuru Muigai Kenyatta and the case of William Samoei Ruto and Joshua Arap Sang were withdrawn in 2015[573] and terminated in 2016[574], respectively. The investigations have been focused on alleged crimes committed in the context of post-election violence in Kenya between 2007 and 2008.[575]

Arrest warrants by Pre-Trial Chamber II

The execution of arrest warrants issued for Mr. Walter Osapiri Barasa (on 2 August 2013), and Mr. Paul Gicheru and Mr. Philip Kipkoech Bett (on 10 March 2015) was still pending during the reporting period. The above arrest warrants were issued based on

---

[569] In cooperation with the Office of the United Nations High Commissioner for Human Rights.

[570] Available at: https://unsmil.unmissions.org/sites/default/files/n1725784.pdf.

[571] OTP, Statement of the Prosecutor of the International Criminal Court, Fatou Bensouda, to the United Nations Security Council on the situation in Libya, 9 May 2017, available at: https://www.icc-cpi.int/Pages/item.aspx?name=170509-otp-stat-lib.

[572] *Situation in the Republic of Kenya*, Corrigendum of the Decision Pursuant to Article 15 of the Rome Statute on the Authorization of an Investigation into the Situation in the Republic of Kenya, ICC-01/09-19-Corr, 31 March 2010.

[573] *The Prosecutor* v. *Uhuru Muigai Kenyatta*, Decision on the withdrawal of charges against Mr. Kenyatta, ICC-0l/09-02/11, 13 March 2015.

[574] *The Prosecutor* v. *William Samoei Ruto and Joshua Arap Sang*, Public redacted version of Decision on Defence Applications for Judgments of Acquittal, ICC-01/09-01/11, 5 April 2016.

[575] Statement of the Prosecutor of the International Criminal Court, Fatou Bensouda, regarding the unsealing of Arrest Warrants in the Kenya situation, 10 September 2015, available at: https://www.icc-cpi.int/Pages/item.aspx?name=otp-stat-10-09-2015-2.

charges of interference with the Court's witnesses pursuant to article 70(1)(*c*) of the Rome Statute.

- *The Prosecutor* v. *Walter Osapiri Barasa*, ICC-01/09-01/13 (Execution of arrest warrant pending).
- *The Prosecutor* v. *Paul Gicheru and Philip Kipkoech Bett*, ICC-01/09-01/15 (Execution of arrest warrant pending).

(ix) *The Situation in Darfur, Sudan*

Sudan is not a State Party to the Rome Statute. The situation was referred to the Court by the United Nations Security Council with Resolution 1593 on 31 March 2005. Therefore, the Court has both territorial and personal jurisdiction over crimes committed in Darfur, Sudan from 1 July 2002 onwards. As of 8 June 2017, in four cases the execution of arrest warrants following the investigation process was still pending.[576]

- *The Prosecutor* v. *Ahmad Muhammad Harun and Ali Muhammad Ali Abd-Al-Rahman*, ICC-02/05-01/07 (Execution of arrest warrant pending).
- *The Prosecutor* v. *Omar Hassan Ahmad Al Bashir*, ICC-02/05-01/09 (Execution of arrest warrants pending).[577]
- *The Prosecutor* v. *Abdallah Banda Abakaer Nourain*, ICC-02/05-03/09 (Execution of arrest warrant pending).
- *The Prosecutor* v. *Abdel Raheem Muhammad Hussein*, ICC-02/05-01/12 (Execution of arrest warrant pending).

Non-Compliance with the Execution of Arrest Warrants

The Court relies on the cooperation of States to carry out the arrest and surrender of suspects and may refer the non-compliance of a State Party with a request to cooperate to the Assembly of State Parties (ASP) or to the United Nations Security Council, by virtue of article 87(7) of the Rome Statute. On 6 July 2017, PTC II decided, bearing in mind its discretional power, that a referral of South-Africa's non-compliance with the execution of the arrest warrant of Omar Al-Bashir to the ASP and the United Nations Security Council was not warranted.[578] With regard to the same arrest warrant, on 11 December 2017, PTC II decided to refer the non-compliance of the Hashemite Kingdom of Jordan.[579]

[576] Statement before the United Nations Security Council on the Situation in Darfur, pursuant to UNSCR 1593 (2005), 8 June 2017, available at: https://www.icc-cpi.int/Pages/item.aspx?name=170608-otp-stat-UNSC.

[577] The first arrest warrant was issued on 4 March 2009 on counts of war crime and crimes against humanity; the second arrest warrant was issued on 12 July 2010 on counts of genocide.

[578] *Prosecutor* v. *Omar Hassam Ahmand Al Bashir* (ICC-02/05-01-09), Decision under article 87(7) of the Rome Statute on the non-compliance by South Africa with the request by the Court for the arrest and surrender of Omar Al-Bashir, 6 July 2017.

[579] *Prosecutor* v. *Omar Hassam Ahmand Al Bashir* (ICC-02/05-01/09-309), Decision under article 87(7) of the Rome Statute on the non-compliance by Jordan with the request by the Court for the arrest and surrender of Omar Al-Bashir, 11 December 2017.

(x) *The Situation in Uganda*

In June 2002, Uganda acceded to the Statute and in January 2004 it referred the situation in its territory since 1 July 2002 to the Court. The focus of the investigations to date has been alleged war crimes and crimes against humanity committed in the context of a conflict between the Lord's Resistance Army (LRA) and the national authorities in Northern Uganda since 1 July 2002. Two cases are currently before the Court:

- *The Prosecutor* v. *Dominic Ongwen*, ICC-02/04-01/15 (Trial phase).
- *The Prosecutor* v. *Joseph Kony and Vincent Otti*, ICC-02/04-01/05 (Execution of arrest warrant pending).

(xi) *The Situation in the Democratic Republic of the Congo*

In April 2002, the Democratic Republic of Congo (DRC) ratified the Rome Statute and in April 2004 it referred the situation on its territory for crimes committed since 1 July onwards. The Court may exercise both territorial and personal jurisdiction for these crimes. The investigation to date has been focused on war crimes and crimes against humanity in Eastern DRC, in the Ituri region and the North and South Kivu Provinces. Four cases are currently before the Court:

Case before Trial Chamber II

On 15 December 2017, Trial Chamber II issued a decision completing the order for reparations of March 2015.

- *The Prosecutor* v. *Thomas Lubanga Dyilo*, ICC-01/04-01/06 (Reparation/compensation phase).

Case before Trial Chamber VI

Trial Chamber VI found on 4 January 2017 that it has jurisdiction over counts 6 and 9 (referring to the alleged war crimes or rape and sexual slavery of child soldiers). That was confirmed by the Appeals Chamber on 15 June 2017 with a rejection of the appeal of Mr. Ntaganda. TC VI concluded, and the Appeals Chamber concurred, that members of the same armed group are not excluded as potential victims of war crimes or rape and sexual violence.

- *The Prosecutor* v. *Bosco Ntaganda*, ICC-01/04-02/06 (Second Decision on the Defence's challenge to the jurisdiction of the Court in respect of Counts 6 and 9).
- *The Prosecutor* v. *Bosco Ntaganda*, ICC-01/04-02/06 OA5 (Appeal against the Second Decision on the Defence's challenge).
- *The Prosecutor* v. *Bosco Ntaganda*, ICC-01/04-02/06 (Trial phase).

Case before Trial Chamber II

- *The Prosecutor* v. *Germain Katanga*, ICC-01/04-01/07 (Reparation/compensation phase).
- *The Prosecutor* v. *Sylvestre Mudacumura*, ICC-01/04-01/12 (Execution of arrest warrant pending).

(*d*) Victims' participation in the proceedings: recent developments

One of the fundamental mandates of the ICC is the participation of victims in the judicial proceedings as well as their possibility to receive reparations in case of a conviction of an accused.

The Victims Participation and Reparations Section (VPRS) in the Registry acts as the main liaison body between victims and the ICC; a small team of lawyers and data processing specialists act as the entry point for victims' applications and liaison with the Chamber.

In 2017, the VPRS received a total of 2254 applications for participation in the proceedings and/or for reparations, as well as a number of victim representations under article 15(3) of the Rome Statute related to the situation in the Islamic Republic of Afghanistan (Afghanistan).[580] The largest number of applications received related to: (i) ongoing investigations in the situation in the Republic of Côte d'Ivoire (1737 application forms for participation and/or reparations); (ii) to the reparations phase of the case against Mr. Thomas Lubanga Dylio in the situation in the Democratic Republic of Congo (323 application forms); and (iii) to the reparations phase of the case against Mr. Ahmad Al Faqi Al Mahdi in the situation in Mali (154 applications forms). In 2017, a total of 722 victims were recognised as beneficiaries of reparations in the cases against Mr. Germain Katanga (297) and Mr. Thomas Lubanga Dylio (425). The VPRS also provided observations to Chambers on several occasions in ongoing article 15(3) and reparations proceedings, marking another important assistance function of the Section to Chambers in judicial proceedings. It compiled and organised data relevant to representations, participation in proceedings and reparations from thousands of applications received. The VPRS also assisted experts appointed by Chambers in the reparation process in different cases and transmitted their reports to the Chambers.

The VPRS, despite being part of the ICC Headquarters in The Hague, also actively supported victims' representations, participation and reparations-related activities in a number of situations before the ICC. Notably, the VPRS collected victims' views and opinions on a potential investigation by the ICC Prosecutor in Afghanistan and conveyed these to the Pre-Trial Chamber. The VPRS carried out a number of missions and video conferences in order to provide information about the ICC, victims' rights, the article 15(3) process and its possible outcomes. The security situation in Afghanistan did not allow for much direct interaction with victims within the affected communities on the ground; therefore, with a view to reaching out to as many victims as possible, the VPRS also strengthened its online dissemination of relevant information and representation forms. In order to mitigate some of the security risks that victims and their representatives could encounter when submitting their representations, the VPRS developed, by way of a pilot project in the ICC, an online process which allowed potential victims to fill in the form online without downloading any file, and with the benefit of being able to send it to the Registry without any trace at the users' end.

Other relevant activities related to victim participation in the proceedings and reparations, including the liaison with a range of internal and external actors aimed at

580 When the Prosecutor intends to commence an investigation on her own volition, she needs to seek a Pre-Trial Chamber's authorisation. As part of this process, victims may make so-called 'representations' to the Pre-Trial Chamber on the matter. This process is facilitated by the VPRS. Altogether, several hundreds of such representations were received, the majority thereof in early 2017.

building support networks for the VPRS mandate; identifying pools of relevant experts in the field; supporting victims' legal representatives and providing relevant observations to the Chambers related to judicial developments. The VPRS's field activities in reaching out to affected victims' communities focused on providing accurate information on victim participation and reparations before the ICC; conducting consultations with victims and key civil society actors; as well as preparing and, as appropriate, delivering key messages in the field in response to judicial developments.

In relation to activities relating to potential new investigations by the Prosecutor, the VPRS continued the preliminary mapping of communities of potentially affected persons in relevant situations. It also engaged in further developing networks of reliable local partners and contact points for potential future victim participation and/or reparations proceedings before the ICC.

The VPRS has continued, throughout 2017, to develop objectives as well as key performance indicators of its activities and output which are in line with the Registry strategic goals. Notably, internal processes and communications with the Chambers have been refined in order to contribute to expeditious and fair proceedings.

In 2017, the VPRS also started developing the VPRS Mobile Application (VMA), an application form for victims regarding participation in judicial proceedings and/or reparations, which in the future will be delivered through various mediums, including a web-based version and an application for secured, ICC-issued mobile devices. In practice, this will allow ICC staff to take relevant statements and information from victims in the field through a tablet device, adding significantly to the security of information and the efficiency of workflows. In addition, victims of ICC crimes will be able to submit relevant information and, importantly, application forms online. This does not make the direct human interaction less important, but adds to the efficient and secure data flow and general accessibility of the ICC for victims, and allows the Registry to better focus its resources in order to reach out to *all* affected communities as good as possible. The VMA represents a significant technological investment that has the potential to considerably enhance the efficiencies associated with the current victim application processes.

(*e*) Developments concerning the relationship between the ICC and the United Nations

In 2017, the ASP to the Rome Statute issued the following resolutions regarding the Court's relationship with the United Nations:

In resolution ICC-ASP/16/Res.2[581] ("Resolution on cooperation"), the ASP:

- *Emphasizes* the importance of timely and effective cooperation and assistance from States parties and other States under an obligation or encouraged to cooperate fully with the Court pursuant to Part 9 of the Rome Statute or a United Nations Security Council resolution, as the failure to provide such cooperation in the context of judicial proceedings affects the efficiency of the Court and *stresses* that the non-execution of cooperation requests has a negative impact on the ability of the Court to execute

[581] *Official Records of the Assembly of States parties to the Rome Statute of the International Criminal Court,* 16th session, The Hague, 4–14 December 2017 (ICC-ASP/16/2), vol. I, part III, ICC-ASP/16/Res.2.

its mandate, in particular when it concerns the arrest and surrender of individuals subject to arrest warrants (para. 1); and

- *Urges* States parties to explore possibilities for facilitating further cooperation and communication between the Court and international and regional organizations, including by securing adequate and clear mandates when the United Nations Security Council refers situations to the Court, ensuring diplomatic and financial support; cooperation by all United Nations Member States and follow-up of such referrals, as well as taking into account the Court's mandate in the context of other areas of work of the Security Council, including the drafting of Security Council resolutions on sanctions and relevant thematic debates and resolutions (para. 26).

In resolution ICC-ASP/16/Res.6[582] ("Strengthening the ICC and the Assembly of States Parties"), the ASP:

- *Recognizes* the need for enhancing the institutional dialogue with the United Nations, including on Security Council referrals (para. 32);
- *Recognizes* that ratification or accession to the Rome Statute by members of the United Nations Security Council enhances joint efforts to combat impunity for the most serious crimes of concern to the international community as a whole (para. 34);
- *Also recognizes* the Security Council's call regarding the importance of State cooperation with the Court and *encourages* further strengthening of the Security Council's relationship with the Court (para. 35);
- *Recalls* the report of the Court on the status of ongoing cooperation with the United Nations, including in the field (para. 36);
- *Encourages* all United Nations Offices, funds and programmes to strengthen their cooperation with the Court, and to collaborate effectively with the Office of Legal Affairs as focal point for cooperation between the United Nations system and the Court (para. 37);
- *Notes with concern* that, to date, expenses incurred by the Court due to referrals by the Security Council continue to be borne exclusively by States parties, and *notes* that, to date, the approved budget allocated so far within the Court in relation to the referrals made by the Security Council amount to approximately €58 million (para. 41);
- *Stresses* that, if the United Nations is unable to provide funds for the Court to cover the expenses incurred due to referrals by the Security Council, this will, among other factors, continue to exacerbate resource pressure on the Court (para. 42);
- *Encourages* the Court to further engage with the relevant Sanctions Committees of the United Nations Security Council with a view to improving their cooperation and achieving better coordination on matters pertaining to areas of mutual concern (para. 44);
- *Notes* that all cooperation received by the Court from the United Nations is provided strictly on a reimbursable basis (para. 45).

---

[582] *Official Records of the Assembly of States parties to the Rome Statute of the International Criminal Court*, 16th session, The Hague, 4–14 November 2017 (ICC-ASP/15/5), vol. I, part III, ICC-ASP/16/Res.6.

Chapter IV

TREATIES CONCERNING INTERNATIONAL LAW CONCLUDED UNDER THE AUSPICES OF THE UNITED NATIONS AND RELATED INTERGOVERNMENTAL ORGANIZATIONS

A. Treaties concerning international law concluded under the auspices of the United Nations

In 2017, the Treaty on the Prohibition of Nuclear Weapons, New York, 7 July 2017, was concluded under the auspices of the United Nations.[1]

B. Treaties concerning international law concluded under the auspices of intergovernmental organizations related to the United Nations

1. World Health Organisation

Mozambique ratified the World Health Organisation (WHO) Framework Convention on Tobacco Control in 2017, bringing the total number of parties to 181.

Costa Rica, Cyprus, Germany, Guinea, Madagascar, Montenegro, Niger, Serbia and Slovakia ratified the Protocol to Eliminate Illicit Trade in Tobacco Products in 2017. By the end of 2017, there were 34 parties to the Protocol.

2. International Criminal Court

Exchange of letters for the prevention of torture and inhuman or degrading treatment between the International Criminal Court (ICC) and the European Committee for the Prevention of Torture and Inhuman or Degrading Treatment, Council of Europe (ICC-PRES/24-06-17),[2] which entered into force on 9 November 2017.

---

[1] Not reproduced herein. For the text of the Treaty, see Multilateral Treaties Deposited with the Secretary General, chapter XXVI.9.

[2] *Exchange of letters between ICC and the European Committee for the Prevention of Torture and Inhuman or Degrading Treatment of Punishment, and the Council of Europe*, 7 November 2017, ICC-PRES/24-06-17, available at https://www.icc-cpi.int/itemsDocuments/Exchange_of_letters_november2017.pdf [Last access: 10/10/2018].

On 24 April 2017 the ICC and the Government of Sweden concluded an Agreement on the Enforcement of Sentences of the ICC (ICC-PRES/20-02-17).[3]

On 18 April 2017, the ICC and the Argentine Republic concluded an Agreement on the Enforcement of Sentences of the ICC (ICC-PRES/19-01-17).[4]

[3] *Agreement between the Government of Sweden and the International Criminal Court on the enforcement of sentences of the International Criminal Court*, 24 April 2017, ICC-PRES/20-02-17, available at https://www.icc-cpi.int/itemsDocuments/170424-oj-sa-Sweden.pdf [Last access: 10/10/2018].

[4] *Agreement between the Argentine Republic and the International Criminal Court on the enforcement of sentences of the International Criminal Court*, 18 April 2017, ICC-PRES/20-02-17, available at https://www.icc-cpi.int/itemsDocuments/170424-oj-sa-Sweden.pdf [Last access: 10/10/2018].

Chapter V

DECISIONS OF THE ADMINISTRATIVE TRIBUNALS OF THE UNITED NATIONS AND RELATED INTERGOVERNMENTAL ORGANIZATIONS[1]

A. United Nations Dispute Tribunal

In 2017, the United Nations Dispute Tribunal ("UNDT" or "Tribunal") in New York, Geneva and Nairobi issued a total of 100 judgments.[2] Summaries of six selected judgments are reproduced below.[3]

1. *Judgment No. UNDT/2017/018 (10 March 2017): Wondimu v. Secretary-General of the United Nations*[4]

Non-reassignment—Revocation of appointment—Removal from post—Readvertisement of post

The Applicant challenged the decisions of the United Nations High Commissioner for Refugees ("UNHCR") to remove him from the post of Deputy Representative in South Sudan and to re-advertise his post. At the time of the contested decision, the Applicant was serving at the P-5 level. In March 2013, the Applicant's substantive post as Assistant Representative ("Operations") was reclassified to Deputy Representative, South Sudan. The Applicant participated in a competitive selection process for the reclassified position.

On 15 December 2013, a conflict broke out in South Sudan while the Applicant and the UNHCR Representative for South Sudan ("Country Representative") were on leave. The Applicant returned to South Sudan on 23 December 2013 to support UNHCR's operations during the conflict. He learned the same day through a UNHCR broadcast that he had been selected for the post of Deputy Representative, South Sudan, and that his new appointment was to take effect on 1 January 2014. On 29 December 2013, the Applicant e-mailed female staff members who were on leave not to return to South Sudan due to

---

[1] For general information on the administration of justice at the United Nations, see chapter III, part A, section 16 (*n*) of this publication. In view of the large number of judgments rendered by the administrative tribunals of the United Nations and related intergovernmental organizations, only those judgments which address significant issues of United Nations administrative law or are otherwise of general interest have been summarized in the present edition of the Yearbook.

[2] The 100 judgments disposed of 113 applications. See A/73/217, table 6, p. 9.

[3] The summaries provided are for illustrative purposes only and are not authoritative, representative or exhaustive. Some UNDT judgments summarized may have been overturned on appeal by UNAT. For the full list of judgments by the UNDT and the latest developments, consult the website of the Office of the Administration of Justice at https://www.un.org/en/internaljustice.

[4] Judge Nkemdilim Izuako (Nairobi).

the escalation of gender-based violence at the time. On 30 December 2013, the Applicant departed to Ethiopia due to a family emergency. The Country Representative had still not returned from leave at the time but the Applicant informed the acting Representative in South Sudan who in turn informed the UNHCR leadership in Geneva.

On 7 January 2014, the Country Representative wrote to the High Commissioner requesting the reversal of the Applicant's appointment as the Deputy Representative. On 8 January 2014, the Applicant was informed of the High Commissioner's decision to review assignments for the reconfiguration of UNHCR's response to the crisis. He was also informed that his job description and functions would be revised and that his new position would be re-advertised to reflect the changed operational realities. The Country Representative told the Applicant on 14 January 2014 that the UNHCR leadership was unhappy with him for leaving South Sudan on 30 December 2013. The Applicant immediately emailed the UNHCR leadership to apologize for leaving South Sudan prior to the Representative's arrival.

By memorandum dated 13 January 2014, the High Commissioner removed the Applicant from the post of Deputy Representative and assigned another staff member to the post. By memorandum dated 23 January 2014, UNHCR provided the Applicant with information related to his departure from South Sudan.

UNDT noted that the Applicant had properly competed for and had been selected for the Deputy Representative post. UNDT determined that the Country Representative failed to conduct a proper and detailed analysis of the refugee emergency in South Sudan, which would have shown what new skill set was required and how that of the Applicant was not suitable in the circumstances, before requesting the Applicant's removal from the Deputy Representative post on 7 January 2014. UNDT held that a mere statement by the Country Representative that there had been "dramatic developments" in the country that required adjustment to the profile of the Deputy Representative was not a reasoned request and could not, without more, constitute a sufficient basis for the exercise of the High Commissioner's discretion to remove the Applicant.

UNDT held that the alleged unauthorized departure of the Applicant from South Sudan on 30 December 2013 and his unilateral advisory to female staff members not to return to the country during the emergency were the reasons for his removal from the Deputy Representative post. The decision of the High Commissioner to remove the Applicant was not based on any operational reasons but was simply "disciplinary action by stealth". UNHCR ought to have called for an explanation from the Applicant regarding his departure from the duty station and then determined whether removal was justified in light of his explanations and the United Nations' policy on staff balancing their personal and professional lives. UNDT concluded that the manner in which UNHCR removed the Applicant from the Deputy Representative position violated UNHCR's Policy and Procedures on Assignments and Promotions.

UNDT awarded the Applicant four months' net base salary as compensation for UNHCR's failure to follow its own rules and procedures, which resulted in the Applicant's unlawful removal from his position as Deputy Representative and for harm to his career prospects.

2. *Judgment No. UNDT/2017/062 (4 August 2017): Chama* v. *Secretary-General of the United Nations*[5]

PROPOSED ABOLITION OF POST—RECEIVABILITY OF APPLICATION—DOWNSIZING

The Applicant challenged the "procedures used to arrive at the decision to abolish his post and sought rescission of the abolition." On 19 January 2015, the Report of the Secretary-General A/69/731 (Budget for the United Nations Interim Force in Lebanon ("UNIFIL") for the period from 1 July 2015 to 30 June 2016) was issued. Paragraph 37 of the Report proposed to convert one of two FSlevel posts in the Joint GIS ("JGIS") section to a national post. By letter dated 21 April 2015, the Applicant was informed that his post in the JGIS section was being abolished/nationalized in the 2015/2016 budget and that his contract would not be extended beyond 30 June 2015.

UNDT considered that the fact that UNIFIL's decision to designate a post for abolition was premised on the anticipated resolution of the General Assembly approving UNIFIL's restructuring. However, in the view of UNDT, a proposed budget was irrelevant for the issue of receivability *ratione materiae*, just as it would be irrelevant for any other justification or motive for an administrative decision.

In this respect, it would be incorrect to distil from UNAT's holding in 2014-UNAT-481 that only administrative acts which are subsequent to regulatory acts of the General Assembly or the Secretary-General may be contested before the UNDT. The gist of the issue contemplated in the UNAT judgment was to distinguish regulatory acts from individual administrative decisions when they remain in a normative or other causal relation. However, whether an individual administrative decision would be taken in advance of the General Assembly's resolution or after, or whether it implements it correctly or incorrectly are matters valid for the question of legality of an administrative decision and not for the question of its receivability for review.

Rather, the issue material for receivability was in UNDT's view whether a designation of a specific post for abolition is *per se* capable of being reviewed for compliance with the staff member's terms of appointment. In this respect, UNDT noted that UNAT took a firm stance that acts prefatory to the abolition of a post have no direct effect on the conditions of employment as these only occur when the abolition is being implemented. UNDT observes, however, that applying the UNAT judgment to deny the staff an ability to autonomously challenge a decision on designation of his or her individually identified post for abolition in the proposed budget effectively removes the matter of legality of abolition of that post from UNDT's cognizance. This is because: a) subsequent decisions of the General Assembly which approve the abolition of that specific post are not subject to review before UNDT; b) administrative decisions on non-extension are validated by the General Assembly, which renders the review of legality largely irrelevant since, as held by UNAT in 2015-UNAT-530, paragraph 35, "decisions of the General Assembly are binding on the Secretary-General and therefore, the administrative decision under challenge must be considered lawful."

It would be for the parties to test through appellate processes whether the outcome of 2014-UNAT-481 might be revisited by UNAT in relation to the designation of a specific post for abolition, considering that it is a decision of individual application and final in

[5] Judge Agnieszka Klonowiecka-Milart (Nairobi).

the administrative course of the matter, the immediate consequences of which render the status of the appointment precarious. Whereas the abolition of a post is decided with a large margin of discretion, however, judicial review would be warranted to remedy situations where designation of a specific post for abolition would have contradicted the stated criteria or been tainted by cronyism, discrimination, or other arbitrary and unlawful exercise of the discretion, which are criteria for intervention generally accepted by UNAT in situations of restructuring.

As shown by art. 8 of the UNDT Statute, access to recourse before UNDT is conditioned upon requesting a management evaluation of the impugned decision but not upon actually obtaining it. By the same token, a result of management evaluation which does not remove the gravamen of the impugned decision does not bar access to the UNDT. As held by UNAT in 2011-UNAT-135, paragraph 22, an erroneous "[…] refusal by the Management Evaluation Unit to consider a request for management evaluation on the basis that the MEU [MEU] found it not receivable *ratione personae*, must be reviewable by the UNDT and this [UNAT] Court. In the view of UNDT, the same principle applies in a situation where MEU finds the request moot, i.e., non-receivable *ratione materiae*.

3. *Judgment No. UNDT/2017/078 (28 September 2017): Buckley* v. *Secretary-General of the United Nations*[6]

Compensation for loss of or damage to personal effects attributable to service—Duty of care in emergency situations—Negligence

The Applicant challenged the United Nations Claims Board's ("UNCB") recommendation denying his claim for loss of personal effects after all staff in Camp Faouar of the United Nations Disengagement Observer Force ("UNDOF") in Syria, including the Applicant, were relocated/evacuated to Camp Ziouani in the Israeli Occupied Golan Heights on 15 September 2014.

The Applicant was tasked with supervising the transfer of United Nations property and critical equipment, together with the evacuation of up to 200 personnel after the planned relocation transitioned into an emergency due to deteriorating security conditions and imminent threat to the lives of United Nations personnel, its property and equipment. The Applicant described the circumstances as "[a] dangerous situation within which the activity was being performed, which included rockets (whistling overhead), mortar round and live ammunition strikes in proximity of Camp Faouar". The Applicant was among the last to leave and did not manage to bring with him any of his personal effects aside from his so-called "run bag" which contained his passports, credit cards and other documents.

Subsequently, the Applicant filed a claim for compensation for loss of personal effects of USD 14,700 with the UNDOF Local Claims Review Board, which recommended that he be paid USD 7,490 for the total depreciated/payable value of the relevant personal effects. The Applicant then filed a claim with the UNCB, which recommended that it be denied in its entirety, *inter alia*, for lack of credibility due to a "conspicuous resemblance" between the Applicant's claim and those of two other claimants, the Applicant having acted negligently, and/or the relevant articles not being reasonably required for day-to-day life in Camp Faouar. The United Nations Controller approved UNCB's recommendation.

[6] Judge Ebrahim-Carstens (New York).

The Applicant filed a request for management evaluation, and the Under-Secretary-General for Management ("USG/DM") reversed the decision in part, finding that the claimed items related to articles that can be considered to be reasonably required for day-to-day life at Camp Faouar and also finding the Applicant's claim credible as it was based on a previous inventory list. The USG/DM however did not award the Applicant any compensation for his loss of an iPad and a wristwatch, on the basis he had allegedly been negligent in not securing them in his run bag but left them in his residence.

The UNDT held that if the Applicant were to have been required to pack the iPad and wristwatch in his run bag, such instructions would not only have been in direct contravention of the United Nations Security Management System guidelines on what a run bag is to include, but also lead to the absurd or perverse result that, instead of focusing on saving lives and valuable United Nations equipment in a worsening security situation, the Applicant should have prioritized the recovery of these personal items of a relatively miniscule monetary value of USD 2,100. If the Applicant had a duty of care in the given context, it would rather have been not to carry his personal iPad or wristwatch in his run bag, nor to attempt to retrieve them from his residence in the midst of a dangerous emergency evacuation. On the contrary, had the Applicant done so, this may well have amounted to negligence.

Based thereon, the UNDT found that, in the exercise of its discretion, the Administration did not take into account, or give due regard to all the aforesaid circumstances surrounding the loss of the Applicant's property. In particular, there was no requirement, either by law or by reason, or on any reasonable basis, for the Applicant to pack the said items in his run bag; and consequently, in all the circumstances, he could not have been said to have been negligent. Accordingly, the UNDT granted the Applicant's claim in full, to also include the iPad and wristwatch.

4. *Judgment No. UNDT/2017/080 (29 September 2017): Timothy* v. *Secretary-General of the United Nations*[7]

ABOLITION OF POST—INDEFINITE APPOINTMENT—SEPARATION FROM SERVICE—ADMINISTRATION'S OBLIGATION UNDER STAFF RULE 9.6(*E*) AND 9.6(*F*)

The Applicant, a former GS-7 Senior Administrative Associate with the United Nations High Commissioner for Refugees ("UNHCR") challenged the Administration's decision to not make good faith efforts to absorb her on to a new post after it decided to abolish her existing post and to separate her from service as a result.

The Applicant received an indefinite appointment in 2011. On 11 January 2016, the Applicant received a letter from the Director of Liaison Office in New York informing her that, as a result of a comprehensive review of the office structure, a number of posts, including the Applicant's, were proposed to be abolished. The letter also stated that there will be newly created positions for which the Applicant would be encouraged to apply.

Between April and September 2016, the Applicant applied to 18 UNHCR vacancies that she was qualified for. Only one application led to further assessment. However, on 12 August 2016, the Applicant was informed that a former colleague holding a fixed-term appointment was selected for the post instead of her.

[7] Judge Alessandra Greceanu (New York).

On 16 September 2016, the Applicant received a letter from the UNHCR Director of Division of Human Resources Management informing that the Headquarters Assignments Committee met on 25 August 2016 and undertook a review of the availability of suitable positions in the Liaison Office in New York in which her services could be utilized. The letter stated that the Committee had not found any suitable positions for the Applicant. As such, the letter notified the Applicant that her indefinite appointment would be terminated.

On 10 November 2016, the Applicant requested management evaluation of the Administration's decision to not make good faith efforts to absorb her on to a new post after it decided to abolish her existing post. On 8 December 2016, the Deputy High Commissioner informed the Applicant of her decision to uphold the Administration's decision.

The Applicant argued that by failing to make good faith efforts to find her a suitable alternative post upon abolition, the Administration violated its obligation to her as the holder of an indefinite appointment under staff rule 9.6(*e*) and (*f*). The Respondent argued that the Administration fully complied with its obligation under the staff rules and the Applicant failed to establish that the contested decision was unlawful, unfair or otherwise flawed.

UNDT determined that staff rule 9.6(*e*) provides a staff member holding a continuing/indefinite appointment the highest level of legal protection from being terminated as compared to those serving on fixed-term or temporary appointments. The staff member has the right to be retained either in any suitable positions vacant at the same level or at lower level at the date of abolition or reduction of staff, or in any suitable positions occupied at the date of abolition, or reduction of staff. Staff members retained pursuant to staff rule 9.6(*e*) are required to have relative competence for new suitable post. A staff member who is to be retained in the order of preference established in staff rule 9.6(*e*) is therefore not required to be fully competent for the alternative post where s/he is to be retained, but to have a relative competence for the new suitable post. Further the staff member is to be retained in another position(s) on a non-competitive basis without having to go through a full competitive selection process, including by applying, for any of the suitable posts available. For the Administration to fully respect its obligation pursuant to staff rule 9.6(*e*), it has the duty to timely provide staff member(s) affected by abolition of posts or reduction of staff with a list of: (1) all posts, at the staff member's duty station, occupied at the date of abolition by staff members with a lower level of protection than the one of the staff member(s) affected, if any; and (2) all the vacant suitable positions, if any, in order for the staff member to be able to evaluate all the options and to timely express his/her interest.

UNDT found that the Administration did not respect its obligation pursuant to staff rule 9.6(*e*) and 9.6(*f*) to retain the Applicant and the Applicant's correlative right to be retained in any available suitable post at her level (G7 step 10) or at a lower level in UNHCR New York, or at her Professional level or lower in the parent Organization. The UNDT granted the Applicant's claim in part, rescinding the contested decision and ordering the Respondent to retain the Applicant with retroactive effect from 31 December 2016 in any current suitable available post(s), or in alternative, the Respondent to pay compensation of 12 months net-base salary. In addition, the UNDT ordered the Respondent to pay compensation of 3 months of net base salary as moral damages.

5. *Judgment No. UNDT/2017/091 (29 November 2017): Campeau* v. *Secretary-General of the United Nations*[8]

United nations privileges and immunities—Duty to cooperate with national authorities—Exercise discretion—Duty of care

The Applicant challenged the decision to release a United Nations Board of Inquiry ("BOI") report to [name of State] authorities, in relation with the prosecution of an individual involved in his kidnapping in Syria in 2013 ("the accused").

A Headquarters BOI had been constituted and issued a report ("BOI report") around the circumstances surrounding the Applicant's disappearance, abduction and return from captivity. In the context of criminal proceedings against the accused, [name of State] authorities requested the United Nations to provide them with information on whether it had conducted an investigation of the Applicant's abduction and any relevant documents or other elements on this event. At the end of a consultative process, the United Nations Legal Counsel decided to release a partially redacted BOI report to the Permanent Mission of [name of State], for further transmittal to the [name of State] Prosecutor.

The Note Verbale transmitting the report stressed that it was shared on a strictly voluntary basis and requested that it be treated confidentially and not be publicly disclosed to the extent possible under the applicable law. The BOI report contained, *inter alia*, the name of the Applicant's wife, the name of the city where she and their son resided, as well as the city of residence of Applicant's ex-wife, first son and parents.

In 2017, the High Regional Court in [name of city and State], convicted the accused as an accessory to (i) deprivation of liberty; (ii) attempt of extortion under threat of force, and (iii) (aggravated) kidnapping, thus sentencing him to three and a half years of imprisonment.

At the time of the proceedings before UNDT, the Applicant published a book in which he described his captivity in Syria. In its first edition, the name of the Applicant's wife and her city of residence were provided and the book disclosed, *inter alia*, that the Applicant gave his captors his wife's phone number and that they called her as well as the Applicant's parents several times.

The UNDT found that the decision to release the BOI report constituted an administrative decision for the purpose of art. 2.1(*a*) of its Statute. It stressed that despite its obligations under the Convention on Privileges and Immunities of the United Nations ("the Convention"), the Organization could have refused disclosing the BOI report on the basis of the inviolability of its archives. It further noted that, while under the Convention, privileges and immunities are granted to the Organization and not for the benefit of individual staff members, a decision by the Organization to disclose to national authorities a document containing information about a staff member and/or his/her family could potentially affect his/her terms of appointment, to the extent that it may impact on the Applicant's right to safety and security arising from the Organization's duty of care.

With respect to the merits of the case, UNDT examined, *inter alia*, the extent and limits of the Organization's duty to cooperate with judicial authorities of Member States under section 21 of the Convention; how that duty relates to the Organization's duty of

[8] Judge Teresa Bravo (Geneva).

care towards the Applicant; and whether the Organization duly took the latter into account when it decided to disclose the redacted BOI report to the [name of State] authorities.

It noted that the extent and scope of the Organization's duty to cooperate under the Convention is limited first and foremost by the Organization's privileges and immunities, which extend to its assets and archives. As the Note Verbale correctly stated, the BOI report was shared on a "strictly voluntary basis". In sharing the BOI report, the Organization exercised its discretion under the Convention and had to weigh its duty to cooperate against other factors, including its duty of care *vis-à-vis* the Applicant.

The Organization's duty of care towards its staff implies, first and foremost, that it must provide a healthy and safe working environment for and ensure the safety of its staff. That may encompass a duty to protect its staff against outside risks, *e.g.*, when divulging information, including personal data, that may impact on the safety and security of a staff member or her/his immediate family.

After hearing evidence from witnesses involved in the consultation process prior to the release of the BOI report, UNDT was satisfied that the Organization legally exercised its discretion and duly assessed the Applicant's safety, and that of his family, when it decided to share the BOI report, as well as the level of redaction of the BOI report. The UNDT recalled that, in making that risk assessment, the Organization had to balance its duty to cooperate with [name of State] authorities, its duty of care *vis-à-vis* the Applicant, and the interests of the Organization.

On the basis of the evidence heard at the hearing, UNDT was further satisfied that it was a reasonable exercise of discretion not to share other sources of information with the [name of State] authorities, including proof of life videos and names of negotiators, to protect the interests of the Organization and the security of its staff, including those who had acted as negotiators in situations like the one the Applicant endured. Contrary to what the Applicant suggested, the United Nations did not exercise its discretion in an arbitrary way with respect, on the one hand, of the disclosure of the BOI report and, on the other hand, of the non-disclosure of the proof-of-life videos and the names of the negotiators. In light of all the circumstances, UNDT was satisfied that the disclosure of the BOI report, and its level of redaction, were not arbitrary, unreasonable or unfair towards the Applicant.

UNDT was also satisfied from the evidence provided at the hearing that by releasing the BOI report, the Organization had no intention to undermine the Applicant's reputation or credibility and noted that the accused was convicted by the [name of State] Court. Hence, while it may have made it more difficult and stressful for the Applicant to provide his evidence in light of the BOI report, ultimately the conviction of the accused demonstrates that the release of the BOI report had either no impact or a positive one on the outcome of the criminal proceedings against the accused. Within the realm of judicial control of discretionary decisions, the UNDT therefore found that the disclosure of the BOI report was the result of a proper assessment undertaken by the Organization, and did not violate its duty of care towards the Applicant.

Finally, UNDT found that any alleged violation of the internal BOIs policy or the Standard Operating Procedures on BOIs were not relevant for its finding that the decision to share the BOI report was a legal exercise of administrative discretion, which did not violate the Applicant's terms of appointment; it also stressed that the Organization was not obliged to inform or consult with the Applicant before releasing the BOI report. The application was rejected.

6. *Judgment No. UNDT/2017/097 (29 December 2017): Lloret Alcaniz, Zhao, Xie, Kutner and Krings* v. *Secretary-General of the United Nations*[9]

Conversion of a portion of the salary into an allowance—Acquired rights

Five Applicants, who all have a non-dependent spouse and at least one dependent child, challenged the decision to reduce their salary in implementing a new Unified Salary Scale introduced on 1 January 2017 ("USS"). They took issue with the fact that a decision of the Secretary General reduced their salary as of that date by removing the portion that was previously paid to them in view of their entitlement to be paid at the dependency rate (due to fact that they had a dependent child), and that the transitional allowance introduced to mitigate their loss did not fully compensate for the salary reduction.

Prior to the introduction of the new USS on 1 January 2017, the Applicants, as staff members in the Professional and higher categories were paid their net salary at either a single or a dependency rate depending on their family status. Staff members who, like the Applicants, had a non-dependent spouse and at least one dependent child were paid at the dependency rate on account of their first dependent child.

Following a review initiated by the International Civil Service Commission ("ICSC") and its subsequent recommendations, the General Assembly decided to introduce one net USS for all staff members in the Professional and higher categories without regard to family status. Support provided for dependent family members was then separated from the salary and, therefore, the gross and net base salaries of staff members previously paid at the dependency rate were reduced. Changes were also made to the eligibility criteria for the support provided to families.

The Applicants, who were previously paid at the dependency rate on account of their first child because they had a non-dependent spouse, are eligible under the new regime for a child allowance, a fixed amount per annum. Because the amount of the child allowance is less than the reduction in the net base salary provided by the new USS, they are also eligible to receive a six-year transitional allowance. This transitional allowance, calculated at 6% of the net base salary and post adjustment, is equivalent to the difference between the new unified rate of salary and the dependency rate of the previous salary scale. However, over time, the transitional allowance does not fully compensate for the reduction of the Applicants' net base salary as it will be reduced by one percentage point every year, starting from 1 January 2018, and it will be discontinued when the child in respect of whom the transitional allowance is payable is no longer recognized as a dependent child, *e.g.*, upon the child reaching the age of 21.

The Applicants' payslips at the end of January 2017 showed a reduction of their net base salary and the introduction of the transitional allowance which, for the year 2017, compensated for their loss. The Applicant's payslips also showed a slight increase of their net take home pay in 2017. This was not due to the modification of the remuneration scheme but to an adjustment due to inflation and the application of the Noblemaire

[9] Judge Rowan Downing, Presiding, Judge Teresa Bravo and Judge Goolam Meeran Judge Alexander W. Hunter, Jr. (Geneva).

principle, which led to an overall increase of the salary scale in January 2017 as it is regularly the case at the beginning of each year.

According to an estimation tool made available to staff members by the Administration, which factors the impact of the USS, the Applicants will suffer losses over the coming years. Taking into account the yearly reduction of the transitional allowance and its discontinuation when the Applicants' oldest child will turn 21, it was estimated that each of the five Applicants will overall receive between approximately USD 28,598.88 and 65,563.48 less then what they would have been entitled to under the previous regime, depending on their individual situation.

UNDT rejected the Respondent's challenge to the receivability of the applications and found that it had jurisdiction to entertain them insofar as they challenged the implementation of the new USS in the Applicants' individual cases.

In examining the receivability of the applications, UNDT held that it shall take into consideration the Organization's duty to provide access to justice to its staff members in interpreting the jurisdiction that is vested in it by virtue of its Statute, notably in light of the absence of an alternative remedy to address alleged violations of the staff members' contractual rights. UNDT held that the contested decisions constituted "administrative decisions" within the meaning of its Statute, because the reduction of the Applicants' salary and the loss of their entitlement to be paid at the dependency rate negatively impacted their terms and conditions of appointment. The UNDT also took into account that the Applicants were not challenging the legality of the new USS but rather its implementation in their individual situations, which they claimed was in breach of their contracts of employment and their acquired rights.

UNDT further found that it had jurisdiction to review the contested decisions although they stemmed from the implementation by the Secretary-General of regulatory decisions taken by the General Assembly. UNDT acknowledged that the Secretary-General was bound by the General Assembly resolutions adopting the salary scale and the consequent modifications to the Staff Regulations and Rules. However, it found that the Secretary-General was equally bound by his contractual obligations towards staff members and preceding resolutions adopted by the General Assembly that formally protect their acquired rights. The UNDT held that this conflict of norms or obligations can neither be ignored by the Secretary-General nor by UNDT, notably in light of the Applicants' right to have access to justice. It further stressed that the Secretary-General had opportunities, in the process leading to the approval of the new USS, to bring any issues of conflicting obligations before the ICSC and the General Assembly.

Turning to the merits, UNDT held that staff members' acquired rights are protected by staff regulation 12.1, which takes precedence over other regulations and rules governing conditions of employment. Hence, conditions of employment that constitute acquired rights are not to be unilaterally changed by the Organization without the consent of the staff members.

The Applicants' salary was explicitly set out in their letters of appointment and goes to the root of their contract of employment. In UNDT's view, the salary is a fundamental and essential term of the Applicants' employment and thus constitutes an acquired right. Furthermore, the right to salary necessarily extends to its quantum and as the Applicant's salary increased over time, they accrued a right to be paid the newly determined salaries.

As their letters of appointment stated, the Applicants' salary was subject to increase, and thus cannot be reduced unilaterally by the Organization.

As a result of the implementation of the new salary scale, the Applicants lost 6% of their net base salaries on account of their family situation. Because this additional payment made to the Applicants was initially embedded in their salaries, which UNDT deemed an acquired right, it could not be unilaterally reduced or discontinued by the Organization, irrespective of the reason for the change or its impact.

UNDT further found that the introduction of a transitional allowance to mitigate the Applicants' losses is insufficient to safeguard their acquired right as it does not compensate for the financial loss that the Applicants will incur over time, starting from 1 January 2018. Likewise, the child allowance, which will be paid to the Applicants instead of receiving their salary at the dependency rate, is significantly lower. Moreover, the two allowances are not part of the Applicants' salary and may be subject to further change. They will also not be taken into account in the determination of other entitlements in case of separation, such as termination indemnity, repatriation grant, indemnity in case of death and commutation of accrued annual leave, which are all based on the Applicants' net base salary.

UNDT concluded that the Secretary-General's implementation of the new salary scale for the Applicants, which resulted in their being paid reduced gross and net base salaries from 1 January 2017, violated their acquired rights and was thus unlawful.

UNDT then examined the Applicant's claim that the Secretary-General misinterpreted the General Assembly resolution introducing the transitional allowance when he transposed it into the staff rules insofar as the staff rules prevent the transitional allowance to be transferred to a second dependent child when the one in respect of which the transitional allowance is paid turns 21. UNDT found that it was clear from the General Assembly resolution that by granting the transitional allowance, at the moment of the introduction of the new USS, to the child in respect of whom the staff member was paid at the dependency rate as of 31 December 2016 and providing that it would cease when "the child in respect of whom the allowance is payable loses eligibility", which is the case when the child turns 21, the General Assembly intended that it would not be transferable to any other child. UNDT found this matter was beyond the scope of its review powers.

UNDT rescinded the Secretary-General's decisions to pay the Applicants a salary reduced from the portion that was previously paid on the basis that they have a dependent child entitling them to be paid at the dependency rate, and clarified that the effect of the rescission entails that the 6% reduction of the Applicants' net salary plus post adjustment should be reintegrated as part of their salary from 1 January 2017 onwards. It further ruled that this amount should not be subject of reduction as long as the Applicants continue to meet the eligibility criteria for payment at the dependency rate, as defined under the former USS. UNDT also found that this amount shall be considered in the calculation of other entitlements or benefits based on the net base salary. UNDT found that the Applicants will not be entitled to the transitional allowance.

UNDT rejected the Applicants' claim for compensation for harm and retroactive payment of salary as it found that any prejudice is compensated by the rescission of the contested decisions and by their receipt of a transitional allowance for 2017, which will not be subject to recovery.

B. Decisions of the United Nations Appeals Tribunal

The United Nations Appeals Tribunal ("UNAT" or "Appeals Tribunal") issued a total of 152 judgments in 2017.[10] The summaries of seven of those judgments are reproduced below.[11]

1. *Judgment No. 2017-UNAT-742 (31 March 2017): Kallon v. Secretary-General of the United Nations*[12]

Claims for moral damages supported by only the complainant's testimony satisfies the burden of proof if found to be reliable and credible

A staff member at the United Nations Stabilization Mission in Haiti ("MINUSTAH") contested, before the UNDT, two administrative decisions to remove his designation as Chief Procurement Officer ("CPO") at MINUSTAH and to deny him the required designation to take up the post of CPO at another duty station. The UNDT rescinded the two decisions finding that they were taken in reaction to allegations that the staff member failed to properly exercise his delegated authority and without due process or substantiation. The UNDT declined to reinstate the applicant's designations but ordered USD 50,000 in non-pecuniary damages with interest for the stigmatization, reputational damage, stress, anxiety, and moral injury to the staff member.

UNAT, sitting en banc, upheld by majority, the UNDT's findings that the contested decisions were substantively and procedurally flawed. As for the UNDT's moral damages award, the majority noted that the purpose of the amendment to the UNDT's statute Article 10(5)(*b*) made following General Assembly resolution 69/203 is to introduce an express requirement that compensation for harm can be awarded only when there is a sufficient evidentiary basis. The majority held that evidence of moral injury consisting exclusively of the testimony of the complainant if credible, reliable and satisfactory in material respects, may be sufficient to discharge the evidentiary burden. The dissenting and concurring opinions took the view that evidence consisting exclusively of the complainant's testimony is not sufficient without corroboration by independent evidence (expert or otherwise). The majority thus upheld the UNDT's award of moral damages finding that the staff member's testimony was sufficient. While the staff member did not adduce expert or independent evidence to support his allegations of stress and anxiety, the evidence of the applicant, the egregious nature of the violation of his substantive and procedural rights, the self-evident damage to his professional reputation and his career, together provided a sufficient and convincing basis for the reasonable inference that he suffered a significant degree of stress and anxiety.

---

[10] See A/73/217, Table 7, p. 13.

[11] The summaries provided are for illustrative purposes only and are not authoritative, representative or exhaustive. For the full list of judgments by the UNAT and the latest developments, consult the website of the Office of the Administration of Justice at https://www.un.org/en/internaljustice.

[12] Judge Deborah Thomas-Felix, Presiding, Judge Richard Lussick, Judge Rosalyn Chapman, Judge John Murphy, Judge Dimitrios Raikos, Judge Sabine Knierim, and Judge Martha Halfeld.

2. *Judgment no. 2017-UNAT-750, Judgment No. 2017-UNAT-751, Judgment No. 2017-UNAT-752, Judgment No. 2017-UNAT-753, Judgment No. 2017-UNAT-754, Judgment No. 2017-UNAT-755, Judgment No. 2017-UNAT-756 (14 July 2017): Kagizi et al.,*[13] *Wanza et al.,*[14] *Baguma et al.,*[15] *Kiluwe et al.,*[16] *Kisubi et al.,*[17] *Ramzani et al.*[18] *and Nkashama et al.*[19] v. *Secretary-General of the United Nations*

NON-RENEWAL OF APPOINTMENT NOT APPEALABLE WHEN PROPERLY IMPLEMENTED IN CONSEQUENCE OF GENERAL ASSEMBLY'S DECISION TO ABOLISH POSTS

The fixed-term appointments of 51 appellants, all former Language Assistants at the General Service level with the United Nations Organization Stabilization Mission in the Democratic Republic of the Congo, expired on 30 June 2015 and were not renewed because the posts they encumbered had been abolished by a decision of the General Assembly with effect from 1 July 2015. The appellants challenged the non-renewal of their appointments and several ancillary matters before the UNDT.

The UNDT issued 51 individual judgments, dismissing the applications. The UNDT found that the claims regarding the non-renewal of the appointments were not receivable because the appellants had no standing to challenge a decision by the General Assembly and the decision of the General Assembly was binding on the Secretary-General who properly implemented it. The UNDT also held that the re-engaging by UNOPS of the appellants as individual contractors following their separation was not unlawful and that there had been no inequality of treatment in the implementation of the Mission's restructuring efforts.

UNAT consolidated the 51 appeals into seven groups heard by seven panels, the first group being heard by the full bench. UNAT dismissed the appeals. It confirmed the UNDT's finding that the claims regarding the abolition of posts made pursuant to a decision of the General Assembly were not receivable and upheld the UNDT's conclusion that the appellants lacked standing to challenge the non-renewal of their appointments. UNAT further found that the UNDT had no authority to review the re-engaging of the appellants by UNOPS as individual contractors as this was not an administrative decision subject to judicial review.

[13] Judge Deborah Thomas-Felix, Presiding, Judge Richard Lussick, Judge Rosalyn Chapman, Judge John Murphy, Judge Dimitrios Raikos, Judge Sabine Knierim and Judge Martha Halfeld.

[14] Judge Richard Lussick, Presiding, Judge Deborah Thomas-Felix and Judge Dimitrios Raikos.

[15] Judge Rosalyn Chapman, Presiding, Judge Deborah Thomas-Felix and Judge Richard Lussick.

[16] Judge John Murphy, Presiding, Judge Deborah Thomas-Felix, and Judge Sabine Knierim.

[17] Judge Dimitrios Raikos, Presiding, Judge John Murph and Judge Martha Halfeld.

[18] Judge Sabine Knierim, Presiding, Judge Deborah Thomas-Felix and Judge John Murphy.

[19] Judge Martha Halfeld, Presiding, Judge Deborah Thomas-Felix, Judge John Murphy.

3. *Judgment 2017-UNAT-759, Judgment 2017-UNAT-763, Judgment 2017-UNAT-764, Judgment 2017-UNAT-765, Judgment 2017-UNAT-766, Judgment 2017-UNAT-767, and Judgment 2017-UNAT-768 (14 July 2017): Hassanin,[20] Crotty,[21] Zachariah,[22] Fasanella,[23] Alsado,[24] Wrigth,[25] and Smiths[26]* v. *Secretary-General of the United Nations*

UNITED NATIONS' OBLIGATION TO GIVE PRIORITY CONSIDERATION TO PERMANENT STAFF FACING TERMINATION DUE TO ABOLITION OF POST

Several former staff members in the Publishing Division of the Department for General Assembly and Conference Management ("DGACM") filed applications before the UNDT challenging the decision to terminate their permanent appointments following the abolition of posts in DGACM. UNDT ordered compensation for emotional distress and—in all cases in which staff members had not secured another position with the Organization at the time of their application with UNDT—rescission of the termination decision and in-lieu compensation.

UNAT vacated UNDT's compensation orders in the cases in which staff members had secured alternative employment, finding that the applications had become moot. In the remaining cases, UNAT considered that any permanent staff member facing termination due to abolition of post must show an interest in a new position (for which he or she is suitable and qualified) by timely and completely applying for that position. However, once the application process is completed, thes Administration is required by Staff Rule 13.1(*d*) to consider the permanent staff member on a preferred or non-competitive basis for the position in an effort to retain the permanent staff member, which the Administration failed to do in this case.

Accordingly, UNAT upheld UNDT's findings that the termination decisions were unlawful in cases in which the respective staff members had complied with the aforementioned requirement to apply for alternative positions and vacated the UNDT's findings in cases where the staff members had failed to submit timely and complete applications for positions for which they were suitable and qualified. In the former cases, UNAT upheld the award of in-lieu compensation, albeit, unlike the UNDT, not reducing the total amount by the termination indemnity paid but vacated the award of moral damages for lack of evidence of harm; in the latter cases, UNAT vacated UNDT's order of in-lieu compensation and moral damages.

---

[20] Judge Sabine Knierim, Presiding, Judge Rosalyn Chapman and Judge Dimitrios Raikos.

[21] Judge Rosalyn Chapman, Presiding, Judge Dimitrios Raikos and Judge Sabine Knierim.

[22] Judge Rosalyn Chapman, Presiding, Judge Dimitrios Raikos and Judge Sabine Knierim.

[23] Judge Dimitrios Raikos, Presiding, Judge Rosalyn Chapman and Judge Sabine Knierim.

[24] Judge Rosalyn Chapman, Presiding, Judge Dimitrios Raikos and Judge Sabine Knierim.

[25] Judge Sabine Knierim, Presiding, Judge Rosalyn Chapman and Judge Dimitrios Raikos.

[26] Judge Sabine Knierim, Presiding, Judge Rosalyn Chapman and Judge Dimitrios Raikos.

4. *Judgment 2017-UNAT-785 (27 October 2017): Smith* v. *Secretary-General of the United Nations*[27]

TEMPORARY JOB OPENING ANNOUNCED INTERNALLY—RESTRICTION LIMITING RECRUITMENT TO STAFF MEMBERS AT A PARTICULAR DUTY STATION IS UNLAWFUL

A staff member, who at the relevant time worked with the Department of Field Support in New York challenged before the UNDT the Administration's decision that he was not eligible for the Temporary Job Opening ("TJO") he applied for, since the TJO was advertised internally within the United Nations Mission in South Sudan ("UNMISS") and was therefore only open to UNMISS staff.

The UNDT found that the decision to consider the staff member ineligible for the TJO was unlawful and breached his right to be fully and fairly considered. Since the TJO stated that it was open to internal candidates, it was open to all internal candidates, including the staff member, because he was recruited after a competitive examination under Staff Rule 4.16. The UNDT awarded moral damages for loss of career prospect, in that his prospects for career development and opportunities for professional growth were reduced by the restriction.

UNAT found that the Secretary-General had the lawful authority to impose such a restriction, which objectively furthered the operational purposes of efficiency and short-term convenience and was proportional in its effects. It found that the decision of the Administration to limit the appointment to UNMISS staff members was reasonable and that there was insufficient evidence to support a finding of discrimination or improper motive. Accordingly, UNAT vacated the UNDT Judgment.

5. *Judgment 2017-UNAT-787 (27 October 2017): Auda* v. *Secretary-General of the United Nations*[28]

TESTIMONIAL EVIDENCE WITHOUT CORROBORATION BY INDEPENDENT EVIDENCE (EXPERT OR OTHERWISE) IS NOT SATISFACTORY PROOF TO SUPPORT AN AWARD OF MORAL DAMAGES

A staff member within the Department for General Assembly and Conference Management ("DGACM") filed an application before the UNDT contesting an administrative decision to close an investigation of the staff member's complaint filed under [Secretary-General's Bulletin] ST/SGB/2008/5 (Prohibition of discrimination, harassment, including sexual harassment, and abuse of authority). The UNDT concluded that the decision to close the complaint without further action was improper as the investigation was tainted by serious procedural breaches. The UNDT awarded USD 5,000 in moral damages compensation to the staff member for the harm suffered to the staff member's reputation and general well-being.

UNAT found no error and upheld both UNDT's finding that the decision was improper as well as the UNDT's refusal to order rescission on account of the subject of the investigation having separated from the Organization. UNAT, however, vacated the UNDT's moral damages award on grounds that the staff member did not present any evidence, apart from his own unsworn testimony to support the claim. UNAT held that "generally

[27] Judge John Murphy, Presiding, Judge Richard Lussick and Judge Martha Halfeld.

[28] Judge Dimitrios Raikos, Presiding, Judge Richard Lussick and Judge Sabine Knierim.

speaking, the testimony of an applicant alone without corroboration by independent evidence (expert or otherwise) affirming that non-pecuniary harm has indeed occurred is not satisfactory proof to support an award of damages." As the staff member's testimony was the only evidence presented to support his allegation of harm to his reputation and general well-being, the UNDT committed an error of law in stating that this alone was sufficient to sustain an award of compensation under Article 10(5)(*b*) of the UNDT Statute.

6. *Judgment 2017-UNAT-801 and Judgment No. 2017-UNAT-807 (27 October 2017): Faye*[29] *and Rockcliffe*[30] v. *Secretary-General of the United Nations*

STAFF MEMBERS OF THE PENSION FUND DULY ELECTED TO THE UNITED NATIONS PENSION FUND'S STAFF PENSION COMMITTEE HAVE THE SAME RIGHTS/PRIVILEGES AS OTHER ELECTED MEMBERS

Two staff members of the Pension Fund were elected to the United Nations Pension Fund's Staff Pension Committee (UNSPC). Following the elections, they were given two options: i) to remain on the UNSPC and accept to be moved to an appropriate post elsewhere in the Secretariat outside the Fund; or (ii) to continue to work in the Fund's secretariat and resign from the UNSPC and the Pension Board. The staff members rejected both options.

The staff members were subsequently informed that the Pension Board had discussed the conflict of interest arising from the fact that they had been elected to the UNSPC while staff members of the Pension Fund and that it had decided that they would not be given access to the Pension Board documents nor could they participate in any formal preparations for the Pension Board session and meetings until such time the conflict of interest had been resolved. Both staff members appealed the decisions to UNAT.

UNAT considered that at the time of the elections, there was no law which prevented the appellants from being elected to the UNSPC once they met the prerequisite requirements which they did. UNAT held that both staff members were duly elected members of the UNSPC and that as a direct consequence of their election, they had the same rights and privileges which are bestowed upon other elected members and which could not be restricted or denied. UNAT granted the appeals and ordered that the appellants be given access to all relevant Pension Board documents and be allowed to participate and function as elected member in all relevant areas including the preparations for the Pension Board sessions, meetings of the Pension Board and of its constituent groups, committees and working groups.

7. *Judgment 2017-UNAT-802 (27 October 2017): Riecan* v. *Secretary-General of the United Nations*[31]

NO NEED FOR INTERVIEW PANEL TO CONSIDER E-PAS OF APPLICANTS AND REFLECT CONSIDERATION OF E-PAS IN ASSESSMENT REPORT

A staff member challenged before the UNDT the decision not to recommend him for the position he applied for because he was not given a full and fair assessment by the assessment/interview panel.

[29] Judge Deborah Thomas-Felix, Presiding, Judge Richard Lussick and Judge Sabine Knierim.

[30] Judge Deborah Thomas-Felix, Presiding, Judge Richard Lussick and Judge Sabine Knierim.

[31] Judge Dimitrios Raikos, Presiding, Judge Richard Lussick, Judge Sabine Knierim.

UNDT found that there was a material failure by the interview panel to consider the applicant's e-PAS reports which were relevant material, especially in the context of the disparity between its ratings and those of his reporting officers on the same competencies and within the same organization. UNDT concluded that the staff member's application was not given full and fair consideration and awarded compensation.

UNAT vacated UNDT judgment, finding that it erred in law and exceeded its competence by ruling that the interview panel was under a duty to consider the staff member's e-PAS reports and reflect that consideration in its own assessment report, even after the staff member had failed the interview. In finding so, UNDT improperly assumed the role of deciding which evaluation method should have been used and adopted an approach which is not provided for in the existing staff selection system.

C. Decisions of the Administrative Tribunal of the International Labour Organization[32]

In 2017, the Administrative Tribunal of the International Labour Organization adopted a total of 181 judgments at its 123rd (2nd part), 124th and 125th sessions.[33]

D. Decisions of the World Bank Administrative Tribunal[34]

In 2017, the Administrative Tribunal of the World Bank adopted a total of 26 judgments and two orders at its spring and fall sessions: fourteen judgments were rendered on April 21, 2017 at the conclusion of the Tribunal's spring session, and eleven judgments and two orders were rendered on October 25, 2017 at the conclusion of the Tribunal's fall session.[35]

---

[32] The Administrative Tribunal of the International Labour Organization is competent to hear complaints alleging non-observance, in substance or in form, of the terms of appointment of officials and of the staff regulations of international organizations that have recognized the competence of the Tribunal. For a list of those organizations, see http://www.ilo.org/tribunal/membership/lang--en/index.htm. The Tribunal is also competent to hear disputes with regard to the execution of certain contracts concluded by the International Labour Organization and disputes relating to the application of the regulations of the former Staff Pension Fund of the International Labour Organization. For more information about the Administrative Tribunal of the International Labour Organization and the full texts of its judgments, see http://www.ilo.org/tribunal/lang--en/index.htm.

[33] See https://www.ilo.org/dyn/triblex/triblexmain.showlist.

[34] The World Bank Administrative Tribunal is competent to hear and pass judgment upon any applications alleging non-observance of the contract of employment or terms of appointment, including all pertinent regulations and rules in force at the time of the alleged non-observance, of members of the staff of the International Bank for Reconstruction and Development, the International Development Association and the International Finance Corporation, the Multilateral Investment Guarantee Agency and the International Centre for the Settlement of Investment Disputes (collectively "the Bank Group"). The Tribunal is open to any current or former member of the staff of the Bank Group, any person who is entitled to a claim upon a right of a member of the staff as a personal representative or by reasons of the staff member's death and any person designed or otherwise entitled to receive payment under any provision of the Staff Retirement Plan. For more information on the World Bank Administrative Tribunal and full texts of its decisions, see https://tribunal.worldbank.org (accessed on 31 December 2013).

[35] See https://tribunal.worldbank.org/judgments-orders?search_api_fulltext_op=and&search_api_fulltext=&items_per_page=20&sort_bef_combine=field_date_DESC&sort_by=field_date&sort_order=DESC&page=5.

E. Decisions of the Administrative Tribunal of the International Monetary Fund[36]

The summaries of two judgments issued by the Administrative Tribunal of the International Monetary Fund in 2017 are reproduced below as representing significant developments in the jurisprudence of the Tribunal.[37]

1. *Judgment No. 2017-1 (15 November 2017): Mr. "MM"* v. *International Monetary Fund*

Decision of the Staff Retirement Plan (SRP) Administration Committee granting request of former spouse to give effect to divorce judgment awarding marital portion of Applicant's future pension payments—Interpretation of the provisions of SRP Section 11.3 and implementing Rules

The Tribunal rendered a Judgment on an Application brought by Mr. "MM", a staff member of the Fund and participant in the Fund's Staff Retirement Plan ("SRP" or "Plan"). Applicant challenged the decision of the SRP Administration Committee ("Committee"), granting the request of his former spouse to give effect under Section 11.3 of the Plan to a District of [name of District] divorce judgment awarding her one-half of the marital portion of Applicant's future pension payments. Applicant's former spouse participated in the Tribunal proceedings as an Intervenor, as permitted under Rule XIV of the Tribunal's Rules of Procedure.

SRP Section 11.3 provides a mechanism for the Committee to give effect under the Plan to a "legal obligation arising from a marital relationship or pursuant to a legal obligation to make child support payments, evidenced by an order of a court or by a settlement agreement incorporated into a court order". Applicant contended that the District of [name of District] divorce judgment failed to meet the criteria prescribed by the implementing rules ("Section 11.3 Rules"). Those rules require that a court order: (A) is valid by reason that: (1) a reasonable method of notification has been employed and a reasonable opportunity to be heard has been afforded to the persons affected; and (2) the judgment has been rendered by a court of competent jurisdiction … and in accordance with such requirements of the state of [rendition] as are necessary for the valid exercise of power by the court; (B) is the product of fair proceedings; (C) is final and binding on the parties; and (D) does not conflict and is not inconsistent with any other valid court order or decree.

Applying the standard of review applicable when the Tribunal considers a challenge to a decision of the SRP Administration Committee, the Tribunal asked whether the Committee had correctly interpreted the provisions of SRP Section 11.3, and the implementing Rules, and soundly applied them to the facts of the case.

[36] The Administrative Tribunal of the International Monetary Fund became operational on 1 January 1994. The Tribunal is competent to pass judgment upon any application: (*a*) by a member of the staff challenging the legality of an administrative act adversely affecting him; or (*b*) by an enrollee in, or beneficiary under, any retirement or other benefit plan maintained by the Fund as employer challenging the legality of an administrative act concerning or arising under any such plan which adversely affects the applicant. The complete jurisprudence of the IMF Administrative Tribunal may be accessed electronically at http://www.imf.org/tribunal.

[37] The Tribunal rendered three judgments in 2017.

Although Applicant did not dispute that the District of [name of District] divorce judgment met criteria (A) and (B), the Tribunal began by addressing those essential requirements. The Tribunal observed that the District of [name of District] divorce judgment was the result of adversary proceedings in which both Applicant and his former spouse had fully participated. The court had expressly found that it had jurisdiction over the divorce action. Applicant had not alleged otherwise. The Tribunal accordingly concluded that the judgment had been rendered by a court of competent jurisdiction in which the parties were afforded fair process, including notice and an opportunity to be heard. For these reasons, the Tribunal concluded that the Committee had not erred in deciding that the judgment met criteria (A) and (B) of the Section 11.3 Rules.

The Tribunal considered Applicant's argument that the divorce judgment was not "final and binding on the parties" as required by criterion (C) of the Section 11.3 Rules because his appeal of that judgment was pending in the District of [name of District] Court of Appeals at the time that the Committee decided to give it effect under the Plan. The Court of Appeals later denied that appeal. The Tribunal concluded that "[i]n the light of the prevailing law of the District of [name of District], which Applicant has not disputed, the Tribunal cannot say that the Committee erred in determining that the Judgment of Absolute Divorce was 'final and binding on the parties' within the meaning of criterion (C) of the Section 11.3 Rules." (Para. 69.) An important consideration in construing that provision, according to the Tribunal, was that "... were the Committee to require 'final order' to mean 'unappealable order,' then the object of the Plan provision to encourage enforcement of orders for family support and division of marital property ... might be frustrated because, in some legal systems, a retiree could delay implementation of a court order by repeatedly filing appeals against it". (*Id.*) A further consideration was that the Plan provides, and the Committee has created a mechanism, for a Plan participant or affected spouse to return to the Committee with a subsequently rendered court order and Applicant had been so advised by the Committee.

As to criterion (D), which requires that the court order "does not conflict and is not inconsistent with any other valid court order or decree", the Tribunal considered Applicant's assertions that the District of [name of District] divorce judgment was in conflict with the law of the country of which he was a citizen and that proceedings were underway in that jurisdiction to obtain a conflicting court order. No allegedly conflicting court order, however, had been presented to the Committee. In the view of the Tribunal, the Committee could not be said to have erred in failing to take account of a court order that did not exist at the time it rendered its decisions. "Nor did the Committee deny Applicant fair process when it considered only the order that was the subject of his ex-spouse's request, in the absence of being presented with any other court order." (Para. 75.) Furthermore, the "Committee is not authorized to speculate as to the content of future court orders or required to hold the proceedings in abeyance while awaiting the emergence of a new court order, when it finds that the order presented meets the requirements of the Section 11.3 Rules." (*Id.*) It was also significant that the Plan and the implementing Rules provide for the possibility of bringing a subsequent, allegedly inconsistent order to the Committee's attention and that Applicant had been so advised.

Having concluded that the Committee correctly interpreted the provisions of the Plan and soundly applied them to the facts of the case, as those facts were established at the time of the Committee's decisions, the Tribunal turned to the further question whether any developments subsequent to the Committee's Decision on Review precluded the Tribunal from sustaining that decision. These developments included the dissolution of the marriage in the country of Applicant's citizenship and ongoing litigation in that jurisdiction. The Tribunal considered that its authority in relation to the Plan is an appellate one: "[I]t is not within the ambit of the Tribunal's competence to assess *in the first instance* whether any current or future court order may be in conflict or inconsistent with the District of [name of District] divorce judgment that has been given effect by the Committee. That is the province of the Committee to undertake, in accordance with the Tribunal's jurisprudence." (Para. 86.) (Emphasis in original.) The Tribunal accordingly concluded that subsequent developments did not preclude the Tribunal from sustaining the Committee's decision. The Tribunal's Judgment noted that, consistent with the Plan and the implementing Rules, Applicant may return to the Committee with a new court order if he believes that it is in conflict or inconsistent with the District of Columbia divorce judgment. In such case, the Committee would render a decision, which could later be challenged in the Administrative Tribunal if Applicant remained aggrieved.

Accordingly, the Application of Mr. "MM" was denied.

2. *Judgment No. 2017-2 (11 December 2017): Ms. "NN"* v. *International Monetary Fund*

Denial of opportunity to compete for vacancy as a Result of Absence of Pre-screening Interview—Departments discretion to fashion their own Selection Processes—Binding Character of Elected Selection Processes—Prejudgment of Applicant's Suitability for a Vacancy without subjecting her to the Established Process for Making the Selection Decision—Abuse of Discretion by Fund When Deciding not to afford Applicant a Pre-Screening Interview

The Tribunal rendered a Judgment on an Application brought by Ms. "NN", a former limited-term staff member of the Fund, challenging the selection process for a vacancy for which she had applied, a position that was similar in substance to that which she was then occupying on a limited-term appointment. Applicant also raised several other claims.

The Tribunal began by considering Applicant's chief complaint, that she was wrongfully denied the opportunity to compete for a vacancy because, as a Department staff member who met the eligibility requirements for the position, she was entitled to a pre-screening interview in accordance with vacancy selection guidelines adopted by her Department. The necessary result of failing to afford Applicant a pre-screening interview was to eliminate her from the competition altogether, as pre-screening was a prerequisite to a candidate's advancing to the shortlist.

The Fund maintained that the Department's practice of conducting pre-screening interviews of all eligible Departmental candidates did not amount to a Fund recruitment policy applicable in every case. The Tribunal observed, however, that the Fund-wide policy was that departments were given discretion to fashion their own selection processes. In the view of the Tribunal, "once Applicant's Department exercised that discretion and adopted a process that included pre-screening interviews for all internal candidates—a policy that managers testified was consistently applied—it was bound to abide by that process". (Para. 94.) This was so, said the Tribunal, because a "transparent, rules-based vacancy selection process protects against arbitrariness and discrimination". (Para. 95.) The Tribunal additionally observed that such a process "creates expectations among Fund staff members that their applications for vacancies will be fairly considered in accordance with those rules". (*Id.*)

As to the Fund's contentions that the pre-screening interview would not have served the purpose of that practice in Applicant's case (given that the hiring manager was already well-acquainted with her work in a substantially similar job) and that the failure to grant Applicant a pre-screening interview did not prejudice the outcome of the selection process, the Tribunal concluded: "[T]he question is not whether supervisors' concerns about Applicant's performance in her expiring position were well-founded or whether such concerns could be taken into account in deciding whether or not to shortlist or select her for the vacancy. According to the Tribunal, the question was "whether—in light of the Departmental vacancy selection guidelines and the individual assurance Applicant had been given that she could apply to vacancies as they arose—it was fair to Applicant to exclude her from the competition altogether so that her strengths and weaknesses would not be assessed as would those of any other internal candidate…". (Para. 106.) The Tribunal concluded that it was fundamentally unfair of the Fund to prejudge Applicant's suitability for a vacancy without subjecting her to the established process for making the selection decision.

Accordingly, the Tribunal concluded that the Fund abused its discretion when it decided not to afford Applicant a pre-screening interview, thereby excluding her from the competition for the vacancy. Additionally, the Fund failed to inform Applicant of that decision, contrary to Department guidelines and general principles of international administrative law. For these breaches of the Fund's rules and her legitimate expectations, the Fund was ordered to pay Applicant $7,500 as compensation. In setting the quantum of compensation, the Tribunal noted that an aggravating factor was that the impugned decision was a considered choice and that surrounding circumstances raised questions as to the reason for that decision. At the same time, evidence that Applicant had a relatively slim likelihood of success in her application for the vacancy served to mitigate the harm. The Fund additionally was ordered to pay Applicant 50 percent of the total amount of her legal fees and costs.

The following additional complaints raised by Applicant were not sustained by the Tribunal: (i) that the Fund abused its discretion in accepting the Grievance Committee's recommendation not to award Applicant relief after the Committee found procedural faults in the vacancy selection process; (ii) that the Fund was required to provide Applicant special consideration in her job search in light of the Departmental reorganization; and (iii) that Applicant was subjected to abusive written comment to which managers failed to respond.

The case of Ms. "NN" was the second in which the Tribunal convened oral proceedings, which may be held if the Tribunal "deems such proceedings useful". (Rule XIII, para. 1.) Given the structure of the Fund's dispute resolution system and the exhaustion requirement of the Tribunal's Statute, it will be rare for the Tribunal to admit witness testimony in cases arising through the Grievance Committee, in the absence of a showing that such testimony would be useful to clarify a material point at issue before the Tribunal. Ms. "NN"'s request to testify as a witness before the Tribunal did not meet that standard. Accordingly, the proceedings were limited to the oral arguments of the parties' counsel.

Chapter VI

SELECTED LEGAL OPINIONS OF THE SECRETARIATS OF THE UNITED NATIONS AND RELATED INTERGOVERNMENTAL ORGANIZATIONS*

A. Legal opinions of the Secretariat of the United Nations

(Issued or prepared by the Office of Legal Affairs)

Procedural and institutional issues

(*a*) Letter from the Under-Secretary-General for Legal Affairs and United Nations Legal Counsel to the CEO and Chairperson of the Global Environment Facility (GEF), Washington, D.C., regarding the participation of the GEF in meetings of the United Nations

Participation in meetings and conferences convened under United Nations auspices requires decision of relevant intergovernmental organ—Advisory role of the United Nations Secretariat—Status of global environment facility—Subsidiary organ of International Bank for Reconstruction and Development (IBRD) and the United Nations (UN)—Participation as part of delegation of IBRD in United Nations meeting or conference open to participation of United Nations specialized agencies—No participation as a separate entity unless specifically allowed by intergovernmental organ of the United Nations—Participation as observer in meetings of several treaty bodies as serves as financial mechanism—Possibility, in light of this practice, that competent intergovernemental organ of the United Nations grant the right to participate separately in meetings and conferences convened under its auspices to GEF and other operating entities of financial mechanisms for multilateral treaties—Such decision lies with United Nations Member States

23 January 2017

Dear [Name],

I wish to refer to your letter dated 22 November 2016 to the Secretary-General in which you have raised the question of the participation of the Global Environment Facility ("GEF") in meetings of the United Nations.

We would like to first note that it is not the United Nations Secretariat but a competent intergovernmental organ of the United Nations, such as the General Assembly that decides which States and other entities are eligible to participate in meetings and conferences

* This chapter contains legal opinions and other similar legal memoranda and documents.

convened under its auspices. The Secretariat merely advises on whether a particular entity that applies to participate in a United Nations meeting or conference as an observer, falls within the categories of entities that have been allowed to participate as observers by the relevant intergovernmental organ of the United Nations.

For example, with respect to the United Nations Summit for the adoption of the post-2015 development agenda held on 25 September 2015 ("Summit"), which is specifically referred to in your letter, the General Assembly, pursuant to its resolution 69/244 of 29 December 2014 concerning the organization of the Summit, "convened [the Summit] as a high-level plenary meeting of the General Assembly" and decided that "the rules of procedure and established practices of the General Assembly shall apply for the summit unless otherwise decided in the present resolution and the annexes thereto". These provisions allowed the Member States as well as observer States and other entities which have been granted observer status in the General Assembly to participate in the Summit. The General Assembly also "[i]nvite[d] the United Nations funds and programmes and the specialized agencies of the United Nations system, as well as the Bretton Woods institutions, including the World Bank Group and the International Monetary Fund, the World Trade Organization, the regional development banks, the regional commissions of the United Nations and other stakeholders, including parliamentarians, academia, non-governmental organizations, civil society organizations, major groups and the private sector" to participate as observers in the Summit (operative paragraph 7).

As far as GEF is concerned, it was originally established as a subsidiary body of the International Bank for Reconstruction and Development (IBRD) in 1991, which is a United Nations Specialized Agency. Subsequently, the States participating in the GEF accepted the Instrument for the Establishment of the Restructured GEF ("the Instrument") at their meeting in Geneva, Switzerland, held from March 14 to 16 1994. Pursuant to paragraph 1 of the Instrument, the Instrument was adopted by the Implementing Agencies namely the United Nations Development Programme ("UNDP"), the United Nations Environment Programme ("UNEP"), and IBRD. The Office of Legal Affairs previously examined the status of the restructured GEF and concluded that the restructured GEF was a subsidiary body of the IBRD and the United Nations, acting through UNDP and UNEP. Furthermore, in our view, the restructured GEF was not established as a new international organization and therefore does not have legal personality under international law. We attach our legal opinion on this matter[1].

The Instrument has been amended several times since its adoption. However, none of those amendments has changed the status of GEF as a subsidiary body of the IBRD and the United Nations. As a subsidiary body of the IBRD, and the United Nations, the GEF would be in a position to participate as part of the delegation of the IBRD in a meeting or conference convened under the auspices of the United Nations that is open to the participation of United Nations Specialized Agencies but would not be in a position to participate as a separate entity unless specifically allowed to do so by the relevant intergovernmental organ of the United Nations.

However, we note that the GEF is already permitted to participate as an observer in the meetings of several treaty bodies, as it serves as a financial mechanism for certain multilateral treaties.

---

[1] *United Nations Juridical Yearbook*, 1994, p. 469.

For example, Article 11, paragraph 1 of the United Nations Framework Convention on Climate Change ("UNFCCC") entitled "Financial Mechanism" provides that, "[a] mechanism for the provision of financial resources on a grant or concessional basis, including for the transfer of technology, is hereby defined. It shall function under the guidance of and be accountable to the Conference of the Parties, which shall decide on its policies, programme priorities and eligibility criteria related to this Convention. Its operation shall be entrusted to one or more existing international entities". Article 21 (3) of the UNFCCC further provides that "[t]he Global Environment Facility … shall be the international entity entrusted with the operation of the financial mechanism referred to in Article 11 on an interim basis."

The Conference of the Parties ("COP") of the UNFCCC, through its decisions 12/CP.2 of 19 July 1996 and 3/CP.4 of 14 November 1998, has designated the GEF, amongst other entities, with the operation of the financial mechanism. Specifically, rule 6 of the draft rules of procedure provides, *inter alia*, that "any international entity or entities entrusted by the Conference of the Parties pursuant to Article 11 of the Convention with the operation of the financial mechanism" may be represented at sessions of the COP as observers and "upon invitation of the President, participate without the right to vote in the proceedings of any session, unless at least one third of the Parties present at the session object." This rule is also applicable to the Conference of the Parties serving as the meeting of the Parties to the Kyoto Protocol and the Conference of the Parties serving as the Meeting of the Parties to the Paris Agreement.

Consequently, the GEF, as one of the operating entities of the financial mechanism, may participate as an observer in the meetings of the UNFCCC, Kyoto Protocol and the Paris Agreement.

It may therefore be possible given the importance of the work of the GEF that in the future a competent intergovernmental organ of the United Nations, such as the General Assembly, take into account the above-mentioned practice when it considers the participation clause for a particular meeting or conference, and expressly grants the GEF and other operating entities of financial mechanisms for multilateral treaties, the right to participate separately in meetings and conferences convened under its auspices. However, this is a decision that lies within the hands of the Member States of the United Nations and not the Secretariat.

Finally and as explained above, the GEF can currently participate as a part of the delegation of the IBRD in United Nations meetings and conferences that are open to the participation of the representatives of United Nations Specialized Agencies.

[*Signed*]

(*b*) Note to the Chef de Cabinet, Executive Office of the Secretary-General ("EOSG"), regarding the status of the African Union in the United Nations

Status of Regional Organizations in the United Nations—African Union (AU) and European Union (EU) status—Granting of observer status in the General Assembly—Rights and modalities of participation of the EU—Procedure by which the EU obtained its current status

The purpose of this note is to explain the status of the African Union ("AU") in the United Nations and to highlight the differences with the status of the European Union ("EU") in the United Nations. It will also briefly explain the procedure by which the EU obtained its current status.

The African Union is an international organization which was established by the Constitutive Act of the African Union of 11 July 2000, and is legally separate and independent from the United Nations.

Within the United Nations, the AU has been an observer in the General Assembly since 1965. The General Assembly resolution granting the AU observer status (resolution 2011 (XX) of 11 October 1965) does not set out the specific rights of participation of the AU, but, as a matter of practice, the AU has been given a seat with a nameplate in the General Assembly, allowed to attend plenary meetings, and allowed to make statements in such meetings after Member States and observer States. It does not have the right to vote, to sponsor or co-sponsor draft decisions and resolutions, or raise procedural motions, such as points of order.

Organizations with observer status in the General Assembly, including the AU, have also been permitted to participate as observers in other United Nations organs, such as the Economic and Social Council and the Main Committees of the General Assembly, as well as in United Nations conferences, pursuant to the applicable rules of procedure and practice. In these organs and conferences, the AU has been given the same facilities and rights as in the General Assembly.

The European Union has been an observer in the General Assembly since 1974 pursuant to General Assembly resolution 3208 (XXIX) of 11 October 1974. Subsequently, the General Assembly accorded additional rights of participation to the EU by its resolution 65/276 of 3 May 2011. Pursuant to this resolution, the EU is allowed, in relevant United Nations meetings and conferences:

— to be inscribed on the list of speakers among representatives of major groups;

— to participate in the general debate of the General Assembly;

— to have its relevant communications circulated as documents of the General Assembly and relevant meetings and conferences;

— to present proposals and amendments orally;

— to exercise the right of reply; and

— to have assigned seats.

The EU, therefore, has more rights of participation than the AU pursuant to this resolution in the relevant United Nations meetings and conferences. The resolution, however, specifically provides that the EU should not have the right to vote, to cosponsor draft resolutions or decisions, or to put forward candidates for elections.

The proposal on additional rights of participation for the EU was originally made by Member States that were members of the EU in a form of a draft resolution (A/64/L.67), but the consideration on the proposal was deferred due to concerns raised by Member States. A new proposal was subsequently submitted by the same States (A/65/L.64), which was further revised (A/65/L.64/Rev.1) before being adopted on 3 May 2011 as resolution 65/276. The entire process was a Member State-process, and OLA had advised the then Chef de Cabinet that the Secretary-General should remain strictly neutral on the matter. We would advise the same with respect to any proposal on additional participation rights for the AU in the United Nations.

20 April 2017

(*c*) E-mail message to the Secretary, First Committee, and Chief, Disarmament and Peace Affairs Branch, regarding the election of an ambassador accredited to the United Nations Office at Geneva ("UNOG") as Chair of a Main Committee of the General Assembly

Election of a non-resident ambassador as chair of a Main Committee of the General Assembly—Rules of Procedure of the General Assembly appear to presume that a Chair of a Main Committee belongs to a delegation of a Member State to the General Assembly—Ambassador to be included in delegation of Member State concerned as representative or alternate representative—For purposes of accreditation to the General Assembly, credentials to be submitted pursuant to rule 27 of the rules of procedures of the General Assembly.

I refer to your question whether an ambassador accredited to the United Nations Office at Geneva ("UNOG") may be elected Chair of a Main Committee of the General Assembly.

The rules of procedure of the General Assembly provide as follows with respect to the elections of the Chairs of the Main Committees:

Rule 99 (*a*): "All the Main Committees shall, at least three months before the opening of the session, elect a Chairman. Elections of the other officers provided for in rule 103 shall be held at the latest by the end of the first week of the session."

Rule 103: "Each Main Committee shall elect a Chairman, three Vice-Chairmen and a Rapporteur. These officers shall be elected on the basis of equitable geographical distribution, experience and personal competence. The elections shall be held by secret ballot unless the committee decides otherwise in an election where only one candidate is standing. The nomination of each candidate shall be limited to one speaker, after which the committee shall immediately proceed to the election."

As [...] has indicated, these rules do not seem to exclude the possibility of electing a non-resident ambassador as Chair of a Main Committee. In fact, the Permanent Representative of Mexico in Geneva was elected as Chair of the First Committee in 2004 (A/C.1/58/PV.24, p. 1).

However, it is first noted that the rules of procedure of the General Assembly appear to presume that a Chair of a Main Committee belongs to a delegation of a Member State to the General Assembly. Thus, rule 104 provides that "[t]he Chairman of a Main Committee shall not vote, but another member of his delegation may vote in his place" (emphasis added).

Pursuant to rule 25, "[t]he delegation of a Member shall consist of not more than five representatives and five alternate representatives and as many advisers, technical advisers, experts and persons of similar status as may be required by the delegation."

Thus, it seems advisable that the ambassador who is accredited to UNOG be included in the delegation of the Member State concerned to the General Assembly. We would recommend that the ambassador concerned be included in the delegation as a representative or an alternate representative. Rule 101 provides that "[p]ersons of this status [advisers, technical advisers, experts or persons of similar status] shall not, however, unless designated as alternate representatives, be eligible for election as Chairmen, Vice-Chairmen or Rapporteurs of committees or for seats in the General Assembly" (emphasis added). This implies that the person concerned should be either an alternate representative or above, *i.e.* representative, in order to be eligible for election as Chair of a Main Committee.

The accreditation as a representative or alternate representative also seems advisable as the Chair of a Main Committee may be asked to speak in plenary meetings of the General Assembly. Rule 69 of the rules of procedure of the General Assembly envisages such a situation: "The Chairman and the Rapporteur of a committee may be accorded precedence for the purpose of explaining the conclusions arrived at by their committee." If the ambassador concerned is not properly accredited to the General Assembly, it could create an unusual situation where a representative of a Member State makes a statement (although in his or her capacity as the Chair of a Main Committee) in the plenary of the General Assembly without being properly accredited to it.

In order to be accredited to the General Assembly as a representative or an alternate representative, credentials should be submitted pursuant to rule 27 of the rules of procedure of the General Assembly. As OLA is the custodian of the credentials, we could check whether the person is already listed in the credentials, if you could let us know the name of the ambassador and the Member State.

[*Signed*]

(*d*) Note from the Assistant Secretary-General for Legal Affairs to the Chef de Cabinet, Executive Office of the Secretary-General ("EOSG"), regarding the Secretary-General's authority to establish a follow-on mechanism to a Board of Inquiry

Killing of two members of the Group of Experts on the Democratic Republic of the Congo—Limits to the follow-on mechanism the Secretary-General may establish on his own authority—Object and purpose of mechanism—Consent and cooperation of host State to carry out investigations within the host State

1. This responds to your request for our views on the legal aspects of a mechanism that may be established by the Secretary-General on his own authority with respect to the killing of two members of the Group of Experts on the Democratic Republic of the Congo originally established pursuant to Security Council resolution 1533 (2004).

2. As you are aware, on 25 April 2017, the Under-Secretary-General for Safety and Security convened a United Nations Security Management System ("UNSMS") Board of Inquiry into the incident. The Board completed its report and delivered it to the Under-Secretary-General for Safety and Security on 3 August 2017. In accordance with its terms of reference, the Board was mandated to, among other things, identify the attackers to the extent possible and report on any ongoing local or other investigation or proceedings into the incident. We understand that the report is currently being reviewed by the relevant departments and offices.

3. Under his own authority, the Secretary-General may establish a follow-on mechanism to the Board of Inquiry to undertake certain tasks, such as to further establish the facts of the incident [redacted]. The mechanism could also support and cooperate with criminal investigations conducted by relevant State authorities.

4. There are limits to what the Secretary-General may establish on his own authority. For instance, any such mechanism could not displace national criminal investigations or prosecutions. The mechanism could not itself be a criminal investigation, though, as already

noted, it could support and cooperate with criminal investigations conducted by relevant States. On his own authority, the Secretary-General cannot establish a mechanism that would interfere in matters essentially within the domestic jurisdiction of a Member State.

5. The mechanism would need the consent of the host State in order to deploy to its territory and would rely on the cooperation of the host State authorities to be able to carry out any investigations within the host State, including in respect of its freedom of movement and access to information.

6. From a legal point of view, the Secretary-General would have discretion in what a mechanism established on his own authority may be called. Whether it is a "Special Investigation" or a "Commission of Inquiry" or has some other title, however, the limits with respect to the Secretary-General's authority would remain the same.

[...]

4 August 2017

B. Legal opinions of the secretariats of intergovernmental organizations related to the United Nations

1. International Labour Organization

(submitted by the Office of the Legal Adviser of the International Labour Office)

(a) Legal opinions rendered during the 106th session of the International Labour Conference (June 2017)

(i) *Question concerning the status of international labour Recommendations in the Committee on Employment and Decent Work for the Transition to Peace*

International labour law standards, whether legally binding or not, form part of international law

In response to the Government member of [State] seeking clarification as to whether the non-binding Recommendation that was being negotiated constituted international law, the Legal Adviser explained that what the Committee was negotiating was a formal instrument which, if adopted by the Conference, would become part of what was known as international labour law, a distinct body of international law that addressed standards of conduct of sovereign States and other entities enjoying international legal personality in matters of labour and social policy and that comprised both conventions which produced binding legal effect upon ratification and recommendations which offered non-binding policy guidance. In this sense, he expressed the view that international labour standards, whether legally binding or not, formed part of international law.[1]

(ii) *Question concerning the procedure for the adoption of conclusions by the Committee on the Application of Standards*

Committee draws on standing orders of the Conference, as well as its own working methods and long-standing practices—Where government disagrees with conclusions, disagreement is reflected in records of proceedings—Chairperson could proceed on the basis of a very large majority in circumstances where objections were expressed

In response to the Government representative of [State] who had indicated that his Government fully opposed and objected to the totality of the Committee's conclusions concerning his country's compliance with provisions of the Freedom of Association and Protection of the Right to Organise Convention, 1948 (No. 87), the Legal Adviser indicated that the point raised concerned the procedure to be followed for the adoption of the Committee's conclusions on individual cases when the government concerned wished to express objections to the proposed conclusions. In this respect, it was essential to recall that in discharging its supervisory function, the Committee on the Application of Standards drew on the Standing Orders of the Conference but had also developed its own working

[1] Provisional Record No. 13-2 (Rev.), International Labour Conference 106th Session, Geneva, June 2017, para. 238, available at https://www.ilo.org/wcmsp5/groups/public/---ed_norm/---relconf/documents/meetingdocument/wcms_558622.pdf.

methods and long-standing practices over the years. The Committee's conclusions were based on carefully balanced views in order to reflect consensus. It could happen, and had indeed happened in the past, that the government concerned expressed its disagreement with the conclusions. In these cases, the Government's disagreement was always faithfully reflected in the Record of Proceedings. This long-standing and constant practice gave satisfaction to governments that their objections had been faithfully reproduced.

In reply to a further question by another Government representative whether, in the event of an objection as in this case, the Chairperson could still go ahead and declare that the conclusions had been adopted by consensus, the Legal Adviser answered that the Chairperson could proceed on the basis of a very large majority in circumstances where objections were expressed. The main duty of the Chairing Officer was to conduct the debate according to the Standing Orders of the Conference. He could therefore proceed to adopt conclusion despite disagreement expressed by the government concerned as long as all relevant statements were faithfully reflected in the Record of Proceedings.[2]

(*b*) Legal opinions rendered at the Meeting of the Working Group of the Special Tripartite Committee established under Article XIII of the Maritime Labour Convention, 2006 (MLC, 2006)

Question concerning seafarers' contract of employment in high risk areas

Extended validity or deferred termination of a Seafarers' Contract may be provided in national legislation

The Shipowner Vice-Chairperson requested legal advice on how an employment contract that expired could be maintained in force by legal means, and also on the best means of including the definitions of piracy and armed robbery in the proposals. The Legal Adviser, in response, said that, in principle, nothing prevented national legislators from providing that, under certain circumstances, a contract shall remain valid, meaning that it shall continue to produce its effects, or some of its effects, after it had expired, or that under certain circumstances a contract shall expire at a later date, or that it shall be deemed to have been renewed, or that it shall not be deemed to have ended. There were examples of national legislation providing for such "extended validity" or "deferred termination" of a contract, including Article 19(*a*) of Danish Act No. 73, which provided that "employment shall not terminate though the ship is lost in connection with piracy or the shipowner is no longer able to have it at his disposal". Article 6(3) of the same Act provided that "if a time limited service agreement expires while the ship is at sea, the agreement shall remain in force until the ship arrives at a port". Similarly, Article 67 of the Estonian Seafarers' Employment Act of June 2014 provided that "if the date of expiry of a seafarer's fixed term employment contract arrives while a ship is at sea, the contract shall be deemed to be extended until the ship reaches the next port". It should also be noted that, in some cases, the law might implicitly provide that the contract shall remain in force in whole or in part. For example, in accordance with Article 69 of the Indian Bill of 2016 amending the Merchant Shipping Act, "[a] seafarer shall be entitled to continue to receive the wages at the

[2] Provisional Record No. 15, Part Two, International Labour Conference, 106th Session, Geneva, June 2017, p. 130.

same rate till such time he returns home if such seafarer is held in captivity including in case of piracy". He added that collective agreements could also have the same effect, such as the International Transport Workers' Federation (ITF) standard collective agreement of 2015, which recognized that "the seafarer's employment status and entitlements shall continue until the seafarer's release and safe repatriation". Nevertheless, there was always a possibility that provisions in domestic legislation, such as those referred to above, could be challenged before national courts, possibly as being contrary to freedom of contract. The validity of such provisions therefore depended on the national jurisdiction. In the event that an amendment to the Convention was envisaged by the Working Group, it might be advisable to refer to the shipowner's obligation to continue to pay wages, instead of making explicit reference to the seafarer's employment agreement remaining in force, which might raise complex questions (such as whether the employment agreement would remain in force in whole, or only as far as the payment of wages was concerned, or whether the employment agreement could be deemed to be in force if the seafarer were held captive ashore and was no longer physically on board the ship).[1]

In response to the request by the Seafarers' group for a legal opinion on whether the kidnapping of seafarers could qualify as an act of piracy under the definition of piracy set out in Article 101 of UNCLOS, the Legal Adviser recalled that kidnapping was generally understood to mean abducting a person and holding him/her as a hostage without his/her consent, by force or fraud, often for ransom. In accordance with Article 101 of UNCLOS, piracy consisted of any illegal act of violence or detention, committed for private ends by the crew of a ship and directed, on the high seas, against persons on board another ship either on the high seas or in a place outside the jurisdiction of any State. It would therefore appear evident that, based on that definition, kidnapping qualified as an "illegal act of violence or detention", within the meaning of the relevant provision of UNCLOS, on condition that all the remaining constitutive elements of piracy were also present, and in particular that: the act of kidnapping was "committed for private ends", as contrasted to political ends; it was committed "by the crew of another ship", therefore excluding mutiny or acts by terrorists on board the same ship; and it was committed "on the high seas or in a place outside the jurisdiction of any State", which excluded acts committed in the territorial waters of a State. The expression "kidnapping of seafarers" seemed to be widely used in relevant publications, such IMB publications on piracy. Dedicated so-called "kidnap and ransom" marine insurance policies had also been developed to respond to the need to cover ransom demands not explicitly addressed by Protection and Indemnity (P&I) clubs, as the modus operandi of pirates had changed from raiding and looting ships to boarding and taking the crew hostage for ransom. In conclusion, present day acts of piracy did involve the kidnapping of seafarers, but not all acts of the kidnapping of seafarers would automatically qualify as piracy. He added that the definitions of "piracy" in UNCLOS and of "armed robbery against ships" under IMO Resolution A.1025(26) were practically identical, and only differed in their spatial scope of application. Piracy covered illegal acts of violence or detention committed for private ends and directed against persons on board a ship on the high seas or in a place outside the jurisdiction of a State, whereas armed robbery referred to illegal acts of violence or detention also committed for private ends, but

[1] Final report, Meeting of the Working Group of the Special Tripartite Committee established under Article XIII of the Maritime Labour Convention, 2006 (MLC, 2006), STCMLC/WG/2017/5 , paras. 64-65.

only when the ship was in the territorial waters of a State. Consequently, the abduction of a seafarer would qualify as an act of piracy if it occurred on the high seas or in a place outside the jurisdiction of a State, and as an act of armed robbery against ships if it occurred within the territorial waters of a coastal State.[2]

2. United Nations Industrial Development Organization

(Submitted by the Legal Adviser of the United Nations Industrial Development Organization)

(*a*) Internal e-mail message to the Officer-in-Charge of the UNIDO Department of Operational Support Services concerning the responsibility for fire insurance at the [United Nations Headquarters]

FIRE INSURANCE FOR THE BUILDINGS COMPRISING THE UNITED NATIONS HEADQUARTERS—SCOPE OF THE OBLIGATIONS OF THE UNITED NATIONS HEADQUARTERS-BASED ORGANIZATIONS FOR ROUTINE OPERATION AND MAINTENANCE OF THE UNITED NATIONS HEADQUARTERS

1. This is with reference to your email of 20 December 2016 concerning the issue of fire insurance for the buildings comprising the [UN Headquarters]. It appears that the [Conference Centre], which oversees [Host Country] responsibilities in respect of the [UN Headquarters], is currently paying some € […] per year for such insurance coverage. The question that arose at the 53rd meeting of the [Joint Committee of the UN-based organizations], held in November 2016, is *whether the cost of fire insurance can be passed on to the [UN Headquarters]-based organizations as an operating expense.*

2. The obligations of the [UN Headquarters]-based organizations for routine operation and maintenance of the [UN Headquarters] derive from their respective headquarters agreements. Section 6 of the Headquarters Agreement of UNIDO stipulates that:

> "The UNIDO shall be responsible at its own expense for the *orderly operation and adequate maintenance* of the buildings and facilities forming part of the headquarters seat and of the installations located therein and for minor repairs and replacements for the purpose of keeping them in good working order, and for any repairs or replacements which may be made necessary by faulty operation and inadequate maintenance." [Emphasis added.]

3. Section 6 does not refer to fire insurance for the buildings and facilities forming part of the headquarters seat. Nor can the phrase "orderly operation and adequate maintenance" be interpreted to mean that UNIDO has an implied duty to take out fire insurance or to pay the premiums for fire insurance taken out by or on behalf of the [Host Country]. Other insurance matters are regulated expressly and in detail in the Headquarters Agreement (see, for example, Section 9). Had the Parties wished to make UNIDO liable for such an important matter as fire insurance, they would have done so expressly.

4. Established practice supports the above interpretation. Fire insurance has always been treated as the sole concern of the [Host Country] as owner of the [UN Headquarters].

---

[2] *Ibid.*, para. 66.

This practice was reinforced during the handover of the [Name A]-building in 2009, when the parties undertook a careful review of risks and insurance arrangements in connection with the transfer. Our files contain a report from [Name B], then Head of the General Legal Section at the [UN Organization], on a meeting held at the foreign ministry on 25 February 2009. In relevant part, the report reads as follows:

> *We discussed ongoing issues such as building insurance (it was agreed that as the [Name A]-Building is and will remain [Host Country]-owned, this is an issue for [Host Country]),* and injuries to our staff members in the [Name A]-Building (it was noted that all [UN organizations] staff members on duty remain the responsibility of the [UN organization]s). *The [nationals of the Host Country] consider that these issues, often raised by [Conference Centre], do not warrant further attention and [Conference Centre] will be informed accordingly.* [Email from [Name B] to the members of the Committee on Common Services and the legal advisers, dated 25 February 2009; emphasis added.]

5. In my opinion, there is no legal basis for suggesting that the cost of fire insurance for the [UN Headquarters] is an operating expense for which UNIDO and the other [UN Headquarters]-based organizations are responsible. Whether the Government is obliged to retain such insurance is a different question that should be answered by the [Host Country] authorities themselves. From the perspective of the [UN Headquarters]-based organizations, adequate fire insurance remains important given that major repairs and replacements – including those that may result from fire damage – are co-funded by the organizations pursuant to the provisions of the [Name C] Agreement of 1981, as amended in 2002.

6 January 2017

(*b*) Internal e-mail message to the Investigator of the UNIDO Office of Internal Oversight and Ethics concerning the unauthorized registration of UNIDO trademark regarding a project

Registration of trademarks in connection with UNIDO projects—
Legal framework for UNIDO projects

I wish to refer to your email of 1 February 2017, which raised ... questions concerning the registration of trademarks in connection with UNIDO projects. My answers are as follows:

...

Whether there are guidance notes that assist [Project Managers]/governs registration of trademarks (or other intellectual properties) created under UNIDO projects.

In short, the answer is No. That said, it has been the case for a very long time that UNIDO projects require a proper legal framework. Such a framework is established through the recipient country's signature of the UNIDO Standard Basic Cooperation Agreement, or its acceptance to apply the terms of the agreement that it signed with [UN Organization] (or with the UN) to the specific UNIDO project. The aforementioned agreements contain a clause along the following (or substantially similar) terms: "Patent rights, copyrights and other similar rights to any discoveries or work resulting from [the UN Agency] assistance under this Agreement shall belong to [the UN Agency]. Unless otherwise agreed by the Government and [the UN Agency] in each case, however, the Government shall have the right to use any such discoveries or work within the country free of royalty or any charge of similar nature."

Furthermore, to ensure that ownership of intellectual property rights (IPRs) created by UNIDO staff, consultants or contractors belong to the Organization, the following should be noted. As concerns regular staff, see Staff Rule 101.05 (All rights, including title, copyright and patent rights, in any work performed by a staff member as part of his or her official duties shall be vested in the Organization); for project staff, see Staff Rule 201.04 (All rights, including title, copyright and patent rights, in any work performed by project personnel as part of their official duties shall be vested in the Organization). As concerns consultants (Individual Service Agreement holders), please refer to the terms of the ISA, paragraph 6 (The title rights, copyrights, patents and all other rights of whatsoever nature in any material produced under the provisions of this Agreement shall be vested exclusively in UNIDO unless an original copyright or other right is already applicable).

...

UNIDO contractors are subject to the General Terms and Conditions of Contract (GTC), see article 19 (The United Nations or UNIDO, as the case may be, shall be entitled to all property rights including but not limited to patents, copyrights and trademarks, with regard to material which bears a direct relation to, or results from the services provided to the United Nations or UNIDO by the Contractor under this Contract. At the request of UNIDO, the Contractor shall take all necessary steps, prepare and process all necessary documents and assist in securing such property rights and transferring them to the United Nations and UNIDO in compliance with the requirements of the applicable law).

...

Finally, I would like to comment on the statement from the Project Manager, that "the UNIDO project has no legal status in [State]". The [State] is a Member State of UNIDO and, therefore, it has accepted to grant UNIDO "such legal capacity" in the territory of [State] "as [is] necessary for the exercise of its functions and for the fulfilment of its objectives". See Constitution of UNIDO, art. 21, paragraph 1. Moreover, consistent with article 21, paragraph 2 (*b*), of the Constitution, [State] has agreed that the legal capacity of UNIDO in the territory of [State] shall be as defined in the Convention on the Privileges and Immunities of the United Nations. Pursuant to the foregoing, it is the legal position that UNIDO enjoys juridical personality in [State] and, in particular, the legal capacity to contract and acquire property, whether movable, immovable or intangible (such as IPRs). In my opinion, whilst the UNIDO project itself probably did not have a separate legal personality from UNIDO, there was, in principle and as a matter of international law, no obstacle for UNIDO to register the mark in question under its own name.

13 February 2017

(*c*) Internal e-mail message to the UNIDO Senior Human Resource Officer concerning the status of the [NGO] at the [United Nations Headquarters]

STATUS OF THE EMPLOYEES OF NON-GOVERNMENTAL ORGANIZATIONS—RELATIONSHIP BETWEEN UNIDO AND NON-GOVERNMENTAL ORGANIZATIONS—CONSULTANTS OF UNIDO HAVE THE STATUS OF INDEPENDENT CONTRACTORS *VIS-À-VIS* UNIDO AND FOR THE PURPOSES OF FUNCTIONAL PRIVILEGES AND IMMUNITIES, THEY ALSO HAVE THE STATUS OF EXPERTS ON MISSION FOR UNIDO—REJECTION OF REQUEST TO EXEMPT EMPLOYEES OF NON-GOVERNMENTAL ORGANIZATIONS FROM SCREENING UPON ENTERING THE UNITED NATIONS HEADQUARTERS

This is with reference to your email of 23 January 2017 asking for a meeting to discuss the status of [NGO] employees. Your request relates to a letter from the Director General of [NGO], dated 25 November 2016, seeking UNIDO's assistance in a number of areas. I have prepared the following advice on the issue, which may obviate the need for a meeting. If you would still like to meet, please let me know.

1. In his letter dated 25 November 2016, the Director General of [NGO] asks UNIDO to implement the following "administrative requirements":

(1) UNIDO should communicate with all other parties when required that [NGO]'s headquarters are based at the [UN Headquarters] and that [NGO] is an executing partner of UNIDO;

(2) UNIDO should recognize with all parties concerned that [NGO] is a quasi-international organization as of 1 July 2016; and

(3) [NGO] staff should be given the same status at the [UN Headquarters] as full-time consultants (without daily screening requirements).

2. According to the records of LEG, [NGO] is an international non-governmental organization established under the laws of [State]. The relationship between UNIDO and [NGO] is governed by two instruments: (i) a Memorandum of Cooperation (MoC) of 2013, pursuant to which [NGO] became a partner organization of UNIDO, and (ii) a rental contract, which was last extended in 2016, in terms of which UNIDO provides [NGO] with office space in the [UN Headquarters]. The MoC of 2013 was concluded for an initial period of two years. It is unclear whether the MoC has been renewed.

3. Even if [NGO] is a partner organization of UNIDO and rents office space from the Organization, UNIDO is not under a legal obligation to provide [NGO] with the assistance it has requested. Each request should be assessed on its own merits.

4. *Request (1)*: It would be inappropriate for UNIDO to confirm the location of [NGO] or any other partner organization. Such confirmation should be provided by the partner organization concerned. Provided the MoC with [NGO] is in force, the responsible UNIDO project manager could confirm that [NGO] is a partner organization of UNIDO.

5. *Request (2)*: The exact purport of this request is unclear. However, it is not for UNIDO to recognize or otherwise attest to the legal status of entities established under national law. The preamble to the MoC of 2013 describes [NGO] as "a non-profit association organized under the laws of [State]". If that status has changed as a result of changes in [State] legislation, an appropriate amendment may be made to the MoC if and when it is formally renewed.

6. *Request (3)*: Consultants of UNIDO (*i.e.* holders of Independent Service Agreements) have the status of *independent contractors vis-à-vis* UNIDO. For the purposes of functional privileges and immunities in [State], they also have the status of *experts on mission for UNIDO*. Employees of [NGO], on the other hand, have no contractual or other association with UNIDO. They therefore cannot have the same official status, whether at the [UN Headquarters] or for any other purpose, as consultants of UNIDO. The *Manual for UNIDO Partner Organizations* specifically clarifies that:

> "Neither the Partner Organization nor any of its directors, staff, personnel, consultants or sub-contractors shall be considered an official, staff member or agent of UNIDO, nor shall they be entitled to any privileges, immunities, compensation or reimbursements, nor be authorized to commit UNIDO to any expenditure or other obligation not explicitly provided for herein." (Director General's Administrative Instruction 20/Rev.1, Annex F, para. 2.7)

7. In addition, [NGO]'s request that its staff should not be subjected to daily security screening upon entering the [UN Headquarters] is a request that UNIDO has no power to grant. The screening requirements for occupants of the [UN Headquarters] who are neither officials nor consultants are a security matter falling under the responsibility and authority of the Safety and Security Service (SSS) [City]. If UNIDO considers that the current access policy is overly restrictive as applied to [NGO], the issue could be raised with SSS [City] or the Committee on Common Services. Bearing in mind that the employees of [NGO] are not vetted by any [UN Headquarters]-based organization, the final decision should be left to SSS [City].

13 February 2017

(*d*) Internal e-mail message to the Officer-in-Charge of the UNIDO Department of Operational Support Services

Relationship agreement between UNIDO and the United Nations—As a rule, the policies, decisions and instructions of the United Nations Department of Safety and Security are not directly applicable to, or legally binding on UNIDO

This is with reference to your email of 3 March 2017 seeking advice on the Organization's implementation of the revised UN System Programme Criticality Framework. [UNIDO Office of Legal Affairs] answers to your questions are as follows:

1. Is UNIDO legally obliged to implement a United Nations Department of Safety and Security (UNDSS) policy, decision or instruction as is? Or do we have some discretion and flexibility?

As a rule, the policies, decisions and instructions of UNDSS are not directly applicable to, or legally binding on, UNIDO. Accordingly, UNIDO has no legal obligation to implement a UNDSS policy, decision or instruction unless it agrees to do so. UNIDO has, for example, agreed to follow the policies, decisions and instructions of UNDSS relating to safety and security, which is a common service at the [UN Headquarters].

2. Is UNIDO legally obliged to implement a Chief Executive Board (CEB) or High-level Committee on Management (HLCM) or United Nations Development Group (UNDG) policy? Or do we have some discretion and flexibility?

Under article 2 of the relationship agreement between UNIDO and the United Nations, UNIDO has agreed to coordinate and cooperate with the United Nations and to participate in the work of the CEB and other United Nations bodies. The relationship agreement does not provide or imply that policies approved by the CEB, HLCM or UNDG are binding on UNIDO or that UNIDO is legally obliged to implement such policies. While UNIDO must coordinate and cooperate with the United Nations in good faith, the Organization enjoys some discretion in giving effect to CEB, HLCM or UNDG policies. Appropriate adjustments may thus be made to accommodate the Organization's requirements and practice. This discretion may be contrasted with the legal obligation to implement decisions of the General Assembly and the ICSC on the salaries and entitlements of staff, a legal obligation that emanates from adherence to the Statute of the ICSC.

…

17 March 2017

(*e*) External e-mail message to the Legal Adviser of the [UN Organization] concerning the scope of Section 21 of the Convention on the Privileges and Immunities of the Specialized Agencies

Convention on the Privileges and Immunities of the Specialized Agencies—Diplomatic status is conferred on the Director General or the acting Director General

I refer to your email of 21 March 2017 regarding Section 21 of the Convention on the Privileges and Immunities of the Specialized Agencies.[1]

In the practice of UNIDO, diplomatic privileges and immunities have never been extended to regional directors or heads of country offices pursuant to the provisions of Section 21 of the Specialized Agencies Convention. Diplomatic privileges and immunities are only accorded to such officials in their countries of accreditation if an appropriate provision is included in the applicable bilateral office agreement.

Our reading of Section 21 tends towards the one taken by the [UN Organization]. In the context of UNIDO, Section 21 means that diplomatic status is conferred on the Director General and, in his or her absence from duty, the acting Director General (appointed by the governing bodies) or the Officer-in-Charge of the Secretariat (appointed by the Director General or acting Director General). The nature of the Director General's absence from duty is, in our view, irrelevant.

…

28 March 2017

---

[1] Section 21. In addition to the immunities and privileges specified in sections 19 and 20, the executive head of each specialized agency, including any official acting on his behalf during his absence from duty, shall be accorded in respect of himself, his spouse and minor children, the privileges and immunities, exemptions and facilities accorded to diplomatic envoys, in accordance with international law.

(*f*) Internal e-mail message to a UNIDO consultant concerning childcare allowance

HEADQUARTERS AGREEMENT OF UNIDO—PRIVILEGES AND IMMUNITIES OF EXPERTS ON MISSION FOR UNIDO—CHILDCARE ALLOWANCE PAID BY NATIONAL AUTHORITIES TO A UNIDO EXPERT ON MISSION

I refer to your email of 2 May 2017 regarding your ongoing dispute with the [Host Country] authorities. The dispute concerns the childcare allowances that you received from the state in 2012 in respect of your daughter, who has [Host Country] nationality, which the authorities are claiming back on the basis that you held an individual service agreement (ISA) with UNIDO at the time.

Attached to your email was a letter from the [regional social security institution] to the labour and social court of [City], dated 24 April 2017. The letter sets out supplementary arguments as to why the allowances, amounting to € [...], must be repaid. In brief, the [regional social security institution] takes the position that, as a non-[national of the Host Country], you were precluded from receiving the allowances under the provisions of the Headquarters Agreement of UNIDO. The [regional social security institution] also argues that EU Council directive 2003/109/EC of 25 November 2003 concerning the status of third-country nationals who are long-term residents, on which you had sought to rely, does not apply to you because your status is regulated by the Headquarters Agreement.

Your question to the Office of Legal Affairs is whether Council directive 2003/109/EC is "applicable on" the Headquarters Agreement of UNIDO. In its letter, the [regional social security institution] uses the term ... (*i.e.* to superimpose), concluding that the law of the European Union is not "superimposed on" the Headquarters Agreement. I accordingly understand your question to be whether the directive is hierarchically "superimposed on" the Headquarters Agreement of UNIDO; in other words, whether the directive supersedes or takes precedence over the Headquarters Agreement in the event of a conflict between the two.

The answer to your question is that, as far as UNIDO is concerned, the directive is not "superimposed on" the Headquarters Agreement. The Headquarters Agreement has been incorporated into [Host Country] law and is not governed by, or subject to, the provisions of EC directives.

At issue in your case is Section 39(*b*) of the Headquarters Agreement, which provides that "[o]fficials of the UNIDO and the members of their families living in the same household to whom this Agreement applies shall not be entitled to payments out of the Family Burden Equalization Fund or an instrument with equivalent objectives, unless such persons are [Host Country] nationals or stateless persons resident in [Host Country]". Section 39(*b*) seems to be the sole basis on which the authorities are demanding repayment of the childcare allowances you received in 2012. Although this Office generally refrains from becoming involved in private legal matters, your case concerns the interpretation of a number of provisions of the Headquarters Agreement. I would therefore like to make the following brief observations:

1. You are correct to conclude that you are not an official of UNIDO within the meaning of the Headquarters Agreement. As an ISA-holder or consultant, your official status under the Headquarters Agreement is that of an expert on mission for UNIDO. The privileges and immunities of experts on mission are set out in Article XIII, Sections 42

to 44, of the Headquarters Agreement. Section 42 defines experts on mission for UNIDO to include experts "consulting at its request in any way with, the UNIDO". If the question of your status comes up again in court, the court can request the [Federal Ministry] (Protocol Department) to obtain confirmation from UNIDO of your status in 2012.

2. Section 39(*b*) of the Headquarters Agreement forms part of Article XII on officials. As noted above, the section regulates the situation of "[o]fficials of the UNIDO and the members of their families living in the same household to whom this Agreement applies". Since you are not an official, Section 39(*b*) does not apply to you and does not affect your rights, obligations or status in [Host Country]. In my opinion, Section 39(*b*) cannot serve as the basis for withdrawing childcare allowances to which you would otherwise be entitled under [Host Country] law.

3. There is another aspect of the analysis by the [regional social security institution] that calls for comment. The [regional social security institution] argues that, had the parties so wished, Section 39(*b*) could have referred, in addition to "[Host Country] nationals or stateless persons resident in [Host Country]", to "persons of other nationality granted equivalent status by European Union legislation". According to the [regional social security institution], the fact that the additional clause is found in the Headquarters Agreement of the [International organization] of 2011 but not in the Headquarters Agreement of UNIDO implies that the parties intentionally omitted it from the latter. In my opinion, this argument is incorrect. The additional clause in the Headquarters Agreement of the [International organization] takes account of [Host Country]'s obligations under Council directive 2003/109/EC, amongst other obligations. The Headquarters Agreement of UNIDO, on the other hand, was concluded in 1995, well before the adoption of the directive. The question of equivalence of national treatment was not an issue in 1995 and the parties did not intend to regulate it one way or the other in Section 39(*b*).

4. Furthermore, [Host Country] state agencies normally interpret the country's various headquarters commitments in a manner that does not place UNIDO or its officials or experts at a comparative disadvantage. In terms of Section 55 of the Headquarters Agreement of UNIDO, [Host Country] has undertaken to extend to UNIDO the most favourable treatment it accords to any organization. Section 55 stipulates that, "[i]f and to the extent that the Government shall enter into any agreement with any intergovernmental organization containing terms or conditions more favourable to that organization than similar terms or conditions of this Agreement, the Government shall extend such more favourable terms or conditions to the UNIDO, by means of a supplemental agreement". If the authorities interpret the headquarters agreement of the [International organization] in such a way as to grant the [International organization] better treatment than that enjoyed by UNIDO, then the Organization will be entitled to invoke the provisions of Section 55 in order to secure the same treatment for itself.

Finally, if you would like this Office to raise your case with the responsible authorities *via* the foreign ministry, kindly let me know what its current status is from a procedural point of view. Any action by UNIDO would not, however, replace the need for you to exercise your rights under [Host Country] law.

10 May 2017

(*g*) External e-mail message to the Legal Adviser of the [United Nations Organization] concerning claims by private domestic helpers against UNIDO officials

Private claims against UNIDO officials—Duty of the UNIDO staff to respect private legal obligations—Possible disciplinary or administrative action—Waiver of official immunity

Kindly refer to your email of 17 May 2017 asking me to inform you about UNIDO's practice in cases involving claims by private domestic helpers against UNIDO officials. Further to our telephone conversation of earlier this afternoon, the relevant practice of UNIDO may be summarized as follows:

1. In principle, claims by household help against officials of UNIDO are private in nature.

2. UNIDO staff are required to respect their private legal obligations. Failure to do so may lead to disciplinary or other administrative action.

3. From time to time, the foreign ministry intervenes with UNIDO concerning private legal matters involving officials, with a view to protecting the interests of [Host Country] persons or entities or ensuring respect for [Host Country] law.

4. In such situations, the official concerned is requested to state his or her position on the matter, which is then generally relayed to the foreign ministry.

5. Waiver of an official's immunity may be considered if he or she has diplomatic status and the dispute has to be adjudicated before a [Host Country] court.

17 May 2017

(*h*) Note verbale to the [Federal Ministry] concerning the residency issues of retirees and officials in [Host Country]

Headquarters Agreement of UNIDO—Exemption of the organization and from the application of the laws on social insurance of the Host Country

The Secretariat of the United Nations Industrial Development Organization ("UNIDO"), on its own behalf and on behalf of the United Nations Office at [City], presents its compliments to the [Federal Ministry] of the [Host Country] and has the honour to bring the following important matter to the attention of the Federal Ministry.

The Secretariat has received several reports that officials and retirees applying for residency in [Host Country] are being notified that their organizational health insurance is inadequate for the purposes of an [Host Country] residency permit. Some officials and retirees have also been asked to produce the relevant insurance policy of UNIDO for inspection. In order to correct any misunderstanding regarding the health insurance arrangements of UNIDO, it would be appreciated if the Federal Ministry could notify the competent authorities, including [local authority], of the following:

1. The [Host Country] recognizes that UNIDO is entitled to establish its own health insurance scheme. The Headquarters Agreement of UNIDO stipulates, for example, that the Organization and its officials are exempt from the application of all laws of the

[Host Country] on social insurance, except as provided in the supplemental agreement on social security of 23 April 2010.

2. The health insurance scheme of UNIDO is an official, organizational scheme and is not a private health insurance.

3. The Organization's *Headquarters Medical Insurance Plan* provides worldwide coverage to officials of UNIDO and [UN organization] and their families and eligible retirees. The insurance is at least equivalent to that provided by a [State health insurance scheme] and in some instances exceeds that coverage…

4. The *Headquarters Medical Insurance Plan* is currently operated by [Health Insurance Company]. The contract of insurance between UNIDO and [Health Insurance Company] is a confidential document, which cannot be made available to officials or retirees. Officials and retirees who participate in the Plan receive a membership card and, when required, an official certificate from UNIDO attesting to their membership of the Plan.

The Secretariat of the United Nations Industrial Development Organization wishes to express its appreciation to the [Federal Ministry] of the [Host Country] for its assistance in this matter and avails itself of this opportunity to renew to the Federal Ministry the assurances of its highest consideration.

19 May 2017

(*i*) External e-mail message to the Legal Adviser of the [United Nations Organization] concerning tax exemption on United Nations pensions in [Host Country]

Headquarters Agreement of UNIDO—Privileges and immunities of the officials of UNIDO—Legal basis of the exemption from taxation on United Nations pensions—The exemption from taxation applies to all recipients of pensions from the United Nations Joint Staff Pension Fund who reside in the Host Country

I refer to your emails of 1 and 15 May 2017 concerning the above subject. You ask whether UNIDO has any information on the rationale used by the government of [Host Country] in deciding to exempt United Nations pensions from taxation. This exemption was first expressly included in article XII of the old Headquarters Agreement of UNIDO of 1967 and is now found in the Headquarters Agreement of 1995, as well as in other headquarters agreements, such as those of the [UN organizations].

In relevant part, article XII reads:

Article XII

Officials of the UNIDO

Section 27

Officials of the UNIDO shall enjoy within and with respect to the [Host Country] the following privileges and immunities:

…

(*d*) Exemption from taxation in respect of the salaries, emoluments, indemnities and *pensions paid to them by the UNIDO for services past or present or in connexion with their service with the UNIDO*... [Emphasis added]

We have researched the question and have been able to locate some relevant material in our archives and on [Host Country] state websites. The material includes official correspondence and decisions, as well as the government's submission to parliament in 1967. I can also confirm that the stenographic records of the [Host Country] parliament reveal that the issue of tax exemption was not discussed in parliament at the time.

The government's position is that the legal basis of the exemption from taxation on United Nations pensions is article V, section 18(*b*) of the Convention on the Privileges and Immunities of the United Nations of 1946 and article VI, section 19(*b*) of the Convention on the Privileges and Immunities of the Specialized Agencies of 1947. The [Host Country] acceded to both conventions in the 1950s and incorporated them into its domestic law. The exemption in article XII and in the corresponding provisions of other headquarters agreements thus reflects the country's existing legal obligations under the two conventions. Accordingly, the exemption is not limited to retirees of organizations with their seat in [City] but extends, through direct application of the two conventions in [Host Country] law, to all recipients of pensions from the United Nations Joint Staff Pension Fund who reside in [Host Country].

...

18 May 2017

(*j*) Note verbale to the [Federal Ministry] concerning a dispute between a UNIDO consultant and [regional social security institution] on childcare allowance

Dispute concerning childcare allowance paid by national authorities to a UNIDO consultant—Differences in status between consultants and officials of UNIDO—Interpretation of Headquarters Agreement of UNIDO

The Secretariat of the United Nations Industrial Development Organization ("UNIDO") presents its compliments to the [Federal Ministry] of the [Host Country] and has the honour to request the assistance of the Federal Ministry in connection with a dispute that has arisen between [Name], a national of [State] born on [date], and the [regional social security institution]. [Name] is a consultant with UNIDO who has the status of an expert on mission for UNIDO in terms of the Headquarters Agreement of UNIDO.

At issue are children's allowances (...) in the amount of € [...] paid to [Name] between September and December 2012 in respect of her daughter, who has [Host Country] nationality. From the documentation submitted to the Office of Legal Affairs, ... the [regional social security institution] is demanding the return of the allowances in the mistaken belief that [Name] was an official of UNIDO at the time she received them. To correct any misunderstanding regarding the status of [Name] and to facilitate proper consideration of the case, the Federal Ministry is kindly requested to notify the [Court] [City], the [regional social security institution] and any other competent [Host Country] authority of the position of UNIDO, which is as follows:

1. Authority to appoint an individual as an official of UNIDO (...) rests solely with the Director General of UNIDO. In the present case, and contrary to the conclusion of the

[regional social security institution] and the court, [Name] was not appointed as, and did not enjoy the status of, an official of UNIDO at the material time. As a consultant or holder of an individual service agreement, [Name]'s status was that of an expert on mission for UNIDO (...) within the meaning of Section 42 of the Headquarters Agreement.

2. Section 39(*b*) of the Headquarters Agreement is being applied incorrectly in [Name]'s case. Section 39(*b*) stipulates that "Officials of the UNIDO and the members of their families living in the same household to whom this Agreement applies shall not be entitled to payments out of the Family Burden Equalization Fund or an instrument with equivalent objectives, unless such persons are [Host Country] nationals or stateless persons resident in [Host Country]". Since [Name] is not, and has never been, an official of UNIDO, the section does not apply to her and cannot be relied upon to determine her status, rights or obligations in [Host Country].

3. The Secretariat understands that [Name] possesses an [Host Country] residency card (...) and is a long-term resident of [Host Country] within the meaning of EU Council Directive 2003/109/EC of 25 November 2003. Article 11(1) of that Directive provides that "[l]ong-term residents shall enjoy equal treatment with nationals as regards ... social security, social assistance and social protection as defined by national law". In its communication of 24 April 2017, the [regional social security institution] cites Article 3(2)(*f*) of the Directive, which stipulates that "this Directive does not apply to third-country nationals who ... enjoy a legal status governed by the Vienna Convention on Diplomatic Relations of 1961, the Vienna Convention on Consular Relations of 1963, the Convention of 1969 on Special Missions or the Vienna Convention on the Representation of States in their Relations with International Organisations of a Universal Character of 1975". The [regional social security institution] also refers to the judgment of the European Court of Justice in the case of *Evans* (ECLI:EU:C:2015:12), which concerned the case of a national of an EU Member State whose status was regulated under the Vienna Convention on Consular Relations of 1963. Considering that [Name]'s status in [Host Country] is not governed by the provisions of any of the foregoing conventions, the arguments of the [regional social security institution] are without merit and should be rejected by the court.

4. The [regional social security institution] suggests that, had the parties so wished, Section 39(*b*) of the Headquarters Agreement could have referred to "persons of other nationality granted equivalent status by European Union legislation". According to the [regional social security institution], the fact that this clause is found in the Headquarters Agreement of the [International organization] of 2011 but not in the Headquarters Agreement of UNIDO implies that the parties intentionally omitted it from the latter. This argument is likewise unfounded given that the current Headquarters Agreement of UNIDO was concluded in 1995, long before the Directive 2003/109/EC entered into force. Moreover, if the Headquarters Agreement of the [International Organization] is interpreted so as to afford the [International Organization] better treatment than that afforded to UNIDO, UNIDO would be entitled to invoke the provisions of Section 55 of its own Headquarters Agreement in order to secure the same treatment for itself.

The Secretariat of the United Nations Industrial Development Organization wishes to express its appreciation to the [Federal Ministry] of the [Host Country] for its assistance in this matter and avails itself of this opportunity to renew to the Federal Ministry the assurances of its highest consideration.

26 May 2017

(*k*) External e-mail to the United Nations Legal Counsel in relation to Criminal accountability of United Nations officials and experts on mission

Criminal accountability of United Nations officials and experts on mission—Referral to national authorities—In the event that an investigative report recommends referral of a case to national authorities for possible prosecution, the UNIDO Office of Legal Affairs is responsible for advising the Director General of UNIDO on whether the referral is appropriate and, if so, to which national authorities—The UNIDO Office of Legal Affairs may also make a recommendation for referral in the absence of an internal investigation, if credible information is otherwise brought to its attention

I refer to [the UN Legal Counsel]'s letter of 16 January 2017 (LA/COD/50/2) regarding General Assembly resolution 71/134 (*Criminal accountability of United Nations officials and experts on mission*), paragraph 27 of which requests the Secretary-General to submit a report to the General Assembly setting out all relevant existing policies and procedures of the United Nations system regarding allegations referred to in paragraphs 17 and 18 of the resolution, namely "credible allegations that reveal that a crime may have been committed by United Nations officials or experts on mission". This email furnishes the information requested by [the UN Legal Counsel] in his letter, including information on relevant policies and procedures of UNIDO and a short narrative describing the activities of the Office of Legal Affairs of UNIDO in relation to matters raised in paragraph 27 of the resolution.

The mandate of the [UNIDO] Office of Legal Affairs is summarized as follows in the programme and budgets of UNIDO for the biennium 2016–2017:

The Programme provides legal advisory services to all organs of UNIDO. Core activities include advising on international agreements, contracts, employment matters, external relations, and technical assistance projects; defending UNIDO's interests in contractual or litigation matters before international tribunals and other fora; and furthering the development of international law and the harmonization of rules, procedures and policies in the United Nations common system. (Document IDB.43/6, p. 35)

Concerning the activities of the Office of Legal Affairs in the area of criminal accountability, I would like to provide the following overview. Firstly, it should be noted that allegations of criminal conduct on the part of officials or experts on mission are rare at UNIDO. The Office of Legal Affairs has referred a suspected serious offense by an official to the authorities of the Host State for possible prosecution on only two occasions since UNIDO became a specialized agency in 1985. Both cases related to financial crimes and both resulted in the conviction of the individual concerned. The number of referrals to the authorities of other States is likewise negligible, as is the number of notifications received from States concerning the investigation or prosecution of officials or experts on mission. The Organization has accordingly not found it necessary to promulgate formal policies or procedures governing these matters.

The practice of the [UNIDO] Office of Legal Affairs with respect to referral to national authorities is well settled. Allegations of criminal conduct necessitating referral typically result from investigations by the Office of Internal Oversight and Ethics, which is mandated to investigate allegations of wrongdoing within the Secretariat. In the event that an investigative report recommends referral of a case to national authorities for possible prosecution, the [UNIDO] Office of Legal Affairs is responsible for advising the Director

General of UNIDO on whether the referral is appropriate and, if so, to which national authorities. The [UNIDO] Office of Legal Affairs may also make a recommendation for referral in the absence of an internal investigation, if credible information is otherwise brought to its attention.

The [UNIDO] Office of Legal Affairs has developed an informal check-list of questions and considerations to assist it in fulfilling its advisory function in relation to possible referrals. The check-list is included [below]. It should be noted that referral of allegations of criminal conduct to national authorities is discretionary and not automatic. The final decision on whether to authorize a particular referral rests with the Director General of UNIDO as chief administrative officer of the Organization.

If an alleged crime is thought to have occurred at Headquarters in [City], the referral is made to the authorities of the Host State only, regardless of the nationality of the individual involved. [Host Country] criminal law is applicable within the Headquarters Seat of UNIDO and [Host Country] criminal courts retain jurisdiction over crimes committed therein, provided of course that any issues of immunity are settled beforehand. If the official or expert on mission is not present in [Host Country], or if the alleged offence occurred outside of the territory of [Host Country], the referral may be made to the authorities of the State in which the offence occurred or to the authorities of the State of nationality of the individual, whichever is considered closest from a jurisdictional perspective.

Referrals are made by the [UNIDO] Office of Legal Affairs using the diplomatic channel; that is, by means of note verbale initialed by the Legal Adviser and addressed to the foreign ministry or permanent mission of the State concerned. The investigative report and any relevant documentary evidence in the possession of the Secretariat are normally handed over at the same time. If necessary, the immunity of the official or expert is waived in the note vebale making the referral, thereby ensuring that such immunity is not an impediment to investigation and prosecution. Alternatively, the note verbale may confirm that no immunity is enjoyed in respect of the act in question. If the matter proceeds to trial, the Office of Legal Affairs may send a representative to court and facilitate the attendance of witnesses who are in the employ of the Organization.

...

All in all, we believe that the legal framework of UNIDO is more than adequate to assist national authorities in appropriate cases.

I trust that the information provided will be of use to the Codification Division [in its capacity as Secretariat of the Sixth Committee] and remain at your disposal should you require further clarification.

Referral of Alleged Criminal Conduct to National Authorities for Investigation and Possible Prosecution

Check-list

The purpose of the following check-list of questions and considerations is to assist in deciding whether it is in the best interests of UNIDO to refer a case of alleged criminal conduct on the part of a staff member to national authorities for investigation and possible prosecution. The relevance and importance of each question or consideration may vary depending on the facts of the case.

i. The nature and gravity of the alleged crime;

ii. The identity of the victim(s);

iii. The harm suffered by UNIDO, including financial loss;

iv. The degree to which the alleged crime has been established internally (*e.g.* is there a finding by the Internal Oversight Section (IOS), the Joint Appeal Board or the International Labor Organisation Administrative Tribunal (ILOAT)?);

v. The action already been taken by UNIDO against the staff member;

vi. The resource implications of referral (*e.g.* the time required of Human Resources Management (HRM), IOS and the UNIDO Office of Legal Affairs (LEG); the need to release staff to act as witnesses; and the cost of local counsel to advise on local law or to oversee the interests of UNIDO);

vii. The possibility that UNIDO may be able to seek redress as a civil party during criminal proceedings;

viii. The staff member's presence in or absence from the jurisdiction;

ix. The reputational risk of referral;

x. The reputational risk of non-referral;

xi. The desirability of making confidential Secretariat documents available to national authorities in original or redacted form (*e.g.* the IOS report);

xii. The criminal justice system in the country concerned (*e.g.* referral may be inappropriate if there are no assurances of a fair trial or humane sentence);

xiii. The existence of extenuating circumstances and/or humanitarian factors;

xiv. Possible political considerations, such as the potential impact of referral on relations between a Member State and UNIDO.

1 June 2017

(*l*) Note verbale to the [Federal Ministry] of [Host Country] concerning a former member of an association, being denied access to the [United Nations Headquarters]

Denial of access to the United Nations Headquarters—Scope of requests for information—Rejection of requests for information relating to an individual's access to the United Nations Headquarters as inconsistent with UNIDO's privileges and immunities

The Secretariat of the United Nations Industrial Development Organization ("UNIDO") presents its compliments to the [Federal Ministry] of [Host Country] and has the honour to refer to the Federal Ministry's note [...] of 10 May 2017 requesting, on behalf of the [Regional Court for Civil Matters] [City], that the Secretariat inquire from the administrative centre (...) of the [United Nations Headquarters] and from the Safety and Security Service about the reasons and circumstances [Name], a former member of the association [Name], is being denied access to the [United Nations Headquarters] and on the basis of which information this occurred.

The Secretariat wishes to inform the Federal Ministry that an administrative centre of the [UN Headquarters] does not exist. If the Federal Ministry is referring to the Buildings Management Services ("BMS") of the [UN Headquarters], the Secretariat wishes to clarify that BMS is a common service of the [City]-based Organizations of the [UN Headquarters] without responsibility to control access to the [UN Headquarters]. Concerning the Safety and Security Service, the Secretariat wishes to refer to the information shared with the Federal Ministry by note verbale dated 17 November 2016. In addition, the Secretariat further wishes to inform the Federal Ministry that [Name]'s access to the [UN Headquarters] has been denied on security grounds based on information provided to the Safety and Security Service.

The Secretariat wishes to recall that UNIDO has responded to requests for information and even made available its personnel to give evidence as a result of [Name]'s various actions in the local courts despite the fact that UNIDO is not a party to these proceedings. UNIDO extended its cooperation voluntarily, in the interests of the administration of justice in [Host Country], and without prejudice to its rights under the Headquarters Agreement of UNIDO and the Convention on the Privileges and Immunities of the United Nations of 1946 as applied to UNIDO. The requests initiated by [Name]'s actions are disruptive and threaten to interfere with the full and efficient discharge of UNIDO's responsibilities. The Federal Ministry is therefore requested to inform the [Regional Court for Civil Matters] [City] that UNIDO rejects any further requests for information relating to [Name]'s access to the [UN Headquarters] as inconsistent with UNIDO's privileges and immunities.

The Secretariat of the United Nations Industrial Development Organization avails itself of this opportunity to renew to the [Federal Ministry] of [Host Country] the assurances of its highest consideration.

2 June 2017

(*m*) External e-mail to the Legal Adviser of the [UN Organization] concerning the selection and appointment of the Executive Head

Appointment process of the executive head of the organization—Competent organ for the selection and appointment of the executive head—Majority required by the rules of the organization for the appointment of the executive head—Situation in the event the selected candidate does not achieve the required majority to be appointed

I refer to your e-mail of 2 June 2017, in which you requested information concerning the appointment of the executive head in our organization. In UNIDO the executive head is denominated Director General. Please see below our response to your questions:

1. *In your Organization, which organ is competent for the selection and appointment of the executive head?*

Under Article 11.2 of the Constitution of UNIDO and Rule 103.1 of the Rules of Procedure of the General Conference, the Director General shall be appointed by the General Conference upon recommendation of the Industrial Development Board. The procedures for recommendation and appointment are described, respectively, in Rule 61 of the Rules of Procedure of the Industrial Development Board and Rule 104 of the Rules of Procedure of the General Conference.

2. *What is the required majority for the appointment of the executive head established in the rules of your Organization?*

Rule 104.2 of the Rules of Procedure of the General Conference provides that the decision to appoint the Director General shall require a simple majority of those present and voting, but no fewer than two fifths of the Members participating in the current session of the Conference.

3. *Is there any procedure foreseen in your rules in case the selected candidate does not achieve the required majority to be appointed? If yes, please specify.*

In this case, Rule 104.3 of the Rules of Procedure of the General Conference stipulates that, "If a candidate recommended by the Board does not obtain the majority specified in paragraph 2 above [*i.e.* Rule 104.2], the Board shall reconsider the matter and present a new recommendation to the Conference."

4. *Have you encountered this situation before and if yes, what was the procedure followed for the appointment of the executive head?*

No, this situation has not been encountered before in UNIDO. Since 1985 all the Directors General of UNIDO have been appointed by acclamation.

5. *In accordance with the applicable legal framework of your Organization, what would you advise if the situation was to arise?*

In terms of Rule 104.3 of the Rules of Procedure of the General Conference, the matter must be reconsidered by the Industrial Development Board with a view to presenting a new recommendation to the General Conference. A special session of the Industrial Development Board may have to be convened for this purpose. It is up to the Industrial Development Board to decide how it wishes to reconsider the matter. The Board could, for example, take fresh ballots among the nominated candidates (provided they are still available), hold consultations among the Member States, organize a hearing for the selected candidate so that interested States ask questions or re-start the procedure from scratch by calling for new nominations from Governments for the post of Director General.

The basic legal documents of UNIDO may be consulted on UNIDO's public website: http://www.unido.org/legal/basic-legal-documents.html

16 June 2017

(*n*) Internal e-mail to the UNIDO Programme Officer concerning a letter of credentials of UNIDO Representative in the [State]

Letter of credentials of UNIDO Representative—Privileges and immunities of UNIDO representatives—As a general rule, UNIDO country representatives enjoy the same functional privileges and immunities as are enjoyed by all other officials of the Organization

1. Kindly refer to your emails of 18 and 19 July 2017 concerning the above-mentioned subject. Attached to your email was an email from [Name], Industrial Development Officer, asking you to add the following statement to her credentials as the new country representative of UNIDO in the [State]:

> "The appointment of UNIDO Country Representative is consistent with Article III of the Basic Cooperation Agreement between UNIDO and the Government of the [State]."

2. She explains that the addition of the above-mentioned sentence "should help in [her] accreditation and also to minimize ambiguities in the conferment of immunities and privileges, and other confusion …".

3. I wish to inform you that, under Article X (3) of the Basic Cooperation Agreement of 26 February 1993 between UNIDO and the [State], the UNIDO Country Director "shall enjoy the same privileges and immunities as the Government accords to diplomatic envoys in accordance with international law."

4. [Name] is a newly appointed country representative who is a national of the [State]. Given that she does not have the rank of director, her appointment did not follow the procedure set out in Article III of the Basic Cooperation Agreement (*i.e.*, UNIDO may appoint, where appropriate upon consultation with the United Nations Development Programme, a UNIDO Country Director in the [State]).

5. Further, as [Name] is a national of the [State], UNIDO does not expect the Government to grant her the privileges and immunities of a diplomatic envoy. The principle that states do not grant diplomatic immunity to their own nationals is well recognized in international law, including in the Vienna Convention on Diplomatic Relations of 18 April 1961 and in the Headquarters Agreement of UNIDO.

6. In this regard, it should be noted that there is no general legal obligation on member states to grant diplomatic privileges and immunities to UNIDO country representatives. As a rule, UNIDO country representatives enjoy the same functional privileges and immunities as are enjoyed by all other officials of the Organization. [Name]'s privileges and immunities in the [State] will therefore be those set forth in the Convention on the Privileges and Immunities of the United Nations, to which the [State] acceded on 28 October 1947.

7. In the light of the above, the following sentence may be added to [Name]'s credentials:

The UNIDO Country Representative fulfills the functions and responsibilities set forth in the Basic Cooperation Agreement between UNIDO and the Government of the [State] of 26 February 1993.

21 July 2017

(*o*) Internal e-mail to the UNIDO Director of the Office of Internal Oversight and Ethics concerning the position of the ILO Administrative Tribunal on burden of proof required for misconduct

Burden of proof for misconduct—Uniform Principles and Guidelines for Investigations—Scope of the discretionary authority of the Executive Head is not limited to the choice of proceeding or not proceeding with a disciplinary case—Depending on the circumstances of the case and the best interests of the Organization, the Executive Head may decide to deal with the matter in a non-disciplinary manner—The standard of proof in disciplinary cases is beyond a reasonable doubt, which is higher than the standard used by the Office of Internal Oversight and Ethics

I wish to refer to your email of 21 July 2017, which sought my views on the burden of proof for misconduct as set out in two ILOAT judgments (Judgment Nos. 3848 and 3880).

I understand your query's motivation to be as follows. In the *Uniform Principles and Guidelines for Investigations*, the burden of proof to determine whether a complaint is substantiated "is defined for the purposes of an investigation as information that, as a whole, shows that something is more probable than not". This professional standard, however, differs from the burden of proof that the ILOAT requires to uphold a disciplinary decision. As Judgment No. 3880 at Consideration 17 makes clear, "for a finding of misconduct to withstand scrutiny, each of the elements of the alleged misconduct must be proved beyond a reasonable doubt".

The two standards of proof differ due to the functions that are served by two different, albeit related, processes. The investigative process has the function of examining and determining the truth of allegations, *e.g.*, of corrupt or fraudulent practices and misconduct on the part of staff. The investigative process is primarily and essentially a fact-finding process, whose object and purpose is to ascertain the facts. The other process is disciplinary. The function of the disciplinary process is to determine whether or not a disciplinary sanction should be imposed for an act of misconduct. See Judgment No. 3848 at Consideration 6 ("A finding of misconduct is one that is only made in the context of a disciplinary process") (emphasis supplied). The object and purpose of the disciplinary process is to establish and enforce discipline in the secretariat.

Because of the heightened risk to the staff member's career and reputation, the Administrative Tribunal of the ILO demands the highest standard of proof before a staff member can be sanctioned with a disciplinary measure. The due process requirements are correspondingly enhanced in order to protect the rights of staff. There must be a charge laid against the staff member, followed by an adversarial proceeding. As the Tribunal put it in Judgment No. 3848 at Consideration 7:

> "The case law consistently states that even if an organization's regulations, rules and other relevant documents do not provide for formal disciplinary procedures, the disciplinary process requires that before deciding a disciplinary sanction the concerned staff

member must be given ample opportunity to take part in adversarial proceedings, in the course of which he is given the opportunity to express his point of view, put forward evidence and participate in the processing of the evidence submitted in support of the charges against him (see Judgment 3682, consideration 12)." [Internal quotations omitted]

There is no inherent or logical reason why the standard of proof applicable to the Office of Internal Oversight and Ethics ("IOE")'s investigating function should be identical to the Tribunal's standard of review of a disciplinary decision. The Executive Head's discretionary authority is not limited to the choice of proceeding or not proceeding with a disciplinary case. Depending on the circumstances of the case and the best interests of the Organization, the Executive Head may decide to deal with the matter in a non-disciplinary manner, *e.g.*, through the performance management system or a recovery action pursuant to staff rule 101.06, for which the preponderance of the evidence standard is sufficient. In any event, it is worth recalling the recent UNIDO case of *in re* [Name] (Judgment No. 3725), which the Tribunal recently decided at its 123rd session. As I explained to the Director General when reporting on the outcome of the [Name] case, the "Tribunal confirmed that the standard of proof in disciplinary cases is beyond a reasonable doubt, which is higher than the standard used by IOE. The task of the Joint Disciplinary Committee ("JDC") is to determine whether the evidence of misconduct uncovered by IOE meets the standard of proof beyond a reasonable doubt."…

1 August 2017

(*p*) Internal e-mail to the UNIDO consultant concerning tax status of [Host Country] consultants

HEADQUARTERS AGREMENT OF UNIDO—TAX STATUS OF CONSULTANTS

I refer to your e-mail of 12 September 2017 seeking [the Legal Adviser]'s advice on whether UNIDO has concluded an agreement granting [consultants], including those who are [Host Country] nationals, exemption from income tax in [Host Country].

Relations between UNIDO and the [Host Country] are governed by the Headquarters Agreement of 1995. As a consultant, your status is regulated under article XIII of the Headquarters Agreement, which concerns experts on mission for UNIDO. On the issue of taxation, article XIII effectively grants all consultants exemption from [Host Country] income tax on their official income, except if they are [Host Country] nationals.

Article XIII, section 43, of the Headquarters Agreement reads as follows:

(*a*) Where the incidence of any form of taxation depends upon residence, periods during which the persons designated in Section 42 may be present in the [Host Country] for the discharge of their duties shall not be considered as periods of residence. In particular, such persons shall be exempt from taxation on their salaries and emoluments received from the UNIDO during such periods of duty and shall be exempt from all tourist taxes.

(*b*) Except as otherwise provided, persons designated in Section 42 who are [Host Country] nationals or stateless persons resident in [Host Country], shall enjoy only those privileges and immunities provided for in the General Convention [*i.e.* the Convention on the Privileges and Immunities of the United Nations of 1946], it being understood, nevertheless, that such privileges and immunities include exemption from taxation on pensions paid to them by the Pension Fund.

The Headquarters Agreement and the Convention on the Privileges and Immunities of the United Nations are both published on the Intranet: https://intranet.unido.org/intra/Legal_Resources.

13 September 2017

(*q*) Internal e-mail to the UNIDO Officer-in-Charge of the UNIDO Department of Operational Support Services concerning a Joint Inspection Unit ("JIU") study on administrative support services

Administrative support services by UNIDO to other organizations in the United Nations system—Mutual recognition in the area of procurement

Reference is made to your email of 5 September 2017, which requested our inputs to the JIU's Questionnaire on "Opportunities to improve efficiency and effectiveness in administrative support services by enhancing inter-agency cooperation". It is noted that the JIU defines "administrative support services" as embracing services in relation to finance, human resources, information and communications technology, logistics, procurement and facility (buildings management) services. In view of the Questionnaire's subject, the [UNIDO] Office of Legal Affairs inputs are necessarily limited.

Nevertheless, the following questions give rise to legal comments:

Question No. 9.

UNIDO has a mandate to provide administrative support services to other United Nations system organizations (namely, buildings management and catering services) in the Headquarters seat. The arrangement is based on an inter-agency Memorandum of Understanding, and the related funding and work programmes are approved by the Governing Bodies of UNIDO as part of the biennial programme and budgets cycle. The provision of administrative support services to UN system organizations outside the Headquarters seat area would most likely require the approval of the UNIDO Governing Bodies as well.

Question Nos. 25 to 28.

"Mutual recognition" is not defined in the Questionnaire; however, a UNDG position paper from May 2016 states as follows: "Mutual recognition entails recognizing and enabling use of other agencies' processes such as a hiring of staff. It is based on the premise that all UN agencies meet international audit and internal control standards and are regularly assessed against these standards. Therefore using each other's systems and processes should not pose a risk to the agencies" (p. 5).

Mutual recognition is already possible in the area of procurement. In the exercise of delegated procurement authority under UNIDO's financial rules, the Managing Director, PPS, may cooperate with other organizations of the United Nations system to meet the procurement requirements of UNIDO, provided that the regulations and rules of those organizations are compatible with those of UNIDO. The Managing Director, PPS, may, as appropriate, enter into agreements for such purposes. Such cooperation may include carrying out common procurement actions together or UNIDO may enter into a contract relying on a procurement decision of another organization or may request another organization to carry out procurement activities on its behalf. See *Financial Rule 109.5.3(b).*

Further information on the application of this rule may be found on pages 42–43 of the *UNIDO Procurement Manual.*

More generally, UNIDO has relied on [UN Organization] for the provision of various administrative support services at the country level. In such cases, UNIDO relies on [UN Organization]'s rules and procedures for the provision of requested services. The services are usually rendered on the basis of a global agreement, which was signed with [UN Organization], in 2003…

September 2017

(*r*) Internal e-mail to the Managing Director of the UNIDO Department concerning a request for UNIDO's endorsement

ENDORSEMENT BY UNIDO OF BID TO HOST FORUM EVENT—INCOMPATIBILITY WITH THE RULES OF UNIDO—UNIDO CONSTITUTION—POSSIBLE DISCRIMINATION AMONG BIDDERS AND UNINTENDED REPERCUSSIONS

This is in response to your email dated 18 September 2017 asking for advice on [National Organization]'s request for a letter endorsing its bid to host the "World Forum on Energy Regulation" in [City] in 2021.

Your view is that "expressing support to one particular bid in an international competition amongst public entities might compromise the neutrality expected of an international organization". We agree. On the face of it, supporting [National Organization]'s bid would be incompatible with the rules of UNIDO, including article 11(4) of the Constitution, staff relegations 1.1-1.3, and Section II(*e*) of the UNIDO Code of Ethical Conduct (*UNIDO/DGB/(M).115*).[1] Supporting the bid would also discriminate against oth-

---

[1] Article 11(4) of the Constitution of UNIDO:

In the performance of their duties the Director-General and the staff shall not seek or receive instructions from any government or from any authority external to the Organization. *They shall refrain from any action that might reflect on their position as international officials responsible only to the Organization.* Each Member undertakes to respect the exclusively international character of the responsibilities of the Director-General and the staff and not to seek to influence them in the discharge of their responsibilities.

Regulation 1.1:

Staff are international civil servants. Their responsibilities are not national but exclusively international. *By accepting appointment, they pledge themselves to discharge their functions and to regulate their conduct with only the interests of the Organization in view.*

Regulation 1.2:

In the performance of their duties staff shall neither seek nor accept instructions from any Government or from any other authority external to the Organization. Staff should note that Member States have on their part undertaken to respect the exclusively international character of the responsibilities of the Director-General and the staff and not to seek to influence them in the discharge of their responsibilities.

Regulation 1.3:

Staff shall conduct themselves at all times in a manner befitting their status as international civil servants. They shall not engage in any activity that is incompatible with the proper discharge of their duties with the Organization. *They shall avoid any action and in particular any kind of public pronouncement which may adversely reflect on their status, or on the integrity, independence and impartiality which are required by that status.* While they are not expected to give up their national sentiments or their political and religious convictions, they shall at all times bear in mind the reserve and tact incumbent upon them by reason of their international status."

Section II(e) of the UNIDO Code of Ethical Conduct:

er bidders and could have unintended repercussions for UNIDO. If the Director General were to support this bid he would indirectly open the floodgates for similar requests. Our advice is to refrain from endorsing the bid.

28 September 2017

(*s*) Internal e-mail to the Chief of the UNIDO Financial Management of Technical Cooperation Division concerning a proposed amendment to Staff Regulation 6.8

Mitigation of financial risk incurred in connection with the income tax reimbursement to staff members currently on board as well as for the future recruited staff members—Proposed amendment to the staff regulations—Role of tax reimbursement agreements

1. Reference is made to your email of 11 September 2017 requesting advice on a proposed amendment to Staff Regulation 6.8. The proposal is the result of an enquiry by the External Auditor as to "how UNIDO is planning to mitigate the financial risk incurred in connection with the income tax reimbursement to staff members currently on board as well as for the future recruited staff members". Our advice is as follows.

2. The main amendment under consideration is the addition of a clause, underlined below, at the end of staff regulation 6.8(*c*):

> "(*c*) … the Director-General is authorized to refund to the staff member an amount representing the tax paid for the year on his or her organization salary and emoluments *to the extent it is reimbursed to UNIDO through a tax reimbursement agreement between the Organization and the State levying such taxes.*"

3. The proposed amendment would clearly contravene the Organization's legal obligations and should not be pursued. UNIDO is under a duty to comply with general principles of international administrative law, which are implied terms of the contracts of all staff. The general principles jeopardized by the amendment include the principle of equal treatment, the principle of equal pay for equal work, the principle of tax exemption, and the principle of respect for acquired rights.

4. The ILOAT has decisively rejected the notion that an international organization can rely on the terms of a tax reimbursement agreement or its staff regulations to limit the amount of the tax it refunds to a staff member. Of particular relevance is Judgment No. 2256, delivered in July 2003, which is worth quoting at length:

> "8. The Organisation raises various arguments with regard to its refusal to reimburse all of the taxes that staff members pay on OPCW income. It relies specifically on the terms of the [Tax Reimbursement Agreement (TRA)] which it has negotiated with the [State]. *It also invokes Staff Regulation 3.3(b) which, it says, prohibits it from reimbursing the complainant unless and until it has itself received an equivalent payment from the [State] Government. These arguments beg the question: if the Organisation is under a duty to protect its employees from national taxation of their earnings as international civil*

In all countries and regions where UNIDO operates, personnel are called upon to exercise special care in maintaining their independence. *At times, personnel may receive requests from the government of the host country or from other partners, but this should not compromise their independence.* […]

servants, it cannot rely on the TRA and the provisions of its Staff Regulations as an excuse for abdicating its responsibilities to its staff members under international law. In Judgment 2032, the Tribunal made it abundantly clear that the principle of tax exemption is fundamental; that it is ultimately the Organisation's responsibility to ensure that staff members are fully reimbursed for any income tax paid on their OPCW income; and that the last-income method is the only appropriate method for determining tax reimbursements.

....

11. While the existence of a Tax Reimbursement Agreement with the [State] makes the present case marginally different from Judgment 2032, it is impossible to see how the Organisation could be said to have acted in conformity with the fundamental principles of tax exemption and non-discrimination in concluding such an agreement. Paragraphs 3 and 5 of the TRA, and its Annex excluding Provident Fund part B contributions as income, in combination with Staff Regulation 3.3(*b*), make the Organisation's position clear: it does not accept that it should include Provident Fund contributions as income for the purpose of tax reimbursements. It will calculate the reimbursements using the first-income method. It will not reimburse the staff member more than it itself is reimbursed by the State Party. These positions have not been forced upon the Organisation; it has voluntarily embraced them, and this, notwithstanding the Tribunal's clear holding in Judgment 2032 to which the Organisation was itself a party.

12. *The Organisation does not dispute the principle of tax exemption or that such principle is fundamental to the law of the international civil service. It nonetheless argues that, despite its acknowledged submission to that principle, it can derogate from its obligations by creating limiting provisions in bilateral agreements and in its Staff Regulations. The argument is unacceptable and if adopted would lead to anarchy and the destruction of the rule of law.*

13. In Judgment 2032, the Tribunal stated the following:

"If the Organisation does not (and clearly now it cannot) contest the exempt status of the complainant, it is its duty to protect him against the claims of the authorities of a member State, to reimburse him the amount of tax he has paid to the State, and to employ its own considerable power, authority and influence to have the [national] authorities change their position. *Exemption from national taxes is an essential condition of employment in the international civil service and is an important guarantee of independence and objectivity. It cannot be made to depend upon the whim of national taxing authorities who will be understandably reluctant to admit any exceptions to their claims.*"

14. With regard to the role of a tax reimbursement agreement, the Tribunal stated the following:

"It would be strange indeed if the absence of such an agreement could be invoked by an international organisation or its member States to deprive some staff members and not others of their tax-exempt status. *If a member State in breach of its international obligations taxes the exempt income of a staff member, the reimbursement of that tax cannot be made to depend upon the grace and favour of that State.*"

15. The evident corollary of that statement is that it would similarly be strange if the existence of an agreement could be invoked by an international organisation to deprive some staff members and not others of their tax exempt status. Such an agreement is meant to set the terms of a member State's commitment to refund an organisation for tax reimbursements. It must, however, conform with international law and cannot be used to undermine the fundamental principles of tax exemption recalled by the Tribunal. Thus,

even if the text of the TRA had the reach which the Organisation contends for it, which may be doubted, it would simply be unenforceable as being contrary to law.

16. *It is likewise with the provisions of the Staff Regulations which, in the Organisation's submissions, would limit the complainant's right to tax reimbursement to the amounts actually paid to the Organisation by the [State] under the TRA. Like the TRA itself, the Staff Regulations must be in conformity with the requirements of the law and where they are not, they are simply unenforceable.*

....

20. *The Tribunal ... does not accept that the problem of states which refuse to recognise their legal obligations can be dealt with by organisations at the expense of their own staff and in violation of the law.*" [Emphasis added]

As far as the [UNIDO] Office of Legal Affairs is aware, the only state taxing the official income of its nationals or permanent residents is the [State]. Considering that the [State] is no longer a member of UNIDO, the financial risk associated with the obligation to refund taxes on official income should be containable through the following measures:

(i) to continue to restrict the hiring of new staff members who are nationals or permanent residents of the [State] (except at the Office in [City]);

(ii) to promulgate an administrative instruction informing staff that the Director General will generally not authorize the acquisition of residency in the [State];

(iii) to institute appropriate administrative or disciplinary action against any staff member who obtains residency in the [State] without permission or without disclosing such residency to UNIDO; and

(iv) to propose the conclusion of an appropriate tax reimbursement agreement with any other state that imposes taxes on official income.

6 October 2017

(*t*) Internal e-mail to the Chief of the UNIDO Department of Finance concerning the Interpretation of Financial Regulation 4.2 on unencumbered balance of the appropriations

References to "members" in UNIDO financial regulations and rules—Management of unencumbered balance of payment by members

I refer to your email of 25 October 2017 asking for my interpretation of certain provisions of financial regulation 4.2 on current and future bienniums. I understand that the matter is urgent and therefore provide summary answers to your questions below.

(1) Does "Members" refer to active Members at the given time of surrendering (i.e. 2017) of the unencumbered balance, or also to ex-Members active at the time of the budget appropriations?

Although not defined, the term "the Members" (or sometimes "the members") is used in various contexts in the financial regulations and rules. The ordinary meaning of the term in each of these contexts is "the member states of UNIDO". The term encompasses those states that are members of UNIDO *at the time of application of the regulation or rule in question*, in other words, current member states of the Organization. This is the meaning that should also be given to "the Members" in financial regulation 4.2. Had the drafters of the financial regulations intended the term to have a different meaning in financial regulation 4.2 (for example, to include some former members), they would have expressly stated as much.

(2) Can "surrendering" be interpreted as "allocated", but with withheld payment/refund to the Members, to temporarily finance cash-flow of unpaid contributions for the current biennium?

The expression "surrendered to the Members" appears in paragraphs (*b*) and (*c*) of financial regulation 4.2. Read together, paragraphs (*b*) and (*c*) foresee a two-stage process of surrendering the unencumbered balance of the appropriations for a biennium: crediting the amount *pro rata* to the member states at the end of the first financial year following the biennium (paragraph (*a*)) and surrendering or returning the remaining balance *pro rata* at the end of the second financial year following the biennium (paragraph (*b*)). Before being surrendered or returned, the unencumbered balance remains with UNIDO and is subject to the treatment specified in the regulation, which includes satisfying outstanding regular budget obligations of individual member states. As financial regulation 4.2 expressly lays down how the unencumbered balance may be utilized, it should not be used for any other purpose, such as to pre-finance contributions for the next biennium. (The relevant principle of interpretation is known by its Latin maxim *Expressio unius est exclusion alterius.*) Authorization to utilize the unencumbered balance for that purpose would, in my opinion, require an amendment of the regulations or a decision of the policymaking organs.

27 October 2017

(*u*) External e-mail to a certified auditor and tax consultant of [Host Country] concerning the interpretation of 24 (c) of Headquarters Agreement regarding valued added taxes (VAT)

Headquarters Agreement of UNIDO—Privileges and immunities of UNIDO consultants

This is with reference to your email of 23 October 2017 regarding the applicability of Section 24(*c*) of *the Headquarters Agreement of UNIDO* (which deals with exemption from tax on all transactions by UNIDO) to individual service agreements of consultants working for UNIDO. The question you have asked is as follows:

As there is no legal regulation in the relevant VAT law (...) I am wondering if paragraph 24c is the legal basis to charge this kind of services (consultancy of services for a foreign country, based on an individual service agreement) without [Host Country] VAT?

Generally speaking, UNIDO pays VAT as part of the price of goods and services purchased in [Host Country]. The Organization then claims the VAT back from the ministry of finance pursuant to Section 24(*b*) of the Headquarters Agreement. Although the interpretation you suggest is an interesting one, the tax status of consultants serving under individual service agreements is normally determined with reference to other provisions of the Headquarters Agreement.

From a legal perspective, consultants are considered to be "experts on mission for UNIDO", whose privileges and immunities are those defined in Article XIII (Sections 42–44) of the Headquarters Agreement. In terms of Section 43(*a*), experts on mission enjoy exemption from [Host Country] taxation on their official salaries and emoluments while working at Headquarters. This exemption from [Host Country] income tax does not, however, apply to [Host Country] nationals (and possibly permanent residents). In terms of Section 43(*b*), experts on mission who are [Host Country] nationals or stateless persons resident in [Host Country] enjoy only those privileges and immunities provided for in *the Convention on the Privileges and Immunities of the United Nations of 1946* (see Article VI), which do not include exemption from taxation on organizational income.

6 November 2017

(*v*) Internal e-mail to the Chief of the UNIDO Financial Management of Technical Cooperation Division concerning taxation of UNIDO in [State]

Taxation of UNIDO—Exemption from withholding tax—Submission of tax returns—Fiscal privileges and immunities of the United Nations—Delays in issuance of tax exemption certificates

I refer to your email of 27 October 2017 regarding the withholding tax in [State]. I also refer to the subsequent emails from [Name] and to the letter from the [State] tax authorities dated 2 March 2016, which seems to require UNIDO to submit tax returns for the period 2006 to 2016.

In my view, UNIDO is exempt from the withholding tax in [State] and should not be asked to fill out and submit tax returns. In terms of the Constitution of UNIDO and the Basic Cooperation Agreement of 1994, the Government is under an obligation to accord to UNIDO and its officials the privileges and immunities set forth in the Convention on the Privileges and Immunities of the United Nations of 1946. As is well known, these privileges and immunities include, for UNIDO, exemption from all direct taxes and, for officials, exemption from taxes on official income and emoluments. These instruments are available on the Intranet under *Basic Legal Documents*.

I note that the Country Office has, correctly, already reminded the foreign ministry that UNIDO enjoys the fiscal privileges and immunities of the United Nations. If the tax authorities continue to demand the submission of tax returns, the Country Office should restate the Organization's position and ask the foreign ministry to facilitate observance of the provisions of the Constitution of UNIDO and the Basic Cooperation Agreement. In this regard, the Country Office may wish to coordinate with other United Nations agencies represented in [City]. In the event that formal and informal interventions with the tax authorities and the foreign ministry prove unsuccessful, the Country Office should revert to Headquarters. If possible, however, the matter should be settled at the country level.

As concerns the delay in issuing tax exemption certificates, the Country Office may wish to remind the responsible authorities of the provisions of Article XI(1)(*b*) of the Basic Cooperation Agreement, which requires "*Délivrance rapide et gratuite des visas, permis et autorisations nécessaires*". This matter should be raised again with the foreign ministry if the problem persists.

7 November 2017

(*w*) Note verbale to the [Federal Ministry] of [Host Country] concerning issuance of a legitimation card for a senior official of UNIDO

Issuance of legitimation cards for UNIDO senior officials—Headquarters Agreement of UNIDO—Privileges and Immunities of UNIDO

The Secretariat of the United Nations Industrial Development Organization ("UNIDO") presents its compliments to the [Federal Ministry] of the [Host Country] and has the honour to refer to the Secretariat's note verbale dated 6 September 2017 requesting issuance of a legitimation card for a senior official of UNIDO of [State] nationality who enjoys diplomatic privileges and immunities in [Host Country]. In view of the condition subsequently set by the authorities for issuance of the legitimation card, the Secretariat wishes to recall that Section 40(*b*) of the Headquarters Agreement of UNIDO stipulates as follows:

The Government shall furnish the UNIDO for each official within the scope of this Article with an identity card bearing the photograph of the holder. This card shall serve to identify the holder in relation to all [Host Country] authorities.

The Secretariat notes that Section 40(*b*) establishes a clear legal obligation for the Government to furnish UNIDO with a legitimation card for each official of the Organization. The Secretariat notes further that the practice of issuing legitimation cards to officials of UNIDO upon official request dates back to 1967. In order to facilitate the cost-effective operations of the Secretariat, it would be appreciated if the service-provider contracted to issue legitimation cards on behalf of the Government could implement Section 40(*b*) in accordance with its terms.

Finally, the Secretariat wishes to record that important matters concerning the privileges and immunities of UNIDO are customarily brought to the attention of the Legal Counsel of the United Nations.

23 November 2017

(*x*) Internal e-mail to the UNIDO Director of Policymaking Organs concerning the acceptance of new agenda items and draft resolution to the seventeenth session of the UNIDO General Conference

The acceptance of new agenda items and draft resolution of the UNIDO General Conference

I refer to your interoffice memorandum dated 24 November 2017 on the subject "*Acceptance of new agenda items and draft resolutions to GC.17*", in which you request my advice on certain procedural questions that have arisen in relation to a proposal submitted by the Western European and Other States Group (WEOG) and a draft resolution submitted by the [Intergovernmental Organization] and its Member States. The Secretariat received both documents on 17 November 2017.

Proposal of WEOG to move [State A] to List B of Annex I of the Constitution

You indicate that this proposal will be brought to the attention of the General Committee at its first meeting on Monday afternoon. In this regard, you ask (1) whether the General Committee must agree by consensus to forward the matter to the General

Conference for an oral decision; and (2) whether the proposal qualifies as a new agenda item or whether it could fall under agenda item 2 [Election of officers], which has been used in the past for similar decisions. I would like to answer these questions briefly as follows:

1. The General Committee's functions, as set out in rule 42(1)(*a*) of the rules of procedure of the General Conference, give the Committee the authority to "examine the provisional agenda, together with any supplementary list, and make recommendations to the Conference with regard to each item proposed concerning its inclusion in the agenda, the rejection of the request for inclusion or the inclusion of the item in the provisional agenda of a future session".

2. Footnote 1 of the provisional agenda (GC.17/1/Add.1) states that, "account has to be taken of the latest lists of States to be included in Annex I to the Constitution". It also states that the Conference will have to decide, before proceeding to elections, in which list of States to include [State B]. Footnote 1 relates to agenda item 2 [Election of officers] and agenda item 7 [Election to organs].

3. In view of agenda items 2 and 7 and footnote 1, the proposal of WEOG need not be considered as a proposal to add a new agenda item. Cf. rule 18 and rule 42(1)(*b*). The General Committee may thus recommend to the Conference that, in addition to the decision on [State B], the Conference may wish to make a decision to move [State A] to List B of Annex I.

4. If the General Committee cannot reach consensus on such a recommendation, the Committee can vote on the question whether to recommend to the Conference to take a decision to move [State A] to List B of Annex I. Cf. rule 49(*d*) ("Decisions of committees and working groups shall be taken by a majority of the members present and voting…").

5. The Conference is expected to take up agenda item 2 (and hence footnote 1) before the General Committee meets. The President of the Conference could therefore inform delegates that the Conference will revert to the topic of the Lists of States in Annex 1 following consideration by the General Committee of the proposal of WEOG. The Conference's authority in this regard is derived from paragraph 2 of Annex I, which states, "The Conference may at any time, after appropriate consultations, change the classification of a Member as listed below".

Draft resolution of the [Intergovernmental Organization] and its Member States on PCPs (agenda item 13)

You note that the Secretariat received the draft resolution of the [Intergovernmental Organization] and its Member States late and that there may be no consensus in the General Committee to forward the draft resolution to the Main Committee. If consensus is not possible, you ask whether this means that the draft resolution will not be forwarded to the Main Committee under any circumstances. You also point out that the rules of procedure of the General Conference set no deadline for the submission of draft resolutions and ask whether the deadlines set by the IDB and the informal consultations (3 and 13 November 2017, respectively) can override the rules of procedure. My advice is as follows:

1. Concerning the need for consensus in the General Committee, please refer to my comments above. If consensus is not possible, the General Committee can vote. Cf. rule 49(*d*).

2. As a legal matter, it is unclear why the General Committee is expected to make a recommendation on whether the draft resolution should be forwarded to the Main Committee. Rule 42(1) of the rules of procedure lists functions of the Committee relating to the adoption of the agenda and the allocation of agenda items. The rule does not seem to

provide for the Committee to make recommendations on the allocation to sessional bodies of draft decisions or resolutions submitted under agenda items.

3. On the question of the deadline, it bears noting that the IDB's decision is purely *hortatory* (*i.e.*, strongly advising): it "[u]rged Member States to submit to the informal consultations any proposed draft decisions or resolutions by 3 November 2017". Cf. IDB.45/Dec.14. The IDB did not prohibit Member States from submitting draft decisions or resolutions after 3 November 2017. At any rate, the IDB cannot suspend the authority or the rules of procedure of the General Conference.

4. In terms of rule 84 of the rules of procedure, a Member State participating in the Conference may clearly submit the draft resolution in question for consideration by the Conference. Once the Conference has allocated agenda item 13 to the Main Committee, the draft resolution may be taken up by that committee. Cf. rule 47.

26 November 2017

3. Universal Postal Union

(Submitted by the Legal Adviser of the Universal Postal Union)

Legal Affairs Directorate memorandum No. 01/2017 to the Council of Administration—Legal assessment of issues arising from certain measures announced by the designated operator of the [name of State]*

The UPU as an intergovernmental organization and a specialized agency of the United Nations—The UPU Constitution and General Regulations—The UPU Convention and Regulations—The obligation to provide basic and mandatory supplementary international postal services—The principle of designation of offices of exchange by a member country (or its designated operators)—The principle of non-discrimination—The principle of freedom of transit (including *transit à découvert*)—The "office-of-exchange-to-office-of-exchange" principle—Bilateral agreements (as special agreements defined under article 8 of the UPU Constitution)—Quality of service—The authority and mandate of the Council of Administration—Ancillary considerations potentially stemming from the General Agreement on Trade in Services—Potential consequences in case of violation of the Acts of the Union

A. Introduction and factual considerations

1. On 5 December 2016, the designated operator (DO) of the [name of State], the Federal State Unitary Enterprise "[State] Post" ([State] Post), sent a notification to the DOs of UPU member countries, informing them of several changes to its network of offices of exchange (OEs). In particular, [State] Post informed them that, as of 1 January 2017:

— All inbound letter-post mail should be sent to the [name of city] through the OE MIRNYJ (international mail processing centre—IMPC—code RUMJZA);

* The memorandum was submitted together with a series of annexes, which were not reproduced herein.

— Delivery of letter-post mail to all other OEs would be performed only in accordance with the terms pro-posed by [State] Post (bilateral agreement).

2. Following the notification issued by [State] Post, the Council of Administration (CA) instructed the International Bureau (IB) to: i) undertake a study of the legal problems arising in relation to the measures taken by [State] Post and report back to the Postal Operations Council (POC) as well as the CA at their respective S1 sessions in March/April 2017; and ii) withdraw any action taken to date, and temporarily suspend any action to register, process or publish requests to change IMPC codes insofar as they relate to this matter.

3. In the meantime, on 8 December 2016, [State] Post sent an e-mail to a number of DOs, in which it provided additional details on the scope of the aforementioned notification, notably in the sense that EMS, parcel-post and letter-post items without goods (*i.e.* not requiring CN 22 forms) would not be subject to any changes in existing operational and financial models—nevertheless, non-priority small packets would still have to be sent to a new OE in [name of city].

4. On 12 January 2017, [State] Post issued another letter to DOs in an effort to further clarify the exact scope of the intended measures. This notification comprised the following main elements:

— [State] Post will continue operations in all existing OEs;

— There will be no changes for the admission and registration of incoming EMS and parcel traffic into the [name of State];

— For priority small packets (letter-post items), there will be new procedures for pre-sorting and data exchange, aimed at further accelerating the process of acceptance, sorting and transportation of such items through the territory of the [name of State];

— Non-priority (non-registered) small packets (letter-post items) may be accepted at other OEs (other than [name of city]) in accordance with bilaterally-agreed conditions.

5. In February 2017, [State] Post representatives visited the IB in order to orally explain that the instruction to route all ordinary letter-post small packets to [name of city] concerned only inbound items addressed to the [name of State], and would have no impact whatsoever on transit operations that might take place through the territory of that member country. [State] Post also shared more detailed information on the actual and/or intended scope of the operation of OEs on the territory of the [name of State].

6. In addition, on 7 March 2017, [State] Post (through its Director for Legislative, Corporate and International Affairs) sent the IB a letter containing a number of considerations aimed at reiterating [State] Post's opposition to the aforementioned CA decision, notably on the basis of the following main arguments:

— Such a decision was contrary to the Acts of the Union and exceeded the authority of the CA;

— The Acts of the Union do not define or prescribe any kind of limitation for the establishment of OEs and IMPCs on the territory of a member country; it is solely up to member countries to decide on the geographical location of those offices;

— The CA decision violates the sovereign rights of a UPU member country.

7. Finally, on 13 March 2017, [State] Post (again, through its Director for Legislative, Corporate and International Affairs) confirmed in writing to the IB that "the new OE in [name of city] would not be used for transit operations of letter-mail items through the territory of the [name of State]". [State] Post also confirmed that, for transit operations of

letter-mail items under the C category (surface mail/non-priority mail) through the territory of the [name of State], the OEs in [name of city] and [name of city] would be used.

8. In fulfilment of the instructions issued by the CA and in view of the additional developments and clarifications highlighted above, the IB (through its Legal Affairs Directorate) proceeded to examine the situation with regard to the legal framework of the Union and other general principles of international law, as summarized in the considerations presented herein.

B. Applicable legal principles and provisions

i. The UPU as an intergovernmental organization and a specialized agency of the United Nations

9. The UPU is an intergovernmental organization and a specialized agency of the United Nations whose membership currently comprises 192 member countries.[1] As such, it contributes to the development of United Nations policies and activities which have a direct link with its mandate and mission as defined in the UPU Constitution ("Constitution").

10. In the light of the above, the UPU is set up and bound by international law and the treaties that constitute it. This is reflected *inter alia* in the Acts of the Union, which not only establish the basic legal framework applicable to the organization but also regulate the operation of the international postal network and of the postal services defined in those Acts, insofar as they are provided by the various DOs of member countries.

11. For that reason, one needs to examine the language contained in the Acts of the Union, consistently with the fundamental public international law tenet of literal interpretation of treaties (article 31 of the Vienna Convention on the Law of Treaties—"VCLT"), by which "[a] treaty shall be interpreted in good faith and in accordance with the ordinary meaning to be given to the terms of the treaty in their context and in the light of its object and purpose".

ii. The UPU Constitution and General Regulations

12. The Constitution constitutes the basic act of the UPU and outlines the most fundamental principles and organic rules applicable to the organization, such as the mission of the Union as presented in its Preamble:[2]

> The mission of the Union is to *stimulate the lasting development of efficient and accessible universal postal services of quality* in order to facilitate communication between the inhabitants of the world by:
>
> — *guaranteeing the free circulation of postal items over a single postal territory composed of interconnected networks;*
>
> — encouraging the adoption of fair common standards and the use of technology;
>
> — *ensuring cooperation and interaction among stakeholders;*
>
> — promoting effective technical cooperation;
>
> — *ensuring the satisfaction of customers' changing needs.*

[1] In more specific terms, 190 sovereign states as well as two non-self-governing territories to which earlier Congresses had granted the status of member countries.

[2] In that regard, it may be noted that one of the general rules of interpretation referred to in article 31 of the Vienna Convention on the Law of Treaties states that the context for the purpose of the interpretation of a treaty includes, *inter alia*, the preamble and annexes to a treaty.

13. The mission of the Union is complemented by article 1 of the Constitution, which sets out the main scope and objectives of the Union as being the establishment of a "*single postal territory* for the *reciprocal exchange* of letter-post items", to which the essential guarantee of freedom of transit shall apply. Moreover, the same article states that the aim of the Union shall be "to *secure the organization and improvement of postal services and to promote in this sphere the development of international collaboration*".

14. Likewise, article 1bis of the Constitution further specifies the concepts of "single postal territory" and "freedom of transit", which, when taken together, place an obligation, on all member countries, to provide for the *reciprocal exchange* of letter-post items[3] and to treat postal items in transit from other countries like their own postal items, without discrimination. In specific relation to freedom of transit, any intermediate member country is required to "ensure the transport of postal items passed on to it *in transit for another member country, providing similar treatment to that given to domestic items*".

15. Fulfilment of such an obligation is evidently undertaken in accordance with article 1bis.1.7 of the Constitution, which provides the definition of a DO, namely "any governmental or non-governmental entity officially designated by the member country to operate postal services and to fulfil the related obligations arising out of the Acts of the Union on its territory". In other words, and notwithstanding the fact that the respective member country is the actual member and signatory to the Acts of the Union, DOs are mandated to fulfil part of the obligations arising out of the Acts on behalf of their respective member countries, regardless of the specific setup within a given member country (given that some DOs may operate as private companies, while others may constitute a governmental entity belonging to the public sector).

16. In addition, article 8 of the Constitution determines that "member countries, or their designated operators if the legislation of those member countries so permits, may [...] make Special Agreements concerning the *international postal service, provided always that they do not introduce provisions less favourable to the public than those provided for by the Acts* to which the member countries concerned are parties".

17. Within the context of Special Agreements, it is also necessary to highlight the provisions of article 135 of the UPU General Regulations (General Regulations), which defines a mechanism for communication and verification of such agreements by the IB and the CA:[4]

> 1. Two copies of the Acts of Restricted Unions and of Special Agreements concluded under article 8 of the Constitution *shall be sent to the International Bureau* by the offices of such Unions, or failing that, by one of the contracting parties.
>
> 2. The International Bureau shall see that the Acts of Restricted Unions and *Special Agreements do not include conditions less favourable to the public than those which are provided for in the Acts of the Union. It shall notify the Council of Administration of any irregularity discovered through applying this provision.*
>
> 3. The International Bureau shall inform member countries and their designated operators of the existence of the Restricted Unions and the Special Agreements mentioned above.

[3] It is worth noting that the 26th Congress (Istanbul) adopted an important amendment to article 1 of the Constitution, namely to extend the concept of single postal territory to basically all postal items.

[4] Nevertheless, it may be noted that such a mechanism, which constitutes a mandatory provision of the General Regulations, has seldom been applied in practice as far as verification of Special Agreements is concerned.

iii. The UPU Convention and Regulations

18. Similarly to the Constitution, the Convention provides, in its article 1.1.9, for the definition of a DO. This is further detailed in article 2 of the Convention, whereby "member countries shall notify the International Bureau [...] of the name and address of the governmental body responsible for overseeing postal affairs. [...] Member countries shall also provide the International Bureau with the name and address of the operator or operators officially designated to operate postal services and to fulfil the obligations arising from the Acts of the Union on their territory".

19. Following the above provision, it is worth reiterating that the operation of international postal services (whose scope is determined by the Acts of the Union), as well as the fulfilment of the various obligations arising from those Acts, shall be guaranteed by the member country and executed by its respective DO(s). These obligations relate to the various basic and supplementary postal services established and regulated by member countries, as well as a wide range of legal and operational aspects which a member country and its DO(s) shall respect in order to be able to comply with the international treaty obligations reflected in the Acts of the Union.

20. Moreover, the Convention refers on multiple occasions[5] to the Letter Post or Parcel Post Regulations (RL and RC respectively), which stipulate more detailed provisions concerning the description of postal services, as well as the applicable charges and operational requirements.[6] Within this context, the Regulations also define the concept of OE as the required point of contact for international mail exchanges, as exemplified in article RL 173, §§ 3 and 4:[7]

> 3. The *exchange of mails shall be carried out by offices called "offices of exchange"*. Wherever an office of exchange needs to be specified on a postal form, this shall be done in accordance with the rules set out in UPU Technical Standard S34 (Registration of International Mail Processing Centres). This encompasses:
>
> 3.1 The six-character code of the office of exchange;
>
> 3.2 The name of the office of exchange;
>
> 3.3 The code and name of the designated operator responsible for the office of exchange.
>
> 4. Each office of exchange shall be registered in the International Mail Processing Centre code list *by the designated operator responsible for that office*. This list is published on the UPU website.

21. The stipulation quoted above is particularly important for the purposes of this analysis, as it introduces the basic principle whereby any exchange of international mail (be it letter post, parcel post or even EMS), including its sub-categories, shall be carried out by and between OEs.[8] Such a principle (that DOs exchange international postal items between OEs) is, for instance, highlighted in the definition of tracking and tracing, since the departure from the

---

[5] See for instance article 13 of the Convention.

[6] This is also reflected in article 22.3 of the Constitution, which states that the "Universal Postal Convention, the Letter Post Regulations and the Parcel Post Regulations shall embody the rules applicable throughout the international postal service and the provisions concerning the letter-post and postal parcels services"; likewise for the Regulations applicable to postal payment services, as per article 22.4 of the Constitution.

[7] The same provision exists, mutatis mutandis, in article RC 166.3 of the Parcel Post Regulations. It may be noted that, from 1 January 2018 onwards, a consolidated set of Regulations will enter into force with the same or similar provisions.

[8] Once more, the same provision is mirrored in article RC 166 of the Parcel Post Regulations and appears in articles 16-114 and 16-214 of the consolidated Regulations which will shortly be adopted by the POC. This fundamental principle (*i.e.* that exchanges of mail take place between offices of exchange)

outward office of exchange (event EMC) and the arrival at the inward office of exchange (event EMD) are necessary and chronologically placed requirements (see articles RL 190 and RC 168).

22. Likewise for articles RL 197 and RC 186, which emphasize the need for "every office [of exchange] receiving a mail" to check the origin and destination of the receptacles making up the mail and entered on the delivery bill, among other formalities.

23. Consequently, it stems from the above regulatory provisions that all DOs have the obligation to ensure (whether directly or through their transportation agents and partners) due exchange of international mail between offices of exchange—this also means that international mail shall always be made available at the actual, mandatory point of handover, *i.e.*, the OE at transit or destination.

C. SPECIFIC ISSUES ARISING FROM THE APPLICABLE LEGAL PRINCIPLES AND PROVISIONS

i. On the obligation to provide basic and mandatory supplementary international postal services

24. From the outset, it is essential to note that the general obligations mentioned in the preceding paragraphs are closely associated with the universal requirement for member countries and their DOs to provide[9] *basic and mandatory supplementary* international postal services as currently outlined in articles 13 and 15 of the Convention (subject only to a very limited scope of possible treaty reservations). Within the context of OEs, this means that no member country is allowed to require prior and *exclusive* signature of bilateral agreements to ensure acceptance, handling, conveyance and delivery of postal items covered by such basic and mandatory supplementary international postal services.

25. This aspect is particularly relevant given the terms of the *initial* notifications issued by [State] Post, which could have been interpreted as restricting freedom of transit (more detailed considerations provided below) or even limiting the scope of acceptance by the [name of State] of basic and mandatory supplementary international postal services. In this regard, it is necessary to stress that, except as otherwise authorized in the form of a member country *reservation* duly adopted and inserted in the relevant Final Protocol, *basic* UPU-defined obligations cannot simply be "contracted out" through bilateral agreements signed between member countries or their DOs; nor can they be derogated from in the form of unilateral requirements (including operational and technical procedures *not yet* incorporated as *obligations* in the Acts of the Union).

26. Nevertheless, the additional assurances and clarifications made by [State] Post on the exact scope of its measures would lead to a conclusion that there is *no breach of the minimum obligation to provide basic international postal services* as referred to above.

ii. On the principle of designation of offices of exchange by a member country (or its designated operators)

27. With reference to the designation of OEs, it may be remarked that, apart from the basic elements out-lined in articles RL 171 and RC 166 (as indicated above), the Acts of the Union do not describe any detailed procedure which specifically regulates or somehow

---

is equally reflected in other provisions of the Letter Post and Parcel Post Regulations, such as articles RL 181, RL 184, RC 155 and RC 168).

[9] For the purposes of this memorandum, the term "provide" refers to a general obligation to "accept, handle, convey and deliver" postal items as per articles 13 and 15 of the Convention.

limits the possibility of such a designation by a member country or its DO(s). In fact, the Acts of the Union leave an unambiguously wide margin of discretion for member countries and their DOs to define the location and the scope of operations of OEs on their territory. This can be verified in articles such as RL 184 ("Transmission of IBRS items"), which endorses the role of the destination DO in defining the OE or OEs that shall specialize in the handling of IBRS dispatches:

> *Designated operators operating the service shall designate the office of exchange of destination specializing in handling mails containing IBRS items.* If justified by operational reasons, designated operators *may designate several offices of exchange for this purpose.*

28. In other words, nowhere in the Acts of the Union is there any condition prescribing whether an OE shall be located within a certain distance from a member country's international airport, whether it shall be required to accept or handle all kinds of international postal services, or whether its location shall be associated with or driven by specific mail traffic thresholds.

29. Indeed, one may confirm such a statement by checking the current list of open OEs and their respective IMPC codes as currently managed by the IB (in accordance with Doha Congress resolution C 6/2012). This list corroborates the extremely *diverse* scope of coverage and operation of OEs among DOs of member countries (including not only service limitations but also country—and region-based restrictions), as per the various examples provided below:

— ARMDZA (Mendoza)—Import and export only—Letter post only, no merchandise

— ATSZGA (Salzburg)—Import, export and transit—Letter post, bilateral agreement required

— AUPERD (Perth)—Import and transit—Letter post and parcel post, non-priority, restricted to imports destined for delivery within Western Australia only

— BYMSQF (Minsk)—Import and export—Only for letter post coming from China (including Hong Kong) and Singapore

— CUHAVE (Havana)—Import, export and transit—EMS only

— DEGUGA (Guenzburg)—Import, export and transit—Parcel post and letter post (small packets) exchanged with European partners only

— DKCPHI (Copenhagen)—Import—Letter post and parcel post concerning only Finland, Iceland, Norway and Sweden

— FRDINA (Divonne-Les-Bains)—Import—Letter post; non-dutiable items only from Switzerland

— GRATHC (Athens)—Import and export—Parcel post, import/export, European Parcel Group mem-ber countries only

— TRISTA (Istanbul)—Export and transit—Letter post, parcel post and EMS, inbound mail not accepted

— UZTASC (Tashkent)—Import, export and transit—Parcel post, CIS countries only

30. Nevertheless, as already outlined in the preceding sections, the Acts of the Union do contain a number of fundamental principles which apply to the situation at hand as well as to the operation of OEs by member countries and their DOs.

iii. On the principle of non-discrimination

31. The mandatory Acts of the Union[10] (the Constitution and General Regulations, and the Convention and its Regulations), as defined in article 22 of the Constitution, are agreed upon by all member countries and have binding force on them. As a result, all member countries are obliged to comply with the principles, provisions and obligations that arise from their adherence to those Acts.

32. The fundamental principles stipulated in the Constitution are, from an operational standpoint, further complemented by the Convention. In accordance with article 2 of the latter Act, member countries shall designate the operator or operators responsible for fulfilling the obligations arising from the Acts of the Union. This requirement stems from the fact that, even though postal markets may have been liberalized in many member countries, a member country must still transfer part of the obligations and responsibilities arising from its adherence to the Acts of the Union (mostly for operational duties) to its DO(s). Regardless of the UPU's specific character as an intergovernmental organization within the United Nations system, such DOs are subsidiarily bound to comply with the abovementioned principles, provisions and related obligations when operating as part of the UPU network and providing UPU-defined international postal services.

33. Moreover, the Acts of the Union are based on the principle of sovereign equality of member countries. This means that all member countries shall be regarded as equal members of the UPU community and the international postal network it comprises, notwithstanding any differences of an economic, social or political character. Essentially, such a principle of sovereign equality of states, which can be found not only in the Acts of the Union but also in customary international law, entitles member countries to be treated equally (unless otherwise specifically provided for in the relevant treaty) in international treaty relations. Thus, sovereign equality would relate to equality of legal status, a principle which the Constitution indirectly enshrines in order to ensure free movement of international postal items. Just as it is the case in other international treaties,[11] a freedom of this kind is generally ensured through a general prohibition of discrimination.

34. This principle of non-discrimination is often narrowed down to the matter of "treating equals on equal terms, and non-equals on unequal terms". Despite this basic notion, it is a well-established fact and a logical consequence that non-discrimination may not necessarily guarantee certain results and outcomes; it rather aims at safeguarding an intent to regulate international issues from undue restrictions imposed either by governments or, as far as the UPU is concerned, DOs as well.

35. With particular regard to international mail exchanges, this principle (which is associated with the fundamental concept of a "single postal territory") involves an obligation upon all member countries and their DOs to provide for the reciprocal exchange of

[10] The Convention, similar to the Constitution, constitutes an international treaty which sets forth the relevant rules applicable to international postal services as agreed by member countries. Compared to the Constitution, the Convention focuses more on the operational process as such.

[11] Reference may be made, for instance, to the principle of freedom of movement in the Treaty on the Functioning of the European Union.

letter-post items,[12] including freedom of transit, *and to treat postal items in transit from other countries like their own postal items, without discrimination.*

36. Accordingly, it needs to be noted that the recent measures announced by [State] Post in relation to its OE network would apply to all member countries, thus placing them under the same legal and operational framework regardless of national characteristics. Indeed, the fact that a member country may opt to place itself "in a better situation" by entering into a bilateral agreement which affords preferential treatment would not violate the principle of non-discrimination per se, since member countries and their DOs are in principle free to conclude bilateral agreements under the aegis of the UPU, insofar as this neither entails an undue restriction on the provision and acceptance of basic and mandatory supplementary international postal services *with regard to transit operations*, nor infringes upon the "no less favourable" requirement outlined in article 8 of the Constitution.

37. In the light of the foregoing, it may be concluded that the recent measures announced by [State] Post *would not infringe the principle of non-discrimination* contained in the Acts of the Union. Nevertheless, a number of associated considerations must still be presented with regard to freedom of transit.

iv. On the principle of freedom of transit (including transit à découvert)

38. In the light of the measures announced by [State] Post, it is now necessary to assess whether they may infringe the principle of freedom of transit as outlined in the Acts of the Union.

39. As earlier referred to in this memorandum, the term "freedom of transit" is broadly defined in article 1bis.1.4 of the Constitution:

> "Freedom of transit: obligation for an intermediate member country to ensure the transport of postal items passed on to it in transit for another member country, providing similar treatment to that given to domestic items."

40. In addition to the definition contained in the Constitution, article 4.1 of the Convention provides more specifically that:

> "The principle of the freedom of transit is set forth in article 1 of the Constitution. It shall carry with it the obligation for each member country to ensure that its *designated operators forward, always by the quickest routes and the most secure means which they use for their own items*, closed mails and à découvert letter-post items which are passed to them by another designated operator [...]."

41. As may be seen from the above provisions, the principle of freedom of transit comprises the obligation on member countries and their DOs to prevent any measures that delay or prevent international transit by placing greater restrictions on international mail than on domestic items.

42. Thus, any measures which might lead to such a restrictive outcome with regard to forwarding postal items by "the quickest routes and the most secure means" could potentially constitute an infringement of the obligation to provide uniform treatment of postal items in transit as per the obligations mentioned herein. However, in the light of the additional clarifications and assurances provided by [State] Post to the IB in February and

---

[12] Once more, this is soon to be basically extended to all "postal items", as recently decided by the 26th Congress (Istanbul).

March 2017 (*i.e.* that the new OE in [name of city] would accept and process only a specific class and category of inbound items addressed to the [State] Federation, thus having no impact on transit operations that might take place through the territory of the [name of State]), the situation at hand would not lead to infringement of the fundamental principle of freedom of transit.

43. In this context, it must be noted that the 1964 Vienna Congress, considering that freedom of transit was one of the essential and fundamental principles of the UPU, had already appealed, through resolution C 23/1964, to the good faith and solidarity of all member countries to ensure, in all circumstances, strict respect for the application of this principle, without which the UPU cannot completely fulfil its mission.

44. Notwithstanding the foregoing assurances, another mail transit aspect may necessitate additional legal clarification, namely that of transit à découvert as defined in article 1.1.5 of the Convention:

> "transit à découvert: open transit through an intermediate country, of items whose number or weight *does not justify the make-up of closed mails for the destination country.*"

45. As stipulated in article RL 176, transit à découvert concerns a situation where the making up of closed mails for the country of destination is not justified:

> 1. The transmission of à découvert items to an intermediate designated operator shall be *strictly limited to cases where the making up of closed mails for the country of destination is not justified.* À découvert transmission shall not be used to countries of destination for which the weight of the mail exceeds three kilogrammes per mail or per day (when several dispatches are made in a day) and shall not be used for M bags.
>
> 2. *In the absence of a special agreement, items for transit à découvert weighing more than three kilogrammes per mail or per day (when several dispatches are made in a day), dispatched to a particular country of destination, shall be considered as missent items* and the intermediate designated operator shall be authorized to claim from the dispatching designated operator the relevant charges calculated in accordance with article RL 211.1.5 for the entire quantity of mail concerned.
>
> 3. *The dispatching designated operator shall consult in advance the intermediate designated operators as to the suitability of using them for à découvert items to the destinations concerned. The dispatching designated operator shall notify the designated operators concerned of the date on which dispatch of mail in transit à découvert commences, providing at the same time the estimated annual volumes for each final destination.* [...] Items in transit à découvert shall, as far as possible, be sent to a designated operator which makes up mails for the designated operators of destination.
>
> 4. *For items sent à découvert without prior consultation to an intermediate designated operator, destined for countries other than those notified by the intermediate country in the Transit Compendium, the charge provided for in article RL 211.1.5 may be applied.*

46. As can be seen from the above regulatory excerpts, as well as the OE examples provided in § 29 of this document, one may identify several instances of existing OEs that *do not admit any form of transit* (including transit à découvert); yet this would seem to be in line with the advance consultation obligation contained in § 3 of article RL 176. However, it must be emphasized that this does not mean that a member country may simply *refuse* applicability of transit à découvert on its territory, as the IB commentary to article RL 176.3 clarifies:

"Transit à découvert services are a means to guarantee the freedom of transit as defined in [article 1 of the Constitution and article 4 of the Convention]. The purpose of the consultation with the intermediate DO, provided for in RL 176.3, is to *identify the most suitable route for sending items à découvert.* It does not affect the mandatory character of transit à découvert."

47. Accordingly, the [name of State] (or any other member country for that matter) is always required to ensure that *forwarding* of closed mail dispatches as well as transit à découvert dispatches takes place "by the quickest routes and the most secure means which they use for their own items". Nevertheless, in accordance with the principle of designation of OEs, a member country (or DO) would still be entitled to define the scope of operation of its own OEs, as long as the general obligation to provide transit through other OEs is not impaired by artificially restrictive conditions or bilateral agreement demands.

48. It is also necessary here to highlight one aspect which may often be overlooked when studying the concept of freedom of transit under the Acts of the Union: the obligation to provide freedom of transit is always a *forwarding obligation* whereby the "quickest routes and the most secure means" used for domestic items shall be employed.

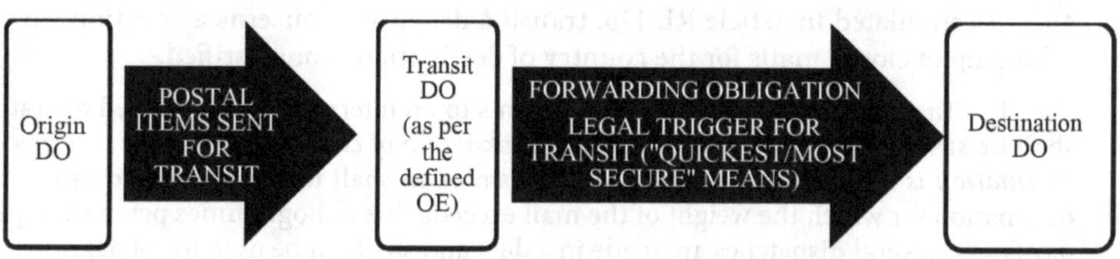

49. In conclusion, *and subject to due incorporation and formalization of the additional assurances and clarifications made by [State] Post on the exact scope of operation of its OE in [name of city], the revised measures would not seem to infringe the principle of freedom of transit* as defined in the Acts of the Union.[13]

v. On the "office-of-exchange-to-office-of-exchange" principle

50. As already mentioned in section B iii above, the Acts of the Union provide for the mandatory exchange of international mail between OEs. In this regard, it must be reiterated that such OEs essentially constitute the *entry and exit* points for international mail on the territory of a member country. As far as the UPU legal framework is concerned, this specifically means that international mail exchanges under the Acts of the Union shall take place between OEs of the respective member countries or DOs. Therefore, sending DOs have an obligation to ensure the exchange of international mail between the actual OEs, and not only to any physical point of entry within a member country's territory (in this case, the member country of the DO of transit or destination).

[13] However, it must be stressed that, in the absence of such additional assurances and clarifications, and solely bearing in mind the original language of the announcement made by [State] Post, freedom of transit would, in principle, be infringed upon, notably if: i) international letter-post items (including items in transit) were to be necessarily routed to the OE in [name of city] under conditions dissimilar to those afforded to domestic items; or ii) transit à découvert for such specific mail classes and categories could be assured by [State] Post through other OEs.

51. In other words, the transportation legs between a physical point of entry and the actual OE of the DO of transit or destination would have to be covered by the DO of origin (either directly or with the help of a transportation agent); it would not be sufficient for the DO of origin to simply notify the DO of transit or destination that international mail is available at any point other than the actual, mandatory point of handover, in this case the OE at transit or destination.

52. However, while the DO of transit or destination is expected to publicly announce, in advance, any changes in this regard through the relevant UPU databases and publications, *the legal attribution to define and determine an OE as entry/exit point for all or certain classes and categories of international mail rests solely with the member country concerned and/or its DO*. This fact results as a necessary conclusion from the application of the principle of *sovereignty of countries*, which is not only a basic principle within the Acts of the Union (especially in the absence of more specific designation procedures agreed upon by member countries), but also a corollary of international treaty law.

53. *Accordingly, the recent measures by [State] Post would not seem to infringe the principle of OE-to-OE exchanges*, as these considerations are not only in line with the Acts of the Union (regardless of its location, any designated entry point into/exit point from the [name of State] still constitutes an OE), but also with the previously mentioned article 31 of the VCLT, according to which "*[a] treaty shall be interpreted in good faith and in accordance with the ordinary meaning to be given to the terms of the treaty in their context and in the light of its object and purpose*."

54. Yet it would be necessary for the IB to *assess and validate, prior to any IMPC registration action, whether the OE in [name of city] (or any other OE around the world, for that matter) is duly in place and equipped with the necessary facilities and infrastructure to appropriately handle international mail dispatches* (even if they concern a limited set of mail classes and categories).

vi. On the issue of bilateral agreements (as special agreements defined under article 8 of the UPU Constitution)

55. As the notification by [State] Post suggests, in the event that a DO of another member country wishes to make use of another OE for the dispatching of non-priority small packets (in line with the additional clarifications provided by [State] Post), the respective DO will be required to agree to a bilateral agreement subject to different conditions in terms of remuneration, among other aspects.

56. Based on the *raison d'être* of the UPU and the international postal network it establishes, it must be clarified that all aspects of the postal services provided through this international network, including documentation, as well as operational and technical elements (such as specific postal-customs arrangements agreed by the World Customs Organization in Specific Annex J of the International Convention on the Simplification and Harmonization of Customs Procedures, or IB-registered IMPC codes) shall be considered as subsets of the wider UPU legal framework, including its principles and conditions defined in the Acts of the Union. The intent of the above can be clearly identified as an attempt to prevent so called "cherry-picking policies" by member countries and their DOs, whereby they reap only the benefits of the UPU international network while disregarding its relevant obligations.

57. Accordingly, when it comes to the Acts of the Union and the establishment of special agreements, the provisions of article 8 of the Constitution shall apply. As a rule, these special agreements may have the aim of facilitating the operation of international postal services between two member countries or DOs (more commonly the latter), or define more comprehensive multilateral conditions between various entities.

58. In addition, it should be noted that the general clause of article 8.1 of the Constitution clearly relates to special agreements concerning the international postal service which, given the specific setup of the UPU (with operators designated by member countries), might comprise additional or distinct features when compared to those defined in the Acts of the Union—*however, insofar as they make use of the UPU network, such features shall neither run counter to nor deviate from the fundamental principles and provisions contained in the Acts of the Union, particularly so as to avoid any provisions being introduced that are less favourable to the public than those provided for in the Acts of the Union.* In addition, they may not impact upon the mandate and obligations imposed on the different UPU bodies through the relevant decisions adopted by the organization and its member countries.

59. Therefore, in order to be deemed acceptable within the UPU legal framework, any such bilateral agreements must contain provisions which are, at the very least, equal to or better than those provided for in the Acts of the Union as far as the general public is concerned.

60. As a result of the constitutional principle above, DOs may not curtail the benefits, rights and service features provided to the general public under the Acts of the Union, even though the same DOs do have the possibility of negotiating specific terms among themselves to the extent that they, once again, do not touch upon the aforementioned benefits, rights and service features.[14]

61. Therefore, in a scenario where bilateral agreements are proposed *prior* to the use of a certain OE (as would be the case for the dispatching of non-priority small packets to other OEs outside [name of city]), it would be necessary to assess whether such conditions are in line with the relevant provisions of article 8 of the Constitution.[15] *Yet, since the designation of an OE for specific international mail classes and categories is possible under the current UPU regulatory framework, it may be concluded that the recent measures announced by [State] Post would not, in principle, infringe article 8 of the Constitution.*

vii. On the issue of quality of service

62. Another issue to be briefly examined pertains to the potential impact of such OE designation measures on the overall goal of achieving increasingly higher quality of service within the framework of the UPU. As already quoted in the preceding sections of this memorandum, the aim of the Union as defined in article 1 of the Constitution is "to secure the *organization and improvement of postal services* and to promote in this sphere the development of international collaboration". This aim is further detailed through various

---

[14] It is worth emphasizing that the legal analysis presented herein does not apply to a situation where DOs wish to regulate the provision of non-UPU services and solutions, thus falling completely outside the scope of the Acts of the Union (*i.e.* no access to UPU documentation, IMPC code registration, WCO-specific customs procedures, etc.). In such cases, DOs are evidently free to act as they deem fit under their appropriate domestic legal frameworks.

[15] For information, at least 484 out of the 1,926 OEs/IMPCs currently listed and registered by the IB require the signature of a bilateral agreement.

articles in the Convention and Regulations, as well as a number of Congress decisions and resolutions issued over the years (such as resolution C 40/2012, which: i) implemented a Quality of Service Programme for the period 2013–2016; ii) maintained a global quality of service standard at J+5 and the target for attainment of this standard at 85%; and iii) determined that this standard should apply to the "international priority letter post between those areas and/or cities that are most important in terms of inter-national postal exchanges in each member country").[16]

63. Nevertheless, it is important to stress that, in strict legal terms, only the provisions of the Acts of the Union are binding on member countries (and their DOs); any other Congress decision not enshrined in the Acts of the Union (such as the resolution referred to above) is solely binding on the bodies of the Union, in this case specifically as a set of "programmatic" instructions aimed at ensuring gradual implementation of those quality of service objectives.

64. This fundamental aspect leads to the conclusion that any potentially negative effects arising from country-specific OE designations may only be challenged once they lead to an infringement of obligations contained in those Acts (for example, in a *hypothetical* scenario where: i) the J+5 standard were unambiguously set in the Convention or Regulations as a minimum quality of service threshold for end-to-end non-priority letter-post dispatches; and ii) the [name of city] OE designation adversely impacted the achievement of that target by the [name of State]).

65. Otherwise, and without prejudice to a potential[17] risk of performance degradation in the concrete case of inbound non-priority small packet dispatches, it may be concluded that the recent measures announced by [State] Post *would not, in principle, infringe any binding provisions pertaining to quality of service of letter-post dispatches.*

viii. On the authority and mandate of the Council of Administration

66. Finally, in view of the positions expressed by [State] Post in its letter of 7 March 2017, it is appropriate to assess whether the instructions issued by the CA in its decision CA 2/2016.2 exceeded the authority of that Council.

67. As extensively discussed in this memorandum, it may be reiterated that, apart from the basic elements outlined in articles RL 171 and RC 166, the Acts of the Union do not define or prescribe any kind of additional limitation for the establishment of OEs and IMPCs on the territory of a member country; it is solely up to member countries to decide on the geographical location of those offices. And, as per the terms of resolution C 63/2008, it is equally true that a DO "may continue to request registration of IMPCs established for its own purposes and on its own national territory" (as is the case for the OE in [name of city]).

68. Moreover, as acknowledged by [State] Post, the IB is responsible, *inter alia*, for managing the IMPC registration process in liaison with the POC, as per Congress resolution C 6/2012.

69. Nevertheless, it may be stated that the aforementioned CA decision follows from its main functions as delineated in article 107 of the General Regulations, particularly in terms of supervising all the activities of the Union between Congresses, studying questions with respect to governmental policies on postal issues, considering and approving,

---

[16] A similar set of Congress instructions for the 2017–2020 period is specifically outlined in work proposal 021 of the draft Istanbul Business Plan (adopted by the Istanbul Congress through resolution C 24/2016), subject to finalization by the CA in line with the UPU Programme and Budget.

[17] In the sense that such a risk may be legitimately expected, but not assumed or proven in legal terms.

within the framework of its competence, any action considered necessary to safeguard and enhance the quality of the international postal service, studying administrative, legislative and legal problems concerning the Union or the international postal service, and providing control over the activities of the IB.[18]

70. So, even if the IB is directly responsible for managing IMPC registration procedures, such a Congress instruction must be carried out in observance of the standing provisions of the Constitution and General Regulations, which not only define the CA as the governing body responsible for ensuring the continuity of the work of the Union in accordance with the provisions of the Acts of the Union, but also subject the IB to the authority of the latter Council, especially since the exact scope of the measures announced by [State] Post was not entirely clear from the outset.

71. As a result, it may be concluded that the CA *did not exceed its authority and mandate* when issuing the relevant instructions to the IB.

D. Ancillary considerations potentially stemming from the General Agreement on Trade in Services

72. Having examined the relevant legal points arising directly from the Acts of the Union, it might be worth assessing, for informational purposes, whether other sources of international law may also contain principles or provisions that might touch upon the situation at hand.

73. In that regard, the General Agreement on Trade in Services ("GATS") forms part of Annex 1 to the World Trade Organization ("WTO") Agreement. It constitutes an international agreement which is binding on all WTO members and establishes a multilateral framework of principles and rules to govern trade in services and to progressively liberalize existing barriers to trade in services. Yet it must be emphasized that article I of the GATS explicitly excludes its application for any services that are supplied in the "exercise of governmental authority" (*i.e.* supplied neither on a commercial basis nor in competition with other suppliers).

74. The GATS itself consists of three main elements: the first element is a basic framework agreement and includes the general obligations applicable to all members and services sectors; the second consists of a number of annexes to the agreement that establish special or different rules for particular types of services; and the third element consists of schedules of commitments that set out each member's specific market access concessions.

75. The most fundamental obligation with regard to all services is the so-called most-favoured-nation ("MFN") Treatment. This trade principle is accorded to the country that is treated most favourably by stating that: "With respect to any measure covered by this Agreement, each Member shall accord immediately and unconditionally to services and service suppliers of any other Member, treatment no less favourable than that it accords to like services and service suppliers of any other country". Essentially, this means that the country which is the recipient of MFN treatment must, nominally, receive equal trade advantages as the "most favoured nation" from the country granting such treatment. As a result, a country that has been accorded MFN status may not be treated less advantageously than any other

[18] See article 107 of the General Regulations, §§ 1.1, 1.17, 1.18 and 1.23.

country with MFN status by the according country; nevertheless, derogations to this principle are possible, in the form of what are defined as "Article II exemptions".[19]

76. In line with the above, postal services are generally deemed to be covered by the GATS, as they fall within the respective "services" domain (subject to the general MFN principle and country-specific schedules of commitment). However, as far as the [name of State] is concerned, its schedule of commitments only sets out specific engagements in terms of market access and national treatment for some "courier services", which in any case do not extend to any services assigned as an exclusive right to [State] Post as "national postal operator". In fact, even if one were to assume a hypothetical scenario where postal services were fully liberalized in the [name of State], the recent measures concerning OEs on [State] territory would have no bearing on the MFN principle or any sectoral commitments under the GATS.

77. Even then, a question may arise as to whether the adherence of the [name of State] to the Acts of the Union awards these treaties (Constitution, Convention, etc.) a position of priority in comparison to a country's adherence to the GATS.

78. In international law, especially in cases where international treaties and agreements may potentially contradict each other in terms of their application, two main principles are generally used regarding the determination of primacy in application. These principles are namely: i) that *the most recent agreement generally prevails* over the older one (as per article 30 of the VCLT); and ii) that, as per the general rules of customary international law, special provisions would prevail over general ones, also known as the principle of *lex specialis*.[20]

79. When it comes to the first of these principles, and in accordance with article 30 of the VCLT, each member country would have to determine when its respective memberships of the two frameworks in question entered into force. Keeping in mind that not all member countries are members of the WTO and the respective revision procedures of each agreement (for example, neither the GATS nor the Convention is permanent), the determination of a most recent agreement might be difficult and can only be solved on a case-by-case basis.

80. With regard to the second principle, the lex specialis rule is a commonly accepted methodology under public international law. In this regard, it needs to be noted that the general principles of the GATS, in particular the abovementioned MFN treatment, would also apply, *inter alia*, to postal services. On the other hand, the Acts of the Union do constitute international treaties which are intended to apply specifically and exclusively to international postal services. Accordingly, it can be said that, while the Convention may be considered a

---

[19] In the case of the [name of State], these article II exemptions are contained in document GATS/EL/149 of 5 November 2012; one example concerns the movement of natural persons supplying services, whereby parties to the Partnership and Cooperation Agreement between the [name of State and International Organization and their Member States] signed on 24 June 1994 with future supplements, and also CIS countries may benefit from more advantageous conditions. There is no specific exemption defined for postal or courier services.

[20] This principle is, as noted by the United Nations' International Law Commission, a "generally accepted technique of interpretation and conflict resolution in international law". See "Conclusions of the work of the Study Group on the Fragmentation of International Law: Difficulties arising from the Diversification and Expansion of International Law", International Law Commission, 2006.

multilateral agreement aimed at the accomplishment of a single purpose (namely the definition and regulation of international postal services), the GATS rather pursues the establishment of a multilateral framework of principles and rules for trade in all services sectors.

81. As a result, in what pertains to the specific OE situation studied herein and on the basis of not only i) the absence of a nexus between GATS obligations and such [State] measures, but also ii) the lex specialis rule (since the Convention would prevail over the GATS as a more specific agreement), there would be no additional conclusions to report other than those already discussed in this memorandum.

E. Potential consequences in case of violation of the Acts of the Union

82. While no specific violation of the Acts of the Union or any other relevant principle of international law could be identified by the IB with regard to the situation at hand, the potential consequences of a theoretical violation of the Acts of the Union should nevertheless be addressed for the sake of completeness.

83. Such consequences in general fall within the sovereignty of member countries, as well as the letter and practice of public international law, especially the VCLT.

84. With specific respect to the legal framework of the UPU, the Convention and Regulations contain few provisions in this regard. However, it is established that, if a member country fails to observe the provisions regarding the principle of freedom of transit, other member countries may discontinue their postal service with that member country (recalling once more that the 1964 Vienna Congress had, through resolution C 23/1964, already stressed the fundamental character of freedom of transit).

85. As a result, should the situation at hand be deemed to violate the involved member country's obligation to guarantee freedom of transit for postal items destined for other countries (in the sense that these measures delay or prevent this transit, or place greater restrictions on international mail than on domestic items as far as transit is concerned), those measures could potentially be identified as an infringement of the international obligations mentioned above.

86. Accordingly, failure by a member country to ensure the provision of freedom of transit by its DO(s) is, from an operational viewpoint, complemented by articles RL 102 and RC 103 (in line with article 4.5 of the Convention), which again provide a member country with the possibility of discontinuing "the postal service with a member country that fails to observe freedom of transit [...]".

87. Furthermore, it may be noted that, when exceptional circumstances oblige a DO to temporarily suspend its services wholly or in part, it shall immediately inform the other DOs concerned (articles RL 171.2 and RC 166.2). In addition, article RL 202 (as well as article RC 171) contains similar provisions and sets out the steps to be taken in the event of temporary suspension and resumption of services.

88. With reference to the above, article RC 201 also defines the application of new rates due to unforeseeable changes in routing. In more specific terms, reasons of *force majeure* or any other unforeseeable occurrence may oblige a DO to use, for the conveyance of its own parcels, a new dispatch route which causes additional sea or land conveyance costs.

In such a case, it shall be required to inform immediately by telecommunications all the DOs whose parcel-post items or à découvert parcels are sent in transit through its country. From the fifth day following dispatch of this information, the intermediate DO shall be authorized to charge the DO of origin the land and sea rates corresponding to the new route.

89. Therefore, temporary suspension of the service on the grounds of *force majeure* or an unforeseeable event is not contrary to the Acts of the Union. However, in compliance with the obligations arising from the Acts of the Union, DOs should, if necessary, forward the mail by means other than air if the latter becomes unusable for reasons beyond the control of the DO.

F. Conclusions and possible recommendations

90. In summary, the following conclusions and recommendations may be drawn from the above considerations:

(*a*) Several principles and provisions contained in the Acts of the Union are related to the issue at hand, notably in terms of the intergovernmental character of the UPU; the concept of "single postal territory"; the obligation to provide basic and mandatory supplementary international postal services; the designation of OEs; non-discrimination; freedom of transit; "OE-to-OE" obligations; and special agreements under article 8 of the Constitution;

(*b*) All member countries and their DOs are required to provide basic and mandatory supplementary international postal services as currently outlined in articles 13 and 15 of the Convention (unless otherwise exceptionally stipulated through treaty reservations); within the context of OEs, no member country may require prior and *exclusive* signature of bilateral agreements to ensure the acceptance, handling, conveyance and delivery of postal items covered by those *basic and mandatory supplementary* international postal services;

(*c*) The additional assurances and clarifications made by [State] Post on the exact scope of its measures would lead to a conclusion that there is no breach of the minimum obligation to provide international postal services as referred to above;

(*d*) The Acts of the Union neither contain nor describe any detailed procedure which specifically regulates or somehow limits the possibility of designation of OEs by a member country or its DO(s);

(*e*) Any exchange of international mail under the Acts of the Union (be it letter post, parcel post or EMS), including its sub-categories, shall be carried out by and between OEs;

(*f*) The measures announced by [State] Post *would not infringe the principle of non-discrimination*, to the extent that such announced measures neither entail an undue restriction on the provision and acceptance of basic and mandatory supplementary international postal services *with regard to transit operations*, nor infringe upon the "no less favourable" requirement outlined in article 8 of the Constitution;

(*g*) Subject to due formalization of the additional assurances and clarifications made by [State] Post on the exact scope of operation of its office of exchange in [name of city], the measures announced by [State] Post *would not, in principle, infringe the principle of freedom of transit* as defined in the Acts of the Union;

(*h*) Since the designation of an OE for specific international mail classes and categories is possible under the current UPU regulatory framework, it may be concluded that the recent measures announced by [State] Post *would not, in principle, infringe article 8 of the Constitution*;

(*i*) Notwithstanding a potential risk of performance degradation in the case of non-priority small packets addressed to the [name of State], the recent measures announced by [State] Post *would not*, in principle, infringe any binding provisions pertaining to quality of service of letter-post dispatches;

(*j*) The CA did not exceed its authority and mandate when issuing the relevant instructions to the IB;

(*k*) For information, there does not seem to be any nexus between the GATS obligations currently undertaken by the [name of State] and the measures announced by [State] Post on international mail operations;

(*l*) *Recommendation 1*: bearing in mind the conclusions above, the CA would be in a position to *lift the suspension on registration of the relevant IMPC code for [name of city]* with immediate effect, subject to:

— Due incorporation and formalization, into the relevant IMPC registration request, of the additional assurances and clarifications made by [State] Post on the exact scope of operation of its OE in [name of city]; and
— Confirmation by the IB (upon provision of the necessary information by [State] Post) that the OE in [name of city] is in place and effectively equipped with the necessary facilities and infrastructure to appropriately handle international mail dispatches (even if for a restricted mail class/category, *i.e.* non-priority small packets).

(*m*) *Recommendation 2*: given the sensitivity of the matter and potential impact on international mail operations (notably since changes to current provisions may lead to a comprehensive review of current registrations of OEs and IMPCs across the world), any proposed amendments to the Acts of the Union that might be submitted by member countries or UPU bodies should be carefully studied by both the POC and CA before their final adoption;

(*n*) *Recommendation 3*: finally, one may note that, in line with Istanbul Congress–Doc 39, and as per the relevant amendment to the Regulations already adopted by the POC in December 2016 (proposal 25.16–107.1), all small packets containing goods shall require a unique S10 barcode identifier as of 1 January 2018. This also means that the bulk of the customs—and security-related concerns originally expressed by the [name of State] as the main rationale for the announcements referred to herein will already be dealt with following the entry into force of the new Regulations.

[*Signed*]

Part Three

JUDICIAL DECISIONS ON QUESTIONS RELATING TO THE UNITED NATIONS AND RELATED INTERGOVERNMENTAL ORGANIZATIONS

Chapter VII

DECISIONS AND ADVISORY OPINIONS OF INTERNATIONAL TRIBUNALS

A. International Court of Justice[1]

The International Court of Justice is the principal judicial organ of the United Nations. It was established in June 1945 by the Charter of the United Nations and began work in April 1946.

1. Judgments

(*a*) *Maritime Delimitation in the Indian Ocean (Somalia* v. *Kenya)*, Judgment on the preliminary objections raised by the Respondent, 2 February 2017.

2. Advisory Opinions

No advisory opinions were delivered by the International Court of Justice in 2017.

3. Pending cases and advisory proceedings as at 31 December 2017

(*a*) *Legal consequences of the separation of the Chagos Archipelago from Mauritius in 1965* (request for an advisory opinion) (2017–).

(*b*) *Request for Interpretation of the Judgment of 23 May 2008 in the case concerning* Sovereignty over Pedra Branca/Pulau Batu Puteh, Middle Rocks and South Ledge (Malaysia/Singapore) (*Malaysia* v. *Singapore*) (2017–).

(*c*) *Jadhav Case (India* v. *Pakistan)* (2017–).

(*d*) *Application for revision of the Judgment of 23 May 2008 in the case concerning* Sovereignty over Pedra Branca/Pulau Batu Puteh, Middle Rocks and South Ledge (Malaysia/Singapore) (*Malaysia* v. *Singapore*) (2017–).

[1] The texts of the judgments, advisory opinions and orders are published in the *ICJ Reports*. Summaries of judgments, advisory opinions and orders of the Court are provided in English and French on its website http://www.icj-cij.org. In addition, the summaries can be found in all six official languages of the United Nations on the website of the Codification Division of the United Nations Office of Legal Affairs, http://www.un.org/law/ICJsummaries/. For more information about the Court's activities, see Report of the International Court of Justice, *Official Records of the General Assembly, Seventy-first Session, Supplement No. 4* (A/71/4) and *Seventieth-second Session, Supplement No. 4* (A/72/4), for the periods of 1 August 2015 to 31 July 2016 and 1 August 2016 to 31 July 2017, respectively.

(*e*) *Application of the International Convention for the Suppression of the Financing of Terrorism and of the International Convention on the Elimination of All Forms of Racial Discrimination (Ukraine* v. *Russian Federation)* (2017–).

(*f*) *Land Boundary in the Northern Part of Isla Portillos (Costa Rica* v. *Nicaragua)* (2017–).

(*g*) *Certain Iranian Assets (Islamic Republic of Iran* v. *United States of America)* (2016–).

(*h*) *Immunities and Criminal Proceedings (Equatorial Guinea* v. *France)* (2016–).

(*i*) *Dispute over the Status and Use of the Waters of the Silala (Chile* v. *Bolivia)* (2016–).

(*j*) *Maritime Delimitation in the Indian Ocean (Somalia* v. *Kenya)* (2014–).

(*k*) *Maritime Delimitation in the Caribbean Sea and the Pacific Ocean (Costa Rica* v. *Nicaragua)* (2014–).

(*l*) *Alleged Violations of Sovereign Rights and Maritime Spaces in the Caribbean Sea (Nicaragua* v. *Colombia)* (2013–).

(*m*) *Question of the Delimitation of the Continental Shelf between Nicaragua and Colombia beyond 200 nautical miles from the Nicaraguan Coast (Nicaragua* v. *Colombia)* (2013–).

(*n*) *Obligation to Negotiate Access to the Pacific Ocean (Bolivia* v. *Chile)* (2013–).

(*o*) *Certain Activities carried out by Nicaragua in the Border Area (Costa Rica* v. *Nicaragua)* (2010–).

(*p*) *Armed Activities on the Territory of the Congo (Democratic Republic of the Congo* v. *Uganda)* (1999–).

(*q*) *Gabčíkovo-Nagymaros Project (Hungary/Slovakia)* (1993–).

B. International Tribunal for the Law of the Sea[2]

The International Tribunal for the Law of the Sea is an independent permanent tribunal established by the United Nations Convention on the Law of the Sea, 1982.[3] The Agreement on Cooperation and Relationship between the United Nations and the International Tribunal for the Law of the Sea,[4] signed by the Secretary-General of the United Nations and the President of the Tribunal on 18 December 1997, establishes a mechanism for cooperation between the two institutions.

1. Judgments and Orders

Case No. 23—Dispute Concerning Delimitation of the Maritime Boundary between Ghana and Côte d'Ivoire in the Atlantic Ocean (Ghana/Côte d'Ivoire), Judgment, 23 September 2017.

---

[2] For more information about the Tribunal's activities, including relating to orders and judgments rendered in 2016, see the Annual report of the International Tribunal for the Law of the Sea for 2016 (SPLOS/304) and the Tribunal's website at http://www.itlos.org.

[3] United Nations, *Treaty Series*, vol. 1833, p. 3.

[4] *Ibid.*, vol. 2000, p. 468.

2. Pending cases and proceedings as at 31 December 2017

(*a*) *Case No. 25—The M/V "Norstar" Case (Panama* v. *Italy)* (2015–).

C. International Criminal Court[5]

The International Criminal Court is an independent permanent court established by the Rome Statute of the International Criminal Court, 1998.[6] The Relationship Agreement between the United Nations and the International Criminal Court, signed by the Secretary-General of the United Nations and the President of the Court on 4 October 2004, outlines the relationship between the two institutions.[7]

In 2017, the following situations were under investigation by the Office of the Prosecutor: Uganda,[8] Democratic Republic of the Congo,[9] Central African Republic,[10] Darfur (the Sudan),[11] Kenya,[12] Libya,[13] Côte d'Ivoire,[14] Mali,[15] Central African Republic II,[16] Georgia,[17] and Burundi.[18]Additionally, in 2017, the Office of the Prosecutor continued

---

[5] For more information about the Court's activities, see Report of the International Criminal Court, for the period 1 August 2016 to 31 July 2017 (A/72/349) and the period 1 August 2017 to 31 July 2018 (A/73/334), as well as the Court's website at http://www.icc-cpi.int.

[6] United Nations, *Treaty Series*, vol. 2187, p. 3.

[7] *Ibid.*, vol. 2283, p. 195.

[8] The situation was referred to the Court by Uganda in January 2004.

[9] The situation was referred to the Court by the Democratic Republic of the Congo in April 2004.

[10] The situation was referred to the Court by the Central African Republic in December 2004. The referral pertains to crimes within the jurisdiction of the Court committed anywhere on the territory of the Central African Republic since 1 July 2002.

[11] On 31 March 2005, the Security Council referred the situation in Darfur, the Sudan, to the Prosecutor of the Court by Security Council resolution 1593 (2005), adopted on 31 March 2005.

[12] On 31 March 2010, Pre-Trial Chamber II granted the Prosecutor's request to open an investigation *proprio motu* into the situation in Kenya.

[13] On 26 February 2011, the Security Council referred the situation in Libya to the Prosecutor of the Court by Security Council resolution 1970 (2011), adopted on 26 February 2011.

[14] On 3 October 2011, Pre-Trial Chamber III granted the Prosecutor's request to open an investigation *proprio motu* into the situation in Côte d'Ivoire.

[15] The situation was referred to the Court by Mali in July 2012.

[16] The situation was referred to the Court by the Central African Republic in May 2014. The referral pertains to crimes allegedly committed on the Central African Republic territory since 1 August 2012.

[17] On 27 January 2016, Pre-Trial Chamber I granted the Prosecutor's request for authorization to open an investigation *proprio motu* into the situation in Georgia.

[18] On 25 October 2017, Pre-Trial Chamber III granted the Prosecutor's request for authorization to open an investigation *proprio motu* into the situation in Burundi.

its preliminary examinations[19] in Afghanistan[20], Colombia[21], Gabon[22], Guinea[23], Iraq/United Kingdom[24], Nigeria[25], the State of Palestine[26] and Ukraine[27].

On 16 July 2015, following a request for review presented by the Government of the Union of the Comoros, Pre-Trial Chamber I requested the Prosecutor to reconsider her decision, dated 6 November 2014, to close the preliminary examination regarding the situation on Registered Vessels of Comoros, Greece and Cambodia, due to the lack of a

---

[19] Before the Office of the Prosecutor opens an investigation in a certain situation, it conducts a preliminary examination in order to determine whether a situation meets the legal criteria established by the Rome Statute and if there is a reasonable basis to proceed with an investigation. Pre-Trial Chamber III has interpreted "reasonable basis" as a "sensible or reasonable justification for a belief that a crime falling within the jurisdiction of the Court has been or is being committed" (see *Situation in the Republic of Burundi*, Public Redacted Version of "Decision Pursuant to Article 15 of the Rome Statute on the Authorization of an Investigation into the Situation in the Republic of Burundi", ICC-01/17-X-9-US-Exp, 25 October 2017 (ICC-01/17-9-Red), 9 November 2017, para. 30.

[20] On 20 November 2017, the Prosecutor requested authorization from the Court's Judges to initiate an investigation into alleged war crimes and crimes against humanity, committed in the context of the ongoing armed conflict in Afghanistan.

[21] Among other developments, the Prosecutor conducted her first visit to Bogota in September 2017, where she met senior officials from the executive and the judiciary, including President Juan Manuel Santos. Upon invitation by the President of the Constitutional Court of Colombia, on 18 October 2017, the Prosecutor submitted to the Constitutional Court an *Amicus Curiae* brief summarising the Office's views on certain aspects of the Legislative Act 01 of 2017 and Law 1820 ("Amnesty Law").

[22] In June 2017, the Office of the Prosecutor conducted its first mission to Libreville, where it met with political and judicial authorities, as well as with the Prosecutor General and the Public Prosecutors of Libreville.

[23] Among other developments, in March 2017, the Office of the Prosecutor conducted its fourteenth mission to Conakry to obtain detailed information on the investigative steps taken by the panel of judges and gauge the prospect of organising a trial within a reasonable timeframe.

[24] In 2017, the Office of the Prosecutor continued to engage with the relevant national authorities, including through high level meetings of the Prosecutor and Deputy Prosecutor. As part of its close scrutiny of relevant developments at the national level, the Office conducted its third mission to the UK from 13 to 14 February 2017.

[25] In 2017, the Office of the Prosecutor continued to gather information on Nigerian national proceedings related to the identified potential cases involving the commission of alleged crimes against humanity and war crimes, respectively, by Boko Haram and Nigerian security forces. To this end, it engaged with the Nigerian authorities as well as other relevant stakeholders to identify any pending impunity gaps. In May 2017, the Prosecutor also travelled to Abuja, where she met with Acting President Yemi Osinbajo and relevant civil and military authorities, including the Minister of Foreign Affairs and the Minister of Defence.

[26] In 2017, the Office of the Prosecutor continued to analyse information pertaining to the Court's jurisdiction in Palestine, as well as crimes allegedly committed by both parties to the 2014 Gaza conflict and crimes allegedly committed in the West Bank, including East Jerusalem since 13 June 2014. It also continued to closely follow relevant developments in the region, and held multiple meetings with relevant stakeholders at the seat of the Court, including government officials and civil society representatives.

[27] In 2017, the Office of the Prosecutor continued its analysis of whether alleged crimes relating to the situation in Crimea and the fighting in eastern Ukraine fall within the jurisdiction of the Court, as well as analysed new information and allegations received concerning the crimes allegedly committed in the context of the Euromaidan events. It also continued engaging with a variety of relevant stakeholders, both through consultations held at the seat of the Court and during two missions to Ukraine, in April and September 2017.

reasonable basis to proceed with an investigation.[28] On 6 November 2015, the Appeals Chamber of the International Criminal Court (ICC) decided by majority to dismiss, *in limine* and without discussing its merits, the Prosecutor's appeal against the decision of Pre-Trial Chamber I requesting the Prosecutor to reconsider the decision.[29] Consequently, the Prosecutor was required to review its decision as soon as possible pursuant to rule 108(2) of the Rules of Procedure and Evidence of the ICC. On 29 November 2017, the Prosecutor notified Pre-Trial Chamber I of her "final decision", as required by rule 108(3). Having carried out a thorough review of all the submissions made and all the information available, including information newly made available in 2015–2017, the Prosecutor remained of the view that the information available did not provide a reasonable basis to proceed with an investigation. The final decision filed with the Court provided extensive reasoning in support of this conclusion.[30]

Situations and cases before the Court as at 31 December 2017

(*a*) Situation in Uganda

Pending cases and proceedings

(*a*) *The Prosecutor* v. *Joseph Kony and Vincent Otti*, Case No. ICC-02/04-01/05.

(*b*) *The Prosecutor* v. *Dominic Ongwen*, Case No. ICC-02/04-01/15.

(*b*) Situation in the Democratic Republic of the Congo

Pending cases and proceedings

(*a*) *The Prosecutor* v. *Thomas Lubanga Dyilo*, Case No. ICC 01/04-01/06.

(*b*) *The Prosecutor* v. *Bosco Ntaganda*, Case No. ICC-01/04-02/06.

(*c*) *The Prosecutor* v. *Germain Katanga*, Case No. ICC-01/04-01/07.

(*d*) *The Prosecutor* v. *Sylvestre Mudacumura*, Case No. ICC-01/04-01/12.

(*c*) Situation in Darfur, the Sudan

Pending cases and proceedings

(*a*) *The Prosecutor* v. *Ahmad Muhammad Harun ("Ahmad Harun") and Ali Muhammad Ali Abd-Al-Rahman ("Ali Kushayb")*, Case No. ICC-02/05-01/07.

---

[28] *Situation on Registered Vessels of the Union of the Comoros, the Hellenic Republic and the Kingdom of Cambodia*, Pre-Trial Chamber I, Decision on the request of the Union of the Comoros to review the Prosecutor's decision not to initiate an investigation, 16 July 2015, No. ICC-01/13-34.

[29] *Situation on Registered Vessels of the Union of the Comoros, the Hellenic Republic and the Kingdom of Cambodia*, Appeals Chamber, Decision on the admissibility of the Prosecutor's appeal against the "Decision on the request of the Union of the Comoros to review the Prosecutor's decision not to initiate an investigation", 6 November 2015, No. ICC-01/13 OA.

[30] *Situation on Registered Vessels of the Union of the Comoros, the Hellenic Republic and the Kingdom of Cambodia*, Notice of Prosecutor's Final Decision under Rule 108(3), 29 November 2017, No. ICC-01/13-57 30-11-2017 1/3 EC PT.

(*b*) *The Prosecutor* v. *Omar Hassan Ahmad Al Bashir*, Case No. ICC-02/05-01/09.

(*c*) *The Prosecutor* v. *Abdallah Banda Abakaer Nourain*, Case No. ICC-02/05-03/09.

(*d*) *The Prosecutor* v. *Abdel Raheem Muhammad Hussein*, Case No. ICC-02/05-01/12.

(*d*) Situation in the Central African Republic

(i) *Judgments delivered by the Trial Chambers*

The Prosecutor v. *Jean-Pierre Bemba Gombo, Aimé Kilolo Musamba, Jean-Jacques Mangenda Kabongo, Fidèle Babala Wandu and Narcisse Arido*, Case No. ICC-01/05-01/13, Decision on Sentence pursuant to Article 76 of the Statute, 22 March 2017.

(ii) *Pending cases and proceedings*

(*a*) *The Prosecutor* v. *Jean-Pierre Bemba Gombo*, Case No. ICC-01/05-01/08.

(*b*) *The Prosecutor* v. *Jean-Pierre Bemba Gombo, Aimé Kilolo Musamba, Jean-Jacques Mangenda Kabongo, Fidèle Babala Wandu and Narcisse Arido*, Case No. ICC-01/05-01/13.

(*e*) Situation in Kenya

Pending cases and proceedings

(*a*) *The Prosecutor* v. *Walter Osapiri Barasa*, Case No. ICC-01/09-01/13.

(*b*) *The Prosecutor* v. *Paul Gicheru and Philip Kipkoech Bett*, Case No. ICC-01/09-01/15.

(*f*) Situation in Libya

Pending cases and proceedings

(*a*) *The Prosecutor* v. *Saif Al-Islam Gaddafi*, Case No. ICC-01/11-01/11.

(*b*) *The Prosecutor* v. *Al-Tuhamy Mohamed Khaled*, ICC-01/11-01/13.

(*c*) *The Prosecutor* v. *Mahmoud Mustafa Busyf Al-Werfalli*, ICC-01/11-01/17-2.

(*g*) Situation in Côte d'Ivoire

Pending cases and proceedings[31]

(*a*) *The Prosecutor* v. *Laurent Gbagbo and Charles Blé Goudé*, Case No. ICC-02/11-01/15.

(*b*) *The Prosecutor* v. *Simone Gbagbo*, Case No. ICC-02/11-01/12.

[31] On 11 March 2015, Trial Chamber I joined the Gbagbo case (ICC-02/11-01/11) and the Blé Goudé case (ICC-02/11-02/11).

(*h*) Situation in Mali

Pending cases and proceedings

The Prosecutor v. *Ahmad Al Faqi Al Mahdi*, Case No. ICC-01/12-01/15.

D. International Criminal Tribunal for the former Yugoslavia[32]

The International Criminal Tribunal for the former Yugoslavia was a subsidiary body of the United Nations Security Council, established by Security Council resolution 827 (1993), adopted on 25 May 1993.[33] The Tribunal closed on 31 December 2017.[34] In line with Security Council resolution 1966 (2010), the International Residual Mechanism for Criminal Tribunals continued its jurisdiction, rights and obligations and essential functions.

1. Judgement delivered by the Appeals Chamber

Prosecutor v. *Jadranko Prlić, Bruno Stojić, Slobodan Praljak, Milivoj Petković, Valentin Ćorić and Berislav Pusić*, Case No. IT-04-74, Judgment, 29 November 2017.

2. Judgements delivered by the Trial Chambers

Prosecutor v. *Ratko Mladić*, Case No. IT-09-92-T, Judgment, 22 November 2017.

3. Pending cases and proceedings as at 31 December 2017

The Tribunal ended its mandate on 31 December 2017. [35]

---

[32] The texts of the indictments, decisions and judgements are published in the *Judicial Reports/Recueils judiciaires* of the International Criminal Tribunal for the former Yugoslavia. The texts are also available in English and French on the Tribunal's website at http://www.icty.org. For more information about the Tribunal's activities in 2017, see the Twenty-fourth annual report of the International Tribunal for the Prosecution of Persons Responsible for Serious Violations of International Humanitarian Law Committed in the Territory of the Former Yugoslavia since 1991, for the period from 1 August 2016 to 31 July 2017 (A/72/266–S/2017/662), as well as the Letter dated 29 November 2017 from the President of the International Tribunal for the Prosecution of Persons Responsible for Serious Violations of International Humanitarian Law Committed in the Territory of the Former Yugoslavia since 1991, addressed to the President of the Security Council (S/2017/1001).

[33] The Statute of the Tribunal is annexed to the report of the Secretary-General pursuant to Security Council resolution 808 (1993) of 22 February 1993 (S/25704 and Add.1).

[34] Pending cases of the International Criminal Tribunal for the former Yugoslavia were transferred, where appropriate, to the Mechanism for International Criminal Tribunals (see Letter dated 29 November 2017 from the President of the International Tribunal for the Prosecution of Persons Responsible for Serious Violations of International Humanitarian Law Committed in the Territory of the former Yugoslavia since 1991, addressed to the President of the Security Council (S/2017/1001)).

[35] *Ibid.*

E. Mechanism for International Criminal Tribunals[36]

The Mechanism for International Criminal Tribunals was established in 2010 by Security Council resolution 1966 (2010), adopted on 22 December 2010.[37] The Mechanism was created to carry out certain residual functions of the International Criminal Tribunal for the former Yugoslavia[38] and the International Criminal Tribunal for Rwanda,[39] including trial and appellate proceedings, the supervision and enforcement of sentences, and tracking the remaining fugitives.

No judgements were delivered by the Mechanism for International Criminal Tribunals in 2017.

Pending cases and proceedings as at 31 December 2017

(*a*) *Prosecutor* v. *Petar Jojić and Vjerica Radeta*, Case No. MICT-17-111 (2017–)[40].

(*b*) *Prosecutor* v. *Ratko Mladić*, Case No. MICT-13-56 (2017–).

(*c*) *Prosecutor* v. *Vojislav Šešelj*, Case No. MICT-16-99 (2016–).

(*d*) *Prosecutor* v. *Augustin Ngirabatware*, Case No. MICT-12-29 (2016–).

(*e*) *Prosecutor* v. *Radovan Karadzić*, Case No. MICT-13-55 (2016–).

(*f*) *Prosecutor* v. *Mićo Stanišić and Stojan Župljanin*, Case No. MICT-13-53 (2016–).

(*g*) *Prosecutor* v. *Jovica Stanišić and Franko Simatović*, Case No. MICT-15-96 (2015–).

(*h*) *Prosecutor* v. *Félicien Kabuga*, Case No. MICT-13-38 (2012–).

F. Extraordinary Chambers in the Courts of Cambodia[41]

The Agreement between the United Nations and the Royal Government of Cambodia concerning the prosecution under Cambodian law of crimes committed during the period

---

[36] The texts of the orders, decisions and judgments are available on the Mechanism's website at http://www.unmict.org/. For more information about the Mechanism's activities, see the Fourth and Fifth annual reports of the International Residual Mechanism for Criminal Tribunals, for the period 1 July 2016 to 30 June 2017 (A/72/261–S/2017/661) and 1 July 2017 to 30 June 2018 (A/73/289–S/2018/559), respectively.

[37] The Statute of the Mechanism is contained in the annex to the resolution.

[38] See footnote 34 above.

[39] The International Criminal Tribunal for Rwanda was a subsidiary body of the United Nations Security Council, established by Security Council resolution 955 (1994), adopted on 8 November 1994. The Statute of the Tribunal is in the annex to the resolution. The Tribunal closed on 31 December 2015. The texts of the orders, decisions and judgements are published in the *Recueil des ordonnances, decisions et arrêts/Reports of Orders, Decisions and Judgements* of the International Criminal Tribunal for Rwanda. The texts are also available in English and French on the Legacy website of the International Criminal Tribunal for Rwanda at https://unictr.irmct.org/en.

[40] Proceedings against Jovo Ostojić, who was among the accused in the ICTY Case No. IT 03-67-R77.5, were terminated on 17 August 2017, following Ostojić's death.

[41] The texts of the judgements, decisions and orders of the Extraordinary Chambers in the Courts of Cambodia are available on its website at http://www.eccc.gov.kh. For more information on the Court's activities, see the Report of the Secretary-General on the Request for a subvention to the Extraordinary Chambers in the Courts of Cambodia of 16 August 2017 (A/72/341).

of Democratic Kampuchea, signed in Phnom Penh on 6 June 2003,[42] entered into force on 29 April 2005 and established the Extraordinary Chambers in the Courts of Cambodia to prosecute crimes committed during the period of Democratic Kampuchea.

No judgements were delivered by the Extraordinary Chambers in the Courts of Cambodia in 2017.

1. Judgement delivered by the Supreme Court Chamber

No judgements were delivered by the Supreme Court Chamber in 2017.

2. Pending cases and proceedings as at 31 December 2017

(*a*) *Khieu Samphân and Nuon Chea*, Case No. 002/01 (2010–).

(*b*) *Khieu Samphân and Nuon Chea*, Case No. 002/02 (2010–).

(*c*) *Meas Muth*, Case No. 003 (2009–).

(*d*) *Yim Tith*, Case No. 004 (2009–).

(*e*) *Im Chaem*, Case No. 004/01 (2009–).

(*f*) *Ao An*, Case No. 004/02 (2009–).

G. Special Tribunal for Lebanon[43]

The Special Tribunal for Lebanon was established in 2007 pursuant to the Agreement between the United Nations and the Lebanese Republic on the establishment of a Special Tribunal for Lebanon, dated 22 January and 6 February 2007,[44] and to the Security Council resolution 1757 (2007) adopted on 30 May 2007 to prosecute persons responsible for the attack of 14 February 2005 resulting in the death of former Lebanese Prime Minister Rafiq Hariri and in the death or injury of other persons.

Pending cases and proceedings as at 31 December 2017

(*a*) *Salim Jamil Ayyash, Mustafa Amine Badreddine, Hassan Habib Merhi, Hussein Hassan Oneissi and Assad Hassan Sabra*, Case No. STL-11-01 (2011–).

(*b*) *Al Jadeed [CO.] S.A.L./NEW TV S.A.L. and Karma Mohamed Tahsin Al Khayat*, Case No. STL-14-05 (2014–).

(*c*) *Akhbar Beirut S.A.L. and Ibrahim Mohamed Ali Al Amin*, Case No. STL-14-06 (2014–).

---

[42] United Nations, *Treaty Series*, vol. 2329, p. 117.

[43] The texts of the indictments, decisions and orders of the Special Tribunal for Lebanon are available at an archived version of the Tribunal's website at: https://exhibits.stanford.edu/virtual-tribunals/catalog/nb441sq7196. For more information on the Tribunal's activities, see the Eighth and Ninth Annual Reports of the Special Tribunal for Lebanon, for the periods 1 March 2016 to 29 February 2017 and 1 March 2017 to 28 February 2018, respectively, available from https://swap.stanford.edu/was/20231017155108/https://www.stl-tsl.org/en/documents/annual-reports.

[44] United Nations, *Treaty Series*, vol. 2461, p. 257.

H. Residual Special Court for Sierra Leone[45]

The Special Court for Sierra Leone[46] was an independent court established by the Agreement between the United Nations and the Government of Sierra Leone on the Establishment of a Special Court for Sierra Leone, 2002.[47] The Special Court was mandated to try those who bore the greatest responsibility for serious violations of international humanitarian law and Sierra Leonean law committed in the territory of Sierra Leone since 30 November 1996.

As the Special Court completed its mandate and finished its judicial activities in 2013, the Residual Special Court for Sierra Leone superseded the Special Court. The Residual Special Court was established pursuant to an Agreement between the United Nations and the Government of Sierra Leone on the Establishment of a Residual Special Court for Sierra Leone,[48] signed in 2010 and entered into force in 2012.

The purpose of the Residual Special Court is to carry out the continuing obligations of the Special Court after its closure in 2013, such as witness protection, supervision of prison sentences, and management of the Special Court's archives. Johnny Paul Koroma is the only indicted person by the Special Court who is not in custody. Should he be arrested, the Residual Special Court will have jurisdiction to try him.

No judgements were delivered by the Residual Special Court for Sierra Leone in 2017.

---

[45] The texts of the decisions delivered by the Residual Special Court for Sierra Leone are available at the Residual Special Court's website at http://www.rscsl.org. For more information on the Residual Special Court's activities, see the Third Annual Report of the President of the Residual Special Court for Sierra Leone, available from http://www.rscsl.org/Documents/AnRpt2017.pdf.

[46] The texts of the judgements and decisions delivered by the Special Court for Sierra Leone are available at the Residual Special Court's website at http://www.rscsl.org. For more information on the Court's activities, see the Eleventh and Final Report of the President of the Special Court for Sierra Leone, available from http://www.rscsl.org/Documents/AnRpt11.pdf.

[47] For the text of the Agreement and the Statute of the Special Court dated 26 January 2002, see United Nations, *Treaty Series*, vol. 2178, p. 137.

[48] The Agreement and the Statute of the Residual Special Court were registered with the United Nations under No. 50125 (see also S/2012/741).

Chapter VIII

DECISIONS OF NATIONAL TRIBUNALS

[No decision or advisory opinion from national tribunals on questions relating to the United Nations and related intergovernmental organizations to be reported for 2017.]

Part Four

BIBLIOGRAPHY

A. International organizations in general

1. General

Block-Lieb, S., and Halliday, T.C., *Global Lawmakers: International Organizations in the Crafting of World Markets* (Cambridge, UK; New York: Cambridge University Press, 2017). 250 p.

Boisson de Chazournes, L., *Interactions between Regional and Universal Organizations: A Legal Perspective* (Leiden: Brill Nijhoff, 2017). 384 p.

Cahin, G., L'exécution des decisions juridictionnelles internationales rendues à l'encontre des organisations internationales, *Revue générale de droit international public*, vol. 121 (2017): p. 613–644.

Cimiotta, E., 'Triangular' Relationships between the United Nations and African Regional and Sub-Regional Organizations in Maintaining Peace, *International Organizations Law Review*, vol. 14 (2017): p. 321–345.

Dannenberg, G., Quelques remarques sur la coordination conventionnelle entre organisations internationales, *Revue générale de droit international public*, vol. 121 (2017): p. 335–359.

Ferstman, C., *International Organizations and the Fight for Accountability: The Remedies and Reparations Gap. First ed.* (New York, NY: Oxford University Press, 2017). 200 p.

Fioretos, O. (ed), *International Politics and Institutions in Time.* (1st ed.) (Oxford: Oxford University Press, 2017). 352 p.

Gasbarri, L., The Dual Legality of the Rules of International Organizations, *International Organizations Law Review*, vol. 14 (2017): p. 87–119.

Hathaway, O.A., and Shapiro, S.J., *The Internationalists: And Their Plan to Outlaw War* (London: Allen Lane, 2017). 581 p.

Johns, F., Data, Detection, and the Redistribution of the Sensible in International Law, *American Journal of International Law*, vol. 111 (2017): p. 57–103.

Kunz-Hallstein, H.P., Views from Practice: Paralysing the Functioning of International Organisations' Internal Appeals Boards, *International Organizations Law Review*, vol. 14 (2017): p. 196–203.

Lall, R., Beyond Institutional Design: Explaining the Performance of International Organizations, *International Organization*, vol. 71 (2017): p. 245–280.

Lemay-Hébert, N. Exploring the Effective Authority of International Administrations to the United Nations. *Journal of Intervention and Statebuilding*, vol. 11, iss. 4 (2017): p. 468–489.

Schifano, A., Distribution of Power within International Organizations, *International Organizations Law Review*, vol. 14 (2017): p. 346–401.

Schmitt, P., *Access to Justice and International Organizations: The Case of Individual Victims of Human Rights Violations* (Cheltenham, UK: Edward Elgar Publishing, 2017). 400 p.

2. Responsibility of international organizations

Barros, A.S., Ryngaert, C. and Wouters, J., (eds), *International Organizations and Member State Responsibility: Critical Perspectives* (Leiden; Boston: Brill Nijhoff, 2017). 232 p.

García Segura, C., "Westfalia, Worldfalia, Eastfalia": el impacto de las transformaciones de la estructura de poder interestatal en el orden internacional, *Revista española de derecho internacional*, vol. 69 (2017): p. 45–70.

Galetto, A. Immunities and Responsibilities of International Organizations: Two Sides of the Same Coin or Two Separate Coins? in Besson, S. (ed), *International Responsibility: Essays in Law, History and Philosophy* (Genève: Schulthess; LGDJ Lextenso Éditions, 2017): p. 199–219.

Kihara-Hunt, A., *Holding UNPOL to Account: Individual Criminal Accountability of United Nations Police Personnel* (Leiden; Boston: Brill Nijhoff, 2017). 433 p.

Klabbers, J., Reflections on Role Responsibility: The Responsibility of International Organizations for Failing to Act, *European Journal of International Law*, vol. 28 (2017): p. 1133–1161.

McGaughey, F., Advancing, Retreating or Stepping on each Other's Toes?: The Role of Non-Governmental Organisations in United Nations Human Rights Treaty Body Reporting and the Universal Periodic Review, *Australian Year Book of International Law*, vol. 35 (2017): p. 187–216.

Moelle, M.P., *The International Responsibility of International Organisations: Cooperation in Peacekeeping Operations* (Cambridge, United Kingdom; New York, NY: Cambridge University Press, 2017). 373 p.

Nollkaemper, A. (ed), *The Practice of Shared Responsibility in International Law* (Cambridge, United Kingdom: Cambridge University Press, 2017). 1198 p.

Young, C., The Limits of International Organization Immunity: An Argument for a Restrictive Theory of Immunity Under the IOIA, *Texas Law Review*, vol. 95 (2017): p. 889–913.

B. United Nations

1. General

Becker, M.A., Commissions of Inquiry: Problems and Prospects, *European Journal of International Law*, vol. 28 (2017): p. 1418–1422.

Doyle, M.W., The UN Charter and Global Constitutionalism? in Lang, A.F., and Wiener, A. (eds), *Handbook on Global Constitutionalism* (Cheltenham, UK: Edward Elgar Publishing, 2017): p. 338–354.

Klabbers, J., Functionalism, Constitutionalism and the United Nations, in Lang, A.F. and Wiener, A. (eds), *Handbook on Global Constitutionalism* (Cheltenham, UK: Edward Elgar Publishing, 2017): p. 355–367.

Nesbitt, M., Re-Purposing UN Commissions of Inquiry, *Journal of International Law and International Relations*, vol. 13, (2017): p. 83–122.

Nolan, A., Freedman, R., and Murphy, T., *The United Nations Special Procedures System* (Leiden: Brill Nijhoff, 2017). 472 p.

Patel, G., How 'Universal' is the United Nations' Universal Periodic Review Process? An Examination of the Discussions Held on Polygamy, *Human Rights Review*, vol. 18 (2017): p. 459–483.

Rashkow, B., Above the Law? Innovating Legal Responses to Build a More Accountable U.N.: Where is the U.N. Now? *Journal of International & Comparative Law*, vol. 23 (2017): p. 345–371.

Schaus, F., The Privileges and Immunities of the United Nations: Some Challenges After 70 Years of Existence, in Vaz Patto, S., *et al.* (eds), *Anuario de direito internacional 2016* (Lisboa: Ministério dos Negócios Estrangeiros, 2017): p. 87–102.

Spijkers, O., Global Values and the Institutions of the United Nations, *ICL Journal*, vol. 11 (2017): p. 211–255.

von der Schulenburg, M., *On Building Peace: Rescuing the Nation-State and Saving the United Nations* (Amsterdam: Amsterdam University Press, 2017). 282 p.

2. Principal organs and subsidiary bodies

General Assembly

Ramsden, M., Uniting for MH17, *Asian Journal of International Law*, vol. 7 (2017): p. 337–360.

Ramsden, M., and Hamilton T., 'Uniting Against Impunity: The UN General Assembly as a Catalyst for Action at the ICC', *International and Comparative Law Quarterly*, vol. 66 (2017): p. 893–921.

Whiting, A., An Investigation Mechanism for Syria: The General Assembly Steps into the Breach, *Journal of International Criminal Justice*, vol. 15 (2017): p. 231–237.

Zavoli, I., Peacekeeping in Eastern Ukraine: The Legitimacy of a Request and the Competence of the United Nations General Assembly, *Journal of Conflict and Security Law*, vol. 22 (2017): p. 147–173.

Security Council

Aitken, H., The Security Council and International Law Enforcement: A Kelsenian Perspective on Civilian Protection Peacekeeping Mandates, *Journal of Conflict and Security Law* (2017): p. 1–38.

Ayeni, V.O., and Olong, M.A., Opportunities and Challenges to the UN Security Council Referral Under the Rome Statute of the International Criminal Court, *African Journal of International and Comparative Law*, vol. 25 (2017): p. 239–260.

Boon, K., D. Hovell, The Power of Process: The Value of Due Process in Security Council Decision-Making, *Netherlands International Law Review*, vol. 64 (2017): p. 177–181.

Couzigou, I., Enforcement of UN Security Council Resolutions and of ICJ Judgments: The Unreliability of Political Enforcement Mechanisms, in Jakab, A., and Kochenov, D. (eds), *The Enforcement of EU Law and Values: Ensuring Member States' Compliance* (Oxford, United Kingdom: Oxford University Press, 2017): p. 363–378.

Elgebeily, S., *The Rule of Law in the United Nations Security Council Decision-Making Process: Turning the Focus Inwards* (London; New York: Routledge, Taylor & Francis Group, 2017). 207 p.

Galand, A.S., Was the Residual Mechanism's Creation Falling Squarely within the Chapter VII Power of the Security Council? *Questions of International Law*, vol. 40 (2017): p. 5–20.

Gehring, T., Dorsch, C., and Dörfler, T., Precedent and Doctrine in Organisational Decision-Making: The Power of Informal Institutional Rules in the United Nations Security Council's Activities on Terrorism, *Journal of International Relations and Development* (2017): p. 1–29.

Harrington, J., The Working Methods of the United Nations Security Council: Maintaining the Implementation of Change, *International and Comparative Law Quarterly*, vol. 66, (2017): p. 39–77.

Moeckli, D., and Fasel, R.N., A Duty to Give Reasons in the Security Council: Making Voting Transparent, *International Organizations Law Review*, vol. 14 (2017): p. 13–86.

Proulx, V., An Incomplete Revolution: Enhancing the Security Council's Role in Enforcing Counterterrorism Obligations, *Journal of International Dispute Settlement*, vol. 8 (2017): p. 303–338.

Ralph, J., and Gifkins, J., The Purpose of United Nations Security Council Practice: Contesting Competence Claims in the Normative Context Created by the Responsibility to Protect, *European Journal of International Relations, vol. 23* (2017): p. 630–653.

Runjic, L., Reform of the United Nations Security Council: The Emperor has no Clothes, *Revista de Direito Internacional*, vol. 14 (2017): p. 267–284.

Sicilianos, L., The European Court of Human Rights Facing the Security Council: Towards Systemic Harmonization, *International and Comparative Law Quarterly*, vol. 66 (2017): p. 783–804.

van den Herik, L. (ed), *Research Handbook on UN Sanctions and International Law* (Cheltenham, UK: Edward Elgar Publishing, 2017). 544 p.

Werner, W., Recall it again, Sam. Practices of Repetition in the Security Council, *Nordic Journal of International Law*, vol. 86 (2017): p. 151–169.

International Court of Justice

Abalde Cantero, Ó., *Naturaleza jurídica de las decisiones de la Corte Internacional de Justicia: fuerza obligatoria y fuerza ejecutiva* (Cizur Menor: Thomson Reuters Aranzadi, 2016). 510 p.

Abraham, R., The Role of the ICJ in the Promotion of the Rule of Law, *Japanese Yearbook of International Law*, vol. 60 (2017): p. 339–349.

Andenas, M., and Leiss J.R., The Systemic Relevance of "Judicial Decisions" in Article 38 of the ICJ Statute, *Zeitschrift für ausländisches öffentliches Recht und Völkerrecht = Heidelberg Journal of International Law*, vol. 77 (2017): p. 907–972.

Bonafé, B.I., Establishing the Existence of a Dispute before the International Court of Justice: Drawbacks and Implications. *QIL: Questions of International Law: QDI: Questions de droit international*, December (2017): p. 3–32.

Chao, Y.Y., Power, Jurisdiction and Admissibility: Reconceptualizing Procedural Legal Issues in the Interpretative Proceedings Under Article 60 of the ICJ Statute, *Journal of East Asia and International Law*, vol. 10 (2017): p. 511–534.

Couvreur, P., *The International Court of Justice and the Effectiveness of International Law* (Leiden; Boston: Brill Nijhoff, 2017). 278 p.

d'Aspremont, J., The International Court of Justice and the Irony of System-Design, *Journal of International Dispute Settlement*, vol. 8 (2017): p. 366–387.

Garrido-Muñoz, A., Managing Uncertainty: The International Court of Justice, 'Objective Reasonableness' and the Judicial Function, *Leiden Journal of International Law*, vol. 30 (2017): p. 457–474.

Keith, K.J., Challenges to the Independence of the International Judiciary: Reflections on the International Court of Justice, *Leiden Journal of International Law*, vol. 30 (2017): p. 137–154.

Koua, S., Plaidoyer pour une réforme de la Cour internationale de justice (CIJ), *Revue juridique et politique des états francophones*, vol. 71 (2017): p. 252–275.

Kovács, P., Les mesures conservatoires dans la pratique de la Cour internationale de Justice et de la Cour Pénale Internationale, *Revue générale de droit international public*, vol. 121 (2017): p. 575–596.

Lusa Bordin, F., Procedural Developments at the International Court of Justice, *The Law & Practice of International Courts and Tribunals*, vol. 16 (2017): p. 307–353.

Olorundami, F., Objectivity Versus Subjectivity in the Context of the ICJ's Three-Stage Methodology of Maritime Boundary Delimitation, *The International Journal of Marine and Coastal Law*, vol. 32 (2017): p. 36–53.

Palchetti, P., Responsibility for Breach of Provisional Measures of the ICJ: Between Protection of the Rights of the Parties and Respect for the Judicial Function, *Rivista di diritto internazionale*, vol. 100 (2017): p. 5–22.

Petersen, N., The International Court of Justice and the Judicial Politics of Identifying Customary International Law, *European Journal of International Law*, vol. 28 (2017): p. 357–385.

Pomson, O., The Obligations Concerning Negotiations Cases and the "Dispute" Requirement in the International Court of Justice, *Law and Practice of International Courts and Tribunals*, vol. 16 (2017): p. 373–397.

Sarmiento Lamus, A., and Arévalo Ramírez, W., Non-Appearance before the International Court of Justice and the Role and Function of Judges Ad Hoc, *Law and Practice of International Courts and Tribunals*, vol. 16 (2017): p. 398–412.

Stoppioni, E., Decentring the ICJ: A Critical Analysis of the Marshall Islands Judgments, *QIL: Questions of International Law: QDI: Questions de droit international*, December (2017): p. 65–75.

Wellens, K., The International Court of Justice, Back to the Future: Keeping the Dream Alive, *Netherlands International Law Review*, vol. 64 (2017): p. 193–212.

Xue, H., *Jurisdiction of the International Court of Justice* (Leiden: Brill Nijhoff, 2017). 252 p.

Zamuner, E., The Temporal Scope of Application of the Genocide Convention: A Retrospective Assessment of the ICJ Case Law, *Diritti umani e diritto internazionale*, vol. 2 (2017): p. 361–374.

Secretariat

Axworthy, L. and Rock, A., Memorandum to the New UN Secretary-General, *Global Responsibility to Protect*, vol. 9 (2017): p. 5–14.

Gastaut, T., L'élection du neuvième Secrétaire général des Nations Unies, *Annuaire français de relations internationales*, vol. 18 (2017): p. 817–834.

Higgins, R., *et al.*, The United Nations Secretariat and Secretary-General, in Higgins, R., *et al.* (eds), *Oppenheim's International Law: United Nations* (Oxford, UK: Oxford University Press, 2017): p. 495–543.

Ponzio, R., and Schroeder, M.B., A Fool's Errand? The Next Secretary-General and United Nations Reform, *Global Policy*, vol. 8 (2017): p. 263–269.

Ravndal, E.J., "A Force for Peace": Expanding the Role of the UN Secretary-General Under Trygve Lie, 1946–1953, *Global Governance*, vol. 23 (2017): p. 443–459.

Terlingen, Y., A Better Process, a Stronger UN Secretary-General: How Historic Change was Forged and What Comes Next, *Ethics & International Affairs*, vol. 31 (2017): p. 115–127.

Thakur, R., Choosing the Ninth United Nations Secretary-General: Looking Back, Looking Ahead, *Global Governance*, vol. 23 (2017): p. 1–13.

Weiss, T.G., and Carayannis, T., Windows of Opportunity for UN Reform: Historical Insights for the Next Secretary-General, *International Affairs*, vol. 93 (2017): p. 309–326.

Zappalà, S., Le palais de verre est-il devenu plus transparent? La nomination d'Antonio Guterres comme neuvième Secrétaire général de l'ONU, *Annuaire français de droit international*, vol. 62 (2016): p. 252–264.

C. Intergovernmental organizations related to the United Nations

1. Food and Agricultural Organization

Organisation for Economic Co-operation and Development, Food and Agriculture Organization of the United Nations, and United Nations Capital Development Fund, *Adopter une approche territoriale dans les politiques de sécurite alimentaire et nutritionnelle* (Paris: OCDE, 2017). 176 p.

Food and Agricultural Organization, *Analyse comparative des cadres juridiques régissant la gestion de la faune par les collectivités locales en Afrique centrale—Diversités et Limites*, Document prepared by E. Sartoretto, A. Tomassi and P. Karpe, FAO Legal Papers No. 103. http://www.fao.org/3/a-i7824f.pdf.

Food and Agricultural Organization, *Review and Analysis of International Legal and Policy Instruments Related to Deep-Sea Fisheries and Biodiversity Conservation in Areas Beyond National Jurisdiction*, Document prepared by J. Harrison, T. Lobach, E. Morgera and P. Manoa, http://www.fao.org/3/a-i7009e.pdf.

Food and Agricultural Organization, *Legal aspects of contract farming agreements—Synthesis of the UNIDROIT/FAO/IFAD Legal Guide on Contract Farming*, Document prepared by FAO, IFAD and UNIDROIT, http://www.fao.org/3/a-i6711e.pdf.

Food and Agricultural Organization, *Contract farming and the law: What do regulators need to know?* http://www.fao.org/3/a-i7580e.pdf.

Food and Agricultural Organization, Contract farming and the law: what do farmers need to know? http://www.fao.org/3/a-i7581e.pdf.

Food and Agricultural Organization, How existing legal frameworks shape forest conversion to agriculture. A study of the Congo Basin. Document prepared by E. Sartoretto, C. Henriot M-M. Bassalang and S. Nguiffo, FAO Legal Papers No. 102, http://www.fao.org/3/a-i7947e.pdf.

Food and Agricultural Organization, Legal pluralism, women's land rights and gender equality in Mozambique, Document prepared by M. Bicchieri and A. Ayala, FAO Legal Papers No. 104, http://www.fao.org/3/a-i7825e.pdf.

Rastouin, J., and Ferault, C., *La sécurité alimentaire mondiale: état des lieux et prospectives* (Paris: L'Harmattan, 2017). 312 p.

2. General Agreement on Tariffs and Trade

Hoekman, B.M., and Mavroidis, P.C., MFN Clubs and Scheduling Additional Commitments in the GATT: Learning from the GATS, *European Journal of International Law*, vol. 28 (2017): p. 387–407.

Santana, R., 70th Anniversary of the GATT: Stalin, the Marshall Plan, and the Provisional Application of the GATT 1947, *Trade, Law and Development*, vol. 9 (2017): p. 1–20.

Sarmah, A., Renewable Energy and Article III:8(A) of the GATT: Reassessing the Environment-Trade Conflict in Light of the 'Next Generation' Cases of Trade, *Trade, Law and Development*, vol. 9 (2017): p. 197–220.

Suttle, O., What Sorts of Things are Public Morals? A Liberal Cosmopolitan Approach to Article XX GATT, *The Modern Law Review*, vol. 80 (2017): p. 569–599.

3. International Atomic Energy Agency

El Jadie, A., *L'énergie nucléaire et le droit international public* (Université François-Rabelais de Tours, France, 2017). 557 p.

Getmansky, A., Who Gets What from International Organizations? The Case of the International Atomic Energy Agency's Technical Cooperation, *International Studies Quarterly*, vol. 61 (2017): p. 596–611.

Handl, G., The IAEA Nuclear Safety Conventions: An Example of Successful Treaty Management? *Environmental and Energy Law*, vol. 1 (2017): p. 621–641.

Kerr, P., The JCPOA and Safeguards: Model or Outlier? *The Non-proliferation Review*, vol. 24 (2017): p. 261–273.

Taipale, I., and Taipale, V. (eds), *Nuclear Exits: Countries Foregoing the Nuclear Option* (Oxon: Taylor and Francis, 2017). 106 p.

4. International Centre for Settlement of Investment Disputes

Baltag, C., *ICSID Convention After 50 Years Unsettled Issues* (Alphen aan den Rijn: Wolters Kluwer, 2017). 620 p.

Brown, C.M., A Multilateral Mechanism for the Settlement of Investment Disputes: Some Preliminary Sketches, *ICSID Review: Foreign Investment Law Journal*, vol. 32 (2017): p. 673–690.

Calamita, N.J., The Challenge of Establishing a Multilateral Investment Tribunal at ICSID, *ICSID Review: Foreign Investment Law Journal*, vol. 32 (2017): p. 611–624.

Cantelmo, T., The Inherent Power of Reconsideration in Recent ICSID Case Law, *The Journal of World Investment & Trade*, vol. 18 (2017): p. 232–270.

Cazala, J., La défiance étatique à l'égard de l'arbitrage investisseur-État exprimée dans quelques projets et instruments conventionnels récents, *Journal du droit international*, vol. 144 (2017): p. 81–97.

Cleis, M.N., *The Independence and Impartiality of ICSID Arbitrators: Current Case Law, Alternative Approaches, and Improvement Suggestions* (Leiden; Boston: Brill Nijhoff, 2017). 292 p.

Cortesi, G.A., ICSID Jurisdiction with Regard to State-Owned Enterprises—Moving Toward an Approach Based on General International Law, *Law and Practice of International Courts and Tribunals*, vol. 16 (2017): p. 108–138.

Descours-Karmitz, R., The Role of ICSID Tribunals in the Combat Against Corruption, *World Arbitration & Mediation Review*, vol. 11 (2017): p. 1–44.

Dias Simões, F., Myopic Amici: The Participation of Non-Disputing Parties in ICSID Arbitration, *North Carolina Journal of International Law and Commercial Regulation*, vol. 42 (2017): p. 791–821.

Diel-Gligor, K., *Towards Consistency in International Investment Jurisprudence: A Preliminary Ruling System for ICSID Arbitration* (Leiden; Boston: Brill Nijhoff, 2017). 590 p.

Footer, M.E., Umbrella Clauses and Widely-Formulated Arbitrated Clauses: Discerning the Limits of ICSID Jurisdiction, *The Law and Practice of International Courts and Tribunals: A Practitioners' Journal*, vol. 16 (2017): p. 87–107.

García Matamoros, L.V., and Arévalo Ramírez, W., Procedimiento para la solución de diferencias en el arbitraje de inversión: El Centro Internacional de Arreglo de Disputas relativas a Inversiones (CIADI), in García Matamoros, L.V., and Ávila Medina, D.C. (eds), *Procedimiento, litigio y representación ante tribunales internacionales*. (Bogotá: Editorial Universidad del Rosario, 2017): p. 445–535.

Gazzini, T., and Kolb, R., Provisional Measures in ICSID Arbitration from "Wonderland's Jurisprudence" to Informal Modification of Treaties, *The Law & Practice of International Courts and Tribunals*, vol. 16 (2017): p. 159–184.

Hafner-Burton, E.M., Puig, S., and Victor, D.G., Against Secrecy: The Social Cost of International Dispute Settlement, *The Yale Journal of International Law*, vol. 42 (2017): p. 279–343.

Huber, M., and Tereposky, G., The WTO Appellate Body: Viability as a Model for an Investor–State Dispute Settlement Appellate Mechanism, *ICSID Review*, vol. 32 (2017): p. 545–594.

Kidane, W.L., Culture and the Legal Infrastructure of Investment Arbitration, in Kidane, W.L. (ed), *The Culture of International Arbitration* (Oxford: Oxford University Press, 2017): p. 133–176.

Maric, E., Dawn of the New Era in Investment Arbitration: The Growing Significance of Issue Conflict Towards Restructuring and Reshaping of ICSID? *International Arbitration Law Review*, vol. 20 (2017): p. 91–105.

Mullen, S., and Whitsitt, E., ICSID and Legislative Consent to Arbitrate: Questions of Applicable Law, *ICSID Review: Foreign Investment Law Journal*, vol. 32 (2017): p. 92–115.

Pivnichny, D., Treaty-Based Claims Against Subdivisions of ICSID Contracting States, *Washington University Global Studies Law Review*, vol. 16 (2017): p. 125–172.

Reisenfeld, K.B., and Robbins, J.M., Finality Under the Washington and New York Conventions: Another Swing of the Pendulum? *ICSID Review: Foreign Investment Law Journal*, vol. 32 (2017): p. 371–384.

Thomas, J.C., and Dhillon, H.K., The Foundations of Investment Treaty Arbitration: The ICSID Convention, Investment Treaties and the Review of Arbitration Awards, *ICSID Review*, vol. 32 (2017): p. 459–502.

Treves, E.P., Investment Treaty Arbitration: Dual Nationals are Now Welcome: A Way Out of ICSID's Dual Nationality Exclusion, *New York University Journal of International Law & Politics*, vol. 49 (2016): p. 607–618.

Viktorova, N.N., Interpretation of the Convention on the Settlement of Investment Disputes between States and Nationals of Other States (1965) by ICSID Tribunals, *Czech Yearbook of International Law*, vol. 8 (2017): p. 367–385.

Zarra, G., Orderliness and Coherence in International Investment Law and Arbitration: An Analysis through the Lens of State of Necessity, *Journal of International Arbitration*, vol. 34 (2017): p. 653–678.

Zarra, G., The Relevance of State Interests in Recent ICSID Practice, *The Italian Yearbook of International Law*, vol. 26 (2017): p. 487–512.

5. International Civil Aviation Organization

Abeyratne, R., ICAO's Involvement in the Sustainable Development Goals—The Aviation Connection, *European Transport Law: Journal of Law and Economics*, vol. 52 (2017): p. 129–144.

Erling, U.M., International Aviation Emissions Under International Civil Aviation Organization's Global Market Based Measure: Ready for Offsetting? *Air & Space Law*, vol. 42 (2017): p. 1–12.

Huang, J., 7 Security Regulations in Dempsey, P.S. and Jakhu, R.S. (eds), *Routledge Handbook of Public Aviation Law*, 2017: p. 137–161.

Nyampong, N., 9 Aircraft and Airport Noise in Dempsey, P.S. and Jakhu, R.S. (eds), *Routledge Handbook of Public Aviation Law*, 2017: p. 180–194.

Trigeaud, B., L'OACI «Autorité mondiale des airs»?: Étude de la formation du droit dérivé de l'Organisation de l'aviation civile internationale, *Revue française de droit aérien et spatial*, vol. 284 (2017): p. 365–384.

6. International Criminal Court

Abd, I.A., Mustaqbal al-Mahkamah al-Jinaiyah al-Duwaliyah, *Cihan University-Erbil Scientific Journal*, vol. 1, iss. 3 (2017): p. 20–29.

Abd-Allah, Y.M., Muawiqat tahqiq al-Adala al-Jinaiyah al-duwaliyah amama al-Mahkamah al-Jinaiyah al-Duwaliyah, *Journal of College of Law for Legal and Political Sciences*, vol. 6, iss. 20/part 1 (2017): p. 253–298.

Aksenova, M., Human Rights at the International Criminal Court: Testing the Limits of Judicial Discretion, *Nordic Journal of International Law*, vol. 86, iss. 1 (2017): p. 68–90.

Al-Abidi, K.A.H., Al-difa al-sharai fi itar al-Mahkamah al-Jinaiyah al-Duwaliyah, *Tikrit University Journal for Rights*, vol. 1, iss. 3 (2017): p. 203–241.

Al-Saleh, R.M., Taqnin al-jaraim al-duwaliyah khutwah nahwa aadala jinaiyah duwaliyah: al-Mahkamah al-Jinaiyah al-Duwaliyah al-daimah namouthajan, *Majallat al-Mufakkir*, iss. 16 (2017): p. 263–289.

Alobwede, J., *The Future of the ICC & the ICC of the Future* (Saarbrücken: LAP LAMBERT Academic Publishing, 2017). 136 p.

Avila Jaimes, L. and Benavides Vanegas, F.S., Crímenes internacionales in *Manual de Derecho Penal Internacional: Temas Básicos* (Bogotá: Legis Editores, 2017). 334 p.

Baraybar, J.P., The International Criminal Court and the Need for a Scientific Advisory Unit, in Bergsmo, M., Rackwitz, K., and Tianying, S., *Historical Origins of International Criminal Law* (Brussels: Torkel Opsahl Academic EPublisher, vol. 5, 2017): p. 179.

Barmet, C., Contre-interroger la Cour pénale, *Politique de sécurité: analyses du CSS*, iss. 214 (2017).

Barreto, A.J.A., Parada Trujillo, A., and Aguilar Barreto, C.P., Delitos de lesa humanidad: posturas de la Corte Penal Internacional. In Graterol Rivas, M.E., *et al.* (eds) *Derechos Humanos desde una Perspectiva Socio-Jurídica*. (Maracaibo, República Bolivariana de Venezuela: Ediciones Astro Data, 2017): p. 247–265.

Baylis, E., The Persuasive Authority of Internationalized Criminal Tribunals, *American University International Law Review*, vol. 32, iss. 3 (2017): p. 611–643.

Bekou, O., *International Criminal Court* (London: Taylor & Francis, 2017).

Belik, V.N., Международный уголовный суд: состояние и проблемы организационно-правовой деятельности, *Уголовно-исполнительное право*, vol. 12, iss. 1 (2017): p. 45–47.

Bensouda, F., The Arc of Justice: From Nuremberg to the International Criminal Court, in Agrast, M.D., *et al.* (eds), *Proceedings of the Tenth International Humanitarian Law Dialogs*: September 29–30, 2016 at Nuremberg, Germany. (Washington, DC: The American Society of International Law, 2017).

Bergsmo, M. and V. Tochilovsky, Measures Available to the International Criminal Court to Reduce the Length of Proceedings, in Bergsmo, M., Rackwitz, K., and Tianying, S., *Historical Origins of International Criminal Law*. (Brussels: Torkel Opsahl Academic EPublisher, vol. 5, 2017): p. 651–593.

Birdsall, A. and A.F. Lang Jr., The International Criminal Court and Global Constitutionalism, in Lang Jr., A.F., and Wiener, A., *Handbook on Global Constitutionalism*. (Cheltenham, UK: Edward Elgar Publishing, 2017): p. 383–394.

Bower, A., States Parties and the International Criminal Court, in *Norms Without the Great Powers: International Law and Changing Social Standards in World Politics*. (Oxford: Oxford University Press, 2017).

Burneo Labrín, J., El Estatuto de Roma de la Corte Penal Internacional (1998), in *Derecho Penal Internacional: genealogía de los crímenes internacionales más graves*. (Lima: Pontificia Universidad Católica del Perú, Fondo Editorial, 2017). 368 p.

Carey, F. and Mitchel, S., *Understanding International Law through Moot Courts: Genocide, Torture, Habeas Corpus, Chemical Weapons, and the Responsibility to Protect*. (Maryland: Lexington Books, 2017). 386 p.

Cerda Dueñas, C., Incidentes y riesgos de involución en la Corte Penal Internacional. *Revista Criminalidad*, vol. 59, iss. 2 (2017): p. 125–138.

Chapman, T. and Chaudoin, S., Public Reactions to International Legal Institutions: the ICC in a Developing Democracy [Conference Paper]. (Madison, Wisconsin: The Political Economy of International Organization, 2017).

Chazal, N., The International Criminal Court, Human Rights and Intervention Narratives, in Weber, L., Fishwick, E., Marmo, M., *The Routledge International Handbook of Criminology and Human Rights* (London; New York; Routledge, Taylor & Francis Group, 2017). 617 p.

Coco, A. and M.E. Cross. The ICC on the Yellow Brick Road. Journal of International Criminal Justice, vol. 15, iss. 3 (2017): p. 593–596.

Cotte, B., La Cour pénale internationale. L'expérience d'un magistrat français, *La Revue des droits de l'homme*, vol. 11 (2017): p. 1–15.

Cour pénale internationale, *Enquêtes financières et recouvrement des avoirs*. (The Hague: International Criminal Court, 2017).

Cour pénale internationale, *Règlement de la Cour*. (The Hague: International Criminal Court, 2017).

Cour Pénale Internationale, *Rejoindre la Cour pénale internationale: Pourquoi est-ce important ?* (The Hague: International Criminal Court, 2017).

Cowell, F., Inherent Imperialism: Understanding the Legal Roots of Anti-imperialist Criticism of the International Criminal Court, *Journal of International Criminal Justice*, vol. 15, iss. 4 (2017): p. 667–687.

Davidson, C., How to Read International Criminal Law: Strict Construction and the Rome Statute of the International Criminal Court, *St. John's Law Review*, vol. 91 (2017): p. 37–103.

Demaria, T., Nouveaux développements relatifs à l'article 98-1 du Statut de Rome, *Revue québécoise de droit international*, vol. 2017 Special Edition (2017): p. 125–142.

de Hoon, M., The Future of the International Criminal Court, On Critique, Legalism and Strengthening the ICC's Legitimacy. *International Criminal Law Review*, vol. 17, iss. 4 (2017): p. 591–614.

De Silva, N., Intermediary Complexity in Regulatory Governance: the International Criminal Court's Use of NGOs in Regulating International Crimes, *Annals of the American Academy of Political and Social Science*, vol. 670, iss. 1 (2017): p. 170–188.

DePiazza, J., Denial of Fair Trial as an International Crime: Precedent for Pleading and Proving it under the Rome Statute, *Journal of International Criminal Justice*, vol. 15, iss. 2 (2017): p. 257–289.

Deprez, C., Article 21 (3) of the ICC Statute and 'Internationally Recognised Human Rights' as a Source of Mandatory Judicial Dialogue, in Lobba, P., and Mariniello, T. (eds), *Judicial Dialogue on Human Rights: The Practice of International Criminal Tribunals* (Martinus Nijhoff, 2017): p. 90–108.

Deprez, C., *La Cour pénale internationale à l'épreuve du droit de la liberté* (Bruxelles: Nemesis Anthemis, 2017). 378 p.

Dezalay, S., Weakness as Routine in the Operations of the Intentional Criminal Court, *International Criminal Law Review*, vol. 17, iss. 2 (2017): p. 281–301.

Dukalskis, A., Foreign Policy Change and the International Criminal Court, *International Politics*, vol. 54, iss. 6 (2017): p. 698–713.

Dutton, Y.M., Bridging the Legitimacy Divide: The International Criminal Court's Domestic Perception Challenge, *Columbia Journal of Transnational Law*, vol. 56, iss. 1 (2017): p. 71–122.

Eboibi, F.E., The Pre-Trial Procedures and Principles of the International Criminal Court, *Nnamdi Azikiwe Unitersity Journal of International Law and Jurisprudence*, vol. 8, iss. 1 (2017): p. 74–88.

Eiroa, P.D., El impacto de las jurisdicciones penales internacionales en la finalización de un conflicto de violencia grave y la consolidación de la paz, in Gil, A., and Maculan, E., *La influencia de las víctimas en el tratamiento jurídico de la violencia colectiva* (Madrid: Editorial Dykinson, 2017): p. 81–117.

Fernández Doblado, L. and Azuela Güitrón, M., *La Suprema Corte de Justicia de la Nación y la Corte Penal Internacional* (México: Suprema Corte de Justicia de la Nación, 2017).

Galand, A.S., A Global Public Goods Perspective on the Legitimacy of the International Criminal Court, *Loyola of Los Angeles International and Comparative Law Review*, vol. 41, iss. 2 (2017): p. 125–389.

García Ruiz, R., El papel de las ONGs en el sistema de la Corte Penal Internacional, *Anuario Español de Derecho Internacional*, vol. 33, (2017): p. 309–336.

Geoff, G. and Wouter, W., Between the Dog and the Divine: Resistance and Conventionalism in Cosmopolitanism, *Utrecht Law Review*, vol. 13, iss. 2 (2017): p. 28–36.

Guariglia, F., The ICC Appeals SectionBergsmo, M., Rackwitz, K., Song, T. (eds), *Historical Origins of International Criminal Law* (Brussels: Torkel Opsahl Academic EPublisher, vol. 5, (2017): p. 275–291.

Gyuljyan, G.G., Особенности реализации международного уголовного правосудия: международно-правовой аспект, in Усова, Е.В. (ed) *Юридическая наука: история, современность, перспектив: сборник материалов VIII Международной научно-практической конференции, посолщенной Дню российской науки и 25-летию Международного юридического института.* (Астрахань: Астраханский филиал Международного юридического института, 2017): p. 33–37.

Khamidova, M.F., Создание Международного уголовного суда и правовые вопросы ответственности за международные преступления. Вестник Санкт-Петербургского университета, *Серия 14. Право*, vol. 8, iss. 3 (2017): p. 337–348.

Hayashi, N., Comparative Law in the Work of the International Criminal Court, in Bergsmo, M., Rackwitz, K., and Song, T. (eds), *Historical Origins of International Criminal Law* (Brussels: Torkel Opsahl Academic EPublisher, vol. 5, 2017): p. 546–555.

Higgins, N., *Cultural Defences at the International Criminal Court* (London: Routledge, 2017). 132 p.

Hunter, M., All Roads Lead to the Rome Statute? *Without Prejudice*, vol. 17, iss. 3 (2017): p. 27–28.

Hurd, I., The International Criminal Court. In *International Organizations: Politics, Law, Practice* (Cambridge: Cambridge University Press, 2017): p. 226–254.

Ingadóttir, T., The Implementation of the Rome Statute of the International Criminal Court in the Nordic Countries: A New Comprehensive Criminalization of Serious Crimes, in Kjeldgaard-Pedersen, A. (ed), *Nordic Approaches to International Law* (Leiden: Brill, 2017): p. 115–146.

International Bar Association, *Offences against the Administration of Justice and Fair Trial Considerations before the International Criminal Court.* (London: International Bar Association, 2017).

International Criminal Court, *Financial Investigations and Recovery of Assets* (The Hague: International Criminal Court, 2017).

International Criminal Court, *Joining the International Criminal Court: Why Does it Matter? / International Criminal Court.* (The Hague: International Criminal Court, 2017).

International Criminal Court, *Regulations of the Court* (The Hague: International Criminal Court, 2017).

Keith, C., Prosecutorial Policy, Strategy and External Relations, in Bergsmo, M., Rackwitz, K., and Song, T. (eds), *Historical Origins of International Criminal Law,* (Brussels: Torkel Opsahl Academic EPublisher, vol. 5, 2017): p. 293–372.

Kenny, C., Prosecuting Crimes of International Concern: Islamic State at the ICC? *Utrecht Journal of International and European Law,* vol. 33, iss. 84 (2017): p. 120–145.

Klamberg, M., *Commentary on the Law of the International Criminal Court,* (Brussels: Torkel Opsahl Academic Epublisher, 2017). 775 p.

Köchler, H., Justice and Realpolitik: The Predicament of the International Criminal Court, *Chinese Journal of International Law,* vol. 16, iss. 1 (2017): p. 1–9.

Kovács, P., Les mesures conservatoires dans la pratique de la Cour internationale de Justice et de la Cour pénale internationale, *Revue générale de droit international public: droit des gens histoire diplomatique, droit pénal, droit fiscal, droit administratif,* vol. 121, iss. 3 (2017): p. 575–596.

—, Références à la jurisprudence de la Cour européenne des droits de l'homme et de la Cour interaméricaine des droits de l'homme dans la pratique de la Cour pénale internationale, in "Bidault, M., *et al. Reciprocité et universalité: sources et régimes du droit international des droits de l'homme: Mélanges en l'honneur du Professeur Emmanuel Decaux.* (Paris: Éditions Pedone, 2017): p. 245–262.

Lafontaine, F., Regards critiques de jeunes chercheurs sur certains des grands enjeux de la justice internationale pénale, *Revue québécoise de droit international,* vol. 2017, Special Edition (2017): p. 1–8.

Leonard, E.K., *The Onset of Global Governance: International Relations Theory and the International Criminal Court* (London: Routledge, 2017). 241 p.

Li, G., 浅谈联合国与国际刑事法院的关系, ("An Introduction to the Relationship between the United Nations and the International Criminal Court"), *Legality Vision,* iss. 18 (2017): p. 133–134.

Lingsma, T., *All Rise: The High Ambitions of the International Criminal Court and the Harsh Reality* (Utrecht, the Netherlands: Ipso Facto, 2017). 448 p.

Lohne, K., Claiming Authority In the Name of the Other: Human Rights NGOs and the ICC, in Hayashi, N. and Bailliet, C. (eds), *The Legitimacy of International Criminal Tribunals*. (Cambridge: Cambridge University Press, 2017): p. 449–472.

Mariniello, T., The Impact of International Commissions of Inquiry on the Proceedings before the International Criminal Court, in Henderson, C., (then continues with *Commissions of Inquiry*) *Commissions of Inquiry—Problems and Prospects*. (Portland: Hart Publishing, 2017): p. 171–196.

Margariti, S., State Sovereignty, Cosmopolitanism and the International Criminal Court, in *Defining International Terrorism: Between State Sovereignty and Cosmopolitanism*. (The Hague: Asser Press; Berlin: Springer, 2017): p. 27–61.

Matus Acuña, J.P., El mecanismo de cambio de la teoría del delito en el derecho penal internacional: La jurisprudencia de la Corte Penal Internacional, in *Estudios sobre derecho penal internacional: su aplicación e implementación en el derecho nacional*. (Santiago de Chile: Ediciones Jurídicas Olejnik, 2017): p. 84–125.

Matus Acuña, J.P., El tratamiento del error en el Estatuto de Roma y sus efectos en el ordenamiento nacional, in *Estudios sobre derecho penal internacional: su aplicación e implementación en el derecho nacional*. (Santiago de Chile: Ediciones Jurídicas Olejnik, 2017): p. 143–167.

Matus Roa, K., Algunas consideraciones en torno a la Corte Penal Internacional, *Encuentro*, vol. 57, (2017): p. 134–141.

McCormack, T., Who's Afraid of the International Criminal Court?, in Gaita, R. and Simpson, G.J. (eds), *Who's Afraid of International Law?* (Clayton, Victoria: Monash University Publishing, 2017): p. 43–76.

McManus, P., Enemy of Mankind or Just No Powerful Friends Left? Insights from International Relations about the Efficacy of the ICC, *International Criminal Law Review*, vol. 17, iss. 2 (2017): p. 302–324.

Mendeloff, D., Punish or Persuade? The Compellence Logic of International Criminal Court Intervention in Cases of Ongoing Civilian Violence, *International Studies Review*, vol. 20, iss. 3 (2018; Published December 2017): p. 395–421.

Mistry, H., The Significance of Institutional Culture in Enhancing the Validity of International Criminal Tribunals, *International Criminal Law Review*, vol. 17, iss. 4: p. 703–727.

O'Keefe, R., The International Criminal Court, in *International Criminal Law* (Oxford, UK: Oxford University Press, 2017) p. 529–584.

Olásolo, H., The Triggering Procedure as an Autonomous Procedure in the International Criminal Court Criminal Justice System: Subject, Parties and ProceedingsBergsmo, M., Rackwitz, K. and Song, T. (eds), *Historical Origins of International Criminal Law*. (Brussels: Torkel Opsahl Academic EPublisher, vol. 5, 2017): p. 423–486.

Pechegin, D.A., *Состязательная и розыскная модели судопроизводства в Международном уголовном суде* (Москва: Юрлитинформ, 2017).

Pellet, A., Nouveau regard sur les sources du droit applicable par la Cour pénale internationale Stahn, C., van den Herik, L and Schrijver, N., *International Law and the Protection of Humanity: Essays in Honor of Flavia Lattanzi*, (Leiden, The Netherlands: Brill Nijhoff, 2017): p. 453–487.

Pérez-León Acevedo, J.P., The Close Relationship between Serious Human Rights Violations and Crimes against Humanity: International Criminalization of Serious Abuses, *Anuario Mexicano De Derecho Internacional*, vol. 17 (2017): p. 145–186.

Pezeshki, A. and Asadzadeh, M., A Survey on the Position of the Principle of Proportionality in the International Criminal Court, *International Journal Series in Multidisciplinary Research*, vol. 1, iss. 1 (2017): p. 12–26.

Politi, M., *The Rome Statute of the International Criminal Court: A Challenge to Impunity.* (London: Routledge, 2017). 340 p.

Popalzai, G. and Thobani, H., The Complexities of the Gravity Threshold in the International Criminal Court: A Practical Necessity or an Insidious Pitfall? *Max Planck Yearbook of United Nations Law Online*, vol. 20, iss. 1 (2017): p. 150–169.

Prorok, A.K., The (in)compatibility of Peace and Justice? The International Criminal Court and Civil Conflict Termination, *International organization*, vol. 71, iss. 2 (2017): p. 213–243.

Ramsden, M. and Hamilton, T., Uniting Against Impunity: The UN General Assembly as a Catalyst for Action at the ICC, *International and Comparative Law Quarterly*, vol. 66, iss. 4 (2017): p. 893–921.

Ransdell, J., Power of the Purse: A Macro-Survey of Recent Financing at International Criminal Courts and Tribunals with Special Emphasis on the International Criminal Court, *International Judicial Monitor*, Summer (2017).

Rastan, R., What is 'Substantially the Same Conduct'? *Journal of International Criminal Justice*, vol. 15, iss. 1 (2017): p. 1–29.

Rodríguez, B., Las sanciones selectivas del Consejo de Seguridad y la Corte Penal Internacional, in Cuadrado, J., El nuevo entorno de seguridad de Europa (Madrid: Instituto Universitario General Gutiérrez Mellado, 2017): p. 273–292.

Royer, C., International Criminal Justice Between Scylla and Charybdis-the 'Peace Versus Justice' Dilemma Analysed through the Lenses of Judith Shklar's and Hannah Arendt's Legal and Political Theories, *Human Rights Review*, vol. 18, iss. 4 (2017): p. 395–416.

Rudolph, C., *Power and Principle: The Politics of International Criminal Courts* (Ithaca: Cornell University Press, 2017). 232 p.

Sadushaj, M. *et al.*, Interpretation and Application of Article 98 of the Rome Statute, *Academic Journal of Interdisciplinary Studies*, vol. 6, iss. 1 (2017): p. 141–147.

Salcedo, A. and Garrocho, M., Imprudencia y derecho penal internacional: algunas consideraciones sobre su previsión en el Estatuto de la Corte Penal Internacional, *Revista Electrónica de Ciencia Penal y Criminología*, vol. 19 (2017): p. 1–27.

Sandoval Mesa, J., Formas de autoría en la persecución de crímenes internacionales, *Prolegómenos: Derechos y valores*, vol. 40 (2017): p. 11–26.

Schabas, W., An *Introduction to the International Criminal Court* (Cambridge: Cambridge University Press, 2017). 612 p.

Scheipers, S., *Negotiating Sovereignty and Human Rights: International Society and the International Criminal Court* (Manchester, UK: Manchester University Press, 2017). 176 p.

Schense, J. and Carter, L., Assessing Deterrence and the Implications for the International Criminal Court Schense, J. and Carter, L. (eds), *Two Steps Forward, One Step Back: The Deterrent Effect of International Criminal Tribunals*. (Brussels: Torkel Opsahl Academic EPublisher, 2017): p. 13–59.

Schrag, M. Goals of the International Criminal Tribunal for the Former Yugoslavia and International Criminal Court, in Bergsmo, M., Rackwitz, K., and Song, T., *Historical Origins of International Criminal Law* (Brussels: Torkel Opsahl Academic EPublisher, vol. 5, 2017): p. 392–397.

Schwöbel-Patel, C., Commissions of Inquiry: Courting International Criminal Courts and Tribunals Henderson, C. (ed), Commissions of Inquiry—Problems and Prospects (Oxford; Portland, Oregon: Hart Publishing, 2017) p. 145–170.

Simbeye, Y., *Immunity and International Criminal Law* (London: Taylor and Francis Ltd.; Routledge, 2017). 184 p.

Stepanchenko, R.F. and Sito-Obong, U., Роль Международного уголовного суда в защите прав человека: общетеоретические аспекты, *Современные тенденции развития науки и технологий*, iss. 3–7 (2017): p. 131–133.

Stolk, S., Imagining Scenes of Mass Atrocity from Afar: Maps and Landscapes at the International Criminal Court, *London Review of International Law*, vol. 5, iss. 3 (2017): p. 425–451.

Stover, E., Peskin, V., and Koenig, A., International Criminal Court: At the Mercy of States, in *Hiding in Plain Sight: The Pursuit of War Criminals from Nuremberg to the War on Terror* (Oakland, California: University of California Press, 2017) p. 279–332.

Sullo, P., The International Criminal Court Reparation System: Punishment, Retaliation, Restoration, in Turner, B., and Schlee, G., *On Retaliation: Towards an Interdisciplinary Understanding of a Basic Human Condition*. (New York: Berghahn Books, 2017) p. 257–272.

Tan, J., Where next for the ICC? *Socialist Lawyer*, iss. 76 (2017): p. 6–7.

Tarāwinah, M. Al-mahkamah al-jinaiyah al-duwaliyah: al-tandhim—usul al-muhakamah al-ithbat. In Huqūq al-insān bayna al-nass wa-al-tatbīq. (ʻAmmān: ʻAmmān: Markaz ʻAmmān li-Dirāsāt Huqūq al-Insān, 2017), p. 153–163.

Teles, P.G., The ICC at the Centre of an International Criminal Justice System: Current Challenges, *Janus.Net: E-Journal of International Relations*, vol. 8, iss. 1 (2017): p. 61–73.

Valeev, A.A. and Konovalova, E.A., Статут Международного уголовного суда. Роль и место информационных технологий в современной науке: сборник статей Международной научно-практической конференции 28 декабря 2017 г., vol. 4, (Уфа: Омега Сайнс, 2017): p. 46–49.

Van Regemorter, M., *The International Criminal Court and the Right to Interim Release* (Bruxelles: Bruylant, 2017). 256 p.

Vega, S.D. and A. Linnarsson. La competencia de la Corte Penal Internacional sobre desapariciones forzadas, *Foro Jurídico*, vol. 4 (2017): p. 173–177.

Wallace, D., International Criminal Court (ICC), in Silander, D., Wallace and Janzekovic, J., *International Organizations and the Rise of ISIL: Global Responses to Human Security Threats* (Abingdon, Oxon; New York, NY: Routledge, 2017): p. 121–136.

Werle, G. *et al.*, Consolidación: El Estatuto de Roma y el establecimiento de la Corte Penal Internacional, in *Tratado de derecho penal internacional* (Valencia: Tirant lo Blanch, 2017): p. 62–78.

Werle, G. *et al.*, Persecución de crímenes contra el derecho internacional por tribunales internacionales e "internacionalizados", in *Tratado de derecho penal internacional* (Valencia: Tirant lo Blanch, 2017): p. 184–213.

Woolaver, H. and Palmer, E., Challenges to the Independence of the International Criminal Court from the Assembly of States Parties, *Journal of International Criminal Justice*, vol. 15, iss. 4 (2017): p. 641–665.

7. International Fund for Agricultural Development

Phillips, L.M., Policy Engagement and Civil Society: The Case of IFAD, in Marchetti, R. (ed), *Partnerships in International Policy-Making: Civil Society and Public Institutions in European and Global Affairs* (London: Palgrave Macmillan, 2017): p. 89–105.

8. International Labour Organization

Adrien-Kirby, A., *Migrant women workers and overt migration policies in Nepal: a law and policy baseline study* (Geneva: ILO, 2017). 22 p.

Alix, N., *Migrant domestic and garment workers in Jordan: A baseline analysis of trafficking in persons and related laws and policies* (Geneva: ILO, 2017). 58 p.

Bodeau-Livinec, P., Thévenot-Werner, AM., Activité et jurisprudence des Tribunaux administratifs des Nations Unies et de l'OIT (2016), *Annuaire français de droit international;* vol. 62 (2016): p. 303–345, 2017.

Castro Méndez, M., *La reforma procesal laboral de Costa Rica: guide pour les travailleurs et les travailleuses*, 1st ed. (San José, Costa Rica: OIT, 2017). 90 p.

De Stefano, V., Non-Standard Work and Limits on Freedom of Association: A Human Rights-Based Approach, *Industrial Law Journal*, vol. 46, iss. 2 (2017): p. 185–207.

Dennis, M.J., The ILO Convention on the Worst Forms of Child Labor, in Stark, B. (ed), *Human Rights and Children* (Cheltenham, UK; Northampton, MA, USA: Edward Elgar Publishing, 2017): p. 469–474.

Dražen, P. (ed), *Une Contribution de 90 ans du Tribunal Administratif de l'Organisation Internationale du Travail à la création d'un droit de la fonction publique internationale = 90 Years of Contribution of the Administrative Tribunal of the International Labour Organization to the Creation of International Civil Service Law* (Geneva: ILO Administrative Tribunal, 2017). 215 p.

Errico, S., *The rights of indigenous peoples in Asia: human rights-based overview of national legal and policy frameworks against the backdrop of country strategies for development and poverty reduction* (Geneva: ILO, 2017). 87 p.

Fenwick, C.F., Goethem, V. van, and International Labour Office, *Regulating for equitable and job-rich growth* (Cheltenham, UK; Geneva: Edward Elgar Publishing; ILO, 2017). 244 p.

Freyens, B., and Verkerke, J.H., *Mapping employment dismissal law: a leximetric investigation of EPL stringency and regulatory style* (Geneva: ILO, 2017). 48 p.

Galli, R., *The role of investment incentives for structural transformation: a comparative analysis of investment incentives legislations in Sub-Saharan African, South-Asian and South-East Asian developing countries* (Geneva: ILO, 2017). 65 p.

Giuseppe, M.M., *El trabajo forzoso en Argentina: avances y desafíos*, 1st ed. (Buenos Aires: OIT, 2018). 99 p.

Hanania L.R., The Social Dimension of Sustainable Development in EU Trade Agreements: Strengthening International Labour Standards, *German Yearbook of International Law*, vol. 59 (2016): p. 435–465.

ILO Global Employment Injury Programme, International Labour Office. Enterprises Department and ILO Country Office for the United Republic of Tanzania, Kenya: Technical Memorandum, *Report to the Government: Legal Governance and Compliance Issues Concerning the Development of a Comprehensive Work Injury Compensation Legislation in Kenya* (Geneva: ILO, 2017). 12 p.

International Labour Conference, *Acabar con la violencia y el acoso contra las mujeres y los hombres en el mundo del trabajo*, 1st ed. (Ginebra: OIT, 2017). 147 p.

International Labour Conference, *Empleo y trabajo decente para la paz y la resiliencia: revisión de la Recomendación sobre la organización del empleo (transición de la guerra a la paz), 1944 (núm. 71)*, 1st ed. (Ginebra: OIT, 2017). 19 p.

International Labour Conference, *Employment and decent work for peace and resilience: revision of the Employment* (Transition from War to Peace) Recommendation, 1944 (No. 71), 1st ed. (Geneva: ILO, 2017). 44 p.

International Labour Conference, *Ending violence and harassment against women and men in the world of work*, 1st ed. (Geneva: ILO, 2017d). 23 p.

International Labour Conference, *Mettre fin à la violence et au harcèlement contre les femmes et les hommes dans le monde du travail*, 1st ed. (Genève: BIT, 2017e). 147 p.

International Labour Office, Fundamental Principles and Rights at Work Branch and International Labour Office Labour, Migration Branch, *Principes généraux et directives opérationnelles concernant le recrutement équitable* (Genève: BIT, 2017a). 37 p.

International Labour Office, Fundamental Principles and Rights at Work Branch and International Labour Office, Labour Migration Branch, *Principios generales y directrices para la contratación equitativa* (Ginebra: OIT, 2017). 37 p.

International Labour Office, International Labour Standards Department, and International Labour Office. *Employment Policy Department, Guide to international labour standards and rights at work concerning young people* (Geneva: ILO, 2017). 107 p.

International Labour Office, Labour Administration, Labour Inspection and Occupational Safety and Health Branch, *ILO approach to strategic compliance planning for labour inspectorates* (Geneva: ILO, 2017). 12 p.

International Labour Office, Labour Administration, Labour Inspection and Occupational Safety and Health Branch, and International Labour Office, Fundamental Principles and Rights at Work Branch, *Optimizing compliance with child labour legislation through strategic collaboration of labour inspection and child labour monitoring programmes* (Geneva: ILO, 2017). 8 p.

International Labour Organization, *Implementation of international labour standards for domestic workers* (Geneva: ILO, 2017). 5 p.

International Labour Organization, and ILO Country Office for Ethiopia, Djibouti, Somalia, Sudan and South Sudan, *The Ethiopian overseas employment proclamation No. 923/2016: a comprehensive analysis* (Addis Ababa: ILO, 2017). 53 p.

International Labour Organization, Research Department, *Réglementer le recours des entreprises au travail temporaire* (Genève: BIT, 2017). 4 p.

International Labour Organization, Research Department, *Regulating the use of temporary contracts by enterprises* (Geneva: ILO, 2017). 4 p.

Judd, J., Checkley, J.C., Land-Kazlauskas, C., Nogami, N., and ILO Liaison Officer for Myanmar, *ILO guide to Myanmar labour law* (Yangon: ILO, 2017). 53 p.

Kagan, S., Byrne, M., and Leighton, M., Organizational perspective from the International Labour Organization, in Mayer, B., and Crépeau, F. (eds), *Research Handbook on Climate Change, Migration and the Law* (Cheltenham, UK; Northampton, MA, USA: Edward Elgar Publishing, 2017): p. 288–315.

Kunz-Hallstein, H.P., Views from Practice: Paralysing the Functioning of International Organisations' Internal Appeals Boards, *International Organizations Law Review*, vol. 14 (2017): p. 196–203.

McDougall, P., Keynes, Sen, and Hayek: Competing Approaches to International Labor Law in the ILO and the WTO, 1994–2008, *Northwestern University Journal of International Human Rights*, vol. 15 (2017): p. 32–90.

Nunes, J.P., Christian, A., Barbero, J., and International Labour Office. Labour Administration Labour Inspection and Occupational Safety and Health Branch, *Le contrôle des chantiers de construction par l'inspection du travail: guide à l'intention des inspecteurs du travail, 1ère éd.* (Genève: BIT, 2017). 83 p.

Nunes, J.P.P., Christian, A., Barbero Marcos, J., and International Labour Office. Labour Administration, Labour Inspection and Occupational Safety and Health Branch, *Conducting labour inspections on construction: a guide for labour inspectors* (Geneva: ILO, 2017). 79 p.

Ozkan, U.R., Translating from multiple sources: labour legislation reform in Turkey, *International Labour Review*, vol. 156, iss. 2 (2017): p. 287–302.

Reynaud, E., *The International Labour Organization and the living wage: a historical perspective* (Geneva: ILO, 2017). 37 p.

Rombouts, S.J., The Evolution of Indigenous Peoples' Consultation Rights under the ILO and U.N. Rights: A Comparative Assessment of Participation, Consultation, and Consent Norms Incorporated in ILO Convention No. 169 and the U.N. Declaration on the Rights of Indigenous Peoples and their Application by the Inter-American Court of Human Rights in the Saramaka and Sarayaku Judgments, *Stanford Journal of International Law*, vol. 53, iss. 2 (2017): p. 169–224.

Servais, J.-M., *International Labour Law*, 5th ed. (Alphen aan den Rijn: Kluwer Law International, 2017). 398 p.

Stumbitz, B., Kyei, A., Lewis, S., and Lyon, F., *Maternity protection and workers with family responsibilities in the formal and informal economy of Ghana: practices, gaps and measures for improvement* (Geneva: ILO, 2017). 109 p.

Van Haasteren, F.C.A., *Decent Flexibility: The Impact of ILO Convention 181 and the Regulation on Temporary Agency Work* (Den Haag: Kluwer Law International, 2017). 544 p.

Van Panhuys, C., Kazi Aoul, S., and Binette, G., *Migrant access to social protection under Bilateral Labour Agreements: a review of 120 countries and nine bilateral arrangements* (Geneva: ILO, 2017). 81 p.

9. International Maritime Organization

Basaran, I., The Future of Arctic Navigation: Cooperation between the International Maritime Organization and Arctic Council, *Journal of Maritime Law and Commerce*, vol. 48 (2017): p. 35 –64.

Beckman, R., and Sun, Z., The Relationship between UNCLOS and IMO Instruments, *Asia-Pacific Journal of Ocean Law and Policy*, vol. 2 (2017): p. 201–246.

Clarenc Bicudo, N., L'OMI et l'air impur du large: La vie juridique des règles relatives à la pollution atmosphérique des navires, *Revue générale de droit international public*, vol. 121 (2017): p. 361–392.

Gambardella, S., La stratégie de réduction des émissions maritimes internationales de gaz à effet de serre après l'accord de Paris. Réflexions sur la pertinence de l'Organisation maritime internationale en tant qu'échelle d'action, *Revue juridique de l'environnement*, vol. 42 (2017): p. 201–213.

Shi, Y., *Climate Change and International Shipping: The Regulatory Framework for the Reduction of Greenhouse Gas Emissions* (Leiden: Brill Nijhoff, 2017). 498 p.

10. International Monetary Fund

Bal Gündüz, Y., and Crystallin, M., Do IMF Programs Catalyze Donor Assistance to Low-Income Countries? *Review of International Organizations*, vol. 13 (2017): p. 359–393.

Casper, B.A., IMF Programs and the Risk of a Coup d'État, *The Journal of Conflict Resolution*, vol. 61 (2017): p. 964–996.

Feibelman, A., Law in the Global Order: The IMF and Financial Regulation, *New York University Journal of International Law and Politics*, vol. 49 (2017): p. 687–745.

Güven, A.B., Defending Supremacy: How the IMF and the World Bank Navigate the Challenge of Rising Powers, *International Affairs*, vol. 93 (2017): p. 1149–1166.

Martin, A., and Mercurio, B., The IMF Mandate on Capital Controls: Legal Analysis of the Article IV Byroad and of the Institutional View of 2012, *Arizona Journal of International and Comparative Law*, vol. 34 (2017): p. 529–556.

Murillo López, S., Legal Legitimacy of Tax Recommendations Delivered by the IMF in the Context of 'Article IV Consultations, *Erasmus Law Review*, vol. 10 (2017): p. 106–118.

Reinold, T., The Path of Least Resistance: Mainstreaming "Social Issues" in the International Monetary Fund, *Global Society: Journal of Interdisciplinary International Relations*, vol. 31 (2017): p. 392–416.

de Stefano, C., Reforming the Governance of International Financial Law in the Era of Post-Globalization, *Journal of International Economic Law*, vol. 20 (2017): p. 509–533.

Tsikata, D.A., The International Public Corporation: A Concept More Relevant than Ever? *International Organizations Law Review*, vol. 14 (2017): p. 120–153.

11. Organisation for the Prohibition of Chemical Weapons

Kelle, A., Power in the Chemical Weapons Prohibition Regime and the Organisation for the Prohibition of Chemical Weapons, *International Politics*, vol. 55 (2017): p. 403–420.

Walker, P.F., A Century of Chemical Warfare: Building a World Free of Chemical Weapons, in Friedrich, B., *et al.* (eds), *One Hundred Years of Chemical Warfare: Research, Deployment, Consequences* (Cham: Springer, 2017): p. 379–399.

12. Preparatory Commission for the Comprehensive Nuclear-Test-Ban Treaty Organization

Fukui, Y., CTBT: Legal Questions Arising from its Non–Entry into Force Revisited, *Journal of Conflict & Security Law*, vol. 22 (2017): p. 183–200.

13. United Nations Educational, Scientific and Cultural Organization

Gagliani, G., Regards croisés sur les conventions UNESCO et le droit international de l'économie: entre interactions pratiques et gouvernance mondiale, in Monti, A., Carreau, D., and Dordi, C. (eds), *Éthique globale, bonne gouvernance et droit international économique.* (Turin: G. Giappichelli, 2017): p. 57–82.

Lempereur, F., Le rôle de l'UNESCO et de sa Convention pour la sauvegarde du PCI, in Lempereur, F., and Khaznadar, C. (eds), *Le patrimoine culturel immatériel* (Paris: Harmattan, 2017): p. 231–245.

Papathanassiou, A., Protecting Cultural Property in the Event of Armed Conflict: New Challenges and Recent Developments in the Context of UNESCO, *Art, Antiquity and Law*, vol. 22 (2017): p. 257–272.

Seatzu, F., and Lai, A., Mission Impossible? Revitalising the Role of UNESCO as a Human Rights Organization, *Human Rights & International Legal Discourse*, vol. 11 (2017): p. 222–264.

14. Universal Postal Union

Caflisch, L., Statut juridique en Suisse de l'Union postale universelle, *La pratique suisse en matière de droit international public*, vol. 27 (2017): p. 591–592.

—, Immunité de juridiction des organisations intergouvernementales. Notification de documents de caractère judiciaire à des organisations internationales établies en Suisse, *La pratique suisse en matière de droit international public*, vol. 27 (2017): p. 592–594.

15. World Bank Group

Borson, F., Reforms Under the World Bank Procurement and the Policy Implications for Developing Countries, *European Procurement & Public Private Partnership Law Review*, vol. 12 (2017): p. 146–154.

Carvajal Martínez, J.E. and Guzmán Rincón, A.M., Economía de mercado y democracia: elementos para una crítica al discurso del desarrollo promovido por las Instituciones Financieras Internacionales, *Justicia*, vol. 22 (2017): p. 116–134.

Dorlig, U., Legality of the World Bank's Informal Decisions to Expand into the Tax Field, and Implications of these Decisions for its Legitimacy, *Erasmus Law Review*, vol. 2017 (2017): p. 119–133.

Güven, A.B., The World Bank and Emerging Powers: Beyond the Multipolarity-Multilateralism Conundrum, *New Political Economy*, vol. 22 (2017): p. 496–520.

McLean, E.V., The Politics of Contract Allocation in the World Bank, *Review of International Organizations*, vol. 12 (2017): p. 255–279.

Passoni, C., Rosenbaum, A., and Vermuni, E., Empowering the Inspection Panel: The Impact of the World Bank's New Environmental and Social Safeguards, *New York University Journal of International Law & Politics*, vol. 49 (2017): p. 921–958.

Qureshi, W.A., The Indus Waters Treaty and the Role of World Bank as Mediator, *Willamette Journal of International Law & Dispute Resolution*, vol. 24 (2017): p. 211–232.

Reinsberg, B., Organizational Reform and the Rise of Trust Funds: Lessons from the World Bank, *Review of International Organizations*, vol. 12 (2017): p. 199–226.

Sciso, E., *Accountability, Transparency and Democracy in the Functioning of Bretton Woods Institutions* (Cham: Springer, 2017). 262 p.

Tang, Y.S., The International Politics of Legal Reforms: Hard Bilateralism, Soft Multilateralism and the World Bank's "Doing Business" Indicators, *Revista Brasileira de Política Internacional*, vol. 60 (2017): p. 1–17.

Van Den Meerssche, D., The Evolving Mandate of the World Bank: How Constitutional Hermeneutics Shaped the Concept and Practice of Rule of Law Reform, *Law and Development Review*, vol. 10 (2017): p. 89–118.

Vazquez, A., Is the BRICS New Development Bank a Fledgling Alternative to the World Bank? *BRICS Law Journal*, vol. 4 (2017): p. 6–34.

16. World Health Organization

Acharya. B., Ekstrand. M., Rimal. P., Ali, M., Swar, S., Srinivasan. K., Mohan, V., Untzer. J. & Chwastiak. L., "Collaborative Care for Mental Health in Low- and Middle-Income Countries: A WHO Health Systems Framework Assessment of Three Programs", *Psychiatric Services*, vol. 68. no. 9 (2017): p. 870–872.

Alirol. E., Kuesel, A., Guraiib, M., dela Fuente-Nunez, Y., Saxena, A. & Gomes, M., "Ethics review of studies during public health emergencies—the experience of the WHO ethic review committee during the Ebola virus disease epidemic", *BMC Medical Ethics*, vol. 18, no. 1 (2017): p. 43.

Amann, M., Purohit, P., Bhanarkar, A.D., Bertok, I., Borken-Kleefeld, J., Cofala, J., Heyes, C., Kiesewetter, G., Klimont, Z., Liu. J., Majumdar, D., Nguyen, B., Rafaj, P., Rao, P.S., Sander, R., Schopp, W., Srivastava, A. & Vardhan, B.H., "Managing future air quality in megacities: A case study for Delhi", *Atmospheric Environment*, vol. 161 (2017): p. 99–111.

Clinton, C., and Sridhar, D.L., *Governing Global Health: Who Runs the World and Why?* (New York, NY: Oxford University Press, 2017). 282 p.

Cooper. R., "Commentary on WHO Gate Initiative", *Journal of Spinal Cord Medicine*, vol. 40, no. 1 (2017): p. 2–4.

Cordes, K., Cookson, S., Boyd, A., Hardy, C., Malik, M., Mala, P., El Tahir. K., Everard, M., Jasiem, M. & Husain, F., "Real-Time Surveillance in Emergencies Using the Early Warning Alert and Response Network", *Emerging Infectious Diseases*, vol. 23, no. 13 (2017): p. S131-S137.

Deluca, L., "United Nations: Online data repositories and resources" *College & Research Library News*, Vol. 78 (2017): p. 41–45. Retrievable at http://crln.acrl.org/content/78/1/41.full.

Ellis, H. & Schoenberger, E., "On the Identification of Associations between Five World Health Organization Water, Sanitation and Hygiene Phenotypes and Six Predictors in Low and Middle-Income Countries", *Plos One*. vol. 12, no. 1: e0170451 (2017), p. 1–19.

Frau, R., Combining the WHO's International Health Regulations (2005) with the UN Security Council's Powers: Does it make Sense for Health Governance?, in Vierck, L., Villarreal, P., and Weilert, A.K. (eds), *Governance of Disease Outbreaks: International Health Law: Lessons from the Ebola Crisis and Beyond* (Baden-Baden: Nomos, 2017): p. 327–348.

Friedlich, M.J., "Global Health", *JAMA, The Journal of the American Medical Association*, vol. 317, no. 19 (2017): p. 1941.

Giné-Garriga, R., Flores-Baquero, O., Jiménez-Fdez de Palencia, A. & Perez-Foguet, A., "Monitoring sanitation and hygiene in the 2030 Agenda for Sustainable Development: A review through the lens of human rights", *Science of the Total Environment*, vol. 580 (2017): p. 1108–1119.

Gisslen, M., Svedhem, V., Lindborg, L., Flamholc, L., Norrgren. H., Wendahl, S., Axelsson. M. & Sonnerborg, A., "Sweden, the first country to achieve the Joint United Nations Programme on HIV/AIDS (UNAIDS) World Health Organization (WHO) 90–90–90 continuum of HIV care targets", *HIV Medicine*, vol. 18, no. 4 (2017): p. 305–307.

Gostin. L.O., Abou-Taleb. H., Roache, S.A. & Alwan, A., "Legal priorities for prevention of non-communicable diseases: innovations from WHO's Eastern Mediterranean region", *Public Health*, vol. 144 (2016; 2017): p. 4–12.

Gostin, L., Magnusson, R., Krech, R., Patterson, D., Solomon, S., Walton, D., Burci, G., O'Cathaoir, G., Roache, S. & Kieny, M., "Advancing the Right to Health—The Vital Role of Law", *American Journal of Public Health*, vol. 107, no. 11 (2017): p. 1755–1756.

Hanrieder, T., and Zurn, M., Reactive Sequences in Global Health Governance, in Fioretos, O. (ed), *International Politics and Institutions in Time* (Oxford: Oxford University Press, 2017): p. 93–116.

Horton, R., "Offline: The tasks facing Dr. Tedro", *The Lancet*, vol. 390, no. 10112 (2017): p. 2538.

Kabra, R., Ali, M. & Kiarie, J., "Design and initial implementation of the WHO FP umbrella project to strengthen contraceptive services in the sub-Saharan Africa", *Reproductive Health*, vol. 14, no. 1 (2017): p. 74.

Kerr, Y., Mailhot, M., Williams, A., Swezy, V., Quick, L., Tangermann, R., Ward. K., Benke, A., Callaghan, A., Clark, K., Emery, B., Nix, J., Aydlotte. E., Newman, C. & Nkowane, B., "Lessons Learned and Legacy of the Stop Transmission of Polio Program", *Journal of Infectious Diseases*, vol. 216, no. suppl. 1 (2017): p. S316–S323.

Lancet, T., "Law: an underused tool to improve health and wellbeing for all", *Lancet, The*. vol. 389, no. 10067 (2017): p.331.

Lee, S.G., "Assessing impacts of the WHO FCTC on national legislations: A case study of the Republic of Korea", *Health Policy*, vol. 121, no. 6 (2017): p. 604–612.

Lydon, P., Schreiber, B., Gasca. A., Dumolard, L., Urfer, D. & Senouci, K., "Vaccine stockouts around the world: Are essential vaccines always available when needed?", *Vaccine*, vol. 35, no. 17 (2017): p. 2121–2126.

Sekalala, S., *Soft Law and Global Health Problems: Lessons from Responses to HIV/AIDS, Malaria and Tuberculosis* (Cambridge: Cambridge University Press, 2017). 312 p.

"The International Health Regulations (IHR) 10 years of global public health security", *Relevé épidémiologique hebdomadaire*, vol. 92, no. 51–52 (2017): p. 781.

"Tobacco control boosts economies", *Bulletin of World Health Organization*, vol. 95, no. 1 (2017): p. 4.

Villarreal, P., The World Health Organization's Governance Framework in Disease Outbreaks: A Legal Perspective, in Vierck, L., Villarreal, P., and Weilert, A.K. (eds), *Governance of Disease Outbreaks: International Health Law: Lessons from the Ebola Crisis and Beyond* (Baden-Baden: Nomos, 2017): p. 243–272.

17. World Intellectual Property Organization

Batanga, M., L'adhésion des États membres de l'OAPI aux traités internationaux régissant la propriété intellectuelle administrés par l'OMPI, in Edou Edou, P. (ed), *Regards sur la propriété intellectuelle en Afrique: mélanges en l'honneur de l'action du DR Paulin Edou Edou pour l'OAPI* (Paris: Juriscope, 2017): p. 131–142.

Gazzola, M., Multilingualism and the International Patent System: An Assessment of the Fairness of the Language Policy of WIPO, *Journal of Industry, Competition and Trade*, vol. 17 (2017): p. 349–369.

Robinson, D.F., Roffe, P., and Abdel-Latif, A., *Protecting Traditional Knowledge: The WIPO Intergovernmental Committee on Intellectual Property and Genetic Resources, Traditional Knowledge and Folklore* (London: Routledge, Taylor & Francis Group, 2017). 366 p.

Strandburg, K.J., Evolving Innovation Paradigms and the Global Intellectual Property Regime in Ghosh, S., and Melvin, C. (eds), *Intellectual Property and Innovation* (Cheltenham, UK: Edward Elgar Publishing, 2017): p. 218–277.

18. World Trade Organization

Adaeze, O.V., The Decision-Making Process of the WTO in Relation to Developing Countries, *Manchester Journal of International Economic Law*, vol. 14 (2017): p. 115–138.

Allee, T., Elsig, M., and Lugg, A., The Ties between the World Trade Organization and Preferential Trade Agreements: A Textual Analysis, *Journal of International Economic Law*, vol. 20 (2017): p. 333–363.

Baroncini, E., The WTO Case-Law on the Relation between the Marrakesh System and Regional Trade Agreements, in Hilpold, P. (ed), *Europa Im Umbruch*. (Baden-Baden: Nomos Verlagsgesellschaft, 2017): p. 57–76.

Daku, M., and Pelc, K.J., Who Holds Influence Over WTO Jurisprudence? *Journal of International Economic Law*, vol. 20 (2017): p. 233–255.

Elsig, M., and Hoekman, B., *Assessing the World Trade Organization: Fit for Purpose? World Trade Forum* (Cambridge: Cambridge University Press, 2017). 445 p.

García Matamoros, L.V., A.C. Restrepo Escobar, and Arévalo Ramírez, W., Procedimiento Procedimiento ante el Órgano de Solución de Diferencias de la Organización Mundial del Comercio (OMC), in García Matamoros, L.V., and Ávila Medina, D.C. (eds), *Procedimiento, litigio y representación ante tribunales internacionales* (Bogotá: Editorial Universidad del Rosario, 2017): p. 537–586.

Garcia, T., Règlement des différends juridictionnels et respect des règles procédurales fondamentales à l'OMC, *Revue de droit international et de droit comparé*, vol. 94 (2017): p. 487–503.

Gehring, M., and Genest, A., Disputes on Sustainable Development in the WTO Regime, in Cordonier Segger, M., and Weeramantry, C.G. (eds), *Sustainable Development Principles in the Decisions of International Courts and Tribunals: 1992–2012* (London: Routledge, 2017): p. 357–383.

Hahn, M., *et al.* The Jurisprudence of the World Trade Organization in 2016, *Schweizerische Zeitschrift für internationales und europäisches Recht*, vol. 27, iss. 2 (2017): p. 265–298.

Hepburn, J., The Principle of Good Governance in WTO Disputes, in Cordonier Segger, M., and Weeramantry, C.G. (eds), *Sustainable Development Principles in the Decisions of International Courts and Tribunals: 1992–2012* (London: Routledge, 2017): p. 384–397.

Keene, A., The Incorporation and Interpretation of WTO-Style Environmental Exceptions in International Investment Agreements, *The Journal of World Investment & Trade*, vol. 18 (2017): p. 62–99.

Lanyi, P.A., and Steinbach, A., Promoting Coherence between PTAs and the WTO through Systemic Integration, *Journal of International Economic Law*, vol. 20 (2017): p. 61–85.

Marceau, G., and Marquet, C., La jurisprudence de l'OMC et la recherche d'un équilibre entre développement économique et considérations non-commerciales: le cas de l'environnement, *Revue québécoise de droit international*, vol. 30 (2017): p. 119–149.

Melo Araujo, B.A., Setting the Rules of the Game: The Rise (and Fall) of Mega-Regionals, Deep Integration and the Role of the WTO, *UCLA Journal of International Law and Foreign Affairs*, vol. 21 (2017): p. 151–203.

Mitchell, A.D., Sanctions and the World Trade Organization, in Van den Herik, L. (ed), *Research Handbook on UN Sanctions and International Law* (Cheltenham, UK: Edward Elgar Publishing, 2017): p. 283–303.

Müller, W., *WTO Agreement on Subsidies and Countervailing Measures a Commentary* (Cambridge, UK; New York, NY: Cambridge University Press, 2017). 780 p.

Rosso, C., *Les mécanismes de flexibilité dans le droit de l'OMC* (Bruxelles: Bruylant, 2017). 638 p.

Shongwe, M.N., The Fragmentation of the Multilateral Trading System: The Impact of Regionalism on WTO Law, *Amsterdam Law Forum*, vol. 9 (2017): p. 3–41.

Warikandwa, T.V., and Osode, P.C., Exploring the World Trade Organisation's Trade and Environment/Public Health Jurisprudence as a Model for Incorporating a Trade-Labour Linkage into the Organisation's Multilateral Trade Regime: Should African Countries Accept a Policy Shift? *African Journal of International and Comparative Law*, vol. 25 (2017): p. 47–65.

Zekos, G.I., An Investigation of WTO Arbitration Mechanism, in International Centre for Dispute Resolution (ed), *ICDR Handbook on International Arbitration and ADR* (Huntington, NY: Juris, 2017): p. 371–391.

19. World Tourism Organization

Kala, N., *et al.*, The World Tourism Organization for Countering Terrorist Threats, *Journal of East Asia and International Law*, vol. 10 (2017): p. 549–550.

D. Other legal issues

1. Aggression

Cowell, F., and Magini, A.L., Collapsing Legitimacy: How the Crime of Aggression Could Affect the ICC's Legitimacy, *International Criminal Law Review*, vol. 17 (2017): p. 517–542.

Dannenbaum, T., Why have we Criminalized Aggressive War? *Yale Law Journal*, vol. 126 (2017): p. 1242–1319.

Hajdin, N., The Nature of Leadership in the Crime of Aggression: The ICC's New Concern? *International Criminal Law Review*, vol. 17 (2017): p. 453–566.

Kress, C., and Barriga, S. (eds), *The Crime of Aggression: A Commentary* (Cambridge: Cambridge University Press, 2017). 1,583 p.

Pietri, D.d., La agresión: ¿crimen internacional del Estado o crimen del individuo? in Campione, R., and Ruschi, F., *Guerra, derecho y seguridad en las relaciones internacionales* (Valencia: Tirant lo Blanch, 2017): p. 211–229.

Ruys, T., Justiciability, Complementarity and Immunity: Reflections on the Crime of Aggression, *Utrecht Law Review*, vol. 13 (2017): p. 18–33.

Trahan, J., From Kampala to New York—The Final Negotiations to Activate the Jurisdiction of the International Criminal Court Over the Crime of Aggression, *International Criminal Law Review*, vol. 18 (2018): p. 197–243.

2. Aviation Law

Cheng, B., and Cheng, J., *Studies in International Air Law: Selected Works of Bin Cheng* (Leiden: Brill Nijhoff, 2017). 1,219 p.

Gonçalves, V.K., Climate Change and International Civil Aviation Negotiations, *Contexto Internacional*, vol. 39 (2017): p. 443–458.

Dempsey, P.S., and Jakhu, R.S. (eds), *Routledge Handbook of Public Aviation Law* (London; New York: Routledge, 2017). 360 p.

Reuleaux, P., Tang, M., and Chong, L.C., Lightning Doesn't Strike Twice: The Tragedy and Challenges of the MH370 and MH17 Losses, *Air & Space Law*, vol. 42 (2017): p. 423–442.

3. Collective Security

Breen, C., *Economic and Social Rights and the Maintenance of International Peace and Security* (New York, NY: Routledge, 2017). 212 p.

Guillermet Fernández, C., and Fernández Puyana, D., Countering Terrorism and Violet Extremism while Promoting the Right of Peoples to Peace and Security in Africa, *Strathmore Law Journal*, vol. 3 (2017): p. 39–64.

Karim, S., and Beardsley, K., *Equal Opportunity Peacekeeping: Women, Peace, and Security in Post-Conflict States* (New York, NY: Oxford University Press, 2017). 297 p.

Koskenniemi, M., The Place of Law and the Role of Legal Advisers in Collective Security, in Zidar, A. and Gauci, J.P. (eds), *Role of Legal Advisers in International Law* (Leiden; Boston: Brill Nijhoff, 2017): p. 327–336.

Renzulli, I., Women and Peace: A Human Rights Strategy for the Women, Peace and Security Agenda, *Netherlands Quarterly of Human Rights*, vol. 35 (2017): p. 210–229.

Thakur, R.C., *The United Nations, Peace and Security: From Collective Security to the Responsibility to Protect* (Cambridge: Cambridge University Press, 2017). 444 p.

von der Schulenburg, M., *On Building Peace: Rescuing the Nation-State and Saving the United Nations* (Amsterdam: Amsterdam University Press, 2017). 282 p.

4. Commercial Arbitration

Balcerzak, F., *Investor-State Arbitration and Human Rights* (Leiden, Netherlands: Brill Nijhoff, 2017). 323 p.

Becker, M.A., and Rose, C. Investigating the Value of Site Visits in Inter-State Arbitration and Adjudication, *Journal of International Dispute Settlement*, vol. 8 (2017): p. 219–249.

Boisson de Chazournes, L., Environmental Protection and Investment Arbitration: Yin and Yang? *Anuario Colombiano de Derecho Internacional*, vol. 10 (2017): p. 371–399.

Bonnitcha, J., International Investment Arbitration in Myanmar: Bounded Rationality, But Not as We Know It, *The Journal of World Investment & Trade*, vol. 2017 (2017): p. 974–1000.

Bonnitcha, J., Poulsen, L.N.S., and Waibel, M., *The Political Economy of the Investment Treaty Regime* (Oxford: Oxford University Press, 2017). 325 p.

Bungenberg, M., and De Mestral, A, L.C., *Second Thoughts: Investor-State Arbitration between Developed Democracies* (Waterloo, Ontario: Centre for International Governance Innovation, 2017). 552 p.

Cleis, M.N., *The Independence and Impartiality of ICSID Arbitrators* (Leiden: Brill Nijhoff, 2017). 292 p.

Diel-Gligor, K., *Towards Consistency in International Investment Jurisprudence: A Preliminary Ruling System for ICSID Arbitration* (Leiden, Netherlands: Brill Nijhoff, 2017). 590 p.

Fernández de Buján, A., *La deuda histórica del arbitraje moderno* (Madrid, Spain: Dykinson, S. L, 2017). 205 p.

Fontanelli, F., and Tanzi, A., Jurisdiction and Admissibility in Investment Arbitration. A View from the Bridge at the Practice, *The Law and Practice of International Courts and Tribunals*, vol. 16 (2017): p. 3–20.

Gaillard, E., and Bermann, G.A., *Guide on the Convention on the Recognition and Enforcement of Foreign Arbitral Awards: New York, 1958* (Leiden: Brill/Nijhoff, 2017). 399 p.

Gattini, A., Jurisdiction *Ratione Temporis* in International Investment Arbitration, *The Law and Practice of International Courts and Tribunals*, vol. 16 (2017): p. 139–158.

Grisel, F., Treaty-Making between Public Authority and Private Interests: The Genealogy of the Convention on the Recognition and Enforcement of Foreign Arbitral Awards, *European Journal of International Law*, vol. 28 (2017): p. 73–87.

Hepburn, J., *Domestic Law in International Investment Arbitration* (Oxford: Oxford University Press, 2017). 320 p.

Kidane, W.L., *The Culture of International Arbitration* (New York, NY: Oxford University Press, 2017). 337 p.

Kulick, A., Investment Arbitration, Investment Treaty Interpretation, and Democracy, *Cambridge International Law Journal*, vol. 4 (2017): p. 441–460.

Langford, M., Behn, D., and Lie, R.H., The Revolving Door in International Investment Arbitration, *Journal of International Economic Law*, vol. 20 (2017): p. 301–331.

Lookofsky, J.M., *Understanding the CISG: A Compact Guide to the 1980 United Nations Convention on Contracts for the International Sale of Goods* (Alphen aan den Rijn, The Netherlands: Kluwer Law International B.V, 2017). 337 p.

McLachlan, C., Shore, L., and Weiniger, M., *International Investment Arbitration: Substantive Principles* (Oxford: Oxford University Press, 2017). 520 p.

Meshel, T., The Croatia v. Slovenia Arbitration: The Silver Lining, *The Law and Practice of International Courts and Tribunals*, vol. 16 (2017): p. 288–306.

Orawiec, B., The Public Policy Exception Under the New York Convention on the Recognition and Enforcement of Foreign Arbitral Awards (The UK Perspective), *Comparative Law Review*, vol. 21 (2017): p. 55–78.

Ostrove, M., and Emery, C., L'exécution des mesures conservatoires prononcées par les tribunaux arbitraux, *Revue générale de droit international public*, vol. 121 (2017): p. 807–835.

Rensmann, T. (ed), *Small and Medium-Sized Enterprises in International Economic Law* (Oxford: Oxford University Press, 2017). 370 p.

Stone Sweet, A., and Grisel, F., *The Evolution of International Arbitration: Judicialization, Governance, Legitimacy* (Oxford: Oxford University Press, 2017). 273 p.

Sullivan, J., and Kirsey, V., Environmental Policies: A Shield or a Sword in Investment Arbitration? *The Journal of World Investment & Trade*, vol. 2017 (2017): p. 100–130.

5. Consular Relations

Rea Falcón, M.E., Los extranjeros en Estados Unidos de América y el cumplimiento del Artículo 36 de la Convención de Viena sobre Relaciones Consulares = Foreigners in the United States of America and Compliance with Article 36 of the Vienna Convention on Consular Relations, *Revista de Derecho UNED*, iss. 20 (2017): p. 527–557.

Veneziano, S., The Right to Consular Notification: The Cultural Bridge to a Foreign National's Due Process Rights, *Georgetown Journal of International Law*, vol. 49 (2017): p. 501–551.

6. Diplomatic Protection

Arredondo, R., "Wikileaks", Assange y el futuro del asilo diplomático, *Revista española de derecho internacional*, vol. 69 (2017): p. 119–144.

7. Diplomatic Relations

Behrens, P. (ed), *Diplomatic Law in a New Millennium* (Oxford: Oxford University Press, 2017). 448 p.

Behrens, P., Diplomats Bearing Presents: Diplomatic Funding Under International Law, *Houston Journal of International Law*, vol. 39 (2017): p. 645–694.

Subramanian, S.R., Abuse of Diplomatic Privileges and the Balance between Immunities and the Duty to Respect the Local Laws and Regulations Under the Vienna Conventions: The Recent Indian Experience, *The Chinese Journal of Global Governance*, vol. 3 (2017): p. 182–233.

8. Disarmament

Amoroso, D., Jus in Bello and Jus Ad Bellum Arguments Against Autonomy in Weapons Systems: A Re-Appraisal, *QIL: Questions of International Law: QDI: Questions de droit international*, October (2017): p. 5–31.

Ancelin, J., *La lutte contre la prolifération des armes légères et de petit calibre en droit international* (Bruxelles: Bruylant, 2017). 790 p.

Becker, M.A., The Dispute that Wasn't there: Judgments in the Nuclear Disarmament Cases at the International Court of Justice, *Cambridge Journal of International and Comparative Law*, vol. 6 (2017): p. 4–26.

Cançado Trindade, A.A., *The Universal Obligation of Nuclear Disarmament* (Brasilia: Fundação Alexandre de Gusmão, 2017). 234 p.

Chakravorty, A., A New Nuclear Age: An Exclusionary Global Order? *Groningen Journal of International Law*, vol. 5 (2017): p. 191–202.

Coppen, T., *The Law of Arms Control and the International Non-Proliferation Regime: Preventing the Spread of Nuclear Weapons* (Leiden: Brill Nijhoff, 2017). 377 p.

Ekelhof, M.A.C., Complications of a Common Language: Why it is so Hard to Talk about Autonomous Weapons, *Journal of Conflict and Security Law*, vol. 22 (2017): p. 311–331.

Fukui, Y., CTBT: Legal Questions Arising from its Non Entry into Force Revisited, *Journal of Conflict and Security Law*, vol. 22 (2017): p. 183–200.

Kello, L., *The Virtual Weapon and International Order* (London: Yale University Press, 2017). 336 p.

Popp, R., Horovitz, L., and Wenger, A., *Negotiating the Nuclear Non-Proliferation Treaty: Origins of the Nuclear Order* (Milton Park, Abingdon, Oxon; New York, NY: Routledge, 2017). 249 p.

9. Environmental Questions

Al-Abdulrazzak, D., *et al.*, Opportunities for Improving Global Marine Conservation through Multilateral Treaties, *Marine Policy*, vol. 86 (2017): p. 247–252.

Atapattu, S., Climate Change, International Environmental Law Principles, and the North-South Divide, *Transnational Law & Contemporary Problems*, vol. 26 (2017): p. 247–261.

Bodansky, D., Brunnée, J., and Rajamani, L., *International Climate Change Law* (Oxford, United Kingdom: Oxford University Press, 2017). 374 p.

Boisson de Chazournes, L., Environmental Protection and Investment Arbitration: Yin and Yang? *Anuario Colombiano de Derecho Internacional*, vol. 10 (2017): p. 371–399.

de Castro, D., The Colonial Aspects of International Environmental Law: Treaties as Promoters of Continuous Structural Violence, *Groningen Journal of International Law*, vol. 5 (2017): p. 168–190.

Costi, A., and Ross, N.J., The Ongoing Legal Status of Low-Lying States in the Climate-Changed Future, in Butler, P., and Morris, C., *Small States in a Legal World* (Cham, Switzerland: Springer, 2017): p. 101–138.

Dellinger, M., Rethinking Force Majeure in Public International Law, *Pace Law Review*, vol. 37 (2017): p. 455–506.

Dowd, R., and McAdam, J., International Cooperation and Responsibility Sharing to Combat Climate Change: Lessons for International Refugee Law, *Melbourne Journal of International Law*, vol. 18 (2017): p. 180–218.

Elliott, L., Cooperation on Transnational Environmental Crime: Institutional Complexity Matters, *Review of European, Comparative & International Environmental Law*, vol. 26 (2017): p. 107–117.

Fernández Liesa, C.R., Transformaciones del Derecho internacional por los objetivos de desarrollo sostenible = Sustainable Development Goals and Changes of International Law, *Anuario español de derecho internacional*, vol. 32 (2016): p. 49–81.

Fitzmaurice, M., Legitimacy of International Environmental Law. the Sovereign States Overwhelmed by Obligations: Responsibility to React to Problems Beyond National Jurisdiction? *Zeitschrift für ausländisches öfentliches Recht und Völkerrecht, ZAORV =Heidelberg Journal of International Law*, vol. 77 (2017): p. 339–370.

Fitzmaurice, M., Tanzi, A., and Papantoniou, A. *Multilateral Environmental Treaties* (Cheltenham, UK: Edward Elgar Publishing, 2017). 512 p.

Hassan, P., Role of the South in the Development of International Environmental Law, *Chinese Journal of Environmental Law*, vol. 1 (2017): p. 133–157.

Juvelier, B., When the Levee Breaks: Climate Change, Rising Seas, and the Loss of Island Nation Statehood, *Denver Journal of International Law and Policy*, vol. 46 (2017): p. 21–44.

Kim, Y., Tanaka, K., and Matsuoka, S., Institutional Mechanisms and the Consequences of International Environmental Agreements, *Global Environmental Politics*, vol. 17 (2017): p. 77–98.

Klein, D., *et al.* (eds), *The Paris Agreement on Climate Change: Analysis and Commentary* (Oxford: Oxford University Press, 2017). 328 p.

Kolleck, N., *et al.*, The Power of Social Networks: How the UNFCCC Secretariat Creates Momentum for Climate Education, *Global Environmental Politics*, vol. 17 (2017): p. 106–126.

Malby, S., The Rule of Law and Sustainable Development, *Commonwealth Law Bulletin*, vol. 43 (2017): p. 521–532.

Manou, D., *et al.* (eds), *Climate Change Migration and Human Rights: Law and Policy Perspectives* (Milton Park, Abingdon, Oxon: Routledge, 2017). 268 p.

Michaelowa, K., and Michaelowa, A., The Growing Influence of the UNFCCC Secretariat on the Clean Development Mechanism, *International Environmental Agreements: Politics, Law and Economics*, vol. 17 (2016): p. 247–269.

Montini, M., Some Critical Reflections on the Paris Agreement on Climatic Changes, *Rivista di diritto internazionale*, vol. 100 (2017): p. 719–755.

de Paor, R., Climate Change and Arbitration: Annex Time before there won't be A Next Time, *Journal of International Dispute Settlement*, vol. 8 (2017): p. 179–215.

Sanderson, J., *Plants, People and Practices: The Nature and History of the UPOV Convention* (Cambridge, United Kingdom; New York, NY: Cambridge University Press, 2017). 356 p.

Stahn, C., Iverson, J., and Easterday, J.S. (eds), *Environmental Protection and Transitions from Conflict to Peace*. First ed. (Oxford: Oxford University Press, 2017). 450 p.

Stua, M., *From the Paris Agreement to a Low-Carbon Bretton Woods: Rationale for the Establishment of a Mitigation Alliance* (Cham, Switzerland: Springer, 2017). 239 p.

Tehan, M., *et al.*, *The Impact of Climate Change Mitigation on Indigenous and Forest Communities: International, National and Local Law Perspectives on REDD+.* (Cambridge: Cambridge University Press, 2017). 440 p.

van Wyk, S., *The Impact of Climate Change Law on the Principle of State Sovereignty Over Natural Resources* (Baden-Baden: Nomos, 2017). 383 p.

Viñuales, J.E., La protección ambiental en el Derecho consuetudinario internacional. *Revista española de derecho internacional*, vol. 69 (2017): p. 71–91.

10. Financing

Bayram, A.B., and Graham, E.R., Financing the United Nations: Explaining Variation in How Donors Provide Funding to the UN, *Review of International Organizations*, vol. 12 (2016): p. 421–459.

Coleman, K.P., Extending UN Peacekeeping Financing Beyond UN Peacekeeping Operations? the Prospects and Challenges of Reform, *Global Governance*, vol. 23 (2017): p. 101–120.

Ege, J.ö., and Bauer, M.W., How Financial Resources Affect the Autonomy of International Public Administrations, *Global Policy*, vol. 8 (2017): p. 75–84.

Wade, L., Can You Pay for Peace?: The Role of Financing Frameworks in Effective Peace Operations, *Journal of International Peacekeeping*, vol. 21 (2017): p. 152–175.

11. Friendly Relations and Cooperation among States

Boisson de Chazournes, L., *Interactions between Regional and Universal Organizations: A Legal Perspective* (Leiden: Brill Nijhoff, 2017). 384 p.

12. Human Rights

Atrey, S., Fifty Years on: The Curious Case of Intersectional Discrimination in the ICCPR, *Nordic Journal of Human Rights*, vol. 35 (2017): p. 220–239.

Barnabas, S.G., The Legal Status of the United Nations Declaration on the Rights of Indigenous Peoples (2007) in Contemporary International Human Rights Law, *International Human Rights Law Review*, vol. 6 (2017): p. 242–261.

de Beco, G., Protecting the Invisible: An Intersectional Approach to International Human Rights Law, *Human Rights Law Review*, vol. 17 (2017): p. 633–663.

Ben-Natan, S., Constitutional Mindset: The Interrelations between Constitutional Law and International Law in the Extraterritorial Application of Human Rights, *Israel Law Review*, vol. 50 (2017): p. 139–176.

Brems, E., Desmet, E., and Vandenhole, W., *Children's Rights Law in the Global Human Rights Landscape: Isolation, Inspiration, Integration?* (Abingdon, Oxon UK; New York: Routledge, 2017). 312 p.

Caflisch, L., Attribution, Responsibility and Jurisdiction in International Human Rights Law, *Anuario Colombiano de Derecho Internacional*, vol. 10 (2017): p. 161–203.

Carpenter, D., So Made that I Cannot Believe: The ICCPR and the Protection of Non-Religious Expression in Predominantly Religious Countries, *Chicago Journal of International Law*, vol. 18 (2017): p. 216–244.

Carraro, V., The United Nations Treaty Bodies and Universal Periodic Review: Advancing Human Rights by Preventing Politicization? *Human Rights Quarterly*, vol. 39 (2017): p. 943–970.

Dancy, G., and Fariss, C.J., Rescuing Human Rights Law from International Legalism and its Critics, *Human Rights Quarterly*, vol. 39 (2017): p. 1–36.

Deva, S., and Bilchitz, D. (eds), *Building a Treaty on Business and Human Rights Context and Contour* (Cambridge: Cambridge University Press, 2017). 536 p.

Estrada Tanck, D., Seguridad humana y derecho internacional público = Human Security and Public International Law, *Anuario español de derecho internacional*, vol. 32 (2016): p. 373–404.

Ezeizabarrena, X., *Derecho de libre determinación y derecho a decidir: nueva soberanía y derechos humanos en el siglo XXI* (Bilbao: Universidad de Deusto, 2017). 109 p.

Fortin, K., *The Accountability of Armed Groups Under Human Rights Law* (Oxford, United Kingdom: Oxford University Press, 2017). 448 p.

Freedman, R., and Houghton R., Two Steps Forward, One Step Back: Politicisation of the Human Rights Council, *Human Rights Law Review*, vol. 17 (2017): p. 753–769.

Gammeltoft-Hansen, T., and Vedsted-Hansen J. (eds), *Human Rights and the Dark Side of Globalisation: Transnational Law Enforcement and Migration Control* (London; New York: Routledge, 2017). 366 p.

Glarou, D., *The Impact of Naturalistic and Legal Positivist Doctrines on the Implementation of International Human Rights Treaty Law: The Case of Reservations to Human Rights Treaties* (Baden-Baden, Germany: Nomos, 2017). 387 p.

Harris-Short, S., International Human Rights Law: Imperialist, Inept and Ineffective? Cultural Relativism and the UN Convention on the Rights of the Child, in Stark, B. (ed), *Human Rights and Children* (Cheltenham, UK; Northampton, MA, USA: Edward Elgar Publishing, 2017): p. 300–351.

Heupel, M., and Zürn, M., *Protecting the Individual from International Authority: Human Rights in International Organizations* (Cambridge: Cambridge University Press, 2017). 370 p.

Keane, D. and Waughray, A. (eds), *Fifty Years of the International Convention on the Elimination of all Forms of Racial Discrimination: A Living Instrument* (Manchester: Manchester University Press, 2018). 336 p.

Langford, M., and Russell, A.F.S. (eds), *The Human Right to Water: Theory, Practice and Prospects* (Cambridge, United Kingdom: Cambridge University Press, 2017). 300 p.

Leonés Salido, J.M., *Inmigración irregular y derechos fundamentales: ¿hay límites?* (Barcelona: José María Bosch, 2017). 248 p.

Lindkvist, L., *Religious Freedom and the Universal Declaration of Human Rights* (Cambridge, United Kingdom: Cambridge University Press, 2017). 186 p.

Lobba, P., and T. Mariniello., *Judicial Dialogue on Human Rights: The Practice of International Criminal Tribunals* (Leiden; Boston: Brill Nijhoff, 2017). 304 p.

Lundy, L., and Byrne, B., The Four General Principles of the United Nations Convention on the Rights of the Child: The Potential Value of the Approach in Other Areas of Human Rights Law, in Brems, E., Desmet, E., and Vandenhole, W. (eds), *Children's Rights Law in the Global Human Rights Landscape: Isolation, Inspiration, Integration?* (London: Routledge, 2017): p. 52–70.

Maisley, N., The International Right of Rights? Article 25(*a*) of the ICCPR as a Human Right to Take Part in International Law-Making, *European Journal of International Law*, vol. 28 (2017): p. 89–113.

McGaughey, F., Advancing, Retreating Or Stepping on each Other's Toes? The Role of Non-Governmental Organisations in United Nations Human Rights Treaty Body Reporting and the Universal Periodic Review, *Australian Year Book of International Law*, vol. 35 (2017): p. 187–216.

McQuigg, R.J.A., The CEDAW Committee and Gender-Based Violence Against Women, *International Human Rights Law Review*, vol. 6 (2017): p. 263–278.

Namakula, C.S., The Human Rights Mandate of a Prosecutor of an International Criminal Trial, *International Criminal Law Review*, vol. 17 (2017): p. 935–959.

Nesbitt, M., Due Process in UN Commissions of Inquiry: A Legal Analysis of the Procedures of Goldstone's Gaza Inquiry, *German Law Journal*, vol. 18 (2017): p. 127–187.

Nifosi-Sutton, I., *The Protection of Vulnerable Groups Under International Human Rights Law* (Abingdon, Oxon [UK]; New York: Routledge, 2017). 292 p.

Principi, K.F., United Nations Individual Complaint Procedures: How do States Comply? A Categorized Study Based on 268 Cases of "Satisfactory" Implementation Under the Follow-Up Procedure, mainly regarding the UN Human Rights Committee, *Human Rights Law Journal*, vol. 37 (2017): p. 1–31.

Rachovitsa, A., The Principle of Systemic Integration in Human Rights Law, *International and Comparative Law Quarterly*, vol. 66 (2017): p. 557–588.

Reif, L.C., The UN Guiding Principles on Business and Human Rights and Networked Governance: Improving the Role of Human Rights Ombudsman Institutions as National Remedies, *Human Rights Law Review*, vol. 17 (2017): p. 603–632.

Rombouts, S.J., The Evolution of Indigenous Peoples' Consultation Rights Under the ILO and U.N. Regimes, *Stanford Journal of International Law*, vol. 53 (2017): p. 169–224.

Schabas, W.A., Reservations to the Convention on the Rights of the Child, in Stark, B. (ed), *Human Rights and Children* (Cheltenham, UK; Northampton, MA, USA: Edward Elgar Publishing, 2017): p. 280–299.

Schmitt, P., *Access to Justice and International Organizations: The Case of Individual Victims of Human Rights Violations* (Cheltenham, UK: Edward Elgar Publishing, 2017). 400 p.

Shelton, D. (ed), *International Protection of Human Rights* (United Kingdom: Brill Nijhoff, 2017). 797 p.

Smart, S., Cambio de foco en la priorización de casos de la Corte Penal Internacional: Los delitos ambientales = Changing the Scope in the Prioritization of the International Criminal Court: Environmental Crimes, *Anuario de derechos humanos*, vol. 13 (2017): p. 123–133.

Soirila, U., Persons and Things in International Law and Law of Humanity, *German Law Journal*, vol. 18 (2017): p. 1163–1182.

Sosa, L., *Intersectionality in the Human Rights Legal Framework on Violence Against Women: At the Centre Or the Margins?* (Cambridge, United Kingdom: Cambridge University Press, 2017). 304 p.

Stark, B. (ed), *Human Rights and Children* (Cheltenham, UK; Northampton, MA, USA: Edward Elgar Publishing, 2017). 960 p.

Subedi, S.P., *The Effectiveness of the UN Human Rights System: Reform and the Judicialisation of Human Rights* (Abingdon, Oxon; New York, NY: Routledge, 2017). 288 p.

Torroja, H. (ed), *Public International Law and Human Rights Violations by Private Military and Security Companies* (Cham: Springer, 2017). 158 p.

Touzé, S., L'exécution des constatations des comités conventionnels des Nations Unies, *Revue générale de droit international public*, vol. 121 (2017): p. 645–659.

von Stein, J., Exploring the Universe of UN Human Rights Agreements, *Journal of Conflict Resolution*, vol. 62 (2017): p. 871–899.

13. International Administrative Law

Kunz-Hallstein, H.P., Views from Practice: Paralysing the Functioning of International Organisations' Internal Appeals Boards, *International Organizations Law Review*, vol. 14 (2017): p. 196–203.

Petrović, D., and International Labour Office, *Une contribution de 90 ans du Tribunal Administratif de l'Organisation Internationale du Travail à la création d'un droit de la fonction publique internationale* (Geneva: International Labour Office, 2017). 215 p.

Silverstein, R., Revisiting the Legal Basis to Deny International Civil Servants Access to a Fundamental Human Right, *Michigan State International Law Review*, vol. 25 (2017): p. 375–428.

14. International Commercial Law

Alvarez, J.E. (ed), *International Investment Law* (Leiden: Brill Nijhoff, 2017). 1,334 p.

Dawar, K., The Government Procurement Agreement, the Most-Favored Nation Principle, and Regional Trade Agreements, in Georgopoulos, A., Hoekman, B.M., and Mavroidis, P.C. (eds), *The Internationalization of Government Procurement Regulation* (Oxford: Oxford University Press, 2017): p. 111–139.

Gonzalez-Perez, M., and Leonard, L., The UN Global Compact, in de Jonge, A. and Tomasic, R. (eds), *Research Handbook on Transnational Corporations* (Cheltenham, UK; Northampton, MA: Edward Elgar Publishing, 2017): p. 117–138.

Kadner Graziano, T., The Hague Solution on Choice-of-Law Clauses in Conflicting Standard Terms: Paving the Way to More Legal Certainty in International Commercial Transactions? *Uniform Law Review*, vol. 22 (2017): p. 351–368.

Nicholas, C., UNCITRAL and the Internationalization of Government Procurement Regulation, in Georgopoulos, A., Hoekman, B.M., and Mavroidis, P.C. (eds), *The Internationalization of Government Procurement Regulation* (Oxford: Oxford University Press, 2017): p. 86–110.

Soopramanien, R., International Trade in Indigenous Cultural Heritage: What Protection does International Law Provide for Indigenous Cultural Goods and Services in International Commerce? *Stanford Journal of International Law*, vol. 53 (2017): p. 225–248.

15. International Criminal Law

Ahmad, H., Context at the International Criminal Court, *Pace International Law Review*, vol. 29 (2017): p. 132–201.

Aksenova, M., Symbolism as a Constraint on International Criminal Law, *Leiden Journal of International Law*, vol. 30 (2017): p. 475–499.

Alija Fernandez, R.A., and Saura Estapa, J., Towards a Single and Comprehensive Notion of "Civilian Population" in Crimes against Humanity, *International Criminal Law Review*, vol. 17 (2017): p. 47–77.

Bergsmo, M., Rackwitz, K.U., and Song, T. (eds), *Historical Origins of International Criminal Law* (Brussels: Torkel Opsahl Academic EPublisher, 2017). 1141 p.

Beshah Abebe, Z., The African Court with a Criminal Jurisdiction and the ICC: A Case for Overlapping Jurisdiction, *African Journal of International and Comparative Law*, vol. 25 (2017): p. 418–429.

Bonafé, B.I., Sentencing Practice and the Contribution of International Criminal Tribunals to the Maintenance of Peace, *Diritti umani e diritto internazionale*, vol. 11 (2017): p. 101–113.

Botte-Kerrison, A., Responsibility for Bystanders in Mass Crimes: Towards a Duty to Rescue in International Criminal Justice, *International Criminal Law Review*, vol. 17 (2017): p. 879–908.

Bufalini, A., On the Power of a State to Waive Reparation Claims Arising from War Crimes and Crimes Against Humanity, *Zeitschrift für ausländisches öffentliches Recht und Völkerrecht (ZaöRV)*, vol. 77 (2017): p. 447–470.

Byczyk, M., A Breach of the Norms of Cautiousness as Fundament for Criminal Responsibility, *European Journal of Comparative Law and Governance*, vol. 4 (2017): p. 211–245.

Çakmak, C., *A Brief History of International Criminal Law and International Criminal Court* (New York: Palgrave Macmillan, 2017). 305 p.

Christensen, M.J., Crafting and Promoting International Crimes: A Controversy among Professionals of Core-Crimes and Anti-Corruption, *Leiden Journal of International Law*, vol. 30 (2017): p. 501–521.

Combs, N.A., Grave Crimes and Weak Evidence: A Fact-Finding Evolution in International Criminal Law. *Harvard International Law Journal*, vol. 58 (2017): p. 47–125.

Dancy, G., Searching for Deterrence at the International Criminal Court, *International Criminal Law Review*, vol. 17 (2017): p. 625–655.

Dancy, G., and Montal, F., From Law Versus Politics to Law in Politics: A Pragmatist Assessment of the ICC's Impact, *The American University International Law Review*, vol. 32 (2017): p. 645–705.

Dancy, G., and Montal, F., Unintended Positive Complementarity: Why International Criminal Court Investigations May Increase Domestic Human Rights Prosecutions, *American Journal of International Law*, vol. 111 (2017): p. 689–723.

Du Plessis, M., and Mettraux, G., South Africa's Failed Withdrawal from the Rome Statute: Politics, Law, and Judicial Accountability, *Journal of International Criminal Justice*, vol. 15 (2017): p. 361–370.

Egan, B.J., International Law and Stability in Cyberspace, *Berkeley Journal of International Law*, vol. 35 (2017): p. 169–180.

Elliot, I. 'A Meaningful Step Towards Accountability'?: A View from the Field on the United Nations International, Impartial and Independent Mechanism for Syria. *Journal of International Criminal Justice*, vol. 15 (2017): p. 239–256.

Ellis, M.S., The ICC's Role in Combatting the Destruction of Cultural Heritage, *Case Western Reserve Journal of International Law*, vol. 49 (2017): p. 23–62.

Fairlie, M.A., The Abiding Problem of Witness Statements in International Criminal Trials, *New York University Journal of International Law and Politics*, vol. 50 (2017): p. 77–158.

Fehr, C., Domestic Detention Under Article 78(2) of the ICC Statute, *Journal of International Criminal Justice*, vol. 15 (2017): p. 31–50. Fyfe, S., Tracking Hate Speech Acts as Incitement to Genocide in International Criminal Law, *Leiden Journal of International Law*, vol. 30 (2017): p. 523–548.

Gendron, S., Sub Silentio: The Sexual Assault of Women in International Law, in Abbenhuis, M., Barber, C.E., and Higgins, A.R. (eds), *War, Peace and International Order? The Legacies of the Hague Conferences of 1899 and 1907* (London: Routledge, 2017): p. 103–120.

Gilbert, G., Undesirable but Unreturnable: Extradition and Other Forms of Rendition, *Journal of International Criminal Justice*, vol. 15 (2017): p. 55–74.

Hafetz, J., Fairness, Legitimacy, and Selection Decisions in International Criminal Law, *Vanderbilt Journal of Transnational Law*, vol. 50 (2017): p. 1133–1171.

Hamilton, L., Beyond Ballot-Stuffing: Current Gaps in International Law regarding Foreign State Hacking to Influence a Foreign Election, *Wisconsin International Law Journal*, vol. 35 (2017): p. 179–204.

Heller, K.J., What is an International Crime: (A Revisionist History), *Harvard International Law Journal*, vol. 58 (2017): p. 353–420.

Höfner, S., and Terwolde-Berhan, Z., Crimes Against Humanity: The Commission of Inquiry on Eritrea, in van Reisen, M., and Mawere, M., *Human Trafficking and Trauma in the Digital Era: The Ongoing Tragedy of Trade in Refugees from Eritrea* (Mankon, Bamenda: Langaa, 2017): p. 350–369.

Irving, E., When International Justice Concludes: Undesirable but Unreturnable Individuals in the Context of the International Criminal Court, *Journal of International Criminal Justice*, vol. 15 (2017): p. 115–131.

Jalloh, C.C., and Bantekas, I. (eds), *The International Criminal Court and Africa* (Oxford, United Kingdom: Oxford University Press, 2017). 416 p.

Jain, N., Radical Dissents in International Criminal Trials, *European Journal of International Law*, vol. 28 (2017): p. 1163–1186.

Jarvis, M., The Practice of International Criminal Law: Some Reflections from an ICTY Prosecutor, *International Criminal Law Review*, vol. 17 (2017): p. 398–415.

Kantorowicz-Reznichenko, E., Misidentification of Victims Under International Criminal Law: An Attempted Offence? *Journal of International Criminal Justice*, vol. 15 (2017): p. 291–318.

Kastner, P., *International Criminal Law in Context* (New York, NY: Routledge, 2017). 346 p.

Kavran, O., International Criminal Courts and the Right to Information, *Journal of International Criminal Justice*, vol. 15 (2017): p. 953–983.

Kellman, B., Targeted Killings—Never Not an Act of International Criminal Law Enforcement, *Boston College International and Comparative Law Review*, vol. 40 (2017): p. 27–62.

Kittichaisaree, K., *Public International Law of Cyberspace* (Switzerland: Springer International Publishing, 2017). 376 p.

Kolieb, J., Through the Looking-Glass: Nuremberg's Confusing Legacy on Corporate Accountability Under International Law, *American University International Law Review*, vol. 32 (2017): p. 569–604.

Koskenniemi, M., Between Impunity and Show Trials, in Bell, C. (ed), *Transitional Justice* (Abingdon, Oxon: Routledge, Taylor & Francis Group, 2017): p. 189–223.

Labuda, P.I., The Special Criminal Court in the Central African Republic: Failure or Vindication of Complementarity? *Journal of International Criminal Justice*, vol. 15 (2017): p. 175–206.

Lugano, G., Counter-Shaming the International Criminal Court's Intervention as Neocolonial: Lessons from Kenya, *International Journal of Transitional Justice*, vol. 11 (2017): p. 9–29.

Magliveras, K.D., Substituting International Criminal Justice for an African Criminal Justice? *International Organizations Law Review*, vol. 14 (2017): p. 291–320.

Marrero Rocha, I., Nuevas dinámicas en las relaciones entre crimen organizado y grupos terroristas, *Revista española de derecho internacional*, vol. 69 (2017): p. 145–169.

McCausland, C., From Tolerance to Tactic: Understanding Rape in Armed Conflict as Genocide, *Michigan State International Law Review*, vol. 25 (2017): p. 149–191.

McDermott, Y., The International Criminal Court's Chambers Practice Manual: Towards a Return to Judicial Law Making in International Criminal Procedure? *Journal of International Criminal Justice*, vol. 15 (2017): p. 873–904.

Medawatte, D.S., Legal Regimes to Enforced Disappearances, *Florida Journal of International Law*, vol. 29 (2017): p. 227–251.

Morris, N., and Knaap, A., When Institutional Design is Flawed: Problems of Cooperation at the United Nations War Crimes Commission, 1943–1948, *European Journal of International Law*, vol. 28 (2017): p. 513–534.

Nicholson, J., Strengthening the Effectiveness of International Criminal Law through the Principle of Legality, *International Criminal Law Review*, vol. 17 (2017): p. 656–681.

Nyawo, J., *Selective Enforcement and International Criminal Law: The International Criminal Court and Africa* (Mortsel: Intersentia, 2017). 288 p.

Okafor, O.C., and Ngwaba, U., Between Tunnel Vision and a Sliding Scale: Power Normativity and Justice in the Praxis of the International Criminal Court, *Temple International and Comparative Law Journal*, vol. 31 (2017): p. 179–193.

O'Sullivan, A., *Universal Jurisdiction in International Criminal Law: The Debate and the Battle for Hegemony* (Milton Park, Abingdon, Oxon; New York, NY: Routledge, Taylor & Frances Group, 2017). 222 p.

Patel, P., Expanding Past Genocide, Crimes Against Humanity, and War Crimes: Can an ICC Policy Paper Expand the Court's Mandate to Prosecuting Environmental Crimes, *Loyola University Chicago International Law Review*, vol. 14 (2016–2017): p. 175–197.

Pichou, M., Between Pragmatism and Normativity: Legal Standards for Issuing Subpoenas and Witnesses Summonses in International Criminal Procedure, *International Criminal Law Review*, vol. 17 (2017): p. 135–160.

Pimenta de Souza, F., and de Oliveira Machado, D., La doble naturaleza de la recuperación de activos por la Corte Penal Internacional: disuasión de la práctica delictiva y reparación de las víctimas, *Anuario Iberoamericano de Derecho Internacional Penal*, vol. 5 (2017): p. 62–93.

Pocar, F., International Criminal Justice and the Unifying Role of Customary Law, *Uniform Law Review*, vol. 21 (2016): p. 171–176.

Power, J., *Ending War Crimes, Chasing the War Criminals* (Leiden; Boston: Brill Nijhoff, 2017). 136 p.

Prorok, A.K., The (In)Compatibility of Peace and Justice? The International Criminal Court and Civil Conflict Termination. *International Organization*, vol. 71 (2017): p. 213–243.

Pues, A., Discretion and the Gravity of Situations at the International Criminal Court. *International Criminal Law Review*, vol. 17 (2017): p. 960–984.

Qinmin, S., Lingering Issues of Foreign Official Immunity in Enforcing Prohibition Against Torture in Domestic Courts: Pinochet's Reasoning Reassessed, *Chinese Journal of International Law*, vol. 16 (2017): p. 311–350.

Quénivet, N., Does and should International Law Prohibit the Prosecution of Children for War Crimes? *European Journal of International Law*, vol. 28 (2017): p. 433–455.

Rankin, M., Investigating Crimes Against Humanity in Syria and Iraq: The Commission for International Justice and Accountability, *Global Responsibility to Protect*, vol. 9 (2017): p. 395–421.

Rauter, T., *Judicial Practice, Customary International Criminal Law and Nullum Crimen Sine Lege* (Cham: Springer International Publishing, 2017). 261 p.

Richardson, L., Offences Against the Administration of Justice at the International Criminal Court: Robbing Peter to Pay Paul? *Journal of International Criminal Justice*, vol. 15 (2017): p. 741–774.

Robinson, D., A Justification of Command Responsibility, *Criminal Law Forum*, vol. 28 (2017): p. 633–668.

Rohan, C., and Zyberi, G., *Defense Perspectives on International Criminal Justice* (Cambridge: Cambridge University Press, 2017). 609 p.

Rossi, P., The Al Mahdi Trial before the International Criminal Court: Attacks on Cultural Heritage between War Crimes and Crimes Against Humanity, *Diritti umani e diritto internazionale*, vol. 11 (2017): p. 87–100.

Schwartz, S., Wartime Sexual Violence as More than Collateral Damage: Classifying Sexual Violence as Part of a Common Criminal Plan in International Criminal Law, *University of New South Wales law journal*, vol. 40 (2017): p. 57–88.

Schuerch, R., *The International Criminal Court at the Mercy of Powerful States: An Assessment of the Neo-Colonialism Claim made by African Stakeholders* (The Hague, The Netherlands: Asser Press, 2017). 305 p.

Sperfeldt, C., Rome's Legacy: Negotiating the Reparations Mandate of the International Criminal Court *International Criminal Law Review*, vol. 17 (2017): p. 351–377.

Ssenyonjo, M., African States Failed Withdrawal from the Rome Statute of the International Criminal Court: From Withdrawal Notifications to Constructive Engagement, *International Criminal Law Review*, vol. 17 (2017): p. 749–802.

Stahn, C., Daedalus Or Icarus? Footprints of International Criminal Justice Over a Quarter of a Century, *Zeitschrift für ausländisches öfentliches Recht und Völkerrecht, ZAORV = Heidelberg Journal of International Law*, vol. 77 (2017): p. 371–408.

Stahn, C., Damned if You do, Damned if You Don't: Challenges and Critiques of Preliminary Examinations at the ICC, *Journal of International Criminal Justice*, vol. 15 (2017): p. 413–434.

Trahan, J., The International Criminal Court's Libya Case(s)—The Need for Consistency with International Human Rights as to Due Process and the Death Penalty, *International Criminal Law Review*, vol. 17 (2017): p. 803–843.

Urueña, R., Prosecutorial Politics: The ICC's Influence in Colombian Peace Processes, 2003–2017, *American Journal of International Law*, vol. 111 (2017): p. 104–125.

Valiani, S., Genocide Left Unchecked: Assessing the ICC's Difficulties Detaining Omar Al-Bashir, *Berkeley Journal of International Law*, vol. 35 (2017).

Werle, G., and Vormbaum, M., *The African Criminal Court: A Commentary on the Malabo Protocol*, (The Hague: Asser Press, 2017). 347 p.

Wierczyńska, K., and Jakubowski, A., Individual Responsibility for Deliberate Destruction of Cultural Heritage: Contextualizing the ICC Judgment in the Al-Mahdi Case*, *Chinese Journal of International Law*, vol. 16 (2017): p. 695–721.

Yogendran, S., Did the ICC Fail Child Victims in the Lubanga Reparations Order? *Amsterdam Law Forum*, vol. 9 (2017): p. 65–83.

Zafra, R.d.P. and Valle, P., La "neutralidad" del crimen de guerra de violación sexual en el Derecho penal internacional = The "Neutrality" of the War Crime of Rape in International Criminal Law, *Anuario de derechos humanos*, vol. 13 (2017): p. 63–84.

Zakerhossein, M.H., *Situation Selection Regime at the International Criminal Court: Law, Policy, Practice* (Cambridge: Intersentia, 2017). 439 p.

Zemach, A., Indeterminacy in the Law of War: The Need for an International Advisory Regime, *Brooklyn Journal of International Law*, vol. 43 (2017): p. 1–74.

16. International Economic Law

Anderson, R.D., and Muller, A.C., The Revised WTO Agreement on Government Procurement (GPA): Key Design Features and Significance for Global Trade and Development, *Georgetown Journal of International Law*, vol. 48 (2017): p. 949–1008.

Bäumler, J., Implementing the No Harm Principle in International Economic Law: A Comparison between Measure-Based Rules and Effect-Based Rules, *Journal of International Economic Law*, vol. 20 (2017): p. 807–828.

Beckers, A., Legalization Under the Premises of Globalization: Why and Where to Enforce Corporate Social Responsibility Codes, *Indiana Journal of Global Legal Studies*, vol. 24 (2017): p. 15–42.

Beckers, A., and Kawakami, M.T., Why Domestic Enforcement of Private Regulation Is (Not) the Answer: Making and Questioning the Case of Corporate Social Responsibility Codes, *Indiana Journal of Global Legal Studies*, vol. 24 (2017): p. 1–13.

Decreux, Y., and Fontagné, L., What Next for Multilateral Trade Talks? Quantifying the Role of Negotiation Modalities, *World Trade Review*, vol. 14 (2015): p. 29–43.

Gu, B., Chinese Multilateralism in the AIIB, *Journal of International Economic Law*, vol. 20 (2017): p. 137–158.

Howard, D.M., Creating Consistency through a World Investment Court, *Fordham International Law Journal*, vol. 41, iss. 1 (2017): p. 1–52.

Kamphuis, C., Litigating Indigenous Dispossession in the Global Economy: Law's Promises and Pitfalls, *Revista de Direito Internacional*, vol. 14 (2017): p. 164–224.

Kotiswaran, P., *Revisiting the Law and Governance of Trafficking, Forced Labor and Modern Slavery* (New York, NY, USA: Cambridge University Press, 2017). 606 p.

Nam, J., Model Bit: An Ideal Prototype or a Tool for Efficient Breach? *Georgetown Journal of International Law*, vol. 48 (2017): p. 1275–1308.

Rensmann, T. (ed), *Small and Medium-Sized Enterprises in International Economic Law* (Oxford: Oxford University Press, 2017). 370 p.

Tams, C.J., Schill, S.W., and Hofmann, R., *International Investment Law and the Global Financial Architecture* (Cheltenham, UK; Northampton, MA, USA: Edward Elgar Publishing, 2017). 384 p.

Travis, K., A Plurilateral Investment Treaty: Marrying Trade and Investment to Re-Establish a Customary International Norm, *Vanderbilt Journal of Transnational Law*, vol. 50 (2017): p. 499–533.

Trommer, S., The WTO in an Era of Preferential Trade Agreements: Thick and Thin Institutions in Global Trade Governance, *World Trade Review*, vol. 16 (2017): p. 501–526.

Wang, Y., Central and Peripheral Reforms of Global Trade Governance, *China and WTO Review*, vol. 3 (2017): p. 289–318.

17. International Terrorism

Ackermann, T., and Fenrich, K., Motion and Rest—International Law's Responsiveness Towards Terrorism, Mass Surveillance, and Self-Defence, *Zeitschrift für ausländisches öfentliches Recht und Völkerrecht, ZAORV = Heidelberg Journal of International Law*, vol. 77 (2017): p. 745–807.

Alvarez-Jiménez, A., From Al-Qaida in 2001 to ISIL in 2015: The Security Council's Decisions on Terrorism and their Impact on the Right to Self-Defense Against Autonomous Non-State Actors, *Minnesota Journal of International Law*, vol. 26 (2017): p. 345–418.

Black-Branch, J., Nuclear Terrorism by States and Non-State Actors: Global Responses to Threats to Military and Human Security in International Law, *Journal of Conflict and Security Law*, vol. 22 (2017): p. 201–248.

Burchardt, D., and Gulati, R., International Counter-Terrorism Regulation and Citizenship-Stripping Laws—Reinforcing Legal Exceptionalism, *Journal of Conflict and Security Law*, vol. 23 (2018): p. 203–228.

Campusano Droguett, R.F., and Acevedo Espínola, L.H., Naturaleza jurídica de los atentados en París. ¿Terrorismo o crímenes de guerra? = Legal nature of the crimes at Paris. Terrorism or war crimes? *Revista tribuna internacional*, vol. 6 (2017): p. 1–20.

Colombo, A., El terrorismo entre legalidad y legitimidad: el insostenible monopolio de los Estados sobre la noción de violencia ilegítima, in Campione, R., and Ruschi, F. (eds), *Guerra, derecho y seguridad en las relaciones internacionales* (Valencia: Tirant lo Blanch, 2017): p. 77–110.

Gasser, H., Acts of Terror, Terrorism and International Humanitarian Law, in Cryer, R., and Henderson, C. (eds), *Law on the Use of Force and Armed Conflict* (Cheltenham, UK: Edward Elgar Publishing, 2017): p. 443–466.

Ludvik, J., *Nuclear Asymmetry and Deterrence: Theory, Policy and History* (London; New York: Routledge, Taylor & Francis Group, 2017). 184 p.

Margariti, S., *Defining International Terrorism: Between State Sovereignty and Cosmopolitanism* (The Hague: T.M.C. Asser Press, 2017). 186 p.

Qureshi, W.A., Combating International Terrorism, *Florida Journal of International Law*, vol. 29 (2017): p. 1–39.

de la Rasilla, I., An International Terrorism Court in Nuce in the Age of International Adjudication, in Rehman, J., Shahid, A. and Dickinson, M. (eds), *The Asian Yearbook of Human Rights and Humanitarian Law* (Leiden; Boston: Brill Nijhoff, 2017): p. 76–108.

Saul, B., The Legal Relationship between Terrorism and Transnational Crime, *International Criminal Law Review*, vol. 17 (2017): p. 417–452.

Walker, C., The War of Words with Terrorism: An Assessment of Three Approaches to Pursue and Prevent, *Journal of Conflict and Security Law*, vol. 22 (2017): p. 523–551.

18. International Trade law

Kawharu, A., Punctuated Equilibrium: The Potential Role of FTA Trade Commissions in the Evolution of International Investment Law, *Journal of International Economic Law*, vol. 20 (2017): p. 87–113.

Morin, J., Pauwelyn, J. and Hollway, J., The Trade Regime as a Complex Adaptive System: Exploration and Exploitation of Environmental Norms in Trade Agreements, *Journal of International Economic Law*, vol. 20 (2017): p. 365–390.

Nyombi, C., and Mortimer, T., Is a Multilateral Treaty on Business and Human Rights Justified? *International Trade Law & Regulation*, vol. 23 (2017): p. 126–136.

Schéré, L., The Culture War: A Look at the Cultural Exception Principle in International Trade Law, *Fordham International Law Journal*, vol. 40 (2017): p. 561–582.

Vidigal, G., Why is there so Little Litigation Under Free Trade Agreements? Retaliation and Adjudication in International Dispute Settlement, *Journal of International Economic Law*, vol. 20 (2017): p. 927–950.

19. International Tribunals

Aloisi, R., and Meernik, J.D., *Judgment Day: Judicial Decision Making at the International Criminal Tribunals* (New York: Cambridge University Press, 2017). 254 p.

Alter, K.J., The Evolution of International Law and Courts, in Fioretos, O. (ed.), *International Politics and Institutions in Time* (Oxford: Oxford University Press, 2017): p. 251–273.

Bachvarova, T., *The Standing of Victims in the Procedural Design of the International Criminal Court* (Leiden; Boston: Brill, Nijhoff, 2017). 258 p.

Baylis, E., The Persuasive Authority of Internationalized Criminal Tribunals, *American University International Law Review*, vol. 32 (2017): p. 611–643.

Benvenisti, E., and Downs, G.W., *Between Fragmentation and Democracy: The Role of National and International Courts* (Cambridge: Cambridge University Press, 2017). 244 p.

Birdsall, A., and Lang, A.F., The International Criminal Court and Global Constitutionalism, in Lang, A.F., and Antje, W., *Handbook on Global Constitutionalism* (Cheltenham, UK: Edward Elgar Publishing, 2017): p. 383–394.

Boisson de Chazournes, L., Plurality in the Fabric of International Courts and Tribunals: The Threads of a Managerial Approach, *European Journal of International Law*, vol. 28 (2017): p. 13–72.

Carcano, A., Of Efficiency and Fairness in the Administration of International Justice: Can the Residual Mechanism Provide Adequately Reasoned Judgments? *Questions of International Law*, vol. June (2017): p. 21–38.

Cotte, B., *et al.* (eds), *70 ans après Nuremberg: juger le crime contre l'humanité* (Dalloz, 2017). 240 p.

De Souza Dias, T., 'Interests of Justice': Defining the Scope of Prosecutorial Discretion in Article 53(1)(*c*) and (2)(*c*) of the Rome Statute of the International Criminal Court, *Leiden Journal of International Law*, vol. 30 (2017): p. 731–751.

DePiazza, J., Denial of Fair Trial as an International Crime Precedent for Pleading and Proving it Under the Rome Statute, *Journal of International Criminal Justice*, vol. 15 (2017): p. 257–289.

Deprez, C., The Gravity of International Crimes as a Challenge to the (Full) Protection of Human Rights before International Criminal Tribunals? A Strasbourg Perspective, *Nordic Journal of International Law*, vol. 86 (2017): p. 499–524.

Ford, S., What Investigative Resources does the International Criminal Court Need to Succeed: A Gravity-Based Approach, *Washington University Global Studies Law Review*, vol. 16 (2017): p. 1–70.

Gallus, N., *The Temporal Jurisdiction of International Tribunals* (Oxford, United Kingdom: Oxford University Press, 2017). 158 p.

García Matamoros, L.V., and Ávila Medina, D.C. (eds), *Procedimiento, litigio y representación ante tribunales internacionales* (Bogotá: Editorial Universidad del Rosario, 2017). 592 p.

Grey, R., The ICC's First Forced Pregnancy Case in Historical Perspective, *Journal of International Criminal Justice*, vol. 15 (2017): p. 905–930.

Hassanein, A.S., Self-Referral of Situations to the International Criminal Court: Complementarity in Practice—Complementarity in Crisis, *International Criminal Law Review*, vol. 17 (2017): p. 107–134.

Hayashi, N., and Bailliet, C. (eds), *The Legitimacy of International Criminal Tribunals* (Cambridge: Cambridge University Press, 2017). 524 p.

Heinze, A., The Kosovo Specialist Chambers' Rules of Procedure and Evidence: A Diamond made Under Pressure? *Journal of International Criminal Justice*, vol. 15 (2017): p. 985–1009.

Imoedemhe, O.C., The Complementarity Regime of the International Criminal Court: National Implementation in Africa (Cham: Springer, 2017). 229 p.

Jia, B.B., International Case Law in the Development of International Law, *Collected Courses of the Hague Academy of International Law / Recueil des cours de l'Académie de Droit International de la Haye*, vol. 382 (2017): p. 175–397.

Kent, A., and Trinidad, J., The Management of Third-Party Amicus Participation before International Criminal Tribunals: Juggling Efficiency and Legitimacy, *International Criminal Law Review*, vol. 17 (2017): p. 728–747.

Kielsgard, M.D., and Gee-Kin, K., Prioritizing Jurisdiction in the Competing Regimes of the International Criminal Court and the African Court of Justice and Human Rights: A Way Forward, *Boston University International Law Journal*, vol. 35 (2017): p. 285–335.

King, K.L., and Meernik, J.D., *The Witness Experience Testimony at the ICTY and its Impact* (Cambridge: Cambridge University Press, 2017). 220 p.

Kopylova, E.A., The Offence of Giving False Testimony Under Solemn Declaration in the Rome Statute, *Criminal Law Forum*, vol. 28 (2017): p. 669–708.

Le Moli, G., Vishvanathan, P.S., and Aeri, A., Whither the Proof? The Progressive Reversal of the Burden of Proof in Environmental Cases before International Courts and Tribunals, *Journal of International Dispute Settlement*, vol. 8 (2017): p. 644–672.

May, L., and Fyfe, S., *International Criminal Tribunals: A Normative Defense* (Cambridge, United Kingdom; New York, NY: Cambridge University Press, 2017). 217 p.

McDermott, Y., Fairness before the Mechanism for the International Criminal Tribunals, *Questions of International Law*, vol. June (2017): p. 39–55.

McDermott, Y., Strengthening the Evaluation of Evidence in International Criminal Trials, *International Criminal Law Review*, vol. 17 (2017): p. 682–702.

Miles, C.A., Provisional Measures before International Courts and Tribunals (Cambridge; New York, NY: Cambridge University Press, 2017). 592 p.

Mistry, H., The Significance of Institutional Culture in Enhancing the Validity of International Criminal Tribunals, *International Criminal Law Review*, vol. 17 (2017): p. 703–727.

Mujuzi, J.D., The African Court on Human and Peoples' Rights and its Protection of the Right to a Fair Trial, *Law and Practice of International Courts and Tribunals*, vol. 16 (2017): p. 187–223.

Rastan, R., What is 'Substantially the Same Conduct'? Unpacking the ICC's 'First Limb' Complementarity Jurisprudence, *Journal of International Criminal Justice*, vol. 15 (2017): p. 1–29.

Sarzo, M., *Res Judicata, Jurisdiction Ratione Materiae* and Legal Reasoning in the Dispute between Nicaragua and Colombia before the International Court of Justice, *The Law & Practice of International Courts and Tribunals*, vol. 16 (2017): p. 224–244.

Schabas, W.A., and Murphy S. (eds), *Research Handbook on International Courts and Tribunals* (Cheltenham, UK; Northampton, MA, USA: Edward Elgar Publishing, 2017). 576 p.

Schense, J., and Carter, L.E. (eds), *Two Steps Forward, One Step Back: The Deterrent Effect of International Criminal Tribunals* (Nuremberg; Brussels: International Nuremberg Principles Academy, 2017). 491 p.

Schultz, T., and Ridi, N., Comity and International Courts and Tribunals, *Cornell International Law Journal*, vol. 50 (2017): p. 577–610.

Theiring, R., The Policy of Truth: A Comparative Study of Transitional Justice between the Rwandan Gacaca Court and the Extraordinary Chambers in the Courts of Cambodia, *California Western International Law Journal*, vol. 48 (2017): p. 159–188.

van der Wilt, H., Unconstitutional Change for Government: A New Crime within the Jurisdiction of the African Criminal Court, *Leiden Journal of International Law*, vol. 30 (2017): p. 967–986.

20. International Waterways

Barraud, R., and Germaine, M., *Démanteler les barrages pour restaurer les cours d'eau: controverse environnementale et représentations* (Versailles, France: Éditions Quae, 2017). 253 p.

Kinna, R., and Rieu-Clarke, A., *The Governance Regime of the Mekong River Basin: Can the Global Water Conventions Strengthen the 1995 Mekong Agreement?* (Leiden; Boston: Brill, 2017). 92 p.

Murthy, S.L., and Mendikulova, F., Water, Conflict, and Cooperation in Central Asia: The Role of International Law and Diplomacy, *Vermont Journal of Environmental Law*, vol. 18 (2017): p. 400–454.

Tanzi, A., *The Consolidation of International Water Law: A Comparative Analysis of the UN and UNECE Water Conventions* (Napoli: Editoriale scientifica, 2017). 266 p.

21. Intervention and humanitarian intervention

Bartels, R., Discrepancies between International Humanitarian Law on the Battlefield and in the Courtroom: The Challenges of Applying International Humanitarian Law during International Criminal Trials, in Cryer, R., and Henderson, C. (eds), *Law on the use of Force and Armed Conflict* (Cheltenham, UK: Edward Elgar Publishing, 2017): p. 643–682.

Bellamy, A.J. (ed), *Humanitarian Intervention: Critical Concepts in Military, Strategic and Security Studies* (London; New York, NY: Routledge, Taylor & Francis Group, 2017). 1508 p.

Bitensky, S.H., For Recognition of a Peoples' Right to U.N. Authorized Armed Intervention to Stop Mass Atrocities, *Washington University Global Studies Law Review*, vol. 16 (2017): p. 245–294.

Breslin, A., A Reflection on the Legal Obligation for Third States to Ensure Respect for IHL, *Journal of Conflict and Security Law*, vol. 22 (2017): p. 5–37.

Chang, Z., Cyberwarfare and International Humanitarian Law, *Creighton International and Comparative Law Journal*, vol. 9 (2017): p. 29–53.

Díaz Santis, B., *La ambientalización del derecho internacional humanitario* (Valencia: Tirant lo Blanch, 2017). 348 p.

Dowd, R., and McAdam, J., International Cooperation and Responsibility-Sharing to Protect Refugees: What, Why and How? *International and Comparative Law Quarterly*, vol. 66 (2017): p. 863–892.

Geiss, R., Zimmermann, A., and Haumer, S., *Humanizing the Laws of War: The Red Cross and the Development of International Humanitarian Law* (Cambridge, United Kingdom; New York, NY: Cambridge University Press, 2017). 266 p.

Glanville, L., The Responsibility to Protect Beyond Borders in the Law of Nature and Nations, *European Journal of International Law*, vol. 28 (2017): p. 1069–1095.

Henderson, S., The Arms Trade Treaty: Responsibility to Protect in Action? *Global Responsibility to Protect*, vol. 9 (2017): p. 147–172.

Henry, E., *Le principe de nécessité militaire: histoire et actualité d'une norme fondamentale du droit international humanitaire* (Paris: Editions A. Pedone, 2017). 826 p.

Hill-Cawthorne, L., Rights Under International Humanitarian Law, *European Journal of International Law*, vol. 28 (2017): p. 1187–1215.

Hofer, A., The Developed/Developing Divide on Unilateral Coercive Measures: Legitimate Enforcement or Illegitimate Intervention, *Chinese Journal of International Law*, vol. 16 (2017): p. 175–214.

Lesser, S., Early Non-Military Intervention to Prevent Atrocity Crimes, *Cardozo Journal of Conflict Resolution*, vol. 19 (2017): p. 129–162.

Liebermann, J., The Scope of Application of International Humanitarian Law in Non-International Armed Conflicts—Analysing State Practice from Colombia, *Humanitäres Völkerrecht: Informationsschriften*, vol. 29 (2016): p. 146–158.

Longobardo, M., (New) Cyber Exploitation and (Old) International Humanitarian Law, *Zeitschrift für ausländisches öfentliches Recht und Völkerrecht, ZAORV = Heidelberg Journal of International Law*, vol. 77 (2017): p. 809–834.

Mull, N.W., A Critique of the ICRC's Updated Commentary to the First Geneva Convention: Arming Medical Personnel and the Loss of Protected Status, *Georgia Journal of International and Comparative Law*, vol. 45 (2017): p. 495–511.

O'Meara, C., Should International Law Recognize a Right of Humanitarian Intervention? *International and Comparative Law Quarterly*, vol. 66 (2017): p. 441–466.

Orakhelashvili, A., Kosovo and Intersecting Legal Regimes: An Interdisciplinary Analysis, *Global Constitutionalism*, vol. 6 (2017): p. 237–264.

Paust, J.J., R2P and Protective Intervention, *Temple International and Comparative Law Journal*, vol. 31 (2017): p. 109–121.

Rim, Y., The Role of the International Criminal Court in Implementing the Responsibility to Protect, *Florida Journal of International Law*, vol. 29 (2017): p. 69–98.

Saul, B., Enhancing Civilian Protection by Engaging Non-State Armed Groups Under International Humanitarian Law, *Journal of Conflict and Security Law*, vol. 22 (2017): p. 39–66.

Todeschini, V., The ICCPR in Armed Conflict: An Appraisal of the Human Rights Committee's Engagement with International Humanitarian Law, *Nordic Journal of Human Rights*, vol. 35 (2017): p. 203–219.

Townley, S., Indiscriminate Attacks and the Past, Present, and Future of the Rules/ Standards and Objective/Subjective Debates in International Humanitarian Law, *Vanderbilt Journal of Transnational Law*, vol. 50 (2017): p. 1223–1279.

Tzeng, P., Humanitarian Intervention at the Margins: An Examination of Recent Incidents, *Vanderbilt Journal of Transnational Law*, vol. 50 (2017): p. 415–461.

Warren, A., and Grenfell, D. (eds), *Rethinking Humanitarian Intervention in the 21st Century* (Edinburgh, Scotland: Edinburgh University Press, 2017). 332 p.

22. Jurisdiction

Bonafe, B., I., Maritime Delimitation in the Indian Ocean (Somalia v Kenya). Preliminary Objections. International Court of Justice, February 2, 2017, *The American Journal of International Law*, vol. 111 (2017): p. 725–731.

Liivoja, R., *Criminal Jurisdiction Over Armed Forces Abroad* (Cambridge, United Kingdom: Cambridge University Press, 2017). 332 p.

Reeves, A.R., Liability to International Prosecution: The Nature of Universal Jurisdiction, *European Journal of International Law*, vol. 28 (2017): p. 1047–1067.

Svantesson, D.J.B., *Solving the Internet Jurisdiction Puzzle* (Oxford: Oxford University Press, 2017). 265 p.

23. Law of Armed Conflict

Aldrich, G.H., Progressive Development of the Laws of War: A Reply to Criticisms of the 1977 Geneva Protocol I: Commentary, in Hulme, K., *Law of the Environment and Armed Conflict* (Cheltenham, UK: Edward Elgar Publishing, 2017): p. 693–720.

Blank, L.R., The Limits of Inviolability: The Parameters for Protection of United Nations Facilities during Armed Conflict, *International Law Studies*, vol. 93 (2017): p. 45–101.

Bradley, M.M., Expanding the Borders of Common Article 3 in Non-International Armed Conflicts: Amending its Geographical Application through Subsequent Practice? *Netherlands International Law Review*, vol. 64 (2017): p. 375–406.

Brilmayer, L., Giorgetti, C. and Charlton, L., *International Claims Commissions: Righting Wrongs After Conflict* (Cheltenham, UK: Edward Elgar Publishing, 2017). 272 p.

Cameron, L., *et al.*, The Updated Commentary on the First Geneva Convention—A New Tool for Generating Respect for International Humanitarian Law, *International Law Studies*, vol. 93 (2017): p. 157–178.

Chehtman, A., Revisionist Just War Theory and the Concept of War Crimes, *Leiden Journal of International Law*, vol. 31 (2017): p. 171–194.

Chinkin, C., and Kaldor, M., *International Law and New Wars* (Cambridge, United Kingdom; New York, NY: Cambridge University Press, 2017). 592 p.

Clapham, A., Detention by Armed Groups Under International Law, *International Law Studies*, vol. 93 (2017): p. 1–44.

Crawford, E., Tracing the Historical and Legal Development of the Levée En Masse in the Law of Armed Conflict, *Journal of the History of International Law*, vol. 19 (2017): p. 329–361.

Cusato, E., Back to the Future? Confronting the Role(s) of Natural Resources in Armed Conflict through the Lenses of Truth and Reconciliation Commissions, *International Community Law Review*, vol. 19 (2017): p. 373–400.

Erdem, M., Enforcing Conventional Humanitarian Law for Environmental Damage during Internal Armed Conflict, *Georgetown Environmental Law Review*, vol. 29 (2017): p. 435–480.

Evangelista, M., and Tannenwald, N. (eds), *Do the Geneva Conventions Matter?* (New York, NY: Oxford University Press, 2017). 376 p.

Haque, A.A., Whose Armed Conflict? Which Law of Armed Conflict? *Georgia Journal of International and Comparative Law*, vol. 45 (2017): p. 475–493.

Henckaerts, J., Study of Customary International Humanitarian Law: A Contribution to the Understanding and Respect for the Rule of Law in Armed Conflict, in Cryer, R., and Henderson, C. (eds), *Law on the Use of Force and Armed Conflict* (Cheltenham, UK: Edward Elgar Publishing, 2017): p. 508–545.

Hulme, K. (ed), *Law of the Environment and Armed Conflict* (Cheltenham, UK; Northamton, Massachusetts: Edward Elgar Publishing, 2017). 904 p.

John-Hopkins, M., Extrapolation of Criminal Law Modes of Liability to Target Analysis Under International Humanitarian Law: Developing the Framework for Understanding Direct Participation in Hostilities and Membership in Organized Armed Groups in Non-International Armed Conflict, *Journal of Conflict and Security Law*, vol. 22 (2017): p. 275–310.

Kassoti, E., The Normative Status of Unilateral *Ad Hoc* Commitments by Non-State Armed Actors in Internal Armed Conflicts: International Legal Personality and Lawmaking Capacity Distinguished, *Journal of Conflict and Security Law*, vol. 22 (2017): p. 67–96.

Marxsen, C., Violation and Confirmation of the Law: The Intricate Effects of the Invocation of the Law in Armed Conflict, *Journal on the Use of Force and International Law* (2017): p. 1–32.

Murray, D., Non-State Armed Groups, Detention Authority in Non-International Armed Conflict, and the Coherence of International Law: Searching for a Way Forward, *Leiden Journal of International Law*, vol. 30 (2017): p. 435–456.

Newton, M.A., Contorting Common Article 3: Reflections on the Revised ICRC Commentary, *Georgia Journal of International and Comparative Law*, vol. 45 (2017): p. 513–527.

Seatzu, F., Revitalizing the International Legal Protection of Humanitarian Aid Workers in Armed Conflict, *Revue des droits de l'homme*, vol. 11 (2017): p. 1–12.

Shun Ming Yau, S., Blurring the Beginning of Non-International Armed Conflict: The Frustration of Legal Paradigms in Response to Terrorism, *Groningen Journal of International Law*, vol. 5 (2017): p. 241–254.

Todeschini, V., The ICCPR in Armed Conflict: An Appraisal of the Human Rights Committee's Engagement with International Humanitarian Law, *Nordic Journal of Human Rights*, vol. 35 (2017): p. 203–219.

Zamir, N., *Classification of Conflicts in International Humanitarian Law: The Legal Impact of Foreign Intervention in Civil Wars* (London: Edward Elgar Publishing, 2017). 288 p.

24. Law of the Sea

Acikgonul, Y.E., Equitable Delimitation of Maritime Boundaries: The Uncontested Supremacy of Coastal Geography in Case Law, *Ocean Yearbook*, vol. 31 (2017): p. 173–196.

Aksenova, M., and Burke, C., The Chagos Islands Award: Exploring the Renewed Role of the Law of the Sea in the Post-Colonial Context, *Wisconsin International Law Journal*, vol. 35 (2017): p. 1–38.

Anderson, D., Some Aspects of the Regime of Islands in the Law of the Sea, *The International Journal of Marine and Coastal Law*, vol. 32 (2017): p. 316–331.

Bikundo, E., Artificial Islands, Artificial Highways and Pirates, *Asia-Pacific Journal of Ocean Law and Policy*, vol. 2 (2017): p. 140–166.

Courmont, B., Lasserre, F., and Mottet, E. (eds), *Assessing Maritime Disputes in East Asia: Political and Legal Perspectives* (Milton Park, Abingdon, Oxon; New York, NY: Routledge, 2017). 244 p.

Dupont, P., and Solomou, A., Provisional Measures in Maritime Delimitation Cases, in Crawford, J., *et al.* (eds), *The International Legal Order: Current Needs and Possible Responses: Essays in Honour of Djamchid Momtaz* (Leiden; Boston: Brill Nijhoff, 2017): p. 312–333.

Fernández Sánchez, P.A. (ed), *New Approaches to the Law of the Sea: (in Honor of Ambassador José Antonio De Yturriaga-Barberán)* (New York: Nova Science Publisher's, 2017). 475 p.

Forteau, M., and Thouvenin, J. (eds), *Traite de droit international de la mer* (Paris: Pedone, 2017). 1322 p.

Gates, D.W., International Law Adrift: Forum Shopping, Forum Rejection, and the Future of Maritime Dispute Resolution, *Chicago Journal of International Law*, vol. 18 (2017): p. 287–320.

Harrison, J., *Saving the Oceans through Law: The International Legal Framework for the Protection of the Marine Environment,* First ed. (Oxford: Oxford University Press, 2017). 300 p.

Hossain, K., and Morris, K., Protecting Arctic Ocean Marine Biodiversity in the Area Beyond National Jurisdiction, in Andreone G. (ed), *The Future of the Law of the Sea: Bridging Gaps between National, Individual and Common Interests* (Cham, Switzerland: Springer, 2017): p. 105–126.

Jaeckel, A.L., *The International Seabed Authority and the Pre-Cautionary Principle: Balancing Deep Seabed Mineral Mining and Marine Environmental Protection* (Boston: Brill Nijhoff, 2017).

Kamto, M., Considérations actuelles sur la méthode de délimitation maritime devant la Cour internationale de Justice: de charybde en scylla?, in Crawford, J., *et al.* (eds), *The International Legal Order: Current Needs and Possible Responses: Essays in Honour of Djamchid Momtaz* (Leiden; Boston: Brill Nijhoff, 2017): p. 383–420.

Klein, N., The Vicissitudes of Dispute Settlement Under the Law of the Sea Convention, *The International Journal of Marine and Coastal Law*, vol. 32 (2017): p. 332–363.

Korger, N., Going Boldly Where no Country has Gone before: UNCLOS and the Russian Federation's Claim to the Arctic Circle, *Wisconsin International Law Journal*, vol. 34 (2017): p. 731–754.

Kunoy, B., Assertions of Entitlement to the Outer Continental Shelf in the Central Arctic Ocean, *International and Comparative Law Quarterly*, vol. 66 (2017): p. 367–409.

Lando, M., Delimiting the Continental Shelf Beyond 200 Nautical Miles at the International Court of Justice: The Nicaragua v. Colombia Cases, *Chinese Journal of International Law*, vol. 16 (2017): p. 137–173.

Lando, M., Judicial Uncertainties Concerning Territorial Sea Delimitation Under Article 15 of the United Nations Convention on the Law of the Sea, *International and Comparative Law Quarterly*, vol. 66 (2017): p. 589–623.

Le Floch, G., L'exécution des décisions ordonnant la mainlevée des navires devant le Tribunal international du droit de la mer, *Revue générale de droit international public*, vol. 121 (2017): p. 597–611.

Liao, X., Evaluation of Scientific Evidence by International Courts and Tribunals in the Continental Shelf Delimitation Cases, *Ocean Development and International Law*, vol. 48 (2017): p. 136–157.

Lodge, M.W., Segerson, K., and Squires, D., Sharing and Preserving the Resources in the Deep Sea: Challenges for the International Seabed Authority, *The International Journal of Marine and Coastal Law*, vol. 32 (2017): p. 427–457.

Moore, J.N. (ed), *Common Resources: Law of the Sea, Outer Space, and Antarctica* (Brill Nijhoff, 2017). 758 p.

Nordquist, M.H., Moore, J.N., and Long, R.J. (eds), *International Marine Economy: Law and Policy* (Leiden; Boston: Brill Nijhoff, 2017). 445 p.

Oral, N., The South China Sea Arbitral Award: Casting Light on Article 121 of UNCLOS, *The Law and Practice of International Courts and Tribunals*, vol. 16 (2017): p. 354–364.

Pappa, M., The Impact of Judicial Delimitation on Private Rights Existing in Contested Waters: Implications for the Somali-Kenyan Maritime Dispute, *Journal of African Law*, vol. 61 (2017): p. 393–418.

Peiris, N., Advisory Opinion on Fisheries in the Exclusive Economic Zone from the International Tribunal for the Law of the Sea: The Birth of Regional Treaty-Based Advisory Jurisdiction, *Ocean Yearbook Online*, vol. 31 (2017): p. 250–288.

Ros, N., La gouvernance des mers et océans, entre mythes et réalités juridiques, *Journal du droit international*, vol. 144 (2017): p. 757–812.

Scanlon, Z., Taking Action Against Fishing Vessels without Nationality: Have Recent International Developments Clarified the Law? *The International Journal of Marine and Coastal Law*, vol. 32 (2017): p. 54–68.

Talmon, S., The South China Sea Arbitration and the Finality of 'Final' Awards, *Journal of International Dispute Settlement*, vol. 28 (2017): p. 388–401.

Telesetsky, A., The Global North, the Global South, and the Challenges of Ensuring due Diligence for Sustainable Fishing Governance, *Transnational Law & Contemporary Problems*, vol. 26 (2017): p. 435–470.

Toman, R.G., Jurisdictional Requirements for Arbitration Under UNCLOS: Does the South China Sea Decision Bring Long Sought Clarity to the Scope of Historic Claims? *New York University Journal of International Law and Politics*, vol. 49 (2017): p. 619–634.

Tzevelekos, V.P., and Proukaki, E.K., Migrants at Sea: A Duty of Plural States to Protect (Extraterritorially)? *Nordic Journal of International Law*, vol. 86 (2017): p. 427–469.

Warner, R., Strengthening Governance Frameworks for Conservation and Sustainable use of Marine Biodiversity in Areas Beyond National Jurisdiction: Southern Hemisphere Perspectives, *The International Journal of Marine and Coastal Law*, vol. 32 (2017): p. 607–634.

Williams, L.C., An Ocean between Us: The Implications of Inconsistencies between the Navigational Laws of Coastal Arctic Council Nations and the United Nations Convention on the Law of the Sea for Arctic Navigation, *Vanderbilt Law Review*, vol. 70 (2017): p. 379–411.

Yang, R.K. (ed), *The South China Sea Disputes Flashpoints, Turning Points and Trajectories* (Singapore: World Scientific Publishing, Co., 2017). 509 p.

Yiallourides, C., Senkaku/Diaoyu: Are they Islands? *The International Lawyer*, vol. 50 (2017): p. 347–365.

Zou, K. (ed), *Sustainable Development and the Law of the Sea* (Leiden; Boston: Brill Nijhoff, 2017). 306 p.

25. Law of Treaties

Beckman, R., and Sun, Z., The Relationship between UNCLOS and IMO Instruments, *Asia-Pacific Journal of Ocean Law and Policy*, vol. 2 (2017): p. 201–246.

Berman, F., Why do we Need a Law of Treaties? Inaugural Lecture, *Recueil des cours*, vol. 385 (2017): p. 9–31.

Broude, T., Haftel, Y.Z., and Thompson, A., The Trans-Pacific Partnership and Regulatory Space: A Comparison of Treaty Texts, *Journal of International Economic Law*, vol. 20 (2017): p. 391–417.

Elsig, M., and Milewicz K., The Politics of Treaty Signature: The Role of Diplomats and Ties that Bind, *International Negotiation*, vol. 22 (2017): p. 521–543.

Gillette, C.P., and Walt, S.D., Judicial Refusal to Apply Treaty Law: Domestic Law Limitations on the CISG's Application, *Uniform Law Review*, vol. 22 (2017): p. 452–491.

Grisel, F., Treaty-Making between Public Authority and Private Interests: The Genealogy of the Convention on the Recognition and Enforcement of Foreign Arbitral Awards, *European Journal of International Law*, vol. 28 (2017): p. 73–87.

Kammerhofer, J., Taking the Rules of Interpretation Seriously, but Not Literally? A Theoretical Reconstruction of Orthodox Dogma, *Nordic Journal of International Law*, vol. 86 (2017): p. 125–150.

Klučka, J., The Significance of Principles of International Law for Interpretation and Application of International Treaties, *Czech Yearbook of International Law*, vol. 8 (2017): p. 145–194.

Lo, C., *Treaty Interpretation Under the Vienna Convention on the Law of Treaties: A New Round of Codification* (Singapore: Springer, 2017). 361 p.

López Martín, A.G., Aplicación de tratados sucesivos concernientes a la misma materia: Análisis del artículo 30 de la Convención de Viena sobre Derechos de los Tratados, *Anuario colombiano de derecho internacional*, vol. 10 (2017): p. 51–84.

Nyombi, C., and Mortimer, T., Tackling the Legitimacy Crisis in International Investment Law through Progressive Treaty-Making Practices, *International Arbitration Law Review*, vol. 20 (2017): p. 162–172.

Prislan, V., Domestic Explanatory Documents and Treaty Interpretation, *International and Comparative Law Quarterly*, vol. 66 (2017): p. 923–962.

Safta, M., Constitutional Review of International Treaties, *Czech Yearbook of International Law*, vol. 8 (2017): p. 307–326.

Shereshevsky, Y., and Noah, T., Does Exposure to Preparatory Work Affect Treaty Interpretation: An Experimental Study on International Law Students and Experts, *European Journal of International Law*, vol. 28 (2017): p. 1287–1316.

Wyraz, E., The Application of International Conventions and Treaties to Third States, *Czech Yearbook of International Law*, vol. 8 (2017): p. 387–399.

26. Membership and Representation

Higgins, R., *et al.*, Membership, In Higgins, *et al.* (eds), *Oppenheim's International Law: United Nations* (Oxford, UK: Oxford University Press, 2017): p. 260–319.

27. Most Favored Nation Clause

Batifort, S., and Heath, J.B., The New Debate on the Interpretation of MFN Clauses in Investment Treaties: Putting the Brakes on Multilateralization, *The American Journal of International Law*, vol. 111 (2017): p. 873–913.

Hoekman, B., and Mavroidis, P.C., MFN Clubs and Scheduling Additional Commitments in the GATT: Learning from the GATS, *European Journal of International Law*, vol. 28 (2017): p. 387–407.

Johnson, J.P., The Agency Model and MFN Clauses, *The Review of Economic Studies*, vol. 84 (2017): p. 1151–1185.

Perez-Aznar, F., The Use of Most-Favoured-Nation Clauses to Import Substantive Treaty Provisions in International Investment Agreements, *Journal of International Economic Law*, vol. 20 (2017): p. 777–805.

Sharmin, T., Should the MFN within Investment Treaties Exclude Dispute Resolution? An Evaluation of the Australian Approach, *Australian Year Book of International Law*, vol. 35 (2017): p. 123–155.

Schill, S.W., MFN Clauses as Bilateral Commitments to Multilateralism: A Reply to Simon Batifort and J. Benton Heath, *The American Journal of International Law*, vol. 111 (2017): p. 914–935.

Wüstenberg, M., Back to the Future: MFN Treatment in an Era of Protectionism, *Nordic Journal of International Law*, vol. 86 (2017): p. 525–546.

28. Narcotic Drugs

Riedel, B., I'd like to make a Reservation: Bolivian Coca Control and Why the United Nations Should Amend the Single Convention on Narcotic Drugs, *The George Washington International Law Review*, vol. 49 (2017): p. 711–747.

29. Natural Resources

Eckstein, G., *The International Law of Transboundary Groundwater Resources* (London; New York: Routledge, Taylor & Francis Group, 2017). 174 p.

Mushkat, R., Exploring International Environmental Governance Regimes: The Asian Way, *Wisconsin International Law Journal*, vol. 34 (2017): p. 585–667.

30. Non-Governmental Organizations

Ahmed, S., Accountability of International NGOs: Human Rights Violations in Healthcare Provision in Developing Countries and the Effectiveness of Current Measures, *Annual Survey of International and Comparative Law*, vol. 22 (2017): p. 33–71.

Bernaz, N., and Pietropaoli, I., The Role of Non-Governmental Organizations in the Business and Human Rights Treaty Negotiations, *Journal of Human Rights Practice*, vol. 9 (2017): p. 287–311.

Breen, C., The Role of NGOs in the Formulation of and Compliance with the Optional Protocol to the Convention on the Rights of the Child on Involvement of Children in Armed Conflict, in Stark, B. (ed), *Human Rights and Children* (Cheltenham, UK; Northampton, MA, USA: Edwar Elgar Publishing, 2017): p. 604–632.

De Silva, N., Intermediary Complexity in Regulatory Governance: The International Criminal Court's use of NGOs in Regulating International Crimes, *The Annals of the American Academy of Political and Social Science*, vol. 670 (2017): p. 170–188.

Dezalay, S., The Role of International NGOs in the Emergence of Transitional Justice: A Case Study of the International Center for Transitional Justice, in Lawther, C., Moffett, L. (ed), *Research Handbook on Transnational Justice* (Cheltenham, UK; Northampton, MA, USA: Edward Elgar Publishing, 2017): p. 202–220.

Guimezanes, M., Mastor, W., and Pellet, A., *Organisations non-gouvernementales, financement étatique et efficacité de l'aide au développement: une illustration des rôles des ONG en droit international* (Issy-les-Moulineaux: LGDJ, 2017). 364 p.

31. Non-self-governing Territories

Clapton, W., Pluralism, Decolonization and International Society, *Cambridge Review of International Affairs*, vol. 30 (2017): p. 350–367.

Ojeda García, R., *Global, Regional and Local Dimensions of Western Sahara's Protracted Decolonization: When a Conflict Gets Old* (New York, NY: Palgrave Macmillan, 2017). 355 p.

Smith, A.W.M., and Jeppesen, C., *Britain, France and the Decolonization of Africa: Future Imperfect?* (London, England: UCL Press, 2017). 254 p.

32. Outer Space Law

Blanchette-Séguin, V., Reaching for the Moon: Mining in Outer Space, *New York University Journal of International Law & Politics*, vol. 49 (2017): p. 959–970.

Butler, D.A., Who Owns the Moon, Mars, and Other Celestial Bodies: Lunar Jurisprudence in Corpus Juris Spatialis, *Journal of Air Law and Commerce*, vol. 82 (2017): p. 505–517.

Hobe, S., and de Man, P., National Appropriation of Outer Space and State Jurisdiction to Regulate the Exploitation, Exploration and Utilization of Space Resources. *Zeitschrift fur Luft und Weltraumrecht = German Journal of Air and Space Law = Revue allemande de droit aérien et spatial*, vol. 66 (2017): p. 460–475.

Jakhu, R.S., Steer, C., and Chen, K., Conflicts in Space and the Rule of Law. *Zeitschrift für Luft- und Weltraumrecht: German Journal of Air and Space Law*, vol. 66 (2017): p. 657–692.

Mizushima, A., Fujii, K., and Ishido, S., What is an Appropriate Interaction between International Law and Domestic Legal Systems to Promote Space Resources Development? *Air & Space Law*, vol. 42 (2017): p. 543–570.

Su, J., Legality of Unilateral Exploitation of Space Resources Under International Law, *The International and Comparative Law Quarterly*, vol. 66 (2017): p. 991–1008.

Sun, R., Legal Issues of Space Colonization, *Zeitschrift fur Luft und Weltraumrecht = German Journal of Air and Space Law = Revue allemande de droit aérien et spatial*, vol. 66 (2017): p. 476–490.

Vecchio, V., Customary International Law in the Outer Space Treaty: Space Law as Laboratory for the Evolution of Public International Law, *Zeitschrift fur Luft und Weltraumrecht = German Journal of Air and Space Law = Revue allemande de droit aérien et spatial*, vol. 66 (2017): p. 491–502.

33. Peaceful Settlement of Disputes

McGarry, B., The Development of Custom in Territorial Dispute Settlement, *Journal of International Dispute Settlement*, vol. 8 (2017): p. 339–365.

Swinehart, M.W., Reliability of Expert Evidence in International Disputes, *Michigan Journal of International Law*, vol. 38 (2017): p. 287–347.

34. Peacekeeping and related activities

Boutin, B., Attribution of Conduct in International Military Operations: A Causal Analysis of Effective Control, *Melbourne Journal of International Law*, vol. 18 (2017): p. 154–179.

Cameron, L., *The Privatization of Peacekeeping: Exploring Limits and Responsibility Under International Law* (Unite Kingdom: Cambridge University Press, 2017). 410 p.

Campione, R., and Ruschi, F. (eds), *Guerra, derecho y seguridad en las relaciones internacionales* (Valencia: Tirant lo Blanch, 2017). 329 p.

Crowe, J., and John, A., The Status of Private Military Security Companies in United Nations Peacekeeping Operations Under the International Law of Armed Conflict, *Melbourne Journal of International Law*, vol. 18 (2017): p. 16–44.

Giles, S.A., Criminal Prosecution of UN Peacekeepers: When Defenders of Peace Incite Further Conflict through their Own Misconduct, *The American University International Law Review*, vol. 33 (2017): p. 147–185.

Mathias, S., UN Peacekeeping Today: Legal Challenges and Uncertainties, *Melbourne Journal of International Law*, vol. 18 (2017): p. 138–153.

Nakamura, E., Monitoring Accountability for UN Peacekeeping Under ICCPR, *Nordic Journal of International Law*, vol. 86 (2017): p. 341–365.

Perova, N., Disentangling 'Effective Control' Test for the Purpose of Attribution of the Conduct of UN Peacekeepers to the States and the United Nations, *Nordic Journal of International Law*, vol. 86 (2017): p. 30–67.

Sprik, L., Command Responsibility in Peacekeeping Missions: Normative Obligations of Protection in a Criminal Law Environment, *Journal of Conflict and Security Law*, vol. 22 (2017): p. 1–26.

Von Billerbeck, S., UN Peace Operations and Conflicting Legitimacies, *Journal of Intervention and Statebuilding*, vol. 11 (2017): p. 286–305.

35. Piracy

Fernández Sanz, J.C., Piratería marítima: Una Amenaza Actual, *Política y estrategia*, iss. 122 (2017): p. 101–140.

Dubner, B.H., and Vargas, L.M., On the Law of "Pirate" Fishing and its Connection to Human Rights Violations and to Environmental Degradation—A Multi-National Disaster, *Journal of Maritime Law and Commerce*, vol. 48 (2017): p. 103–154.

Paige, T.P., The Impact and Effectiveness of UNCLOS on Counter-Piracy Operations, *Journal of Conflict and Security Law*, vol. 22 (2017): p. 97–123.

Scharf, M., and Taylor, M., A Contemporary Approach to the Oldest International Crime, *Utrecht Journal of International and European Law*, vol. 33 (2017): p. 77–89.

36. Political and Security Questions

Allen, S., *The Chagos Islanders and International Law* (Portland: Hart Publishing, 2017). 336 p.

Asaala, E.O., Rule of Law or Realpolitik? The Role of the United Nations Security Council in the International Criminal Court Processes in Africa, *African Human Rights Law Journal*, vol. 17 (2017): p. 265–293.

Bering, J., The Prohibition on Annexation: Lessons from Crimea, *New York University Journal of International Law and Politics*, vol. 49 (2017): p. 747–832.

Buchan, R., and Tsagourias, N.K., The Crisis in Crimea and the Principle of Non-Intervention, *International Community Law Review*, vol. 19 (2017): p. 165–193.

Carisch, E., Rickard-Martin, L., and Meister, S.R., *The Evolution of UN Sanctions: From a Tool of Warfare to a Tool of Peace, Security and Human Rights* (Cham, Switzerland: Springer, 2017). 501 p.

Caytas, J.D., Sanctions, Real and Imaginary: Experiences with Russia in the Ukraine Crisis, *Amsterdam Law Forum*, vol. 9 (2017): p. 26–47.

Chibundu, M.O., International Law and the Legitimation of External Coercive Measures in Aid of International Change, *Temple International and Comparative Law Journal*, vol. 31 (2017): p. 123–144.

Gross, A., *The Writing on the Wall: Rethinking the International Law of Occupation* (Cambridge, United Kingdom; New York, NY: Cambridge University Press, 2017). 447 p.

Henderson, C. (ed), *Commissions of Inquiry: Problems and Prospects* (Oxford; Portland, Oregon: Hart Publishing, 2017). 392 p.

Kettemann, M.C., Ensuring Cybersecurity through International Law, *Revista española de derecho internacional*, vol. 69 (2017): p. 281–289.

Ott, N., Conflict in Cyberspace: How International Legal Norms Can Reduce Military Escalation in Cyberspace Policy, *Fletcher Security Review*, vol. 3 (2017): p. 67–76.

Polański, P.P., Cyberspace: A New Branch of International Customary Law? *Computer Law & Security Review*, vol. 33 (2017): p. 371–381.

Schmitt, M.N., Peacetime Cyber Responses and Wartime Cyber Operations Under International Law: An Analytical Vade Mecum, *Harvard National Security Journal*, vol. 8 (2017): p. 239–282.

Segura Serrano, A., Cybersecuridad y Derecho internacional, *Revista española de derecho internacional*, vol. 69 (2017): p. 291–299.

Tucker, J.E., The Targeting of Non-State-Affiliated Civilians in Cyberspace: Lagging LOAC Principles Cause Uncertainty on Both Sides, *North Carolina Journal of International Law and Commercial Regulation*, vol. 42 (2017): p. 1013–1059.

Tzimas, T., Examination of the 'Assad must Go' Doctrine: Evaluation of Regime Legitimacy and De-Legitimisation from an International Law Perspective, *International Community Law Review*, vol. 19 (2017): p. 485–517.

Vaccaro-Incisa, G.M., Crimea's Secession from Ukraine and Accession to the Russian Federation as an Instance of North(-West) v. South(-East) Divide in the Understanding of International Law, *Santa Clara Journal of International Law*, vol. 15 (2017): p. 125–156.

Wenaweser, C., and Cockayne, J., Justice for Syria? The International, Impartial and Independent Mechanism and the Emergence of the UN General Assembly in the Realm of International Criminal Justice, *Journal of International Criminal Justice*, vol. 15 (2017): p. 211–230.

37. Progressive Development and Codification of International Law

Abashidze, A., and Shatalova, S., International Crimes Exception to the Immunity of State Officials from Foreign Criminal Jurisdiction: The Russian Perspective on the Work of the International Law Commission, *Netherlands International Law Review*, vol. 64 (2017): p. 213–236.

Abbenhuis, M., Barber, C.E., and Higgins, A.R., *War, Peace and International Order: The Legacies of the Hague Conferences of 1899 and 1907* (London: Routledge, 2017). 230 p.

Aldrich, G.H., Progressive Development of the Laws of War: A Reply to Criticisms of the 1977 Geneva Protocol I: Commentary, in Hulme, K., *Law of the Environment and Armed Conflict* (Cheltenham, UK: Edward Elgar Publishing, 2017): p. 693–720.

Alland, D., A titre de conclusions: qu'est-ce que l'exécution d'une décision juridictionnelle internationale et qui l'assume? *Revue générale de droit international public*, vol. 121 (2017): p. 863–873.

Almeida, P.W., Beyond Compliance: Law-Making through Latin American Cases before the World Court, *The Law & Practice of International Courts and Tribunals*, vol. 16 (2017): p. 245–263.

Arajärvi, N., The Requisite Rigour in the Identification of Customary International Law, *International Community Law Review*, vol. 19 (2017): p. 9–46.

Bandeira Galindo, G.R., and Yip, C., Customary International Law and the Third World: Do Not Step on the Grass, *Chinese Journal of International Law*, vol. 16 (2017): p. 251–270.

Bartolini, G., The ILC Draft Articles on the Protection of Persons in the Event of Disasters, *Rivista di diritto internazionale*, vol. 100 (2017): p. 677–718.

Bassiouni, M.C., Codification of International Criminal Law, *Denver Journal of International Law and Policy*, vol. 45 (2017): p. 333–364.

Bennouna, M., Le droit international entre la lettre et l'esprit: Cours général de droit international public, *Recueil des cours*, vol. 383 (2017): p. 9–231.

Benvenisti, E. and Nolte, G. (eds), *Community Interests Across International Law* (Oxford, United Kingdom: Oxford University Press, 2018).

Besson, S., and D'Aspremont, J. (eds), *The Oxford Handbook on the Sources of International Law* (Oxford: Oxford University Press, 2017). 900 p.

Bhabba, J., A Progressive Development, Children's Rights and the ILC Draft Articles on the Expulsion of Aliens, *Harvard Human Rights Journal*, vol. 30 (2017): p. 15–27.

Bialosky, J., Non-Refoulement in the ILC Articles on Expulsion of Aliens and its Practical Value for U.S. Immigration Law, *Michigan State International Law Review*, vol. 25 (2017): p. 1–30.

Blokker, N., International Organizations and Customary International Law: Is the International Law Commission Taking International Organizations Seriously? *International Organizations Law Review*, vol. 14 (2017): p. 1–12.

Carrillo-Santarelli, N., The Possibilities and Legitimacy of Non-State Participation in the Formation of Customary Law, *International Community Law Review*, vol. 19 (2017): p. 98–125.

Chigara, B.A., The Administration of International Law in National Courts and the Legitimacy of International Law, *International Criminal Law Review*, vol. 17 (2017): p. 909–934.

Chow, P.Y.S., Reservations as Unilateral Acts? Examining the International Law Commission's Approach to Reservations, *International and Comparative Law Quarterly*, vol. 66 (2017): p. 335–365.

Costelloe, D., *Legal Consequences of Peremptory Norms in International Law* (Cambridge: Cambridge University Press, 2017). 374 p.

Crawford, J., *et al.*, *The International Legal Order: Current Needs and Possible Responses: Essays in Honour of Djamchid Momtaz* (Leiden: Brill, 2017). 700 p.

Cryer, R., Of Custom, Treaties, Scholars and the Gavel: The Influence of the International Criminal Tribunals on the ICRC Customary Law Study, in Cryer, R., and Henderson, C. (eds), *Law on the Use of Force and Armed Conflict* (Cheltenham, UK: Edward Elgar Publishing, 2017): p. 604–628.

Cullen, H., Harrington, J., and Renshaw, C. (eds), *Experts, Networks and International Law* (Cambridge: Cambridge University Press, 2017). 308 p.

Dawidowicz, M., *Third-Party Countermeasures in International Law* (Cambridge, United Kingdom: Cambridge University Press, 2017). 431 p.

Dehaussy, J., *Propos sur les sources du droit international: l'exercice de la fonction normatrice dans un ordre juridique singulier* (Paris: Éditions Pedone, 2017). 360 p.

Deplano, R., Assessing the Role of Resolutions in the ILC Draft Conclusions on Identification of Customary International Law, *International Organizations Law Review*, vol. 14 (2017): p. 227–253.

Dienelt, A., and Sjöstedt, B., Is the ILC's Work Enhancing Protection for the Environment in Relation to Warfare? A Reply to Stavros-Evdokimos Pantazopoulos and Karen Hulme, *Questions of International Law*, vol. July (2017): p. 43–56.

Diller, J.M., Economic, Social and Cultural Human Rights: The Journey Towards Peremptory Norms in International Law, *Nordic Journal of Human Rights*, vol. 36 (2018): p. 19–37.

Droubi, S., Institutionalisation of Emerging Norms of Customary International Law through Resolutions and Operational Activities of the Political and Subsidiary Organs of the United Nations, *International Organizations Law Review*, vol. 14 (2017): p. 254–290.

Droubi, S., The Role of the United Nations in the Formation of Customary International Law in the Field of Human Rights, *International Community Law Review*, vol. 19 (2017): p. 68–97.

Druzin, B.H., Why does Soft Law have any Power Anyway? *Asian Journal of International Law*, vol. 7 (2017): p. 361–378.

Dumberry, P., Has the Fair and Equitable Treatment Standard Become a Rule of Customary International Law? *Journal of International Dispute Settlement*, vol. 8 (2017): p. 155–178.

Forteau, M., A New 'Baxter Paradox'? Some Observations on the ILC Draft Articles on the Expulsion of Aliens, *Harvard Human Rights Journal*, vol. 30 (2017): p. 29–47.

Gaita, R., and Simpson, G. (eds), *Who's Afraid of International Law?* (Clayton: Monash University Pub, 2017). 240 p.

Gastorn, K., Defining the Imprecise Contours of Jus Cogens in International Law, *Chinese Journal of International Law*, vol. 16 (2018): p. 643–662.

Giacco, L.L., Swinging between Finding and Justification: Judicial Citation and International Law-Making, *Cambridge Journal of International and Comparative Law*, vol. 6 (2017): p. 27–42.

Goldsmith, J., and Posner, E.A., A Theory of Customary International Law, in Wiessner, S. (ed), *General Theory of International Law* (Leiden; Boston: Brill Nijhoff, 2017): p. 427–465.

Guan, S.S., Jus Cogens: To Revise a Narrative, *Minnesota Journal of International Law*, vol. 26 (2017): p. 461–499.

Hakimi, M., Constructing an International Community, *American Journal of International Law*, vol. 111 (2017): p. 317–356.

Hakimi, M., The Work of International Law, *Harvard International Law Journal*, vol. 58 (2017): p. 1–46.

Hameed, A., Some Misunderstandings about Legislation and Law, *Chinese Journal of International Law*, vol. 16 (2017): p. 475–514.

Helmersen, S.T., Scholarly-Judicial Dialogue in International Law, *Law and Practice of International Courts and Tribunals*, vol. 16 (2017): p. 464–482.

Iovane, M., L'influence de la multiplication des jurisdictions internationales sur l'application du droit international, *Recueil des cours*, vol. 383 (2017): p. 233–446.

Ireland-Piper, D., *Accountability in Extraterritoriality: A Comparative and International Law Perspective* (Northampton, MA: Edward Elgar Publishing, 2017). 208 p.

Jeutner, V., *Irresolvable Norm Conflicts in International Law: The Concept of a Legal Dilemma* (Oxford, United Kingdom; New York, NY: Oxford University Press, 2017). 208 p.

Kanstroom, D., Deportation as a Global Phenomenon: Reflections on the ILC Draft Articles on the Expulsion of Aliens, *Harvard Human Rights Journal*, vol. 30 (2017): p. 49–75.

Kassoti, E., The Constitutionalization of International Law and the Challenge of Non-State Actors, *ICL Journal*, vol. 11 (2017): p. 177–210.

Kidane, W., Missed Opportunities in the International Law Commission's Final Draft Articles on the Expulsion of Aliens, *Harvard Human Rights Journal*, vol. 30 (2017): p. 77–88.

Kjeldgaard-Pedersen, A., *The International Legal Personality of the Individual* (Oxford, UK: Oxford University Press, 2018). 304 p.

Kolb, R., *Good Faith in International Law* (Oxford, UK; Portland, Oregon: Hart Publishing, 2017). 280 p.

Lepard, B.D. (ed), *Reexamining Customary International Law* (New York, NY: Cambridge University Press, 2017). 438 p.

Merkouris, P., Interpreting the Customary Rules on Interpretation, *International Community Law Review*, vol. 19 (2017): p. 126–155.

Meron, T., The Geneva Conventions as Customary Law in Cryer, R., and Henderson, C. (eds), *Law on the Use of Force and Armed Conflict* (Cheltenham, UK: Edward Elgar Publishing, 2017): p. 485–507.

Morris-Sharma, N.Y., The ILC's Draft Articles before the 69th Session of the UNGA: A Reawakening? *Asian Journal of International Law*, vol. 7 (2017): p. 1–12.

Neuman, G.L., Human Rights and the International Law Commission's Draft Articles on the Expulsion of Aliens, *Harvard Human Rights Journal*, vol. 30 (2017): p. 3–14.

Odermatt, J., The Development of Customary International Law by International Organizations, International and Comparative Law Quarterly, vol. 66 (2017): p. 491–511.

Ōnuma, Y., *International Law in a Transcivilizational World* (Cambridge, United Kingdom; New York, USA: Cambridge University Press, 2017). 711 p.

Peters, A., The Refinement of International Law: From Fragmentation to Regime Interaction and Politicization, *International Journal of Constitutional Law*, vol. 15 (2017): p. 671–704.

Pirker, B., and Smolka, J., Making Interpretation More Explicit: International Law and Pragmatics, *Nordic Journal of International Law*, vol. 86 (2017): p. 228–266.

Prost, M., Hierarchy and the Sources of International Law: A Critique, *Houston Journal of International Law*, vol. 39 (2017): p. 285–330.

Rao, P.S., The Identification of Customary International Law: A Process that Defies Prescription, *Indian Journal of International Law*, vol. 57 (2017): p. 221–258.

Rubin, E.L., The Role of Federalism in International Law, *Boston College International and Comparative Law Review*, vol. 40 (2017): p. 195–243.

Ryngaert, C., Non-State Actors in International Law: A Rejoinder to Professor Thirlway, *Netherlands International Law Review*, vol. 64 (2017): p. 155–162.

Sadat, L.N., and Falconer, K., The UN International Law Commission Progresses Towards a New Global Treaty on Crimes Against Humanity, *ASIL Insights*, vol. 21 (2017): p. 1–10.

Sand, P.H., The Discourse on 'Protection of the Atmosphere' in the International Law Commission, *Review of European, Comparative & International Environmental Law*, vol. 26 (2017): p. 201–209.

Schabas, W., DeGuzman, M.M., and Amann, D.M., *Arcs of Global Justice: Essays in Honour of William A. Schabas* (New York: Oxford University Press, 2018). 592 p.

Sivakumaran, S., Techniques in International Law-Making: Extrapolation, Analogy, Form and the Emergence of an International Law of Disaster Relief, *European Journal of International Law*, vol. 28 (2017): p. 1097–1132.

Slawotsky, J., The Clash of Architects: Impending Developments and Transformations in International Law, *The Chinese Journal of Global Governance*, vol. 3 (2017): p. 83–159.

Thirlway, H., The Role of Non-State Actors: A Response to Professor Ryngaert, *Netherlands International Law Review*, vol. 64 (2017): p. 141–153.

Tladi, D., The International Law Commission's Draft Articles on the Protection of Persons in the Event of Disasters: Codification, Progressive Development or Creation of Law from Thin Air? *Chinese Journal of International Law*, vol. 16 (2017): p. 425–451.

von Bogdandy, A., Goldmann, M., and Venzke, I., From Public International to International Public Law: Translating World Public Opinion into International Public Authority, *European Journal of International Law*, vol. 28, iss. 1 (2017): p. 115–145.

38. Recognition of States

Alexandrowicz, C.H., Pitts, J., and Armitage, D., *Law of Nations in Global History* (Corby: Oxford University Press, 2017). 432 p.

Longobardo, M., The Self-Proclaimed Statehood of the Islamic State between 2014 and 2017 and International Law, *Anuario Español de Derecho Internacional*, vol. 33 (2017): p. 205–228.

Naticchia, C., *A Law of Peoples for Recognizing States: On Rawls, the Social Contract, and Membership in the International Community* (Lanham; Boulder; New York; London: Lexington Books, 2017). 281 p.

Riegl, M., and Doboš, B. (eds), *Unrecognized States and Secession in the 21st Century* (Cham: Springer International Publishing, 2017). 225 p.

Santiago Pagliari, A., and Benítez, O.C., Secesión: una incógnita en el Derecho Internacional contemporáneo, *Anuario hispano-luso-americano de derecho internacional*, vol. 23 (2017): p. 237–264.

39. Refugees and internally displaced persons

Aguelo Navarro, P., and Granero Sánchez, H.V., Mécanismos jurídicos de intervención ante los grandes desplazamientos de refugiados y migrantes, *Revista de derecho migratorio y extranjería*, iss. 44 (2017): p. 167–217.

Goldenziel, J.I., Displaced: A Proposal for an International Agreement to Protect Refugees, Migrants, and States, *Berkeley Journal of International Law*, vol. 35 (2017): p. 47–89.

Li, Y., *Exclusion from Protection as a Refugee: An Approach to a Harmonizing Interpretation in International Law* (Leiden: Brill, 2017). 415 p.

McAdam, J., The Enduring Relevance of the 1951 Refugee Convention, *International Journal of Refugee Law*, vol. 29 (2017): p. 1–9.

Moreno-Lax, V., and Papastauridēs, E. (eds), *'Boat Refugees' and Migrants at Sea: A Comprehensive Approach Integrating Maritime Security with Human Rights* (Leiden; Boston: Brill Nijhoff, 2017). 462 p.

Nanda, V.P., Migrants and Refugees are Routinely Denied the Protection of International Human Rights: What does the Future Hold? *Denver Journal of International Law and Policy*, vol. 45 (2017): p. 303–331.

Noussia, K., The Rescue of Migrants and Refugees at Sea: Legal Rights and Obligations, *Ocean Yearbook Online*, vol. 31 (2017): p. 155–170.

Schloenhardt, A., and Macdonald, H., Barriers to Ratification of the United Nations Protocol Against the Smuggling of Migrants, *Asian Journal of International Law*, vol. 7 (2017): p. 13–38.

Türk, V., Edwards, A., and Wouters, C.W. (eds), *In Flight from Conflict and Violence: UNHCR's Consultations on Refugee Status and Other Forms of International Protection* (Cambridge, UK; New York: Cambridge University Press, 2017). 322 p.

Verhellen, J., La portabilité transfrontalière du statut personnel des réfugiés: situer les interactions entre le droit international privé et le droit international des réfugiés, *Revue critique de droit international privé*, vol. 106 (2017): p. 173–189.

Wall, P., A New Link in the Chain: Could a Framework Convention for Refugee Responsibility Sharing Fulfil the Promise of the 1967 Protocol? *International Journal of Refugee Law*, vol. 29 (2017): p. 201–237.

40. Right of Asylum

Battjes, H., Territoriality and Asylum Law: The use of Territorial Jurisdiction to Circumvent Legal Obligations and Human Rights Law Responses, *Netherlands Yearbook of International Law 2016*, vol. 47 (2017): p. 263–286.

Li, Y., *Exclusion from Protection as a Refugee: An Approach to a Harmonizing Interpretation in International Law* (Leiden, Netherlands: Brill Nijhoff, 2017). 396 p.

Moreno Lax, V., *Accessing Asylum in Europe Extraterritorial Border Controls and Refugee Rights Under EU Law* (Oxford: Oxford University Press, 2017). 568 p.

Rikhof, J., Prosecuting Asylum Seekers Who Cannot be Removed: A Feasible Solution? *Journal of International Criminal Justice*, vol. 15 (2017): p. 97–113.

41. Rule of Law

Gogarty, B., and Lawrence, P., The ICJ Whaling Case: Missed Opportunity to Advance the Rule of Law in Resolving Science-Related Disputes in Global Commons? *Zeitschrift für ausländisches öffentliches Recht und Völkerrecht = Heidelberg Journal of International Law*, vol. 77 (2017): p. 161–197.

Huang, Z., and Mačák, K., Towards the International Rule of Law in Cyberspace: Contrasting Chinese and Western Approaches, *Chinese Journal of International Law*, vol. 16 (2017): p. 271–310.

John-Hopkins, M., *The Rule of Law in Crisis and Conflict Grey Zones: Regulating the Use of Force in a Global Information Environment* (London, England; New York, New York: Routledge, 2017). 334 p.

McCarthy, A.H., Erosion of the Rule of Law as a Basis for Command Responsibility Under International Humanitarian Law, *Chicago Journal of International Law*, vol. 18 (2018): p. 553–593.

42. Self-defence

Akermark, S.S., The Puzzle of Collective Self-Defence: Dangerous Fragmentation or a Window of Opportunity? an Analysis with Finland and the Åland Islands as a Case Study, *Journal of Conflict & Security Law*, vol. 22 (2017): p. 249–274.

Arias, G.J., Están las reglas del derecho a la legítima defensa obsoletas para solucionar conflictos actuales como ataques de agentes no-estatales y ciberataques? *Revista Tribuna Internacional*, vol. 6 (2017): p. 1–19.

Brandis, G., The Right of Self-Defence Against Imminent Armed Attack in International Law, *Australian Year Book of International Law*, vol. 35 (2017): p. 55–66.

Green, J.A., The 'Additional' Criteria for Collective Self-Defence: Request but Not Declaration, *Journal on the Use of Force and International Law*, vol. 4 (2017): p. 4–13.

Grimal, F., and Sundaram, J., Cyber Warfare and Autonomous Self-Defence, *Journal on the Use of Force and International Law*, vol. 4 (2017): p. 312–343.

Hayward, R.J., Evaluating the "Imminence" of a Cyber Attack for Purposes of Anticipatory Self-Defense, *Columbia Law Review*, vol. 117 (2017): p. 399–434.

Kliem, T., You Can't Cyber in Here, This is the War Room! A Rejection of the Effects Doctrine on Cyberwar and the Use of Force in International Law, *Journal on the Use of Force and International Law*, vol. 4 (2017): p. 344–370.

O'Meara, C., The Relationship between National, Unit and Personal Self-Defence in International Law: Bridging the Disconnect, *Journal on the Use of Force and International Law*, vol. 4 (2017): p. 273–311.

Paddeu, F.I., Use of Force Against Non-State Actors and the Circumstance Precluding Wrongfulness of Self-Defence, *Leiden Journal of International Law*, vol. 30 (2017): p. 93–115.

Peters, A., and Marxsen, C., Self-Defence Against Non-State Actors: Impulses from the Max Planck Trialogues on the Law of Peace and War, *Zeitschrift für ausländisches öffentliches Recht und Völkerrecht = Heidelberg Journal of International Law*, vol. 77 (2017): p. 1–93.

Schaller, C., Beyond Self-Defense and Countermeasures: A Critical Assessment of the Tallinn Manual's Conception of Necessity, *Texas Law Review*, vol. 95 (2017): p. 1619–1638.

Wilenmann von Bernath, J., La Legítima Defensa Sin Contención Material: Sobre La Defensa Frente a Agresiones Incorporales y Omisivas, *Lus et Praxis*, vol. 23 (2017): p. 419–464.

Zamani, M., and Nikouei, M., Intervention by Invitation, Collective Self-Defence and the Enigma of Effective Control, *Chinese Journal of International Law*, vol. 16 (2017): p. 663–694.

43. Self-determination

Allen, S., *The Chagos Islanders and International Law* (Oxford, United Kingdom: Hart Publishing, 2017). 315 p.

Baran, D., Does "Self-Determination" Right Grant the Right for Unilateral Independence? *Al Sharq Forum* (2017): p. 1–9.

Cunningham, K.G., and Sawyer, K., Is Self-Determination Contagious? A Spatial Analysis of the Spread of Self-Determination Claims, *International Organization*, vol. 71 (2017): p. 585–604.

Ezeizabarrena, X., *Derecho de libre determinación y derecho a decidir: nueva soberanía y derechos humanos en el siglo XXI* (Bilbao: Universidad de Deusto, 2017). 109 p.

Hilpold, P., Self-Determination and Autonomy: Between Secession and Internal Self-Determination, *International Journal on Minority and Group Rights*, vol. 24 (2017): p. 302–335.

Pentassuglia, G., Self-Determination, Human Rights, and the Nation-State, *International Community Law Review*, vol. 19 (2017): p. 443–484.

Watson, I., *Indigenous Peoples as Subjects of International Law* (Abingdon, Oxon UK: Routledge, 2017). 236 p.

44. State Immunity

Bradlow, D.D., Using a Shield as a Sword: Are International Organizations Abusing their Immunity? *Temple International and Comparative Law Journal*, vol. 31 (2017): p. 45–68.

Ekpo, S., Jurisdictional Immunities of the State (Germany v. Italy): The Debate Over State Immunity and *Jus Cogens Norms, Queen Mary Law Journal*, vol. 8 (2017): p. 151–164.

Goh, N., 'Court-Ordered Interim Relief Against States in Aid of Arbitration: Sovereign Immunity, Waiver and Comity', *Journal of International Arbitration*, vol. 34 (2017): p. 679–709.

González Vega, J.A., Otra etapa en "la lucha contra las inmunidades del poder": derechos humanos versus inmunidad de los Estados, *Rivista ordine internazionale e diritti umani*, iss. 4 (2017): p. 485–506.

Quinn, P.S., "Head-of-State-Owned Enterprise" Immunity, *Vanderbilt Journal of Transnational Law*, vol. 50 (2017): p. 1065–1090.

Saint-James, V., and Plas, P. (eds), *L'immunité* (Bayonne: Institut Universitaire Varenne, 2017). 200 p.

45. State Responsibility

Abeyratne, R., State Responsibility for Exogenous Interference with Air Navigation: Some Legal and Regulatory Issues, *Air & Space Law*, vol. 43 (2018): p. 61–75.

Arangio-Ruiz, G., State Responsibility Revisited the Factual Nature of the Attribution of Conduct to the State, *Rivista di diritto internazionale*, vol. 100 (2017): p. 1–162.

Barros, A.S., Ryngaert, C. and Wouters, J. (eds), *International Organizations and Member State Responsibility: Critical Perspectives* (Leiden: Brill Nijhoff, 2017). 232 p.

Luterstein, N.M., Judicial Interpretation of the Convention for the Prevention and Punishment of the Crime of Genocide: What Rules Apply when Determining State and Individual Responsibility? *Groningen Journal of International Law*, vol. 5 (2017): p. 223–240.

Mayer, B., Climate Change Reparations and the Law and Practice of State Responsibility, *Asian Journal of International Law*, vol. 7 (2017): p. 185–216.

Risso Ferrand, M., *et al.* Jurisprudencia sobre responsabilidad del Estado, *Revista de Derecho de la Universidad Católica del Uruguay*, iss. 16 (2017): p. 197–238.

46. State Sovereignty

Bocchese, M., Odd Friends: Rethinking the Relationship between the ICC and State Sovereignty, *New York University Journal of International Law and Politics*, vol. 49 (2017): p. 339–387.

Contipelli, E., Soberanía, gobernanza global y mega-regionalismos: perspectivas latinoamericanas, *Revista Eletrônica Direito e Política*, vol. 12 (2017): p. 1046–1062.

Enyew, E.L., Application of the Right to Permanent Sovereignty Over Natural Resources for Indigenous Peoples: Assessment of Current Legal Developments, *Arctic Review on Law and Politics*, vol. 8 (2017): p. 222–245.

Kadelbach, S., and Roth-Isigkeit, D., The Right to Invoke Rights as a Limit to Sovereignty-Security Interests, State of Emergency and Review of UN Sanctions by Domestic Courts Under the European Convention of Human Rights, *Nordic Journal of International Law*, vol. 86 (2017): p. 275–301.

Kim, S., Non-Refoulement and Extraterritorial Jurisdiction: State Sovereignty and Migration Controls at Sea in the European Context, *Leiden Journal of International Law*, vol. 30 (2017): p. 49–70.

Mikalsen, K.K., No Cosmopolitan Morality without State Sovereignty, *Philosophy & Social Criticism*, vol. 43 (2017): p. 1072–1094.

Montgomery, J.D., and Glazer, N., *Sovereignty Under Challenge: How Governments Respond* (London, England: Routledge, 2017). 413 p.

Van Wyk, S., *The Impact of Climate Change Law on the Principle of State Sovereignty Over Natural Resources* (Baden Baden, Germany: Nomos, 2017). 383 p.

47. State Succession

Grzybowski, J., To Be or Not to Be: The Ontological Predicament of State Creation in International Law, *European Journal of International Law*, vol. 28 (2017): p. 409–432.

48. Transitional Justice

Aciru, M., Rethinking Post-Truth Commissions: Empowering Local Capacities to Shape the Post-Truth Commission Discourse, *Human Rights & International Legal Discourse*, vol. 11 (2017): p. 71–82.

Bell, C., *Transitional Justice* (London; New York: Routledge, 2017). 629 p.

Dyzenhaus, D., Judicial Independence, Transitional Justice and the Rule of Law, in Mcevoy, K., and Mallinder, L. (eds), *Transitional Justice: Critical Concepts in Law* (London: Routledge, 2017): p. 245–270.

Garfunkel, I., Verdad y justicia: ¿Términos incompatibles en la justicia transicional? *American University International Law Review*, vol. 32 (2017): p. 409–436.

Kaapama, P., The Enduring Colonial Legacies of Land Dispossessions and the Evolving Property Rights Legal Discourses: Whither Transitional Justice? *Human Rights & International Legal Discourse*, vol. 11 (2017): p. 108–119.

Lawther, C., Moffett, L., and Jacobs, D. (eds), *Research Handbook on Transitional Justice* (Cheltenham, UK: Edward Elgar Publishing, 2017). 576 p.

Marxsen, C., Unpacking the International Law on Reparation for Victims of Armed Conflict, *Zeitschrift für ausländisches öffentliches Recht und Völkerrecht (ZaöRV)*, vol. 78 (2018): p. 521–540.

McAuliffe, P., *Transformative Transnational Justice and the Malleability of Post-Conflict States* (Cheltenham, UK; Northampton, MA, USA: Edward Elgar Publishing, 2017). 348 p.

Moffett, L., Reparations in Transitional Justice: Justice or Political Compromise? *Human Rights & International Legal Discourse*, vol. 11 (2017): p. 59–70.

Robins, S., Failing Victims? the Limits of Transitional Justice in Addressing the Needs of Victims of Violations. *Human Rights & International Legal Discourse*, vol. 11 (2017): p. 41–58.

Sarkin, J.J., How Conditional Amnesties Can Assist Transitional Societies in Delivering on the Right to the Truth: Are Such Processes Compatible with International Law? *International Human Rights Law Review*, vol. 6 (2017): p. 143–175.

Steinl, L., *Child Soldiers as Agents of War and Peace a Restorative Transitional Justice Approach to Accountability for Crimes Under International Law* (T.M.C. Asser Press, 2017). 421 p.

Sullo, P., The ICC as a Transitional Justice Actor: New Space for Victims? *Diritti umani e diritto internazionale*, vol. 11 (2017): p. 239–275.

van der Wilt, H. and Paulussen, C. (eds), *Legal Responses to Transnational and International Crimes Towards an Integrative Approach* (Cheltenham, UK; Northampton, MA, USA: Edward Elgar Publishing, 2017). 336 p.

Zoli, C., Bassiouni, M.C., and Khan, H., Justice in Post-Conflict Settings: Islamic Law and Muslim Communities as Stakeholders in Transition, *Utrecht Journal of International and European Law*, vol. 33 (2017): p. 38–61.

49. Use of Force

Abuhamoud, A., *La démocratie en droit international: étude critique sur le statut juridique de la démocratie en droit international et la légitimité de l'imposer par la force* (Paris: Harmattan, 2017). 405 p.

Alshdaifat, S.A., *International Law and the Use of Force Against Terrorism* (Newcastle upon Tyne: Cambridge Scholars Publis, 2017). 370 p.

Boddens Hosang, J.F.R., The Effects of Paradigm Shifts on the Rules on the Use of Force in Military Operations, *Netherlands International Law Review*, vol. 64 (2017): p. 353–373.

Chehtman, A., The Ad Bellum Challenge of Drones: Recalibrating Permissible Use of Force, *European Journal of International Law*, vol. 28 (2017): p. 173–197.

Cryer, R., and Henderson, C., *Law on the Use of Force and Armed Conflict*, (Cheltenham, UK; Northampton, MA, USA: Edward Elgar Publishing, 2017). 2,832 p.

Kliem, T., You can't Cyber in here, this is the War Room! A Rejection of the Effects Doctrine on Cyberwar and the Use of Force in International Law, *Journal on the Use of Force and International Law*, vol. 4 (2017): p. 344–370.

Lanovoy, V., The Use of Force by Non-State Actors and the Limits of Attribution of Conduct, *European Journal of International Law*, vol. 28 (2017): p. 563–585.

Pourcel, É., Interdiction du recours à la force: où en est-on? *Revue défense nationale*, iss. 803 (2017): p. 47–55.

Wrange, P., Does Who Matter? Legal Authority and the Use of Military Violence, *Ethics & International Affairs*, vol. 31 (2017): p. 191–212.